NEW ESSAYS ON THE FISH-DWORKIN DEBATE

This book considers the seminal debate in jurisprudence between Ronald Dworkin and Stanley Fish. It looks at the exchange between Dworkin and Fish, initiated in the 1980s, and analyses the role the exchange has played in the development of contemporary theories of interpretation, legal reasoning, and the nature of law.

The book encompasses four key themes of the debate between these authors: legal theory and its critical role, interpretation and critical constraints, pragmatism and interpretive communities, and some general implications of the debate for issues like the nature of legal theory and the possibility of objectivity. The collection brings together prominent legal theorists and one of the protagonists of the debate: Professor Stanley Fish, who concludes the collection with an interview in which he discusses the main topics discussed in the collection.

Volume 15 in the series Law and Practical Reason

Law and Practical Reason

The intention of this series is that it should encompass monographs and collections of essays that address the fundamental issues in legal philosophy. The foci are conceptual and normative in character, not empirical. Studies addressing the idea of law as a species of practical reason are especially welcome. Recognising that there is no occasion sharply to distinguish analytic and systematic work in the field from historico-critical research, the editors also welcome studies in the history of legal philosophy. Contributions to the series, inevitably crossing disciplinary lines, will be of interest to students and professionals in moral, political, and legal philosophy.

General Editor

Prof George Pavlakos (Glasgow)

Advisory Board

Prof Robert Alexy (Kiel)
Prof Samantha Besson (Collége de France and Fribourg, CH)
Prof Emilios Christodoulidis (Glasgow)
Prof Sean Coyle (Birmingham)
Prof Mattias Kumm (New York and Berlin)
Prof Stanley Paulson (St Louis and Kiel)
Prof Arthur Ripstein (Toronto)
Prof Scott Shapiro (Yale Law School)
Prof Victor Tadros (Warwick)

Previous members of the Advisory Board

Neil MacCormick†
Joseph Raz†

Recent titles in the series

Volume 9: Freedom and Force: Essays on Kant's Legal Philosophy
Edited by Sari Kisilevsky and Martin J Stone

Volume 10: The Nature and Value of Vagueness in the Law
Hrafn Asgeirsson

Volume 11: Law's Humility: Enlarging the Scope of Jurisprudential Disagreement
Triantafyllos Gkouvas

Volume 12: Rightful Relations with Distant Strangers: Kant, the EU, and the Wider World
Aravind Ganesh

Volume 13: The Making of Constitutional Democracy: From Creation to Application of Law
Paolo Sandro

Volume 14: New Essays on the Nature of Legal Reasoning
Edited by Mark McBride and James Penner

Volume 15: New Essays on the Fish-Dworkin Debate
Edited by Thomas Bustamante and Margaret Martin

New Essays on the Fish-Dworkin Debate

Edited by
Thomas Bustamante
and
Margaret Martin

·HART·
OXFORD · LONDON · NEW YORK · NEW DELHI · SYDNEY

HART PUBLISHING

Bloomsbury Publishing Plc

Kemp House, Chawley Park, Cumnor Hill, Oxford, OX2 9PH, UK

1385 Broadway, New York, NY 10018, USA

29 Earlsfort Terrace, Dublin 2, Ireland

HART PUBLISHING, the Hart/Stag logo, BLOOMSBURY and the Diana logo are trademarks of Bloomsbury Publishing Plc

First published in Great Britain 2023

Copyright © The editors and contributors severally 2023

The editors and contributors have asserted their right under the Copyright, Designs and Patents Act 1988 to be identified as Authors of this work.

All rights reserved. No part of this publication may be reproduced or transmitted in any form or by any means, electronic or mechanical, including photocopying, recording, or any information storage or retrieval system, without prior permission in writing from the publishers.

While every care has been taken to ensure the accuracy of this work, no responsibility for loss or damage occasioned to any person acting or refraining from action as a result of any statement in it can be accepted by the authors, editors or publishers.

All UK Government legislation and other public sector information used in the work is Crown Copyright ©. All House of Lords and House of Commons information used in the work is Parliamentary Copyright ©. This information is reused under the terms of the Open Government Licence v3.0 (http://www.nationalarchives.gov.uk/doc/open-government-licence/version/3) except where otherwise stated.

All Eur-lex material used in the work is © European Union, http://eur-lex.europa.eu/, 1998–2023.

A catalogue record for this book is available from the British Library.

Library of Congress Cataloging-in-Publication data

Names: Bustamante, Thomas da Rosa de, 1976- editor. | Martin, Margaret (Law teacher), editor.

Title: New essays on the Fish-Dworkin debate / edited by Thomas Bustamante and Margaret Martin.

Description: Oxford ; New York : Hart Publishing, An Imprint of Bloomsbury Publishing, 2023. | Series: Law and practical reason; 15 | Includes bibliographical references and index. | Summary: "This book considers the seminal debate in jurisprudence between Ronald Dworkin and Stanley Fish. It looks at the exchange between Dworkin and Fish, initiated in the 1980s, and analyses the role the exchange has played in the development of contemporary theories of interpretation, legal reasoning, and the nature of law. The book encompasses 4 key themes of the debate between these authors: legal theory and its critical role, interpretation and critical constraints, pragmatism and interpretive communities, and some general implications of the debate for issues like the nature of legal theory and the possibility of objectivity. The collection brings together prominent legal theorists and one of the protagonists of the debate: Professor Stanley Fish, who concludes the collection with an interview in which he discusses the main topics discussed in the collection"—Provided by publisher.

Identifiers: LCCN 2023011765 | ISBN 9781509961795 (hardback) | ISBN 9781509961832 (paperback) | ISBN 9781509961818 (pdf) | ISBN 9781509961801 (Epub)

Subjects: LCSH: Law—Philosophy. | Law—Methodology. | Fish, Stanley Eugene. | Dworkin, Ronald.

Classification: LCC K235 .N485 2023 | DDC 340/.1—dc23/eng/20230504

LC record available at https://lccn.loc.gov/2023011765

ISBN:	HB:	978-1-50996-179-5
	ePDF:	978-1-50996-181-8
	ePub:	978-1-50996-180-1

Typeset by Compuscript Ltd, Shannon

To find out more about our authors and books visit www.hartpublishing.co.uk. Here you will find extracts, author information, details of forthcoming events and the option to sign up for our newsletters.

Table of Contents

List of Contributors vii

Introduction 1
Thomas Bustamante and Margaret Martin

PART ONE
LEGAL THEORY AND ITS CRITICAL ROLE

1. *Reasoning Within and About (Legal) Practices* 17
   Brian H Bix

2. *Fish versus Dworkin: Sound and Fury, But …?* 27
   Larry Alexander

3. *Explaining Us to Ourselves* 35
   Jeremy Waldron

4. *Law, Reason and Celestial Music* 51
   NE Simmonds

5. *The Game Goes On: Why Legal Theorists Can Never Admit that Stanley Fish is Right* 75
   David Kenny

PART TWO
INTERPRETATION AND CRITICAL CONSTRAINTS

6. *Reenchanting Practice: Stanley Fish and the Challenge of Virtue Ethics* 99
   Maria Cahill and Patrick O'Callaghan

7. *The Law in Quest of Integrity: Interpretation, Invention and Internal Critique* 119
   TRS Allan

8. *The Relevance of Literary Interpretation* 141
   Barbara Baum Levenbook

9. *Clash of the Titans: Hercules vs Dennis Martinez (Reflections on the Fish-Dworkin Debate)* 159
   Charles L Barzun

10. *Social, Moral or Ameliorative? Understanding Constraints on Legal Interpretation* 183
    Natalie Stoljar

PART THREE
PRAGMATISM AND INTERPRETIVE COMMUNITIES

11. *Revisiting the 'Fish-Dworkin Debate'* 205
    Dennis Patterson

12. *Almost Naturalism: The Jurisprudence of Ronald Dworkin* 217
    Dan Priel

13. *Interpreting Community: Agency, Coercion, and the Structure of Legal Practice* 239
    Nicole Roughan and Jesse Wall

14. *Fish versus Dworkin: A Comparison between Two Versions of Legal Pragmatism* 259
    Thomas Bustamante

15. *Making it Objective: Dworkin, Inferentialism, and the CLS Critique* 291
    Thiago Lopes Decat

PART FOUR
IMPLICATIONS

16. *Dworkin, Fish, and Radically Defective Constitutions* 317
    Sanford Levinson

17. *The Problem of Immoral Integrity* 343
    Lars Vinx

18. *What Makes Law? Dworkin, Fish, and Koskenniemi on the Rule of Law* 363
    David Lefkowitz

19. *Is Hercules a Natural?* 381
    Margaret Martin

20. *Interview with Professor Stanley Fish* 405
    Thomas Bustamante and Margaret Martin

Index 429

List of Contributors

TRS Allan is Professor Emeritus of Jurisprudence and Public Law at the University of Cambridge, Fellow of Pembroke College, Cambridge, and Fellow of the British Academy. His publications include *The Sovereignty of Law: Freedom, Constitution, and Common Law* (Oxford, Oxford University Press, 2013), *Constitutional Justice: A Liberal Theory of the Rule of Law* (Oxford, Oxford University Press, 2001) and *Law, Liberty, and Justice: The Legal Foundations of British Constitutionalism* (Oxford, Clarendon Press, 1993).

Larry Alexander is Warren Distinguished Professor of Law and Co-Executive Director of the Institute for Law & Religion, at the University of San Diego. His scholarship includes the books *Crime and Culpability: A Theory of Criminal Law* (with Ferzan, and Morse) (Cambridge, Cambridge University Press, 2009), *Demystifying Legal Reasoning* (with Sherwin) (Cambridge, Cambridge University Press, 2008), *Is There a Right of Freedom of Expression?* (Cambridge, Cambridge University Press, 2005), and *The Rule of Rules: Morality, Rules, and the Dilemmas of Law* (with Sherwin) (Durham, NC, Duke University Press, 2001). He has contributed, among others, to the volumes *Oxford Handbook of Distributive Justice* (Olsaretti, ed, Oxford, Oxford University Press, 2018), *Moral and Legal Ignorance* (Peels, ed, London, Routledge, 2017), *Legal, Moral, and Metaphysical Truths: The Philosophy of Michael Moore* (Ferzan, and Morse, eds, Oxford, Oxford University Press, 2016), *Precedent in the United States Supreme Court* (Peters, ed, Dordrecht, Springer, 2013), *Essays on Criminal Law* (with Ferzan) (Christopher, ed, Oxford, Oxford University Press, 2012), and *Institutionalized Reason: The Jurisprudence of Robert Alexy* (Klatt, ed, Oxford, Oxford University Press, 2012), as well published as articles on *Northwestern Law Review, University of Chicago Law Review, Harvard Law Review, Philosophy and Public Affairs*, and *University of Pennsylvania Law Review*, and other journals.

Charles L Barzun is the Horace W Goldsmith Professor of Law at the University of Virginia. He received a JD/MA (History) degree from Virginia in 2005. During law school, he served as notes development editor of the *Virginia Law Review* and won the Best Note Award for his student note, 'Common Sense and Legal Science'. After graduating, he clerked for Judge Robert D Sack of the US Court of Appeals for the Second Circuit. Prior to joining the faculty, Charles was a Climenko Fellow and lecturer at Harvard Law School. He writes in the areas of constitutional theory, jurisprudence, and the history of legal thought.

Brian H Bix is the Frederick W Thomas Professor of Law and Philosophy at the University of Minnesota. He holds a D. Phil. (doctorate) from Oxford University, and a JD from Harvard University. He has published over 180 works, primarily in the areas of Jurisprudence, Family Law, and Contract Law. His books include *Jurisprudence: Theory and Context*, 9th edn (London, Sweet & Maxwell and Carolina Academic Press, 2023); *A Dictionary of Legal Theory* (Oxford, Oxford University Press, 2004); and *Law, Language and Legal Determinacy* (Oxford, Oxford University Press, 1993). His works have been translated into eight languages.

Thomas Bustamante is Professor of Legal Theory and Philosophy of Law at the Federal University of Minas Gerais, Brazil, and Senior Research Productivity Fellow of the National Council for Scientific and Technological Development (CNPq), Brazil. He was Visiting Research Fellow at the following institutions: New York University (2020–22), with a Grant from the Fulbright Commission; King's College London (2022–23), with a Grant from CAPES Foundation; and University of São Paulo (2016–17), with a Grand from FAPESP. He holds a PhD from the Pontifical Catholic University, Rio de Janeiro. He has edited the books *Philosophy of Law as an Integral Part of Philosophy: Essays in the Jurisprudence of Gerald J Postema* (with Thiago L Decat, Oxford, Hart Publishing, 2020), *Democratizing Constitutional Law: Perspectives on Legal Theory and the Legitimacy of Constitutionalism* (with Bernardo Fernandes, Cham, Springer, 2016), *Argument Types and Fallacies in Legal Argumentation* (with Christian Dahlman, Cham, Springer, 2015) and *On the Philosophy of Precedent* (with Carlos Bernal Pulido, 2012).

Maria Cahill is Professor of Law at University College Cork, and a graduate of Trinity College, Dublin, and the European University Institute, Florence, Italy. She has been a Visiting Fellow at the Institute of European and Comparative Law at the University of Oxford in 2015 and a Kathleen Fitzpatrick Visiting Fellow at the Centre for Comparative Constitutional Studies at the University of Melbourne in 2019 as well as a Research Associate at the Programme for the Foundations of Law and Constitutional Government at the University of Oxford. She is currently an Irish Research Council Laureate Scholar as Principal Investigator of a four-year project researching comparative doctrinal approaches to and the philosophical foundations of the right to freedom of association.

Thiago Lopes Decat is Professor of Philosophy and Theory of Law at the Federal University of Minas Gerais (UFMG), Brazil. He got his Master's Degree in Philosophy, at UFMG, in the field of 'Logic, Science, Mind and Language', and his PhD in Theory of Law at the Pontifical Catholic University of Minas Gerais. He has had books and articles published in the areas of Legal Theory and Philosophy, and researches subjects concerning rationality, agency, normativity and metaethics applied to law understood as a social practice. His publications in English include the book *Philosophy of Law as an Integral Part* *of Philosophy: Essays on the Jurisprudence of Gerald Postema* (coedited with Thomas Bustamante, Oxford, Hart Publishing, 2020).

Stanley Fish is Professor of Law at Florida International University. He previously served as Dean of the College of Liberal Arts and Sciences at the University of Illinois at Chicago. He holds a BA from the University of Pennsylvania (1959) and an MA and PhD from Yale University (1960; 1962). He has previously taught at the University of California at Berkeley (1962–74); Johns Hopkins University (1974–85), where he was the Kenan Professor of English and Humanities; and Duke University, where he was Arts and Sciences Professor of English and Professor of Law (1986–1998). From 1993 through 1998 he served as Executive Director of Duke University Press. Professor Fish was named Chicagoan of the Year for Culture by the Chicago Tribune in 2001 and was given a lifetime achievement award by Yale University in 2011. To date he has written 22 books. His latest, *Law at the Movies: Turning Legal Doctrine into Filmic Art*, will be published by Oxford University Press in the near future.

David Kenny is an Associate Professor of Law and Fellow at Trinity College Dublin, where he teaches and researches comparative constitutional law, critical legal theory, and law and literature. He has published critical scholarship on comparative constitutional law in leading journals such as the American Journal of Comparative Law, Public Law, and the International Journal of Constitutional Law (ICON). He has also published on legal readings of Hilary Mantel, Seamus Heaney, and Star Wars in leading journals Law and Literature and Law and Humanities. He is currently working on a book entitled Pragmatism in Law and Literature, and on a project about the crucial role of culture in constitutional law.

David Lefkowitz is Professor of Philosophy and the founding Coordinator of the Program in Philosophy, Politics, Economics, and Law (PPEL) at the University of Richmond. His scholarship focuses largely on conceptual and normative questions in international law, and the morality of obedience and disobedience to law. He is the author of *Philosophy and International Law: A Critical Introduction* (Cambridge, Cambridge University Press, 2020), as well as more than 40 journal articles and book chapters. Lefkowitz has held fellowships at Princeton University, the US Naval Academy, and the National University of Singapore, and served as a visiting research scholar at Pompeu Fabra University.

Barbara Baum Levenbook is Professor Emerita in the Department of Philosophy and Religious Studies at the North Carolina State University. She has been writing and publishing on topics of legal philosophy for over 40 years. Her articles on legal philosophy have appeared in *Legal Theory*, *Law and Philosophy*, *The Canadian Journal of Philosophy*, *Jurisprudence* and law reviews. In other journals, she has published articles on social and political philosophy, on normative ethics and on its intersection with metaphysics. In addition, she has contributed and continues to contribute to philosophical anthologies, including *Oxford Studies in Philosophy of Law* (vol 2), *The Cambridge Companion to Legal*

Positivism, a volume in the Routledge Studies in Contemporary Philosophy series (for intersection of legal philosophy and philosophy of language) and a volume in the Cambridge Topics in Contemporary Philosophy series. She is a contributing editor to Jotwell: *Jurisprudence*. She holds a BA and an MA in philosophy from the University of Rochester and a PhD in philosophy from the University of Arizona.

Sanford Levinson is the W. St. John Garwood and W. St. John Garwood Jr. Centennial Chair in Law at the University of Texas Law School and a Professor of Government at the University of Texas at Austin. Among his books are *Constitutional Faith* (1988, winner of the Scribes Award, 2nd edn, New Jersey, Princeton University Press, 2011); *Written in Stone: Public Monuments in Changing Societies* (Duke University Press, 1998); *Wrestling With Diversity* (Duke University Press, 2003); *Our Undemocratic Constitution: Where the Constitution Goes Wrong (and How We the People Can Correct It)* (New York, Oxford University Press, 2006); *Framed: America's 51 Constitutions and the Crisis of Governance* (New York, Oxford University Press, 2012); *An Argument Open to All: Reading the Federalist in the 21st Century* (New Haven, Yale University Press, 2015); and, with Cynthia Levinson, *Fault Lines in the Constitution: The Framers, Their Fights, and the Flaws that Affect Us Today* (Atlanta, Peachtree, 2017). He was elected to membership in the American Academy of Arts and Sciences in 2001.

Margaret Martin is Associate Professor at the Faculty of Law at Western University, in Canada. She holds a PhD from the University of Cambridge, a MSL from the University of Toronto and got her BA (Hons) and MA from McMaster University. She has held fellowships at the University of Toronto and at Corpus Christi College at the University of Cambridge. Martin is co-editor of the *Canadian Journal of Law and Jurisprudence* and on the editorial board for *Jurisprudence* and the *American Journal of Jurisprudence*. Her monograph, *Judging Positivism*, was published by Hart Publishing in 2014. She has also published in the area of criminal theory, the theory of international criminal law, and political philosophy.

Patrick O'Callaghan is a member of faculty at the School of Law, University College Cork, Ireland, where he teaches jurisprudence and tort law. Previously he was a senior lecturer at Newcastle University (UK) and a researcher at the Centre for European Law and Politics, Universität Bremen.

Dennis Patterson is Board of Governors Professor of Law and Philosophy at Rutgers University and Professor of Legal Philosophy at Surrey Law School, Guildford, UK.

Dan Priel is a Professor at Osgoode Hall Law School, at York University, Canada. He joined Osgoode's full-time faculty in 2011. Prior to that, he was a Visiting Professor at Osgoode during the 2010–11 academic year and an

Assistant Professor at the University of Warwick in the UK. From 2005 to 2007, he was Oscar M. Ruebhausen Fellow-in-Law at Yale Law School, and before that a postgraduate student at the University of Oxford, where he wrote his doctoral dissertation. He served as law clerk in the Israeli Supreme Court, and was co-editor-in-chief of the student-edited law journal at the Hebrew University Law Faculty. His current research interests include legal theory, private law (especially tort law and restitution), and he is also interested in legal history and in the application of the social sciences, in particular psychology, to legal research. His published work appeared in *Law and Philosophy*, *Legal Theory*, *Oxford Journal of Legal Studies*, and *Texas Law Review*.

NE Simmonds is Emeritus Professor of Jurisprudence in the University of Cambridge, and Life Fellow of Corpus Christi College. His principal book is *Law as a Moral Idea* (2007).

Natalie Stoljar is Professor of Philosophy and Director of the Institute for Gender, Sexuality and Feminist Studies at McGill University. She holds a joint appointment in the Department of Equity, Ethics and Policy, Faculty of Medicine. Her research expertise is in feminist philosophy, social and political philosophy, and the philosophy of law. She has published numerous articles and book chapters in these areas and is also co-editor (with C Mackenzie) of *Relational Autonomy. Feminist Perspectives on Autonomy, Agency and the Social Self* (Oxford, OUP, 2000) and (with K Voigt) of *Autonomy and Equality. Relational Approaches* (London, Routledge, 2021).

Nicole Roughan is an Associate Professor at the Faculty of Law, University of Auckland, a Rutherford Discovery Fellow of the Royal Society Te Apārangi, and co-Director of the NZ Centre for Legal Theory. Nicole's research in general jurisprudence includes work on theories of law's authority, law's persons (both officials and subjects of law), and pluralist jurisprudence. Her book publications include a monograph, *Authorities: Conflicts, Cooperation, and Transnational Legal Theory* (Oxford, Oxford University Press, 2013) and a co-edited volume (with Andrew Halpin), *In Pursuit of Pluralist Jurisprudence* (Cambridge, Cambridge University Press, 2017).

Lars Vinx is Associate Professor in the Faculty of Law at the University of Cambridge, and a Fellow at Hughes Hall. He works in legal and political philosophy as well as in constitutional theory. Vinx currently investigates the question whether robust forms of constitutional control of legislative and executive power are justifiable by appeal to the notion of popular sovereignty. He also has a strong interest in the history of political and constitutional thought – with a focus on the constitutional theory of the Weimar Republic – and has published on the legal-theoretical and political-theoretical writings of Hans Kelsen and Carl Schmitt. Before coming to Cambridge, Vinx was a Max Weber Fellow at the European University Institute in Florence, Italy, and then taught in the Department of Philosophy at Bilkent University in Ankara, Turkey. He received his PhD in philosophy from the University of Toronto and holds an MA in history, philosophy and political science from the University of Heidelberg.

Jeremy Waldron is University Professor at New York University. He teaches legal and political philosophy at NYU School of Law. Until recently, he was also Chichele Professor of Social and Political Theory at Oxford University (All Souls College). Waldron has written extensively on jurisprudence and political theory, including numerous books and articles on theories of rights, constitutionalism, the rule of law, democracy, property, torture, security, homelessness, and the philosophy of international law. His books include *Dignity, Rank, and Rights* (New York, Oxford University Press, 2012), *Partly Laws Common to All Mankind: Foreign Law in American Courts* (New Haven, Yale University Press, 2012), *The Harm of Hate Speech* (Cambridge, MA, Harvard University Press, 2012), *Torture, Terror, and Trade-offs: Philosophy for the White House* (Oxford, Oxford University Press, 2010), *Law and Disagreement* (Oxford, Clarendon, 1999), and *The Dignity of Legislation* (Cambridge, Cambridge University Press, 1999). Elected to the American Academy of Arts and Sciences in 1998 and a fellow of the British Academy since 2011, Waldron has given many prestigious academic lectures, such as the Tanner Lectures at Berkeley in 2009, the Holmes Lectures at Harvard Law School in 2009, the Hamlyn Law Lectures in England in 2011, and the Gifford Lectures in Edinburgh in 2015.

Jesse Wall is an Associate Professor/Ahonuku at the Faculty of Law, University of Auckland. He was previously a Junior Research Fellow at Merton College, University of Oxford, and a Senior Lecturer at the University of Otago. Wall completed his undergraduate degrees in law and philosophy at Otago, and the BCL and DPhil at Oxford, where he was studying as a Rhodes Scholar. His research focuses on methodology in the philosophy of law, property law theory, and consent in intimate contexts. Wall's main works include monographs *Being and Owning* (Oxford, Oxford University Press, 2015) and *Sex and the Other* (forthcoming) in addition to articles published in the *Oxford Journal of Legal Studies*, the *Cambridge Law Journal*, the *Journal of Legal Philosophy*, and the *Canadian Journal of Law and Jurisprudence*.

Introduction

THOMAS BUSTAMANTE AND MARGARET MARTIN

THE EXCHANGE BETWEEN Ronald Dworkin and Stanley Fish in the beginning of the 1980s, where Dworkin first introduced the analogy between law and literature in his philosophy of law, constitutes an important chapter in the history of jurisprudence and continues to attract the interest of legal scholars. Nevertheless, to our knowledge, there has never been a volume dedicated to this debate. The current collection of essays provides an exciting opportunity to fill this gap in the literature.[1]

The Fish/Dworkin debate is much more than a relic in jurisprudential history. Bound up in this debate is a host of important questions, and potential answers, that remain central to jurisprudential thought. The heated exchanges between these two famed jurisprudence scholars focused on the questions of the nature of interpretation, the role of moral values in legal interpretation, the status of moral norms, and the nature of philosophy more generally. Both authors eschew the common moves found in natural law jurisprudence wherein theorists attempt either to locate authority in the divine or to derive the normative force of law from a basic set of transcendental values. They seek, instead, to make sense of the human source of value. Dworkin maintains that 'the practices of interpretation and morality give these [moral] claims all the meaning they need or could have',[2] while Fish insists that 'values do not exist independently of socially organized activities but emerge simultaneously with the institutional and conventional structures within which they are intelligible'.[3]

---

[1] The secondary literature is rich and insightful, although it regrettably vanished in more recent years. See, among the most representative works, M Robertson, *Stanley Fish on Philosophy, Politics and Law: How Fish Works* (Cambridge, Cambridge University Press, 2014); M Moore, *Educating Oneself in Public: Critical Essays in Jurisprudence* (Oxford, Oxford University Press, 2000) chs 10 and 11; P Schlag, 'Normativity and Politics of Form' (1991) 139 *University of Pennsylvania Law Review* 801; P Schlag, 'Theory and the Uses of Dennis Martinez' (1987) 76 *Georgia Law Review* 53; S Winter, 'Bull Durham and the Uses of Theory' (1990) 42 *Stanford Law Review* 639; JM Schelly, 'Interpretation in Law: The Dworkin-Fish Debate (Or, Soccer Amongst the Gahuku-Gama)' (1985) 73 *California Law Review* 158; N Stavropoulos, *Objectivity in Law* (Oxford, Oxford University Press, 1996) esp chs 5 and 6; A Marmor, *Interpretation and Legal Theory*, 2nd edn (Oxford, Hart Publishing, 2005) 47–64; as well as the contributions from authors included in this collection, viz., D Patterson, *Law and Truth* (Oxford, Oxford University Press, 1996); S Levinson, 'Law as Literature' (1982) 60 *Texas Law Review* 373; and B Bix, *Law, Language and Determinacy* (Oxford, Oxford University Press, 1993) 54–55, 75.

[2] R Dworkin, *Law's Empire* (Cambridge, MA, Harvard University Press, 1986) 80–81.

[3] S Fish 'Anti-Professionalism' in his collection *Doing What Comes Naturally* (Durham, NC, Duke University Press, 1989) 215, 232.

Furthermore, both thinkers offer different views about the relationship between theory and practice. Fish is a self-proclaimed 'theory minimalist', whereas Dworkin sees theory as an essential part of the act of judging. Contra Fish, Dworkin famously, and controversially, argues that 'jurisprudence is the general part of adjudication, silent prologue to any decision at law'.[4] This should not be taken to mean, however, that Dworkin is suggesting a role for metaphysical concepts in legal argumentation, inasmuch as he regards theories as embedded in practices,[5] as it were. Dworkin, after all, famously denies the distinction between first-order moral or legal concepts and second-order statements that purport to be *about*, rather than *within*, the practice they seek to describe. Hence, both Fish and Dworkin can be regarded as committed to a methodological priority of social practices. Perhaps this explains why both thinkers anchor their accounts in claims about interpretation in the literary world – Fish with the idea of interpretive communities and Dworkin with the metaphor of a chain novel. Nonetheless, there is a limit to their agreement, because they end with divergent visions of the human condition and different conclusions about the character of social practices.

A case can be made that Fish is the foremost polemicist of our age. His influence takes us far beyond the debate in jurisprudence: he also left his mark on the world of literary criticism. He is famous for declaring, 'there is no text in this class'.[6] Meaning, Fish insisted, resides neither in the words of the text nor in subjective intentions of the author; rather, it is always the product of assumptions, rules, conventions and protocols of the interpretive community where they are read. 'Interpretive communities' emerge as a result of tacit and shared assumptions that are never fully articulable or intentionally alterable.[7]

Fish takes one of the seemingly simple truths about our classroom experience – that there is a text in the class and our job is to acquire meaning from it – and calls it into question. He asks us to rethink everything we thought we knew. It is, of course, far from clear whether he can achieve this end without asserting the very thing that he denies – the denial of the existence of incontrovertible

---

[4] Dworkin (n 2) 90.
[5] R Dworkin, *Justice in Robes* (Cambridge, MA, Harvard University Press, 2006) 49ff.
[6] S Fish, *Is There a Text in This Class? The Authority of Interpretive Communities* (Cambridge, MA, Harvard University Press, 1980).
[7] According to Fish, 'Interpretive communities are made up of those who share interpretive strategies not for reading (in the conventional sense) but for writing texts, for constituting their properties and assigning their intentions. In other words, these strategies exist prior to the act of reading and therefore determine the shape of what is read rather than, as is usually assumed, the other way around. If it is an article of faith in a particular community that there are a variety of texts, its members will boast a repertoire of strategies for making them. And if a community believes in the existence of only one text, then the single strategy its members will employ will be forever writing it. The first community will accuse the members of the second of being reductive, and they in turn will call their accusers superficial. The assumption in each community will be that the other is not correctly perceiving the 'true text;, but the truth be that each perceives the text (or texts) its interpretive strategies demand and call into being'. ibid 171.

truths takes the form of a truth claim. Fish's critics frequently take aim at this particular target. They also insisted that Fish was unable to assign interpretive communities a status that was more than provisional. Of course, when pressed, even this idea seems to disintegrate into an idea so fragile, it is barely recognisable. The best Fish can do is to suggest that a nod of agreement (without words that can be interpreted) is the only communal bond we can find. But even nodding may, in fact, be the product of a misunderstanding.

Nevertheless, it is also the case that Fish's anti-foundationalism, when articulated in literary circles, is either revelatory or frustrating, depending on your point of view. But in the legal sphere, it is anxiety-inducing: if we cannot have objective judgments, then who is imprisoned, and who is set free, will be the result of the exercise of power alone. The perpetual fear that judges make decisions on the basis of their subjective value judgements will make those who want more understandably nervous. But if Fish is right – if we simply cannot have more – then the idea of an interpretive community will provide sufficient resources to understand a text, legal or otherwise. From the perspective of the average citizen – or, indeed, almost all of us – the stakes appear to be very high. Fish boldly counters: the stakes are not high (or, indeed, low). For 'law as integrity' is not, in his view, 'a special practice engaged in only by gifted or Herculean judges'. Judges, Fish insists, are doing what they have always done, and they do it *naturally*.[8]

To take Fish seriously, even if only temporarily, requires one to let go of many metaphysical intuitions and common-sense assumptions about the locus of meaning in the world. The sense of vertigo that Fish can call forth in any dedicated reader echoes the challenge Plato's Socrates posed to his many interlocutors: if they stay and continue to take his questions seriously, they are at risk of losing their bearings in a world that seemed, but moments before, so secure and so familiar. The discomfort experienced is exacerbated if one takes Fish's account seriously. Plato, at least according to the common reading of his works, is trying to call into question everything we think we know in order to get us to see beyond conventional views where more permanent values reside. The pain of the loss of all that is familiar is softened by the hope of discovery. Fish does not offer us this consolation prize, or any other. The loss of the familiar is permanent, and, as mentioned, Fish thinks it matters little. Fish takes away all the things we think we know then tells us not to get upset that our world is gone. On this view, humans are no different from a hive of bees (to draw upon an example from Hobbes), except unlike bees, we continually deceive ourselves into thinking we can harness reason and transcend the world of causality. Fish is quick to offer a psychological appraisal of those who protest: we all have a bad case of wishful thinking. It is no wonder that the debates are often cantankerous and that few escape without scars.

---

[8] S Fish, 'Still Wrong After All These Years', in *Doing What Comes Naturally* (n 3) 367–368.

Of course, Fish's story is not one Dworkin is willing to endorse (nor will he accept Fish's contention that he is *already* endorsing Fish's worldview, as Fish claims). While Fish has a point – at times, Dworkin speaks as if judges always and inevitably adopt the lens of integrity – Dworkin nevertheless does not wish to follow Fish into the abyss. Like Fish, Dworkin is operating within a fallen world, locating ideals in the human world alone; however, he has not lost faith in reason's ability to anchor judgements, including judgments offered by judges in a courtroom. In Dworkin's ground-breaking paper 'Objectivity and Truth: You'd Better Believe It', he locates objective value within our shared human world. While Fish is part of a tradition of thought that traces back to Thrasymachus, Dworkin echoes Plato, insisting that values form a unity and that we can access them through reason. In the last book he published in his lifetime, Dworkin argues that both Plato and Aristotle can be construed as 'particularly instructive examples of *interpretive* moral philosophy', in the sense he specifies.[9] Although Dworkin's account of objectivity purports to justify our judgements from the internal point of view of existing social practices, rather than some transcendental ideal, Dworkin shares with the classics the holistic ambition to construct a 'mutually supportive network of value'.[10] Judges can make responsible value judgments and ought to do so in a specific way: he famously refers to this judicial approach as 'law as integrity'. But integrity is not only a virtue for judges and officials. It is important, for Dworkin, because it requires that each citizen 'must accept demands on him', and 'make demands on others, that share and extend the moral dimension of any explicit political decisions'.[11] In Dworkin's words: 'Integrity fuses citizens' moral and political lives'.[12] Our legal rights do not exist in positive law alone – they are located in a morally sound interpretation of the practice that is implied in, and transcends, mere black-letter law.

Notice that Dworkin has not completely escaped anxiety-inducing elements that permeate Fish's account: whether force is used in a justifiable way will turn on whether judges are able to emulate Hercules. Success is never guaranteed. Hence, we are left pondering whether state coercion is, in fact, being used at the whims of judges' personal proclivities. In fact, some critics have worried whether Dworkin fails to attend to the intersubjective dimensions of legal practice and ends up locking judges in the world of 'subjective' value judgements instead of focusing on collective touchstones provided by shared practices.[13] Dworkin, on this objection, encourages judges to turn inward towards their sense of moral correctness, rather than outward towards shared practices. While Dworkin insists that there is a world outside subjective value judgements, these

---

[9] R Dworkin, *Justice for Hedgehogs* (Cambridge, MA, Harvard University Press, 2011) 184 (emphasis added).
[10] ibid.
[11] Dworkin (n 2) 189.
[12] ibid.
[13] See, for instance, Patterson (n 1) 71–127.

critics argue that he moves participants precariously close to Fish when his 'Protestantism' is emphasised. Dworkin's belief that integrity requires that each participant in the practice makes *her own judgement* about the moral point of the practice of law is regarded, by these critics, as insufficiently intersubjective and insufficiently political, because 'while he regards the activity of the [legal] practice as public and collective, he seems to regard the enterprise of understanding that activity as private and individual'.[14] Whether Dworkin is guilty of this charge has been the topic of sustained debate.[15] The point, at this juncture, is to demonstrate that Fish and Dworkin spark similar worries for readers, which has led some to speculate that the shared ground accounts for the pointed nature of the exchanges, at least in part. Fish always spies these points of intersection in Dworkin's account and works to regain the upper hand with every turn of the interpretive screw. In the process, Fish brings all of us to the precipice. In our view, there is value in staring into this particular void: it generates a sense of urgency that can, and often does, infuse debates with purpose and passion.

The debate is also ripe for reconsideration because Dworkin's scholarship still occupies a central role in legal philosophy. Dworkin has been in a long-standing debate with his formidable adversary, HLA Hart. But one should not ignore the significant (but often unacknowledged) influence that the Fish–Dworkin debate produced in the development of Dworkin's most significant contributions to legal and moral philosophy. Although in his last book, *Justice for Hedgehogs*, Dworkin expresses (in the preface) the 'unmatched good fortune' to have as friends and interlocutors 'three of the greatest philosophers of our time: Thomas Nagel, Thomas Scanlon and the late Bernard Williams', whose impact on Dworkin's thoughts is promptly acknowledged,[16] Dworkin sometimes does not recognise the crucial role that his adversaries played in the development of his own thoughts. In his first response to Fish, for instance, Dworkin calls Fish's response 'incompetent' in the very first sentence.[17] In a more recent exchange, after *Law's Empire*, Dworkin argues that the complaints of Fish and other pragmatists against his theory are 'quarrels no one needs', 'pointless metaphysical theater', 'fierce campaigns against invented fools',

---

[14] GJ Postema, 'Protestant Interpretation and Social Practices' (1987) 6 *Law and Philosophy* 283, 288–89.
[15] For more recent developments in this debate on the notion of 'protestant' interpretation, see the contributions of Thomas Bustamante, Dennis Patterson, and Brian Bix in T Bustamante and TL Decat (eds), *Philosophy of Law as an Integral Part of Philosophy: Essays in the Jurisprudence of Gerald J Postema* (Oxford, Hart Publishing, 2020); and, in this volume, the analyses of Trevor Allan, Dennis Patterson, and Nicole Roughan and Jesse Wall. For a defence of Dworkin's position, see T Bustamante, 'Is Protestant Interpretation an Acceptable Attitude Toward Normative Social Practices? An Analysis of Dworkin and Postema' (2021) 66 *American Journal of Jurisprudence* 1–25.
[16] Dworkin (n 9) xi.
[17] R Dworkin, 'My Reply to Stanley Fish (and Walter Benn Michaels): Please Don't Talk about Objectivity Any More' in WJT Mitchel (ed), *The Politics of Interpretation* (Chicago, University of Chicago Press, 1983) 287.

'misleading', and 'spuriously shocking dramas about interpretive truth being only interpretive power'.[18] Dworkin is one of the most clever jurisprudence scholars of his generation, but none of this appears to be fair. One cannot fully appreciate the development of Dworkin's own views without looking at Fish. In fact, we believe that Dworkin took Fish more seriously than he would admit. In the very first exchange with Fish, Dworkin presented for the first time the core of his theory of moral objectivity, which later developed into the seminal article 'Objectivity and Truth: You'd Better Believe It' and into the central thesis of his masterpiece *Justice for Hedgehogs*.[19] Although Dworkin mocked Fish and asked him 'not to talk about objectivity any more', he spent the rest of his career making insightful philosophical claims about it, and it was precisely with *this* kind of talk that Dworkin earned the admiration and respect of his intellectual heroes, including, ironically, moral philosophers like Scanlon, whose recent work is evidently inspired by Dworkin's views on moral objectivity.[20]

Furthermore, *Law's Empire*, Dworkin's most influential legal work, can be partly interpreted as one of the products of his early debate with Stanley Fish. A foundational commitment of Dworkin's most famous book can be found, indeed, in chapter two, where Dworkin carefully explains the difference between deferring to the interpretation of others (including legislators or even interpretive communities) and making one's own *responsible judgements* about the correct interpretation of a purposeful social practice.[21] One can see in Dworkin's sophisticated reasoning a *permanent concern* to distinguish between interpreting and inventing a practice without collapsing into the legal positivist distinction between creating and applying a law, which was the very first objection Fish presented against Dworkin in his earliest piece.[22] Regardless of whether Fish played a role in determining Dworkin's thoughts on this matter, we can be sure that Fish anticipated all these difficulties and turned a spotlight onto the very heart of the arguments and controversies that made Dworkin's jurisprudence attain the philosophical endurance it now has.

---

[18] R Dworkin, 'Pragmatism, Right Answers, and True Banality' in M Brint and W Weaver (eds), *Pragmatism in Law & Society* (Boulder, CA, Westview Press, 1991) 357, 382.

[19] Consider, for instance, the following excerpt, which anticipates some of the most important claims of Dworkin's future work in moral philosophy: 'I see no point in trying to find some *general* argument that moral or political or legal or aesthetic or interpretive judgments are objective. Those who ask for an argument of that kind want something different from the king or arguments I and they would make for particular examples or instances of such judgments. I have no arguments for the objectivity of moral judgments, except moral arguments, no arguments for the objectivity of interpretive judgments except interpretive arguments, and so forth.' Dworkin (n 17) 297.

[20] TM Scanlon, *Being Realistic about Reasons* (Oxford, Oxford University Press, 2016).

[21] Dworkin (n 2) 49–67. According to Dworkin, deferring to interpretive communities does not solve the problem of distinguishing between good and bad interpretations of a social practice, but it just adds another mental state or intention that cannot be understood without a new interpretive judgement of the assessor. Interpretations should seek, therefore, to determine what the practice 'really requires', instead of what a previous interpreter said it does (see ibid 65).

[22] Fish (n 3) 'Working on the Chain Gang: Interpretation in Law and Literature' in *Doing What Comes Naturally* (n 3).

While we are confident that this volume will be an important addition to the mainstream ideas in the field, we anticipate that it will also add to the intrigue. In 'A Drama of Development: Gary Olson on Stanley Fish', Richard Mullendert relays the story of Fish's first on-stage encounter with Dworkin:

> Olson tells us that 'Dworkin deftly cut [Fish] to ribbons'. He adds that '[n]ever before – and never since – had [Fish] been so unable to gain the upper hand'. In this moment, Fish resolved to 'get' Dworkin in print.[23]

This memorable interaction, which took place at a conference in Chicago, instigated a series of philosophically deft exchanges, punctuated by piercing and memorable titles. Fish's contributions include: 'Wrong Again', 'Still Wrong After All These Years' and 'Almost Pragmatism'.[24] Dworkin replies in kind, as we saw above. The next chapter in the debate, which this volume aims to bring about, will also be the next act in this unfolding jurisprudential drama. The fact that Fish is now often classified as an originalist is a plot twist that matters little from our perspective: the goal of this volume is broader than this.

The main questions addressed in the volume are divided into four sections, which are followed by an interview with Professor Stanley Fish. The first section discusses the role and the nature of legal theory, as well as the relationship between theory and practice.

Chapter one, by Brian Bix, provides a general analysis of the debate, centred on the distinction between arguing *with* and *about* legal practices. By looking to the shared assumptions and theses that inform the debate between Dworkin and Fish, including metaphysical ones, Bix aims to 'explore the different, and occasionally convergent, views of Fish and Dworkin', acknowledging the relevance of their jurisprudences and locating an important disagreement about the capacity of legal theory to impose constraints on the development of a normative practice.

Chapter two, by Larry Alexander, provides a historical contextualisation of the debate and challenges the point of departure of their interchange. Alexander, who is also an originalist, is uniquely positioned to situate Fish's current views in the context of the original exchange. He argues, however, that it is time to depart from the jurisprudence of Fish and Dworkin: 'Dworkin was arguing based on a view of law that is defective, and Fish was arguing from a postmodern perspective that supports anything and nothing.'

In chapter three, Dworkin's position is defended by one of his most renowned and influential doctoral students, Jeremy Waldron, who sides with Dworkin over Fish in reference to the value of philosophical reflection. In his contribution, Waldron insists that Fish's critique ignores the point that in philosophy,

---

[23] R Mullender, 'A Drama of Development: Gary Olson on Stanley Fish' [2018] *Cardozo L Rev De-Novo* 47 (footnote omitted).

[24] See S Fish's essays 'Working on the Chain Gang: Interpretation in Law and Literature', 'Wrong again', and 'Still Wrong After all These Years', all in S Fish, *Doing What Comes Naturally* (n 3).

we often set out to explain things even though no one disputes them. He concedes that no one has to instruct lawyers to look to the past to justify their behaviour, but nevertheless, 'the wider community certainly cries out for a theory that addresses the role of legal practice and the place of its peculiarity in a society ruled by law'. This leads Waldron to reject Fish's claim that Dworkin's task is pointless, because Dworkin identifies a feature of the legal practice (its justificatory role) that is 'bound up with the idea of *the rule of law*'.

Chapter four, by NE Simmonds, provides an insightful analysis of Fish's well-known essay 'Force', to locate an important absence in this work, which is the role of reason in normative practices. While Fish assumes an 'illusory character of reason, when "reason" is understood as a critical standard capable of standing in judgment upon human reasoning', Simmonds replies with a social and historically oriented understanding of reason. While settled practices are necessarily structured by ideals, Simmonds believes that these ideals emerge also from concrete social practices. In order to re-establish the critical force of reason, over and against Fish's insistence that reason is the same as belief, Simmonds emphasises 'reason's immanence rather than transcendence', while arguing that such immanence 'does not reduce reason's critical power'. A re-engagement with Fish's work prompted Simmonds to consider the concept of reason as conceptualised in our secular age.

In the opposite direction, in chapter five, David Kenny argues not only that Fish's position against the role of theory in legal practice is right, but also that it shows, to the despair of traditional legal theorists, that 'the whole enterprise of legal theory is wrongheaded and, indeed, on its own terms, redundant'. In contraposition to Dworkin, Fish rejects the idea that theoretical thinking can drive legal interpretation and play a role in constraining it. Nevertheless, despite being fully committed to Fish's position, Kenny still contemplates a 'general rhetorical function' for legal theory, which is to 'lend law intellectual credibility in a world that demands that many of its social processes have apparent intellectual rigor and prestige'. Kenny's point is not that the law resolves disputes in a consistent and conceptually coherent way, but that theory can help people *believe* it does. Kenny calls that capacity the law's 'amazing trick', which is its capacity to gain authority by enabling its subjects to satisfy their desire for integrity and consistency.

The second section discusses one of the most enduring disagreements between Fish and Dworkin, which is the possibility of relying on an internal structure to distinguish between 'right' and 'wrong' interpretations of a given practice.

Still on the question of the relationship between theory and practice, in chapter six, Maria Cahill and Patrick O'Callaghan seek to identify a way to counter Fish's interpretive scepticism. Like Waldron, they reject Fish's distinction between arguing about a practice and within a practice and offer, instead, a reply to Fish's correlative claims 'that practice is not generated by theory and that theory does not offer a genuine account of how practice unfolds'.

A more fruitful jurisprudence should, in their view, 'reframe' the practice, to *re-enchant* it in light of recent developments in virtue ethics.

In chapter seven, in turn, TRS Allan comes to Dworkin's defence with a critical assessment of the debate. Allan begins by identifying an ambiguity at the core of Dworkin's account of the connection between law and morality: 'It is not quite clear [in Dworkin's theory] whether political morality demands an appropriate response to institutional actions, viewed largely as matters of social fact, or whether instead such actions are themselves identifiable for practical purposes only by exercise of moral judgment.' In other words,

> Do statutes and judicial precedents impose external *constraints* on legal interpretation in virtue of their existence as authoritative texts? Or are there implications for the law's content internal to interpretation in the sense of being wholly dependent on the best theory of legal practice viewed as a whole?

In response to that ambiguity, Allan proposes to place the second alternative – wherein Dworkin envisions a conception of law as a branch of political morality – in sharper focus in order to see the extent to which Dworkin can withstand Fish's challenge. 'The unity of law and morality that Dworkin defends in his last major work, *Justice for Hedgehogs*', he argues, 'is a more promising version of anti-positivism'.

In chapter eight, Barbara Baum Levenbook offers a less optimistic take on the viability of an assumption shared by both Dworkin and Fish – namely, that interpreting law is akin to interpreting literary texts. After revisiting the mainstream interpretation of Wittgenstein, which assumes that guidance by law depends on a capacity to understand the meaning of legal or linguistic acts *without* the need for interpretation, she argues that 'the debate between Dworkin and Fish is somewhat peripheral to the nature of law' because Fish and Dworkin are committed to the implausible assumption that understanding is always dependent on interpretation. Moreover, even in the cases in which interpretation is required to overcome the vagueness of some concepts, Dworkin and Fish fail because their analogy between literary and legal interpretation is premised on the misleading assumption 'that literary interpretation is so closely analogous to legal interpretation that the dissimilarities are irrelevant'. Through a series of counterexamples, she aims to undermine this assumption and hence to reject the conclusion that the analogy between law and literature can contribute to clarifying the interpretive task of participants in the practice of legal reasoning.

Chapter nine, by Charles Barzun, argues in the alternative. Barzun begins by dismissing the worry that Fish and Dworkin are talking past each other and then locates a genuine philosophical disagreement about whether law is an *intellectual* practice, which requires Herculean interpreters committed to a reflected inquiry (as Dworkin suggests), or whether interpretation relies on intuitions and implicit dispositions that fall beyond the scope of any theory or general account (as Fish's criticism seems to imply). It is this theoretical disagreement, in Barzun's view, that constitutes the gist of the Fish–Dworkin debate, and there seem to be reasons to recognise that Dworkin has a better claim. Nevertheless, Barzun is not satisfied with Dworkin's advocacy of an intrinsic connection between law and philosophy because his insistence on keeping interpretive (including legal) practices 'out of reach of the natural and social sciences' makes it 'oddly disconnected from actual human experience'.

This takes us to chapter ten, which closes this section. Here Natalie Stoljar presents another argument in support of Dworkin's position that there is an internal structure that provides standards for the critical appraisal of legal provisions. Nonetheless, Stoljar's argument does not challenge Fish's claim that the constraints of a practice are constituted by 'interpretive communities' that generate the 'rules of the game' that 'participants in interpretive practices necessarily follow'. Her argument is more subtle, since it claims only that 'while Fish's notion of natural constraints is compelling, natural constraints *underdetermine* the activity of interpretation and thus permit the possibility of constructive interpretation'. In contrast to Fish, Stoljar argues that Dworkin's account of constructive interpretation provides a way for the 'conceptual amelioration' of legal provisions, because it offers 'a strategy that "improves" legal concepts along epistemic, semantic and sometimes moral dimensions'.

The third section, in turn, discusses the concept of 'interpretive' communities and the commitment of Fish and Dworkin to philosophical pragmatism.

Dennis Patterson, in chapter eleven, revisits his historical scepticism about Fish's and Dworkin's jurisprudential views. Patterson and Fish engaged in a testy exchange in 1993: Patterson penned this memorable shot across the bow with his essay 'The Poverty of Interpretive Universalism', in which he tackled both Fish and Dworkin and claimed that they have no real disagreement at all.[25] Fish replied with his predictable flare in 'How Come You Do Me Like You Do',[26] which was followed by another adversarial title: 'You Made Me Do It: My Reply to Stanley Fish'.[27] In this volume, Patterson argues that Fish and Dworkin are 'the product of an era that has largely been left behind in legal philosophy', which failed to provide an interesting account of meaning because it can sustain neither a metaphysical commitment to moral realism, in the case of Dworkin, nor a persuasive version of conventionalism, in the case of Fish. 'Like Heidegger, Gadamer, Foucault and Derrida, Fish and Dworkin think that something must come between signs and meaning', blurring the crucial difference between 'directly accessible meaning (understanding) and meaning that is accessible only by way of inference (interpretation)'.

Following a different line of reasoning, chapter twelve, by Dan Priel, uses the exchange between Fish and Dworkin as an entrance point into a novel and

---

[25] D Patterson, 'The Poverty of Interpretive Universalism: Toward the Reconstruction of Legal Theory' (1993) 72 *Texas Law Review* 1.
[26] S Fish, 'How Come You Do Me Like You Do? – A Response to Dennis Patterson' (1993) 72 *Texas Law Review* 57.
[27] D Patterson, 'You Made Me Do It: My Reply to Stanley Fish' (1993) 72 *Texas Law Review* 67.

provocative reading of Dworkin's position – one that explains how important aspects of Dworkin's work are attractive to naturalists, especially WF Quine. According to Priel, if one drops the common misunderstanding that Dworkin's jurisprudence falls smoothly into the categories of 'natural law', 'formalism' and 'moral realism', one can see that Dworkin adopts a pragmatic perspective of legality that can provide an interesting contribution to developing a naturalist account of law, morality and the world. Regardless of the fierce resistance that jurisprudence scholars associated with philosophical naturalism have offered to Dworkin's thought, Priel believes that Dworkin's responses to Fish provide a more promising path to a naturalist jurisprudence than most of his positivist interlocutors do.

In chapter thirteen, Nicole Roughan and Jesse Wall bring up an important question concerning the concepts of 'interpretive community', in Fish, and 'community of principle', in Dworkin. According to Roughan and Wall, there might be relevant differences between these views, inasmuch as for Fish 'legal practice entails the rhetoric of force', while for Dworkin 'it entails the justification of force'. Nonetheless, both appear to miss a relevant aspect of the relationship between agency, interpretation and coercion, which concerns the answers to the question 'Who does what in a community of interpreters?' Once this question is taken seriously, both Fish's account of interpretive communities and Dworkin's account of a community of principles become problematic. Fish is in trouble, on the one hand, because by his account, 'the interpreters, themselves, cannot be reflective about their own practice, not even the practice of interpreting their responsibilities'. And Dworkin is in trouble, on the other hand, because his account of a community of principles ignores the 'hierarchical and differentiated role responsibilities', for these are special responsibilities that Dworkin's account of 'protestant interpretation' and 'political responsibility' fails to explain.

In chapter fourteen, Thomas Bustamante argues that the similarities and differences between Fish's and Dworkin's jurisprudences can be explained by their commitment to different versions of philosophical pragmatism. In his debate with Fish, Dworkin treated legal judgments as 'thick ethical concepts' in Putnam's sense. This brought Dworkin to Fish's province, since both can be classified as philosophical pragmatists. They accept, to begin, what Brandom described as '*fundamental* pragmatism' (the view that to understand a practice, one requires a special know-how or practical ability). And they accept, further, a '*normative* pragmatism' (the view that we resort to implicit norms to determine what counts as a reasonable interpretation within a practice). What distinguishes them is the character of these implicit norms: Fish subscribes to a version of the 'belief–desire' model of cognition and thinks the implicit norms embedded in social practices are only 'instrumental norms', whereas Dworkin eschews any kind of instrumentalism. Nonetheless, Dworkin can still be classified as a pragmatist (in a wider sense) because he believes legal principles are norms implicit in social practice that play the role of providing a rational structure to distinguish between correct and incorrect applications of a set of norms. It is the possibility of inconsistency between implicit norms and interpretive judgements that accounts for the possibility of legal mistakes, regardless of whether these mistakes are made by a single agent or by the interpretive community to which we belong.

At the end of the section, in chapter fifteen, Thiago Lopes Decat builds upon the previous chapter and considers an objection that Critical Legal Scholars presented against Dworkin's interpretivism. Bustamante argues, at the end of chapter fourteen, that Dworkin responds to Fish with a claim that legal objectivity is a sort of 'domain objectivity', because it is 'a *special type* of objectivity' appropriate to the legal domain: 'The law is a distinctive type of interpretive practice, in which the truth-claims of interpretive propositions are responsive to a normative point that underlies the explicit decisions of past political authorities.' Nonetheless, Decat believes that this assumption can sometimes be vulnerable to an objection presented by the supporters of Critical Legal Studies. According to the *Crits*,

> the law of certain jurisdictions – like, it is argued, the United States of America – is an incoherent compromise of inconsistent ideologies, in which 'law as integrity' cannot do its interpretive work because the 'articulate consistency' among principles presupposed by Dworkin's theory of adjudication is an unachievable goal.

The right way to respond to this objection, on Decat's view, is to take up a general inferentialist theory of meaning, of the sort developed by Robert Brandom, which provides a more resistant explanation of the rationality of social practices and appears to be 'fully consistent with Dworkin's theory of legal interpretation'.

Section four, finally, draws some implications of the assumptions and conclusions of the Fish–Dworkin debate.

In chapter sixteen, Sanford Levinson expresses his conviction that Fish gets the upper hand in his debate with Dworkin and that Dworkin's assumption of a right answer about interpretive controversies in legal disputes is an implausible metaphysical fiction. Nonetheless, Levinson intimates that it is time to move beyond the Fish–Dworkin debate, albeit for reasons that are very different from the proponents of analytical jurisprudence. While legal philosophers often present their claims as time-independent truths, Levinson seeks to draw attention to the way in which philosophical debates can emerge from concerns that are highly contextual. This shift in focus, and indeed in Fish's own thinking, prompts Levinson to explore the extent to which philosophical debates are forever wedded to particular cultural moments: constitutional scholarship should move from interpretation to other domains, like, first, the domain of institutional design and, second, the domain of what he called a 'constitution of settlement' – that of the '"hard-wired" structural features of the Constitution – or perhaps of *any* written constitution –that do not lend themselves to litigation and concomitant debate about meaning'. Perhaps one can appeal to these features to identify certain undisputed facts and provisions any lawyer (or, perhaps, any government or citizen) must accept in order to display fidelity to the rule of law.

Lars Vinx shares Levinson's view that the value of philosophical theories must be assessed, at least in part, by their ability to explain real-world examples. In chapter seventeen, instead of focusing on current scholarly debates, he critically assesses the Fish–Dworkin exchange by turning to an historical example. Vinx wonders whether, or to what extent, either thinker can explain the legal system Germany endured during Nazi rule. Vinx maintains that this famous example either forces us to concede that Dworkin was wrong to hold that a notion of integrity built on a theory of interpretation alone has justificatory purchase or to reject Fish's claim that all legal practices, by virtue of being interpretive, invariably exhibit integrity. Theory must, on this account, answer to practice. And it is far from clear that either Fish or Dworkin will pass this test. In effect, Vinx argues that there is a possibility of 'morally perverted integrity' and that the legal practice of Nazi Germany might be regarded as a sample case:

> Nazi legal thought and practice was methodologically interpretivist. Nazi judges did not blindly submit to wicked statutory enactments. They were engaged, rather, in developing a constructive interpretation of the positive legal material, one that aimed to show the law of Nazi Germany in its best light, though their views as to what interpretation would show the law in its best moral light were catastrophically misguided.

Vinx maintains that the example of Nazi law undermines, therefore, the conclusion that there is a necessary connection between integrity and justification.

Already approaching the end of the book, chapter eighteen, by David Lefkowitz, challenges the traditional reading of the Fish–Dworkin debate, according to which Fish is committed to a description of legal argument as an unreflective and purely intuitive practice. After considering Dworkin's account of interpretation in *Law's Empire*, Fish's comments on Posner and Rorty, and Koskenniemi's writings on legality and international law, Lefkowitz finds more connections than disagreement among these three authors and classifies 'each of them' as committed to identifying law 'with a practice of government informed by fidelity to the ideal of the rule of law, or legality'. In Lefkowitz's interpretation,

> all three theorists conceive of legality as an attitude, mindset, or approach to constructing the social world, one that is most fully developed in members of the legal profession, or what is the same, those who have been habituated into a culture devoted to the ideal of government in accordance with the rule of law.

Finally, in chapter nineteen, Margaret Martin considers Fish's idea of what it means to do something 'naturally', in order to make room for a critical role for philosophy (recall that Fish famously insists that philosophy has no consequences). Fish uses the phrase that we interpret the law 'naturally' to signal that judges cannot act otherwise: they have no choice. Significantly, he robs the term 'natural' of its critical force – a point that comes into view when we return to the ways in which the term 'natural' was employed in the history of philosophy. Martin is also worried about the manner in which Dworkin presupposes that judges are naturally Herculean. Fish, she argues, is right to draw attention to the deep ambiguity in *Law's Empire*: pragmatism and conventionalism collapse into Dworkinian constructive interpretation. Judges, and indeed citizens, are always interpreting in accordance with Dworkin's vision of integrity. Instead of conceding the point that judges do what they do naturally, Martin resurrects options within the category of 'constructive interpretation' and argues that Dworkin must say more about his own view, which will, at least in some contexts, require him to take sides in a longstanding political debate within liberal theory. Contra Fish, she insists that the stakes in this debate may prove to be higher than many believe. Philosophy, it turns out, is more than a game.

To finish the volume, the editors have conducted an interview with Professor Stanley Fish, in which he recollects some of the memories of his exchange with Dworkin and answers a set of questions about some of the central claims presented in the chapters of this collection of essays. We hope that this book provides another chapter in the intriguing jurisprudential debate between Fish and Dworkin, and that it can keep alive the insights and ideas that motivated the memorable interactions between these two great exponents of contemporary philosophy of law.

Part One

Legal Theory and its Critical Role

1
Reasoning Within and About (Legal) Practices

BRIAN H BIX

I. INTRODUCTION

IN THE 1980s and early 1990s, Stanley Fish and Ronald Dworkin held a debate of sorts – always provocative and occasionally a little sharp[1] – through a series of published articles, books, and book chapters. In revisiting this debate, one difficulty is in pinning down whether the two scholars were in fact disagreeing, and, if so, what the nature and content of the disagreement was. That initial problem is raised because the two scholars, in their exchanges: (a) often seemed to be talking past one another, or arguably mis-characterised the other's views, rather than responding substantively to one another's arguments; and (b) their positions, on close inspection, often seemed more similar than different.

One interesting aspect of the debate is the similarity of their views on a number of important matters, amid the sharp exchanges regarding their differences. As will be discussed, both theorists avoided arguments that might be characterised as 'metaphysical' or 'ontological', and both emphasised the extent to which our actions and arguments occur within practice communities, analysing the way that this fact shapes how arguments (eg, about law, literature, or morality) could be made and characterised.[2]

---

[1] Fish's titles were sometimes less than respectful: eg, S Fish, 'Wrong Again' (1983) 62 *Texas Law Review* 299; S Fish, 'Still Wrong After All These Years' (1987) 6 *Law & Philosophy* 401. Dworkin, for his part, kept the lack of charity mostly to the texts of his articles: eg, 'His [Fish's] "reading" of my own essay … is incompetent'. R Dworkin, 'My Reply to Stanley Fish (and Walter Benn Michaels): Please Don't Talk about Objectivity Any More' in WJT Mitchell (ed) *The Politics of Interpretation* (Chicago, University of Chicago, 1983) 287, 287.

[2] In another context, Brian Leiter characterises views of this kind as 'Domain Separatism', summarising it as the idea that 'metaphysical and epistemological criteria vary with the subject-matter of cognitive domains'. B Leiter, 'Normativity for Naturalists' (2015) 25 *Philosophical Issues* 64, 69. Leiter reported the following works as falling within that category: R Dworkin, 'Objectivity and Truth: You'd Better Believe It' (1996) 25 *Philosophy & Public Affairs* 87; T Nagel, *The Last Word* (Oxford, Oxford University Press, 1997); D Parfit, *On What Matters* (Oxford, Oxford University Press, 2011); and TM Scanlon, *Being Realistic About Reasons* (Oxford, Oxford University Press, 2014).

The focus on practices may be clearest in Dworkin's rejection of (most forms of) external scepticism and in Fish's argument that judges can never really act in unconstrained or unjudicial ways. Fish ultimately goes further than Dworkin along these lines, arguing that there is no possible interaction between a practice and the theory of a practice, while Dworkin makes the modification or correction of a practice in light of its purpose or theory central to his view. This chapter will explore the different, and occasionally convergent, views of Fish and Dworkin, focusing on the extent to which analysis and critique are confined within and by a practice.

In what follows, section II will look at Dworkin's discussions regarding arguing within a practice, section III will look at Fish's discussions on the same topic, and section IV will offer a critical overview of the points of agreement and disagreement between the two.

II. DWORKIN ON ARGUING WITHIN A PRACTICE

Dworkin consistently argued that criteria regarding arguments and conclusions occur within a discourse.[3] Many of the themes in his discourse-centred or practice-centred approach can be seen in the following quotation, in which Dworkin is criticising another scholar's ideas about literary interpretation:

> Interpretation is an enterprise, a public institution, and it is wrong to assume, a priori, that the propositions central to any public enterprise must be capable of validity. It is also wrong to assume much about what validity in such enterprises must be like – whether validity requires the possibility of demonstrability, for example. It seems better to proceed more empirically here. We should first study a variety of activities in which people assume that they have good reasons for what they say, which they assume hold generally and not just from one or another individual point of view. We can then judge what standards people accept in practice for thinking that they have reasons of that kind.[4]

There is both a focus on the particular discourse (or, one prefers, 'enterprise' or 'institution') and the reluctance to speak *generally* about all discourses. Each is to be investigated on its own terms, to discover its own rules, standards, criteria, and conventions.

One prominent manifestation of Dworkin's approach was his well-known discussion in *Law's Empire* of the difference 'between skepticism within the enterprise of interpretation, as a substantive position about the best interpretation of some practice or work of art, and skepticism outside and about that

---

[3] At one point, Dworkin speaks dismissively of 'the currently fashionable idea of a practice', Dworkin (n 1) 292, but, as discussed in this chapter, it is hard to see his own approach as anything much different from a practice-centred (or, if one prefers, 'discourse-centred') approach.
[4] R Dworkin, 'Law as Interpretation' (1982) 60 *Texas Law Review* 527, 535.

enterprise'.[5] His primary focus in that text – and later in his piece, 'Objectivity and Truth'[6] – was external scepticism *about morality*, but, as will be seen, he generalised his response to external challenges to interpretation, and, indeed, to all external challenges to areas of discourse. Dworkin argued that assertions about the nature of some area of discourse (eg, that it does or does not contain objective truths and right answers) 'offer[] no reason to retract or modify' claims *within* the discourse (eg, that slavery is wrong, or that a particular interpretation of a statute is correct). 'Unlike the global form of internal skepticism, … genuine external skepticism cannot threaten any interpretive project.'[7] (Dworkin was open to the possibility of internal scepticism, but thought that the arguments of that sort that have been offered in relation to law and interpretation could be answered. External scepticism, by contrast, is dismissed as 'a metaphysical theory, not an interpretive or moral position'.[8])

Dworkin's later response to some arguments by Richard Rorty nicely summarised his (Dworkin's) views:

> Rorty and his followers apparently all distinguish … between two levels at which people supposedly think and speak. The first is the internal level at which some enterprise like law or science … is carried on. This is the level at which people use the vocabulary that is useful to them: the level at which people rightly say, because that *is* useful, that science describes how the world really is and that the law is not just what it would be useful to think it is. The second is the external level at which philosophers and other theorists talk *about* these enterprises rather than participate in them. That is the level at which, according to Rorty and the others, some bad philosophers of science claim that science discovers how the world really is, and bad legal philosophers say that lawyers and judges try to discover … what the law really is. … Rorty says the triumph of pragmatism has only cleared the conceptual ground so that actual practice can continue liberated from that [external level] kind of confusion. [] The difficulty with this defense, however, is that the external level that Rorty hopes to occupy does not exist.[9]

Dworkin offers a Wittgensteinian-toned argument: that words get their meaning from use, and that there is no distinctive 'external' or 'philosophical' use of (say)

---

[5] R Dworkin, *Law's Empire* (Cambridge, MA, Harvard University Press, 1986) 78. In his later writings, Dworkin developed his argument against external scepticism about one particular area of discourse – morality – that moved from saying that such scepticism was generally *irrelevant* to saying (at least regarding external scepticism about moral matters) that it was *nonsensical*. D Smith, 'Ronald Dworkin and the External Sceptic' (2006) 19 *Canadian Journal of Law & Jurisprudence* 433.

[6] Dworkin (n 2).

[7] Dworkin (n 5) 80.

[8] The distinction between internal and external scepticism, and the rejection of the latter, is one of the few topics where Fish expressly endorses and praises Dworkin's arguments. Fish, 'Still Wrong' (n 1) 417–18. Fish, though, immediately follows that endorsement with an argument that Dworkin's position undercuts his (Dworkin's) views elsewhere. ibid 418: '"[E]xternal skepticism" and "law as integrity" are … philosophical practices … and the mistake is to assume that as philosophical practices they have anything to say about practices internal to disciplines other than philosophy'.

[9] R Dworkin, 'Pragmatism, Right Answers, and True Banality' in M Brint and W Weaver (eds), *Pragmatism in Law and Society* (US, Westview Press, 1991) 359, 361–62.

the description of legal statements as 'true' or 'false', different from the way lawyers would make the same claim in mundane legal argumentation.[10] Along similar lines, he asserted that his own 'right answer thesis' should be understood the same way, as 'a claim made within legal practice rather than at some supposedly removed, external, philosophical level'.[11]

Dworkin brings basically the same line of analysis and objection when discussing arguments of 'global' incommensurability,[12] 'external scepticism', and allegations about 'objectivity': arguments within a discourse are acceptable, and arguments external to a discourse are suspect – perhaps irrelevant, perhaps nonsensical. He writes that one should not bring an 'a priori theory of objectivity to the enterprise of interpretation; [one should] tak[e] it from the enterprise'.[13]

III. FISH ON ARGUING WITHIN A PRACTICE

The discussion of Dworkin's views, above, began with a quotation in which Dworkin disclaimed any general view about areas of discourse. One can find a similar disclaimer from Fish, responding to an article which purported to discuss his (Fish's) 'theory of interpretation':

> I don't have a theory of interpretation, or, rather, my argument concerning interpretation is that it is not the kind of thing you could have a theory about, if by 'theory' you mean some general account of the process such that anyone persuaded of it would have some notion of what to do – how to proceed, how to make decisions or evaluate evidence – the next time a task of interpretation was called for. I certainly have something to say about interpretation, and while I think that what I have to say is true – it is an accurate description of what interpretation is – it is not helpful; it does not give you any direction in addition to or superior to the direction you already have by virtue of being a situated member of a practice. That is why it is not a theory; most people who look to theories look to them for guidance and my account of interpretation offers none.[14]

---

[10] Dworkin (n 9) 362–63. (Earlier in the same article, Wittgenstein is named, alongside WVO Quine and Donald Davidson, as theorists cited by Rorty as 'pragmatists', but who 'have not so much supported as refuted Rorty's version of that tradition'. ibid 360.).

[11] Dworkin (n 9) 365. One caution here: in passing, Dworkin seems to concede that John Mackie's well-known error-theory about morality, if correct, 'would also defeat the possibility of right answers'. ibid 366 (footnote omitted); see JL Mackie, *Ethics: Inventing Right and Wrong* (London, Penguin, 1977). Dworkin refers to Mackie's theory as 'defending a kind of internal moral scepticism', Dworkin (n 9) 366, but that is a strange characterisation. Under Dworkin's approach, Mackie's views seem better characterised as an *external* sceptical argument, an argument that comes from outside the (moral) discourse, arguing that the alleged moral facts could not exist. In a different work, Dworkin seemed to treat Mackie's ideas, more conventionally, as a form of external scepticism. Dworkin (n 2) 112–16.

[12] See, eg, R Dworkin, 'On Gaps in the Law' in P Amselek and N MacCormick (eds), *Controversies about Law's Ontology* (Edinburgh, Edinburgh University Press 1991) 84, 89–90.

[13] Dworkin (n 1) 291.

[14] S Fish, 'Response: Interpretation is Not a Theoretical Issue', (1999) 11 *Yale Journal of Law & the Humanities* 509.

Stanley Fish once half-jokingly summarised his works as reducing 'to an argument in which the troubles and benefit of interpretive theory are made to disappear in a solvent of an enriched notion of practice'.[15] But, then, how should we understand a practice – or a discipline? Again, Fish's views are stated in a way that portrays matters in a less than laudatory manner:

> [A] discipline achieves its distinctiveness when it manages to carve out for itself a place at the table of disciplines, not by matching up to something in the sky or in the mind of God but by elaborating a vocabulary which produces the need it then fulfills. Rather than it being the case that there is an antecedent model or template prior to actual practices, there are, in this view, only actual practices, which maintain their share of the franchise by ceaseless acts of self-promotion that are also and chiefly acts of self-creation.[16]

In one of his responses to Dworkin, 'Dennis Martinez and the Uses of Theory',[17] Fish again expresses strong views against guidance by theory. The example referred to in the title is a professional baseball pitcher, Dennis Martinez, being spoken to by his famous coach, Earl Weaver. When later asked by a reporter, Ira Berkow, what Weaver told him, Martinez stated that Weaver said: "'Throw strikes and keep 'em off the bases,'" Martinez then added: "'What else could he say?'"[18]

Fish imagines Martinez explaining matters to Berkow:

> 'Look, it may be your job to characterize the game of baseball in terms of overriding theories, but it's my job to play it; and playing it has nothing to do with following words of wisdom, whether they are Weaver's or Aristotle's, and everything to do with already being someone whose sense of himself and his possible actions is inseparable from the kind of knowledge that words of wisdom would presume to impart.' In short, what Weaver says amounts to 'Go out and do it,' where 'do it' means go and play the game.[19]

Fish's ultimate point, as he later summarises it, 'is that performing an activity – engaging in a practice – is one thing and discoursing on that practice another.

---

[15] S Fish, *Doing What Comes Naturally* (Oxford, Oxford University Press, 1989) ix; the reference to 'enriched notion of practice' also appears in S Fish, 'Dennis Martinez and the Uses of Theory' (1987) 96 *Yale Law Journal* 1773, 1789, and S Fish, 'Almost Pragmatism: The Jurisprudence of Richard Posner, Richard Rorty, and Ronald Dworkin' in M Brint and W Weaver (eds), *Pragmatism in Law and Society* (US, Westview Press 1991) 47, 73.
[16] S Fish, 'On Legal Autonomy' (1993) 44 *Mercer Law Review* 737, 741.
[17] Fish, 'Dennis Martinez' (n 15).
[18] Fish, 'Dennis Martinez' (n 15) 1773. In a later work (on the First Amendment and free expression), Fish clarifies that listening to him might have no more effect in the world than pitchers listening to coaches: '[H]earkening to me will lead to nothing. Hearkening to me, from my point of view, is supposed to lead to nothing. ... All I have to recommend is the game, which, since it doesn't need my recommendations, will proceed on its way undeterred and unimproved by anything I have to say.' S Fish, *There's No Such Thing as Free Speech and It's a Good Thing, Too* (Oxford, Oxford University Press, 1993) 307.
[19] Fish, 'Dennis Martinez' (n 15) 1774.

[Additionally], the practice of discoursing on practice does not stand in a relationship of superiority or governance to the practice that is its object.'[20]

For Fish (at least during the time these works were written),[21] meaning was also a matter 'within the discourse'. In a review of Dworkin's book, *Law's Empire*,[22] in the course of deconstructing Dworkin's distinction between a conventionalist and a pragmatist approach to legal interpretation, Fish wrote that

> the possibility of *being* a conventionalist ... depends on the assumption that explicit or literal meanings do in fact exist, and it is my contention that they do not. ... Meanings only become perspicuous against a background of interpretive assumptions in the absence of which reading and understanding would be impossible. A meaning that seems to leap off the page ... is a meaning that flows from interpretive assumptions so deeply embedded that they have become invisible.[23]

According to Fish, Dworkin's conventionalist has confused 'literal meaning' with the meaning of one among many possible interpretive structures. Under this argument, Dworkin's pragmatist is similarly deluded about the ability to escape interpretive structures – in this case, 'any form of consistency with the past'.[24] Fish writes:

> The very ability to formulate a decision in terms that would be recognizably legal depends on one's having internalized the norms, categorical distinctions, and evidentiary criteria that make up one's understanding of what the law is. ... These are not materials the legal actor thinks *about*; they are the material with which and within which he thinks, and therefore whether he "knows" it or not, whether he likes it or not, his very thinking is irremediably historical, consistent with the past in the sense that it flows from the past.[25]

Fish was insistent on the separation between theory and practice, for example, describing 'the mistake of assuming a direct and causal relationship between one's account of one's practice and the actual shape of that practice'.[26] As he writes elsewhere, 'describing a practice' is itself a practice, and one that (whatever its value otherwise) cannot justify the practice in question.[27]

---

[20] ibid 1777–78 (footnote omitted).

[21] Fish was later to reject many of these views and become an intentionalist about meaning. See, eg, S Fish, 'Intention is All There Is: A Critical Analysis of Aharon Barak's Purposive Interpretation in Law' (2008) 29 *Cardozo Law Review* 1109; see also S Fish, 'The Intentionalist Thesis Once More' in G Huscroft and B Miller (eds), *The Challenge of Originalism* (Cambridge, Cambridge University Press, 2011) 105.

[22] Dworkin (n 5).

[23] Fish, 'Still Wrong' (n 1) 403. But notice the parallel argument form, in a passage from Fish's later intentionalist work: 'no piece of language, no matter how "concrete" it may seem, is self-declaring; rather it declares within, and as the product of, an intention ...'. Fish, 'Intention is All There Is' (n 21) 1112, fn 15.

[24] Dworkin (n 5) 92.

[25] Fish, 'Still Wrong' (n 1) 406 (emphasis in original).

[26] Fish, 'Still Wrong' (n 1) 406.

[27] Fish, 'Almost Pragmatism' (n 15) 67.

As regards judicial decision-making and theories about the judicial process, Fish initially seems to make a concession: 'as a practice judging is one of those that includes as a part of its repertoire self-conscious reflection on itself'.[28] However, he goes on to maintain that any references judges make to theory only 'justify a decision reached on other grounds'.[29]

Where many might part company with Fish's approach (during this period) is his characterisation of the way agents are caught in and constructed by their institutional context. For example, Fish discounts Dworkin's worry that judges might want to reach their own preferred outcome to a question (eg, regarding a tortfeasor's possible 'emotional distress' liability to a relative of an accident victim) rather than the outcome required by (the 'law as integrity' reading of) precedent. Fish writes: '*Any* reason that finds its way into a judge's calculation will be per force a *legal* one, and therefore one whose very existence is a function of that history (that is, some view of it) – a history he could not possibly discount even if he declared himself to be doing so.'[30] One can concede much of the power of Fish's point – that we (as lawyers or judges or literary theorists) are deeply marked by our training, our socialization, and the expectations of our communities,[31] and likely can never entirely escape the assumptions and conventions of that background[32] – without entirely denying Dworkin's starting position, that there can be distance between our preferred outcome[33] and the outcome we would consider the 'right' or 'best' by the criteria of our community. To say otherwise would simply be to deny the lived experience of many legal officials without much justification.

A different concern arises if one sees Fish's basic point as one about the importance of tacit knowledge for discovering the truth within one's area of discourse. As Michael Moore points out, 'recipes for discovery are not necessarily

---

[28] Fish, 'Dennis Martinez' (n 15) 1779.

[29] ibid 1781. By contrast, as part of his cultural study of law, Paul Kahn seems to make the opposite point: that theories about law (and doctrinal areas of law) are central to the practice of law, an integral part of how law changes (reforms) over time. Kahn writes: '[T]he study of law is itself a part of the practice of law. An openness to reform is characteristic of the legal order, and a significant source of reform is the study of legal rules and institutions that occurs within the law school. ... Law professors, for the most part, are not studying law, they are doing law.' PW Kahn, 'Freedom, Autonomy, and the Cultural Study of Law' in A Sarat and J Simon (eds), *Cultural Analysis, Cultural Studies, and the Law: Moving beyond Legal Realism* (North Carolina, Duke University Press, 2003) 154, 154.

[30] Fish, 'Still Wrong' (n 1) 412. In the same text, Fish writes that we are 'always in the grip of some vision that is at once the content and the set of practices of the enterprise that in which we are embedded'. ibid 416.

[31] Elsewhere, Fish writes: 'To think within a practice is to have one's very perception and sense of possible and appropriate action issue "naturally" – without further reflection – from one's position as a deeply situated agent.' Fish, 'Dennis Martinez' (n 15) 1788.

[32] And Fish is, of course, correct that 'an insight into the source of our convictions ... will [not] render them less compelling'. Fish, 'Dennis Martinez' (n 15) 1796.

[33] Again, to give due credit to Fish's general point, what a lawyer (or even a law student) might prefer might differ sharply from the views that same person would have had she never gone through the training/indoctrination of legal education.

justifications showing such discoveries to be true; still less are such recipes to be regarded as theories of what there is, [or] what "true" means'.[34]

IV. COMPARE AND CONTRAST

As the above summary of the views of Dworkin and Fish during the time of their debate indicates, the convergence of the two scholars often seems much greater than their disagreements.[35] They were both suspicious of, and found little need for, metaphysical claims. They both urged arguments within a discourse or practice and rejected efforts to bring wholesale challenges to the practice from outside.

However, there *are* clearly differences, though most observers would find these to be fewer and less significant than was at times portrayed in the published exchanges. One point of divergence is the question of the extent to which theory can constrain or guide our actions within a practice. Dworkin takes the conventional view that it can, while Fish (at least during the period of these exchanges) denied it. Here, though, as Michael Moore points out, one could use one of Fish's anti-metaphysical argument moves against him: 'From what viewpoint, context, or situation is Fish making his confident pronouncements about what is possible, what there is, and what makes sense?'[36]

Consider, also, one of the passages where Fish attacks the idea of judges having a '"personal' reason", or a deep psychological bias, causing them to prefer one side in a dispute to another.[37] Fish writes:

> But think of what he would have to do in order to 'work' such 'reasons' into his decision. He could not, of course, simply declare them, because they are not legal reasons and would be immediately stigmatized as inappropriate. Instead, he would be obliged to find recognizably legal reasons that could lead to an outcome in harmony with his prejudices; but if he did that he would not be ruled by those prejudices, but by the institutional requirement that only certain kinds of arguments ... be employed.[38]

Most people would say that judges whose decisions came out one way rather than another because of prejudices, but who worked to make it look like the

---

[34] MS Moore, 'The Interpretive Turn in Modern Theory: A Turn for the Worse' (1989) 41 *Stanford Law Review* 871, 910.

[35] Of course, I am far from the first person to note the similarities of the two scholars' positions. See, eg, Moore (n 34) 908; D Patterson, 'The Poverty of Interpretive Universalism: Toward the Reconstruction of Legal Theory' (1993) 72 *Texas Law Review* 1, 3 ('Dworkin and Fish are allied at the deepest level of philosophical conviction'.).

[36] Moore (n 34) 912. The closest Fish comes to offering a response to such a challenge is in Fish, 'Dennis Martinez' (n 15) 1784, fn 28: eg, 'The thesis of anti-foundationalism is not that there are no foundations, but that whatever is taken to be foundational has to be established in the course of argument and debate and does not exist to the side of argument and debate.' As Moore notes, Fish's response here appears to conflate epistemology and metaphysics. Moore (n 34) 912–14.

[37] Fish, 'Still Wrong' (n 1) 412.

[38] ibid.

decisions were required by the legal sources, were being 'ruled' *both* by institutional norms *and* their prejudices, with the two *combining* to produce the final product.[39]

Fish emphasises how much of our thinking and actions are already constrained and determined by our taking up a particular practice.[40] And he argues persuasively that there is a kind of understanding that informs and shapes how rules are understood, rather than itself (the understanding) being the product of rules.[41] In partial contrast, it is central to Dworkin's view that social practices can and should be modified in line with a better understanding (ie, a better theory) of the practice's purpose(s). Of course, there are occasions where it can be shown that the principles that we think are guiding us may not in fact be doing so.[42] But there are also numerous examples of – for example – great athletes testifying that small adjustments to how they perform, adjustments based on theories and coaching, have had real effects.[43] And Fish gives us little reason to question that theory/teaching/coaching can affect performance other than conclusory statements to that effect.[44]

Both Fish and Dworkin emphasised the importance of thinking within (and not criticising from outside) a practice or discourse. If one might, upon reflection, still prefer Dworkin's view about the potential role that reflection and theory might play within a practice, one should not ignore Fish's insights, that theory is often a separate activity, whose impact on our actions and decisions is easy to overstate.

---

[39] When Fish writes (later in the same discussion) that 'if I am deeply enough embedded in some principled enterprise, the conflict [between personal preference and principle] will never be actualized because some preferences simply will not come into play', ibid 413, he is ignoring or downplaying his own example of how institutional actors can, through their actions and decisions, often serve *both* personal preference and principle. On that point, see also JC Hutcheson, Jr, 'The Judgment Intuitive: The Function of the "Hunch" in Judicial Decision' (1929) 14 *Cornell Law Quarterly* 274; D Kennedy, *A Critique of Adjudication (fin de siècle)* (Cambridge, Mass, Harvard University Press, 1997). A similar objection to Fish is made by Dworkin in Dworkin (n 9) 386, fn 23.

[40] As Fish writes: 'Those who move within these contexts [baseball, law school, classrooms in general, marriages, halfway houses] do so with almost no freedom because their actions flow from the categories of understanding – stipulated definitions – and deeply assumed senses of purpose they have internalized as a condition of entry and informed participation.' S Fish, 'How Come You Do Me Like You Do – A Response to Dennis Patterson' (1993) 72 *Texas Law Review* 57, 58.

[41] S Fish, 'Fish v. Fiss' (1984) 36 *Stanford Law Review* 1325, 1330.

[42] See, eg, DA Farber, 'Do Theories of Statutory Interpretation Matter? A Case Study' (2000) 94 *Northwestern University Law Review* 1409 (offering empirical evidence that theories of statutory interpretation 'adopted' by judges do not affect their decisions on cases).

[43] See, eg, T Williams and J Underwood, *The Science of Hitting* (New York, Simon & Schuster 1982) (advice on hitting used by, and passed along by, one of baseball's best hitters). As Dworkin writes in response to Fish, and referencing T Williams: 'The last player who hit .400, fifty years ago, was the greatest hitter of modern times, and he built a theory before every pitch.' Dworkin (n 9) 382 (footnote omitted).

[44] Eg, Fish (n 41) 1347, fn 44: 'It is my position that theory has no consequences, at least on the level claimed for it by its practitioners.'

2
Fish versus Dworkin: Sound and Fury, But ...?

LARRY ALEXANDER

I. INTRODUCTION

I AM GOING to look back at the Fish/Dworkin exchange in the 1980s and ask: 'What were the presuppositions of the antagonists?', 'Are these presuppositions defensible?', and 'How should we think about the issues on which the antagonists locked horns?' My conclusion is that Dworkin was arguing based on a view of law that is defective, and Fish was arguing from a postmodern perspective that supports anything and nothing.

II. THE FISH/DWORKIN EXCHANGE IN A NUTSHELL

The first shot in the Fish/Dworkin scholarly 'war' was fired by Dworkin in his 1982 'Law as Interpretation',[1] an article that mentioned Fish only in passing.[2] In the article Dworkin was developing a theory of law that he had begun developing in Chapter Four, 'Hard Cases', of *Taking Rights Seriously*,[3] and that he would fully elaborate in 1986 in *Law's Empire*.[4] He would call that theory 'law as integrity'. But its development in 'Law as Interpretation' is far more than embryonic.

One point about Dworkin's theory that is frequently overlooked is that it is a doctrinal theory, a theory about how to determine the truth of propositions of law, such as whether a tortfeasor who causes a death is liable for the emotional injury suffered by one who observed the incident, or whether the Equal Protection Clause of the Fourteenth Amendment bans preferential treatment of members of minority races by state governments. Although Dworkin is

---

[1] R Dworkin, 'Law as Interpretation' (1982) 9 *Critical Theory* 179.
[2] ibid 199.
[3] R Dworkin, *Taking Rights Seriously* (Cambridge, MA, Harvard University Press, 1977) ch 4.
[4] R Dworkin, *Law's Empire* (Cambridge, MA, Harvard University Press, 1986).

opposed to legal positivism as a jurisprudential theory, positivists are primarily interested in how to identify 'law' and distinguish it from other normative systems, and not in answering doctrinal questions such as those just mentioned. Dworkin does not deny that positivists' law – constitutions, statutes, administrative rules, judicial decisions, and the like – is really law. Rather, Dworkin claims that positivists' law is inadequate for determining what the law is on this or that controversy and thus what judges *should* decide is the law.

One way to understand Dworkin in claiming that law is interpretation is that he views positivists' law as fixing the domain of materials to be interpreted. In *Law's Empire* he refers to the positivists' law as pre-interpretive legal materials.[5] True propositions of law are, however, the product of the best interpretation of these pre-interpretive materials.

And what makes an interpretation of these materials a good interpretation? For Dworkin, it is an interpretation that posits a 'principle' that fits with (most of) these materials diachronically and synchronically and renders them the most morally attractive they can be. In other words, it is an interpretation that displays these materials as exemplifying an attractive principle, that shows them to have the virtue of integrity.

Dworkin analogises judges to authors of a chain novel who must make their chapter 'fit' with previous chapters and make them into the best novel possible. They must interpret the previous chapters in the most attractive way and then make their contributions to the novel's continuation accordingly. And judges likewise must take the positivists' law, interpret it in a way that makes it as morally desirable as possible, and rule accordingly.

Fish replied to Dworkin's 1982 article in 'Working on the Chain Gang.'[6] His basic point was that there are no pre-interpretive materials for judges to interpret. These materials will already themselves be the products of interpretation. In other words, the axis of 'fit' is already itself the product of interpretation, not a matter of brute, uninterpreted facts constraining interpretation. As Fish puts it, in referring to the history with which a legal ruling is supposed to fit:

> The distinction between a 'found' history and an 'invented' one is finally nothing more than a distinction between a persuasive interpretation and one that has failed to convince. One man's 'found' history will be another man's invented history, but neither will ever be, because it could not be, either purely found or purely invented.[7]

As Fish says, referring to Dworkin's desire to forge a middle ground between the judicial freedom that legal realists claim exists and the judicial constraint that legal positivists claim positivists' law imposes,

> As one reads Dworkin's essay the basic pattern of his mistakes becomes more and more obvious. He repeatedly makes two related and mutually reinforcing assumptions: he assumes that history in the form of a chain of decisions has, at some level,

---

[5] ibid 65–66.
[6] S Fish, 'Working on the Chain Gang' (1982) 60 *Texas Law Review* 551.
[7] ibid 559.

the status of a brute fact; and he assumes that wayward or arbitrary behavior in relation to that fact is an institutional possibility. Together these two assumptions give him his project, the project of explaining how a free and potentially irresponsible agent is held in check by the self'-executing constraints of an independent text. Of course by conceiving his project in this way – that is, by reifying the mind in its freedom and the text in its independence – he commits himself to the very alternatives he sets out to avoid, the alternatives of legal realism on the one hand and positivism on the other. As a result, these alternatives rule his argument, at once determining its form and emerging, again and again, as its content.[8]

One can see in Fish's critique of Dworkin the postmodernism orientation for which he is well known. Our view of the world will be a function of the categories we impose on it, categories that come from our language, culture, and experience. There is no view from nowhere, no pure, unfiltered Archimedean perspective available to us. But as Fish well knows, and often says, postmodernism has absolutely no normative valence. One cannot employ it to refute an argument – moral, legal, political, historical, or scientific. As I have said, and as Fish has repeated with approval, if one enlists postmodernism in a debate, one has brought an unarmed soldier to the battle.[9]

The Fish/Dworkin exchange entered a second round with Dworkin responding to Fish[10] followed by a Fish response to Dworkin.[11] Dworkin denies that he is assuming brute, uninterpreted facts – legal, historical, or aesthetic, and Fish replies with examples that Fish claims belie Dworkin's denial. Fish points out several passages in which Dworkin asks what an interpreter must believe to believe his interpretation is correct.[12] But Fish argues that if an interpreter has an interpretation, then he must be convinced of it, else he would not hold it.[13]

Toward the end of Fish's article replying to Dworkin's reply to him, the topic turns to authorial intentions. Fish states that an author's intention is always a matter of the reader's interpretation of the author's text.[14] This looks like Fish's reader response theory of interpreting texts, for which he was well known, but which he later abandoned. (More on this below.) But the section is ambiguous on this point because further along he says the following:

> If we are convinced that the meaning of *Hamlet* is psychodynamic but that Shakespeare intended no such meaning, then we are attributing the meaning to an intentional agent other than Shakespeare, perhaps to the spirit of the age, to some trans-historical truth about human nature, or to the intentional structure of language. And if we are convinced both that Shakespeare intended no psychodynamic meaning

---
[8] ibid.
[9] L Alexander, 'What We Do, and Why We Do It' (1993) 45 *Stanford Law Review* 1885, 1897.
[10] R Dworkin, 'My Reply to Stanley Fish (and Walter Benn Michaels): Please Don't Talk about Objectivity Any More' in W Mitchel (ed), *The Politics of Interpretation* (Chicago, University of Chicago Press, 1983) 287.
[11] S Fish, 'Wrong Again' (1983) 62 *Texas Law Review* 299.
[12] ibid 312 (quoting Dworkin (n 10), 289, 292, 296, and 297).
[13] ibid.
[14] ibid 314.

and that the play displays no such meaning, but decide nevertheless to read it psychodynamically, then we have simply set aside what we know to be the play's meaning and Shakespeare's intention for something else. In neither case, however, will we have sundered meaning or interpretation from intention; we just will have demonstrated, first, that one can conceive of intention as something other than the possession of a 'particular historical person,' and, second, that there are things one can do with texts that are not interpretations of them.[15]

The final salvo in the Fish/Dworkin exchange was fired by Fish several years after his last one.[16] In this article, Fish evaluates what Dworkin says in his 1986 *Law's Empire*[17] that bears on the previous exchanges. Dworkin had contrasted his law as integrity with two other approaches: law as conventionalism and law as pragmatism. The former, essentially the view of legal positivists, has it that law consists of authoritative rules found in constitutions, statutes, administrative rules and judicial precedents and orders. The latter, perhaps a form of natural law theory, would have judges 'do the right thing' as they see it irrespective of what the positivists' laws would command.

Fish argues that neither conventionalism nor pragmatism, as Dworkin conceives of them, is a real possibility. Conventionalism founders on the impossibility of clear guidance from rules that themselves do not depend on the interpretive assumptions of their interpreters. He points out that even the seemingly unambiguous constitutional command that the President be at least 35 years of age could mean the President must be sufficiently mature rather than have lived 35 years since birth.[18] Literalism free of interpretive assumptions, which Fish believes Dworkin's conventionalism requires, is an impossibility.

Pragmatism founders on the fact that no one could decide what was best for the future and jettison, in Dworkin's words, 'any form of consistency with the past'.[19] Fish denies that any person could judge what would be 'best' without a sense of history and of historical arguments about what is 'best'.[20]

Fish argues that Dworkin's law as integrity, rather than being an improvement on conventionalism and pragmatism, itself depends on both of those flawed stances. Dworkin's axis of fit assumes the fixity of uninterpreted brute legal facts – conventionalism. Dworkin's other axis – rendering those synchronic and diachronic legal facts as the expression of the most morally attractive set of principles – will not constrain a judge nor free her from her education, her interpretation of history, her sense of institutional role, and so on. As Fish puts his critique,

> What this means is that 'law as integrity' is not the name of a *special* practice engaged in only by gifted or Herculean judges, but the name of the practice engaged

---

[15] ibid 315–16.
[16] S Fish, 'Still Wrong after All These Years' (1987) 6 *Law & Philosophy* 401.
[17] Dworkin (n 4) 4.
[18] Fish (n 16) 404.
[19] ibid 405 (quoting Dworkin (n 17) 95).
[20] ibid 405–06.

in 'naturally' – without any additional prompting – by any judge whose ways of conceiving his field of action are judicial, that is, by any judge. The moment he sees a case *as* a case, a judge is already seeing it as an item in a judicial history, and at the same moment, he is already in the act of fashioning (with a view toward later telling) a story in which his exposition of the case exists in a seamless continuity with his exposition (and understanding) of the enterprise as a whole. In one of the many places at which he recommends 'law as integrity' as a *method*, Dworkin declares that it is 'possible for any judge to confront fresh and challenging issues as a matter of principle, and this is what law as integrity demands of him' (p.258). My point is that it is impossible for a judge to do anything else and still be acting and thinking like a judge, and that therefore the demands of integrity are always and already being met. Dworkin's conditional clause, 'if he accepts integrity' (p. 177) is superfluous, since acceptance is simultaneous with his acceptance of his role.[21]

And as Fish sums up,

> To summarize, *Law's Empire* has a negative and positive argument. The negative argument warns us against the dangers of conventionalism and pragmatism, but since these are not forms of possible judicial practice, the warning is unnecessary. The positive argument urges us to adopt 'law as integrity', but since that is the form our judicial practice already and necessarily takes, the urging is superfluous. Behind both arguments lies the ideal of inhabiting a forum where principle is pure and personal and political appeals have been eliminated, but since that ideal is either empty or already filled with everything it would exclude, a book commending it to us is finally a book with very little to say.[22]

III. THE FISH/DWORKIN EXCHANGE: A POST-MORTEM

In my opinion, the best way to evaluate the debate in terms of legal theory is to ask two questions: First, what are the implications of their views for cases in which the interpretation of some authoritative legal text is at issue? And second, what are the implications of their views for cases not governed by any authoritative legal text?

A. Cases Governed by Authoritative Legal Texts

Dworkin's view of how to interpret authoritative legal texts is quite unclear. Although Dworkin always claimed that he was not an originalist, I was never sure that his conception of originalism was correct. If, as I would argue, originalism is nothing more than giving legal texts the meaning that their authors intended, then Dworkin at times seems to endorse originalism. For example, in his famous exchange with Justice Scalia, Dworkin pointed out that divorced

---

[21] ibid 414 (emphases and page citations in original).
[22] ibid 417.

from the authors' semantic intentions – the meanings that the authors intended as their audience's uptake – texts can mean anything.[23] That is an argument with which originalists like me would concur.[24] Dworkin then went on to claim that the intended meanings of the clauses of section one of the Fourteenth Amendment[25] were more abstract than Scalia thought[26] – though he provided no evidence to support this.[27]

Perhaps Dworkin rejected originalism because he equated it with a call to adhere to how the authors of the texts would themselves have applied them (original applications originalism). But no originalist that I know of endorses original applications originalism, nor should they. If the legislature passes a law banning poisons, they almost assuredly mean by poisons substances toxic to the human body. If they mistakenly believed tomatoes are toxic, that does not mean an originalist interpreter should interpret the statute to ban tomatoes. In any event, in rejecting original applications originalism, Dworkin would not be rejecting a proper version of originalism. So it remains arguable that Dworkin was himself an originalist in interpreting authoritative legal texts.

At least by 2005, when I invited Fish to a conference on legal interpretation, he was squarely in the camp of giving texts the meanings intended by their authors.[28] In other words, he was now in the intentionalist, not reader response, camp. Of course, in trying to figure out an author's intended meaning, the interpreter will necessarily bring all the conceptual baggage that postmodernists cite. They cannot do otherwise. Still, their quarry is what the actual author of a set of symbols intended as the audience's uptake.

So, it is possible that when matters are sufficiently clarified, Dworkin and Fish are actually on the same page with respect to authoritative legal texts. And in my view, that would be the correct page on which to be.

B. Cases Not Governed by Authoritative Legal Texts

When we turn to cases that come before a court and which no authoritative text appears to govern, what do Fish and Dworkin propose? As far as I can discern, nowhere in his 1980s exchanges with Dworkin does Fish issue prescriptions for

---

[23] See R Dworkin, 'Comment' in A Scalia, *A Matter of Interpretation: Federal Courts and the Law* (New Jersey, Princeton University Press 1997) 115–27.
[24] See LA Alexander, 'Was Dworkin an Originalist?' in WJ Waluchow and S Sciaraffa (eds), *The Legacy of Ronald Dworkin* (Oxford, Oxford University Press, 2016) 299–321.
[25] See U.S. Const., amend. XIV, sect. 1; 'No state shall … deprive any person of life, liberty, or property, without due process of law; nor deny to any person within its jurisdiction the equal protection of the laws.'
[26] He claimed that the authors of the Fourteenth Amendment intended that section one be read to constitutionalise the true conceptions of equality and due process, even if these differed from the authors' conceptions of them. See Dworkin (n 23) 122–23.
[27] See Alexander (n 24) 304–05.
[28] S Fish, 'There Is No Textualist Position' (2005) 42 *San Diego Law Review* 629.

such cases. (Indeed, he offers no prescriptions for cases that *are* governed by authoritative texts; and his intentionalist position with respect to their interpretation does not clearly surface until later). Instead, Fish's emphasis is to deny, contra Dworkin, the existence of pre-interpretive legal data.

Dworkin, on the other hand, did have a prescription, one that is well known. He would have had the court survey all the legal decisions – constitutional, statutory, administrative, and judicial – sychronically and diachronically, and formulate the most morally attractive principle that fits with (most of) those decisions. That principle would show that the government was acting with 'integrity' in its coercive measures. And that principle would be the 'law' that governs the case at hand.

Over a quarter century ago, Kenneth Kress and I wrote a lengthy article criticising Dworkin's account of legal principles, the account that he developed most fully in *Law's Empire*.[29] We argued that principles as Dworkin understood them – norms with the dimension of weight – could not be derived from the array of legal decisions in the manner Dworkin described. Moreover, the most morally attractive approach to existing legal materials would be to apply correct moral norms in the cases not governed by authoritative texts. Correct moral norms would take account of the effects of past legal decisions but would not be deformed by having to 'fit' with those that were morally mistaken. In Dworkin's terms, we were arguing for conventionalism in cases covered by authoritative texts and pragmatism in cases not so covered.

Dworkin had raised an objection to applying moral norms rather than legal norms to these cases. He argued that if a plaintiff could not show that she possessed a *legal* right to recover, the defendant had a *legal* right that he not be held liable to the plaintiff. That legal right of the defendant showed that there was always 'law' available to dispose of a case, even if there were no authoritative texts, including precedent court decisions, that governed it.[30]

As Michael Bayles and I demonstrated, in an article critical of *Taking Rights Seriously*, this 'defendant's right' argument was untenable.[31] We hypothesised a case in which the boundary between A's and B's property was described as the midpoint of the river than ran between the properties. Years later, the river altered its course, as rivers tend to do. Its new midpoint gave A more property and B less property than before. A wants to claim the boundary is the new midpoint of the river; B wants to claim the boundary is the old midpoint (which would give him land across the river). The jurisdiction has never had a law or a case dealing with this issue. How would Dworkin's 'defendant's right' apply in a lawsuit over the boundary dispute?

---

[29] L Alexander and K Kress, 'Against Legal Principles' in A Marmor (ed), *Law and Interpretation* (Oxford, Oxford University Press, 1995) 279–327, reprinted in (1997) 82 *Iowa Law Review* 739.
[30] R Dworkin, 'Seven Critics' (1977) 11 *Georgia Law Review* 1202, 1215–16.
[31] L Alexander and M Bayles, 'Hercules or Proteus? The Many Theses of Ronald Dworkin' (1980) 5 *Social Theory and Practice* 267, 282–83.

What we showed is that if A sued B to quiet title to the accretion on A's side of the river, then because there was no law in the jurisdiction for A to rely on, B, invoking Dworkin's defendant's right, should prevail. The law would then be that the old midpoint is the boundary. On the other hand, if B sued A to quiet title to the accretion, A would have the defendant's right on his side and would prevail. The law would then be that the new midpoint is the boundary. So the law dealing with accretion due to rivers' changing course would depend on who sued whom to quiet title, a completely arbitrary basis for determining the law.

So Dworkin's objection to pragmatism – that it amounts to retroactive laws – could not be saved by positing a pre-existing 'defendant's right' law. Pragmatism can take into account any unfairness of surprise and misplaced reliance without the legerdemain of an artificial defendant's right.

IV. CONCLUSION

What can we take away from the Fish/Dworkin exchange of the 1980s? I think very little. Fish successfully scored his postmodernist points against Dworkin's assumption of pre-interpretive legal (and aesthetic) materials. Dworkin was working towards his elaboration of law as integrity that reached full flower in *Law's Empire*. Neither had much to say in the exchange about the interpretation of authoritative legal texts. Although the exchange was interesting and provocative, for me, at least, it left legal theory pretty much untouched.

3

Explaining Us to Ourselves

JEREMY WALDRON

I. DO JUDGES NEED THEORY?

RONALD DWORKIN THINKS they do. He says that jurisprudence (which is another word for legal theory) is the 'silent prologue to any decision at law'. Any argument made by a judge in a courtroom, says Dworkin, 'assumes the kind of abstract foundation jurisprudence offers, and when rival foundations compete, a legal argument assumes one and rejects others'.[1]

What sort of theory do judges need? Well, according to Dworkin, they need at least the following. They need an account of legality or, as it is sometimes called, 'the Rule of Law' – an account of what it is for a society to be governed under the auspices of legal practice rather than in some other way. 'Each judge's interpretive theories,' says Dworkin, 'are grounded in his own convictions about the "point" – the justifying purpose or goal or principle – of legal practice as a whole.'[2] They need such convictions because legal decision-making has a peculiar character. It decides the issues it addresses – political issues, important issues, issues about the use of force in society for good or for ill – by reference to the way things are being done already and the way they have been done in the past. Dworkin sums this up in a proposition that I shall label 'Λ' (*lambda*, for law), because I am going to refer to it many times:

> (Λ) Law insists that force not be used or withheld, no matter how useful that would be to ends in view, ... except as licensed or required by individual rights and responsibilities flowing from past political decisions about when collective force is justified.[3]

One imagines that decisions might be made in other ways than this. Many people think political decision-making should look simply to the future, not to whether there is a warrant in the past for the decision being taken. They think of it as proceeding in a pragmatic forward-looking spirit to advance 'ends in view' like general prosperity or social justice. But according to Λ, legal decisions do

---

[1] R Dworkin, *Law's Empire* (Cambridge, MA, Belknap 1986) 90.
[2] ibid 88–9.
[3] ibid 93.

not and should not proceed in this manner. Legal practice looks to 'past political decisions of the right sort' and it insists that any present decision it licenses must flow from that past in the right sort of way.

That is what law does. Why? Well, that is the key question for legal theory. A theory of law tries to explain *why* we organise the justification of coercive decisions in this way. According to Dworkin, we have to ask: 'Is there any point to requiring public force to be used only in ways conforming to rights and responsibilities that "flow from" past political decisions? ... [I]f there is such a point, what is it?' Is it a matter of predictability, or fairness, or the protection of expectations? Or what? And what reading of 'flow from' – what notion of consistency with past decisions – best serves the point of this approach to political decision-making?[4]

I propose we take this set of questions and the answers we might come up with as our paradigm of legal theory and use it to examine a contention Stanley Fish has put forward, that theory in law is unnecessary. I want to anchor the Fish/Dworkin argument from beginning to end in the challenge posed by the distinctive character of legal practice. Why does legal decision-making have the character it does? How can we make sense of Λ? And here is a broader dimension for legal theory: why does the ideal we call 'the Rule of Law' aim to extend that kind of decision-making to the exercise of public power generally? These questions call for public argumentation, not the dismissal of theory.

II. SOME MISUNDERSTANDINGS

Let me begin by addressing a couple of preliminary issues with Dworkin's formulation. In *Law's Empire*, Dworkin characterises the sort of theory he is looking for as an *interpretation* of legal practice. Λ is our focus; Dworkin says we should try to *interpret* this thing that judges and lawyers do. Is 'interpret' the right word? Judges and lawyers also have to interpret legal texts – precedents, statutes, and the Constitution – in order to decide the cases that come before them (pursuant to the account of legal practice that we are considering). Is this the same sense of 'interpretation'? Dworkin thinks it is. He thinks that the stages of interpretation – a pre-interpretive identification of the object to be interpreted; the interpretive attribution of a point or purpose to that object; and a post-interpretive stage at which we reconceive the object under interpretation in light of that point or purpose[5] – are the same for texts and for practices. Many jurists disagree: they understand the idea of interpreting a text, but they think that confusion results from describing an investigation into the point of a practice – like the practice described in Λ – as 'interpretation'.[6] I do not want to get into

---

[4] ibid 94.
[5] ibid 45–73.
[6] See M Moore, 'The Interpretive Turn in Modern Theory: A Turn for the Worse?' (1989) 41 *Stanford Law Review* 871.

this debate. I shall occasionally make reference to Dworkin's framing of his inquiry as 'interpretation' of Λ. Mostly, I shall use the less controversial phrase 'inquiry into the point' of Λ.

The inquiry into the peculiar character of legal decision-making that Dworkin invited us to undertake is sometimes misunderstood. Alani Golanski reads Dworkin's Λ as saying that 'law's main point [is] to justify political coercion'.[7] But the questions for jurisprudence that Dworkin identifies in *Law's Empire* are not about coercion's justification as such. Λ is about the point of the particular *approach* law takes to the justification of coercion. Why does justifying the use of coercive force have to have this character of being oriented in a backwards-looking way to past political decisions? That is the question. And a theory of law is, in the first instance, a theory of *that*.

Golanski's reading treats Dworkin's inquiry as though it sets out to produce straightforwardly normative political philosophy. That is a mistake, for the reason I have just stated. But political philosophy is never very far away from the Dworkinian inquiry, and it is important to understand its presence. The feature of legal practice that Dworkin identifies in Λ is, as he argues in a later essay, bound up with the idea of *the Rule of Law*.[8] Now, the Rule of Law is not an easy idea to make sense of.[9] When it erupts into politics, as it did in the most recent American election and as it did also in the 2000 election, it presents us with an array of difficult and controversial questions about the role played by state and federal judges in our politics.[10] The answers to these questions do not come naturally. Both on electoral issues and in constitutional issues, judges have to think about how their distinctive style of decision-making takes its place in the overall process of governance. How do legal argument and judicial decision-making fit with the democratic character of our polity? How is law's backward-looking character consistent with the progressive and forward-looking character of our politics? Fish says that judges by and large do not articulate anything about these challenging aspects of their craft. But even if he is right about that – and I am convinced he is not – other people, who are not in the first instance engaged in professional legal practice, do need to wrestle with these challenges. The Rule of Law is a leading element of our political morality, and many who put their faith in it and try to make sense of it are not judges or lawyers but voters and politicians. They need to understand the demands that legality places upon them and the reasons they have for submitting their policy proposals to the discipline of Λ. In other words, whatever the professionals say, the wider community cries out for a theory that addresses the role of legal practice and the place of its peculiarity in a society ruled by law.

---

[7] A Golanski, 'Legal Theory from the Regulative Point of View' (2014) 44 *Cumberland Law Review* 1, 38 and 51.
[8] R Dworkin, 'Hart's Postscript and the Character of Political Philosophy' (2004) 24 *Oxford Journal of Legal Studies* 1, 23ff.
[9] See, eg, T Bingham, *The Rule of Law* (London, Penguin, 2010) 5.
[10] See J Waldron, 'Is the Rule of Law an Essentially Contested Concept (in Florida)?' (2002) 21 *Law and Philosophy* 137.

III. STANLEY FISH ON THE ISSUE OF CONSTRAINT

So, first: do *judges* need the sort of theory Dworkin is looking for? Stanley Fish says they do not. As we shall see in section IX of this chapter, Fish's position is not entirely consistent. But much of the time he says judges have no need of any theory at all. They have their role, which they fill, and their craft, which they exercise almost unthinkingly whenever they put on a robe and enter a courtroom or whenever they open a set of law reports – in leather-bound volumes or on their computers – to read the authorities relevant to a case that has been briefed before them. They are not puzzled by Λ, ie, by what I have called the peculiarity of legal practice, says Fish. They just go right ahead doing what Λ requires, looking for a solution that will mesh with prior authority. If asked what a judge does, Fish's answer is: '[A] judge thinks about cases by inserting them into a history of previous cases that turn on similar problems.'[11]

Most importantly, judges do not need to be told to do this. Such a demand would be uncalled-for, says Fish, because already there is not a man or woman in the legal profession, not a man or woman in the judiciary, who does not think it important to locate their understanding of any case that comes before them in the context of past decisions by earlier judges, legislators, or constitution-framers. '[N]o competent legal practitioner could act in a way that did not attend to institutional history'.[12]

Suppose Fish is right about this. Would that be an embarrassment for Dworkin? Did Dworkin think, as Fish says over and over again, that judges needed to be *urged* or *constrained* to follow Λ (urged by a theorist, constrained by a theory)?[13] Not at all. That most judges follow Λ – indeed (if Fish is right) that most of them do it almost instinctively – is the settled practice of theirs that requires explanation, not something we need to bring into existence. Dworkin would say the practice is *given* at what he calls the pre-interpretive stage.[14] This is what requires interpretation; this is the practice whose point or purpose we have inquired into. So no, judges do not need to be argued into it. The point about their needing or not needing constraint is a red herring. We still need to make sense of it even in its character as something they 'naturally' do.

---

[11] S Fish, *There's No Such a Thing as Free Speech: And It's a Good Thing, Too* (Oxford, Oxford University Press, 1994) 225. See also S Fish, 'Still Wrong after All These Years' (1987) 6 *Law and Philosophy* 401, 414: 'The moment he sees a case as a case, a judge is already seeing it as an item in a judicial history, and at the same moment he is already in the act of fashioning (with a view to later telling) a story in which his exposition of the case exists in a seamless continuity with his exposition (and understanding) of the enterprise as a whole.'

[12] M Robertson, *Stanley Fish on Philosophy, Politics and Law: How Fish Works* (Cambridge, Cambridge University Press, 2014) 255.

[13] Fish, 'Still Wrong' (n 11) 408 et passim.

[14] Dworkin (n 1) 65–6.

For consider this: the fact that something is taken for granted is not a reason for exempting it from philosophical consideration. Many of the things we set out to explain in philosophy are things that no one disputes. We want to get an articulate sense of what it is that we are (unanimously and/or implicitly) committed to, in order to understand ourselves better and in order to explore some of the implications that such understanding of our practice may yield. Sometimes things we do not understand cannot be understood without a more articulate sense of the things we think we do understand. Philosophers often affect puzzlement about common practice and they ponder it as though it were unfamiliar, as though they had no common sense. That is how they do their work: they make the implicit explicit. And it is their vocation to persevere in that long after the point when a man of the world would have put down his logic and gone home to play backgammon. Unless their speculations appear, by ordinary standards, 'cold, and strain'd and ridiculous', they are not doing philosophy.[15]

IV. PRAGMATISM AS DEFAULT

Even if the judges are just doing what comes naturally, what they are doing naturally is quite peculiar: looking over their shoulder all the time, rather than just looking forward, when they make a decision. It can be done; it is done; it may even be done naturally; but it does not seem to make any sense. Every so often someone points this out. It may be a critic of the judiciary or it may be a judge who styles him- or herself as a pragmatist. Judge Richard Posner claimed to be a pragmatist and he accepted this self-description: 'a pragmatist judge always tries to do the best he can do for the present and the future, unchecked by any felt duty to secure consistency in principle with what other officials have done in the past'.[16] Stanley Fish has doubts about whether Judge Posner ever lived up to this.[17] Let us put that question aside. If such a jurist did not exist, we might have to invent him or her, to get the measure of what we are committed to.

Certainly, this is what Dworkin had in mind when he invoked the figure of the pragmatist in *Law's Empire*. We are to imagine a judge, a jurist, a politician, or a citizen who not only refuses to give an account of Λ but repudiates Λ altogether.

---

[15] See J Waldron, 'What Plato Would Allow' in I Shapiro and JW DeCew (eds), *Nomos 37: Theory and Practice* (New York, New York University Press, 1995) 138, 171, quoting D Hume, *A Treatise of Human Nature* (L. A Selby–Bigge ed, 1888) 269.

[16] R Posner, 'Pragmatic Adjudication' (1996) 18 *Cardozo Law Review* 1, 4. This is a modified version of an attribution by Dworkin (at *Law's Empire* (n 1) 161), which Posner says he is willing to accept.

[17] S Fish, 'Almost Pragmatism: Richard Posner's Jurisprudence' (1990) 57 *University of Chicago Law Review* 1447.

He rejects the idea of limiting political decisions to those that can be based on legal rights flowing from past political decisions about when collective force is justified. Pragmatism is a 'skeptical conception' of Λ.[18] Now, what Dworkin said about this possible position is telling:

> The fact that a true pragmatist rejects the idea of legal rights is not a decisive argument against that conception [i.e. against pragmatism]. For it is not self-evident that the idea of legal rights is attractive. Or even sane. On the contrary, it is quite easy to make that idea seem foolish.[19]

Why this preoccupation with the past? Why not just try to make things the best they can be for the future? Of course, people will disagree about that, ie, they will disagree about what makes one outcome better or more reasonable than another. But so what?

> It is not a good objection to [the pragmatist position] that different pragmatist judges will make different decisions .... [T]hey will, but in hard cases judges must make controversial judgments whichever conception of law they hold. ... Pragmatism claims to risk error at least about the right issue. If judicial divisions and controversial judgments are in any case inevitable, the pragmatist asks, why should the controversy not be about what really matters ....[20]

Dworkin appears to be acknowledging here that, in a sane and decent polity devoted to making things better for its citizens, pragmatism will be the default position, one that we should have to be argued out of if we are to give our allegiance to Λ. And so the task of legal theory – now a quite forbidding task rather than a complacent one – is to understand the shift away from that default.

Here is the point. Fish seems to think that Dworkin's concern is to rein in the pragmatist, to constrain him to follow the law rather than just make things better by his own lights. As one of Fish's followers puts it: 'The fear of the unconstrained legal actor looms large ... and Dworkin feels compelled to find a way to bring him under control.'[21] Fish thinks this is a fool's errand, for he does not believe there can possibly be a judge in need of such constraint. But that misconceives Dworkin's concern. Dworkin's concern is not that the pure pragmatist, if such a jurist existed, needed to be restrained. His point is: *the pragmatist needs to be answered.* Why should we not all be pragmatists? The challenge is to make sense of our allegiance to Λ in light of the possibility that pragmatism defines. Intellectually, the pragmatist position is the one that must be displaced. So even if we follow Fish's advice and abandon any sense of the need for constraint, there is still a need for us to articulate and reflect on our theory.

---

[18] Dworkin (n 1) 95.
[19] ibid 162.
[20] ibid 163.
[21] Robertson (n 12) 253.

V. DENNIS MARTINEZ

Fish suggests that such inquiries always involve a mistake. He famously cites as a sort of analogy some remarks by a pitcher in baseball, Dennis Martinez.[22] When Martinez was asked by a sportswriter what words of wisdom his manager had imparted to him before he went to the mound in a particular game, the pitcher said he had been told to 'throw strikes and keep 'em off the bases'. Martinez added: 'And I said, "O.K."' Fish is very excited by this laconic response, which he calls brilliant, 'both as an account of what transpires between fully situated members of a community and as a wonderfully dead-pan rebuke to the outsider who assumes the posture of an analyst'.[23] Martinez, he says, drove 'the lesson home with a precision Wittgenstein might envy: "What else could I say? What else could he say?"' There is no theory available here, says Fish. What the manager told Martinez 'amounts to "Go out and do it," where "do it" means go and play the game. That is why both [the manager]'s counsel and Martinez' response must be without content.'[24]

It is not that there is nothing to it; you or I could not pitch in the major leagues. But having the requisite skills is a matter of know-how; it is not a matter of knowing that some theory is true.[25] The know-how is Martinez's – embedded in his being. Martinez has internalised whatever understanding he has of his role and he keeps it close to his chest. Indeed, Fish sometimes says that Martinez just *is* his knowledge of the game. Or that the knowledge is embedded in the relevant community: it is know-how among ballplayers, of which Martinez partakes simply by being there. He and his team-mates derive all the assistance they need from just taking on their role and exercising it thoughtlessly within the community of those who play the game with them.

Who knows whether this is a good way to think about baseball? Did Dennis Martinez tell the truth to the sportswriter? If he did, is this sort of interaction between pitcher and manager common or exceptional? Is it sensible in all circumstances? What if a bunt is in prospect or a pitch-out is indicated? Same thing? Just 'Go out and do it'? What if we vary the example slightly, so that we raise an issue about the ethics of the game – a pitcher involved in sign-stealing like the Houston Astro's in 2017 and 2018?[26] Again, 'Just go out and do it'?

---

[22] S Fish, 'Dennis Martinez and the Uses of Theory' (1987) 96 *Yale Law Journal* 1773. The story has been told perhaps too often in the Fish/Dworkin debate; certainly, one should look at Steven Winter's debunking of it in 'Bull Durham and the Uses of Theory' (1990) 42 *Stanford Law Review* 639. But, as we shall see, there is no better way of illustrating what is wrong with Fish's position than to compare this anecdote about know-how in baseball with the transparency demands of the Rule of Law.
[23] Fish (n 22) 1773.
[24] ibid 1774.
[25] For the distinction, see, eg, G Ryle, 'Knowing How and Knowing That' (1945–6) 46 *Proceedings of the Aristotelian Society: New Series* 1.
[26] N Vigdor, '"The Houston Astros' Cheating Scandal: Sign–Stealing, Buzzer Intrigue and Tainted Pennants, *New York Times*, 16 July 2020.

Fish's case is less than convincing on its own ground, and it certainly does not generalise when we stop playing games. He seems to think that this celebration of the taciturn and the implicit applies to roles of all sorts: 'Competent members of a practice not only already know what to do – they need no theory to tell them', he says. '[T]hey can do nothing else, at least as long as they think of themselves as occupying this role (lawyer, baker, candlestick maker) rather than another'.[27] And of course he extends it to adjudication. 'Judging,' he says, 'cannot be understood as an activity in the course of which practitioners regularly repair for guidance to an underlying set of rules and principles.'[28] They just use their judicial know-how. That is Fish's view.

To this, Michael Moore puts a telling question: 'Isn't it just dogmatic for Fish to equate judging ... with the exercise of physical skills like [baseball] pitching?'[29] Not all roles can either afford or be permitted the hermetic silence that Fish attributes to Martinez and his manager. Bamboozling sportswriters is one thing. But sometimes articulacy and openness to outsiders are crucial to a given role. In exactly this respect, judging has features that sharply distinguish it from baseball.

Fish's characterisation of Dennis Martinez – persuasive or unpersuasive as it may be – cannot possibly work for a judge. Judges perform a complex *public* function for which they are *publicly accountable*. They may not be electorally accountable, but they owe the public and parties that may possibly come before them an account of what they are doing and how and why. Silence is out of the question; transparency is what their craft requires. Moreover, even apart from judicial accountability, thoughtful members of a society will want to think about how they are ruled and reflect on the legal heritage that informs their political processes. Thinking about what law is, is not just something philosophers do to irritate Fish's judges. As Joseph Raz put it, '"the law" is a concept used by people to understand themselves'.[30] And the quest for such self-understanding is not to be denied in the fashion of Dennis Martinez.

VI. WHO EXACTLY NEEDS THEORY?

The question 'Does X need theory?' is ambiguous. (1) It might refer to what X takes to be necessary for X's pursuit of his own aims? Or (2) it might refer to what we or others need from X (as when a police officer says to X: 'You need to step out of the car'). Fish, I think, adopts understanding (1) of the need-question when he says judges have no need of theory to help them in what they take themselves to be doing. But I think we are in a better position to grasp the importance

---

[27] S Fish, 'Response: Interpretation Is Not a Theoretical Issue' (1999) 11 *Yale Journal of Law and the Humanities* 513.
[28] Fish (n 22) 1785.
[29] Moore (n 6) 915.
[30] J Raz, *Ethics in the Public Domain* (Oxford, Oxford University Press, 1994) 237.

of legal theory, if we adopt understanding (2) of the question. We should ask: do *we* – the rest of us (by which I mean citizens and politicians) – need there to be a theory of adjudication? And if the answer is Yes, then we can approach what is needful for the judges from that direction. Is it necessary – again, necessary for the rest of us – that judges should have a theory in mind as they go about making their decisions?

In a liberal democratic society, adjudication is part of the political process. And the character of adjudication is bound up with political values like the Rule of Law. As Dworkin put it,

> Law is a political concept: people use it to form claims of law, that is, claims that the law of some place or other prohibits or permits or requires certain actions, or provides certain entitlements, or has other consequences. An enormous social practice is built around making, contesting, defending and ruling on such claims.[31]

The point is that the Rule of Law is an ideal for all of us, not only the judges. It is part of our civic ideology (in a good sense of that word). Citizens ask: What gives judges the right to settle various important issues conclusively on the basis of the sort of reasoning that judges typically engage in? What gives them the authority?[32] People need to understand what is going on with adjudication, why judicial power is justified, how we make sense of its peculiarities, what its limits are, and how it ought to be exercised. And that understanding has to be realistic (not mythic). The citizens' theory must satisfy the principle of publicity,[33] which means that it must in some sense match what the judges take themselves to be doing. The judges have their theory: as Dworkin puts it, 'If a judge accepts the settled practices of his legal system ... he must, according to the doctrine of political responsibility, accept some general political theory that justifies those practices.'[34] And the citizens have theirs, and these two bodies of theory must match. There must be a sort of fit between the Rule of Law as a civic ideology and people's understanding of law in the practice of adjudication.

The two theories meet up, for example, in the process whereby judges are appointed – nominated and confirmed. Nominators and senators need to share with candidates an understanding of what judging involves.[35] I believe they need to share an understanding – or at the very least, a set of questions – about Λ.

---

[31] R Dworkin, 'Hart's Postscript and the Character of Political Philosophy' (2004) 24 *Oxford Journal of Legal Studies* 1, 19.

[32] We need to be careful here. Fish is right to observe (in Fish (n 22) 1776–7) that legal theory does not itself claim authority: 'The practice of discoursing on practice does not stand in a relationship of superiority or governance to the practice that is its object.' The point is not that theory aspires to be authoritative. It aspires to produce the best account of such authority as adjudication might have. In other words, an account of X's authority is not necessarily an authority over X.

[33] For the principle of publicity, see J Rawls, *A Theory of Justice,* Revised edition (Cambridge, MA, Harvard University Press, 1000) 397–8.

[34] R Dworkin, *Taking Rights Seriously*, Revised edition (Cambridge, MA, Harvard University Press 1978) 105.

[35] Also, in some American jurisdictions, judges are elected and, in those places, electors need to share with candidates an understanding of adjudicative function.

This is particularly important in a country with strong judicial review, where judges have the authority to strike down decisions by elected branches. But it matters even in systems without strong judicial review. It is important that there be a shared understanding in the community, not that people be somehow assured that the judges know it all in a way they cannot disclose.

Now putting it this way is in one sense too simple. Citizens do not just *have* their theories of governance and the rule of law; these are things they disagree about. And the same is true of judges: they too disagree. I will attend to this at greater length in section VIII. For now, it is enough to note that disagreement does not undermine the importance of theory. People show they take theory seriously when they disagree. And a similar point about *match* can be developed: the citizens' disagreements must make contact with the judges' disagreements; they must share a sense of what is at stake and how those stakes play out. And that will not work if the understanding of one side or the other is held close to the chest as a sort of secret know-how.

VII. FROM THE IMPLICIT TO THE EXPLICIT

We may all need theory. But can we have it? Is it available? The notion that skill is resistant to reflection is all over this debate. Michael Moore talks of Fish's commitment to 'tacit knowledge'.[36] Dworkin says that '[Fish] wants ... to picture lawyers and judges as like natural, unreflective athletes: instinctive craftsmen who react unthinkingly to legal problems, ... obeying the ancient practices of their profession because it would be unthinkable to do otherwise.' And Fish himself says that '[t]o think within a practice is to have one's very perception and sense of possible and appropriate action issue "naturally" – without further reflection – from one's position as a deeply situated agent'.[37]

> The internalized 'know-how' or knowledge of 'the ropes' that practice brings is sufficient unto the day and no theoretical apparatus is needed to do what practice is already doing, that is, providing the embedded agent with a sense of relevancies, obligations, directions for action, criteria, etc.[38]

But is that sense of relevancies, obligations, etc *necessarily* implicit? Phenomenologically, perhaps. Dworkin acknowledged as much: '[A]ny judge's opinion is itself a piece of legal philosophy, even when the philosophy is hidden and the visible argument is dominated by citation and lists of facts'.[39] But Fish needs a stronger position than that. His argument will not work without the assumption 'that an interpretive practice cannot be selfconscious and reflexive'.[40]

---

[36] Moore (n 6) 908.
[37] Fish (n 22) 1788.
[38] ibid 1790.
[39] Dworkin (n 1) 90.
[40] R Dworkin, 'Pragmatism, Right Answers, and True Banality' in M Brint and W Weaver (eds), *Pragmatism in Law and Society* (US, Westview, 1991) 359, 380.

One problem with implicit know-how is the difficulty of articulating it elegantly in a formula that can then be made the object of critical discussion. Someone asks you to set out in a series of statements how to ride a bicycle. It can be done, after a manner, in a halting and unconvincing way. But that ragged statement of cyclist's know-how is embarrassingly clumsy compared to the grace of bike-riding itself. I think it is part of Fish's argument that the implicit know-how of the judge is bound to be distorted and misrepresented when it is brought to the surface for reflection of the kind I have been saying is necessary.

Actually, I am not sure that such inarticulacy is inevitable.[41] There may be a gain rather than a loss when reflection blows some of the cobwebs away from traditional know-how and dispels some of the mystery. But even if Fish is right, a slight loss in fluency may be a price worth paying. The values that Fish's account touts – that he is afraid we might lose by attempting too much reflection – are essentially aesthetic in character: the graceful performance, elegant know-how, noble silence, and so on. There are other things at stake like transparency, accountability, and self-understanding. An attempt to respect these latter imperatives is admirable, not something to be laughed at or dismissed by insiders on account of its initial clumsiness.

We must expect that judges will find it difficult to put their jurisprudence into words for the citizenry, when they are used to having it embedded in the exercise of legal analysis at a case level in the courtroom and in the writing of their opinions. Some will be better at this than others. And citizens, for their part, will not find it easy to dredge up and articulate whatever bits and pieces of legality-lore have made their way into political consciousness. Misunderstandings will be common as well as disagreements. Sometimes the call for a match between the one and the other understanding will seem like a hopeless assignment. (And academic theorists, with their own habits and vocabulary, may sometimes make things better and sometimes make things worse.) None of this is a reason for abandoning the process of reflection that legal theorising involves. On the contrary, this is exactly what we should expect the early and the middle stages of self-understanding to look like in the life of an engaged and opinionated community.

VIII. DISAGREEMENT

The inelegant, stuttering character of our theorising about Λ – judges' theorising, citizens' theorising, scholars' theorising – will of course be compounded by the difficulty of the topic and the controversies that swirl around it.

Any answer to the background question posed concerning Λ has to do with the Rule of Law; and that is a challenging topic, on any account. Judges, citizens, and legal scholars all find it difficult to figure out what the Rule of Law is,

---

[41] But consider the critique of the possibility of making know-how explicit in Winter (n 22) 676.

what it gives us, and what it requires.⁴² Is it a moral ideal in itself or connected essentially to other moral ideals like justice, dignity, democracy, and human rights?⁴³ How is it related to rules and the rule-wielding mentality?⁴⁴ Does it suppress or sponsor thoughtfulness and wise discretion in public administration? Is it responsible for an excess of litigiousness and a preoccupation with proceduralism in public life? How does the contrast between rule by law and rule by men stand in relation to rule by judges.⁴⁵ And how is all of this related to the peculiarity of legal and judicial practice as it is set out in Λ? These are difficult questions and it is to be expected that people will disagree about them, to the extent that they can articulate determinate answers.

Dworkin organised the middle chapters of *Law's Empire* around competing answers that might be given to his questions about Λ: he devoted chapters to the rival answers offered by *conventionalism*, *pragmatism*, and *law as integrity*.⁴⁶ In a later article, he identified a couple of other opposing answers: *accuracy* (about moral ideals) and *efficiency*, as well as his own favoured *integrity*.⁴⁷ He attempted to map these various answers onto familiar positions in jurisprudence, with mixed results: there is considerable debate about whether he was fairly representing legal positivism, for example, in any of these options.⁴⁸ But it is not my purpose here to discuss what Dworkin thought the options were; I just want to note his acknowledgement – indeed his insistence – that the theorising about Λ that he thinks is called for is bound to be contentious. The nature of the issues explains the controversy, and the seriousness of what is at stake explains people's persistence with it. Citizens' concerns and advocacy over the Rule of Law and what it involves will yield a diversity of views – not necessarily phrased in the terms used by Dworkin and other scholars, but addressing in lay terms the importance of law and precedent in our system. Judges too will disagree about this; and they too will articulate their competing views in terms that do not necessarily represent Dworkin's options; they will talk about things like originalism, living-tree constitutionalism, doctrinal formalism, and so on. Judges disagree about how to proceed in interpretation. They talk about it; and in our hearing, they excoriate each other's views.

As I have said several times now, the existence of these layers of disagreement is not a problem for Dworkin's defence of theory; it is just what one should

---

⁴² See, eg, Bingham (n 9) 5. (Tom Bingham was Lord Chief Justice of England).
⁴³ See J Raz, 'The Rule of Law and its Virtue' in his collection *The Authority of Law* (Oxford, Oxford University Press, 1979) 211.
⁴⁴ A Scalia, 'The Rule of Law as a Law of Rules' (1989) 56 *University of Chicago Law Review* 1175.
⁴⁵ For a discussion of these and other themes, see Waldron (n 10).
⁴⁶ Dworkin (n 1) chs 4, 5, and 6.
⁴⁷ Dworkin (n 31) 26–9.
⁴⁸ On his disagreement about positivism with Jules Coleman, for example, see R Dworkin, 'Thirty Years On' (2011) 115 *Harvard Law Review* 1655, 1682–3. See also S Shapiro, *Legality* (Cambridge, MA, Harvard University Press 2011) 261–9 and 288–92.

expect. But it is a problem for Fish and his claims about the unreflective character of adjudication. For if among judges a diversity of inclinations are experienced on matters this important and if those inclinations rival and challenge one another, then judges are bound to feel pressure to bring them to consciousness, articulating them so they can defend their respective positions and (in the best case) consider also what is to be said on the other side. Intelligent people will want to do no less. But then Fish's analogy between the ingenuousness of Dennis Martinez and the character of judicial thought and activity will have to be abandoned.

IX. SCRAMBLED FISH

Has Stanley Fish's position been fairly represented here? Well, it depends. Dworkin maintains that judges, like the rest of us, need to articulate a theory that explains the point of Λ (the proposition about law that we began with). Fish says that such a theory is unavailable because judicial craft is like Dennis Martinez's inarticulate skill at pitching: it is embedded implicitly in adjudication as that is practiced by the community of judges; it need not – indeed it cannot – be made explicit for the purposes of legal philosophy. I have argued that that judges have no choice but to try to make their theory explicit, because they owe an account of it – an account of what they are doing in relation to the Rule of Law – to citizens of the broader community whom they serve. Not only that, but judges disagree with one another about legal practice and about how it relates to the ideals of good governance under the auspices of the Rule of Law. So even if they were not accountable, they would still have to make conscious choices about which elements of their profession's fractured and conflicting self-understandings they want to defend and subscribe to. If these criticisms are sustained, then Fish's account collapses.

Professor Fish is not unaware of these difficulties with his position. And when no one is looking he scrambles to accommodate the force of some of the points that his critics have made. So, for example, he qualifies the Dennis Martinez conception in the following way:

> [T]he fact that interpretation is not a theoretical problem because you engage in it merely by being a member of a practice (it is not an additional or special activity) and because your engagement is not a matter of choice (to opt out of interpretation is to opt out of membership) *does not mean that interpretation is free of problems and disputed questions.*[49]

In other words, he concedes the point about disagreement. Can he reconcile that concession with the claim that 'theory', such as it is, remains implicit? Well,

---

[49] Fish (n 27) 514 (emphasis added).

he tries. He says, without reason or argument, that all the questions that are in dispute

> are empirical – questions of evidence, precedent, injury, remedy – and because they are empirical – shaped by and responsive to the particular histories of self-revising disciplines – there is nothing general to say about them.[50]

There can be no disagreement at the abstract level is what he is implying. Readers can figure out for themselves whether this accurately represents the tendentious theorising about adjudication that one hears from a Scalia, for example, or a Posner.

Much the same may be said about Fish's attempt to cover himself against the accusation of having said that judicial thinking is never reflective, never explicit. 'When I use phrases like "without reflection" and "immediately" and "obviously" I do not mean to preclude self-conscious deliberation on the part of situated agents.'[51] Oh, alright. He is sometimes willing to acknowledge that 'as a practice judging is one of those that includes as a part of its repertoire self-conscious reflection on itself'.[52] How is this reconciled with his broader position? I do not know. I think he hopes that, although these passages are there so he can accuse critics of misrepresentation, they will nevertheless be forgotten when the implications of his broader position are being discussed.

Consider, too, this passage from the end of the 'Dennis Martinez' article in which Fish shows himself anxious not to have argued too broadly.

> I should acknowledge here that what I intend by 'theory' may seem to some to be excessively narrow. I reserve that word for an abstract or algorithmic formulation that guides or governs practice from a position outside any particular conception of practice. … To be sure, the word 'theory' is often used in other, looser ways, to designate high order generalizations, or strong declarations of basic beliefs, or programmatic statements of political or economic agendas, or descriptions of underlying assumptions. Here my argument is that to include such activities under the rubric of theory is finally to make everything theory, and if one does that there is nothing of a general kind to be said about theory.[53]

This is an irritating claim and, if taken at face value, it may mean Fish stipulates he is not really talking about anything that Dworkin is interested in. After all, a judge's interpretation of Λ or a citizen's or scholar's understanding of the Rule of Law may easily be removed from Fish's narrow term 'theory' and crammed into a category such as 'high order generalizations, or strong declarations of basic beliefs, or programmatic statements of political or economic agendas, or descriptions of underlying assumptions'. If the sort of pressure I have been

---

[50] ibid 514–15.
[51] S Fish, 'Fish v. Fiss' (1984) 36 *Stanford Law Review* 1325, 1334n.
[52] Fish (n 22) 1779.
[53] Fish (n 22) 1779. For a suggestion that Fish 'stacks the deck' with his tendentious definition of theory, see Winter (n 22) 646.

adducing is ever applied to Fish's basic position, he will just say he was not talking about that sort of theory.

Indeed, when pressed, Fish has a word for what the rest of us call legal theory. He calls it *rhetoric*. Now this term may be taken more or less seriously. Rhetoric might be viewed as something purely decorative: 'building ... castles ever higher in the non-resisting air', as Fish once described legal philosophy.[54] More seriously, however, Fish cites Aristotle for the proposition that the point of rhetoric is to contribute to political persuasion.[55] And he says judges and lawyers (and presumably also citizens and politicians) resort to it when they want to make their decisions 'presentable'.[56] One can be a cynic and see this as just a matter of salesmanship.[57] Or it may be 'political'[58] in a more respectable sense, where a judge, a politician or a scholar attempts lucidly to connect what is said about the application of law intelligibly to values that everyone knows are important – justice, equality, the common good. Fish is even prepared to say that '[o]nce Dworkin has been recharacterized as a rhetorician rather than a theorist, much of what he says becomes quite acute and to the point',[59] though he doubts whether Dworkin would accept this characterisation 'as someone who is telling us what kinds of stances and poses will best effect our polemical ends'.[60]

I think Fish is quite happy playing back-and-forth with the term 'rhetoric', saying sometimes it is just cover for vanity and polemical self-interest, and saying at other times that he is shocked – shocked! – to hear that anyone might think that is what he meant. His settled position seems to acknowledge that judges are sometimes prisoners of their own rhetoric. They believe in Λ and in the account they give of it. Fish himself, however, shows no inclination to join them in that. He does not accept for a moment that the subject-matter of this legal rhetoric might be worth taking seriously. And my main point has been that legal theory is born of exactly the interplay between those who take it seriously from the bench and those who take it seriously in the processes of the wider political community. Legal theory is an attempt to match one to the other. We need it and I would not denigrate it for the world.

---

[54] Fish (n 27) 514–15 (1999). Maybe some of Dworkin's language answers to this description, as when says: 'The courts are the capitals of law's empire, and judges are its princes.' Dworkin (n 1) 407.

[55] Fish (n 22) 1791: 'Their goal is now persuasion, and they cast around for appropriate means with which to effect it (this is, of course, the traditional Aristotelian definition of rhetoric) and find them, or at least a portion of them, in the rhetorical practice of talking theory.'

[56] ibid 1790.

[57] Robertson (n 12) 268: 'philosophical theory–talk can be used rhetorically to sell that decision to the legal audience being asked to consume it'.

[58] Fish (n 22) 1781: '[T]heory is essentially a rhetorical and political phenomenon'.

[59] ibid 1791.

[60] ibid 1792.

4

Law, Reason and Celestial Music

NE SIMMONDS

> It's not celestial music it's the girl in the bathroom singing
> Brian Patten, *Ode on Celestial Music*[1]

I. INTRODUCTION

STANLEY FISH'S FAMOUS exchanges with Ronald Dworkin provide an important landmark in modern jurisprudence. But they afford us a somewhat restricted understanding of Fish's jurisprudence. A theme of considerable depth informs his critique of Dworkin but does not lie evident upon its surface. Dworkin reacts as one devoid of love for the richness and diversity of nature might react to the pestering of a wasp: he aims to crush. He is frustrated in his efforts because readers discern the troubling resonance of Fish's thought, which disturbs even when it cannot convince. In this chapter, I eschew the spectator sport of watching public figures in gladiatorial combat and try to unearth a deep theme of jurisprudence by examining Fish's well-known essay 'Force'.[2] I question the arguments composing that essay, but my main object is to identify an unarticulated thought that seems to me to provide the essay with much of its fascination. In this way I hope to resurrect an issue that is central to the long history of philosophy of law: reason's suggestion of transcendence, and its relationship to settled human practice.

Reason presents itself as a standard by which all human action and belief must be judged. But herein lies a paradox. The idea of reason can be more than a free-floating *ignis fatuus* only if it is embodied in certain established practices and beliefs. Yet, reason's critical capacity seems to require its independence from all established practices and beliefs. Should reason be conceived as a set of standards with a determinacy that precedes its practice? Must reason appeal to

---

[1] B Patten, *Selected Poems*, (London, Penguin, 2007). I am indebted to Margaret Martin and Joshua Neoh for their comments on an earlier draft of this chapter.
[2] SE Fish, 'Force' (1988) 45 *Washington and Lee Law Review* 883.

a foundation in practice which is somehow self-validating and beyond dispute? Or is reason, in the end, nothing more than established practice, so that, in our ultimate grasp of that fact, 'The awakening of the subject is bought with the recognition of power as the principle of all relationships?'[3] The following pages will offer nothing that could be construed as an answer to these questions. The questions form the background to my reflections rather than their subject matter. For it seems that our practices of reason gain much of their significance from a regulative idea of reason towards which they are oriented: an idea which is intimated but never fully grasped. Here as elsewhere, it seems, a fully human life must be guided by ideas which are imperfectly understood aspirations rather than established givens.

In 'Force', Fish portrays the law as pervasively dependent upon that which it seeks to exclude: 'The force of the law is always and already indistinguishable from the forces it would oppose.'[4] The reader might anticipate in Fish's essay the development of a familiar theme. For it is not at all uncommon to point out that, although we often think of the governance of law as resting on the suppression of violence, legal sanctions (which we might regard as the most obvious manifestation of 'the force of the law') must themselves ultimately rest upon the threat or the use of force. And, while such coercive sanctions are said by some legal theorists to form no part of the concept of law, no one could deny their prominence within virtually all instantiations of that concept. Law, on this account, very clearly depends upon that which it aims to oppose. Indeed, the dependence can seem so prominent that some may come to view law as, not the suppression of force, but rather its systematisation and perfection.

However, if this familiar thesis is present at all in Fish's essay, it is no more than one aspect of a much broader, and much more elusive, theme. Fish's notion of 'force' is one that has little direct connection with physical violence. The closest we get to a general explanation of what he means seems to be this:

> Force is simply a (pejorative) name for the thrust or assertion of some point of view, and in a world where the urging of points of view cannot be referred for adjudication to some independent tribunal, force is just another name for what follows naturally from conviction. That is to say, force wears the aspect of anarchy only if one regards it as an empty blind urge, but if one identifies it as *interest aggressively pursued*, force acquires a content and that content is a complex of goals and purposes, underwritten by a vision, and put into operation by a detailed agenda complete with steps, stages, and directions. Force, in short, is already a repository of everything it supposedly threatens – norms, standards, reasons, and yes, even rules.[5]

There is obviously a lot going on in this account of 'force'. At its core is the equation of 'force' with conviction, or action based upon conviction. Indeed,

---

[3] M Horkheimer and T Adorno, *Dialectic of Enlightenment,* trans E Jephcott, (Palo Alto, Stanford University Press, 2002) 5.
[4] Fish (n 2) 898.
[5] Fish (n 2) 899–900 (italics in original).

force is said to be 'what follows naturally from conviction'. But, within this single passage, for example, we transition (without explanation) from force as a matter of points of view and convictions to force being identified with '*interest aggressively pursued*'. Are there no disinterested convictions? One has the distinct feeling that an entire theory of human action and social order is being smuggled in under the cover of a capacious word. But, for present purposes, all we need to notice is the way in which virtually every significant feature of human society could be encompassed by the notion of 'force', from the threat of violence to the force of a convincing argument or a firmly held conviction. The all-encompassing nature of 'force' is, of course, the main point of the essay, in spite of the fact that the point seems already to be contained within Fish's stipulative definition. But that all-encompassing nature also poses a problem for our understanding of his core thesis regarding law.

To say that the law is indistinguishable from the forces 'it would oppose' is to speak of law anthropomorphically, as if law had aims and wishes. This way of speaking is even more manifest in the title of another one of Fish's essays, where he tells us that 'The Law Wishes to Have a Formal Existence.'[6] In ascribing goals or hopes or wishes to a practice, however, we are not making an unstructured report of observable phenomena: the situation is not comparable to a biographer who ascribes wishes to his subject because the subject repeatedly expressed such wishes in his letters. To ascribe aims or wishes to law, one must identify intelligible aspirations that enable us to make sense of the established features of law. The aspirations must be attractive to us, so that we might ourselves endorse them. Or they must be familiar aspirations that we can recognise as having a wider role within our culture and civilization. The attribution of goals to a practice must be justified by the ability of that attribution to explain features of the practice that are not otherwise easily explicable. And, if the goals so attributed are bizarrely unfamiliar, this will necessarily count (non-conclusively but importantly) against the soundness of the attribution.

Fish faces a difficulty which arises from the great diversity of objects that are grouped together by him as instances of 'force'. It is this great capaciousness of 'force' that enables Fish to claim that 'force' is 'a repository of everything it supposedly threatens – norms, standards, reasons and yes, even rules', and so to sustain his core thesis that law is 'indistinguishable from the forces it would oppose'. But the capaciousness of 'force' poses a problem for the claim that law opposes 'force', or wishes to embody something other than 'force'. For what Quixotic impulse could lead the law to oppose, or seek to transcend, the unavoidable and ubiquitous features of human society? In pursuit of what idea might such opposition be mounted?

---

[6] S Fish, *There's No Such Thing as Free Speech and It's a Good Thing, Too* (Oxford, Oxford University Press, 1994).

For practical purposes, distinctions may of course be made within the domain of 'force'. Thus, the law opposes certain aspects of 'force' (violence and fraud, for example) with such resources as 'norms, standards, reasons' and 'rules'. In doing so, of course, the law does not step outside of the domain of 'force', since the normative resources invoked are themselves just further instances of 'force'. Whatever norms we invoke will be invoked only because they reflect convictions of some sort, and our convictions are themselves contingent, forever entangled with all of the other features making up the realm of 'force'. It is in this sense that the 'force' of law is indistinguishable from 'force' more generally. But it is not obvious that this is a failure on law's part, or that law's object was to 'oppose' force, rather than to oppose one aspect of 'force' by means of another aspect.

Should we worry about the dependence of our norms upon convictions, and the entanglement of all convictions with the empire of 'force'? Surely, we should be anxious to expose the dependence of discrete convictions upon particular and identifiable circumstances of oppression or coercion that may have somehow played a part in the adoption of those convictions. That would suggest an exercise of discrimination wherein we sift through the various aspects of force, provisionally relying on some aspects while scrutinising and perhaps rejecting others. But such an enterprise seems quite at odds with the intellectual posture that Fish adopts, which is precisely one of downplaying or denying the significance of any distinctions between different aspects of 'force'. Indeed, Fish's general stance with regard to the imperial rule of 'force' is conspicuously relaxed. He seems to deny the reflective distance that can be created by historical awareness or philosophical theory. In his view, the insights yielded by theory can make no difference to our practical situation.[7]

Many will be tempted to dismiss Fish's essay as simply an irrelevant display of fireworks. It seems at first to operate by equating the rule of law with the impossible idea of an escape from the unavoidable circumstances of human life. Then, by pointing out that such an escape is indeed impossible, we seem to be implicitly invited to dismiss the rule of law as an illusory idea. Finally, we are offered a dramatic shift in perspective by way of conclusion. Here Fish makes his thesis seem relatively uncontentious or even banal. For he explains his fundamental point as being that the understandings necessary to distinguish law from force are 'an artefact of time, a "mere temporary ascendancy" of one vision or agenda over its rivals'.[8] Meanwhile, he acknowledges, from the more 'short run' perspectives within which we all live our lives, 'the distinction between law and force is unassailable'.[9] Recognition of the temporally contingent nature of our fundamental assumptions will not, Fish tells us, 'lessen their force or make

---

[7] Fish (n 2) 901.
[8] ibid 901.
[9] ibid.

us less likely to surrender to them'.[10] Rejecting the potential critical value of reflective understanding, he adds 'We remain embedded in history even when we know that it is history we are embedded in.'[11]

Fish's thesis therefore seems to reduce to a claim along these lines: The existence of law as a phenomenon which appears to be distinct from, yet dependent on, other features of social life, is itself dependent upon background understandings that are historically contingent and could have been otherwise. This is a remarkably uncontentious, indeed yawn-inducing, conclusion. And it sits very oddly with the intriguing motif that drives the rhetoric of Fish's essay: a motif wherein the law pursues an impossible objective of opposition to the ordinary conditions of human life, and is perpetually doomed to failure because it is forced to rely upon those very conditions.

It is the dramatic motif which provides much of the fascination behind Fish's essay, rather than his somewhat more banal conclusion. And it is the dramatic motif that I hope to address in this chapter. For it can indeed seem that familiar features of our moral, political and juridical life are oriented towards impossible ideals which could never be achieved in the imperfect human world.[12] Perhaps the law has feet of clay but perpetually tries to free itself from that foundation. Perhaps we could not live a fully human life without such ideas.

The central target of Fish's essay, however, is the legal theory of HLA Hart. And we must begin by examining Fish's analysis of that theory.

II. HART AND THE GUNMAN

Fish gives us an unusual picture of Hart's theory of law. We are told that Hart's project involves 'an extended search' for 'a point of resistance' to the rule of 'force', 'an impersonal source that resists the encroaching desires of particular (interpretive) wills'.[13] According to Hart, it seems, 'the law binds members of society to a rule or set of rules that has the character of being general and impartial'.[14] Legal obligations result not from arbitrary power but from power 'that is enabled by an independent and authoritative source'.[15] Hart, we are told, sees rules 'as barriers or walls on which is written "beyond this point interpretation cannot go"'.[16] The rule-follower must be 'compelled, left without choice, deprived of any opportunity to exercise his creative ingenuity' or 'there will be no law'.[17]

---

[10] ibid.
[11] ibid.
[12] See NE Simmonds, 'On the Centrality of Jurisprudence' (2019) 64 *American Journal of Jurisprudence* 1.
[13] Fish (n 2) 885.
[14] ibid 883.
[15] ibid 884.
[16] ibid 885.
[17] ibid 886.

If offered simply as an interpretation of Hart this would be very idiosyncratic. An innocent reader reliant upon Fish's account would be surprised to learn that, far from viewing law as 'impartial', Hart considered it perfectly possible for law to act as a very partial instrument of oppression or exploitation without in any way detracting from its status as law. Nor would they realise that Hart emphasises the scope for innovative interpretation that law leaves open. But Fish would doubtless respond by saying that such ideas as generality, impartiality, and impersonality nevertheless play a significant part in Hart's argument, even if that part is cloaked by Hart's headline doctrines, for they are integral to the notion of a rule. Hart draws upon such connections when, for example, he highlights the close connection between rule-following and formal justice. Rules establish, in his view, a formal kind of impartiality between persons, but one that is 'compatible with very great iniquity' and therefore confers upon the law no moral authority.[18]

Fish begins by highlighting the contrast which Hart draws between law and the situation of a gunman who makes demands backed by the threat of violence. We are told that Hart considers it 'simply counterintuitive' to 'assimilate law to this reductive paradigm', and he quotes the following passage from Hart: 'Mere temporary ascendancy of one person over another is naturally thought of as the polar opposite of law, with its relatively enduring and settled character.'[19] In response, Fish objects that, far from being the 'polar opposite' of 'force', law seems to be in the business, not of 'doing away with force', but of masking it 'by placing it behind a screen or series of screens'. In the end, we are told, there is 'little to distinguish' law from the actions of the gunman, since 'this gunman is merely better camouflaged'.[20]

Contrary to the impression created by Fish, I doubt if Hart would be anxious to disagree very fundamentally with Fish's remarks here. If he did disagree, it might be to point out that Fish seems to equate what may sometimes be the case with what must necessarily be the case (some legal systems resemble the gunman more than do others), and overlooks the fact that resemblances are relative to aspects (legal systems resemble the gunman in some respects but not in others). More importantly, Hart would point out that, even if there is no difference in moral legitimacy between law and the gunman situation, and even if there were no difference in motivations for compliance, it does not follow that there are no important differences. It is Hart's aim to establish that there is a complex web of associated differences between law and the gunman situation, differences which help to explain much of the 'general framework of legal thought'.[21] But, crucially, he wishes to demonstrate that none of those differences need make

---

[18] HLA Hart, *The Concept of Law*, 3rd edn, edn by L Green (Oxford, Oxford University Press, 2012) 207.
[19] ibid 24. Quoted by Fish (n 2) 883.
[20] Fish (n 2) 884.
[21] Hart (n 18) Preface, vi.

much *moral* difference. And they certainly do not, in themselves, confer any moral authority upon the law.

What should strike us most about the passage from Hart that Fish quotes is the final seven-word clause (ie, 'with its relatively enduring and settled character'). We might well agree that 'the temporary ascendancy of one person over another' (ie, the gunman situation) is 'the polar opposite of law'. But does our sense of polar opposition here spring, as Hart's observation seems to suggest, from the fact that the gunman's ascendancy is merely temporary, while the law's ascendancy is 'relatively enduring and settled'? Would that settled and enduring character not make us feel that law is but the deep embedding of coercion, rather than its opposite? Is our sense of polar opposition not, much more fundamentally, the product of some quite different assumptions that we tend to make about law? For example, that the purpose of law is to serve justice, while the gunman's purpose is merely to help himself at the expense of his victim. Or that the purpose of law is to suppress the use of violence and achieve a society based upon peace and mutual respect. Even though we understand that law has sometimes, perhaps often, been employed to exploit or oppress, and even though we may find it hard to reconcile that knowledge with our persisting idealism concerning law's nature, the idealism is nevertheless a real feature of our ordinary attitudes towards law. The fact, then, that Hart does not rely upon such idealism, when he draws his contrast between the ascendancy of the gunman and the situation of governance by law, gives us an early indicator of the trajectory that his theory of law will follow.

Notice that Hart does not tell us that the situation of temporary ascendancy *is* the polar opposite of law: he tells us that it 'is naturally thought of' in that way. And he immediately does a little to debunk that sense of polar opposition by mentioning, not any conceptual connection between law and justice or legitimacy, but rather law's 'relatively enduring' character. Hart's object is not to *sustain* our natural sense of a polar opposition here, but partially to *undermine* it by suggesting that the features of law which appear to support that sense are real, but they do not bear the meaning that we ordinarily attach to them. Or, to put the point somewhat more accurately, the features which distinguish law from the gunman situation are indeed significant, but their jurisprudential significance is entirely a function of their role in explaining the 'general framework of legal thought' (as Hart calls it)[22] while affording no basis on which one might justifiably ascribe inherent moral value to law. By grasping the fact that law is a matter of rules, not of threats, we can understand why reductive analyses of law (ie, analyses that treat propositions of law as statements concerning complex assemblages of past conduct, or predictions of future conduct) are inadequate. And we can also come to understand that the rejection of such reductive analyses should not lead us to endorse the view that law is a branch of moral discourse.

---

[22] ibid.

Law is not, for Hart, an alternative to the exercise of power but a form in which power can be exercised. The particularities of that form are important precisely in so far as they enable us to understand how law can possess a normative character without being grounded in moral ideas of justice or legitimacy. Hart's project is, to that extent, a coldly sceptical one, for it seeks to dispel the air of mystery and sanctity that can sometimes surround the law. The mystery is generated in part by the very structure of legal argument, which is why it can be dispelled by a cool-headed analysis of 'the general framework of legal thought'.

A basic premise underpinning legal argument tends to be that all propositions of law must be supported by authority, usually in the form of some cited enactment or judicial decision. Yet, at the same time, it is assumed that the law's content is not reducible to the content of such sources. Statutes and precedents may be the material from which the law is made, but the law is taken to be the construction that results from them and not the heap of materials in and of itself. The transition from raw materials to finished construction is the enterprise of legal doctrinal argument. In the course of such argument, expert lawyers may disagree about whether or not the law includes some specific principle or doctrine, and those disagreements can persist for decades even though all the participants are equally aware of the relevant enactments and decisions. As Philip Allott elegantly puts it: 'Legislative texts and reported cases are not themselves the law. They do not even contain the law. The law is somewhere else and something else.'[23]

A further mystery underlies the posited materials of statute and precedent. For, while lawyers generally assume that law is created by human decision, they also assume that human decisions can create law only when legally authorised so to do. These two assumptions, however, combine to generate an infinite regress, where each law is created by acts which are themselves authorised by higher laws. Two possible resolutions present themselves. One resolution (legal positivism) suggests that law-making must, in the last analysis, be grounded upon the raw facts of power and compliance: it is the ability of some to secure the compliance of others (whatever the basis of that ability) which is the ultimate foundation of law-making. On this approach, the prescriptions created by such power can constitute laws even though they may possess no moral authority or virtue whatsoever, and that lack of moral value will not detract from their status as law in any way. By contrast with this, a rival approach (stemming from the natural law tradition) holds that the creation of law is ultimately dependent upon the way in which the law can secure certain genuine moral goods, such as justice or civility. Power (understood as the ability to secure compliance) may be as important to law-making on this view as it is on the legal positivist view, but its importance is understood differently. For the natural law position, power is important in so far

---

[23] P Allott, *The Health of Nations: Society and Law Beyond the State* (Cambridge, Cambridge University Press, 2002) 43.

as it may be essential for the attainment of justice, or civil peace, or other moral values. For legal positivism, by contrast, law is simply a form (in itself morally neutral) in which power may be exercised. That form gives rise to a distinctive mode of discourse and of association (a mode centring upon the governance of rules) and it is worth isolating as an object of philosophical reflection and analysis for that reason.

Hart's theory belongs to the legal positivist tradition. His object is to reveal law as simply a form in which power can be exercised: a form which has no necessary moral merit, and certainly no necessary moral authority.[24] To defend this view, he pursues three closely intertwined objectives. The first is to show how the infinite regress can be resolved in a way that supports the positivist approach. The second is to acknowledge that there are significant differences between the gunman situation and the governance of law, but to establish that those differences are not of a kind involving the possession by law of any moral authority. And the third objective is to show how the idea of law as a 'brooding omnipresence in the sky'[25] (law as 'somewhere else and something else') is simply an illusion generated by the open texture of language and the incomplete or revisable character of many legal rules.

III. INTERPRETATION

Much of Fish's essay concerns the interpretation of rules. He tells us that 'If the gunman is the paradigmatic instance of force outside the law, interpretation is the force that resides within the law.'[26] And here our author touches upon a core problem for jurisprudence. For, if law is to be more than an ornamental gloss upon the particularistic exercise of power, judicial decisions must somehow be grounded in the legal rules. Yet a problem in this vicinity is evident in the common insistence of jurists that the application of rules to cases can never be a 'mechanical' task. We naturally find ourselves asking 'If the task is not mechanical, what more does it involve?' Is that supplement to the mechanism compatible with the decision truly being required by the rule? If judgments concerning the applicability of the rules are not determined by the rules alone, is the whole idea of the rule of law not illusory?

This problem was perhaps less pressing for more traditional understandings of law that took for granted law's basis in moral reason. If we regard the nature

---

[24] John Gardner has suggested that my interpretation of Hart 'manufactures' a disagreement between my own position and that of Hart. Those convinced by Gardner's analysis may be inclined to reject the interpretation offered above. For the exchange between Gardner and myself, see J Gardner 'Hart on Legality, Justice and Morality' (2010) 1 *Jurisprudence* 253, and NE Simmonds, 'Reply: The Nature and Virtue of Law' (2010) 1 *Jurisprudence* 277, 281–283.
[25] 'The common law is not a brooding omnipresence in the sky', OW Holmes Jr. dissenting in *Southern Pacific Company v Jensen* (1917) 244 U.S. 205, 222.
[26] Fish (n 2) 885.

of law (including its nature as a body of rules established by positive enactment or decision) as grounded in moral reason, we can view that background of moral reason as informing the content of law. We can then acknowledge that the law is not to be thought of as simply a collection of source-based prescriptions, but as an orderly structure that results from those prescriptions when they are construed as, collectively, a good faith attempt at doing justice and serving the common good. Posited prescriptions can, in this way, lend greater determinacy to our moral understandings while, at the same time, deriving their own meaning in part *from* those understandings. The difference between governance by law and governance by arbitrary power is preserved, in spite of the fact that the enacted provisions cannot in themselves provide what Fish would call a 'barrier or wall' beyond which interpretation cannot go.

This outlook enables us better to understand the significance of many of our ordinary ways of speaking. For example, when considering the claim that statutes are not themselves the law, but are merely sources of law, Hart finds that claim to be (at least at first sight) 'strange and paradoxical'.[27] Yet the idea should not be so unfamiliar to us. For we regularly debate the 'law-making effect' of a statute, and statutes can scarcely have a law-making effect (as opposed to what we might call 'further legal consequences') if they are themselves the law. The legal validity of a statute yields a requirement that we must incorporate the statute's law-making effect in our overall account of the law, always guided by our assumptions concerning the law's aim of serving justice and the common good. While the statute can be identified independently of our understandings of moral reason (and law could not exist in the absence of such easily identifiable sources) the law cannot.[28]

If, however, we wish to defend the picture of law as a rules-based order with no necessary foundation in moral reason (ie, if we wish to defend legal positivism) our problem becomes considerably more acute. Within such a picture, posited verbal formulations must stand alone, without any background of moral reason that is conceived of as intrinsic to their character as law. On this model, the law *can* be interpreted by reference to moral values, but such a mode of interpretation merely represents a choice on the part of the interpreter: it is not itself required by the idea of law. One can go further, by postulating a law that requires the morally guided interpretation of enactments and precedents: but such a law would have to be regarded by the positivist as merely a contingent

---

[27] Hart (n 18) 2, 8.

[28] Law exists in part to overcome our moral uncertainties, and give determinacy to moral understandings. This has often been thought to require a conception of law wherein the law is identifiable independently of morality. But this is obviously incorrect. Laws identified wholly independently of moral understanding would themselves exhibit great practical indeterminacy and would serve only to generate unresolvable dispute. It is in the mutual dependence of posited prescription and background moral understanding that a degree of determinacy can be secured. At its best, doctrinal legal analysis and adjudicative reasoning can foster the forms of detached yet sympathetic reflection that help to construct a shared morality for a tolerant and diverse liberal community. The law thereby helps to sustain the moral foundation upon which it relies for its own determinacy.

feature of some legal systems. (To postulate such a law as a necessary presupposition would simply acknowledge law's necessary basis in moral reason, in violation of the basic positivist thesis.)

Fish places a considerable emphasis upon Hart's suggestion that the rule of recognition identifies laws by some 'authoritative mark',[29] and he associates this with a theory to the effect that 'communication is anchored by ... a level of language immune from contextual variation and therefore resistant to interpretation'.[30] He then tells us that the theory is undermined by the frequency of 'disputes concerning the meaning of supposedly plain or literal language'.[31] Hart, Fish explains, tries to deal with this by means of his distinction between the core and the penumbra: communication is only possible, in Hart's view, if there are standard instances where the appropriate application of a word or a rule is not in doubt.

Admittedly, Hart's discussion of these issues is sparse. His distinction between the 'core' and the 'penumbra' simply notes that, in a very broad range of cases, people will agree about the applicability of a rule, while in other cases they will disagree. This tells us nothing whatever about the 'force' (to borrow Fish's term) which shapes that pattern of convergence and divergence. Indeed, it is with prodigious understatement that Hart tells us that 'it is a matter of some difficulty to give any exhaustive account of what makes a "clear case" clear or makes a general rule obviously and uniquely applicable to a particular case'.[32] But it is far from clear that Hart would see the relevant convergence of judgement as a function of verbal formulae viewed in isolation: indeed, such a view would scarcely be compatible with his acknowledgment of the difficulty in offering an 'exhaustive account' of the contributory factors. Hart could easily acknowledge the role of background cultural assumptions, and an understanding of context, as contributing to that convergence, and therefore to the determinacy of rules. Any such acknowledgement might render problematic some liberal political theories which envisage a society of limitless cultural and ethical diversity that is nevertheless held together by the rule of law. Hart is unconcerned about such issues, in part because he erroneously takes the concept of law to be quite distinct from the liberal value that we call 'the rule of law' (which Hart refers to as 'the requirements of justice which lawyers term principles of legality'[33]).

---

[29] Hart (n 18) 95; Fish (n 2) 887.
[30] Fish (n 2) 887.
[31] ibid 887.
[32] HLA Hart, *Essays in Jurisprudence and Philosophy* (Oxford, Oxford University Press, 1983) 106. Writing from a position much closer to natural law, Alexy is able to cast slightly more light (while nevertheless acknowledging the difficulty) when he says that 'the clarity of a so-called "clear case" is not such a simple matter either', for arguments opposing the proper applicability of the rule are always in principle possible, so that 'the categorization of a case as "clear" constitutes a "negative value judgment" with respect to all potential counter-arguments'. R Alexy, *A Theory of Legal Argumentation,* translated by Ruth Adler and Neil MacCormick, (Oxford, Oxford University Press, 1989) 8.
[33] Hart (n 18) 207.

Hart is equally relaxed about some other features of legal reason that he is careful to point out, such as the fact that binding rules may nevertheless be treated as subject to unspecified exceptions which are 'incapable of exhaustive statement',[34] and the fact that consensus in identifying the *ratio decidendi* of a case may be relative to a particular issue concerning 'the bearing of a precedent on a later case'.[35] Yet these are all issues which some might view as supporting Fish's thesis that the generality of rules is subverted by the particularity of interpretations.

In Hart's opinion, when judicial decisions fall within the penumbra of disagreement, the decisions create new law in virtue of rules empowering the judges and making their decisions binding. But, when penumbral issues arise concerning the most fundamental constitutional rules, no such empowering rules may be available, so that 'Here power acquires authority *ex post facto* from success.'[36] Furthermore, what makes this success possible, Hart points out, is 'the prestige gathered by courts from their unquestionably rule-governed operations over the vast, central areas of the law'.[37] In other words, the courts acquire their power in part from the public error of equating penumbral cases with core cases. Beneath the calm and measured surface of Hart's work, we may be tempted to find a more subversive message than many of his readers acknowledge.

Hart is not in the business of defending law's moral credentials. Evil and exploitative governance is, in Hart's view, fully compatible with governance by law, and does not detract from the legal character of such governance one jot. According to Hart, the 'internal point of view', which sustains the practice of rule-application, might conceivably rest upon nothing more elevated than the concern of officials with their own self-interests, and the population might comply simply from fear. Hart's concerns are clearly quite remote from any desire to demonstrate the deep moral significance of a polar opposition between law and the gunman. Nor does he seem unwilling to acknowledge the flexibility of rules in the context of their interpretation and application, and the potential dependence of their core meanings upon an indefinite context of background understandings. At a superficial level, Fish's critique of Hart therefore looks like a misunderstanding. But, if we dig a little deeper, might we find that it points to a truth?

IV. LAWS AND REASONS

Whatever its possible deficiencies, Fish's interpretation of Hart does leave us with a preliminary sense of what Fish might have in mind when he suggests that

---

[34] ibid 139.
[35] ibid 134.
[36] ibid 154.
[37] ibid 154.

the law opposes 'force'. Hart is portrayed (readers will recall) as seeking in law 'an impersonal source that resists the encroaching desires of particular wills', something that is 'general and impartial', 'independent and authoritative'. The implication seems to be that the realm of 'force' is the realm of particularity, while the law seeks to establish a realm of impartiality, impersonality and independence. That suggestion picks up on Hart's concern with rules, and links that concern to a range of ideas that are indeed closely associated with law. Governance by general rules is central to our ideas of 'the rule of law' as a value.

However, our preliminary sense of Fish's meaning is quickly unsettled. For, after reminding us of the centrality which Hart ascribes to rules, Fish tells us that 'the crucial question', which restores our 'original problem' (he presumably means the problem of the relationship between law and 'force'), is 'Who gets to make the rules?' or perhaps 'Who gets to say who makes the rules?'. He then highlights what he sees as the nub of the issue: for, 'If the answer to these questions is "whoever seizes the opportunity and makes it stick" then there is finally little to distinguish the rule-centered legal system from the actions of the gunman.'[38]

Anyone who regards the rule of law as a value, and adopts a thin or minimal account of the rule of law (as, basically, governance by published, prospective rules), is bound to disagree with Fish's claim that, in the circumstances which he envisages (where law-making power is possessed only in virtue of an act of seizure), there is 'little to distinguish' governance by a 'rule-centered legal system' from the actions of a gunman. For advocates of such a thin version of the rule of law (including me) would say that there is an immensely important difference between the two situations. There are, of course, other ways of thinking about the governance of rules, and about the rule of law. Hart, for example, seems to see no intrinsic moral value in the governance of rules, or at least none that would confer upon the law any moral authority. And a multitude of other theorists have echoed his approach by insisting that governance by rules lacks intrinsic value unless it is associated with a rich array of more substantive values. So, Fish has many allies in thinking that the difference between governance by general rules, and the actions of a gunman, is of no great moral importance.

Once we have (erroneously) dismissed the idea that governance by rules might, in itself, and in some morally significant way, distinguish law from the gunman, we are inevitably led to ask what might provide such a distinction. Fish does not give us a clear and explicit answer, but the implicit suggestion of his essay as a whole seems to be that nothing could ever provide such a distinction. Given his idea of 'force', the conclusion seems obvious. Democratic enactment of the laws, for example, could not distinguish law from the gunman. For democracy, in all circumstances other than those of complete unanimity, might be described in Fish's words as simply a matter of the majority seizing

---

[38] Fish (n 2) 884.

an opportunity and making it stick. Even in circumstances of unanimity, the resulting legislation would simply reflect people's desires, interests, and convictions, all of which are fundamentally shaped by the circumstances of power, and all of which are factors firmly located within the realm of 'force'. And, even if the unanimously enacted legislation directly expressed everyone's ideas of justice, those ideas would merely be their contingently determined 'convictions', shaped by their social context (the realm of 'force') to exactly the same extent as everything else. As Fish puts it (drawing upon his particular reading of Hart) 'those who, like Hart, argue for a neutral space in the world must also argue for a neutral space in the mind, one free of biases, prejudices, and presuppositions'.[39]

I have emphasised the sceptical aspect of Hart's theory, and have suggested that he would not feel particularly anxious to oppose Fish's characterisation of law as simply a variant on the gunman. But there are points in his work where Hart acknowledges features of law that might have led him to a quite different view, had he not been wedded to his agenda of presenting law in a coldly sceptical light. Finnis (considering a somewhat different aspect of Hart's theory) tells us that Hart's method 'points out a land which is left to his readers and hearers to hazard to enter'.[40] This is certainly true. The land in question is the land of reason.

When Hart criticises Austin's reductive theory, he points out that Austin is wrong to treat propositions concerning legal obligations as predictions of sanctions. Rules do not predict sanctions so much as prescribe them, and judges cite legal obligations as reasons or justifications for imposing sanctions.[41] And Hart believes that his theory can easily accommodate this feature, because such normative notions as reason, justification, and obligation can all be seen as features of the 'internal point of view' which Hart ascribes to the 'officials' of the system.

It will be recalled that, as part of his attempt to emphasise law's independence from morality, Hart claims that the officials' 'internal point of view' need not be a moral point of view, but might be grounded in a variety of non-moral considerations, including self-interest. We can quite easily see how self-interest might give the officials good reason for following the rule of recognition. But could self-interest conceivably explain the invocation of the rule of recognition, or the rules stemming from it, as a justification for the imposition of a sanction? Must a justification not invoke considerations which ought to be regarded as good reasons (regardless of whether they are so regarded) by the addressee of the justification? And why should the litigants or defendants (surely the primary

---

[39] ibid 896.

[40] J Finnis, 'Positivism and Authority' in J Finnis, *Philosophy of Law: Collected Papers Vol. 4* (Oxford, Oxford University Press, 2011) 75.

[41] Hart (n 2) 84.

addressees of the judicial judgment) care about the self-interest of the officials?[42] In answer to this type of objection, Hart suggests that, when they invoke the law as a justification for their decisions, judges speak in a 'technically confined way' which merely subsumes the case under the relevant legal rules, without making any assumptions about the wider justifiability of the rules' application.[43] Borrowing a phrase from Fish, but putting it to a different purpose, we might say that the rules constitute a 'barrier or wall' beyond which legal reason need not pass. This is how Hart seeks to secure the law from dependence, not upon 'force', but upon moral reason.[44]

Raz, for one, has acknowledged that Hart's position here is not really satisfactory. He thinks that, when they invoke the law as the basis for their decisions, judges must assume that the law is morally binding or at least pretend to make that assumption. But Raz's position itself is unsatisfactory, for he fails to see that the justification offered by the judge is one that treats as utterly central the status of the relevant rule or obligation as law. Indeed, Raz is so far from grasping this crucial point that he insists that, so far as the judge's duty is concerned, the status as law of the rules applied by the judge 'matters not at all'.[45] What is required for the satisfactory resolution of the difficulties faced by Hart and Raz is a theory of law that recognises the authority that is intrinsic to the nature of law.[46]

Hart comes very close to recognising law's dependence upon moral reason, and perceiving the basis of law's authority, at two points in his book *The Concept of Law*. The first is when he offers us a speculative history of the emergence of a rule of recognition from a regime of primary rules, and presents the rule of recognition as helping to remedy the problem of the uncertainty of the rules. And the second is when he writes of the 'minimum content of natural law'. Here he explains certain permanent features of the human condition which make rules (rules with the general content characteristic of legal systems) necessary for survival. When combined, the two discussions go some way towards acknowledging the law's status as the solution to a fundamental problem of the human condition: we need shared rules; and, in a society of any complexity, this will be possible only with a rule of recognition and a system of law.[47]

---

[42] See NE Simmonds, *Law as a Moral Idea* (Oxford, Oxford University Press, 2007) ch 4.
[43] HLA Hart, *Essays on Bentham* (Oxford, Oxford University Press, 1982) 266.
[44] Simmonds (n 42) ch 4.
[45] J Raz, *Between Authority and Interpretation* (Oxford, Oxford University Press, 2009) 85.
[46] I have discussed this issue elsewhere: NE Simmonds, 'Reflexivity and the Idea of Law' (2010) 1 *Jurisprudence* 1, 13–14. Similar problems detract from MacCormick's suggestion concerning 'underpinning reason' for the rule of recognition: see Simmonds (n 42) 131–133.
[47] Admittedly, Hart's analysis at this point is not very insightful, for it seriously underestimates the range of possibilities revealed to us by anthropology, and thereby fails to see that law may be an attempted solution to a somewhat different problem of the human condition: the problem of how we can enjoy a degree of freedom as independence from the power of another, while living within a human community. See Simmonds (n 42) 182–189.

In discussing his invocation of 'survival' as a relevant value, Hart says:

> (I)t is not merely that an overwhelming majority of men do wish to live, even at the cost of hideous misery, but that this is reflected in whole structures of our thought and language, in terms of which we describe the world and each other.[48]

The idea that certain value concepts might be central to 'whole structures of our thought and language' and therefore the basis on which we understand and describe 'the world and each other' brings us close to a version of natural law, grounded in a kind of world-constituting inter-subjectivity. After all, when Hart speaks in this context of 'the minimum content of natural law', it is the *content* (the selection of 'survival' as the relevant value) which he is describing as minimal, and not the background idea of structures of thought and language which can ground values. That background idea is not minimal but rich and fertile. When this is combined with his discussion of the possible emergence of a rule of recognition, Hart is not far from being able to echo the words of John Finnis, when Finnis says that 'There are human goods that can be secured only through the institutions of human law, and requirements of practical reasonableness that only those institutions can satisfy.'[49] The distance between the two positions is to be found, partly in the goods being invoked as relevant, and partly in Hart's explicit acknowledgment that the appeal to reason and value rests upon our shared structures of thought and language. In the end, even the legal positivist is able to render the law's features intelligible only by relating those features to a shared moral reason. The 'general framework of legal thought' sets us on a path which can be satisfactorily resolved in no other way.

V. FORCE AND REASON

In Fish's picture of the world, we are beings entirely formed by our contexts and we would lack any identity without that formation. There is no space within our being that was not shaped by the realm of 'force' within which it came into being, and therefore no space which is free from the influence of 'force'. Force is coercive, even though it is internal to our identities: 'In the end we are always self-compelled, coerced by forces -beliefs, convictions, reasons, desires – from which we cannot move one inch away.' In fact, while 'there is always a gun at your head', it turns out that 'the gun at your head is your head'.[50]

The questions we asked earlier now become more pressing. For, if 'force' encompasses everything, how can the law be said to oppose 'force'? Clearly, the opposition will fail, for the law itself will be shaped by 'force'. But what idea could render the opposition intelligible? In the name of what value could the effort be mounted? If we cannot answer these questions, the ascription to law

---

[48] Hart (n 18) 192.
[49] J Finnis, *Natural Law and Natural Rights*, 2nd edn (Oxford, Oxford University Press, 2011) 3.
[50] Fish (n 2) 898.

of an effort to oppose 'force' will seem arbitrary and unwarranted. Moreover, if these questions cannot be answered, Fish's thesis reduces to the banal claim that law's distinct existence depends upon common understandings that are historically contingent (ie, the reduction of his thesis that Fish offers by way of conclusion), and the leitmotif of the essay (law's opposition to that upon which it must unavoidably depend) begins to look like an empty decorative feature.

For Fish, 'force' is not a discrete presence. It encompasses everything, and assumes a distinct character only as the mark of a gaping absence. That absence is never explicitly named: it is as if a sanctity surrounds it (compare the name of God within some religious traditions). And the absence is not *merely* an absence. It is an absence that, from what Fish calls 'the long-run point of view', drains everything else of identity and significance, even if 'in the succession of short-runs that make up our lives' everything remains as significant as it has always seemed to the rest of us.[51] Persuasion contrasted with violence, settled rules versus arbitrary demands: all such distinctions, although of considerable importance within our ordinary view of things, are of little significance for Fish's jurisprudence, for each of the supposedly contrasting factors is merely another instantiation of 'force'. Indeed, this erasure of distinctions that are of considerable significance to most of us is really the hallmark of much of Fish's work, enabling him sometimes to emphasise one set of ideas, and sometimes another, while nevertheless insisting that all these seemingly different things are really the same. The world as revealed by Fish is one in which there is no differentiation worthy of note: all is of a uniform character, since everything is eloquent only of an absence. The law's failure to escape from the all-pervasive rule of 'force' is therefore inevitable, but also somewhat unremarkable.

What is the absence which Fish has in mind but does not name? What might conceivably be thought of as relevant to human affairs yet located outside the seemingly all-encompassing realm of 'force'? How might it motivate law's supposed opposition to the rule of force? What is there in our pantheon of values that we might contrast with the rule of persuasion, conviction and desire? These questions are no sooner asked than their answer appears. The unnamed absence is reason.

'Reason' can be understood as the human practice of reasoning, a practice which inevitably falls within the domain of 'force'. But it can also be understood as an independent standard against which all of our efforts at reasoning are to be tested. Within the world of 'force', people act on what they conceive to be reasons, and they engage in reasoning. But they can also ask themselves whether their reasons are *good* reasons, and whether their reasoning is *sound*. Those questions assume the existence of a standard of sound reason which is independent of particular opinions, even when the opinions converge to form a consensus. As Thomas Nagel points out, reason 'is something that each individual can find

---

[51] ibid 901.

within himself, but at the same time it has universal authority'; it 'provides, mysteriously, a way of distancing oneself from common opinion and received practices that is not a mere elevation of individuality – not a determination to express one's idiosyncratic self rather than go along with everyone else'.[52]

This critical aspect of reason certainly represents a deep puzzle. Reason can seem to possess the sublimity of the starry heavens above. Like the heavens, it appears to possess an identity that is independent of the various factors constituting the human realm of 'force'. Once we think of reason that way, we are troubled by the thought that reason may be an impossible illusion. Moreover, if it is indeed an illusion, its absence is so significant that nothing except the absence appears to matter, for there seems to be then no difference between reason and unreason. Yet, at the same time, because it was always an impossible illusion, its absence makes no difference to us at all.

I think it is because Fish is thinking of reason in this way that he picks up on Hart's concern with rules. Fish takes that concern to reflect a deeper impulse within jurisprudential thought: an impulse to discover in law, not simply the impartiality and independence of socially enacted rules, but the law's basis in an impartial and independent reason. Fish sees jurisprudence as an agonised quest for a perhaps unattainable object.

In this he is not entirely mistaken, as we have already seen. Even Hart's austere version of positivism must explain how laws can intelligibly be invoked by the judge as a justification for the judicial decision. To explain this, one needs to explain how laws might be required by moral reason. To deny the need for any such basis in moral reason, Hart is led to insist that legal justifications are 'technically confined', appealing only to the rules without any need implicitly to rely upon any deeper appeal to reason. Perhaps law is uncomfortably placed between the search for an unattainable basis in sublime reason, and the resigned attempts of late modernity to expunge such lofty visions from our practice by construing the practice as merely technical and confined; or as purely instrumental, serving only our arbitrary desires.

To many, it would be reassuring if we could find an account of the human roots of reason: an account which managed to avoid the suggestion of transcendence while nevertheless enabling us to affirm the distinction between reason and unreason. In the absence of such an account, we are haunted by the shadowy thought that our reasoning is a matter of aligning our thought with the *Logos* that was 'in the beginning'.[53] Some philosophers have regarded such ideas as 'the original sin of humanity, the source of its self-enslavement'.[54] They have pursued the attempt to offer a desublimated account of reason.

---

[52] T Nagel, *The Last Word* (Oxford, Oxford University Press, 1997) 3.
[53] St. John's Gospel, 1.1.
[54] F Beiser, *After Hegel: German Philosophy 1840–1900* (New Jersey, Princeton University Press, 2014) 26.

Some of Fish's readers may imagine that such an account is precisely what Fish offers. But one does not achieve a desublimated account of reason by insisting, as post-modernists often appear to, that reason and unreason are much the same. From some lofty pinnacles of disengaged contemplation, distinctions between reason and unreason might seem too small to matter. But, for most of us, the air in those regions is too thin for humans to breathe, and cheerful reassurances from those who claim comfortably to occupy them fail to convince. Do we achieve a desublimated account of reason simply by abandoning, without lament, the idea of reason's transcendence? Or do we require a better understanding of the practices of human reason, their place within the differing forms of association that flourishing communities adopt, and their role in forming us as morally and epistemically responsible beings?

It is ironic that Fish, who perpetually reminds us of our location within a social context, and the inseparability of our identity from that context, takes so little interest in the actual features of the familiar world, at least when he is adopting the 'long-run' view which informs his essay. He seems interested only in the all-encompassing nature of 'force', and the impossibility of any constraint upon its rule. Differences within the domain of 'force', such as different forms that the exercise of power might take, are too footling to concern him, even though they may be of considerable significance for mere mortals inhabiting the sub-lunar world. Indeed, in everything except his jauntily relaxed tone, Fish resembles the disappointed idealist turned sceptic, inhabiting a landscape within which no feature is so striking and important as the evident absence of divinity. By fixing his eyes upon a distant horizon, and pronouncing that horizon to be empty, he forgets to examine the landscape at his feet, and fails to notice the interesting and important features of it within which the rest of us live our lives.

Is the critical face of reason really so distinct from its mundane aspect in our ordinary practices of reasoning? Might our practices not themselves call into being a critical standard by reference to which any instantiation of reasoning (including those self-same practices) can be judged? Might the basis of reason not be found in those 'structures of thought and language' (mentioned by Hart) which render us mutually intelligible and render the world intelligible to us? Fish would doubtless object that such structures merely consist of such things as convictions, desires, prejudices and other mutable and historically contingent aspects of 'force': they are merely aspects of the gun at our head, which turns out to be our head (as he memorably puts it). But some human convictions (or, if you like, 'prejudices') are themselves the expression of our mutual recognition, and constitutive of our status as responsible agents. If they are, in some sense, a gun at our head, they are also the basis of a mode of being that gives that imagery (of guns and coercion) its force: for they are the basis of our freedom and responsibility, and our status as moral persons. A rich and complex strand of philosophical thought (including such highly diverse figures as Fichte,

Hegel, T.H. Green, Strawson and Darwall) explores these ideas.[55] We discern, within that strand of thought, the way in which structures that we have ourselves created may transform us, rendering our beliefs and actions answerable to critical, but nevertheless human, standards.[56]

To understand how all of this is possible, we must seek an account of reason that restores reason to its human habitation and human role, even though the suggestion of transcendence may be an important aspect of reason's identity. We need to acknowledge the way in which even very modest accounts of reason must be suggestive of recognisable ideals: the normative character of reason requires that an adequate account of its nature must encompass the ideal. Thus, identifying what he sees as 'a defining gesture of modernity', Christoph Kletzer has referred to 'the insight that even though reason may not be what we expected or hoped it to be, it is still something'. Reason, on this view, 'may not be able to supply us with an infallible method for producing final values or absolutely sound arguments, but this is not a reason to discharge reason altogether'. The deficiency of reason, however, turns out to underpin an influential political vision. For, 'the fact that we do not possess a substantive philosophical method of finding values *within* the realm of the reasonable … is the hallmark of anti-perfectionism'. Kletzer concludes that, for those who espouse this seemingly modest view of reason within jurisprudence, 'The whole enterprise can be formulated … as an investigation of the structure of liberalism' or as 'as an investigation into the basic structure of the liberal state'.[57] Thus, an austere and demanding political ideal is conjured from the limitations of human reason.

Political ideals may be the cultivated fruits of reason, but they are not its original source, nor are they its nursery. Rather, we need to understand such things as the continuous renewal of moral understanding within 'the talk man holds with week-day man in the hourly walk of the mind's business'.[58] We need to understand the manifestations of reason within our ordinary practices. I have in mind, not only the typical forms of argument and presuppositions of discourse analysed by thinkers such as Robert Alexy and Jurgen Habermas,[59] but also such things as our practice of trying not thoughtlessly to dismiss the

---

[55] See my remarks on this in NE Simmonds, 'Kletzer's Direttissima' (2021) 66 *American Journal of Jurisprudence* 339, 349.

[56] Terry Pinkard describes Hegel's notion of *Geist* as, 'not a metaphysical entity but a fundamental *relation* among persons that mediates their *self-consciousness*'. It is 'a form of life that has developed various social practices for reflecting on what it takes to be authoritative'. T Pinkard, *Hegel's Phenomenology: The Sociality of Reason*, (Cambridge, Cambridge University Press, 1994) 8–9.

[57] C Kletzer, 'Lawyers and Commonplaces' (2007) 13 *Res Publica* 319–20. See also O O'Neill, *Constructing Authorities* (Cambridge, Cambridge University Press, 2015); E Podoksik, *In Defence of Modernity: Vision and Philosophy in Michael Oakeshott* (Exeter, Imprint Academic, 2003).

[58] W Wordsworth, 'I grieved for Bonaparte' in *William Wordsworth: Poetical Works*, edited by T Hutchinson and revised by E De Selincourt (Oxford, Oxford University Press, 1936) 241–42.

[59] See also J Rawls, 'Outline of a Decision Procedure in Ethics' in J Rawls, *Collected Papers* (Cambridge, MA, Harvard University Press, 1999).

arguments offered on some issue currently under discussion (what we call 'keeping an open mind', which should not be equated with what Fish calls a 'neutral space' free from 'presuppositions'); seeking common ground between disputants, without assuming that we already know, independently of the context, where that common ground is located; distinguishing issues that do not need to be conflated, and the conflation of which may make agreement more difficult; not allowing our desires unduly to shape our conclusions regarding the state of the world; and so forth.

The sublimated idea of reason, which perhaps provides for Fish the tacit contrast with the domain of 'force', extends to infinity the implicit rationale of such practices as these, and it may in that way be necessary for the maintenance of the practices. But the point in intellectual space which is thereby constructed should not be mistaken for more than it is. It does not, for example, represent some aspect of being which grounds or underpins our practices of reason. It merely orientates our understanding of their general form and structure. To collapse reason into the undifferentiated domain of 'force', on the grounds that this notional point is not, and cannot be, a real location within the temporal world, is as foolish as (and closely analogous to) dismissing all social contract theories of political legitimacy on the ground that no such historical event as the social contract ever occurred or ever could occur. The relevant question, in each case, is whether the features highlighted by the move into abstraction are the features most serviceable for the values that the practice of abstraction aims to advance (eg, peace and mutual respect). The fact that those features could never exist in isolation, but only in a context characterised by many other circumstances, is not in doubt.

The success of an argument in persuading people is always (in the context of the real world, where discussions must be of finite length) dependent upon the existing beliefs and attitudes of the addressees. This is what encourages Fish to treat the enterprise of giving reasons as but a further manifestation of the universal rule of force, which Fish equates with all those factors which have shaped existing beliefs and desires. But here he simply obscures the basic distinction between 'is' and 'ought'. In responsible and reasoned discussion, we seek to offer arguments which *ought* to persuade, not simply arguments which *are likely to* persuade. Arguments that ought to persuade do not become instances of force simply because they have, in this or that instance, had the effect of persuading, and this is so even though their success may have been achieved as a consequence of factors that Fish would regard as 'force'.

Rational argument is offered in the *hope* of an attainable agreement, but it will be *oriented* towards something different: not towards a here-and-now actual agreement, but towards a normative ideal of ultimate agreement. The attainment of that happy state may be found only at the world's end, but it is the implicit goal that structures rational debate. Clearly, we cannot step outside of all of our convictions and occupy the 'neutral space' of which Fish speaks. But we can most certainly hold up individual convictions for scrutiny, measuring them against all the other things that we currently believe. To 'keep an open mind' is to consider the possibility that our convictions may individually be in error, and to be prepared to subject each conviction to intellectual scrutiny once its veracity has been questioned. Each such investigation will proceed, not in a 'neutral space' stripped of all belief, but in the context of all our other fallible beliefs (beliefs which may themselves, in turn, be called into question). Given the finitude of time, there may come a point where our ordinary practices of reason have done what they can, agreement is for the present impossible, and the time for decision has arrived. Our efforts will not have been in vain, even then: for our willingness to make the effort is itself an expression of civility and of belief in the power of a non-sublime and very human reason. The idea of agreement at the world's end may be essential, not only to the respectful and reasoned character of argument, but also to the values underpinning justice and law.

The absence of the sublime is not the only thing of importance that we need to notice, and one who thinks otherwise is in danger of becoming a bore. Perhaps, as Brian Patten reminds us, there is no celestial music but only the girl in the bathroom, singing. Even if we lament the silence of planetary bodies, it is nevertheless worth asking whether the girl's singing is raucous or lovely. Indeed, it is perhaps worth asking why the silence of the heavens is perceived as a cause for lament, when the human voice is so appealing. The idea of a sublime reason is perhaps never wholly separable from the idea of an ordering of rank within the polity.[60] The de-sublimated reason of ordinary civil discourse, by contrast, embodies mutual respect and mutual intelligibility: the public expression of our common humanity.

Plato envisages the soon-to-be-enlightened prisoner from the Cave being 'forcibly dragged' up the steep ascent to the light. But a voluntary ascent could only be prompted by indications to be found within the phenomena of the cave (indications which suggest the presence of a more perfect and unfailing source of light). It may be the beauty of earthly music that gives rise to our dream of the music of the heavens. There is a dangerous dynamic, identified in part by Feuerbach, wherein such suggestions, although themselves arising from the ordinary phenomena of human life, lead to a needlessly diminished view of those same phenomena, as a consequence of their shortfall from the ideal that they conjure. This is exemplified by some popular moral understandings of the relationship between positive law and perfect justice. Familiarity with the institutions of law fosters a concept of justice as the guiding idea which helps to make the practice what it is. But the possibility of a discrepancy between the practice and the idea (a possibility which is inherent in the role of a guiding idea) leads us to detach justice from institutions, and view it as an entirely abstract requirement, while the law comes to be perceived as a morally inert practice equally serviceable for good and bad purposes.

---

[60] See, eg, L Siedentop, *Inventing the Individual* (London, Allen Lane, 2014) ch 3.

I have emphasised above that Fish's thesis is constantly in danger of seeming banal: the all-encompassing sway of opinion, belief, persuasion and power seems too obvious to require extended argument. Yet, what can lend importance to such a thought is our persisting belief in the possibility of something that transcends these familiar features of our existence. That thing is reason. Only by finding a basis in reason can law claim some independence from the tyranny of 'force'. And jurisprudence is an extended meditation on the possibility of law's basis in reason.

The intellectual culture informing the thought of Socrates and Plato (and, therefore, the context within which philosophy emerges) was fascinated by the potential gulf separating opinion from truth. Seeing that the world was unavoidably shaped by opinion, some Sophists may have abandoned the very idea of truth. But there cannot be opinions of any sort under such a dispensation, so that those who seek to 'go beyond' truth must (like contemporary postmodernists) allow an unearned air of superiority to serve as the totality of their philosophy.[61] Our commitment to the idea of truth is at least as unavoidable for human thought as the role of power, persuasion and all the other manifestations of Fish's 'force.'

From Thrasymachus to the present, those who become transfixed by the absence of transcendence are frequently tempted to vulgarise and simplify the appearances that daily surround us. They believe that any suggestion of such transcendence must be expunged from the earth, lest we become the victims of our own comforting illusions. The enterprise comes at a heavy cost, and whole swathes of modern culture are currently paying the price. Purely personal goals are encouraged, but any suggestion of objective values that might inform the choice of goals is viewed as nothing more than an attempt at the exercise of power. Quotidian social practices of reason are discouraged by a culture that (believing such practices to require an impossible 'neutral space in the mind') chooses instead to emphasise the illusory, and frequently pernicious, ideas of identity and authenticity.

Our practices inevitably fall short of the ideals that guide them; and, sometimes, those guiding ideals may be impossible of realisation. But a valuable practice may nevertheless derive its coherence from its relationship to the ideal. The human world is shaped by our hopes and aspirations, and reflection upon those hopes and aspirations is one of the ways in which we transform our forms of association and ourselves. It is important to acknowledge the *suggestion* of

---

[61] Post-modernism is simply the most recent version of an old dodge whereby empty aesthetic posturing can masquerade as philosophy. Significantly, its most famous appearance is in a disclaimer of responsibility. Writing of Pontius Pilate's question 'What is Truth?', Hegel tells us that the question was asked 'in a superior way' signifying that the 'idea of truth is an expedient which is now obsolete' as 'there is no longer any question about knowing the Truth, seeing that we have gone beyond it'. GWF Hegel, *Lectures on the History of Philosophy*, Vol 1, translated by ES Haldane and FH Simson, (1892) (New Jersey, Humanities Press, 1983) 14–15.

the sublime within our familiar practice if we are to understand ourselves and honour our lives together. The girl's singing will be beautiful only if it resonates to some extent with our idea of heaven and causes us to dream of a peaceful land that we might one day call home. Her voice will not lose its loveliness when we see its origins as purely human and the heaven that it evokes as impossible of attainment. Indeed, from these facts, it gains an added poignancy and power.

5

The Game Goes On: Why Legal Theorists Can Never Admit that Stanley Fish is Right

DAVID KENNY

I. INTRODUCTION

I AM NOT generally an unpopular person, but occasionally I play board games. This usually happens in a house in the west of Ireland with my very closest friends. I enjoy board games – or at least I claim to – and always enthusiastically participate. But I cannot help myself: I always loudly pick apart the rules and mechanics of the various games we play. They do not work the way they say to do, and they do not work the way you think they do. The game says that this or that rule will lead to a competitive and fair experience, that it gives everyone an equal chance to win, but you see, it does not. It is imbalanced because it tends to produce results favouring one side, skewing the experience in one direction. This person may have won, but they did not really deserve to, or their victory was based on a bias in the game. It might seem as though I do this out of some desire to win, but my friends would attest that I do this just as reliably and just as vehemently when I am winning as when I am losing. I just want to promote critical thinking about the games. I have been asked on more than one occasion, after offering a litany of complaints to my companions, if I have any suggestions to improve the course of play, or if I wish to stop playing. No, I say, there is no making it better, and of course we should play on – let's have fun! The incoherence of the rules does not prevent us from enjoying ourselves. We do play on, but I can't help but notice that people seem to have less fun after these interventions, and it is fair to say I am not a popular participant.

My career with board games is an (only slightly imperfect[1]) analogy of the career of Stanley Fish in the realm of legal theory. I am, I maintain, not wrong

---

[1] The imperfections come from that fact that my friends are engaged in the *primary* practice of playing a game; the analogy would be better if they were devoted to the second order practice of explaining and justifying the game's structures, but they are not odd enough to do that. Moreover,

about the problems with these various board games, and Stanley Fish is not wrong about the problems with legal theory. Like me, Fish does not seem to have a dog in the hunt: his contributions do not seem to be directed towards securing a particular victor in the game that is under discussion (the law, or judging), but rather towards proving himself right about the nature of the game. Like me, he has no suggestions to fix the problems he has identified. And our colleagues do not like our interventions because we undermine the game, and then we insist that everyone should keep playing.

In this chapter, I wish to consider legal theorists' reaction to Fish, and why his legal thought – despite having, to my mind, extraordinary perspicacity – is so widely rejected. The Fish-Dworkin debate is the liveliest and most revealing of the exchanges that Fish has had with legal theorists. Dworkin's response to Fish is an extreme but illustrative example of how legal theorists react to Fish's work on the law: with bafflement, hostility, and even dismissiveness. Examining this debate gives us the material and the occasion to consider why Fish elicits this reaction from legal theorists, and why legal theorists seem incapable of taking Fish seriously on his own terms. Forty years on from these exchanges, it does not feel that legal theory has moved on; many of these theories are still the object of great attention, and Fish could make the same arguments, *mutatis mutandis*, against the legal theories that are in vogue today.

The reason for the widespread rejection of Fish's position comes from several facets of Fish's thought, some obvious and some more subtle. Fish undermines legal theory's attempt to justify and uphold the practices of law with an intellectual framework. He does this not by saying some particular intellectual framework is wrong, but by saying there are no intellectual frameworks that can justify the law. The whole enterprise of legal theory is wrongheaded and indeed, on its own terms, redundant. Unlike other critics of legal theory's claims, Fish has no apparent legal cause to advance, and is therefore impossible to attack on the grounds of bias or partisanship, a claim readily levelled against other critiques of legal theory's defence of the status quo. He also does not want to replace legal theory with anything, giving no new directions for future work in the field. And finally, he does not, I think, believe that legal theory should stop because of its incoherence or redundancy; he wants the game to go on, incoherently, because it serves *a* purpose, albeit one that is a far cry from the purpose its proponents wish to advance. This last point raises a crucial but underexplored aspect of this debate: the important (rhetorical) work that legal theory does in a society that demands intellectualised and philosophical justification

---

Fish himself is not really a *participant* in the game that is legal theory, so a better analogy would be if someone who is not playing the game came along to pick it apart, and then left the other players to play on without them. I have not yet done this to my friends, but I could not rule out doing so in future.

of social practices, and whether this sort of justification is something we could live without.

Looked at this way, it is clear why Fish is such a problematic opponent for legal theorists. Fish takes a dim view of the importance and impact of theory and the kind of debates theorists engage in. (He has a similarly modest sense of the importance of his contributions).[2] This lack of importance of theoretical debates is something that legal theorists, seeing themselves as doing crucial work about a highly consequential practice, cannot accept. This is at the heart of Dworkin's reaction to Fish's challenge; Fish is at best incomprehensible and wrong and, at worst, actively dangerous. But he is neither of those things; he is rather, like me with my friends' boardgames, ruining your fun and insisting that the game go on.

I believe, as Fish does, that the law is best understood as existing without foundations; that theory talk has (almost) nothing to do with law; and that we can believe this without collapsing into anarchy, illegitimacy, or despair.[3] Also like Fish, I do not expect that a great many readers will be tempted to step down this road. But for those who might, I think the best way to advance this case is to show why so many legal theorists are opposed to Fish, and why their objections are wrongheaded. That is the task I undertake in this chapter.

II. STANLEY FISH AND LEGAL THEORISTS

I will first consider Fish's arguments with legal theorists, beginning with Dworkin, and then moving on to similar exchanges with other theorists. Mapping these encounters illustrates the nature of these disputes and helps us to locate the source of the hostility of legal theorists to Fish's views.

---

[2] One might ask why, if Fish is unconvinced of the importance of his contributions, he enters the debate at all. I would concede that this is puzzling, but I think I personally understand it. I do not think my boardgame interventions are important; they have no consequences (other than causing irritation); and I know my audience does not want to hear them. But I cannot help myself: I feel compelled to point out the flaws in the game when I see them and to try to convince others that I am right. Perhaps it is the same for Stanley Fish.

[3] I am openly in agreement with Fish in these debates, and have used his arguments in many contexts, including: interpretive communities being the origin of meaning in judging (D Kenny, 'Merit, Diversity and Interpretive Communities: The (Non-party) Politics of Judicial Appointment and Constitutional Adjudication' in L Cahillane et al. (eds), *Judges, Politics and the Irish Constitution* (Manchester, Manchester University Press, 2017) 136); critical self-consciousness and judges understanding their own processes (D Kenny, 'Conventions in Judicial Decisionmaking: Epistemology and the Limits of Critical Self Consciousness' (2015) 38(2) *Dublin University Law Journal* 432); originalism being purely rhetorical (D Kenny, 'Politics all the Way Down: Originalism as Rhetoric' (2017) 31(3) *Diritto pubblico comparato ed europeo (DPCE)* 661); and the extent of the role of the unseen interpretive forces in shaping the legal world (D Kenny, 'Examining Constitutional Culture: Assisted Suicide in Ireland and Canada' (2022) 17(1) *Journal of Comparative Law* 85).

A. Dworkin, Interpretation, and Fish's Critique

Dworkin's thesis in 'Law as Interpretation'[4] – which is an early sketch of the ideas that animate *Law's Empire* – is that all legal statements are interpretive of legal history, and so law as a practice is an exercise in interpreting the past. The motivations behind the project are apparent from the beginning. Dworkin does not believe in a formalist account of law, that the law is 'just there', waiting to be found with ready certainty; it needs interpretation, and interpretation is complex and contested. But the law also must guide a judge's resolution of disputes, or the law will be vulnerable to the sceptic's claim that when judges interpret the law, they 'impose their own view', overriding what is currently there. Dworkin's fear is that the judge 'is actually making new law in the way he or she thinks best' rather than applying a law that is.[5] This seems, at first glance, to suggest that there must be some law that exists outside of interpretation, but Dworkin forcefully denies this. This, as we shall see, is the core of the disagreement with Fish.

Dworkin's project is to explain how the law, if it is not formalist, can avoid the pitfall of the unconstrained judge, and he does this with a theory of interpretation. What we need in law, Dworkin says, is to interpret it in a manner that is 'cut loose from ... associations with speaker's meaning or intentions', as looking to a speaker's intention introduces too much subjectivity into interpretation.[6] To explain how we might interpret properly in law, Dworkin invites us to think of the work of judging as akin to writing a chain novel, with each judge writing a new chapter following from what has gone before. There can be no singular intention after the first chapter ends, and therefore the process is not intention-bound. Writers are duty bound to work 'to create, so far as they can, a single, unified novel' rather than separate stories. Legal cases are like this. Judges

> must read through what other judges in the past have written not simply to discover what these judges have said, or their state of mind when they said it, but to reach an opinion about what these judges have collectively done, in the way that each of our novelists formed an opinion about the collective novel so far written.[7]

The judge can thus not 'strike out in some direction on his own', and is properly restrained by the text.[8]

In proposing this, Dworkin introduces what will become the heart of *Law's Empire*: law as integrity, and the 'fit and justify' thesis.[9] An interpretation of a

---

[4] R Dworkin, 'Law as Interpretation' (1982) 9(1) *Critical Inquiry* 179.
[5] ibid 181.
[6] ibid. If we do not do this – if we interpret by looking to authorial intent instead – then interpretation will not be *about the work*, about the text. It will not treat the text as 'an object in itself'. ibid 190.
[7] ibid 193.
[8] ibid 193–94.
[9] R Dworkin, *Law's Empire* (Cambridge, MA, Harvard University Press, 1986).

work must fit with all that came before the act of interpretation, and must aim to show the work as 'the best work of art it can be'. The crucial distinction is 'between explaining a work of art and changing it into a different one'.[10] The former is the proper role of the judge, making their interpretation of the law cohere with the legal system as they find it, and justifying that system by casting it in its best light. The interpretation 'must both fit that practice and … show the value of that body of law in political terms by demonstrating the best principle or policy it can be taken to serve'.[11] It must fit in with the legal system *as it is*, not make the legal system as they wish it to be.

Dworkin knows that this cannot eliminate disagreement entirely. He admits that the process he is describing requires agreement on what is properly inside the legal system – what we must make our interpretations fit with, and what we should justify – and what is outside of it. He acknowledges that this will be controversial. There will also be disagreement about an interpretation being absolutely right, and its rightness cannot be proven to everyone's satisfaction. But that does not prevent us from saying that a particular interpretation is the best interpretation yet produced.[12]

Dworkin also insists that what guides judges in interpreting is theory, and that 'anyone who interprets … relies on beliefs of a theoretical character'.[13] He acknowledges that these theories or beliefs are to some degree tacit, but not necessarily or fully: they must be amenable to argument or else they are not theories but mere 'reactions'. This is much elaborated on in *Law's Empire*: that what judges have (and must have, to be good judges) is 'coherent theory' and a 'set of principles' to guide them.[14]

Dworkin seems to be driven here by an urgent need to *guide* judges. He is seeking to argue against partisan-political accounts of law that provide 'poor understanding and *even poorer guidance*', and he wants to provide better guidance.[15] He thinks that since law is 'a complex and dramatically important practice',[16] it needs theory to guide it, or it risks illegitimacy by letting loose judges who are not properly constrained.

This, to say the least, is not to Stanley Fish's taste. He says that Dworkin 'repeatedly falls away from his own best insight into a version of the fallacies (of pure objectivity and pure subjectivity) he so forcefully challenges'.[17] What Dworkin fears – radically unconstrained judging – is impossible, Fish says.

---

[10] Dworkin (n 4) 183.
[11] ibid 194.
[12] ibid 186.
[13] ibid 185; *cf* 196.
[14] Dworkin (n 9) 243–245.
[15] Dworkin (n 4) 179 (emphasis added).
[16] ibid 197.
[17] S Fish, 'Working on the Chain Gang: Interpretation in the Law and in Literary Criticism' (1982) 9(1) *Critical Inquiry* 201.

Judges have, from their professional training and experience, already internalised a sense of the enterprise of judging. This internalised set of conventions and suppositions about the law and judging operate as a constraint on how judges perform their task, because it gives them a firm sense of what judges can and cannot do. What Dworkin hopes for – judges constrained in a way stronger than convention – is impossible but also unnecessary, as the conventional constraints already in place are more than enough.

Fish says Dworkin's fundamental mistake in his chain novel analogy is to think that the first writer is free, while the later ones are constrained. The first writer, Fish argues, is just as constrained as those who follow: constrained by the suppositions of the enterprise, by 'the context of a set of practices that at once enables and limits the act of beginning'.[18] It is these same suppositions – rather than the text left by the first writer – that operate to constrain the successors in this practice, shaping their interpretation of what went before and their idea of what can follow. No-one is free or constrained; everyone is equally 'free *and* constrained'.[19] We are all bound by the conventions, suppositions, and practices that give us our understanding of this enterprise and make the task of interpreting possible. Without them, we could not interpret, as we would not even know how to begin the task. If we went outside of these conventions (though it is hard to imagine someone who would, having been intellectually brought up within the enterprise), our actions and utterances would not be heard as a part of the enterprise at all, and would not be taken seriously.[20]

But we are also free in the sense that the things that bind us are not fixed, universal, unchanging, or fully controlling, such that one interpretation is 'inescapable'. They do not 'direct' us in this strong sense.[21] They ebb and flow within and across the community and over time, and we can change, play with, and depart from them, albeit in ways themselves constrained by the enterprise, and included in the enterprise's sense of where it possibly could go.[22] In Dworkin's version of the process, Fish says, both of the things he claims to avoid – full, formalistic constraint, and radical freedom – are in fact taking place: radical freedom at the start, and full constraint at the end. But neither of these things is actually possible. We are bound by our sense of the enterprise of which we are part, and are never fully free. Nevertheless, we are not bound tightly enough by this to make us anything more than partially constrained.

Fish further says that Dworkin is wrong to think that interpretation is not about intention; it is *always* about intention, because you cannot interpret without imagining some volitional author.[23] But this does not, as Dworkin fears,

---

[18] ibid 203.
[19] ibid 203 (emphasis in original).
[20] ibid 207.
[21] ibid 205.
[22] ibid 206.
[23] ibid 213.

prioritise the subjective feelings of the author, or fail to give due reverence to the text as object. The text is never an object, as Dworkin imagines, because texts can only exist in relation to readers and the community of meaning they bring to it.[24] Readers' postulations about the author's intention, not the author's subjective views, are determinative of meaning. Disagreement cannot be settled by reference to text, because it is in the context of interpreting the text that the disagreement arose within the community.[25] Whether an interpretation works or not is a function of the people hearing and considering the interpretation, not some property of the text itself.[26] When Dworkin finds an interpretation he thinks absurd, or a wilful altering of the text, he is just highlighting examples of things that are not within current interpretive bounds.[27]

In short, Fish says, Dworkin is wrong when he thinks a lot is a stake in this debate – when he worries about irresponsible interpretation and the need for constraint. In fact, he is seeking assurance 'he already has and could not possibly be without'.[28] And what we know from our interpretive community – that which guides and constrains us – is not theoretical, but conventional. What seem like theories of judging, or sets of principles, are in fact rhetorical moves designed to make our favoured interpretations persuasive and/or to suggest that people who disagree with us are acting beyond the interpretive pale.[29]

Dworkin was very unhappy with Fish's reading of him. He calls Fish's account of his position 'incompetent' and 'treacherous', saying he has been 'brutally misread'. He writes Fish off as preaching the 'quasi-scepticism' and dogmas of contemporary literary theory.[30] He accuses Fish of giving words like 'intention' and 'finding meaning' new and strained meanings, far removed from what they mean in practice. And then he restates his position in a way that seems (to me at least) to match Fish's description of him in all relevant ways. Though he vociferously denies it is his position, he seems once again to insist at various points that unconstrained interpretation is a risk that must be avoided, and that his account can avoid this risk and provide fixity. Fish, in his response, says Dworkin is wrong again, and that his writings and thought are 'vague and slippery'.[31] Either nothing has changed in Dworkin's position, or – if he has retreated from Fish's reading of his position as he claims he has – he is at the

---

[24] ibid 207.
[25] ibid 204.
[26] ibid 211.
[27] S Fish, 'Wrong again' (1983–1984) 62 *Texas Law Review* 299. Alternatively, they might – as Fish argues is the case with Dworkin's example of reading Agatha Christie as a philosophical treatise on death – just not be to Dworkin's interpretive taste, while the different interpretive community might readily accept them.
[28] Fish (n 17) 212.
[29] ibid 208.
[30] R Dworkin, 'My Reply to Stanley Fish (and Walter Benn Michaels): Please Don't Talk about Objectivity Any More' in WJT Mitchell (ed), *The Politics of Interpretation* (Chicago, University of Chicago Press, 1983) 287–88.
[31] Fish (n 27) 308.

point where he has left 'virtually nothing to say'.[32] When Dworkin expands and refines his position in *Law's Empire*, Fish says he is 'still wrong after all these years'.[33] And the game went on, with blows traded in various other fora.[34]

B. The Real Issue between Dworkin and Fish

The major problem with Dworkin's legal theory, in my view, is that he is astute enough to see its problems, but he is also unwilling to accept the true consequences of those problems. Fish's objections arise because Dworkin sees the problems in formalist theories that claim to provide interpretive objectivity, and tries to offset them with qualifications. But he cannot do this, because he is wedded to aspects of these stronger accounts – the seeming fixity they provide – that he believes he cannot cede. If Dworkin took the qualifications he is making seriously, he and Fish would be on the same page. But he does not and cannot take them seriously, and he almost immediately lapses back into the stronger positions he denies taking.

Dworkin and Fish often sound alike. When Dworkin says judges are guided by 'innumerable decisions, structures, conventions, and practices',[35] it could be a line from Fish. They have a similar project, with the same main antagonists: they both wish to reject that the law is 'just there', or that it is a function of mere personal preference.[36] Fish notes that Dworkin's essay very nearly contains Fish's counterpoints within it,[37] and notes that the differences between them can 'seem small'.[38] It is, however, a significant mistake – though it is commonly made – to think that Fish and Dworkin are the same, or that the differences between them are minor. The differences, though subtle and *seeming* to be small, are profound.

On one level, Dworkin and Fish seem to propose similar solutions to the problems of interpretation. Dworkin's centring of the 'network of beliefs' of the interpreter sounds like Fish's interpretive community. But Dworkin cannot embrace and accept the implications of this position: that because of the network of beliefs, there is no problem of interpretation in the sense that Dworkin thinks, and there is also no way to firmly bind interpreters. Since no one is ever free, there is no problem for Dworkin's method to solve; and since his method in any event does not bind the interpreter tightly, it does not provide the special legitimacy that Dworkin thinks the law requires. Law as integrity could be a Fishian exegesis of what judges are already doing, but then it would

---

[32] ibid 307.
[33] S Fish, 'Still Wrong After All These Years' (1987) 6(3) *Law and Philosophy* 401.
[34] Dworkin critiques Fish's conventionalism (and perhaps pragmatism) in *Law's Empire* (n 9); Fish also comments on Dworkin's work in *Law's Empire* in several other pieces cited below.
[35] Dworkin (n 4) 193.
[36] ibid 196; Fish (n 17) 201.
[37] Fish (n 17) 214.
[38] S Fish, 'Dennis Martinez and the Uses of Theory' (1987) 96 (8) *Yale Law Journal* 1773, 1789.

lack the 'distinct political virtue' which Dworkin wants for it.[39] He cannot say, as Fish would put it, that 'the constraints imposed by practice are as strong as anyone could want'.[40] He cannot accept Fish's version of intention because then intention would, as Dworkin admits, become 'methodologically useless',[41] and we need, he insists, a methodology. For Fish, being bound is not some special condition, or a hallmark of legitimacy; it is just doing what comes naturally, acting as the conventions of community compel you to act. Fish's account offers, at most, an 'enriched notion of practice', a fuller way of seeing practice (but not a fuller way of practicing).[42]

This is why the dispute is so bitter, I think: Dworkin is almost there with Fish – as Fish says, 'almost right'[43] – but since he cannot go the last mile, he repeatedly lapses back into the same errors and veers from the implications of Fish's insight. Dworkin is thus the best of Fish's legal opponents in this sense – he sees more clearly than most that Fish is right – but the worst in another – despite his clarity of vision, he cannot admit it.[44]

C. Fish's Other Quarrels in Legal Theory

While the exchange with Dworkin is the liveliest, Fish's arguments with other legal theorists are very similar, and they, like Dworkin, do not seem to know what to make of him.[45] Take, for example, his exchange with Owen Fiss. Fiss proposed to use Fish's concept of interpretive communities as a way of saving legal interpretation, showing why objectivity in interpretation is possible in law

---

[39] Dworkin (n 9) 166; *cf* discussion in Fish (n 33).
[40] Fish (n 27) 313.
[41] ibid 314.
[42] Fish (n 38) 1787.
[43] Fish (n 33) 410.
[44] I think Dworkin shows this same pattern in other aspects of his legal thought: he takes a position that seems obviously to identify him with some mode of thought, and then strenuously denies this, insisting that he does not hold such a position and/or that his position is different in crucial respects. A vivid example of this is his denial of pragmatism. In *Law's Empire* (n 9) 95, Dworkin spends a great deal of time trying to illustrate that Law as Integrity is not like pragmatism, and is markedly different from it, but as Smith and Nye and others have pointed out, Dworkin is engaged in nothing more than an 'an exercise in veiled pragmatism', and it is not even that veiled; SD Smith, 'The Pursuit of Pragmatism' (1990) 100 *Yale Law Journal* 409, 419. Nye makes a strong case that Dworkin's entire thought is a sort of Peircian pragmatism. H Nye, 'Staying Busy While Doing Nothing? Dworkin's Complicated Relationship with Pragmatism' (2016) 29(1) *Canadian Journal of Law and Jurisprudence* 71. I think Fish has it right when he says Dworkin is 'almost pragmatist', essentially a bad pragmatist. S Fish, 'Almost Pragmatism' in *There's No Such Thing as Free Speech and it's a Good Thing Too* (Oxford, Oxford University Press, 1994) 200. I hope to discuss this question in more detail in a forthcoming book about pragmatism in law and literature. For a fascinating comparison of Dworkin and Fish's pragmatism, distinguishing them based on the idea of 'narrow' and 'broad' pragmatism drawing on Robert B Brandom, see T Bustamante, ch 14 in this volume.
[45] Levinson notes the tendency of legal theorists to misread Fish; DJ Levinson, 'The Consequences of Fish on the Consequences of Theory' (1994) 80 (7) *Virginia Law Review* 1653.

when it is not so in literature.[46] The community of legal interpreters creates 'disciplining rules' of interpretation that can operate quite strictly to restrain judges engaged in interpretation. Fish's interpretive communities seemed like a promising candidate for law: they would acknowledge the community-based nature of legal meaning, but might have the potential to provide a workable, practical constraint on interpretation. This concept could, Fiss thought, save us from the subjectivity and variability that Dworkin so greatly feared in this most consequential of fields. But in doing this, Fiss puts a weight on interpretive communities that the concept cannot bear. As Fish outlines at length, belief in community- or reader-originated meaning cannot solve the problems that legal theorists want to solve.[47] Fiss's position gave the content of the community a privileged position; suggested a conscious knowledge of the content of the community; and suggested an ability to state that content with sufficient precision that we could make it into a set of rules. But the content of the community is not formal in this sense; it comes from a deep sense of the enterprise. When you are actually in the grip of an interpretive community, you cannot state its contents fully and explicitly, but you do not need to; 'explicitness will have been rendered unnecessary'.[48] Fiss's disciplining rules are then just a partial (and necessarily impoverished) account of what the interpreter already knows deep in their bones.

Disciplining rules are also themselves the subject of interpretation that they could not control, as the rule could not conceivably govern a dispute about its own meaning. On Fish's account, such rules – though present – are just another internal feature of interpretation, not an external constraint on it. You have to be a part of the community of interpreters to even understand them; the knowledge you need to engage in interpretation is a 'kind of knowledge that informs rules rather than follows from them'.[49]

Fish's critique was not limited to those who try to find a third way between the extremes of freedom and constraint like Dworkin, Fiss, and others. He applied his insights with equal rigor to originalists and natural law theorists that believe in a more old-fashioned objectivity,[50] and did the same to Critical Legal Studies and strong legal realism that argued that judges were or could be unconstrained.[51] It is probably unnecessary for me to add, following this

---

[46] O Fiss, 'Objectivity and Interpretation' (1982) 34 *Stanford Law Review* 739.
[47] S Fish, 'Fiss v Fish' (1984) 36 *Stanford Law Review* 1325.
[48] ibid 1330.
[49] ibid.
[50] See his commentary on originalists and others in S Fish, 'Play of Surfaces: Theory and the Law' in *There's No Such Thing as Free Speech and it's a Good Thing Too* (Oxford, Oxford University Press, 1994) 180; and on natural law, amongst other things, in Fish (n 38).
[51] He takes on the crits in many fora, including Fish (n 38); S Fish, 'The Law Wishes to Have a Formal Existence' in *There's No Such Thing as Free Speech and it's a Good Thing Too* (Oxford, Oxford University Press, 1994) 141; S Fish, 'Milton and Unger' in *Doing What Comes Naturally* (Durham, NC, Duke University Press, 1989) 398.

sympathetic account, that I agree with Fish on every point. The best way I can add to his case, I think, is to explain why these arguments are taken so badly by legal theorists, and why this reaction is unwarranted. I will try to illustrate this in the rest of this chapter.

III. THE 'PROBLEM' WITH STANLEY FISH

The problem with Stanley Fish – the reason his work does not have broad purchase in legal thought – is not that he is wrong, but the extent to which his thought offers (most[52]) legal theorists *nothing* that they want to hear. He is under no obligation to offer them anything, but it is this, I think, that explains the extreme reaction that Fish received from Dworkin, and the often-hostile response he gets, sometimes being dismissed as nihilistic or jejune. For the legal theorist, Fish's thought offers very little to argue against, nothing to build on, and no agenda to pursue, and therefore reactions to him tend toward either anger or dismissal. In this section, I will discuss which parts of Fish's thought are so hard to accept, and why.

A. Your Project is Wrongheaded, and its Problems cannot be Fixed

The common theme of all this work in legal theory that Fish targets is, as I put it elsewhere, 'wanting to save law and legal interpretation from a common foe: the unrestrained interpreter, the unbound judge who roams freely over the field of pain and death'.[53] Dworkin's project, like the originalists', the natural lawyers', and Fiss's, is one of salvation or redemption for the law from this actor – to bind them, or to be able to firmly distinguish them from those that are doing law legitimately. It is an effort to redeem the law from the perdition and illegitimacy of subjectivity and politics; to perfect the law, or at least reduce its imperfections to tolerable levels. Much of legal theory seems to be justificatory or redemptive of the law in this sense.

---

[52] There are some legal theorists, especially those who offer some deeply critical or sceptical accounts of law, that can deal with Fish on his own terms. Pragmatists can and do usefully engage with and draw on Fish's antifoundationalism (because pragmatism is just an account of what you do in the condition of antifoundationalism) as long as they do not turn pragmatism into a program. See Fish (n 44). Postmodern scholars have usefully critiqued Fish as being insufficiently deconstructive: Schlag, in a pair of short essays, critiques the 'closure' and 'resting place' from deconstruction that Fish's thought offers; P Schlag, 'Fish v Zapp: the case of the relatively autonomous self' (1987–1988) 76 *Georgetown Law Journal* 37.

[53] T Hickey and D Kenny, 'Interpretation in law and literature' in A Hanna and E McNulty (eds), *Law and Literature: The Irish Case* (Liverpool, Liverpool University Press, 2022) 21, 23. The image of the 'field of pain and death' is borrowed from R Cover, 'Violence and the Word' (1985–86) 95 *Yale Law Journal* 1601.

All of Fish's thought runs against this. If there is a unifying theme of his work, it is the imperfectability of social and human affairs. From blind review in academia, to anti-professionalism, to interdisciplinarity, to the legal theory, Fish says that promises to save our enterprises from problems of bias, subjectivity, error, and fault are always false, because to be human is to have perspective, and everything we do is therefore angled, partisan, and partial.[54] Some angled systems will, by our lights, work much better than others for running a society, but that does not make them perfect, and this assessment is just yet another angled and partial position. The goal of these theorists, therefore, is for law to escape the human, but as William James puts it, 'the trail of the human serpent is over everything'.[55]

To put it another way, Fish's work is about 'the irreducibility of difference' in affairs between people.[56] All of his interlocutors' legal theories seek to cabin, contain, or eliminate differences that cause 'political' disputes in the law. But they cannot do this because difference, fundamentally, is the human condition; we all have different experiences that lead us to have different views, goals, and beliefs. When we agree on some matter – contingently and locally – we will find new things, based on our different experiences, to disagree about. Attempts to persuade people to agree with some theory are rhetorical gambits to gain temporary agreement on a point to advance some agenda. It is not some special escape from difference and conflict, but rather a successful move in the unending game of negotiating difference that we are all playing out. To live is to differ, and to paraphrase Justice Robert Jackson, we achieve unanimity only in the graveyard.[57]

This is why Fish knows that his positions, if they are understood, will disturb those who 'seek a jurisprudence in which policy considerations have been either eliminated or subordinated', specifically noting Dworkin as such a person.[58] He is telling legal theorists not just that they have failed in their efforts to cabin or eliminate difference, but that this is never achievable. They are seeking perfection in an imperfectible world, and there is no theory they could offer, or guide for adjudication, that can solve their problem. This, I think, is the first thing that frustrates Fish's legal interlocutors, and it sees him accused of nihilism or scepticism, condemning the law to illegitimacy as nothing more than 'masked power'.

---

[54] See S Fish, 'No Bias, No Merit: The Case against Blind Submission' (1998) 103(5) *Publications of the Modern Language Association of America* 739; S Fish, 'Anti-Professionalism' (1985) 17(1) *New Literary History* 89; S Fish, 'Being Interdisciplinary is so Very Hard to Do' [1988] *Profession* 15; and on legal theory, any and all of Fish's work cited in this chapter.

[55] W James, *Pragmatism* (New York, Dover, 1995) (first published 1907) 14. This always seemed to me to be a good summary of Fish's core insight. Fish also uses the phrase in S Fish, *Versions of Antihumanism* (Cambridge, Cambridge, University Press, 2012) 208.

[56] Fish says this insight is synonymous with antifoundationalism. Fish (n 44) 206.

[57] *West Virginia Board of Education v Barnette* 319 U.S. 624 (1943).

[58] Fish (n 44) 207.

B. That's not a Problem: Your Project does not Matter

Fish, of course, has a response to this charge: it is not in any way nihilistic, and the fear of nihilism or illegitimacy 'is baseless'.[59] There is no such thing as nihilism; everyone is acting to advance some end that they value. And every legal actor is always and already situated in the legal process, embedded in the web of suppositions and assumptions of the legal community, with all its attendant purposes, goals, motivations, and constraints. To be a situated actor of this sort 'is not to be looking about for constraints, or happily evading them (in the mode, supposedly, of nihilism), but to be constrained already'. The 'bogeyman' of the law being no more than 'masked power' is not the problem legal theorists think; the law does not need any more legitimacy than it gets from people's acceptance of it, and it does not need any external source of legitimacy.[60]

This, of course, is his primary point to Dworkin: to be a competent participant in the enterprise is to be restrained already, to 'operate within a strong understanding of what the practice they are engaged in is for'. But none of this comes from theory: what we know from practice is 'not theoretical in any interestingly meaningful way'.[61] Judges may use theory talk to explain what they do – they may have an articulated, self-conscious account of their practice that uses theoretical language – but there is no reason in the world to think that this is an accurate explication of what they do and why.[62] It is a rhetoric that is part of the process of explaining and justifying their actions, rather than being generative of and controlling those actions.

All of this is to say that there is politics in law and judging, but that is simply not a problem.[63] This politics is 'enterprise specific', separate to some degree from your primary political aims and aspirations, operating within the limits of the community-set boundaries and purposes of the law.[64] So there is no need to fear the doom these theorists suggest awaits us without their theories; we are just as restrained as we need to be. To put it more strongly again, the theories are, on their own terms, pointless. The paradoxes and problems that these theorists point out and seek to resolve in fact dissolve the moment we question their assumptions. The legal theorist, Fish says, 'need not even be worried

---

[59] Fish (n 47) 1332.
[60] ibid 1334, 1340.
[61] Fish (n 44) 225.
[62] See Fish (n 38).
[63] I have argued this at length in D Kenny, 'Merit, Diversity and Interpretive Communities: The (Non-party) Politics of Judicial Appointment and Constitutional Adjudication)' in L Cahillane et al. (eds), *Judges, Politics and the Irish Constitution* (Manchester, Manchester University Press, 2017) 136.
[64] Fish (n 47) 1336. As I have put it elsewhere: 'One can be judicially conservative whilst being, say, generally politically liberal: one might favour a liberal result, but be unwilling to reach it judicially. That does not mean judicial politics are neutral; it just means that one's broad political views favour restraint in the specific context of judging.' Kenny (n 63) 148–49.

by the possibility that his account of adjudication might be wrong', because nothing flows from this lack of a strong, principled theory of the law.[65] It is not that I am a nihilist, Fish says; it is that your project is redundant.

So, what motivates these theorists if these fears are so groundless? Their fears are in most or all cases genuinely held; they really believe in them. But this just raises the question of why they hold and maintain these beliefs. One answer is that it is their intellectual disposition, having come up in a particular intellectual community, to hold beliefs of this sort. Another, Fish would say, is that they do so because (subconsciously, perhaps) they know the rhetoric of their theories helps to advance their enterprise-specific politics: deeming in and out of bounds certain interpretive moves, certain legal developments, in a way that suits their preferred vision of the law and judging.

To accept Fish's point, then, legal theorists would have to accept that they are not merely wrong, but that they are engaged in a fool's errand, a task that is not only impossible but, in terms of its stated priorities, entirely pointless. The intellectual project is not motivated by the fears and concerns that they thought guided them. What really guides them is either a baseless fear, and/or a subconscious pursuit of their politics in direct contradiction to their stated aim of objectivity.

That would be a very significant thing to concede, and embracing Fish's position would take a major shift in world view, the legal theory equivalent of falling off your horse on the way to Damascus. Such conversions happen, but they are rare. Few people would have devoted enough time to engage in the enterprise of legal theory – and would have found its pronouncements interesting or worthwhile – without a firm intellectual framework in place that would make a conversion like this very unlikely.

C. No Dog in the Hunt, No Alternatives

Relatedly, Fish has no interest in offering any alternatives, or suggesting future work in the sphere of legal theory. There is no need for an alternative, as theories of this sort matter only in the philosophy seminar, and are not relevant to the actual doing of law.[66] The nature of our philosophical conclusions will not have any effect on the practice of law, which has its own purposes and goals that do not need a philosophical grounding (save in the very limited sense discussed in the next section). Fish's interlocutors are looking for deep knowledge of law, and there is, in short, 'nothing deep to know'.[67]

---

[65] Fish (n 47) 1334–35, 1346.
[66] Fish (n 44) 214; Fish (n 33).
[67] Fish (n 50) 193.

Fish's own (anti)theory is not an alternative legal theory. There is 'nothing to be gained'[68] methodologically from such accounts of the law; if we tried to make it a methodology, what we would be doing would 'no longer be law', as our activity would be dismantling, not advancing, law's authority.[69] It is impossible to try to build on Fish's position to make legal theory better; there are no foundations to support the weight you might put on this position; it gives you no direction to go in; it offers no agenda to pursue. And the insight that there is no foundation cannot, without contradiction, be turned into a foundation. Fish repeatedly takes people to task, inside and outside his debates with lawyers, for this 'theory hope': believing that understanding the reality of contingency can help you evade it.[70] But it cannot, and if you think it can, you show yourself to only partly understand the insight of contingency.

In the same way, Fish's theory has 'no prescription whatsoever'[71] about what direction the law should move in. This is different from the philosophical positions of his interlocutors, which, as discussed previously 'carry a calculable rhetorical weight' in advancing the law in certain directions.[72] Fish has no dog in the hunt; he does not want to move the law in any direction (or at least he has no interest in trying to do this through academic means or philosophical argument). He cannot have a program, a direction for the law to travel in, without betraying the insights of heterogeneity and difference on which his position is based.[73]

I think this is another source of the bafflement and anger that Fish seems to provoke in legal theorists. He offers no work program, and no suggestions for what is to be done. One cannot use his insight as a springboard for further argument. And he is arguing that this is an acceptable outcome, as legal theory is redundant. Fish is also not advancing a particular angle or agenda; this obscures Fish's own politics, and makes him hard to fathom. We are used to theory being angled, and to identifying the agenda that a theory advances; this was regularly used *by* and *against* Critical Legal Studies scholars in debates about the law's

---

[68] ibid 197; *cf* Fish (n 38) on critical legal studies.
[69] Fish (n 51) 176.
[70] Alongside making this point in several of the essays discussed here, he makes it at length in S Fish, 'Consequences' in *Doing What Comes Naturally* (Durham, NC, Duke University Press, 1989) 314.
[71] Fish (n 27) 314.
[72] Fish (n 50) 192. It is this rhetorical weight that differentiates Fish from Hart's positivism, which Hart claimed was morally neutral and sought only to describe, not justify, the law. See HLA Hart, *The Concept of Law*, 2nd edn (Oxford, Clarendon Press, 1997) 240. Fish would say, I think, that Hart's description is not morally neutral, but in fact the product of a (thin) morality. Hart advances and justifies a thin, procedural understanding of the law that hides the centrality of interpretation and the latent force that undergirds the law. In doing so he advanced an agenda nested within that vision of the law that is politically and morally opposed to other, thicker understandings of the law, and the consequences and implications of those other understandings. For a Fish's broader critique of Hart, see S Fish, 'Force' 45 *Washington & Lee Law Review* 883 (1988).
[73] Fish (n 44) 215.

ideology. It is unnerving that Fish's agenda cannot be found; we cannot put him in an ideological box and thus discount his point of view. Ironically, Fish achieves what so many of these theories aspire to: a neutral theoretical perspective. But he can accomplish that only because of the self-confessed unimportance of his position,[74] and the uselessness of what he is saying to any practical agenda. As Fish puts it, his interlocutors

> are alike in thinking that they have something to recommend, something that will make the game better .... All I have to recommend is the game, which, since it doesn't need my recommendations, will proceed on its way undeterred and unimproved by anything I have to say.[75]

D. Keep Playing the (Rhetorical) Game

The game, in this last statement, is the game of the law in practice. But I think the game of legal theory is also one that Fish, for all his complaints about it, is happy to see continue. In the philosophy seminar that is academic writing, Fish is happy to attack and dissect legal theory. But he knows that these attacks will not deter legal theorists; few will be persuaded that the enterprise is pointless. Should he get purchase on some point, and some legal theorists were moved to give up the practice, or if some branch of legal theory were to die, plenty of others would swiftly take their place.[76] He knows the game of legal theory will go on no matter what he says about it, and I think he believes it should.

Fish's core point in all his critiques is that legal theories are rhetorical:[77] they are ways of trying to persuade people of something. They are thus not accurate or true *in terms*, but Fish, who is happy to be called a sophist,[78] would categorically reject the idea that something being rhetorical makes it trivial or unimportant. We live in a rhetorical world, and rhetoric is all we have; it is of the greatest importance. The primary rhetorical purpose of most legal theory (and of all of the legal theory that Fish critiques) is, as previously discussed, to advance various contested and contestable agendas about what law should be. But there is also a more general rhetorical function of legal theory that I think Fish would consider important: it helps to uphold the idea of law as an independent, autonomous, sensible and useful practice. It does this not because legal theories show the law to be so, but because in their elaborate complexity, they

---

[74] He is express about this: 'nothing turns on Fiss's account or, for that matter, on my account either'. Fish (n 47) 1347.
[75] Fish (n 44) 230.
[76] See generally, on this adaptability, P Schlag, 'Law and Phrenology' (1997) 110(4) *Harvard Law Review* 877.
[77] See Fish (n 50) 192.
[78] S Fish, *There's No Such Thing as Free Speech and it's a Good Thing Too* (Oxford, Oxford University Press, 1994) 291.

lend law intellectual credibility in a world that demands that many of its social processes have apparent intellectual rigor and prestige.

In *The Wishes to Have a Formal Existence*, Fish makes essentially this point about the practical legal concepts and principles – mutual agreement, consideration, negligence, causation – that make up the law in action. Looking at contract law, Fish shows the (useful) malleability of supposedly static concepts and principles, and suggests that law's ability to constantly change, while at the same time asserting continuity with that past, is what lets it do its job. To peaceably and authoritatively resolve disputes, the law must respond and adapt to each new context, and transform accordingly in ways that will make it deeply inconsistent and even conceptually incoherent. But to maintain its necessary authority, the law has to obscure this reality, and make it appear that it has conceptual coherence and continuity, as that is part of why people accept the law as a way to resolve disputes. People in general need to believe in the law for it to work. This is the law's 'amazing trick'; laying down new ground as it walks upon it, and then insisting it was there all along.[79] Looked at this way, from a pragmatic point of view, 'the inconsistency of doctrine is what enables law to work'.[80]

It is my case that legal theory of the justificatory sort that Fish critiques is similar. It fulfils the same basic purpose as incoherent legal doctrine – upholding the idea of law as an enterprise that should be respected – but for the more intellectually- and theoretically-inclined crowd. There are two different groups that might be in need of such theoretical validation. First, judges or other legal actors may find it easier to carry on their practices if they feel their practice is intellectually grounded and justified, rather than being a product and function of experience and community. This also helps a great deal with public accountability, and offering public-facing accounts of their actions, which may benefit greatly from the sense of coherence that theoretical vocabulary offers.[81] Second, many people who observe the law or the legal system need to believe it is intellectually coherent for them to be comfortable with the role it plays in their society. As belief in formalism became harder to maintain, people needed some reassurance that something serious and worthwhile is going on with the law in order to maintain their belief in it. They need it to be explained abstractly, comprehensively, or coherently. Or, to be more accurate, they need to *feel* that it is so explained.

For both these groups, it is useful and reassuring to see some very smart and articulate people explaining the law and the legal system in a very complicated way, and legal theorists serve them well in offering an intellectual framework. But legal theorists are also *part* of that group that need to believe in law's intellectual coherence. With their work, they are reassuring themselves in the face of their own doubts about the law.

---

[79] Fish (n 51) 170.
[80] ibid 169.
[81] See generally, on the uses of theoretical vocabulary, Fish (n 38).

I think Fish would acknowledge that legal theory needs to exist to serve this rhetorical purpose, though he has not, as far as I am aware, said so in terms. Law's artifice, its fictive self-presentation, is something Fish says the law cannot do without, and theory is a major part of this artifice. I take him to be saying something similar when he says that various distinctions that make up legal theories are 'constitutive of the law not in the sense of producing it but as components of its intelligibility' and should you take it away, 'you take away the entire basis of the law's current self-presentation'.[82] The law, to put it in Fishian terms, needs to have a theoretical existence.[83]

The requirements for theories that could fulfil this rhetorical role are modest, I think, just as the requirements for the law to have a 'formal existence' are modest: Fish shows that law's principles can allow a great deal of malleability while offering the necessary appearance of consistency.[84] Similarly, a legal theory could fulfil this role once it has enough within it to answer the most pressing challenges posed by sceptics at a given time, and offers the promise of theoretical improvement, paths for further development and iteration.

I should stress that this need for law to have theoretical validation is a contingent rather than an absolute need. It is possible to imagine a legal system similar to ours, in a less intellectually-inclined culture or era, that would not benefit from theory talk in the same way. To put it another way, it is the intellectual and theoretical predisposition of our present legal culture and our culture more broadly, rather than something in the nature of law, that creates the need for theory. Law would not command sufficient respect in our society if it could not offer a robust intellectual (rather than purely pragmatic or force-based) account of itself.[85] This could, in principle, change – our society could cease to demand intellectual justifications of its institutions – but there are few indications that such a turn in our culture is coming, and I do not think it likely.

But this rhetorical necessity for *some* legal theory to exist is a far cry from what legal theorists want for their enterprise. They do not want to offer a theory that rhetorically preserves law's authority in the face of intellectual challenge.

---

[82] Fish (n 50) 193. He elsewhere says 'the law will only work ... in the sense answerable to the desires that impel its establishment' if the 'metaphysical entities' that make up law 'are retained'. See Fish (n 44) 213.

[83] This seems as though it undermines Fish's repeated assertion that theory (in law or literature) does not have consequences, but it does not. (See S Fish, 'Consequences' (1985) 11(3) *Critical Inquiry* 433.) Fish readily acknowledges that theory has *rhetorical* consequences, but these are contingent, and follow from how the theory is received in the culture, not from its theoretical elements. This is not the sort of consequence theorists want from their theories. See Fish (n 51) 181, 191, where he says, contrasting himself to Perry's assertion of the importance of constitutional theory, 'I too shall be arguing that constitutional theory matters, but in terms Perry would regard as weak', and that in this weak sense 'theory matters very much'.

[84] See Fish (n 51).

[85] We can see this in Fish's thought when he says law's artifices will not be done away with 'unless of course society decides that a legal culture is a luxury it can afford to do without', something he thinks possible but deeply unlikely. Fish (n 44) 214; *cf* Fish (n 72).

They want to give accounts that strive towards truth, comprehensive explanations of the law's coherence, better practice of law or judging, etc. As Fish points out, Dworkin is not happy being a rhetorician, but wants to 'link up with a deep epistemological truth' which his theory reflects.[86]

This, then, is the final reason that Fish's position is so difficult for legal theorists to accept. Fish's account does not suggest that legal theory should stop, but that it should continue in this (by the lights of its proponents) fallen and lesser form. As with one my friends' board games after the rules have been picked apart, the game must go on, even if you are no longer having any fun.

IV. CONCLUSION: COULD THE LAW DO WITHOUT THEORY AND ITS OTHER RHETORICAL TRAPPINGS?

Is Fish correct that the law could not successfully continue without its artifices? I think this is one of the underexplored aspects of his thought. It is quite clear that Fish thinks the law could not rid itself of elements like supposedly formal rules and rhetorical theories of judging; he says 'it is hard to imagine it doing without [them]'.[87] But, curiously, he does not devote much argumentative time to explaining why this is the case. He does not think that legal theorists seeing through the law will undermine it: 'it will not fade away because a few guys in Cambridge and Palo Alto are now able to deconstruct it'.[88] So why, then, is he concerned about law's fate if *everyone* were able to deconstruct it? He feels the law could not do its job without its artifices. But is he right about this? Would the actual operations of the law, presented plainly without its conceptual and theoretical trappings, prove unacceptable to people?

I must admit that I have struggled with this question. It is almost certainly a question of degree: it might be possible to be much more open about this than we are now and still preserve the law's authority. But I think Fish is in essence right that we could not radically rid the law of these rhetorical trappings, and I wish to explain why this is so: these artifices are not laid on top of the law, but *baked into* the law, and to remove them would be to remove the law with them.

The law needs an agenda of some sort; it has to advance some direction and tendency for the resolution of disputes. This is angled and partisan in the sense that it advances one agenda and not another. It could not do without this, or the law would be nothing, have no content, and achieve nothing; to purport to resolve disputes is to be partial in a particular direction of resolution. Law's agenda is embedded through its various rules and practices. The agenda of some of these is consciously and deliberately adopted, and overt. But much of

---

[86] Fish (n 38) 1792.
[87] Fish (n 51) 170–71.
[88] Fish (n 38) 1799.

it is not overt, but deeply embedded, and thus invisible; an agenda disguised as principle. (It was perhaps the chief goal and achievement of the Critical Legal Studies movement to illustrate these instances).[89] It would seem possible that this agenda could be plainly stated – we could reveal and debate these nested assumptions, and the law could thus be 'demystified'. But this is not so.

First, this assumes that the agenda *can* be fully stated if we wish to do so, but it cannot. The agenda is baked into the law's myriad rules and practices and is seen only (and even then, partially) in the law's effects. We cannot have full knowledge of what the law is doing in this way; much of it is not consciously known.[90] If, then, we tried to unpack and formalise this agenda, we would attract disagreement, not only because of its substantive politics, but also because of good faith disputes about what the agenda baked into the law actually *is*. To put it another way, the unstated nature of the agenda is part of the law as we know it.

Second, this approach assumes that if we stated the agenda, this would not be encoded, but of course it would be: the statement of agenda would be part of some discursive system,[91] and will rely on coded vocabulary that itself would need to be unpacked. Every decoding is another encoding, and so it is the kind and degree of encoding – not its presence or absence – that is under discussion.

Third, it assumes the agenda stated more baldly is as good – as effective in achieving our purposes – as the agenda encoded. But the encoding serves a purpose: it enables us to endorse not the agenda as articulated and argued for – which might seem self-serving and highly partial – but legal abstractions in which it is nested. The abstraction and nesting of the agenda is a non-trivial component of its appeal, and thus its value.

Finally, and relatedly, the encoding is what allows us to get any agreement on the law at all.[92] Encoded agreements are general. Without the encoding, the primary disagreement about the way to resolve cases would never end. In a large, complex, heterogenous society, it is hard to imagine agreement on such an agenda being reached even provisionally, as anyone to whom the agenda was

---

[89] See, for classic examples of this genre, D Kennedy, 'Legal Education as Training for Hierarchy' in D Kairys (ed), *The Politics of Law* (New York, Pantheon Books, 1982); R Abel, 'A Critique of American Tort Law' (1981) 8(2) *British Journal of Law and Society* 199; JM Feinman and P Gabel, 'Contract Law as Ideology' in D Kairys (ed), *The Politics of Law* (New York, Pantheon Books, 1982). For Fish's critique of the next step in the CLS method – building on these insights to improve the law – see Fish (n 50).

[90] This is also part of the general problem with critical self-consciousness. See S Fish, 'Critical Self-Consciousness, or Can We Know What We're Doing?' in *Doing What Comes Naturally* (Durham, NC, Duke University Press, 1989) 436; D Kenny, 'Conventions in Judicial Decisionmaking: Epistemology and the Limits of Critical Self Consciousness' 2015 38(2) *Dublin University Law Journal* 432.

[91] We would be on 'the already occupied ground of some other line of work no less special, no less hostage to commitments it can neither name nor recognize'. Fish (n 44) 211.

[92] Fish makes this point in respect of doctrinal concepts in Fish (n 51) 171: 'every legal procedure [would be] turned into a debunking analysis of its enabling conditions, decisions would never be reached and the law's primary business would never get done'.

even marginally unfavourable would not wish to acquiesce in it, and there would be no end to specific cases to account for. The uncertainty of the nested agenda allows us to agree at a general level, and hopefully defuse or defer conflict later on when we get down to the specifics.[93] Law's obfuscation lets us accomplish the tasks of resolving disputes and regulating conduct without resort to more forceful means.

Law's authority seems to rest, in the end, on these rhetorical tricks. But this is not a problem; it is just how things are, and it could not be otherwise in the rhetorical world we are in, a world without foundations that transcend language and perspective. All authority is, as Fish says, ultimately rhetorical and political:

> authorities do not come ready made in the form of a pure calculus or a scriptural revelation; rather they are made, fashioned in the course of debate and conflict, established by acts that are finally grounded in nothing firmer than persuasion ... and so finally fashioned and maintained by force.[94]

We have decided that the forces of persuasion and rhetoric are better than more direct types of force to resolve disputes; to help set up a civilization; to let us overcome or defer our inevitable differences just enough so that we can, as a society, find a way to live as the wind rises.[95] The law cannot do without legal theory, and the rhetorical ballast it provides, and so Stanley Fish knows that the game will go on, no matter we say about it.

---

[93] On the value of 'imperfect' pragmatic compromises based on underspecified conditions, see D Kenny, 'The Virtues of Unprincipled Constitutional Compromises: Church and State in the Irish Constitution' (2020) 16(3) *European Constitutional Law Review* 417.
[94] Fish (n 44) 204. On Fish's idea of the law as force, see Fish (n 72).
[95] I am borrowing a phrase here from Paul Valéry's poem 'Le cimetière marin': 'Le vent se lève! ... il faut tenter de vivre!'.

Part Two

Interpretation and Critical Constraints

6

Reenchanting Practice: Stanley Fish and the Challenge of Virtue Ethics

MARIA CAHILL AND PATRICK O'CALLAGHAN*

I. INTRODUCTION

IN THIS CHAPTER, we critique Stanley Fish's essay *Dennis Martinez and the Uses of Theory*,[1] a key contribution to the 'Fish-Dworkin debate'.[2] Our core argument is that Fish's central distinction between engaging in a practice and discoursing on that practice is too sharp, and that the two corollary claims that he makes – that practice is not generated by theory and that theory does not offer a genuine account of how practice unfolds – fail to convince.

Behind Fish's distinction is an attempt to reframe practice: to uncouple it from the sort of abstract theorising that takes place in a vacuum and to throw light on how practitioners actually carry out their activities. In what follows, we also seek to reframe practice, perhaps even to reenchant it, by drawing on the depth and richness of conceptions of practice available in the fields of virtue ethics and virtue jurisprudence.

In section II, we outline the central distinction, while in section III we examine how Fish applies that distinction to the practice of judging. In section IV, we examine how well the distinction stands up against understandings of practice that emerge from the field of virtue ethics. In sections V and VI, we critique Fish's two corollary claims by reference to insights from virtue ethics and virtue jurisprudence.

---

*We wish to thank Bernard Long and Holly Hayes for their research assistance, which was made possible with the support of the Head of Law Strategic Fund at UCC, and the students of the spring 2022 Jurisprudence class with whom some of these ideas were initially tested. We are especially grateful to Barty Begley, Thomas Bustamante, Margaret Martin, Amalia Amaya Navarro, Jeffrey Pojanowski and John Sorabji for their detailed insightful comments on earlier drafts of this paper.
[1] S Fish, 'Dennis Martinez and the Uses of Theory' (1987) 96(8) *The Yale Law Journal* 1773–1800.
[2] See generally, M Robertson, *Stanley Fish on Philosophy, Politics and Law* (Cambridge, Cambridge University Press, 2014) ch 9.

II. THE 'ENGAGING IN A PRACTICE' V. 'DISCOURSING ON A PRACTICE' DISTINCTION

In the 'Dennis Martinez' article, Fish draws a distinction between 'engaging in a practice' and 'discoursing on that practice'.[3] Playing baseball is not the same thing, he says, as explaining or analysing how baseball should be played, and 'in a strict sense ... there is no relationship between them whatsoever'.[4] In fact, no matter what the practice, Fish maintains, there is an ineliminable difference between carrying out the activity in question and analysing or theorising that activity; in short, between the 'doing' and the 'talking about the doing'. This distinction is the essential point of his article,[5] and Fish goes on to apply the distinction to the practice of judging. But having initially articulated this distinction, and before discussing its application in law, Fish makes two further claims. These claims are presented as corollaries of the distinction and therefore help to illuminate the perspective he has in making and articulating the distinction. The first of these, which we will call *the claim of atheoretical generation*, is that practice is not generated by theory, while the second, which we will call *the claim of inauthentic explanation*, is that theoretical discourse about a practice does not provide a genuine account of how that practice unfolds.

A. The Claim of Atheoretical Generation

Fish is keen to clarify that discoursing on practice 'does not stand in a relationship of superiority or governance to the practice that is its object',[6] underscoring that talking is not better than doing, and that talking does not regulate the doing of practice. In particular, Fish argues against an assumption that a good theory is the precursor to or the foundation for developing effective practice. His concern seems to be that we take analysing and theorising too seriously, attributing to them an importance and a power that they do not and should not have. He wants to focus on the actual doing of practice, rather than the talking or theorising about it, and to open our eyes to the ways in which practice stands on its own feet. We think that there is a lot to be said in favour of this effort to shift focus to the importance and power of practice, as will become apparent in the remainder of this chapter, although we dispute the practical feasibility and

---

[3] Fish (n 1) 1777–78.
[4] ibid 1775.
[5] This argument (or arguments of this sort) features not only in this article but also in other essays in which Fish engages with Dworkin's work. See, eg, S Fish, 'Working on the Chain Gang: Interpretation in the Law and in Literary Criticism' (1982) 9 (1) *Critical Inquiry* 201–216; S Fish, 'Wrong Again' (1983) 62(2) *Texas Law Review* 299–316; S Fish, 'Still Wrong After All These Years' Law and Philosophy' (1987) 6(3) *Law and Philosophy* 401–418; S Fish, 'Almost Pragmatism: Richard Posner's Jurisprudence' (1990) 57(4) *The University of Chicago Law Review* 1447–75.
[6] Fish (n 1) 1778.

normative desirability of the claim of atheoretical generation. In Fish's view, theory *never* generates practice:

> Even if the practitioners happen to be in possession of a theory of the activity in which they are engaged, the shape of that activity is not the result of the application of that theory. They do not use their account of what they are doing (assuming that they have one) in order to do it. ... [N]o one follows or consults his formal model of the skill he is exercising in order properly to exercise it.[7]

It is worth noting that by defining theory as 'an abstract or algorithmic formulation that guides or governs practice from a position *outside any particular conception of practice*',[8] Fish is doubling down on the distinction between practice and discoursing on a practice. The basic point seems to be that Fish wants to make space to recognise practice as an immersive experience. Although practitioners may be aware of theory that exists outside the world of practice, it is nevertheless the case that within the world of practice, in his view, it is only the practice that governs:

> While it is certainly the case that the successful performance of a skill will sometimes require the invocation of theory – even of a theory of that particular skill – *it is never the case* that the theory thus invoked is acting as a blueprint or set of directions according to which the performance is unfolding.[9]

Essentially, then, when Fish is articulating the distinction between engaging in a practice and discoursing on a practice, one of the things he wants to say is that practice is not constituted by theory: the claim of atheoretical generation.

B. The Claim of Inauthentic Explanation

Having distinguished between engaging in a practice and discoursing on that practice and having rehabilitated the notion of practice as something to be taken seriously in its own right, Fish then turns to the notion of theory. His definition of theory has placed theory 'outside any particular conception of practice' as noted, and throughout the article, Fish conflates the ideas of 'discoursing on a practice' and 'talking' about a practice and 'theory', and regularly refers to these activities as being undertaken self-consciously and strategically. In one passage, for example, he describes theorising as 'the self-conscious recourse to a theoretical mode of talk, [which] no more generates the shape of [practice] than it generates the shape of what the talk is about'.[10] So when Fish is articulating the distinction between engaging in a practice and discoursing on a practice, the other thing he wants to say is that theorising or discourse on a practice cannot

---

[7] ibid.
[8] ibid 1779 (emphasis added).
[9] ibid (emphasis added).
[10] ibid 1778.

and should not be understood as offering a genuine account of how the practice is unfolding.

On one side, the claim of atheoretical generation asserts that practice is not constituted by theory. On the other side, the claim of inauthentic explanation holds that theory does not truly account for how practice unfolds. Taken together, they sharpen the distinction between engaging in a practice and discoursing on a practice, and they make clearer that Fish wants to reenchant our understanding of the importance of practice and undermine the dominant understanding regarding the contribution of theory. And, of course, Fish has developed these general points about practice and theory in order to tee up some arguments that he wants to make about the practice of judging.[11]

III. THE DISTINCTION AS APPLIED TO JUDGING: THINKING WITHIN A PRACTICE AND THINKING WITH A PRACTICE

Not only Dworkin but 'almost everyone in the legal academy', Fish believes, takes the position that there is overlap between the practice of judging and reflection or theorising on that practice.[12] Fish, however, wants to maintain that judging is like every other practice: there is a sharp distinction to be maintained here, too, between the doing of the practice – that is, the process of reaching a conclusion in a legal dispute – and the talking about the doing – that is, academic theorising about the practice of adjudication or, in the case of judges themselves, the process of using theory to explain a conclusion in a written judgment.

> [W]hat I want to say is that judging or doing judging is one thing and giving accounts or theories of judging is another, and that as practices they are independent, even though the successful performance of the first will often involve engaging with the second. That is, as a practice judging is one of those that includes as a part of its repertoire self-conscious reflection on itself, and therefore it seems counterintuitive to say that such self-reflection – such theorising – is not to some extent at least constitutive of what it is reflecting on; but that is just what I will be asserting, and asserting in direct [1780] opposition to what is assumed by almost everyone in the legal academy.[13]

The nuance of this position must be noted: Fish concedes that successful engagement with the practice of judging often entails invocation of theory and he acknowledges that the practice of judging necessarily includes theorising about judging. But it would appear that, for Fish, such use of theory is merely part of a judge's rhetorical repertoire when seeking to persuade others that her decision is the correct one. Fundamentally, Fish wants to maintain the underlying distinction between engaging in the practice and discoursing or theorising

---

[11] ibid 1779ff.
[12] ibid 1780.
[13] ibid 1779–80.

about the practice. Moreover, at this point in the article, the nomenclature of the distinction changes. Fish now contrasts thinking 'within a practice' and thinking 'with a practice': thinking within a practice maps on to the idea of engaging in a practice while thinking with a practice becomes co-extensive with discoursing about a practice or theorising. Judges who think within the practice of adjudication are the baseball players, while legal academics and those judges who think with a practice are the baseball analysts. Fish explains the new distinction in the following key passage:

> To think *within* a practice is to have one's very perception and sense of possible and appropriate action issue 'naturally' – without further reflection – from one's position as a deeply situated agent. Someone who looks with practice-informed eyes sees a field already organized in terms of perspicuous obligations, self-evidently authorized procedures, and obviously relevant pieces of evidence. To think *with* a practice – by self-consciously wielding some extrapolated model of its working – is to be ever calculating just what one's obligations are, what procedures are 'really' legitimate, what evidence is in fact evidence, and so on. It is to be a theoretician.[14]

Tying the various strands together in the particular context of judging, we can say that judges think within a practice when they are deciding how to rule in any given legal dispute, and they are thinking with a practice when they are discoursing on how they rule in any given legal dispute. Alongside making the distinction between thinking within and thinking with a practice, Fish also re-affirms the claims of atheoretical generation and inauthentic explanation, if anything, even more stridently in the context of the practice of judging, as explained below.

A. The Claim of Atheoretical Generation in Judging

Judges who *think within the practice* of adjudication are so deeply situated in the world of practice that they perform their tasks in an almost automatic way. Such a judge is a 'deeply situated agent' who looks through 'practice-informed eyes', and who is faced with 'perspicuous obligations, self-evidently authorised procedures, and obviously relevant pieces of evidence'.[15] Fish borrows Dworkin's analogy of the chain novel to show how each judge, being a link in the chain, becomes a source of the purposes and values and goals of the law:

> It would follow then that an agent so embedded would not need anything external to what he already carried with him as a stimulus or guide to right – that is, responsible – action; in short, he would not need a theory.[16]

Fish's reading of Dworkin's chain novel analogy is that, rather than explaining the place of theory, it actually confirms his own 'enriched notion of practice',

---

[14] ibid 1788.
[15] ibid 1788.
[16] ibid.

a notion in which practice, rather than being in need of the guidance theory might claim to provide, is itself sufficient, is, in fact, self-sufficient, and in need of nothing additional.[17] For Fish, the chain novel analogy demonstrates that theories of judging do not shape the practice of judging.[18] Even the judge's own self-conscious reflection on her practice does not help to constitute her practice, because practice is a fully immersive experience. A judge reaches her decisions naturally and automatically by engaging in the practice of judging unselfconsciously without needing to have recourse to any external blueprint or benchmark or standards against which they measure their practice. Their practice is their whole world. Nothing else is necessary. Thus, the claim of atheoretical generation – that practice is not governed or generated by theory, or even by self-conscious reflection – holds, as far as Fish is concerned, for the practice of judging.

B. The Claim of Inauthentic Explanation in Judging

If theories and self-reflections do not constitute part of the practice of judging, then why is judging so full of 'theory talk'?[19] Fish's answer is that some judges, knowing 'perfectly well what they are doing',[20] engage in *thinking with the practice* of judging. By this, Fish means that they are instrumentalising theories and self-reflections, and therefore

> engaging in the practice of self-presentation, that is, the practice of offering a persuasive account of why they have done what they have done – decide the case this way rather than that – which is not the same thing (why on earth should it be?) as offering an account of how they actually did it.[21]

The decision reached by a judge is arrived at without the input of theory (the claim of atheoretical generation), but judges subsequently and strategically use 'theory talk' in the form of written judgments to provide highly curated, rhetorical *ex post facto* justification for that decision. According to Fish, judges engage in this process for the following reason:

> [N]ot in order to provide an accurate description of the process by which they came upon their invention, but in order better to dress the product of that process in a garb appropriate to a situation in which their goal – and therefore the ground rules – had changed. Their goal is now persuasion, and they cast around for appropriate means with which to effect it (this is, of course, the traditional Aristotelian definition of rhetoric) and find them, or at least a portion of them, in the rhetorical practice of talking theory.[22]

---

[17] ibid 1787.
[18] ibid.
[19] ibid 1791.
[20] ibid 1790.
[21] ibid.
[22] ibid 1791.

Any use of 'theory talk' in a judgment is simply window dressing.[23] Fish asserts that Dworkin's extensive writings on the practice of adjudication do not uncover the methodology that judges actually use to arrive at their decisions but reveal only 'the complex of rhetorical gestures to which one has recourse when a decision, already made, must be put into presentable form'.[24] In this light, according to Fish, Dworkin should be understood as 'a rhetorician'.[25] Thus, the inauthentic explanation claim – that theorising or discoursing on a practice does not provide a genuine account of how practice unfolds – also holds, on Fish's account, for the practice of judging.

Having given an exposition of the distinction between engaging in a practice and discoursing on a practice, and having discussed how Fish applies this distinction to the practice of judging, and how he sharpens the distinction by adding the claims of atheoretical generation and inauthentic explanation, we now want to analyse the merits of these arguments. We believe that the most serious challenge to any attempt to sharply delineate theory and practice comes from virtue ethics and virtue jurisprudence, because of how these schools of thought conceive of the notion of practice and because of how they understand the relationship between practitioner and practice. The scholars whose work we draw on in the succeeding sections will allow us both to dispute the practical feasibility and normative desirability of Fish's distinction (section IV) and the two corollary claims that he makes (sections V and VI).

IV. THE VIRTUE ETHICS CHALLENGE TO FISH'S DISTINCTION

The first thing to interrogate is the distinction itself. Fish assumes that one can draw a clear line between engaging in a practice and discoursing on a practice: the doing of the practice is entirely unselfconscious and unreflective, the discoursing on the practice is all talk and has no meaningful bearing on action. His aim, as noted above, is to reframe our conceptions of practice, and, as also noted, we support this mission. However, Fish adopts a very thin theory of practice, one that presents practice as quite mechanical and automatic, exclusive of and unresponsive to conscious self-reflection. We believe that a better way to reframe practice or perhaps even to reenchant it is to adopt a deeper, richer and more descriptively accurate definition of practice, such as the one offered by virtue ethics.

Virtue ethics articulates a much thicker understanding of practice that better captures its complexities. Alasdair MacIntyre, for example, defines practice as:

> any coherent and complex form of socially established cooperative human activity through which goods internal to that form of activity are realized in the course of

---

[23] *cf* Hart's discussion of 'window dressing' in the context of rule scepticism: HLA Hart, *The Concept of Law*, 2nd edn (Oxford, Oxford University Press, 1994) 140.
[24] Fish (n 1) 1790.
[25] ibid.

trying to achieve those standards of excellence which are appropriate to, and partially definitive of, that form of activity, with the result that human powers to achieve excellence, and human conceptions of the ends and goods involved, are systematically extended.[26]

For MacIntyre, then, practice is anything but automatic. It is deeply important, hugely ambitious, and necessarily complex for its careful interweaving of activity, conceptualisation and refinement. What is more, self-reflection is a core component of practice, as MacIntyre further explains:

> A practice involves standards of excellence and obedience to rules as well as the achievement of goods. To enter into a practice is to accept the authority of those standards and the inadequacy of my own performance as judged by them. It is to subject my own attitudes, choices, preferences and tastes to the standards which currently and partially define the practice.[27]

If we adapt MacIntyre's understanding of practice to the context of judging, it would be that justice is achieved in individual cases as judges pursue the kinds of professional excellences that are appropriate to and partly definitive of the practice of judging, with the result that the judges' capacity for professional excellence and ability to achieve justice in individual cases as well as conceptions of what justice means become continually more refined and sophisticated. Moreover, self-reflection – thinking about what it means to be a good judge in the light of the standards of excellence and assessing how, as an individual judge, one measures up to those standards – is an essential part of the practice of judging.

On this richer understanding of practice, practice and reflection are bound up together and mutually generating. As we engage in the particular activity, we realise our goals by striving towards standards of excellence that define the activity (meaning that our engagement is shaped by theory and self-reflection). In addition, as we strive for those kinds of excellences, our capacity to achieve them is increased and our understanding of what they mean is refined (meaning that our theory and self-reflection is refined by our practice). Within this perspective, it is not practically possible to separate practice from theory. The doing cannot be done without the reflection. If MacIntyre is correct that standards of excellence partially define a practice, then it surely follows that if practitioners do not attempt to meet those standards of excellence in a systematic way, a point may be reached where the very character of the practice is altered so that it becomes something else, another activity that cannot meaningfully be understood as the practice it purports to be. Moreover, it is not normatively desirable to separate practice from theory, because it is the combination of the two that makes the practice so effective and makes the goods internal to that practice achievable. Adapting this to the context of judging, it is necessarily the case that the

---

[26] A MacIntyre, *After Virtue*, 3rd edn (London, Bloomsbury, 2007) 218.
[27] ibid 221.

practice of adjudication requires that judges are self-reflective, striving towards the standards of excellence that define the practice of judging, and that if there is systematic failure to do this, then the practice that unfolds will not be recognisable as the practice of adjudication.[28]

While MacIntyre's theory offers a counterpoint to Fish's distinction between engaging in a practice and discoursing on that practice, by offering a much richer conception of practice at the macro level, Julia Annas, in her work articulating a compelling account of virtue-as-skill, offers a deeper understanding of practice at the micro level. By conceiving virtue as a skill, she believes that we can better understand how virtues are developed and refined over time, and thus distinguish them more clearly from routines which tend to become ossified over time. In Annas's account, as will be explicated in detail below, this distinction between skill and routine turns on the extent to which the actor must engage her intelligence in order to accomplish the activity, and in this way, like MacIntyre, her work can be used to contest the feasibility of Fish's central distinction which separates doing from reflecting.

First, though, we should understand that Annas' definition of virtue acknowledges that it is 'persisting, reliable and characteristic' of a person.[29] A virtue is persisting because it is 'a lasting feature of a person, a tendency for a person to be a certain way', which persists through challenges and is strengthened by its exercise.[30] A virtue is reliable in that one can count on it as a feature of a person: it is not an accident that she behaves courageously, and we would be surprised if she did not. A virtue is a characteristic when it is 'a *deep* feature of the person' – something which is central to her nature.[31] In being persistent, reliable and characteristic of a person, and for the fact that they can become engrained and reinforced over time, virtues can intelligibly be described as habits. But even if we use the language of habit (and like Annas, we prefer the language of skill), we must be careful not to diminish the level of mental engagement involved. If I am persistently, reliably and characteristically courageous, that is not the same as my being persistently, reliably and characteristically a coffee-drinker.

---

[28] In the field of jurisprudence more generally, this argument bears similarities to Fuller's understanding of the eight principles of legality as a 'morality of aspiration' or 'kinds of legal excellence toward which a system of rules may strive'. L Fuller, *The Morality of Law* (New Haven, Yale University Press, 1964) 41. Should a government fail in 'any one of these eight directions', Fuller insists that the result is not just 'a bad system of law', rather we are left with 'something that is not properly called a legal system at all …' (ibid 39). On the idea of the character of a practice changing so that it becomes something else, consider also Hart's analogy of the role of the 'official scorer' in a game (Hart (n 23) 142–45). Occasional incorrect decisions on the part of the scorer can be tolerated but if these 'aberrations' become too frequent, 'there must come a point when either the players no longer accept the scorer's aberrant rulings or, if they do, the game has changed' (ibid 144).
[29] J Annas, *Intelligent Virtue* (Oxford, Oxford University Press, 2011) 8.
[30] ibid 9.
[31] ibid.

In order to explicate this distinction between routine and skill, Annas lingers on the contrasting examples of driving to work and playing the piano. It is worth quoting Annas at length on this point:

> Here is an example of habit becoming routine. I drive to my university job every day, following the same route to the parking garage. At first, I have to think consciously about the best way to do this, avoiding traffic without going too far from the most direct way, modifying the route at different times of day and so on. Gradually I become used to driving on this route, and it becomes habit with me. I no longer have to think about which way to turn at every corner, where to slow down and the like. My driving has become routine. This does not make it mindless: I am still at some level aware of where I am going, since I stop at red lights, drive at the right speed, and behave cautiously around dangerous drivers. But driving has become detached from my conscious thinking, and my conscious and deliberate thoughts may fail to be properly integrated with it. I may find myself at the garage when I started out intending to go somewhere else en route, or find myself at the usual entrance even when I know it is closed for construction. A decision to act differently from usual has not penetrated the patterns of routine, which carry on unaffected. A change to routine has to be conscious, explicit, and sometimes repeated if it is to have appropriate impact.[32]

Routine is practice that has become so familiar that it no longer requires the kind of fully conscious engagement on the part of the practitioner that virtue must involve. To evoke this aspect of virtue, Annas uses the analogy of playing the piano. The beginner must consciously engage with all the detail of the music, thinking carefully about which notes should be played, in which order and at which speed, but the skilled piano player can play fluidly, without needing to think so much about each individual note. Is the pianist like the commuter, then?

> When we see the speed with which a skilled pianist produces the notes, we might be tempted to think that constant repetition and habit have transformed the original experience, which required conscious thought, into mere routine. But this is completely wrong. The expert pianist plays in a way not dependent on conscious input, but the result is not mindless routine but rather playing infused with and expressing the pianist's [14] thoughts about the piece. Further, the pianist continues to improve her playing. The way she plays exhibits not only increased technical mastery but increased intelligence – better ways of dealing with transitions between loud and soft, more subtle interpretations of the music, and so on. Rather than the rest of the mind being shut off from patterns of routine and proceeding independently, the ability, though a habituated one, is constantly informed by the way the person is thinking.[33]

The skilled pianist could play a piece as a matter of routine, with significantly reduced conscious engagement, failing to attend too carefully to the tempo or

---

[32] ibid 13.
[33] ibid 13–14.

the precision of the notes, and disconnecting from the dynamics and emotional resonance of the piece, but, Annas argues, we would class as a failure, rather than a manifestation, of skill.[34] The difference between routine and skill is in the level of intelligence employed. Virtues are like skills in that their practical mastery is accomplished over time through active intelligent engagement. Thus, from her perspective, Annas's position aligns with MacIntyre's when he posits that it is not practically feasible to distinguish sharply between practice and reflection.

Fish has insisted on such a sharp distinction, and it is instructive here to remember how he described judges as deeply situated agents, who are so immersed in practice that they can perform their tasks almost automatically, deciding naturally and unreflectively by looking through 'practice-informed eyes' at rules and facts without needing to engage in reflection. In his final exchange with Fish, Dworkin reflected on 'Fish's crucial assumption that an interpretive practice cannot be self-conscious and reflexive',[35] which 'leaves actual interpretive practice flat and passive, robbed of the reflective, introspective, argumentative tone that is, in fact, essential to its character'.[36] Read this way, Fish's vision of judging resonates more with Annas's description of driving a car than her account of playing the piano, because of his insistence that judging is done unselfconsciously and unreflectively and her insistence that virtues are exemplified only when there is a significant degree of intellectual engagement. And yet, in other places, Fish underscores that his judges are deeply immersed in practice, so much so that their being becomes shaped by the practice, which resonates with Annas's understanding of how a virtue becomes a persistent, reliable and deep characteristic of a person. Once, in distinguishing his position from Dworkin's, Fish explained that while Dworkin concluded that a judge 'will develop, in the course of his training and experience, a fairly individualised working conception of law on which he will rely, perhaps unthinkingly', Fish's own view is that '[a]ny judge will develop into a working conception of law'.[37] At another point, when discussing Dworkin's vision of law as a 'chain enterprise' and how this actually supports Fish's understanding of practice, Fish noted that a judge becomes a 'repository' of, among other things, the 'values' of that enterprise.[38] All of this resonates with Annas's understanding of how virtues seep into the bones of a person, as it were, so that generosity or courage or wisdom become part of who she is and we can now more accurately explain her behaviour by saying that she is a generous person than by saying that she has done a generous act. In both accounts,

---

[34] ibid 14.
[35] R Dworkin, 'Pragmatism, Right Answers, and True Banality' in M Brint and W Weaver (eds), *Pragmatism in Law and Society* (Boulder, CO, Westview Press, 1991) 380.
[36] ibid.
[37] Fish (n 1) 1789.
[38] ibid 1787–88.

the practice is so immersive that it shapes the identity of the practitioner and in both accounts, this is a process of development that takes place over time. But Fish does not explain the detail of how this development operates. Annas does, by explaining that virtues are learned through exposure to others who are engaged in the same practice and developed through a long process of participating in that practice while *at the same time* carefully reflecting on it, until at a certain point, all the reflections that have been previously undertaken will 'have left their effect in the person's disposition',[39] and therefore the virtue really will have become a persisting, reliable and deep characteristic of that person.[40] At that point, it is no longer necessary that an agent pore over the options as she would have needed to in the past. At that point, she can reliably act instinctively, because her instincts have been (and continue to be) conditioned by participating in the practice and periods of careful reflections thereon. At that point, to use Fish's language, her 'sense of possible and appropriate action [will] issue "naturally" – without further reflection'.

All this is to say that Annas's account of the development of virtues can, in fact, explain how a judge could become one of Fish's 'deeply situated agents', by showing the power of self-reflection to embed virtues in a person over time. Fish's description of judges deciding naturally and unreflectively by looking through practice-informed eyes aligns with Annas's account of persons who exercise virtue effortlessly having allowed that virtue to become part of them over time. Based on the evidence, though, we have to assume that Fish would reject Annas's account of the development process. Fish does not allow that self-reflection could be part of the practice and there are some passages that indicate that he is not enamoured with the discourse of striving for excellence in general.[41] Moreover, Annas's account assumes a richer conception of practice, one which denies a strict separation between practice and theory, and one that marshals the power of self-reflection to explain the development process. Perhaps Fish will offer his own explanation of the development process, in a way that would be compatible with the strict separation between practice and theory to which he is committed, but for now it seems to us that her account of the development process is another reason why Annas's approach – and by extension the virtue ethics approach to the relationship between practice and theory – is more practically feasible and normatively desirable.

---

[39] Annas (n 29) 30.
[40] ibid 8.
[41] For example: 'That is why Dworkin's repeated injunction to arrive at the "best" judgments we possibly can and be the best judges we can possibly be sounds so strange. ... "Be the best you can be" finally means nothing more than "act in the way your understanding of your role in the institution tells you to act" ... Those who are playing the game learn nothing from someone who tells them to be the best they can be. They are the recipients of the verbal equivalent of a pat on the back, and if Dworkin's claim is to be giving direction to judicial decisionmaking, the claim fails, and the best Dworkin can be is a cheerleader. (C'mon fellows, do your best.)' (Fish (n 1) 1793).

Reenchanting Practice: Stanley Fish and the Challenge of Virtue Ethics 111

Together, MacIntyre and Annas dispute not only the practical feasibility of Fish's position that it is possible to separate practice from reflection and theorising on that practice, but also its normative appeal. They hold, to the contrary, that our practice is shaped by our reflections on and theoretical understandings of what that practice should be and that, in turn, our theory is refined by our experience of practice, in the process by which we become more and more skilled at doing whatever it is that our practice entails. Fish's claims of atheoretical generation and inauthentic explanation followed from his strict separation of practice and theory and relied on that distinction holding up. Under a reenchanted conception of practice which denies the sharp distinction between practice and theory, these two claims are deeply contestable.

V. CONTESTING THE CLAIM OF ATHEORETICAL GENERATION

The claim of atheoretical generation holds that, across the board, theory does not generate practice. In the 'Dennis Martinez' article we have been referencing, Fish engages with the work of Michael Moore, Ronald Dworkin and Roberto Unger, arguing that the theories of adjudication that they propose actually do not 'and could not be used to do what [they] want it to do, generate and/or guide practice'.[42] Leaving aside the details and merits of this dispute, we want to argue that a more rigorous test of Fish's arguments would be to consider the claim of atheoretical generation in the light of the theories of adjudication produced by virtue jurisprudence.

Most people, we conject, would prefer to have judges who were intelligent, wise, courageous, fair-minded, empathetic, temperate, perceptive, conscientious, patient, and so on, rather than judges who display the opposite traits. Part of the work of virtue jurisprudence is reflecting on which virtues are especially important for the practice of judging. Different theorists have different lists, and they emphasise different things within those lists. Iris van Domselaar, for example, presents a six-pack of judicial virtues which include: judicial perception; judicial courage; judicial temperance; judicial justice; judicial impartiality; and judicial independency,[43] and she writes particularly compellingly on the importance of perception.[44] Lawrence Solum initially focused on judicial intelligence, judicial integrity and judicial wisdom,[45] but later presented a longer list which includes: judicial temperance; judicial courage; judicial temperament; judicial intelligence; and judicial wisdom.[46] But the theories of adjudication that emerge

---

[42] ibid 1781.
[43] I van Domselaar, 'Moral Quality in Adjudication: on Judicial Virtues and Civic Friendship' (2015) 1 *Netherlands Journal of Legal Philosophy* 24–46.
[44] I van Domselaar, 'The Perceptive Judge' (2018) 9(1) *Jurisprudence* 71–87.
[45] L Solum, 'The Virtues and Vices of Judge: An Aristotelian Guide to Judicial Selection' (1988) 61 *Southern California Law Review* 1735–56, 1740–54.
[46] L Solum, 'Virtue Jurisprudence: A Virtue-centred Theory of Judging' (2003) 34(1/2) *Metaphilosophy* 178–213.

from the field of virtue jurisprudence are not more wordy articulations of the instinct that most of us have that virtues fall into the category of nice-to-have.[47] They are much less tame than that.

The two key figures who present theories of adjudication from the perspective of virtue jurisprudence, Lawrence Solum and Amalia Amaya, set up their own positions by contrasting them with Dworkin's. They want to reject the approach taken by theories of adjudication that focuses on the process of getting to the right answer, and then incidentally saying or implying that a good judge is the one who can arrive at this answer. Dworkin's theory is a good example of this approach, they think, because Dworkin first concentrates on what right answers should look like, by explaining considerations of fit and justification and by deploying the analogy of the chain novel, and so on, after which he posits the figure of Hercules as the superhuman judge who can arrive at the right answer.[48] The problem, for Solum and Amaya, is that these theories assume that the right answer is out there somewhere, antecedent to and existing independently of the virtue of the judge who must find it, and the mythical perfect judge is only a good judge because he finds this right answer.[49] Although Amaya concedes that Hercules can be 'an important heuristic device' to help judges get into the right frame of mind,[50] both Solum and Amaya reject this approach because it fails to appreciate how right answers are actually generated by the virtues practised by the judges. It is against this background that we believe their theories are a more rigorous test of Fish's claim that practice is not constituted by theory or self-reflection.

Instead of starting with the process for finding a right answer and then saying that the good or perfect judge is the one who (climbs up to the heavens, brings down and) presents to us the right answer, Solum and Amaya start with what makes a good judge and then say that the right answer is the one at which the virtuous judge arrives. Solum calls his theory 'a virtue-centred theory' because of the 'claim that judicial virtues are a necessary part of the best theory of judging and that judicial virtue plays a central explanatory and normative role'.[51] The right decisions are 'virtuous decisions', which are

---

[47] Amaya calls this approach one which recognises 'an auxiliary role' for virtues, while Solum terms it a theory of judicial character. A Amaya, 'The Role of Virtue in Legal Justification' in A Amaya and H Hock Lai (eds), *Law, Virtue and Justice* (London, Bloomsbury, 2012) 52; Solum (n 46) 183.

[48] For readings of the 'right answer thesis' that challenge the conventional understandings of it, see D Priel, 'Making Sense of Nonsense Jurisprudence' (21 September 2020), *Osgoode Legal Studies Research Paper*, available at SSRN: ssrn.com/abstract=3696933, 30–32; T Bustamante, 'Between Unity and Incommensurability: Dworkin and Raz on Moral and Ethical Values' (2022) 13(2) *Jurisprudence* 169–93.

[49] Solum calls this 'a decision-centred theory of judging' (Solum (n 46) 184) and Amaya refers to it as granting virtues 'an epistemic role' in legal justification (Amaya (n 47) 52).

[50] Amaya, ibid.

[51] Solum (n 46) 198.

decisions that have been made by virtuous judges acting from judicial virtues in the circumstances relevant to the case.[52] Amaya similarly argues that virtue plays 'a constitutive role' in justifying legal decisions, which means that:

> virtue is not merely a *criterion* of justification, but rather a *condition* of justification. That is to say, it is not merely the case that what a virtuous judge would decide is the best criterion for determining what is right, but rather the claim is that the rightness of the decision itself depends on its being a decision that a virtuous judge might have taken.[53]

Fish's claim of atheoretical generation had insisted that the shape of the practice is never the result of the application of a theory, that a theory never acts as a blueprint or set of directions according to which the practice unfolds, and that a judge's sense of the right decision issues naturally 'without further reflection' from their position. Solum's and Amaya's theories of adjudication are closer to a MacIntyrean-type conception of judicial practice, in which the activity of seeking to deliver justice is shaped by the virtues that judges pursue, those virtues themselves having been articulated by the practice of adjudication, in a process of mutual refinement. On this view, the claim of atheoretical generation is implausible because the practice of adjudication is informed and governed by the judge's theoretical conceptions of the virtues, which operate as a guide to aid their successful engagement with the practice of adjudication, albeit that they are also refined and re-articulated by the practice. These theories of adjudication emanating from virtue ethics contest Fish's claim of atheoretical contestation. At the same time, they reenchant our understanding of practice. This is because they understand practice as being co-constituted with conceptions of virtue rather than merely derivative of rules and routines, and those virtues exercise a greater influence on the agents, drawing them into a secure process of self-reflection which supports their progress in effectively engaging with the practice.

VI. CONTESTING THE CLAIM OF INAUTHENTIC EXPLANATION

Law has long required that judges strive to adjudicate in accordance with the requirements of justice. They are generally required to tell us, in written judgments, the reasons they believe that the outcome they have settled on is

---

[52] Solum (ibid) distinguishes between a virtuous decision (one reached by a virtuous judge) and a lawful decision (one that could have been reached by a virtuous judge even if the judge in question reached that outcome without exemplifying the virtues).

[53] Amaya (n 47) 53. Emphasis in original. Amaya then distinguishes between a causal version of the constitutive theory, which would hold that 'a legal decision is justified if and only if it has been taken by a virtuous decision-maker' and a counterfactual version which holds that 'a legal decision is justified if and only if it is a decision that a virtuous legal decision-maker would have taken in like circumstances'. She defends the counterfactual version (ibid 56).

fair and just. The reasons given in those judgments are kept on record, to be reviewed by future judges, but also future lawyers and law students and legal academics and journalists and interested members of the public. In common law countries, in particular, a lot of work is done by these judgments, and they tend to be lengthy and detailed, because they are a crucial means by which the legal system is refined. The second corollary of Fish's sharp distinction between practice and theory was the claim of inauthentic explanation, which held that when judges hand down written judgments in support of their conclusions, they are not offering us a genuine account of the reasons which explain how they reached their decisions, but rather a highly curated *ex post facto* rationalisation which was written with the aim of persuading us, through rhetoric, that their decision is legitimate. Here again, Fish's deeper aim is to open our eyes so that we are less beguiled by theory and, once again, we believe that Fish is highlighting something important here. Curated, inauthentic reason-giving, and even the idea that 'reasons' might need to be parachuted in because practice cannot account for itself, fails to sufficiently respect the practice of adjudication. To the contrary, we believe that practice does explain practice, more than has been recognised, but only if we adopt the richer conception of practice offered by virtue ethicists.

In order to explore this, we return to Annas's account of virtue-as-skill. As noted above, for Annas, virtues are like skills in that their practical mastery is accomplished over time through active intelligent engagement. When Annas says that virtues require intelligence, and even that virtues are intelligent, several things follow. One is that we can account for the fact that, faced with unexpected danger, the courageous response must be considered, rather than automatic or mechanical, a point reflected on in depth in section V.[54] A second is that we can explain why, faced with acute human need, the same virtue of generosity might be manifested in a variety of creative ways.[55] A third is most pertinent for our purposes. It is that the process of developing virtues is shot through with the need to understand and the need to explain; in other words, as the requirement of 'articulacy'.[56] The novice who wants to become generous needs a model to follow, but the novice will not become a master simply by (mindlessly) mimicking the teacher.[57] Suppose the teacher decides to offer €100 to support a friend in need. The novice cannot robotically replicate this action with every friend she has or every person she knows, or even every friend she has who is currently in need. The novice cannot consider the donation of €100 to be a perspicuous obligation, to use Fish's term. €100 will not be a

---

[54] Annas (n 29) 14.
[55] ibid 15.
[56] ibid 19. For a critique of Annas' position, see M Stichter, 'Philosophical and Psychological Accounts of Expertise and Experts' (2015) 28 *Humana.Mente Journal of Philosophical Studies* 105–28.
[57] *cf* Fish on the 'Charlie Lau Objection' (n 1) 1775, fn 3.

generous response to the need of a friend who has become unexpectedly ill and needs to pay for expensive surgery, and €100 will be a reckless response to the need of a friend who has a gambling addiction. To acquire the virtue of generosity, the novice needs to reflect on and to *understand the reasons* why the teacher thought that it was a good decision to give €100 to the first person, and, having understood those reasons, to begin to self-consciously apply the same kind of reasoning to new situations. This understanding of the reasons is what will free the novice to be a self-directed seeker of virtue. Correspondingly, the teacher needs to be able to explain how she has read the situation and why she has chosen to respond in the way that she has. The teacher must be able to *offer reasons* that help the novice to understand the subtle ways in which the virtue should be manifested. And, over time, both the self-directed novice and the teacher can engage their drive to aspire for continual improvement by articulating, reflecting on, and refining their reasons in a process of self-conscious reflection. Thus, over time, reasons become constitutive of virtue. Reasons therefore play a critical role in Annas's theory of virtue, and virtues can only be accomplished within a context of articulacy. 'Virtue on the above conception is a disposition not just to act reliably in certain ways but to act reliably *for certain reasons*.'[58] These are interesting insights to take to the legal context, because they indicate that reason-giving is baked into the practice of adjudication, if that practice is understood in a richer sense. Fish has critiqued a position in which reasons are flown in from somewhere else to offer a rhetorical defence of a legal decision, but he has not acknowledged the extent to which thoughtful engagement with practice itself necessarily produces reasons which are persuasive. This, of course, is because his conception of practice does not admit of the possibility that practice includes thoughtful engagement with theory and self-reflection.

When it comes to the place of reasons in the process of adjudication, it is possible that written judgments are so much of a feature of our system that we perhaps take them for granted, failing to fully appreciate their value. Mathilde Cohen has tried to guard against this possibility by writing cogently on the relationship between reasons and the rule of law, disambiguating the different reasons why written judgments are beneficial in order to defend her thesis that the rule of law is, in the end, the rule of reasons. She focuses, first, on the fact that reason-giving is an essential component of the procedural aspect of the rule of law, promoting its consistency (by facilitating the ideal that like cases are decided in the same way), its knowability (by making clear how rules should be interpreted and understood, thereby enhancing the clarity and predictability of law) and its contestability (by making clear the grounds for the decision, thereby setting the parameters for future legal disputes). These arguments align with the general sense that written judgments support the rule of law at the most basic level because they facilitate the ideal that like cases should be decided the same way.

---

[58] Annas (n 29) 27. Emphasis added.

Having acknowledged all of this, Cohen moves on to focus on the value of reasons as essential to the substantive aspect of the rule of law. She points out that reason-giving has 'an epistemic value' in that it improves the quality of the decisions that are made. 'A full articulation of public officials' reasons for their decisions is more likely to lead them to sound decisions than the absence of it' because:[59]

> [D]ecisions will be better thought through if decision-makers know that they must substantiate them with reasons. Requiring public officials to give reasons will presumably lead them to reflect on their choices and discuss them with their colleagues. In this process, the argument goes, they will be in a better position to recognise the reasons that should apply to the given instance they must decide upon. The demand for reasons forces decision-makers to revise indefensible claims and enables them to discern more easily weak arguments.[60]

Neil MacCormick has made a similar case that the arguability of law enhances the rule of law over time, because it creates the conditions which effectively corral judges into producing better and better justificatory reasons for the decisions that they make.[61] As lawyers present conflicting arguments before the court, and as the judge sifts through these arguments, she can reach an outcome which is universalisable and therefore produces a kind of certainty about the needs of justice in this situation, albeit that such certainty is always defeasible by a new argument which can be raised in a new case.

Cohen, however, pushes the point farther than MacCormick, by arguing also that 'reasons have a civilising effect', in the following way:

> This [civilising] effect results from the fact that actual reason giving forces decision-makers to articulate their views publicly, be it orally or in writing. The requirement to give reasons pressures decision-makers to find convincing arguments for their position and refrain from using self-interested and immoral arguments. Ideally, in this process, they will change their preferences for the better. You cannot say publicly or put on the record that you have made a given decision 'because it's Monday'. ... [t]he requirement to give reasons, it is hoped, exerts psychological pressures on decision-makers toward self-censorship in anticipation of public disapproval and reproach in case they offer self-centred reasons. Because self-interested reasons carry no weight in the public setting, public officials are led to present other-regarding, rather than self-interested, reasons, to justify their decision.[62]

---

[59] M Cohen, 'The Rule of Law as the Rule of Reasons' (2010) 96(1) *ARSP: Archiv für Rechts- und Sozialphilosophie / Archives for Philosophy of Law and Social Philosophy* 1–16, 11.

[60] ibid.

[61] N MacCormick, *Rhetoric and the Rule of Law: A Theory of Legal Reasoning* (Oxford, Oxford University Press, 2005).

[62] Cohen (n 59) 13. Cohen's idea of the civilising effect is based on Kant's writings. It also resonates with Dworkin's argument that 'political officials must make only such political decisions as they can justify within a political theory that also justifies the other decisions they propose to make'. R Dworkin, *Taking Rights Seriously* (London, Gerald Duckworth & Co Ltd, 1997) 87.

Here Cohen is saying that the effort to give reasons can potentially change the internal disposition of the judge, making her more conscientious, reasonable, fair-minded and just. This echoes Annas's point that the requirement of articulacy helps to constitute the virtues being sought.[63] Applying Annas's concept of the requirement of articulacy to the practice of judging we contend that there is an additional benefit to the requirement of judicial articulacy, one that goes beyond those already listed: it is that the giving of reasons genuinely accounts for the justice being achieved. This provides a context within which experienced judges are encouraged to articulate exactly what the contours of justice are, as well as a context within which novice judges, lawyers, legislators, law students and even members of the public are edified in their growing appreciation of those contours, while at the same time these new conceptions seep into the bones of all the practitioners so that everybody becomes more just. This is, we think, the best way to challenge the claim of inauthentic explanation which assumes that any reference to theory or any attempt at self-reflection in judgments are only window dressing. But this kind of argument also poses an indirect challenge to the claim of atheoretical generation, because as judgments articulate justice more cogently, thereby teaching what justice requires, over time the judgments also become constitutive of the justice that is achieved in later cases. Here again, the distinction Fish articulated between engaging in a practice and discoursing on a practice is implausible, for lack of both practical feasibility and normative desirability.

In summary, Annas's idea of the requirement of articulacy and Cohen's defence of the importance of reason-giving in judgments offer the opportunity to look afresh at the value provided by written judgments and the ways in which articulacy is inextricable from the practice of adjudication. The position that we want to defend here is that reason-giving is important in judgments, not only as a way to sell the outcome, or as a record of the decision that has been made thereby enhancing the knowability of law, and not just because it ensures consistency in the legal system and thereby advances the rule of law. Rather, much more centrally, reason-giving articulates the justice being achieved, thereby allowing judges to reinforce and refine that virtue in themselves and to teach that virtue to those lawyers, legislators, law students, and members of the public who read their decisions. Fish's claim of inauthentic explanation held that theoretical discourse about practice does not provide a genuine account of that practice because the 'reasons' are floated in from outside the practice, but if we adopt the richer account of practice proposed by the virtue ethicists, reason-giving is an inextricable component of the practice of adjudication and the reasons offered in this context are authentic expressions of how the practice is unfolding.

---

[63] Although shortly after stating this, Cohen seems to pull back somewhat from this position (ibid 14): 'This picture of the civilising force of reason giving is attractive, of course, but it might prove too optimistic. It could be doubted that this portrayal is based on plausible factual and psychological assumptions about the potential for decision-makers to start believing reasons that they initially offered as a pure matter of strategy.'

VII. CONCLUSIONS

In the 'Dennis Martinez' essay, Fish stakes out a position that, in his words, is 'in direct opposition to what is assumed by almost everyone in the legal academy, irrespective of doctrinal or political affiliation'.[64] This position, as we have described it, is that one can strictly separate practice from theory with the resulting claims that theory is not generative of the practice of judging and that theory does not provide a genuine explanation of how judges arrive at their decisions.

While we think that his distinction is too sharp and dispute the accuracy of his corollary claims, we think that Fish's instinct that there is a need to reframe our conceptions of practice is exactly right. A theory that comes down from the clouds and is not responsive to the reality of practice is not helpful to anyone. A practice that is becomes a puppet of theory is similarly unappealing.

Turning to the conceptions of practice offered by MacIntyre and Annas helps us to not just reframe but also to reenchant our conceptions of practice. Although the fields of virtue ethics and virtue jurisprudence are still emerging, they already offer rich and deep conceptions of practice and therefore interesting ways to refine our understandings of the practice of adjudication, by telling a story of practice and theory as mutually refining and mutually enriching.

---

[64] Fish (n 1) 1779–1880.

7

The Law in Quest of Integrity: Interpretation, Invention and Internal Critique

TRS ALLAN

I. INTRODUCTION

RONALD DWORKIN'S JURISPRUDENCE involves a close engagement with legal practice. Repudiating detached, descriptive analysis, Dworkin's interpretative method addresses important connections between legal argument and moral or political disagreement. External, 'Archimedean' attempts to define the nature of law, wherever it is found, are displaced by internal, interpretative analysis focused on the experience of legal practice within a familiar political culture.[1] Dworkin's theory of law as 'integrity' is offered not merely as an account of law in Anglophone jurisdictions, reflecting a distinctive legal tradition, but as an attractive political programme, grounded in ideals of equality and fraternity.[2] An interpretation of law, in the sense of an explication of the law applicable in any particular case, is simultaneously an exploration of political morality, attuned or adapted to legal and constitutional history and practice.

An avowedly political approach to law, combining legal and political theory, has important implications, in practice, for the identification and enforcement of the law's requirements. We should not bring moral judgment to bear solely, or even primarily, on the question of whether those requirements ought to be followed or applied. It operates at an earlier stage – when we are determining, in the light of the relevant criteria, what legal rights, powers and duties have

---

[1] See especially R Dworkin, 'Hart's Postscript and the Point of Political Philosophy' in *Justice in Robes* (Cambridge, MA, Belknap Press, 2006) 140–86. Archimedean approaches, whether in moral, political or legal theory, involve an attempt to describe in neutral second-order (or 'meta') discourse the nature of first-order claims within the practice studied. Dworkin denies that such separation between neutral second-order discourse and first-order evaluative claims can be coherently maintained.

[2] See R Dworkin, *Law's Empire* (London: Fontana Press, 1986) especially chs 6,7.

actually been established. The law's content is itself a matter of moral judgment for which the interpreter must bear final responsibility. Sustained and infused by principles of political morality, the law is finally, as a matter of practical reasoning, a reflection of the best reading of those principles as they apply in all the circumstances.[3]

There remains a certain ambiguity, however, concerning the interpretative connection between law and morality, as Dworkin conceives it. It is not quite clear whether political morality demands an appropriate response to institutional actions, viewed largely as matters of social fact, or whether instead such actions are themselves identifiable for practical purposes only by exercise of moral judgment. Do statutes and judicial precedents impose external *constraints* on legal interpretation in virtue of their existence as authoritative texts? Or are their implications for the law's content internal to interpretation in the sense of being wholly dependent on the best theory of legal practice viewed as a whole? The latter view might seem to be implicit in Dworkin's insistence that interpretative claims always reflect the best resolution of competing considerations, each internal to legal or moral or aesthetic judgment – that such claims are 'dependent on aesthetic or political theory all the way down'.[4] A good deal of what Dworkin says about legal practice in *Law's Empire*, however, is only doubtfully consistent with that view.

Stanley Fish exposed that critical ambiguity when he excoriated Dworkin's attempts to locate the limits of interpretation, rejecting his efforts to distinguish interpretation from 'invention'.[5] As Fish observed, the notion that such a distinction could be identified abstractly – outside the specific context of any concrete interpretative issue – supposes a certain factual or non-interpretative legal (or literary) content that is itself beyond dispute. In spite of his antipathy to legal positivism, Dworkin implicitly embraces it by according the facts of legal practice a status that precedes, qualifies and constrains their interpretation. If there were not such a factual, indisputable core, it is hard to see how the distinction between interpretation and invention could be drawn without begging the question. The distinction will in practice vary according to the moral judgments of rival interpreters. One person's interpretation, inspired by his own view of the moral considerations at stake, will be another person's 'invention', neglecting features of legal practice that she treats as having special importance in all the circumstances.

---

[3] Political obligation, accordingly, is 'not just a matter of obeying the discrete political decisions of the community one by one', as political philosophers usually represent it: 'It becomes a more protestant idea: fidelity to a scheme of principle each citizen has a responsibility to identify, ultimately for himself, as his community's scheme'. See Dworkin (n 2) 190.

[4] R Dworkin, *A Matter of Principle* (Oxford, Clarendon Press, 1985) 168.

[5] See S Fish, 'Working on the Chain Gang: Interpretation in Law and Literature' in his collection, *Doing What Comes Naturally: Change, Rhetoric, and the Practice of Theory in Literary and Legal Studies* (Oxford, Clarendon Press, 1989) 87–102, and 'Wrong Again', ibid 103–19.

In his anxiety to narrow the range of possible interpretations of legal practice, as part of his defence of interpretative objectivity, Dworkin arguably violates his own injunctions against external, descriptive jurisprudence.[6] He adopts an Archimedean viewpoint, external to practice, in which distinctions and categories are developed that would make little sense to practice-participants.[7] An interpreter could only hear accusations of 'invention' as allegations of bad faith or incompetence, which she can meet only by further argument in support of the interpretation impugned. If, for example, she has ignored or rejected a familiar paradigm, widely viewed as a test of plausibility, she must show, if possible, that her account is not only consistent with other, equally familiar, paradigms but also a morally superior understanding of legal practice overall.[8]

On the one hand, Dworkin insists on the close connection between law and moral or political theory, denying the possibility of moral neutrality in legal interpretation. On the other hand, however, he seeks an anchor for interpretation in features of practice that sharply curtail, even preclude, interpretative creativity. The tension that characterises interpretation, as we seek to reconcile competing desiderata of 'fit' and justification, threatens an unwelcome divorce between law and morality. What may be the best interpretation of legal practice, all things considered, can apparently contravene political morality. If, however, interpretative objectivity is something different from moral objectivity – moral principle giving way in the face of obdurate facts about historical practice – the moral character of legal reasoning is evidently compromised. The chosen path between legal positivism, on one side, and a more robust natural law stance, on the other, looks quite unstable.

Dworkin's efforts to connect law and morality, forging the critical link between legal reasoning and political obligation, are ultimately undermined by his failure to maintain a consistently internal, interpretative viewpoint. Dworkin recognises only a qualified obligation of obedience to law, accordingly, even when the legal order is properly attuned to the ideal of integrity. Even when the legal order is generally benign, respectful of human dignity and the related demands of equality, its specific prescriptions may nonetheless on some

---

[6] Fish observes that Dworkin's work consistently displays 'the fear of individual or subjective preference', a fear that law as integrity is intended to check or constrain: S Fish, 'Still Wrong After All These Years' in *Doing What Comes Naturally* (n 5) 356–71, 365.

[7] Fish suggests that Dworkin's explanation of the irrelevance of 'external scepticism' has implications for the novelty or distinctiveness of 'law as integrity' itself, both notions being 'stand-ins for the general claim of philosophy to be a model of reflection that exists on a level superior to, and revelatory of, mere practice': ibid 371. Dworkin rightly objects that the external sceptic 'tries to speak from the outside and inside at once and doesn't see that the radical detachment of the one perspective wholly undermines its relevance to the other' (ibid).

[8] Compare *Law's Empire* (n 2) 72–73. As Dworkin observes, paradigms need not be defined by convention. Debate over fundamental practices such as legislation and precedent can proceed by 'contesting discrete paradigms one by one, like the reconstruction of Neurath's boat one plank at a time at sea': ibid 139.

occasions be too wicked to obey. The law's moral integrity may be impaired by regrettable social facts, impervious to interpretative repair or remedy. Even when the law is viewed as whole, underpinned by principles that secure its legitimacy, it may still fall so far short of justice – on Dworkin's questionable account – that political obligation may in some cases be overridden by countervailing requirements of justice.[9]

The unity of law and morality that Dworkin defends in his last major work, *Justice for Hedgehogs*, is a more promising version of anti-positivism.[10] It is not so much a brief encapsulation of the main arguments of *Law's Empire* as a qualified refutation of them. Dworkin's contention that law is itself a segment or department of morality revives an understanding glimpsed briefly at the start of his career but subsequently submerged.[11] He now more clearly recognises that any departures from justice, as anyone might conceive that ideal, are demanded by political morality itself. If we defer to statutes and precedents in determining the requirements of law in particular cases, we do so because they have important implications for moral judgment in all the circumstances. They give crucial guidance to the content of the moral rights and duties applicable.

Dworkin continues to affirm the distinction, usually associated with legal positivism, between the law as it is and the law as it ought to be. There is no guarantee that the law, even when ascertained by exercise of moral judgment, will be beyond reproach.[12] Such reproach, however, can only reflect the complexity of moral judgment, in which competing desiderata must often be duly accommodated. We must reckon with a less than perfect world, adapting our ideals to the circumstances in which we find ourselves. But legal history cannot *curtail* moral judgment by forcing us to accede to measures that violate the principles that animate our conception of the rule of law. The law's content cannot be divorced from a sound grasp of the ideal of legality, a value that operates (as Dworkin himself explains) in harness with other fundamental political values such as liberty and equality.[13]

In the context of legal reasoning and adjudication, then, the law is indeed what it ought to be.[14] When correctly interpreted, consistently with the moral ideals that underpin our allegiance as practice-participants, the law is our true guide to justice. To compare the law with what it ought to be, by recourse to standards borrowed from outside it, we must relinquish the internal, interpretative viewpoint. But from that detached, descriptive stance, external to

---

[9] Political obligation may be defeated in exceptional cases: 'A full political theory of law … speaks both to the *grounds* of law – circumstances in which particular propositions of law should be taken to be sound or true – and to the *force* of law – the relative power of any true proposition of law to justify coercion in different sorts of exceptional circumstance' (ibid 110).
[10] R Dworkin, *Justice for Hedgehogs* (Cambridge, MA, Belknap Press, 2011) ch 19.
[11] See R Dworkin, *Taking Rights Seriously* (London, Duckworth, 1977) ch 3.
[12] Dworkin (n 10) 407–409.
[13] See Dworkin (n 1) especially 168–83.
[14] See also TRS Allan, 'Why the Law is What it Ought to Be' (2020) 11 *Jurisprudence* 574–96.

the practice itself, there is no law at all in the relevant sense – only coercive commands that we must navigate one by one in the manner Dworkin supposedly rejects. We are obliged on that view to accommodate social or institutional facts that constrain rather than *inform* our moral judgment. From the truly internal perspective, by contrast, law is itself an expression of political morality: we must construe the current features of legal practice, in Fish's apt expression, as 'instances of a general and continuing narrative about justice and equality'.[15]

Admittedly, our critical moral judgment may in some circumstances lead us to repudiate state authority altogether: we deny political obligation because the law, as it is widely understood and practised, is morally repugnant. There is no realistic chance of deliberative challenge and reformation. Until such desperate circumstances obtain, however, we must exercise moral judgment internally – trying, as Dworkin often puts it, to make decent legal and political arrangements the best of their kind they can be. If such arrangements are undeniably imperfect, their flaws and failings must be seen, fundamentally, as lapses of consistency and internal coherence. They are moral deficiencies that we must identify and remedy as we proceed, revising and reforming the law in pursuit of its own integrity.[16]

Insofar as integrity falls short of justice, it accommodates the moral disagreement that provides the lifeblood of a flourishing democracy. And insofar as the constraints of due process limit the scope for revision and reform in the context of adjudication, where reasonable expectations and settled assumptions must be accorded their due, the relevant moral considerations are appropriately balanced. But there is here nothing external to the deliberations that morality informs and directs. The objections that Fish levelled at Dworkin's legal theory are best understood as an insistence on the unity and internal integrity of that interpretative debate. No one can deny or defy the law, as Dworkin defines it, without repudiating the interpretative enterprise itself. Personal integrity is in that way aligned with the law's integrity: our commitment, whether as conscientious citizen or state official, is either everything or nothing.

II. ARCHIMEDEAN JURISPRUDENCE

Dworkin's fundamental mistake in *Law's Empire* is to straddle internal and external perspectives, contrary to his own injunction to join the practice

---

[15] S Fish (n 5) 364. Fish contends that Dworkin is wrong to think of that narrative 'as something that must be first constructed and then *added* to a first-level perception of discrete events' (emphasis in original).

[16] Integrity demands consistency of principle: 'It requires that the various standards governing the state's use of coercion against its citizens be consistent in the sense that they express a single and comprehensive vision of justice': Dworkin (n 2) 134.

as participant.[17] His superhuman judge, Hercules, always has one foot inside legal practice, while working out the requirements of integrity, but another outside, while pondering the countervailing demands of justice or fairness. The requirements of integrity may even expire, in the face of an inconsistent or chaotic legal record, obliging Hercules to repair directly to abstract standards of justice or fairness that owe little or nothing to legal tradition or established practice.[18]

Even when the law is conceived on the model of integrity, political obligation may in some circumstances allegedly be overridden. The prevailing conception of equal concern, critical to integrity, may be so defective, in Dworkin's view, that even wicked rules may qualify as valid law, forcing the good citizen to choose between her allegiance to law, on the one hand, and the demands of justice on the other. It is a picture uncomfortably close to legal positivism or conventionalism. When an American judge before the civil war wonders whether he should enforce the Fugitive Slave Act, on the demand of a slave owner, or whether instead he should either lie about the law's requirements or perhaps resign, he has plainly surrendered his interpretative stance.[19] He accords legal status to rules, or purported rules, that lack any moral authority, forcing legal and moral judgment widely apart.

As Jeremy Waldron argues, however, integrity *displaces* justice in the 'circumstances of integrity'.[20] If we do not inhabit a utopia, where there is universal accord, neither do we confront a dystopia in which there is nothing but rancorous discord. While we disagree about what justice requires, our disagreement is not so deeply rooted or our political record so chequered as to preclude all possibility of striving for moral coherence. We have not surrendered, in abject despair, to scepticism.[21] Hercules has no business, then, in reflecting on justice, untethered from the practice in which we join to seek it. When we embrace legal practice as the legitimate framework of our collective endeavour, we must follow where it leads us. We cannot, without unfairness to others, invoke wholly independent political values, drawn from abstract philosophical reflection beyond the reaches of the practice itself.

When legal practice is sensitive to political morality, in the way Dworkin suggests, it subsumes more abstract moral argument, detached from a shared tradition. Practice provides the moral framework for debate over questions of justice as they arise within the innumerable forms of social interaction on which we depend. We serve the basic ideal of legal equality – the principle that all are equally deserving of respect and concern – by seeking systematic moral

---

[17] See Dworkin (n 2) 64: an interpreter of courtesy must '*join* the practice he proposes to understand; his conclusions are then not neutral reports about what the citizens of courtesy think but claims about courtesy *competitive* with theirs' (Dworkin's emphases).
[18] See especially Dworkin's discussion of *McLoughlin* at ibid 240–50.
[19] See ibid 219.
[20] J Waldron, *Law and Disagreement* (Oxford, Oxford University Press, 1999) ch 9.
[21] Dworkin considers the challenge of scepticism in *Law's Empire* (n 2) 76–86.

coherence. Instances of injustice at the hands of the state must be understood, primarily, as ruptures of that coherence. In calling for reform or remedy, then, we are demanding adherence to established practice, correctly conceived. We insist that officials, or the popular majority they represent, should honour their own commitments, or supposed commitments, to legal and constitutional equality. We need not, initially at least, occupy the role of external critic: our critique is primarily *internal*, reminding our fellow citizens of what our common enterprise entails.

In invoking statute and precedent as grounds for decision, a judge upholds the law's integrity. He relies on rules and doctrines that would be equally applicable to other, similar cases; and the criteria of similarity depend not only on the explicit terms of enacted rules or precedents but, more fundamentally, on the moral principles that can best explain and justify those rules or precedents. A judge's adherence to integrity is the closest he can come to justice in a community in which political morality is the subject of lively debate and disagreement. His decision in any particular case follows from his interpretation of the political record, treated as the community's best efforts to *approximate* justice in the circumstances of integrity. It is what morally he ought to decide if he wishes to do justice according to law.[22]

Dworkin's apparent confusion here is closely related to his exaggerated concerns about 'invention', which must be distinguished from genuine interpretation.[23] For Dworkin, robust debate about the point or value of a practice is possible within the practice itself only because the participants fix their attention on the same elements or features. There must be a strong consensus on the objects or domain of the practice even if there is wide divergence about its nature or merits. An interpreter's moral convictions, as regards the best account of the practice, are held in check by the hard reality of its central features: certain 'brute facts of legal history', in the case of legal practice, preclude interpretations that might otherwise be preferred on moral grounds.[24] An interpreter whose convictions about fit too readily adjust themselves to match an attractive moral justification is guilty of cheating: she substitutes her idealised conception of the practice for the real one with all its imperfections.

Insofar, however, as the constraints of fit go beyond the minimal demands of good faith and sincerity, they are surely empty. The true features of the practice, which any successful interpretation must report, can only be identified by reflection on its point or value. They are a *product* of interpretation, sensitive to political morality, rather than elements that exist independently. The constraints of fit are absorbed into the theory of the practice: they are determined by the best account of the practice, which will inevitably identify many otherwise putative

---

[22] Compare GJ Postema, 'Integrity: Justice in Workclothes' (1997) 82 *Iowa Law Review* 821.
[23] See Dworkin (n 2) 65–68.
[24] In Dworkin's account a 'threshold' test of fit excludes certain possibilities automatically: 'the brute facts of legal history will in this way limit the role any judge's personal convictions of justice can play in his decisions' (ibid 255).

elements as mistaken. The 'post-interpretive' or 'reforming' stage, at which we settle the true features of the practice in the light of the point or purposes or value we assign at the 'interpretive' stage, will assume critical importance.[25]

Dworkin concedes this objection, in effect, when he grants that while paradigms play an important role, they need not be grounded in convention. No paradigm is invulnerable to challenge by reference to other paradigms that support a superior interpretation overall – one that shows the paradigm under attack to be misguided, dependent on a rival but inferior view of the practice as a whole. There is all the moral and intellectual freedom anyone might reasonably desire within the scope of the practice itself, provided only that he continues to accept its legitimacy. He retains his faith in the practice, when correctly interpreted, to regulate social and political arrangements fairly in the interests of all those subject to its coercive embrace.

If, as Dworkin maintains, there is a 'threshold' requirement of fit, which any genuine interpretation must satisfy, it can only consist in an interpreter's independent moral judgment. If legal practice is, in his opinion, radically and characteristically unjust or oppressive, or the legal record too hopelessly chaotic or ideologically contradictory to sustain any plausible quest for moral coherence, interpretative reflection must give way to scepticism. The only morally permissible course is to repudiate the practice altogether. In that sense, there is no minimally morally attractive interpretation available that fits. The 'threshold' requirement of fit serves simply to mark the division between allegiance and scepticism. Within the sphere of the practice, from the viewpoint of any committed interpreter, fit is only another name for integrity itself. The supposedly distinct criteria of fit and justification merge in the requirement of moral coherence.[26]

When we are willing to treat legal practice as a legitimate basis for cooperation with our fellow citizens, acknowledging its claims on our allegiance, we will deny any significant difference between law and justice. Our common principles, exhibited and affirmed by the familiar paradigms, equip us to confront egregious injustice by impugning its legality. Grave breaches of fundamental principle, such as infringements of basic rights, can be opposed in the name of the law itself – the law as interpreted in accordance with integrity. Any assertion, even by senior officials, that the law includes a wicked statute, flouting moral standards that we could not in good conscience allow to be infringed, must be rejected as mistaken. We can draw on settled parts of our practice, consistent with basic principles, to show why such offensive state demands (or purported demands) have no authority: they violate principles of justice critical to the law's integrity.

---

[25] For the various stages of interpretation, see ibid 65–68.

[26] Dworkin rightly observes that cases are not decided by following formal canons of theory construction, 'counting the number of precedents explained by competing hypotheses, and contrasting the theoretical elegance of these hypotheses': see Dworkin (n 11) 341. See further TRS Allan, 'Interpretation, Injustice, and Integrity' (2016) 36 *Oxford Journal of Legal Studies* 58, 68–74.

It follows that from an internal, interpretative stance there is no distinction between the 'grounds' and 'force' of law, contrary to Dworkin's view. When the law is correctly identified by recourse to its underpinning moral principles, it will both demand and justify compliance. That is precisely the consequence of taking up the interpretative viewpoint, which integrates these supposedly separate questions of grounds and force. It is only Dworkin's detachment from the practice, or that of his imaginary interpreter, that maintains their separation. There cannot be genuine legal requirements, imposed by statute or precedent in the guise of social or political facts, that violate the first principles of law, as integrity defines them. If such requirements are asserted, whether by a state official or by anyone else, the truth of those assertions must be challenged. We could not acknowledge the authority of such oppressive rules or requirements without abandoning integrity. Any such purported legal authority would be severed from genuine moral authority, turning the committed interpreter perforce into a disillusioned sceptic.

No one can intelligibly stand both within and outside the interpretative enterprise at the same moment, adopting an interpretation of law that meets the demands of integrity while supposing, nonetheless, that the law should be denounced or disobeyed. If there is a legal interpretation capable, in her opinion, of unifying specific rules or requirements with basic principles, there is nothing to deplore even if that interpretation is controversial. The 'protestant' interpreter is legally entitled, and morally bound, to press her own account, emphasising the threat that contrasting views present to fundamental principles. Her judgments of political morality are internal, drawing inspiration from legal practice as she conceives and honours it. She occupies a position similar to that of the dissenting judge, who repudiates the conclusions of her judicial colleagues on explicitly legal grounds – a legality underpinned by the moral vision that informs her allegiance to the law as a whole.[27]

Common law reasoning exemplifies the integration of law and morality that a sound interpretative approach entails. Although the precedents give a certain shape and structure to legal doctrine, which is intended to reflect the requirements of justice, their authority is always vulnerable to challenge. Even a leading precedent, within a particular field, can be brought into question by argument showing its incompatibility with other principles and precedents, perhaps in different but associated fields. Litigants can be treated fairly and equally only if there is moral coherence across legal doctrine in general, differences in the treatment of persons being justified accordingly. Dworkinian integrity encapsulates that idea of fundamental equality, extending a merely formal equality before the law into a richer, more substantive equality of justice.[28]

---

[27] For Dworkin's account of the protestant interpreter, see above, n 3.
[28] See also TRS Allan, 'Principle, Practice, and Precedent: Vindicating Justice, According to Law' (2018) 77 *Cambridge Law Journal* 269.

Law can be understood as a branch of morality, as Dworkin urges in *Justice for Hedgehogs*, in the sense that legal doctrine distils and develops the relevant moral principles, allowing their consistent application to particular cases. The law offers a collective and coordinated response to political morality, forging at least a degree of confidence and provisional consensus that would elude us in its absence. A public conception of political morality thereby displaces a myriad of private notions, each too dependent on individual experience or idiosyncratic opinion to serve as the charter of a just society. A public charter or constitution, attuned to the needs and traditions of a specific jurisdiction, is built on wide recognition of certain basic standards of good governance, illuminated by arrangements or assumptions that serve as paradigmatic examples for purposes of deliberation and debate.

There is, then, no conflict between law and morality – no confrontation between integrity and justice – because the former is only a specification of the latter, adapted to the requirements of time and place. The law, when correctly identified, is always a reflection or approximation of morality, dependent on the efforts of citizens and officials to bring their practice closer to the ideals that animate it. Interpretative disagreement is a stimulus to critical scrutiny and informed debate. Legal doctrine's vulnerability to challenge and reappraisal, even in the context of particular cases, enables legal practice to accommodate changing moral attitudes and foster independent thought and judgment. It is easier to accept an official rule or ruling as binding, even if controversial, when it is understood to be provisional, its authority being open to review and revision in the light of further experience, reflection and argument.

Mark Greenberg's dissatisfaction with Dworkin's jurisprudence leads him to renounce a hermeneutic approach altogether.[29] He doubts whether 'the principles that best fit and justify the actual, often severely morally flawed, practices would be principles one should follow'.[30] But I have argued that considerations of fit collapse, in practice, into those of justification; and severely flawed practices, correctly so described, could provoke only scepticism. If Greenberg cannot understand why we should 'be interested in identifying the principles that best justify the legal practices', or make them the best they can be, it is largely because he takes Dworkin's account at face value, overlooking the necessary adjustments or qualifications.[31] Greenberg's contention that the law is constituted by the moral *effects* or *consequences* of authoritative institutional actions, if truly at odds with a Dworkinian approach, overlooks the possibility that practice can itself be a source of moral insight. It is not always easy to distinguish clearly between our moral ideals, abstractly conceived, and the forms and structures in which they are embodied as settled rules and principles, widely accepted as appropriate public standards.

---

[29] M Greenberg, 'The Moral Impact Theory of Law' (2014) 123 *Yale Law Journal* 1288.
[30] ibid 1302.
[31] ibid 1305.

Greenberg's distinction between official text and its legal effect or consequence, moreover, appears to suggest that the meaning of the text can be ascertained without moral judgment. As Fish contends, however, textual meaning is always the *product* of interpretation rather than a prelude to it, imposing constraints that operate independently. Even if we construe the text as an expression of intention, as Fish recommends, we must suppose or attribute reasonable intentions, consonant with the idea of law as a public scheme or charter of justice. In radically separating textual meaning from its moral significance, if that is what his 'moral impact' theory entails, Greenberg pushes an anti-positivist critique in precisely the wrong direction. An interpretative approach, in contrast, amalgamates social fact and moral judgment – bridging the gap between fact and value by means of a special sensibility, honed by membership of the interpretative community.[32]

It may be objected that textual meaning is always distinct from, and prior to, interpretation in the sense that it depends on linguistic rules and conventions.[33] In that sense, the words clearly constrain the nature and scope of permissible interpretations. As Greenberg himself observes, however, it is very doubtful whether we should identify legal propositions with textual meaning.[34] Whereas a statute is a text, or the enactment of a text, a rule or requirement is normative, giving a reason for action. We should not confuse text and norm by supposing that there is any straightforward correspondence between them. In Dworkin's theory, the law does not consist of the content of authoritative pronouncements, embodied in statute; interpretation is a means of establishing the principles that justify legal practice viewed as a whole. As far as judicial precedent is concerned, moreover, there is no authoritative text to be construed in the manner of a statute. We must interpret the case itself, or more often a line of cases, steered but not irrevocably bound by the reasons offered by way of justification.

III. PROTESTANT INTERPRETATION AND LEGAL PRACTICE

Dworkin's account of legal practice is arguably weakened by reliance on so radical a separation between the object of interpretation, about which all

---

[32] For my critique of Greenberg's theory, see TRS Allan, 'Law as a Branch of Morality: The Unity of Practice and Principle' (2020) 65 *American Journal of Jurisprudence* 1.

[33] That is the main theme of A Marmor, *Interpretation and Legal Theory*, revised 2nd edn (Oxford, Hart Publishing, 2005). Marmor suggests that Dworkin should simply have dismissed Fish's critique as grounded in an implausible view of semantics. But neither Fish nor Dworkin should be understood to deny that ordinary linguistic meaning, subject to the constraints of context, precedes interpretation, which concerns the assignment of legal (or artistic or literary) meaning or significance.

[34] M Greenberg, 'The Standard Picture and its Discontents' in L Green and B Leiter (eds), *Oxford Studies in Philosophy of Law*, vol 1 (Oxford, Oxford University Press, 2011) 39–106. In the 'standard picture', which Greenberg rejects, the law is assumed to consist chiefly of authoritative pronouncements, which generate obligations of obedience.

practitioners must broadly agree, and the purposes or values of the practice, about which there may be almost unlimited controversy. As Gerald Postema observes, we cannot faithfully interpret a common practice by private reflection about our own intentions in choosing to participate.[35] It is not a matter, as Dworkin presents it, of finding an account of the practice with which we feel comfortable.[36] The idea is rather to seek common ground, trying to identify shared purposes and values that illuminate and justify a practice that we can only pursue and develop in collaboration with others. Interpretation cannot be merely, as Dworkin sometimes suggests, a 'conversation with one-self'.[37]

Dworkin is right, of course, to insist on each person's final responsibility for the interpretation she defends. We each bear moral responsibility for the stand we take on contested claims about the demands of the practice. But we acquit that responsibility only by wholehearted adherence to the common endeavour, which may not match – will perhaps rarely match – the arrangements any of us might have designed from scratch in the guise of a benevolent dictator. When we reach outside that endeavour, making judgments that have no secure basis in the common understanding, we act unfairly, subjecting others to our private will in a manner that we would scarcely tolerate if the boot was on the other foot.

Our steadfast adherence reflects our judgment that the practice, regarded in the round, deserves our allegiance. Its paradigms, at any rate, establish the practice as a reasonable basis for cooperation between people who acknowledge their equal moral status. All deserve to be treated with respect as persons entitled to pursue their own interests under conditions that provide a similar freedom for all. Each person belongs to the 'community of principle', entitled to all the benefits of political arrangements that embody that fundamental equality.[38] Even if such a community may be unjust, by anyone's standards of perfect justice – its conception of equal concern is somehow defective or deficient – it nonetheless provides, we suppose, a legitimate basis for cooperation, all things considered. It enforces a recognisable scheme of justice grounded in at least

---

[35] G J Postema, 'Protestant Interpretation and Social Practices' (1987) 6 *Law and Philosophy* 283–319.

[36] According to Dworkin, each interpreter is 'trying to discover his own intention in maintaining and participating in the practice ... in the sense of finding a purposeful account of his behaviour he is comfortable in ascribing to himself': Dworkin (n 2) 58.

[37] As Postema contends, interpretations of a social practice are 'public formulations of collectively meaningful activities'. It does not follow that all participants must agree about the nature of their practice, 'but it does imply that one's own understanding must be addressed to other participants and sensitive to their understanding of it': Postema (n 35) 312–13. Fish mentions his substantial agreement with Postema's critique, observing that an 'interpretive community' takes the form, in Postema's words, 'of a shared discipline and a thick continuity of experience of the common world of the practice': see *Doing What Comes Naturally* (n 5) 580, fn 3.

[38] Integrity requires government to speak with one voice, 'to act in a principled and coherent manner toward all its citizens, to extend to everyone the substantive standards of justice or fairness it uses for some': Dworkin (n 2) 165. For exploration of the Kantian affiliations of Dworkin's legal and moral theory, see L MacInnis, 'The Kantian Core of Law as Integrity' (2015) 6(1) *Jurisprudence* 45.

a *plausible* conception of equal concern. In the absence of legitimate governance, meeting that basic condition, we would have to abandon the interpretative enterprise altogether. We would be internal sceptics, in Dworkin's terms, receptive to the enterprise in principle but unable, in practice, to acknowledge any moral basis on which to proceed in good faith. We would search in vain for any attractive moral justification of legal practice that satisfied the minimal requirements of fit.[39]

Far from displaying wholehearted allegiance, however, Dworkin's interpreter stands somewhat aloof, apparently reluctant to embrace the practice as a source of inspiration or instruction. His allegiance is grudging and infirm, making little or no attempt to accommodate conflicting opinion. If the interpreter recognises the practice of courtesy, in Dworkin's example, he does so only by rejecting the standard view of its purpose and substituting one more congenial to him. Admittedly, he wonders whether his view is too radical, 'too ill-fitting a justification to count as an interpretation at all'.[40] But this is precisely the point at which interpretation teeters on the edge of scepticism. It is a private reflection in which the interpreter wrestles with his conscience, poised on the brink of repudiating the practice altogether. If the practice of courtesy, as the interpreter finds it, is plainly obnoxious, by his own moral standards, he is obliged to urge a radical interpretation as the only means of squaring his allegiance with his own integrity. But it is hardly a standard example of the interpretation of a flourishing practice, where we would usually expect more effort to address the commitments and assumptions of other practice-participants.

I have argued that, as a matter of individual judgment, there are no constraints of fit that exclude a morally attractive interpretation of practice, or at least none beyond the 'threshold' constraint, which marks the boundary between allegiance and scepticism. To that extent, at least, there is a genuine sense in which an interpreter must finally determine for herself the content of the common practice. If, however, the practice is to flourish as a genuinely common endeavour, there must normally be a proper deference to contrary opinion. The committed interpreter must allow for divergent judgments of the demands of the practice, acknowledging that her own understanding can often be enhanced by attention to the experience and arguments of others. A collective practice demands collaboration in the sense that all are willing to learn from the continuing controversy that constitutes its lifeblood. The interpretative freedom enjoyed by one is equally enjoyed by all; and the success of anyone's efforts to justify a common practice must finally depend on their reception by others, who must be persuaded to think afresh, viewing familiar requirements in a new light.

---

[39] The internal sceptic relies on the soundness of a general interpretative stance to call into question all proposed interpretations of a particular object or practice: Dworkin (n 2) 78–79.
[40] ibid 67.

Dworkin imagines, in his discussion of *McLoughlin*, that Hercules might abandon the constraints of fit, in the face of a chaotic legal record, focusing instead on 'more substantive' questions: 'he must decide which interpretation shows the legal record to be the best it can be from the standpoint of substantive political morality'.[41] If, however, the constraints of fit are subsumed by the search for moral coherence, as I have argued, there is no point at which they simply expire, rendering the law indeterminate. A superficially chaotic legal record can usually be interpreted as a more systematic scheme of justice by drawing on principles implicit in significant parts of it. That is surely the faith that integrity assumes and requires. A legal record that really resisted all attempts to secure moral coherence could provoke only scepticism, precluding the law's application to the case at hand. It is only an association of fit with incontrovertible matters of fact, impervious to interpretative judgment, that could support a contrary view.

When Hercules decides that 'the question of fit can play no more useful role in his deliberations', he is in effect abandoning integrity and thereby, in substance, turning his back on the law.[42] We are told that Hercules must weigh the respective demands of justice and fairness, pitting his own convictions against the contrary views of other citizens. His choice of principles to govern the recovery of damages for nervous shock depends

> not only on his beliefs about which of these principles is superior as a matter of abstract justice but also which should be followed, as a matter of political fairness, in a community whose members have the moral convictions his fellow citizens have.[43]

He is now, in effect, a benevolent dictator, moderating his rule out of respect for public opinion.

Even if English legal doctrine concerning recovery of damages for nervous shock were particularly obscure, it is implausible to suppose that Hercules could make no coherent sense of the law of negligence in general or even of the larger domain of tort. A genuine inability to proceed by recourse to more abstract theorising, applicable to a larger sphere of civil liability, would mark the demise of integrity itself. A judge cannot remain faithful to integrity if he ceases to draw inspiration and guidance from the legal record. When Hercules invokes his own independent, 'abstract' views about justice, interpretation really has been supplanted by invention. Hercules has become a lawmaker, legislating to supplement a deficient legal record. He has adopted the stance of the positivist or conventionalist, making law where formerly there was none.[44]

---

[41] ibid 248.
[42] ibid 248.
[43] ibid, 249.
[44] For these contrasting conceptions of law, see ibid, 90–96. Compare G Warnke, *Justice and Interpretation* (Cambridge, Polity Press, 1992) 72–82. Warnke complains that, in practice, Dworkin largely abandons the hermeneutic approach he defends in theory, simply imposing on the legal record the moral principles that reflect the interpreter's political convictions.

In place of law, conceived as the expression of a unified political tradition, Dworkin's model judge has substituted his own will, albeit one informed by private moral reflection. He has, in effect, jettisoned the normal assumption that legal principles, when correctly weighed, dictate a single correct solution to any legal dispute.[45] Integrity ultimately sustains that assumption by treating the law as a reflection of morality, familiar legal principles being a rough approximation, at least, to their moral counterparts, which apply universally.[46] If the law were indeterminate, as a legal positivist or conventionalist must suppose, it would instead be a system of rules dependent, primarily, on its institutional sources. It would only contingently overlap with morality and leave scope for judicial law-making in the absence of determinate rules.

While an interpreter retains her allegiance, she draws on the inherent resources of the practice to determine its demands in particular cases. Moral coherence must be sought from within the practice, building on those primary features that guarantee its legitimacy. These are the familiar paradigms that reflect common assumptions about the proper purposes of authoritative institutions, which in turn rest on deeper commitments to fundamental equality. There is no need to weigh the demands of the practice, correctly conceived, against external considerations that derive from a moral framework that operates independently. And it would be quite unfair to do so, compromising the interpreter's commitment to the practice itself as a reasonable basis for cooperation between mutually respectful persons. The interpreter's moral judgment, while fully engaged, operates through the medium of the practice, which forges the critical link between abstract political ideals and the concrete requirements of the here and now.

Dworkin's analysis goes awry, in large part, because his account of interpretation overlooks the importance of collaboration in a common endeavour. Hercules, accordingly, pays little or no attention to the opinions or reasoning of other lawyers and judges. On Dworkin's account, Hercules concentrates largely on the *results* of previous cases – the precedent decisions, treated as rulings on their particular facts. His radical individualism betrays him.[47] A better judge, being a fully committed participant in legal practice, would instead comb the reasoning of earlier decisions to enrich his sense of how best to develop legal doctrine – extending and articulating it in ways that would be likely to command the assent of other lawyers. Hercules cannot proceed alone, weighing the respective claims of abstract moral principles, detached from the practice in which they find their characteristic shape and resonance. Those principles are

---

[45] For Dworkin's robust defence of this assumption, see Dworkin (n 11) ch 13, and (n 4) ch 5.

[46] For Dworkin's defence of the unity of value, affirming the commensurability of moral values, see Dworkin (n 10) especially 118–20.

[47] Dworkin writes that Hercules wants a theory about legal rights to compensation for emotional injury that supports most of the results the precedents report: 'He begins by setting out various candidates for the best interpretation of the precedent cases even before he reads them' (Dworkin (n 2) 240).

only fully grasped in understanding their application to the cases by the judges who invoked them by way of justification.[48]

The distinction between 'pure' and 'inclusive' integrity, as Dworkin presents it, is based on the idea of conflict between integrity's 'component virtues' of justice, fairness and due process.[49] When we substitute a common understanding for the merely private or personal view, however, the conflict disappears. Fairness is precisely the idea that the pursuit of justice must be a collaborative endeavour: it is the value that underlies the democratic process, giving legal force to statutes intended to cure defects and deficiencies in the public scheme of justice. And justice takes the form, in the 'circumstances of integrity', of integrity itself.[50] If, moreover, due process concerns the procedural requirements of the rule of law, it is intrinsic to the fair administration of justice – a condition of integrity's attainment. Integrity dissolves any conflict between these fundamental values by substituting for their external versions, which belong to ideal theory, internal interpretative counterparts, attuned to legal practice.

Insofar as doctrines of precedent, legislative supremacy and 'local priority' impinge on legal judgment, qualifying an appraisal of the pertinent rights and duties, they lend form and structure to the pursuit of integrity.[51] They permit effective collaboration, allowing everyone access to the relevant knowledge and accumulated experience.[52] We 'bow to justice', as the nerve of pure integrity, because that was our true quest all along. The 'purer law' at the heart of integrity is simply the structure of rules and principles that best exhibits moral coherence, showing each and every rule or requirement to be justified by recourse to a compelling theory of the law as a whole. Pure integrity is as close as the political community can come to justice consistently with the ideal of equal dignity, which must accommodate reasonable doubt and disagreement. Everyone is permitted to join the argument, each contributing to the common endeavour. Legal and moral theory must be constantly tested against experience: principle and practice are mutually reinforcing and interdependent. Fish is right, then, to question the notion that we must leave it to philosophers, rather than thoughtful practitioners, 'to work out law's ambitions for itself'.[53]

---

[48] As Warnke observes, if we dismiss certain readings a priori, in Hercules's manner, we can learn nothing from the material we are trying to interpret. The practice should be a source of insight, not merely a space for the projection of existing theories or principles: see Warnke (n 44) 72–82.

[49] Dworkin (n 2) 404–407.

[50] Waldron (n 20) ch 9.

[51] Dworkin (n 2) 404–405.

[52] Dworkin observes that when the 'legal departments' fostered by the doctrine of 'local priority' match popular opinion, 'they encourage the protestant attitude integrity favours, because they allow ordinary people as well as hard-pressed judges to interpret law within practical boundaries that seem natural and intuitive': ibid 252.

[53] ibid, 407. See Fish (n 6) 368–70.

Practice is open to interpretation at varying levels of abstraction. Herculean adjudication, when correctly performed, embodies the ideal of the rule of law. The requirement that judicial opinions should be fully reasoned, expressing a coherent moral vision, reflects the law's aspiration to enforce the demands of justice. Fish's scepticism goes much too far when he divorces legal practice from legal theory, the latter having merely rhetorical force or significance.[54] The more self-conscious and reflective the practice, the more explicit the link between the law and political morality: thinking *within* the practice includes, by way of internal critique, thinking *about* the practice. A competent practitioner can always offer better or fuller reasons to support her judgment; and that more elaborate response will often be necessary when others misguidedly, or corruptly, threaten injustice in the name of the practice. In those circumstances, interpretation will typically invoke or encompass a theory of good law, inspired by general principle but supported, as appropriate, by familiar example or precedent.[55]

IV. CONCLUSION

The truth of any legal proposition depends on the correct interpretation of legal practice, viewed as a whole. But it is a matter that raises questions of legitimacy as well as moral coherence. For a sceptic, who repudiates legal practice as morally repugnant, there is no law of the kind that imposes genuine obligations. There is only a practice of state officials exerting force against the victims of arbitrary rule. Where political obligation can be sustained, however, the law's requirements must be ascertained by moral reasoning, drawing on principles that honour the equal freedom and dignity of all those subject to the law's authority. Purported rules or requirements that infringe those principles have neither validity nor authority.

Everyone is finally responsible for his own judgment about the truth of any asserted proposition of law: he must either acknowledge or reject the state's authority, imposing the conditions on which, in his considered view, legitimacy depends. Dworkin's wary, semi-detached interpreter, accordingly, illustrates the potential rupture of legal and moral judgment. Even if his interpretation of any legal rule or requirement is idiosyncratic, diverging sharply from the standard view, it may be justifiably so, at least from his perspective. That divergence is necessary to sustain his allegiance. And if he invokes familiar principle

---

[54] Fish, 'Dennis Martinez and the Uses of Theory' in *Doing What Comes Naturally* (n 5) 384–92.
[55] There is a close resemblance here to Rawlsian reflective equilibrium, as defended initially in J Rawls, 'Outline of a Decision Procedure for Ethics' (1951) 60 *Philosophical Review* 177; see further Allan (n 28) 275–78, 280–85. Philosophers can help, as Dworkin observes, by exploring the moral foundations of law, constructing 'self-conscious articulate systems of value and principle out of widely shared but disparate moral inclinations, reactions, ambitions, and traditions': Dworkin (n 10) 109. Kant's moral philosophy affirms the relevant tests of responsibility and authenticity, requiring us to will as well as imagine the universality of a maxim on which we act (ibid 110).

and precedent, framing his arguments in the manner most likely to engender thoughtful debate, there can be no complaint. The protestant interpreter is doing his best to keep the faith, striving to defend the practice as a beneficial collaboration between free and equal citizens. The success of his interpretation, however, must finally depend on other people's responses. No one can impose on the practice an interpretation that fails to command the assent of other reflective participants. If his arguments fall on deaf ears, the dissentient may be forced to conclude that the practice, viewed in the best light now possible, does not deserve his allegiance.

A citizen who declines to obey an official requirement on moral grounds, objecting that compliance would violate her conscience, can usually be understood to make a legal or constitutional claim.[56] Freedom of conscience is an important right that the courts should protect from unwarranted interference: it underpins the rule of law. Even if the dissentient calls for repeal or reform, treating offensive rules or requirements as if they were currently valid, she denies, in effect, that they could be valid in any decent regime – any regime that could command her allegiance. However her objection is framed, it amounts in substance to a legal and constitutional challenge: the requirements impugned derive no authority from the law when correctly interpreted in a manner that preserves its legitimacy. Whether or not she can sustain her challenge ultimately depends on the reactions it elicits. If officials, or a political majority, remain intransigent, dismissing her objections, the dissentient may perforce become a sceptic. She can see no law, exerting moral authority, but only illegitimate force that deserves to be repelled.

The notion that someone might challenge the legitimacy of a rule or requirement, while at the same time granting its legal validity, depends on a conception of political obligation at odds with integrity. Political obligation is conceived as a duty to obey specific rules or requirements, viewed independently – detached from an interpretation of the law as a whole, from which they would otherwise obtain both meaning and force. There is an analogy with the judge who withdraws his allegiance from a wicked regime, however justifiably. He has forsaken law, understood as integrity, not merely when he lies about its content, to forestall iniquity, but also when he acts to protect reasonable expectations generated by official practice in other cases.[57] Divorced from any coherent moral theory of the law as a whole, the good judge's rulings are quintessentially ad hoc, well-intentioned interventions that have no secure foundation in legitimate state law.[58]

---

[56] In Dworkin (n 11) 213–14, Dworkin considers the refusal of students to salute the American flag, a stance finally vindicated by the Supreme Court in *West Virginia Board of Education v Barnette* (1943) 319 US 624.

[57] See Dworkin (n 2) 104–108. If, as Dworkin contends, people may have legal rights because they 'should be protected in relying and planning on law even in wicked places', such rights do not flow from integrity – from 'our interpretive judgments of the system as a whole' (ibid 106).

[58] See further Allan (n 26) 65–67.

For similar reasons, Hercules circumvents the law, in *McLoughlin*, when he shifts his focus away from the precedents and towards universal or 'abstract' ideals of justice and fairness. It is only the steadfast pursuit of integrity, even in hard cases, that distinguishes law from politics, allowing the judge's moral convictions to play a legitimate role within the limits of the practice. Hercules cannot desert the legal record in favour of independent reflection on the respective demands of justice and fairness without aping the deliberations of the conventionalist or the pragmatist, each of whom is free to legislate in a space to which the law supposedly does not extend.[59] Admittedly, Hercules is still seeking the best account of the law as a whole: he has not relinquished the ideal of moral coherence. But by casting the precedents aside, even if they are initially hard to reconcile, he has stepped beyond the practice. His speculations about popular morality, in particular, are no substitute for reflection on what legal tradition would support when studied more closely.

Fish makes a rather similar point in challenging the very possibility of being a conventionalist or pragmatist judge, as Dworkin describes them; legal judgments cannot in practice be separated from institutional history in the way that such approaches would require.[60] These, then, are only straw men, easily brushed aside. The only plausible form of conventionalism, in the context of Anglo-American law, is 'soft' conventionalism, which quickly collapses (as Dworkin observes) into law as integrity.[61] And pragmatism denies the basic idea of the rule of law from which (on Dworkin's account) any genuine interpretative approach begins. It denies the principle that coercion should be used only 'as licensed or required by individual rights and responsibilities flowing from past political decisions about when collective force is justified'.[62] Any concern for interpretative correctness, in identifying legal rights and duties, is merely feigned: it is a trick (we would have to suppose) adopted for reasons of political strategy.[63]

The internal or interpretative viewpoint is quite distinct from the external or detached one, making it impossible to occupy both perspectives simultaneously. When correctly understood, however, integrity forges an important connection, giving an interpreter's moral and political convictions a crucial role in the search for coherence. Legal judgment is underpinned, accordingly, by the same moral judgments that apply to any independent critical appraisal. Its focus on the morally most attractive interpretation of the law as a whole makes legal practice fully a part of moral practice. Any supposed conflict

---

[59] See Dworkin (n 2) chs 4, 5.
[60] Fish (n 6) 357–62.
[61] Whereas 'strict' conventionalism confines the law's content to the explicit extension of accepted conventions, 'soft' conventionalism incorporates all those propositions that follow from the best interpretation of convention. The latter requires, rather than forbids, resort to moral reasoning. See Dworkin (n 2) 120–30.
[62] ibid 93.
[63] ibid 157–60.

between moral and legal obligation, or between the demands of law and those of conscience, is therefore spurious. The law's integrity is perfectly aligned with the interpreter's integrity for as long as he retains his faith in the legal order as a legitimate basis of governance in the general interest. Injustice is properly confronted within the framework that integrity provides: its eradication demands strict adherence to the principles on which the moral unity of legal practice depends.

The boundary between internal and external viewpoints, defining the limits of interpretation, depends largely on interpretative creativity or originality, which is likely to be as well-developed as an interpreter's conscience is lively. Interpretative success, however, is never guaranteed. While the protestant interpreter must stand firm, matching her ingenuity to the scale of any threat she perceives to legitimacy, she can make progress only insofar as others find her arguments persuasive. While it would normally be wrong to repudiate legal practice without fully exploring its inherent moral resources, the interpreter may be finally unable to disturb an orthodoxy that, in her considered view, mars it fundamentally. Legal practice then has no claim on her allegiance: even when regarded in the light of the most favourable interpretation available, it remains radically unjust.

If, however, Dworkin is right to argue that moral truth depends on the correct interpretation of our moral concepts, there is an attractive symmetry between law and morality. The best interpretation of our moral practice – the most compelling account of how moral values can be integrated with a larger theory of ethics – may well diverge from widely accepted opinion about particular instances.[64] Even if moral truth ultimately depends on a shared practice of judgment, which generates the relevant criteria, there is no guarantee that any prevailing consensus on specific issues will turn out to be correct. Moral and legal paradigms are alike open to challenge, even if the challenge is chiefly internal – posing questions of moral or doctrinal coherence.

Legal interpretation, then, stands foursquare with moral interpretation. There is nowhere for the Archimedean to stand, above the fray, the better to understand and resolve either legal or moral controversy. There are neither moral facts nor social facts that must simply be taken as given: they owe their truth or significance, respectively, to the theory on which their existence or relevance depends.[65] If Dworkin's legal theory is vulnerable to criticism, along

---

[64] Dworkin argues that we should defend a conception of justice 'by placing the practices and paradigms of that concept in a larger network of *other* values that sustain our conception'. Any circularity involved is 'global across the whole domain of value': Dworkin (n 10) 162–63 (emphasis in original).

[65] As Dworkin argues, moral facts cannot be barely true, simply in the nature of things. They are true only insofar as they are supported by persuasive argument, which must draw on other moral values and assumptions. Law and morality are pervasively holistic, the truth of each proposition dependent on the truth of the others on which it depends: see ibid ch 7.

the lines that Fish's provocative work suggests, it is because it stands at least partly aloof from the moral theory on which it must draw to be convincing. Dworkin's jurisprudence too often seeks an elusive anchorage in sociological or historical fact, detached from moral argument. It makes too many concessions to the positivist or conventionalist framework that integrity rejects, threatening both the unity and independence of value on which Dworkin so plausibly insists.[66]

---

[66] Legal practice may be understood as a form of social practice in which the relevant rights and duties constitute a distinct domain of (political) morality. Compare G Letsas, 'How to Argue for Law's Full-Blooded Normativity' in D Plunkett, SJ Shapiro, and K Toh (eds), *Dimensions of Normativity* (Oxford, Oxford University Press, 2019) 165–85.

8

The Relevance of Literary Interpretation

BARBARA BAUM LEVENBOOK

I. INTRODUCTION

IF INTERPRETATION IS, at its most general, assigning a meaning or a referent (where one is missing, unclear, or imprecise), then there is plenty in law – and in language – that is not interpretation, but rather, a recognising of meaning (and reference or extension).[1] The ability to recognise full linguistic meaning, to correctly apply the conventions existing in the larger linguistic community to sentences and directive-formulations, is part of competence in the native language in question. Guidance of lay law conduct – as by posting parts of a city ordinance on a sign in a public park– depends upon this ability.

Even if the foregoing restriction on the scope of interpretation is rejected, there are weighty reasons why an interpretive theory of the nature of law – and in particular, Dworkin's version – ought to be rejected. I and others have written about them elsewhere; they need not be recounted here.

The import of these reflections is that the debate between Dworkin and Fish on the nature of interpretation in general and literary interpretation in particular is somewhat peripheral to the inquiry into the nature of law. However, it is clear that sometimes in law there is what is referred to as *interpretation* (and *construction*) – of vague statutes, of unclear constitutional provisions, of apparent inconsistencies in written regulatory instruments such as administrative rules, and so on. Further, there is the phenomena within the common law tradition sometimes called 'reinterpretation' of a precedent. In one common form, distinguishing, the source court ratio decidendi, generally

---

[1] Patterson calls this latter activity 'understanding'. D Patterson, 'Colloquy: The Poverty of Interpretive Universalism: Toward the Reconstruction of Legal Theory' (1993) 72 *Texas Law Review* 1.

taken to be applicable to a current case, is reinterpreted so as to be inapplicable to the current case. So, it is worthwhile to examine the Fish-Dworkin debate on interpretation and inquire if its debate about literary interpretation in general and its inquiry into the chain novel analogy in particular is helpful or illuminating for the nature and structure of legal interpretation, understood more narrowly.

My answer is 'no'. The main reason is that both disputants are misled by the assumption that literary interpretation is so closely analogous to legal interpretation that the dissimilarities are irrelevant. The primary purpose of this chapter is to demonstrate the falsity of this assumption; and thus, to undermine attempts to base contentions about legal interpretation on contentions about literary interpretation.

II. A BRIEF CLARIFICATION OF TERMINOLOGY

By denying, as I do, that the application of local law everywhere is always a matter of interpretation,[2] I am limiting the scope of *legal interpretation*, as I am using that phrase, compared to the scope given to it by Dworkin.

It bears repeating: Legal interpretation, as I will understand it, is neither coextensive with nor required for all (ex ante) law-application (which, I remind the reader, usually is performed by persons other than judges and usually occurs outside of courtrooms[3]). It is only when the ex ante law is in need of clarification or repair, or its application to a particular instance is doubtful or undetermined, that legal interpretation, as I will understand it, has a role.

III. THE ANALOGY BETWEEN LITERARY AND LEGAL INTERPRETATION

I begin by establishing that both Fish and Dworkin hold that literary interpretation and legal interpretation are sufficiently similar to be worth talking about in an investigation of law and adjudication.[4]

---

[2] In a number of publications, I have presented a non-interpretive account of the success of such persons in correctly applying local law to the often mundane situations they encounter (with the resulting successful social coordination achieved by some laws). I will not review my arguments here. See BB Levenbook, 'The Meaning of a Precedent' (2000) 6 *Legal Theory* 185; 'How a Statute Applies' [2006] *Legal Theory* 71; 'The Law of the Street' in M McBride and J Penner (eds), *New Essays on the Nature of Legal Reasoning* (Oxford, Hart, 2020); 'Supplanting Defeasible Rules' in S Lewis, T Endicott, and H Kristjansson (eds), *Philosophical Foundations of Precedent* (Oxford, Oxford University Press, 2023).

[3] Some of it occurs in lawyers' offices. Some of it occurs on a near-daily basis, by registrars of deeds, building inspectors, motor vehicle examiners, tax preparers, realtors, compliance officers in corporations and the like – and ordinary law-abiding subjects.

[4] Though they are discussing legal interpretation broadly conceived, their remarks hold for the more narrow conception I have adopted.

Fish seems to assume so here:

> Dworkin is right, I think, to link his argument about legal practice to an argument about the practice of literary criticism ...[5]

and here, after alleging, at length, the ubiquitous role of interpretation in literary criticism and in simply reading literary work:

> This holds true too when the distinction becomes a judicial one and marks the difference, according to Dworkin, between a judge who feels constrained in his actions by the 'past record of statutes and decisions' and a judge who ignores legal history and decisions 'to decide cases "on a clean slate" instead'. [note omitted] Here the legal history is in the position of ... any ... literary work ... and the judge is in the position of the novelist who is asked to continue the chain and enjoined from breaking it, and the point made in relation to the novelists applies *mutatis mutandis* to the judge: the question of whether the legal history is being ignored or consulted depends upon a prior decision as to what the legal history is, and that decision will be an interpretive one.[6]

Dworkin shares the assumption that there is a useful analogy between literary and legal interpretation: 'I propose that we can improve our understanding of law by comparing legal interpretation with interpretation in other fields of knowledge, particularly literature.'[7] There is also this passage, from the same source:

> [W]e must develop a more inclusive account of what interpretation is. But that means that lawyers must not treat legal interpretation as an activity *sui generis*. We must study interpretation as a general activity, as a mode of knowledge, by attending to other contexts of that activity.
>
> Lawyers would do well to study literary and other forms of artistic interpretation. ... [In particular,] I am interested ... in arguments which offer some sort of interpretation of the meaning of a work as a whole.[8]

And from *Law's Empire*:

> The form of interpretation we are studying – the interpretation of a social practice – is like artistic interpretation .... I shall capitalize on that similarity between artistic interpretation and the interpretation of a social practice.[9]

In looking at such literary arguments, Dworkin contends that 'an interpretation of a piece of literature attempts to show which way of reading ... the text reveals it as the best work of art'.[10] Detailed probing of how, according to

---

[5] S Fish, 'Working on the Chain Gang: Interpretation in Law and Literature' reprinted in S Fish, *Doing What Comes Naturally: Change, Rhetoric, and the Practice of Theory in Literary and Legal Studies* (Durham, NC, Duke University Press, 1989) 87.
[6] S Fish, 'Wrong Again' reprinted in Fish, *Doing What Comes Naturally* (n 5) 109.
[7] R Dworkin, 'Law as Interpretation' (1982) 9 *Critical Inquiry* 179, 179.
[8] ibid 181–82.
[9] R Dworkin, *Law's Empire* (Cambridge, MA, Harvard University Press, 1986) 50.
[10] Dworkin (n 7) 183.

Dworkin, a literary interpreter shows 'which way of reading ... the text reveals it as the best work of art' reveals two dimensions: fit to the text, which in 'Law as Interpretation' he calls 'the constraint of integrity', and a 'more explicitly normative' dimension, which in the case of literary interpretation is a set of beliefs 'about what is good in art'.[11] This alleged feature of literary interpretation Dworkin believes illuminates the two dimensions in legal interpretation: fit (but this time to institutional history) and a normative dimension he describes originally as 'political' and later as 'justification'. Just as an interpretation of a text shows its value as a work of art, 'an interpretation of any body or division of law ... must show the value of that body of law ... by demonstrating the best principle or policy it can be taken to serve'.[12]

IV. WHAT IS THE ROLE OF THE ANALOGY?

The next step is to clarify the role of Dworkin's proffered analogy. As many readers know, the particular form it takes is an analogy between literary interpretation in a chain novel and legal interpretation. Is the analogy used to elucidate Dworkin's claims about legal interpretation? In other words, is it solely a heuristic device that can be offered to help others understand Dworkin's philosophical position? If so, the general claim can be paraphrased as:

> Let us imagine that several authors undertake a chain novel, and that authors after the first engage in a literary interpretation of what has gone before along the two dimensions I have described so as to make their contribution fit well. Now make a few minor adjustments to the story as I direct, and you will understand what I contend judges do in legal interpretation.

In support of this reading, Dworkin says, when introducing the chain novel analogy, 'I want to use literary interpretation as a model for the central method of legal analysis ...'[13] In a review of *A Matter of Principle*, Raz puts the heuristic use this way: '[The analogy] is used to illustrate the complex relations [Dworkin thinks exists] between discovery and creation, and between subjective judgment and objective truth in the law'.[14]

If that is all the analogy is used for, what can the correlative part of the debate between Fish and Dworkin be about? It is not about the aptness of the comparison – on that, we have seen, Fish and Dworkin are in perfect agreement. Is it about the effectiveness of the analogy in this communicative role? That is hardly worth a great deal of philosophical investigation or energy. Is it about the

---

[11] ibid 184–85. Compare with Dworkin (n 9) 66–67.
[12] ibid 194.
[13] Dworkin (n 7) 192. And see ibid 193: 'Deciding hard cases at law is rather like this strange literary enterprise.' Also, see Dworkin (n 9) 228–29.
[14] J Raz, 'Dworkin: A New Link in the Chain [Review of *A Matter of Principle*, by R. Dworkin]' [1986] *California Law Review* 1103, 1117.

accuracy of the first analogue? That is worth philosophical investigation when the topic is literary interpretation. However, when the topic is legal interpretation, at worst inaccuracy about literary interpretation would merely mean that Dworkin has made an unfortunate choice in heuristic device. Inaccuracy about literary interpretation would not challenge his claims about legal interpretation, nor his case for them.

Alternatively, is the analogy intended as part of an argument by analogy, whose conclusion is a claim about legal interpretation? To my knowledge, such an argument is never cohesively formulated in anything Dworkin writes in the period from 1982–86, the period in which he introduced and employed the chain novel analogy. If there is an analogical argument, the assumption being made by Dworkin (and apparently accepted by Fish) is that literary interpretation and legal interpretation in particular are so similar that insights about legal interpretation can be supported by truths about literary interpretation.

One can make a case that Fish relies on his own unformulated argument by analogy from literary interpretation, though he differs at points from Dworkin in his accounts of both literary and legal interpretation. Nonetheless, I will focus on what such an argument would look like coming from Dworkin. (General problems with the strategy, to be explored below, apply to an argument by analogy that might be constructed on Fish's behalf.)

Dworkin's argument by analogy – the argument by analogy intended to support what Dworkin called his 'main thesis, that interpretation in law is essentially political'[15] – would, I suggest, be a compound argument as follows:

1. A judge (faced with a legal decision) is like a new author in a chain novel in that both 'normally recognize a duty [or undertake] to continue ... the practice they have joined'.[16]
2. In order to continue a practice, one must interpret the practice to date.
3. So a judge (faced with a legal decision) is like a new author in a chain novel in that both must engage in interpretation of what has gone before.
4. When a new author in a chain novel engages in literary interpretation, the aim is to find a way of regarding the text that shows it to be 'a single unified novel that is the best it can be'.[17]
5. It follows that an author's literary interpretation in a chain novel rests on that author's assumption of a normative theory of art, or 'background aesthetic convictions'.[18]

---

[15] Dworkin (n 7) 196. Other arguments by analogy for specific components of Dworkin's account of legal interpretation can be constructed from Dworkin's texts.
[16] Dworkin (n 9) 86. See also Dworkin (n 7) 193.
[17] Dworkin (n 9) 229. Note omitted.
[18] ibid 237. See Dworkin (n 7) 185: '... anyone who interprets a work of art relies on beliefs of a theoretical character about ... what is good in art'.

6. Therefore, when a judge rendering a decision engages in legal interpretation, the aim is to find a way of regarding the (local) legal 'practice' or 'process' that has gone before ('as a whole') that shows it in its best light.[19]
7. Therefore, too, a judge's legal interpretation rests on that judge's assumption of a normative political theory, or 'political convictions of different sorts'.[20]

As many readers know, arguments by analogy cannot prove their conclusions. They merely vary on a scale of strength, with good ones relatively strong and bad ones weak. At best, they make their conclusions probable. Therefore, this chain novel analogical argument's conclusions #6 and #7 should begin with 'Probably', or 'It is likely that'. Even if this argument is a strong one, Dworkin will have supported only the likelihood of his characterisation of legal interpretation. I will not, however, press this point in what follows.

If the forgoing argument is the (or a) use of the analogy by Dworkin, then whether or not literary interpretation has been accurately characterised is highly relevant. A case for a contention about legal interpretation hangs upon the accuracy of the proffered account of literary interpretation. That makes debate about literary interpretation germane. (Other aspects of Dworkin's account of literary interpretation – primarily, the claim of increasing constraints as the chain develops – function in another argument by analogy, one that will not be pursued in this chapter. A locus of Fish's challenge to Dworkin is to the accuracy of this expanded account.)

But before entering the debate about literary interpretation and examining the accuracy of Dworkin's characterisation of literary interpretation in the foregoing argument, we must note an independent problem with it.

V. A FIRST DISANALOGY

As many readers know, relevant disanalogies weaken an argument by analogy and can make it a bad argument. Hence, in an analogical argument use of the chain novel analogy, it is important to examine whether legal interpretation is relevantly disanalogous to literary interpretation, as characterised by Dworkin. Curiously, this is a task that neither Fish nor Dworkin undertake.

---

[19] He says as 'an adequate justification for coercion'. Dworkin (n 9) 139. I propose to ignore this point.
[20] Dworkin (n 9) 239. He calls it 'substantive political theory' in 'Law as Interpretation' (Dworkin (n 7) 195), though he also thinks there must also be convictions about the structure of the legal system. Raz summarises the argument I have set out this way: The analogy 'is used to argue for the dependence of judicial decisions on the court's view of substantive moral and political issues'. Raz (n 14).

There is a striking disanalogy in the argument by analogy, and what is more striking is that it is evident from Dworkin's point of view. In the case of the chain novel, the novel has run out when the new author undertakes the task of adding to it. So it is odd that Dworkin should compare this situation to what the judge does in deciding a case. For Dworkin does not maintain that whenever a case (even a 'hard case') comes before the judge for decision, the local law has run out. Dworkin concedes that at least sometimes (and, in his early works, always in a mature legal system) there is ex ante law to be discovered and uncovered by the judge (antecedently true 'legal propositions').[21]

Presumably, Dworkin also thinks judges at least sometimes do this discovering and uncovering successfully. Despite our differences on the scope of the legal interpretation, I agree. (Some *legal interpretation* as I am using the term aims at uncovering and discovering ex ante law – when parts of it are doubtful, difficult to discern, or, to borrow a metaphor from a communication model of law, implicit.)

The objection can be recast this way: there is no implicit novel, or implicit next chapter, for the new author to discover and make explicit in his or her contribution. Yet Dworkin suggests that there is implicit law – an implicit legal right, perhaps – to be discovered by the deciding judge. The activities of the chain novelist and the discovering judge are sufficiently different as to make it highly doubtful that the structure of correct or acceptable reasoning (interpretation) in both cases is significantly the same. The contrary cannot be assumed without begging the question.

This disanalogy may prove decisive, at least for that portion of legal interpretation engaged in (or aimed at) applying ex ante law. When judges legally interpret to uncover and discover ex ante law, the judge is not free to be as creative (or, more precisely, the judge's job is not to be as creative, or perhaps the better word is 'inventive') as the new author of a chain novel. A more precise way to put the point is this: for the new novelist in the chain, there is more than one acceptable 'solution' that will fit with what has gone before. (Dworkin would concede the point about novelists entering the chain perhaps only early on, or early on to midway through.) Choosing among multiple solutions is an act of discretion and creativity. But for the judge or other legal interpreter charged with applying ex ante law, there is always only one acceptable 'solution': the decision that applies, to the situation in hand, the law that exists antecedently

---

[21] See, eg, Dworkin (n 9) 6, 227. See also RM Dworkin, 'No Right Answer?' in PMS Hacker and J Raz (eds), *Law, Morality, and Society* (Oxford, Oxford University Press, 1977). Fish borders on denying that there is ex ante law that can be found or discovered: '[T]here can be no simply "found" [legal] history in relation to which some other history could be said to be "invented"'(Fish (n 5) 94); 'The distinction between a "found" history and an "invented" one is finally nothing more than a distinction between a persuasive interpretation and one that has failed to convince.' (ibid 95). If he denies that ex ante law exists and a fortiori that its discovery can sometimes be the aim of legal interpretation, Fish is deeply mistaken.

to that decision. This, as I have remarked, involves discovering or uncovering, not inventing. So even if creation and invention presuppose a normative theory evaluating not just what moves are permissible or intelligible in a context but which are better or worse, there is room to doubt that uncovering does.

VI. THE LITERARY INTERPRETATION PREMISE

The reader will note that the disanalogy just noted is between (interpretings of) a work of fiction and ex ante law. But some – though not Dworkin – may respond that for judges in, say, appellate courts, what is called by them *legal interpretation* is not always aimed at uncovering ex ante law – even for the statutory interpretation of a single statutory provision. It may then be suggested that the chain novel analogical argument should be employed only when ex ante law runs out. In this situation, a judge must add to it. Surely, it may be thought, this activity is more manifestly creative than uncovering, and so, closer to the chain novel situation.

So suppose that the previous point is granted and that the argument by analogy is amended as follows:

1. A judge faced with a legal decision *when ex ante law runs out* is like a new author in a chain novel in that both have a duty to continue the practice they have joined.
2. In order to continue a practice, one must interpret the practice to date.
3. So a judge faced with a legal decision *when ex ante law runs out* is like a new author in a chain novel in that both must engage in interpretation of what has gone before.
4. When a new author in a chain novel engages in literary interpretation, the aim is to find a way of regarding the text that shows it to be the best unified novel it can be.
5. It follows that an author's literary interpretation in a chain novel rests on that author's assumption of a normative theory of art.
6. Therefore, when a judge rendering a decision engages in legal interpretation *and the ex ante law has run out*, the aim is to find a way of regarding the (local) legal 'practice' or 'process' that has gone before ('as a whole') that shows it in its best light.
7. Therefore, too, a judge's legal interpretation *when ex ante law runs out* rests on that judge's assumption of a normative political theory, or political convictions.

(Italics indicate the changes.) The reader will note that premises #2 and #4 are identical to those in the original argument by analogy (supra, section #3). Note, too, that although the recast analogical argument strays from the direction of the Fish-Dworkin debate, Dworkin can accept the amended argument; though he would assert that it does not go far enough.

Is the argument by analogy rehabilitated if we read it as amended? Note that in this recast argument, Fish's instinct to attack the accuracy of Dworkin's proffered account of literary interpretation is apposite. However, Fish entirely misses the error in the account of literary interpretation that undermines the argument in both its original and amended forms. In other words, the amendments do not rehabilitate the argument.

The account is in premise #4. The relevant parts of it can be paraphrased as follows:

> When a new author in a chain novel engages in literary interpretation, the aim is to find a way of regarding the text *that shows it to be the best it can be.*

This is a curious claim. Fish accepts a version of it:

> All interpretation *does* strive to make an object the best it can be if we understand 'best' to mean nothing more (or less) than the standard of value or relevance that is the defining characteristic of that object. So that, for example, the defining characteristic of a judicial opinion would be that it presented itself as flowing from the principles of justice, of a scientific explanation that it strove to be accurate, of a work of art that it set out to be beautiful or profound or unified.[22]

Why believe premise #4? Authors, we might well imagine, have engaged in chain novels without aiming to make them the best they can be. When, for example, Robert B Parker undertook to finish Raymond Chandler's planned 'Poodle Springs' and inherited only four chapters, it is conceivable that Parker realised that he was free, within constraints of Chandler's style, characters, and fledgling plot, to go in several directions, some of which would have been better than others. Parker might have chosen to experiment – with the plot, for instance – on a path he regarded as (and that was) less stellar than others, for fun or expediency or commercial success.

If chain novel authors must have interpreted what has come before, the Parker-Chandler thought experiment seems a counterexample to premise #4. Dworkin makes a broader claim that 'constructive interpretation is a matter of imposing purpose on an object or practice in order to make of it the best possible example of the form or genre to which it is taken to belong'.[23] Assuming that the interpretation by the new author must be constructive, the Parker-Chandler thought experiment is also a counterexample to that broader claim.

There may be additional counterexamples. Let us assume, for the sake of argument, that understanding conversation always requires interpretation (as Dworkin and Fish appear to believe). There are touchy or suspicious people

---

[22] S Fish, 'Still Wrong After All These Years' reprinted in *Doing What Comes Naturally* (n 5) 364–65. Emphasis in original.
[23] Dworkin (n 9) 52. See also Dworkin (n 7) 183. Compare with Dworkin's suggestion of a 'general account of interpretation in all its forms', Dworkin (n 9) 53: '[A]ll interpretation strives to make an object the best it can be, as an instance of some assumed enterprise, and ... interpretation takes different forms in different contexts only because different enterprises engage different standards of value or success'.

who strive to make an innocent question the worst it can be (inappropriate, for example, or irrelevant). Are these persons not interpreting the utterance? None of them are striving to make the utterance 'the best it can be'.[24] Will Dworkin (and Fish) reply that these people *think* they are making the utterance the best it can be? There are defiant teenagers who sometimes strive to make parental questions and commands unintelligible or ludicrously simple-minded. The teens do not think they are making the utterances the best they can be. Are the teens not interpreting?

Perhaps Dworkin would reply that touchy and suspicious people and defiant teenagers *mis*interpret questions and remarks. Then the claim that all (constructive) interpretation strives to make its object the best it can be is a claim about all accurate or successful interpretation. However, there seem to be counterexamples in the cases of accurately spotting (accurately interpreting?) sarcasm, insincere compliments, humble bragging and the like.

One response to these observations is to exempt conversational interpretation from the sort of interpretation meant by premise #4 – ie, as not constructive. Yet a further counterexample can be derived from another field of artistic interpretation. Consider the plot of the 1967 Mel Brooks film 'The Producers', in which the producers set out to interpret – and present – a particular play ('Springtime for Hitler') in what they conceive of as the worst possible way, in order that it flop. ('The Producers' may also be a counterexample to Fish's contention about interpretations of works of art. The interpreters in question were not striving to make the object beautiful or profound. They need not have been striving to make it unified, either. Is the play not a work of art?[25])

Dworkin might (and perhaps did) insist, however, that the analogy he is relying on is one in which the new authors do adopt the aim of making the resulting novel the best it can be. However, this move eviscerates the argument by analogy. For it amounts to tailoring the description of what duties authors recognise and their goal to suit the desired conclusion about legal interpretation.

This strategy is question-begging. To see this, consider the following counterargument, in which the aim of the chain novelists is specified differently:

1' A judge faced with a legal decision *when ex ante law runs out* is like a new author in a chain novel in that both have a duty to continue the practice they have joined.

---

[24] Not even by 'the standard of value or relevance that is the defining characteristic of that object'.

[25] Fish holds that the text being interpreted is individuated and metaphysically determined by an interpretation (or a series of them, since Fish seems to think that interpretation is 'all the way down'). Fish (n 5) 563, fn 31. On this view, the producers do not interpret their object – which is what? – to be the best it can be. They interpret their object to be the only thing it can be (thus, creating it); there are no possibilities of better or worse. Patterson has done an excellent job of articulating reasons to reject Fish's ontological view. Patterson (n 1).

Fish also holds that all interpretation assigns 'meaning in the light of the motives and purposes and concerns it supposes the' speaker or creator or originator or legislator to have. (Fish (n 22) 365, quoting Dworkin (n 9) 50.) Yet the interpreters in 'The Producers' were not assigning 'meaning in the light of the motives and purposes and concerns it [the interpretation?] supposes the speaker

2'   In order to continue a practice, one must interpret the practice to date.
3'   So a judge faced with a legal decision *when ex ante law runs out* is like a new author in a chain novel in that both must engage in interpretation of what has gone before.
4'   When a new author in a chain novel engages in literary interpretation, the aim is to find a way of contributing to the text so as to make the result a commercial success, acceptable to and accepted by a commercial publisher and the reading public.
5'   It follows that an author's literary interpretation in a chain novel rests on that author's (nonnormative) assumption about consequences of the product that results from the author's contribution.
6'   Therefore, when a judge rendering a decision engages in legal interpretation *and the ex ante law has run out*, the aim is to find a way of contributing to local law so as to make it acceptable to and accepted by other officials in the system (and perhaps the law-abiding).
7'   Therefore, too, a judge's legal interpretation *when ex ante law runs out* rests on that judge's (nonnormative) assumption about consequences of adding a particular decision to the corpus of local law.

As the foregoing discussion illustrates, it is the relevance of the choice of aim of the new author's alleged interpretation that is at issue. That relevance cannot be assumed in an argument by analogy to a conclusion about legal interpretation by judges without begging one of the very questions the argument is designed to establish.

VII. THE SECOND DISANALOGY

Suppose, then, that all of the previous points are conceded. Still, some will protest that there is something that can and should be preserved from the argument by analogy. For the analogy seems apt, persuasive. What may be doing some of the persuasive work in the amended argument by analogy is the recognition that legal systems, and laws that are parts of them, are artifacts, just as novels are.

Artifacts have uses, or purposes.[26] So suppose that the conclusion of the argument by analogy is scaled back to focus on the idea of purpose or, more precisely, unifying purpose. Suppose, that is, that an argument by analogy from a chain novel is recast as follows:

1"   A judge faced with a legal decision when ex ante law runs out is like a new author in a chain novel in that both have a duty to continue the practice they have joined.

[playwright?] to have', but rather going contrary to the motives and purposes and concerns they supposed the playwright had.
[26] See, eg, L Burazin, 'Can There Be an Artifact Theory of Law?' (2016) 29 *Ratio Juris* 385.

2" In order to continue a practice, one must interpret the practice to date.
3" So a judge faced with a legal decision when ex ante law runs out is like a new author in a chain novel in that both must engage in interpretation of what has gone before.
4" When a new author in a chain novel engages in literary interpretation, the aim is to find a way of regarding the text that shows it to *be a unified novel, as if from a single author.*
5" It follows that an author's literary interpretation in a chain novel rests on that author's assumption *of a unifying point, purpose, or value of the text so far.*
6" Therefore, when a judge rendering a decision engages in legal interpretation and the ex ante law has run out, the aim is to find a way to *show the legal history or legal practice so far to be unified, as if from a single lawgiver.*
7" Therefore, too, a judge's legal interpretation *when ex ante law runs out* rests on that judge's assumption *of a unifying point, purpose, or value of the practice, taken as a whole.*

This, of course, is to amend the argument by analogy once again. (The italicised portions indicate the changes.) Note that Dworkin can agree in general with the revised argument, again stipulating that it does not go far enough.[27]

Let us set aside the obvious points that artifacts may have multiple purposes; and that practices in particular may have – and may be construed as having – multiple purposes. Dworkin may well agree;[28] and thus, may not entirely accept the revised conclusion. For present purposes, it is enough that he would conclude that the interpretation must be holistic, assigning something unifying – a point, a value, a scheme of principles – to the entire local legal system.

The main problem is that there is a second disanalogy that undermines this revised argument. Like the first disanalogy, it, too, is independent of debate on the nature of legal interpretation.

The new author of the chain novel is charged with continuing the entire novel, albeit for a chapter. If we conceive of the novel as a time-space worm, the new author will add the current segment. Having responsibility for the entire current segment, it is plausible that the new author has a responsibility to fit it to the whole inherited to date. This makes it plausible that the new author will

---

[27] Dworkin (n 7) 194: '[The judge] must determine, according to his own judgement, what the earlier decisions come to, what the point or theme of the practice so far, taken as a whole, really is'. But see n 28 below.

[28] Dworkin suggests several 'general' points or purposes for law as a whole. ibid 194. ibid 196, he seems to suggest that a legal interpretation need only assign a 'dominant purpose ... [that law] ought to serve'. It follows that a legal interpretation evaluates one of several purposes law performs as the most important. Insofar as this contention depends upon Dworkin's general claim about constructive interpretation examined in section #5, it has been addressed.

need to analyse the entire novel to date (in order to do this well, or to do it as a novel and not as a series of short stories sharing character names). It is not much of a further step to contend, as Dworkin does, that this process will require 'interpreting' the novel to date holistically – for its theme (if determinate, that is), genre, style, and the like.

In contrast, a judge is charged with deciding a particular dispute on a very specific issue (or set of issues raised in a single legal case). What the decision adds to the local law, if anything, depends both on local law (is this judge's decision authoritative for this kind of precedent in a way that transcends the resolution of the particular dispute?) and on the nature and content of precedent. But even when the judicial decision adds to the local law, even when it answers a question of local law (which is not always the case[29]), it adds only a small point to a large and dynamic corpus in a mature legal system. Seldom is the judge's contribution the entire segment of the new part of the local law; there are contemporaneous contributions from other judicial decisions, new legislation, executive orders, administrative orders, and the like. The judge deciding a particular case does not have the responsibility for the entire current segment of local law. So there is not the same story to tell to make it plausible that the judge will need to interpret the entire local law to date holistically (eg, to find its point or purpose).

Have I inflated a difference? One may protest that a judge deciding a particular case cannot (or, more precisely, should not) have tunnel vision. Local law typically occurs in a normative system, in which there are connections (and normative operations such as overriding and excluding) between laws. These connections obtain in a vertical hierarchy of more and less basic laws (or constitutive laws and other sorts), and horizontally. For example, statutes are often understood, interpreted, and applied by officials as if modified by earlier general statutes (or a later general 'interpretive' one[30]), judicial decisions, practices-within-practices (giving rise to claims about unwritten rules, such as the *mens rea* canon of statutory interpretation[31]) and so on. (I will return to this systematicity in the last section of this chapter.) Arguably, some of the modifying standards and judicial decisions are interpretive; and some of these interpretive

---

However, Dworkinian exegesis is not easy. Unity and elevation to a dominant purpose are not mentioned in Dworkin (n 9) 52: 'Interpretation of works of art and social practices ... is ... essentially concerned with purpose .... A participant interpreting a social practice ... proposes value for the practice by describing some scheme of interests or goals or principles the practice can be taken to serve or express or exemplify.'
[29] See the discussions of precedent in Levenbook, 'The Meaning of a Precedent' (n 2) and Levenbook, 'Supplanting Defeasible Rules' (n 2).
[30] See D Smith, 'The Practice-Based Objection to the "Standard Picture" of How Law Works' (2019) 10 *Jurisprudence* 502. See also W Baude and SE Sachs, 'The Law of Interpretation' (2017) 130 *Harvard Law Review* 1079.
[31] Here is one statement of it: 'A statute creating a criminal offense whose elements are similar to those of a common-law crime will be presumed to require a culpable state of mind (*mens rea*) in its commission.' A Scalia and BA Garner, *Reading Law: The Interpretation of Legal Texts* (Eagan, West Publishing, 2012) 303.

legal standards, or interpretive practices-with-legal-status-within-practices, apply to the judge who is adding to the local law. It seems to follow that in order to (properly, at least[32]) add to the law on a point, a judge must take into account (interpret?) and comply with or apply other standards with local legal status that are outside of the particular legal thread at issue in a case.

All of this can be granted. But it does not follow from these observations of systematicity that the judge must take into account, or interpret, all of the local law, developing or assuming a synoptic view of the whole to date.

Nor does this contention follow if one assumes that legal justification always requires legal interpretation. For all justification comes to an end. Moral justification of an act in ordinary circumstances stops well before ascending to the level of commitment to a particular moral theory; many different moral theories can be invoked to support a particular act. So, too, legal justification of an act of law-applying must come to an end. Its ascendancy to a realm of political theory cannot be presupposed.

In short, the necessity for (or the presupposition of) a synoptic interpretation in legal interpretation is in need of (some other) argument. The analogical argument just stated will not do. There is a disanalogy between the new chain novelist and the judge adding to local law.

The relevance of this disanalogy may be challenged. The disanalogy is irrelevant if three controversial and undefended Dworkinian assumptions are true. The first is the persistent premise (2) of the argument by analogy: 'In order to continue a practice, one must interpret the practice to date.' The second is the assumption that one cannot interpret a part of the local law (a sub-practice, such as the decisions on tort recovery for emotional distress) without interpreting the entire practice (the entire local law).[33] The third is this contention: the 'concept of interpretation' is such that an interpretation of anything 'proposes a way of seeing what is interpreted ... as if this were the product of a decision to pursue one set of themes or visions or purposes, one "point," rather than another'.[34]

There are two points to note about this response. The first is that the combination of the three assumptions makes the nature of literary interpretation once again apposite, but only if it is a counterexample to the first or third assumption. (Fish, to my knowledge, does not claim it is.)

The second and more important point is that with the introduction of all three assumptions, reliance on analogy becomes illusory. For the desired conclusion – a judge's legal interpretation when ex ante law runs out rests on

---

[32] Some of these standards might circumscribe the power to add to local law, so that the judge is disabled from adding to the local law if noncompliant. With respect to them, the sentence should begin: 'In order to add to the law, a judge must ....'

[33] Or more: the point of law in general. See Dworkin (n 9) 90: 'Any practical legal argument, no matter how detailed and limited, assumes the kind of abstract foundation jurisprudence offers .... So any judge's opinion is itself a piece of legal philosophy, even when the philosophy is hidden.'

[34] Dworkin (n 9) 58–59.

that judge's assumption of a unifying point or value of (or scheme of principles for) the local legal practice, taken as a whole – follows straightaway with the addition of the contention that a judge faced with a legal decision when ex ante law runs out recognises a duty to continue the practice he or she has joined. The analogy to a chain novel now does no argumentative work. There is a new argument, but it is not an argument by analogy.

Returning to the recently amended argument by analogy, the upshot of these reflections is that the leap to (the necessity of) interpreting holistically – about the point or value of the local law or the scheme of principles it serves as a whole – is unmotivated in that argument. It follows that there is a relevant disanalogy to the new novelist in the chain.

VIII. A LAST AMENDED ARGUMENT BY ANALOGY

Suppose that Dworkin retreats to a portion of the more modest claim quoted in section #2, to wit: '[A]n interpretation of any … *division of law, like the law of accidents*, must show the value of that body of law'.[35] Now the conclusions of the argument by analogy sketched in section #6 may be rendered as follows:

6" Therefore, when a judge rendering a decision engages in legal interpretation and the ex ante law has run out, the aim is to find a way to show *the division of law in which the legal issues of the case are raised* to be unified, as if from a single lawmaker.
7" Therefore, too, a judge's legal interpretation when ex ante law runs out rests on that judge's assumption of a unifying point or value *of the division of law in which the legal issues of the case are raised*.

(Once again, italics indicate the changes.) To legal experts in familiar legal systems, this conclusion may appear perfectly acceptable, if not positively familiar. It seems to explain very well appellate judicial practice in common law systems in which judges are required to submit written rationales for their rulings.[36] (It may also be granted that the following moral claim is true: When a division of law can be plausibly seen to serve – ie, can be interpreted as serving – a sound moral value, a judge adding to that area of law ought, *pro tanto*, to give it this interpretation and decide in a way that serves the moral value in question. This is not, I take it, what Dworkin is attempting to establish.)

Though I will shortly raise a reason to doubt that conclusion #7" (and, by extension, #6") is a (necessary or conceptual) truth about legal interpretation when ex ante law runs out, it bears emphasising that the issue I am raising in this chapter is not the truth of the conclusions of the arguments examined.

---

[35] See n 12. Emphasis added.
[36] See, eg, Dworkin's description of the choices before the judge who is adding to common law decisions about tort liability for emotional distress. Dworkin (n 7) 194.

Nothing I have said in this chapter is intended to show that the Dworkinian-style conclusions are false. Though I do not subscribe to them, I have not been concerned here to criticise these substantive claims about legal interpretation. My primary intention, as I have said, has been to cast doubt on the efficacy of arguing for them by analogy to the literary interpretation, if any, that must be assumed by a chain novelist.

Even in this latest version of the argument by analogy, there is inefficacy. For – and here systematicity re-enters the discussion – unlike chain novels, legal systems typically contain conventions (having legal status) governing how judging is to go in various scenarios.[37] And that creates a potential disanalogy.

We can approach the significance of this point by considering the more general question: what is appealing about the idea that insights into legal interpretation can be gained from and defended on the basis of the chain novelist thought experiment and the literary interpretation involved therein? By definition, a judge aiming at discovering and apply ex ante law is aiming at a continuity with at least some part of the ongoing legal system. Some of the so-called 'canons' of legal interpretation in familiar legal systems, and some of the practices or doctrines applying to judges taken to have legal status, require or privilege continuity and stability. In some legal systems, there is the doctrine of precedent containing standards binding courts to the precedential decisions of other courts. In common law systems, there is a practice of placing a heavy justificatory burden on those few courts authorised to overrule precedent. Moreover, some of the aforementioned canons of statutory interpretation and other interpretive practices arguably apply to a judge adding law. These observations may seem to suggest that a judge doing any sort of legal interpretation is undertaking a task with a necessary aim of continuity with the local law, or with divisions of it. Having such a necessary aim would then appear importantly analogous to the task of the new chain novelist; and then truths about what is presupposed in that latter task would support contentions about necessary presuppositions or commitments of legal interpretation.

However, the leap to 'necessary' in the case of law is unjustified. Those legal canons and legal practices may be contingent, linked to particular legal systems. What is ultimately at issue in Dworkin's argument(s) for his account of legal interpretation is: (1) whether, whenever the judge is adding to the law, setting the aim of a kind of continuity (local or global) is a merely conventional matter, or follows from the very idea of legal interpretation; and (2) whether, whenever the judge is clarifying ex ante law, establishing precisely what kind of continuity

---

[37] Such conventions may set aspirations or create rules imposing requirements, so that a judge grasping them has a belief about 'what judges in his position should do'. Phrase from Dworkin, ibid 199. But this belief may prove to be, in Raz's terms, 'detached'. See J Raz, *Practical Reason and Norms* (Oxford, Oxford University Press, 1975/1990) 171–77. Arguing for this possibility is beyond the scope of this chapter.

(eg, one setting a particular value or point for the relevant part of what came before[38]) is a merely conventional matter, or follows from the very idea of legal interpretation. Selecting 'follows from the very idea of legal interpretation' in both cases – the case of adding to the law, and the case of clarifying ex ante law – is question-begging.[39] This is true even in the restricted sense of 'legal interpretation' used in this chapter.

So if Dworkin's claims about the structure of literary interpretation in the chain novel case are meant to be necessary or conceptual, there is a potential disanalogy in the analogical argument to conclusion 7". Claims about aiming at or presupposing local continuity and strong coherence when adding to the law may be only contingently true of legal interpretation in certain legal systems. One can only dismiss or discount this possibility by begging the question.

In this chapter, I have primarily been casting doubt on the assumption that literary interpretation is so closely analogous to legal interpretation that the dissimilarities are irrelevant. Perhaps there are some respects in which some aspects of legal interpretation might be illuminated, and contentions about them supported, by such an analogy. I do not claim to have exhausted the possibilities. However, the analogy is not so tight as to present anything other than feeble support for principal features of Dworkin's account of legal interpretation.

In sum, these investigations have revealed little reason – indeed, none beyond criticising one of the premises in Dworkin's arguments – why those interested in the nature of legal interpretation should care about literary interpretation.

---

[38] This is what Raz calls 'strong monistic coherence', in R Raz, 'The Relevance of Coherence', reprinted in J Raz, *Ethics in the Public Domain* (Oxford, Clarendon Press, 1994) 320.
[39] As Dworkin does. See Dworkin (n 7) 197, where he writes of 'an explication of the concept of legal interpretation'.

9

Clash of the Titans: Hercules vs Dennis Martinez (Reflections on the Fish-Dworkin Debate)

CHARLES L BARZUN

> I must try to exhibit that complex structure of legal interpretation, and I shall use for that purpose an imaginary judge of superhuman intellectual power and patience who accepts law as integrity. Call him Hercules.
>
> Ronald Dworkin[1]

> That is why Dworkin's repeated injunction to arrive at the 'best' judgments we possibly can and be the best judges we can possibly be sounds so strange. One wants to say, with Dennis Martinez, 'what else could we be or do except what, according to our lights, was the best?'
>
> Stanley Fish[2]

I. INTRODUCTION

MANY SCHOLARLY EXCHANGES produce nothing of lasting intellectual value. The debate between Stanley Fish and Ronald Dworkin that took place over the course of the 1980s and early 90s initially seems to be one such exchange. The two scholars, both giants in their fields, seemed to talk past each other, making it difficult to discern the stakes of their quarrel. It would thus be easy to reach the sceptical conclusion that their debate should be happily forgotten, along with the headbands and mullets that marked the style of the decade in which their debate took place.

That conclusion is half right. There *is* a sense in which Fish and Dworkin talked past each other. In fact, the two theorists offer interpretations of legal

---

[1] R Dworkin, *Law's Empire* (Cambridge, MA, Belknap Press, 1986).
[2] S Fish, *Doing What Comes Naturally: Change, Rhetoric, and the Practice of Theory in Literary and Legal Studies* (Durham, NC, Duke University Press, 1989) 390.

practice that are in some ways the mirror images of each other – two sides of the same methodological coin. But the sceptical conclusion is too quick, because the exchange between them brings out both the question at the heart of their dispute and also why neither theorist offers a satisfying answer to it.

That question is whether law is a genuinely intellectual practice, by which I mean a practice in which ideas matter, both for explaining judicial decisions and legal change over time. Since the law's rhetoric – whether in law-school lectures, legal briefs, or judicial opinions – makes it appear to be an intellectual practice, the question asks whether legal professionals, from lawyers and judges to law students and teachers, are participating in an activity that is either deceptive or self-delusional or both. And for anyone who could lose their life, liberty, or property – or their democracy[3] – through the American legal process (which is to say, everyone in America) its answer in part determines how much confidence they should place in that process.

Neither Fish nor Dworkin offers a satisfying answer to this question. Whereas Fish plays the role of sceptic in the debate, denying that legal reasoning amounts to anything more than rhetoric, Dworkin serves as the defender of law's genuinely intellectual – even philosophical – integrity. But Dworkin's defence fails, and the purpose of this chapter is: (1) to show how and why it does so; and (2) to suggest what a more robust defence requires. What is needed is to abandon the methodological dichotomy, embraced by both Fish and Dworkin, between the methods, sources, and values 'internal' to legal practice and those 'external' to it.

My argument proceeds in three steps. In section II, I first identify what seem to be the main sources of dispute – substantive and methodological – between the two theorists. Both go to the role of ideas in legal practice. I then conduct a thought experiment involving Hercules (Dworkin's mythical judge) and the baseball pitcher Dennis Martinez (Fish's hero of anti-theory). Its purpose is to illustrate the difficulty not only of actually adjudicating the dispute between Fish and Dworkin but of even knowing how one might go about doing so.

It turns out that the impasse reached is hardly surprising once we see how heavily each theorist's claims depend on a dichotomy drawn between 'internal' and 'external' forms of analysis, evaluation, and critique of legal practice. Explaining why that distinction leads to a stalemate in their argument is the task of section III.

The solution to the stalemate is simple (and offered in section IV). It is to drop the internal/external (or inside/outside) dichotomy. Doing so means recognising that law is continuous with other fields of learning, from psychology, sociology, and history to moral and political philosophy. That recognition renders legal practice vulnerable to all sorts of sceptical worries that both Fish's and Dworkin's accounts attempt to defuse. But for precisely that reason it offers

---

[3] As I write, President Trump and his allies (including the Attorneys General of 17 states) have brought over 50 lawsuits in an effort to overturn the 2020 election result.

the only hope for making good on Dworkin's effort to understand legal practice as, at least *sometimes*, a genuinely intellectual enterprise.

II. THE PROBLEM: WHERE'S THE BEEF, EXACTLY?

Let me first briefly summarise the debate with the goal of getting clear what each party's views on the matters in dispute are. Then we can see what the essential disagreement between the two theorists seems to be about. Once the bone of contention is in clear view, we will try to figure out who is right – or how we might know who is right – by conducting a brief thought experiment.

A. Fish and Dworkin: Perfect Strangers?

Ronald Dworkin's theory of law puts questions of interpretation at its centre. Both in his article, 'Law and Interpretation', which was the target of Fish's initial critique, and in *Law's Empire*, Dworkin seeks to offer a rival account of law to legal positivism. He argues that legal propositions are neither purely factual, descriptive statements (as a legal positivist might argue), but nor are they merely 'subjective' expressions of desire (as a legal realist might argue).[4] Rather they are 'interpretive', by which Dworkin means that they are both descriptive *and* evaluative. They aim both to 'fit' the relevant legal materials but also to put them in their best light, just as literary critics aim to make sense of a poem or novel by making the best sense of it (where one's 'best sense' flows from the critic's sense of aesthetic value).[5] In *Law's Empire*, Dworkin calls this process 'constructive interpretation'.[6]

Stanley Fish, too, denies the possibility of 'objective' interpretations of texts, whether legal or literary. There are no literal meanings of words or sentences, according to Fish; rather, meaning is imposed upon texts by the interests, values, and expectations of their readers.[7] But it does not follow that there are no constraints on interpretive possibilities because those readers – and the perceptions, interests, expectations, and values that constitute them – are themselves determined by the 'interpretive communities' to which they belong.[8] Both texts and human agents are *constructed* (not discovered), but they are *socially* (not individually) constructed.[9]

---

[4] R Dworkin, 'Law as Interpretation' (1982) 60 *Texas Law Review* 527–28. I frame the distinction this way because some would argue that the legal realists were also legal positivists.
[5] ibid 531.
[6] Dworkin (n 1) 52.
[7] Fish (n 2) 3.
[8] ibid 25.
[9] ibid 140.

If both Dworkin and Fish see interpretation as neither wholly 'subjective' nor wholly 'objective', what is the difference between them? Arguably, not much.[10] In his first essay on Dworkin, Fish acknowledges that he finds Dworkin's account of interpretation 'attractive' and similar to Fish's own.[11] But he insists there is a difference, and it goes to how each theorist thinks interpretation works. This difference can be seen most clearly in Fish's critique of Dworkin's effort in *Law's Empire* to reinterpret traditional jurisprudential debates about the 'concept' of law as essentially normative debates about how judges ought to decide cases.

There Dworkin distinguishes among three rival 'conceptions' of law, which he dubs conventionalism, pragmatism, and law-as-integrity. According to Dworkin, each conception offers its own 'constructive interpretation' of legal practice, interpreting in different ways the demand that the state's coercive power only be deployed in ways that are 'licensed or required by individual rights and responsibilities flowing from past political decisions about when collective force is justified'.[12] The conventionalist judge is concerned primarily about procedural fairness and predictability and so thinks such rights only exist when they are explicit in those previous decisions. The pragmatist judge, meanwhile, only cares about past political decisions insofar as abiding by them serves some future-looking goal and so does not treat them as genuine constraints at all.

Finally, the judge who subscribes to 'law-as-integrity' sees himself as constrained by the principles of personal and political morality implicit in past political decisions that best fit and justify those decisions.[13] Dworkin's burden in *Law's Empire* is to show that law-as-integrity offers the best constructive interpretation of legal practice. He does so by showing how a 'judge of superhuman intellectual power and patience' would reason through various legal issues. Famously, Dworkin dubs such a judge Hercules.[14]

Fish's critique of Dworkin is not that judges do not practice law as integrity but that they do not do so in the deliberate, reflective way Dworkin imagines them to. Instead, law-as-integrity is the form of 'judicial practice already and necessarily takes' because judges always and necessarily give their 'best' interpretation of the relevant legal materials. A judge's 'constructive interpretation' of a set of materials *just is* whatever that judge believes those materials to mean.[15] Dworkin's mistake is to think that the process by which judges make such judgments is a *theoretical* one in which the judge looks at the materials, makes

---

[10] See D Patterson, *Law and Truth* (Oxford, OUP, 1996) 73.
[11] ibid 87.
[12] Dworkin (n 1) 93.
[13] ibid 94–96.
[14] ibid 239.
[15] ibid 369, 114. Fish also argues that Pragmatism and Conventionalism are impossible (for different reasons) and so do not even warrant Dworkin's normative criticisms of them. Fish (n 2) 356.

an evaluative judgment about what purpose or principle best justifies those materials, and then applies that principle to the case at hand. Instead, the judge practices law-as-integrity 'naturally': since her standards of evaluation are built into her understanding of what the enterprise is when she perceives a case *as a legal case* she is already seeing it as 'the best it could be'.[16]

Fish recounts a story about the pitcher Dennis Martinez to illustrate his point.[17] When asked by a reporter what his manager told him before a game, Martinez responded that the manager had told him to '"[t]hrow strikes and keep 'em off the bases"'. Then he added, 'What else could he say?'[18] As in baseball, so, too, in legal interpretation or any other interpretive activity. To perform competently in any practice depends on craft or tacit knowledge, rather than theoretical knowledge. It requires knowing *how*, not knowing *that*.[19] As Fish explains, '[t]o think within a practice is to have one's very perception and sense of possible and appropriate action issue 'naturally' without further reflection from one's position as a deeply situated agent'.[20] What is true of baseball players is true of judges: they are not engaged in a theoretical and reflective enterprise but instead performing moves in a game.[21]

To Dworkin, Fish's view reflects a stunningly impoverished understanding of legal practice. Fish fails to see that 'in some jobs [like judging] theory itself is second nature. Some things we do are more argumentative than throwing a forkball: Denny Martinez never filed an opinion'.[22] Because Fish fails to appreciate this theoretical, reflective, and introspective character of legal practice, his account, Dworkin explains, 'leaves no room *for puzzle or progress or controversy or revolution*: It cannot explain how lawyers can worry or disagree or change their mind about what the law is'.[23]

So that is the substantive dispute between Fish and Dworkin: is legal reasoning of the kind judges engage in as unreflective as pitching a forkball (as Fish argues)? Or would such a conclusion fail to account adequately for the 'puzzle or progress or controversy or revolution' that actually marks legal practice (as Dworkin argues)?

But that substantive dispute seems to carry even deeper, methodological implications for the legal scholar or would-be theorist. If law is not an intellectual, reflective practice, then efforts like Dworkin's to illuminate and guide it

---

[16] Fish (n 2) 364.
[17] According to Wikipedia, Dennis Martinez, nicknamed 'El Presidente', was the first Nicaraguan to play in Major League Baseball. His career spanned 22 years (1976–98), including 4 years as an all-star: en.wikipedia.org/wiki/Dennis_Mart%C3%ADnez.
[18] ibid 371.
[19] ibid 352.
[20] ibid 385–86.
[21] ibid 387.
[22] R Dworkin, 'Pragmatism, Right Answers, and True Banality' in M Brint and W Weaver (eds), *Pragmatism in Law and Society* (Boulder, CO, Westview Press, 1991) 382.
[23] ibid 388, fn 25 (emphasis added).

are doomed to failure. Thus, in the end, Fish concludes, '[t]hat finally is what is at stake in the debates between us, whether or not Dworkin has a project'.[24]

B. The Greatest American Judge: Hercules or Martinez?

But is there really a difference between these two views of legal practice? How would we know? I propose to answer those questions through a thought experiment. Let us imagine a fictious judge, who has written an opinion in a hard and important case involving statutory interpretation that ends up transforming the law in the area to which it applies. The judge goes by 'Judge Ralph', but he is actually either Hercules or Dennis Martinez (who has changed careers and now decides cases in the way he used to pitch forkballs), but we do not know which. He often seems like the Theoretician, Hercules, but can we rule out the possibility that he is really the Natural, Martinez? How might we do so? Let us see.

i. Form of Argument?

We might start by examining Ralph's written opinion, which seems to reflect the three main stages of 'constructive interpretation' that Dworkin describes.[25] The opinion lays out a series of cases, statutes, and other materials (pre-interpretive stage), ascribes a purpose to the statute in question (interpretive stage), applies that purpose to the facts of the case, yielding a conclusion as to which party wins (post-interpretive stage). Can we conclude that Judge Ralph is Hercules?

Not yet. When judges write their opinions they are, according to Fish, 'engaging in the practice of self-presentation, that is, the practice of offering a persuasive account of why they have done what they have done ... which is not the same thing (why on earth should it be?) as offering an account of how they actually did it'.[26]

ii. Quality of Argument (and Disagreement Over it)?

But it is not just the form of Ralph's argument. His opinion is also novel and bold in that it considers but then dismisses as irrelevant legislative history from the statute's sponsor in Congress that contradicts Judge Ralph's interpretation of the statute. Ralph's colleague makes much of this evidence in a vigorous dissent, but based on our own reading of Ralph's opinion, and related materials,

---

[24] S Fish, 'Almost Pragmatism: The Jurisprudence of Posner, Rorty, and Dworkin' in M Brint and W Weaver (eds), *Pragmatism in Law and Society* (Boulder, CO, Westview Press, 1991) 79.
[25] Dworkin (n 1) 52.
[26] Fish (n 2) 388.

we think Ralph's view superior. It is an ingenious, tightly reasoned opinion; indeed, we think it is *right*. Evidence of Hercules?

Hardly. True, Hercules is not constrained by the subjective intent of legislators. But neither is Martinez.[27] Nor does the brilliance of the opinion help. Fish and Dworkin both deny the existence of any independent standard against which we might compare the opinion in order to judge its correctness.[28] And since we can only make our own interpretive judgments as participants in legal practice, controversies and disagreements (like those with Ralph's dissenting colleague) are inevitable.[29] Ralph could still be either Hercules or Martinez.

iii. Time and Labour?

Then we learn that Ralph spent days on his opinion, pouring over the statute, legislative history, and relevant case law, rarely leaving his office and hoping for further inspiration. His wife was concerned; he was not showering much. Surely that is evidence of a conscious, reflective, *Herculean* effort, no?

Nope. Martinez struggles over cases, too. It is just that he is not struggling for *theoretical* reasons; he feels himself under pressure to figure out the best way to frame what he has already decided (naturally) in a way that will avoid making his colleagues raise their eyebrows.[30]

iv. Brain Scans?

Maybe judging by time and labour alone is inadequate, but surely if we hooked up Ralph to some sort of futuristic brain-scan technology, we could tell whether he is deliberating in the conscious, reflective way that Hercules does or, instead, if he is merely going on instinct, doing what comes naturally. Even current functional magnetic resonance imaging (fMRI) technology may be able to give us a clue as to whether Ralph is 'thinking fast' or 'thinking slow', no?[31]

Not necessarily. Ralph may be Martinez only somewhat self-deluded. The baseball great Ty Cobb, according to Fish, thought that he used a formula to judge when and how to swing at pitches, but there is good reason to think that he was deceiving himself.[32] So Martinez may just be going through the motions of 'constructive interpretation' because he thinks that is what judges are supposed to do, even though the real basis for his decision was just his 'feel' for the relevant materials.[33]

---

[27] ibid 98–99.
[28] ibid 88; Dworkin (n 4) 527–28.
[29] Dworkin (n 1) 14.
[30] Fish (n 2) 356.
[31] D Kahneman, *Thinking, Fast and Slow* (FSG 2011). *cf* B van den Berg, 'Thinking fast or slow? Functional magnetic resonance imaging reveals stronger connectivity when experienced neurologists diagnose ambiguous cases' [2020] *Brain Comms* 1.
[32] Fish (n 24) 78.
[33] ibid.

v. A (Progressive) Revolution?

Suppose we now learn that the case has had an enormous impact on the relevant law. Though considered radical at the time of the decision, within a few years Judge Ralph's view of the statute had been widely adopted. A few years after that, a unanimous Supreme Court validated it. Moreover, the law is much better for it – morally, social, intellectually. Surely only Hercules, or someone of his Calibre – a Holmes, Hand, or Cardozo – could pull that off!?

Not at all. It only shows that Martinez had a good feel for when the time was right – politically, socially, culturally – to make his bold move.[34] There is no reason to think that it was the persuasiveness of Ralph's legal theory that prompted the change.[35] And our judgment that the subsequent legal changes qualify as 'progress' only means that we consider them to be an improvement relative to our own interpretive judgments – as has already been clarified in B.ii, above.

vi. Debunking History?

Perhaps we can try some evidence that cuts the other way to see if we can reveal Ralph to be Martinez. Imagine we turned up evidence that Ralph had massive investments in, and personal ties to, various industries his decision ended up benefiting. If Martinez does not decide cases for the legal reasons expressed in his opinions, then surely these facts would count as at least some evidence that Judge Ralph is Martinez insofar as it suggests another plausible – and discreditable – motivation for the decision?

Unfortunately, this will not work either. Such historical evidence is perfectly consistent with Ralph being Hercules. Remember that Hercules is a mythical hero, not an actual human being. What we are interested in, Dworkin informs us, is the argumentative structure of his legal theories, not some explanation for why he developed those theories.[36] So Ralph's motivations are beside the point.

So where does this leave us? Well, on the one hand, our thought experiment seems to contradict Dworkin's claim that Fish's account of legal practice is so 'flat' and 'passive' that it leaves it robbed of any intellectual integrity. For it appears that Fish can account for all the features that Dworkin thought emblematic of legal practice. Even if all judges are like Martinez, deciding cases and writing opinions 'naturally', they can *puzzle* over decisions (B.i) *disagree* with other judges (B.ii), participate (or even commence) legal *revolutions* we consider *progressive* (B.vi). Anything Hercules can do Martinez can do better.

---

[34] Fish (n 2) 26.
[35] ibid 23.
[36] Dworkin (n 1) 12–13.

On the other hand, it is hard to shake the idea that something is amiss. It is a bit like the experience of attending a zoom cocktail party. True, drinks were imbibed and pleasantries exchanged, so technically it qualified as one. But at the same time, one cannot fight this feeling that a vital element was lacking.[37]

Consider how we would need to interpret these various features under the assumption that Judge Ralph was Martinez. Martinez's 'puzzle' is not really a genuinely intellectual one at all – it is just about how to arrange various terms from the legal lexicon to get the result desired. His disagreement with his colleagues does not actually seem to be about the best reading of the relevant legal materials, but rather an underlying political dispute. The revolution Ralph helped launch was not a revolution *in thought* so much as a rapid shift in societal attitudes.[38] And if we think those changes count as 'progress', that fact simply reveals our own participation in that societal shift. Moreover, our judgment that those changes did constitute progress is immune to any historical or sociological explanation that might undermine the decision's moral or legal stature.

III. THE DIAGNOSIS: BOSOM BUDDIES, AFTER ALL

So what went wrong? Let us take stock of where we are. After acknowledging the superficially similar interpretive approaches of Fish and Dworkin, we identified what seemed to be a real, substantive dispute between the two scholars over whether legal practice was an intellectual practice in which ideas and argument matter in adjudication. Furthermore, that dispute seemed to carry even deeper methodological implications as to the profitability of Dworkinian-style moral and legal theorising. But once we tried to adjudicate the substantive disagreement to see how we might go about vindicating one theorist's view of legal practice over the other's, it became clear that there was no way to do so. Every judicial action or thought that Dworkin might point to as evidence of law's intellectual character, Fish could use as evidence of its essentially rhetorical or 'natural' (ie, non-reflective) quality.

The problem was this: the summary above gets the logical priority of the substantive and methodological issues backwards. Fish's and Dworkin's methodological disagreement as to the existence and value of legal theory does not *grow out of* their substantive dispute over the character of legal practice; rather,

---

[37] While I recognise that the technical philosophical issues raised differ, I see my Hercules/Martinez thought experiment as similar in relevant respects to John Searle's Chinese Room Argument and to arguments for the conceivability of philosophical zombies. The Stanford Encyclopedia of Philosophy has useful entries on both. See D Cole, 'The Chinese Room Argument' in EN Zalta (ed), *The Stanford Encyclopedia of Philosophy* (Palo Alto, CA, Stanford University Press, Winter 2020 edn), plato.stanford.edu/archives/win2020/entries/chinese-room/; R Kirk, 'Zombies' in id (Spring 2021 edn), plato.stanford.edu/entries/zombies/.

[38] Fish (n 2) 23.

their methodological commitments *entail* that substantive dispute. That is because each theorists' methodological stance guarantees at the outset what his evaluation of legal practice will ultimately reveal.

We can say more. Both authors' methodological commitments flow from precisely *the same* assumption. That assumption, which Pierre Schlag detected decades ago,[39] is that one can and should distinguish between those methods, sources, arguments, and values 'internal' to legal practice and those 'external' to it. The difference between Fish and Dworkin, then, is just that Dworkin sees himself as actively operating within legal practice, whereas Fish imagines himself to be passively observing it from the outside.[40]

Let us take Dworkin first. Dworkin insists that law is an argumentative practice, one in which lawyers and judges (and theorists, like himself) argue about what rights and duties people have, what they are legally forbidden and permitted to do.[41] In order to understand the argumentative structure of this practice, the theorist must engage with those arguments rather than simply explain them away. Thus, before expounding his theory of law in *Law's Empire*, Dworkin clarifies that his argument adopts the 'internal point of view', which roughly means the judge's point of view. This point of view is not concerned with the historical or social-scientific explanation of legal practice. Those are 'external'. The reason he does so, he explains, is that judges 'want theories not about how history and economics have shaped their consciousness but about the place of these disciplines in argument about what the law requires them to do or have'.[42]

Dworkin's distinction between internal and external forms of argument is a quite general one that applies to law, morality, and aesthetic forms of interpretation.[43] Its function is to exclude various forms of scepticism that might cast doubt on the sorts of normative judgments those interpretive practices involve. In Dworkin's view, no sceptical challenge to some first-order interpretive claim (whether legal, moral, aesthetic) can get off the ground unless it engages substantively with the claim on its own normative terms. It cannot announce from the 'outside' that all such interpretive judgments within some domain do

---

[39] See P Schlag, 'Normativity and Politics of Form' (1991) 139 *University of Pennsylvania Law Review* 801, 920 (criticising Dworkin's use of the distinction); P Schlag, 'Theory and the Uses of Dennis Martinez' (1987) 76 *George Washington Law Review* 53, 55 (noting Fish's reliance upon it).

[40] As stated below, Dworkin states explicitly that he adopts the 'internal' or 'participant's' point of view when developing his theory of law and adjudication. Dworkin (n 1) 12–13. Meanwhile, Fish occasionally acknowledges that his interpretations of intellectual growth, change, or learning are issued 'from the perspective of neither the one who is newly aware or those who have brought him to his awareness'. Fish (n 2) 461. It almost seems like Fish takes his account to be more *accurate* on account of such detachment.

[41] Dworkin (n 1) 12–13.

[42] ibid.

[43] R Dworkin, 'My Reply to Stanley Fish (and Walter Benn Michaels): Please Don't Talk about Objectivity Any More, in WT Mitchell (ed), in *The Politics of Interpretation* (Chicago 1982) 297.

not have the right kind of metaphysical status or that they are the expression of some more basic, non-normative social phenomenon.[44]

In short, Dworkin's conclusion that law is a reflective, intellectual practice follows necessarily from his requirement that to understand legal practice, one must engage with it from a normative posture (ie, treat it from the 'internal point of view').[45] Other forms of inquiry, which might seek to *explain* law as a social phenomenon, cannot reveal law to be anything else because (by definition) such inquiries are 'external' to law.[46]

Fish, meanwhile, reaches the opposite conclusion from the identical methodological premise. One of Fish's central claims in *Doing What Comes Naturally* is that theory has 'no consequences'. Here is the argument: a theory is a 'set of principles or rules or procedures that is attached to (in the sense of being derived from) no particular field of activity, but is of sufficient generality to be thought of as a constraint on (and an explanation of) all fields of activity'.[47] But there are no rules or principles that belong to 'no particular field of activity'. Therefore, 'there can be no such thing as theory, and something that does not exist cannot have consequences'.[48] In short, 'theory' has no consequences only because Fish defines it out of existence.[49]

But there's more. Even though 'theory', in Fish's thick sense, does not exist, some people *try* to offer such principles and procedures. Those people have even developed a whole practice around such efforts. They call themselves 'philosophers' and their activity 'philosophy'.[50] Even though they cannot actually produce theories (since they do not exist), philosophers can form 'very general' beliefs about various matters, including legal ones.[51] Unfortunately, those very general beliefs will also fail to have any consequences for any practice (such as law or literary criticism) other than the practice of philosophy itself because

---

[44] Dworkin (n 1) 78–83. It is in this sense – and *only* in this sense – that Dworkin insists upon the 'objectivity' of interpretive judgments. See Dworkin (n 43) 297 ('I have no argument for the objectivity of moral judgments except moral arguments, no argument for the objectivity of interpretive judgments except interpretive arguments.'). See also D Priel, Making Sense of Nonsense Jurisprudence, available at: papers.ssrn.com/sol3/papers.cfm?abstract_id=3696933.

[45] Dworkin raises as an objection to his theory the worry that it makes scepticism impossible. See Dworkin (n 43) 301. His response is that scepticism is not ruled out because one can offer a global but 'internal' sceptical account to the effect that judgments within some domain are too 'unstructured and disconnected to count as beliefs within that enterprise'. ibid. But if one concludes that all or nearly all of the judgments made by those within a practice fail to cohere in the way the practice's participants claim they do, then the pressure for an alternative, 'external' explanation of those judgments would be great. It is but a small step to acknowledge that the relative plausibility of rival explanatory accounts bears on the strength of the initial interpretive judgment, which is the point I develop below.

[46] Dworkin (n 1) 13, 273.
[47] Fish (n 2) 13.
[48] ibid.
[49] See Schlag (n 39) 56; T Eagleton, 'The Estate Agent' (Review of Fish, The Trouble with Principle) (2000) 22 *London Review of Books* 2.
[50] Fish (n 2) 396.
[51] ibid 327.

those practices stand outside philosophy and vice versa.[52] In short, philosophers can say anything they would like, but they can have no effect outside their own rhetorical practice.

That is why Dworkin has no project, according to Fish. Dworkin's effort to theorise about law is doomed to fail because any such effort 'emerge[s] from the special context of academic philosophy'. But, just as Dworkin's did, Fish's own conclusion follows necessarily from his own starting premise, namely that 'law is not philosophy'.[53] Anything internal to law is rhetoric, and anything external to law is impotent – because it is outside law.

Fish and Dworkin thus seem to have more in common (as we first suspected) than one might otherwise think. Both see a critical difference between understanding law from the 'inside' and understanding it from the 'outside'. Both treat 'external' critiques of legal practice as ineffectual (or even incoherent), and they both insist that internal forms of analysis and argument are the only kind that matter.[54] No surprise, then, that Fish praises Dworkin's critique of 'external' scepticism,[55] or that Dworkin claims to have anticipated nearly all of Fish's criticisms,[56] or that in the end Fish comes close to acknowledging that the apparent differences between them may have evaporated completely.[57]

In some ways, this should all have been obvious from the start. In *Law's Empire*, Dworkin announces at the outset that 'thoughtful working lawyers and judges' reject the 'plain-fact' or positivist view of law that constitutes Dworkin's main foil. In their 'less guarded moments', these judges – Dworkin here cites Cardozo's *The Nature of the Judicial Process* – tell a 'more romantic story'. They say that 'judging is an art not a science', one in which the judge 'blends analogy, craft, political wisdom' into 'an intuitive decision'. They say that the judge '"sees" law better than he can explain it'.[58]

But after enlisting the '"craft" view' of adjudication in support of his rejection of legal positivism, Dworkin goes on to explain why he finds it wanting. The problem is that it is 'too unstructured, too content with the mysteries it savours' to qualify as a theory of legal argument. Dworkin's aim, he explains, is to 'throw discipline over the idea of law as craft, to see how the structure of judicial instinct' differs from other forms of moral and political theory.[59]

---

[52] ibid 333 (observing that 'philosophy is one thing, and literary criticism is another') and 396 (observing that 'law is not philosophy').
[53] ibid.
[54] For this reason, I am inclined to label both Fish and Dworkin metaphysical *quietists*, by which I mean someone who holds the view that 'metaphysical debates about whether some phenomenon or set of phenomena is "real" or not tend to be fruitless and so should be abandoned'. In that way, Fish's view is similar to Richard Rorty's. See C Barzun, 'Metaphysical Quietism and Functional Explanation in the Law' (2015) 34 *Law & Philosophy* 89, 91. Fish rejects that label, though I am not sure he is using it in the same way I am. Fish (n 2) 463–64.
[55] Fish (n 2) 369.
[56] Dworkin (n 43) 287.
[57] Fish (n 24) 79.
[58] Dworkin (n 1) 10.
[59] ibid 10–11.

The difference between Fish and Dworkin then comes down to this. Both recognise that adjudication *is* in many ways like baseball insofar as experienced judges perform their tasks 'naturally', rather than in a self-conscious, methodical manner. But they draw different lessons from that fact. Because Dworkin sees a logic underlying the judge's craft, his project is to express that underlying logic in normative, theoretical terms. Because Fish thinks there is no knowledge but craft knowledge (for judges, or anyone else), he denies there is any underlying logic there to express. In short, whereas Dworkin seeks to elucidate the 'mystery' of judicial craft, Fish seeks to eliminate it.

But *is there* an underlying logic to judicial craft? Is Dworkin right that law is really a 'reflective' and 'argumentative' practice? Or is Fish right that it is merely 'rhetorical'? Fish maintains that he and Dworkin differ on this question and insists that it is a critical difference.[60] One can see why: it goes to the heart of the issue I suggested at the outset should be of concern to lawyers, judges, legal scholars, and law students.

The problem is that, as we have now seen, neither theorist's methodological approach is well equipped to investigate that question. The reason is that both are impervious to any facts we might learn that might bear on how we should think about the intellectual vitality of legal practice. Consider our failed efforts to discern the true identity of Judge Ralph. None of our evidence or analysis was up to the task. The fact that Ralph's opinion is theoretically sophisticated and morally correct? Dworkin: *See, it's Hercules!* Fish: *No, Martinez is just practiced at the art of persuading people like you (participants in legal practice)*. Our evidence that Judge Ralph stood to gain financially from his decision? Dworkin: *Irrelevant; only the internal point of view matters.* Fish: *Exactly. Such arguments belong to a different interpretive community.*[61] The bottom Line is that for all we know Hercules and Martinez could be constantly trading places, and we would have no way of knowing it. There must be a better way.

IV. THE SOLUTION: GET BACK TO THE FACTS OF LIFE AND LAW

There *is* a better way, and the remedy is simple enough. It is to stop talking (and thinking) about 'internal' and 'external' forms of argument and analysis. It is, after all, just a metaphor; neither legal theory nor literary criticism can literally be physically separated in the way the language of 'inside' and 'outside' suggest. Once that spatial metaphor is abandoned, the question of whether law is an intellectual practice can be investigated as an open question to be answered only after investigation.

---

[60] ibid.
[61] Fish (n 2) 393.

Still, the distinction clearly holds intuitive appeal since Dworkin and Fish are hardly the only ones to invoke it.[62] So let me to try to motivate its abandonment by pointing to some examples of the sort of argument and analysis it has trouble making sense of. These examples alone hardly settle the matter. Not only are they few in number, but some readers may draw the opposite inference, concluding that these sorts of arguments *should* be excluded from the domain of legal practice. Still, they at least offer a taste of a different way of conceptualising the relationship between legal theory and practice. After presenting them, I raise two possible objections, from the perspective of Dworkin and Fish, respectively.

A. Talking about a Revolution (and Actually Experiencing One)

Abandoning inside-outside talk makes room in legal practice 'for puzzle [and] progress [and] controversy [and] revolution', enabling us to 'explain how lawyers can worry or disagree or change their mind about what the law is' in a deeper way than either Fish's *or* Dworkin's account does. Consider the following.

i. Puzzle

Rejecting the dichotomy allows us to explain deeper forms of puzzle and confusion. Take Jerome Frank's famous attack on the legal profession's desire for certainty in law and adjudication. Frank claimed that lawyers' and judges' insistence that the law is and ought to be certain and predictable manifests a psychological hunger. Drawing on the work of the child-psychologist Jean Piaget, Frank suggested that the 'basic legal myth' that the law is certain reflects lawyers' longing for a 'father-figure' that can offer comfort and protection from a risky and unpredictable world.[63] For Frank, the key to improving adjudication was to free judges of this psychological longing, a goal which requires emotional introspection, not logical analysis. Once released from such psychological fixations, judges would be better equipped to their proper task – securing justice in individual cases.[64]

Now one could quarrel with various aspects of this argument, but I mention it only to illustrate two points. First, the kind of confusion or 'puzzle' it potentially gives rise to is real and deep. A lawyer or judge who took the claim seriously would be forced to consider whether one of the central values to which she is professionally committed is a form of illusion from which she needs to be freed. The second point is that on Dworkin's and Fish's view, it is hardly intelligible.

---

[62] See generally C Barzun, 'Inside-Out: Beyond the Internal-External Distinction in Legal Scholarship' (2015) 101 *Virginia Law Review* 1203.

[63] J Frank, *Law & the Modern Mind* (1930) 19–23. See also 'Jerome Frank and the Modern Mind' (2010) 58 *Buffalo Law Review* 1127.

[64] Frank (n 63) 166.

Frank is inquiring into the causes of judges' values and principles, thereby going beyond the scope of what 'constructive interpretation' permits (Dworkin). And, at the time he wrote, Frank was unquestionably attempting to criticise legal practice by deploying the rhetoric of a very different 'interpretive community', with its own values, assumptions, and ways of carving up the world (Fish). Again, perhaps when scrutinised, those differences reveal Frank's argument's to be defective in various respects. But the claim here is just that that conclusion should be a consequence of investigation, not an assumption made prior to it.

ii. Controversy

Abandoning the dichotomy also opens up new forms of disagreement. In particular, it makes relevant to adjudication questions about the origins of traditional legal authorities. Consider the recent Supreme Court case, *Ramos v LA*.[65] In that case, the Court declared unconstitutional laws in Louisiana and Oregon that had authorised criminal convictions based on non-unanimous jury verdicts. Writing for the Court, Justice Gorsuch began his opinion by looking to the history of the non-unanimity requirements in both states. That history revealed that the initial adoption of both statutes was the product of white-supremacist ideology.[66] In dissent, Justice Alito acknowledged that the facts about the origins of the statutes the Court had revealed were 'deplorable', but he considered them irrelevant to the constitutional question the Court faced. By relying on them, the Court was engaging in 'ad hominem' rhetoric.[67]

Again, the point is not to endorse Justice's Gorsuch's argument but just to point out the inconsistency of its assumptions with the approach of Dworkin and Fish. Gorsuch is offering an historical explanation in order to undermine the authority of a legal source. Implicit in such an effort is the suggestion that the authority the statutes in question carry for us today is properly weakened by our discovery of the racist motives that led to it.[68] But, like Justice Alito, Dworkin treats such inquiries into motives as falling 'outside' the domain of legal practice. So does Fish. Historical inquiry may produce some amazing stories, but such stories just reflect the assumptions, methods and values of an entirely different interpretive community – namely that of historians.[69]

iii. Revolutions

Revolutions make more sense once one removes the barricade dividing sociology and law. A good example is Catharine MacKinnon's argument in *Sexual*

---

[65] *Ramos v LA* (2020) (Slip Opinion).
[66] ibid.
[67] ibid.
[68] Evidence of invidious discriminatory intent are relevant to the inquiry under equal-protection clause doctrine, but there was no suggestion that the statutes violated the equal protection clause.
[69] Fish (n 2) 93.

Harassment of Working Women that sexual harassment is a form of sex discrimination under the Civil Rights Act of 1964.[70] The doctrinal argument of that book is in some ways quite traditional and could be easily characterised as just the sort of constructive interpretation Dworkin endorses. But the persuasiveness of MacKinnon's doctrinal analysis is precisely what proves its inadequacy at explaining the enormous impact of her book.[71] For at the time she wrote in 1979, very few courts had recognised sexual harassment as a form of sex discrimination. So, the question is, why had more courts not done so?

As it turns out, MacKinnon herself answers that question in her book. She not only gathers a tremendous amount of empirical data showing how sex-segregated the workforce was in the 1970s; she also argues that (mostly male) judges failed to see sexual harassment as a form of gender oppression because they were blind to the way in which gender itself entrenches forms of sex inequality.[72] In other words, MacKinnon's argument may have transformed the law of sexual harassment in part because she was able to reveal how traditional doctrinal categories had been interpreted in ways that served an oppressive social function (ie, the maintenance of gender hierarchy).[73]

Once again, this kind of argument is not available if one holds fast to the inside/outside dichotomy because MacKinnon both uses legal doctrine *and* steps 'outside' it in order to explain its interpretation as the consequence of forms of social domination to which judges had been blind. We can now see why it is no coincidence that Hercules and Martinez are both men. Neither understands what it means to have one's consciousness raised.[74]

iv. Progress

The arguments just discussed are based on claims about psychology, history, and sociology, respectively. Once such arguments are seen as continuous with, rather than standing outside of, legal practice, we can better understand the concept of progress in the law. For they offer a way of giving that concept

---

[70] CA MacKinnon, *Sexual Harassment of Working Women* (New Haven, Yale University Press, 1979).

[71] The Supreme Court unanimously ratified MacKinnon's theory of sex discrimination in *Meritor Sav. Bank, FSB v Vinson*, 106 S. Ct. 2399 (1986). Professor Reva Siegel describes MacKinnon's book as 'a stunningly brilliant synthesis of lawyering and legal theory' that 'played a crucial role in th[e] process' of making sexual harassment illegal'. RB Siegel, 'Introduction: A Short History of Sexual Harassment' in CA MacKinnon and RB Siegel (eds), *Directions in Sexual Harassment Law* (New Haven, Yale University Press, 2004) 15.

[72] ibid 88.

[73] See C Barzun, 'Catharine MacKinnon and the Common Law', available at: papers.ssrn.com/sol3/papers.cfm?abstract_id=3696540.

[74] Fish is quite explicit about this, insisting that claims of 'raised' consciousness are really just forms of changed consciousness. Fish (n 2) 461.

more meaning than a preference for our current arrangements over previous ones, relative to our own moral convictions. We can now consider explanatory accounts that might buttress our conclusion that our current regime is superior – for instance, by showing that the *process* that led to it was likely to produce a good outcome.

Of course, such explanatory accounts may do the opposite; they may give us reason to doubt a set of assumptions by exposing the social or psychological function those assumptions are serving. To illustrate, consider my own argument in this chapter. I have been challenging Fish and Dworkin's interpretation of legal practice, arguing that an assumption on which they both rely – that we ought to distinguish between 'internal' and 'external' forms of argument and analysis – prevents them from understanding certain aspects of legal reasoning. I could also point out that, though ineffective for investigating legal practice, that distinction might be highly effective at protecting one's disciplinary turf because it makes participation in some practice a prerequisite for critiquing it.[75] If true, pointing to such a self-serving function makes my substantive analytical claims more plausible.

Critical theorists of various stripes have long made arguments of this structure against happy stories of legal or social progress.[76] They purport to reveal the true social function that certain legal regimes serve. Such arguments are indeed threatening. Opening up the question of progress is a risky business, because the term only has meaning if it is possible that one's investigation turns up not progress but instead social stasis, cyclical patterns of injustice, or moral decay.

The law's concern with history and pedigree makes legal practice particularly hospitable to this holistic form of inquiry.[77] Consider the old adage that the common law 'works itself pure' over time. The idea is that something about the process of case-by-case adjudication is likely to produce better rules and principles over time.[78] Unless one is content to leave that process as a complete mystery, trusting entirely our own moral intuitions that approve of the process's current outputs, taking the 'working itself pure' idea seriously demands some judgment about *why* the particular process tends to produce better results – and is likely to continue to do so in the future. And that kind of inquiry requires making not only moral claims, but also explanatory ones, based on claims about human psychology, sociology, or history.[79]

---

[75] See ibid 333 (observing that 'philosophy is one thing, and literary criticism is another').
[76] See, eg, M Horwitz, *The Transformation of American Law, 1780–1860* (Oxford, OUP, 1992); RW Gordon, 'Historicism in Legal Scholarship' (1981) 90 *Yale Law Journal* 1017.
[77] I have developed this point at greater length elsewhere. See, eg, C Barzun, 'Justice Souter's Common Law' (2018) 104 *Virginia Law Review* 655.
[78] See L Fuller, *Law in Quest of Itself* (Foundation, 1940).
[79] Or perhaps economics. See, eg, GL Priest, 'The Common Law Process and the Selection of Efficient Rules' (1977) 6 *Journal of Legal Studies* 65.

176 *Charles L Barzun*

The inability – or, perhaps, unwillingness – of either Dworkin or Fish to authorise such 'external' inquiries is what leaves their accounts of progress so impoverished. So, for instance, although Dworkin gives lip service to the idea that the law 'works itself pure', he can only give an account of why judges might *think* that the law the law works itself pure, not that it *actually does* so.[80] As we have seen, he treats as 'external', and so irrelevant, all inquiry into causal explanation.

Meanwhile, Fish would again likely treat the adage as just a bit of legal mythmaking. It is just one of the many bedtime stories for lawyers. And it may well be exactly that. But the problem for Fish is that – as we have already seen – he has no resources to make *that* sort of sceptical claim since the interpretive community of law is insulated from other interpretive communities and so immune to their challenges.[81] Their theories have 'no consequences' for law.

To restate what I said above, my point in offering these various examples is not to prove that legal practice is in fact an intellectual or philosophical one. I mean only to give some sense of the kinds of arguments and analyses that become available once we abandon the methodological strictures both Dworkin and Fish impose on legal theory. Whether these examples ultimately count in favour of abandoning the inside/outside distinction or against it is ultimately for the reader to decide.

B. A Dworkinian Objection: Get Over the Borderline

I could imagine Dworkin making an objection along the following lines:

> The above examples are best understood as arguments that we draw the borders of legal practice in different places, not that we abandon them altogether. Constructive interpretation requires only that participants in a practice offer interpretations of that practice that best fit and justify it. So if an interpretation of legal practice (or some subset of it) requires making explanatory claims about its historical origins or social function, then that's fine, so long as it can beat out rival interpretations.[82] Indeed, the kind of reasoning described above, in which an explanation of a legal

---

[80] Dworkin (n 1) 400–01. The contrast with how Dworkin treats moral judgments is telling. For one could also say that Dworkin's argument is just about what moral convictions judges might have. In fact, though, Dworkin is quite comfortable making his own substantive moral claims. Yet he does not even attempt to offer any sort of explanation as to why it might be plausible to think that case-by-case adjudication would produce better rules and principles over time.

[81] See Fish (n 2) 393. I take Professor Schlag to be making a similar point when he observes that Fish's view implies that '[y]ou can't talk about whether [interpretive communities] are clans, or cabals, or democratic institutions, or efficient firms, or illegitimate hierarchies .... This sort of constraint, exclusion, ground rule (whatever you want to call it) can really put a crimp in a conversation about the content and structure of social life'. See P Schlag, 'Fish v. Zapp: 'The Case of the Relatively Autonomous Self' (1987) 76 *Georgetown Law Journal* 37, 49.

[82] Dworkin even made occasional gestures in this direction, suggesting that even science might be a domain of constructive interpretation. See Dworkin (n 1) 53. I thank David Plunkett and Dan Priel for raising this objection with me in private conversation.

source purports to undermine its authority, *requires* some kind of internal/external distinction because its logic assumes that some reasons for a decision are legally legitimate and others are not.[83]

There are two things to say about this objection. The first is that if Dworkin were to interpret his own theory this way, I would happily endorse it. My objection to the distinction is not that we ought never distinguish between 'legal' and 'non-legal' forms of argumentation. Indeed, as the objection correctly observes, some such distinction is required in order for debunking (or 'bunking') explanations of legal sources to have any rational force. My objection, rather, is to invoking such a distinction as a *methodological* criterion that excludes certain kinds of argument even from consideration on the basis that it adopts the wrong 'perspective' or 'point of view'.[84] Doing so prevents us from arguing substantively over what forms of reasoning are properly legal ones and why.

The second point is that I doubt Dworkin would interpret his theory so capaciously. The reason for my doubt is that it would require acknowledging the interdependence between factual and evaluative judgments in a way that Dworkin explicitly rejects. One can see this rejection most clearly in Dworkin's magnum opus, *Justice for Hedgehogs*, where he insists that 'interpretation' is the proper method of inquiry over the entire domain of 'value', whereas 'science' governs the domain of 'fact'.[85] Dworkin's moral and intellectual motivation for clinging to this dichotomy was to vindicate the rationality of evaluative judgments without having to question the natural or social sciences. In this way, Dworkin's approach is *compatibilist* about free will, morality, law, and anything else in the 'interpretive' domain.[86] In his view, science threatens nothing we hold dear, so all efforts to 'reconcile' the two domains represent 'bogus philosophical projects'.[87]

Interestingly, Dworkin himself seems to have recognised the sort of objection I have raised at the end of his 1982 article that Fish initially attacked:

> Liberalism ... which assigns great importance to autonomy, may depend upon a particular picture of the role that judgments of value play in people's lives; it may depend on the thesis that people's convictions about value are beliefs, open to argument and review, rather than simply the givens of personality, fixed by genetic and social causes.[88]

---

[83] I thank Thomas Bustamante for raising this point.
[84] See Barzun (n 62) 1237–42.
[85] R Dworkin, *Justice for Hedgehogs* (Cambridge, MA, Harvard University Press, 2011) 152.
[86] ibid 12. Traditionally, compatibilism is understood more narrowly as a position on the philosophical debate over free will. Specifically, compatibilists interpret the requirement of free will in such a way as to maintain its 'compatibility' with causal determinism. M McKenna and D Justin Coates, 'Compatibilism' in EN Zalta (ed), *The Stanford Encyclopedia of Philosophy* (Palo Alto, CA, Stanford University Press, Winter 2020 edn) available at: plato.stanford.edu/archives/win2020/entries/compatibilism.
[87] ibid 9.
[88] Dworkin (n 4) 550.

Having raised the possibility that his particular moral and political commitments might underlie his claims about moral psychology and meta-ethics, though, Dworkin failed to acknowledge just how threatening to his project that admission was. For his assumption that 'convictions about value are beliefs, open to argument and review' and are not fixed by social and genetic causes underlies not just his own preferred theory of law, 'law-as-integrity', but his overarching methodological commitment to the process of constructive interpretation in law, literature, and morality.

C. A Fishy Objection: No Way Out (of Interpretive Communities)

Meanwhile, Fish might make a different sort of objection, though one with similar implications. He might argue thusly:

> You seem to be suggesting that law can be revealed to be an intellectual practice by recognizing the way in which interpretive communities (including law) are not at all monolithic and instead inter-penetrate one another. The thought seems to be that attending to these conflicts and tensions among different disciplines forces reflection and perhaps even stimulates moral and intellectual progress. But that is impossible.

Indeed, in the introduction to *Doing What Comes Naturally*, Fish takes up something like my suggestion and rejects it explicitly:

> However nuanced one's talk about constraint and belief and community may get to be, the nuances will never add up to a moment or a place where consciousness becomes transparent to itself and can at last act freely. Being embedded means just that, being embedded *always*, and one does not escape embeddedness by acknowledging, as I do, that it is itself a fractured, fissured, volatile condition.[89]

Under Fish's view, then, each of the arguments surveyed above has one of two fates. Either it becomes part of legal practice, in which case it just forms part of the set of rhetorical materials available to judges and lawyers, or it stays outside it, in which case it has no consequences for anything in legal practice. True, they may all participate in, or even help create, sub-communities within academic legal practice – perhaps ones with names like 'Law and Society' or 'Legal History' or 'Law and Economics' – but the point is that whatever beliefs those communities end up propagating are just more beliefs. No point is ever reached where consciousness becomes 'transparent' and so capable of genuinely free thought and action.

The first thing to say about this objection is that it is impossible to refute. Any effort to generate a theory, insight, or even a thought is going to be expressed in language and so is always vulnerable to the objection that it, too, is just making

---

[89] Fish (n 2) 31 (emphasis in original).

a move in some language game.[90] But it is also impossible to prove true – a fact that Fish forthrightly acknowledges.[91]

With those dialectical limitations in mind, let me just say that Fish's response strikes me as inconsistent with experience, or at least *my* experience (who else's is there?). The reason is that, once again, Fish frames the issue in binary terms. *Either* we are 'always embedded' in some or other practice *or* we are 'a place where consciousness becomes transparent to itself'. But most of life takes place somewhere in between these poles.

I will not deny that those who purport to be open-minded about some things are often remarkably closed-minded about others. An allegedly cosmopolitan culture can be just as parochial in its attitudes as a provincial one. What passes as diversity on college campuses, for instance, often masks considerable homogeneity of thought. So the sceptical challenges to those who preach liberality and tolerance is a fair and important one.

But just as our thought experiment demonstrated, a sceptical challenge only has bite when an alternative is at least possible. Here, that alternative is the sometimes-mundane phenomenon of seeking second (or third or fourth) opinions. When ordinary people face important decisions, they typically seek out the views of others on the assumption that doing so might help them do the right thing. If your doctor says you need to undergo major surgery, you might seek out a second opinion. If you are having an argument with your spouse over your child's education, you may solicit the advice of friends and family members to get their take and to ensure that you are thinking clearly about the issues.[92]

Now Fish would likely say that such examples all take place 'within' various practices and communities. That is why we seek out other experts in the same field. You do not get a second opinion about open-heart surgery from your accountant. But I do not think that is quite right. We seek another opinion from someone else in the field because: (1) we think she may have had training or experiences different from those of the first expert (ie, that she is constituted by a different configuration of sometimes-conflicting interpretive communities); and (2) we benefit from hearing her perspective precisely *because of those differences*. The utterly banal assumption is that by soliciting multiple views on something – whether the price of a car or the value of a law-school education – we improve our judgments about it.

---

[90] Eagleton makes a related point when he observes that '[t]he felicitous upshot [of Fish's approach] is that nobody can ever criticise Fish, since if their criticisms are intelligible to him, they belong to his cultural game and are thus not really criticisms at all; and if they are not intelligible, they belong to some other set of conventions entirely and are therefore irrelevant'. See Eagleton (n 49).

[91] Fish (n 2) 29.

[92] Of course, some friends may take your side merely *because* it is your side, and if that is why you ask them, you are not genuinely seeking a second opinion; you are seeking reassurance for emotional or strategic reasons. But arguably what it means to be a true friend is to offer honest feedback (if solicited) for just the reasons offered in the text.

Of course, soliciting such views never enables one to become 'transparent' to oneself. In the expert context, sometimes we may not be competent to properly evaluate and compare the opinions solicited.[93] Moreover, we all know that everyone's judgments – whether those of your close friends and family or of the people you crowdsource on Twitter – are shaped by different inborn handicaps and growing pains, different biases and agendas – none of which we can discern clearly. But we often seek out others' views anyway, and we do so because at least *sometimes* we think we can *learn* something as a result.

V. CONCLUSION: HOW WILL I KNOW?

Putting the matter this way allows us to summarise succinctly the problems with both Dworkin's and Fish's account of interpretation. At the end of the day, Fish's account renders genuine learning impossible, whereas Dworkin's merely construes it too narrowly.

Fish seems to follow Socrates's interlocutor, Meno, in concluding that learning is impossible.[94] True, we can improve how we perform specific tasks or develop particular skills 'within' some enterprise. But what it means to be 'always embedded' in one or more practices is to be incapable of ever achieving a vantage point that offers even a marginally wider view or a deeper understanding of oneself or the world. It means we never see things more clearly as a result of experience – by observing, reading, listening, or talking with others. We just replace some beliefs with other ones and modify our vocabularies accordingly.

Of course, the terms I just invoked – 'wider', 'deeper', and 'clearly' – all trade on visual-spatial metaphors, too, and so have no claim of privilege over the 'inside' and 'outside' framing I've criticised throughout this chapter. But abandoning them means giving up a lot. As one example, it requires jettisoning a core aspiration of what is known as 'liberal education'. The guiding thought is that one may gain some knowledge, perhaps even self-knowledge, by engaging with texts written by people at different times, in different circumstances and thus with different experiences of the world. As the philosopher Michael

---

[93] On the difficulty of adjudicating disputes between experts in the fact-finding context, see S Brewer, 'Scientific Testimony and Intellectual Due Process' (1988) 107 *Yale Law Journal* 1535.

[94] The structural similarity between Meno's argument and Fish's is striking. According to Socrates, Meno's argument goes like this: '[A] man cannot enquire either about that which he knows, or about that which he does not know; for if he knows, he has no need to enquire; and if not, he cannot; for he does not know the very subject about which he is to enquire'. Plato, Meno (Benjamin Jowett, trans. Kindle ed) 23. Meanwhile, according to Fish, there is no difference between being genuinely persuaded by an argument and simply changing one's belief: 'Will and deliberation are even more irrelevant to what happens on the other side, the side of the persuadee; you cannot direct yourself to be persuaded; you cannot command your mind to change without already having some idea of what steps you might take to effect that change; and if you have such an idea, you will already have taken them.' Fish (n 2) 462.

Oakeshott wrote, the business of a university is 'the pursuit of learning', which takes the form of an ongoing conversation over time. The enterprise 'has no predetermined course' or even particular goal.[95] Instead, liberal learning is a series of 'adventures in human self-understanding'.[96] But there is no room for *understanding*, let alone *self*-understanding, let alone *adventures* in self-understanding in Fish's account.[97]

Dworkin hits much closer to the mark. He concluded his 1982 article with these words: 'I end simply by acknowledging my sense that politics, art, and law are united, somehow, in philosophy.'[98] Three cheers for that! If law is intrinsically connected to art, politics, and philosophy, then one can see how legal practice could indeed involve genuine learning – perhaps even 'liberal learning' (to borrow Oakeshott's phrase).

But because Dworkin insisted on keeping all of these interpretive practices, including law, out of the reach of the natural and social sciences, his understanding of interpretation, whether legal or literary, was oddly disconnected from actual human experience. Sure, on Dworkin's view interpretation can involve learning, but only insofar as it means that people change their minds and become convinced of their new convictions. Any explanation as to *how* or *why* our mind changed is irrelevant to our judgment that the change constitutes genuine *learning*, as opposed to, say, brainwashing.[99] It is perhaps telling, then, that over his nearly half-century of writing about law and adjudication, Dworkin devoted so little attention to the topic of legal education.

So I would put Dworkin's concluding suggestion slightly differently. I would end simply by acknowledging my sense that politics, art, law, *and* philosophy are united, somehow, as members of what used to be called the *human sciences*.

---

[95] M Oakeshott, *The Voice of Liberal Learning* (New Haven, Yale University Press, 1989) 109–10.
[96] ibid 15.
[97] It is therefore ironic (to put it extremely mildly) that Fish enlists Oakeshott in support of his argument that the humanities need no other defence than an insistence upon the value of studying them 'for its own sake'. S Fish, 'Stop Trying to Sell the Humanities' (17 June 2018) The Chronicle of Higher Education.
[98] ibid.
[99] '[W]e are entitled to no more confidence in our judgment of progress when we can offer [causal historical] explanations than when we can say only that earlier generations did not 'see' some moral truth that we do'. Dworkin (n 85) 87.

10

Social, Moral or Ameliorative? Understanding Constraints on Legal Interpretation

NATALIE STOLJAR*

I. INTRODUCTION

ONE OF THE key topics within the Fish-Dworkin debate is that of the nature of the constraints on legal interpretation. Dworkin thinks that judges and other legal interpreters could in principle be unconstrained – they could in principle 'strike out on their own' to make interpretive decisions on the basis of their subjective interests rather than on the basis of the law.[1] Dworkin aims to provide a theory of legal interpretation that identifies the constraints that ought to bind interpreters. In very broad terms, constraints are (and should be) derived from the moral principles implicit in the history of the legal practice being interpreted: a current interpretation should be coherent with – or preserve 'integrity' with – those moral principles. This is what Dworkin calls 'constructive interpretation': to be coherent with underlying moral principles, an interpretation must both *fit* the history of the relevant area of law and promote *the best justified* moral and political reading of it.

Fish argues that the search for constraints is unnecessary. All interpreters are embedded in social practices and are bound by the norms that apply to participants in those social practices. Legal interpreters could not even in principle engage in purely subjective or unconstrained interpretation because the practice in which they are situated determines their very status as legal interpreters. Hence Fish proposes that there are constraints that bind interpreters, but these are social not moral. They are derived from the interpretive

---

*I am grateful to Thomas Bustamante and Margaret Martin for helpful comments on a previous draft of this chapter.

[1] eg, R Dworkin, 'Law as Interpretation' (1982) 9(1) *Critical Inquiry* 179–200, 193–94. Fish critiques Dworkin's suggestion that judges could, in principle, 'strike out in a new direction of their own', especially in S Fish, 'Working on the Chain Gang: Interpretation in law and literature' (1982) 60 *Texas Law Review* 551–67.

community which generates tacit guidelines, or 'rules of the game' that participants in interpretive practices necessarily follow. These rules of the game operate as constraints 'naturally'. Thus, a judge who strikes out on their own – eg, in making a decision based on a personal religious view or a preference for a defendant's hair colour – would not be conforming to the tacit rules of the legal game. With respect to that decision, the judge would not count as a participant in *legal* practice at all.[2] In short, whereas Dworkin proposes that there are moral constraints on legal interpretation, Fish responds with two claims: there are *always* social constraints on legal interpretation and there are *only* social constraints on legal interpretation.

Commentators have pointed out that there are significant similarities between the two positions. Both argue that the law is a social practice within which interpreters take a participant or 'interpretive' stance; both 'insist that historical experience of practice is crucial';[3] both suggest that laws, like literary works, are 'texts' whose meanings can be illuminated by employing general canons of textual interpretation; both reject the positivist claim that legal systems are comprised exclusively of rules that are laid down by some legal authority; both claim that 'what the law is' is a matter not only of what is explicitly in legal texts but also of 'what sits unnoticed in the background and generates the rules'.[4] However, there are different views in the literature on the Fish-Dworkin debate about its upshot, many of which claim that it ends in a stalemate. For instance, it is said that it is '[played] out ... with opposing enthusiasm but to a tie';[5] that because Dworkin never 'achieved a clear understanding of what Fish was urging upon him ... Fish emerges from their debate as the winner';[6] and that 'declaring a winner is a fraught enterprise. Each scored some good points and at the end of the day, few minds were changed'.[7]

This chapter argues that Dworkin in fact gets the better of the debate. While Fish's notion of natural constraints is compelling, natural constraints *underdetermine* the activity of interpretation and thus permit the possibility of constructive interpretation. Fish's response to Dworkin needs to be separated into two parts: (i) a critique that employs his methodological perspective to undermine certain theoretical assumptions he attributes to Dworkin, and (ii) the repudiation of Dworkin's positive account of interpretation. I will argue that, even if (i) is successful, it does not imply (ii). The flawed methodological

---

[2] S Fish, *Doing What Comes Naturally: Change, Rhetoric and the Practice of Theory in Literary and Legal Studies* (Durham, NC, Duke University Press, 1989) 93.

[3] ibid 388.

[4] M Robertson, *Stanley Fish on Philosophy, Politics and Law: How Fish Works* (Cambridge, Cambridge University Press, 2014) 252. My discussion has benefited from Robertson's comprehensive exposition of the Fish-Dworkin debate in ch 9 of his book.

[5] JM Schelly, 'Interpretation in Law: The Dworkin-Fish Debate (Or, Soccer Amongst the Gahuku-Gama)' (1985) 73 *California Law Review* 158–80, 180.

[6] Robertson (n 4) 253.

[7] D Patterson, ch 11 in this volume.

positions that Fish attributes to Dworkin are not needed to defend constructive interpretation as a theory of interpretation. Further, Fish's specific arguments against constructive interpretation – that it is conceptually flawed because it does not rely on author's intention, and that it is empty or trivial – fail. I argue that constructive interpretation should be understood as legal 'conceptual amelioration' – it is a strategy that 'improves' legal concepts along epistemic, semantic and sometimes moral dimensions.[8] Therefore, the Fish-Dworkin debate is not merely a methodological one but concerns a substantive question about what kind of practice interpreters situated within a legal 'community of interpretation' *are and ought to be* engaged in when they make decisions in particular cases.

The second section of the chapter addresses Fish's methodology, in particular the commitments to natural constraints and to anti-foundationalism. I show that, although there is support from theories of social cognition for Fish's notion of natural constraints, the latter do not determine a particular approach to interpretation within a practice or rule out the constructive mode as an interpretive strategy. In addition, there is no need to resolve the question of anti-foundationalism to evaluate the debate. We can assume anti-foundationalism for the sake of argument, yet constructive interpretation does not collapse. The third section identifies three modes of interpretation: the *subjective*, the *descriptive* and the *constructive*. I argue that the constructive mode is needed due to the existence of interstices or gaps in objects of interpretation that cannot be resolved through descriptive means. The interstices have a number of sources, for instance internal disagreement within communities of interpretation, the open texture of legal language, and vagueness of legal concepts. The fourth section turns to Fish's arguments against constructive interpretation. I reject the position that interpretation conceptually involves author's intention and develop the idea of constructive interpretation as conceptual amelioration to show that it is not trivial or empty of content.

II. FISH'S METHODOLOGY

An important reason that the positions of Dworkin and Fish seem to be irreconcilable (and an explanation of why their ten-year debate did not achieve a rapprochement) is that their methodological outlooks, philosophical dispositions and starting points are opposed: their 'disagreements about law stem

---

[8] For an explanation of epistemic and semantic conceptual amelioration, see S Haslanger, 'Going On, Not in the Same Way' in A Burgess, H Cappelen, and D Plunkett (eds), *Conceptual Engineering and Conceptual Ethics* (Oxford, Oxford University Press, 2020) 230–60. I argue that constructive interpretation corresponds to an ameliorative project in Haslanger's sense in N Stoljar, 'What Do We Want Law to Be? Philosophical Analysis and the Concept of Law' in W Waluchow and S Sciaraffa (eds), *Philosophical Foundations of The Nature of Law* (Oxford, Oxford University Press, 2013) 230–60.

from deeper philosophical disagreements regarding conceptions of the self, epistemology and the role of philosophy'.[9] Dworkin's outlook, which is especially evident in his early work, was that of analytical jurisprudence and political philosophy in the tradition of HLA Hart.[10] His fictional judge, Hercules, occupies a position in legal philosophy analogous to the one occupied in political philosophy by John Rawls' ideal reasoner making decisions behind a 'veil of ignorance'.[11] The notion of constructive interpretation developed in *Law's Empire* is a less obvious exemplification of this methodology because it is congenial to European philosophical hermeneutics in proposing that interpretation takes place within a historical tradition and that there are general canons of interpretation that can be usefully applied to legal practices and 'texts'.[12] Nevertheless, even *Law's Empire* is a contribution to analytical jurisprudence. Fish's starting point is incompatible with this analytical approach. It rejects the very possibility of Hercules, an ideal legal reasoner who is stripped of influences arising from being situated in a historical and social context. It is also committed to the 'anti-foundationalism' that is common in the hermeneutical and poststructuralist traditions, namely that there is no point external to an interpretive practice that provides a standard of objectively correct interpretations: interpretation is 'more fundamental than authorial intentions, texts, etc, and the latter are the products of the former'.[13]

To the extent that Dworkin (especially in his earlier work) referred to 'right' or objectively correct answers in 'hard cases' of legal interpretation, he might be construed as presupposing foundationalism. However, in chapter two of *Law's Empire*, he articulates the idea of an 'interpretive attitude' of 'members of particular communities who share practices and traditions',[14] in particular when they attempt to resolve disputes within the practice:

> [o]nce this interpretive attitude takes hold, the institution [social practice] ceases to be mechanical; it is no longer unstudied deference to a runic order. People now try to impose *meaning* on the institution–to see it in its best light–and then to restructure it in the light of that meaning.[15]

---

[9] Robertson (n 4) 252–53.
[10] HLA Hart, *The Concept of Law*, 3rd edn (Oxford, Oxford University Press, 2012).
[11] J Rawls, *A Theory of Justice*, revised edn (Cambridge, MA, Harvard University Press 1999).
[12] R Dworkin, *Law's Empire* (Cambridge, MA, Harvard University Press, 1986). Dworkin alludes to the hermeneutics of Hans-Georg Gadamer several times (eg, *Law's Empire* 55, 62). For further discussion, see DC Hoy, 'Interpreting the law: Hermeneutical and Poststructuralist Perspectives' (1985) 58 *Southern California Law Review* 136–76.
[13] P Livingston and A Mele, 'Intentions and Interpretations' (1982) 107 *Comparative Literature* (1982) 931–49, 932. Hans-Georg Gadamer famously says that interpretation or 'understanding' is 'not merely a reproductive but always a productive activity as well': H-G Gadamer, *Truth and Method*, 2nd edn (London, Bloomsbury, 2004) 307.
[14] Dworkin (n 12) 46.
[15] ibid 47 (emphasis added).

Dworkin says that 'we need some account of how the attitude I call interpretive works from the inside, from the point of view of interpreters'.[16] His goal therefore is to articulate the interpretative perspective of participants within communities of interpretation. Despite this, Fish claims that Dworkin's discussion involves a 'slide' away from the initially plausible idea of agents embedded within practices.[17] In particular, Dworkin is misguided in treating 'legal pragmatism' as a genuine possibility. Pragmatism claims that 'judges do and should make whatever decisions seem to them best for the community's future, not counting any form of consistency with the past as valuable for its own sake'.[18] Fish argues:

> [Dworkin] repeatedly makes two related and mutually reinforcing assumptions: he assumes that history in the form of a chain of decisions has, at some level, the status of a brute fact; and he assumes that wayward or arbitrary behavior in relation to that fact is an institutional possibility. Together these two assumptions give him his project, the project of explaining how a free and potentially irresponsible agent is held in check by the self-executing constraints of an independent text.[19]

According to Fish, Dworkin's project is flawed because it presupposes an impossibility – a radically unconstrained interpreter. Instead, all interpreters have 'internalized know-how'.[20] They are governed by 'natural' constraints simply in virtue of being embedded in a legal practice. Dworkin also wrongly assumes a kind of foundationalism, namely that institutional history or a legal text has the 'status of brute fact' from which in principle an interpreter could stray. I consider each aspect of Fish's methodological position in turn.

Fish summarises the idea of natural constraints as follows:

> To think within a practice is to have one's very perception and sense of possible and appropriate action issue 'naturally' – without further reflection – from one's position as a deeply situated agent. Someone who looks with practice-informed eyes sees a field already organized in terms of perspicuous obligations, self-evidently authorized procedures, and obviously relevant pieces of evidence … [A]t the moment when a judge sees a case in a certain way – as falling into this category, or requiring that kind of investigation – there would be no point to his consulting institutional history, because it is that history – not consulted but thoroughly internalized – that already constrains what he sees.[21]

Interestingly, these ideas are less contentious now than they may have been in the heyday of the Fish-Dworkin debate. Several movements within philosophy have converged with Fish's view that features of the social contexts in which agents are embedded are often internalised and treated as 'natural'. In

---

[16] ibid 49.
[17] Fish (n 2) 387.
[18] Dworkin (n 12) 95.
[19] Fish (n 2) 95; quoted in Robertson (n 4) 260.
[20] ibid 388.
[21] ibid 387.

political philosophy, feminists and communitarians reject the Rawlsian notion of the 'atomistic' self in favour of a situated *relational* self. In particular, feminists explicate how the social oppression that is responsible for women's subordination can be internalised and become unquestioned, even by women themselves.[22] Further, philosophers working on social cognition have elaborated what it is to 'think within a practice' in ways that support Fish's notion of natural constraints. It has been observed that the existence of social practices presupposes that there is *coordination* among participants. Coordination itself requires 'mindreading', or an ability to posit that there are (hidden) mental states in others' minds to make sense of their behaviour. On one 'standard picture' of cognition, 'we attribute mental states to others ... to try and figure out what others are up to – i.e. to try and explain and predict their behaviour'.[23] This allows rational agents to coordinate with other rational agents, and hence it seems that the mindreading capacity must precede coordination. However, the standard picture has been challenged by an alternative hypothesis of 'mindshaping', a view of cognition congenial to Fish's natural constraints.[24] According to the mindshaping hypothesis, people's psychologies are already prepared for coordination by the linguistic and cultural practices in which they are embedded. Due to being enculturated, they become 'fluent' in the practices that are required for coordination. Hence culture shapes human cognition rather than the other way around. Victoria McGeer argues that attributing mental states to others (engaging in 'folk psychology') is what she calls '*insider expertise*':

> [It is] the 'first person' expertise of someone who is skilled at reading others in accord with shared norms because she is skilled at living herself in accord with those norms, and vice versa ... [N]ormal folk psychological competence [is] a kind of practical know-how ... This attunement does not depend on putting ourselves in others' shoes. We are already in their shoes, as they are in ours.[25]

Fish's description of the way in which judges think, understand and interpret within legal practices broadly corresponds to the mindshaping hypothesis. However, it is not usually thought that mindshaping determines all aspects of how interpretive activity within a social practice does or should proceed. As I suggest in the next section, there are different possible ways of interpreting

---

[22] eg, C Mackenzie and N Stoljar, 'Introduction: Autonomy Refigured' in C Mackenzie and N Stoljar (eds), *Relational Autonomy: Feminist Perspectives on Autonomy, Agency and the Social Self* (Oxford, Oxford University Press, 2000) 3–31.
[23] V McGeer, 'The Regulative Dimension of Folk Psychology' in DD Hutto and M Radcliffe (eds), *Folk Psychology Re-Assessed* (New York, Springer, 2007) 137–56, 139.
[24] ibid; T Zawidzki, *Mindshaping: A New Framework for Understanding Human Social Cognition* (Massachusetts, MIT Press, 2013). Sally Haslanger uses the concept of mindshaping to explain how social oppression can be internalised even by those who are disadvantaged by oppression: S Haslanger, 'Cognition as a Social Skill' (2019) 3(1) *Australasian Philosophical Review* 5–25.
[25] McGeer (n 23) 150–51.

or 'imposing meaning', even *within* an interpretive practice consistently with natural constraints.

The second aspect of the methodological debate concerns foundationalism. Fish thinks that Dworkin's language implicitly commits him to foundationalism, while Fish himself prefers anti-foundationalism. The latter is both a familiar thesis of hermeneutics and poststructuralism and a common position in the analytic philosophical tradition. It is useful to distinguish *epistemological* anti-foundationalism from *metaphysical* anti-foundationalism. The former rejects the position that knowledge rests on incontrovertible foundations such as self-evident truths. Anti-foundationalists often adopt coherentism, 'a holistic picture of justification which does not distinguish between basic or foundational and non-basic or derived beliefs, treating rather all our beliefs as equal members of a "web of belief"'.[26] Metaphysical anti-foundationalism corresponds to anti-realism, the position that there is 'no mind-independent fact of the matter about the world'.[27] According to Fish, Dworkin's position is foundationalist in both senses: the criterion of consistency with institutional history (fit) implies 'brute' or mind-independent facts that obtain independently of the legal practice (a metaphysical claim) to which judges could in principle appeal to justify their decisions (an epistemological claim).

Fish may be right that Dworkin's *rhetoric* is foundationalist. Substantively however, constructive interpretation does not rest on foundationalism. It does not collapse if we assume that anti-foundationalism is true. The facts of institutional history to which constructive interpretation appeals are *social* facts that obtain only relative to the social practice of law. For instance, before the US Supreme Court's decision in the *Dobbs* case, it was an institutional fact that US constitutional law included a right to abortion; now it is a fact that US law no longer contains this right.[28] Constructive interpretation is not committed to metaphysical foundationalism because institutional facts are *mind-dependent*. Similarly, there is no need to posit self-evident truths to defend constructive interpretation. On the contrary, Dworkin's view implies that interpretive decisions are correct when they are generated by the *most coherent* picture of legal practice. It implicitly relies on a coherentist not a foundationalist epistemology. Fish's suggestion that there is 'no point' for judges to 'consult institutional history', or engage in interpretation of that history, does not follow from anti-foundationalism either. To think otherwise would imply that institutional history is univocal and always generates determinate answers to the interpretive questions that judges have to consider within a practice. This is not the case even

---

[26] E Olsson, 'Coherentist Theories of Epistemic Justification', in EN Zalta (ed), *The Stanford Encyclopedia of Philosophy* (Palo Alto, CA, Stanford University Press, Fall 2021 edn), plato.stanford.edu/archives/fall2021/entries/justep-coherence/.
[27] Livingston and Mele (n 13) 932.
[28] *Dobbs v Jackson Women's Health Organization*, 597 U.S. (2022), which overruled both *Roe v Wade*, 410 U.S. 113 (1973) and *Planned Parenthood v Casey*, 505 U.S. 833 (1992).

assuming that there are natural constraints delivered by background interpretive practices. As Robertson explains:

> [I]t is just as possible on Fish's account that the background will deliver disputed factual claims, or ambiguous textual meanings, or conflicting possible courses of action. In short, anti-foundationalism does not rule out uncertainty, ambiguity, or conflicting choices, it only claims that these things will always be 'enterprise-specific' or 'discipline-specific'.[29]

Therefore, as I suggested in the Introduction, Fish's methodological critique of Dworkin's position should be separated from his repudiation of constructive interpretation. We can assume anti-foundationalism for the sake of argument without jeopardising constructive interpretation. Although there are plausible theories of social cognition that hold that there are natural constraints on participants in social practices, the constraints do not determine how interpreters do or should proceed when they attribute meaning to texts and concepts within their practice. Indeed, natural constraints *underdetermine* the activity of interpretation. In the next section, I identify three modes of interpretation that are compatible with natural constraints.

III. THREE MODES OF INTERPRETATION

Fish says that 'I do not mean to preclude self-conscious deliberation on the part of situated agents; it is just that such deliberations always occur within ways of thinking that are themselves the ground of consciousness, not its object.'[30] The question arises then of what modes of 'deliberation' or interpretation are possible for competent interpreters to pursue *within* interpretive communities. In this section, I outline three possible modes: subjective, descriptive and constructive.

Dworkin's summary of legal pragmatism implies that a subjective mode of interpretation is possible. He says that (according to pragmatism) judges 'should make whatever decisions *seem to them* best for the community's future'.[31] However, the phrase 'seem to them' is ambiguous. One sense is that personal judgments inform judges' decisions in the same way that scientific decisions rely on the 'personal judgments of scientists about what the evidence establishes'.[32] Even Fish's work at times seems to endorse this sense of the subjective mode. For instance, he disagrees with Owen Fiss's suggestion that individual interpreters are externally constrained by 'disciplining rules' that derive from an intersubjective consensus within the community of interpretation.[33] The reason is

---

[29] Robertson (n 4) 284.
[30] Fish (n 2) 128, fn 19; quoted in ibid 284.
[31] Dworkin (n 12) 95 (emphasis added).
[32] WJ Waluchow, *A Common Law Theory of Judicial Review. The Living Tree* (Cambridge, Cambridge University Press, 2007) 231.
[33] OM Fiss, 'Objectivity and interpretation' (1982) 4 *Stanford Law Review* 739–63.

that *any* 'external' standards, even intersubjective ones, would 'have to declare their own significance to any observer no matter what his perspective'.[34] This is impossible, because a standard employed by an interpreter is never wholly independent of the interpreter's perspective on it. Fish's criticism of Fiss therefore implicitly claims that an interpreter's personal judgment, like that of the scientist theorising about empirical evidence, will always inform how they view a standard generated by the interpretive community in which they are embedded. Indeed, *all* forms of interpretation would seem to be subjective in this first sense.

There is a second sense of 'seem to them'. Dworkin thinks that pragmatism recommends that individual judges 'strike out in a new direction of their own' and make decisions that promote their subjective values, purposes or policy goals.[35] In doing so, judges would be employing what Samuel Freeman calls 'particular' reasons – reasons that are

> ascertained from our individual perspectives, where we see ourselves as single agents with fixed (final) ends facing a range of options from which we must choose. These reasons are ultimately based on our particular ends, as given by our private, sectarian, and group interests.[36]

The second sense of the subjective mode does not follow from the first, as illustrated by the example of scientific theorising: even if scientific decisions depend on personal judgments by scientists about the evidence, scientific conclusions need not reflect the values or goals of individual scientists.[37] Fish rejects the possibility of subjective interpretation in the second sense because it would be equivalent to radically unconstrained interpretation. Robertson summarises:

> [I]magine a judge who one day experiences a sudden and profound religious conversion, and who thereafter feels compelled to pursue religious goals and values and modes of reasoning in any context he finds himself in, including his judicial role. This ... is a situation in which for this person one practice, religion, has completely taken over the territory formerly occupied by another practice, law. In such a situation, the person acting as a judge is an imposter, a person pretending to be a judge. He can no longer be described as 'thinking within' the tradition of lawyers, for he is now acting as an embedded member of a completely different interpretive community.[38]

Hence, according to Fish, there is no such thing as interpretation based on purely individual perspectives or 'particular' reasons because each of us is embedded in multiple interpretive communities. Judges who employ non-legal religious reasons would be deciding on the basis of natural constraints delivered by a religious social practice. Their decision-making would not count as a competent

---

[34] S Fish, 'Fish v. Fiss' (1984) 36 *Stanford Law Review* 1325–47, 1326.
[35] Dworkin (n 1) 193–94.
[36] S Freeman, 'Original Meaning, Democratic Interpretation, and the Constitution' (1992) 21 *Philosophy and Public Affairs* (1992) 3–42, 21ff.
[37] Waluchow (n 32) 231.
[38] Robertson (n 4) 277.

interpretation of *legal* practice because they would be operating according to the natural constraints of another interpretive practice in which they are also embedded.

The mindshaping hypothesis would agree that there is no such thing as a subjective mode that permits the possibility of radically unconstrained interpreters abstracted from the social or cultural practices in which they are embedded. However, as Fish points out, 'self-conscious deliberation' or interpretation *within* a social practice is not precluded by natural constraints or by the mindshaping framework. There are alternative modes of interpretation – which I call *descriptive* and *constructive* – that are available to interpreters within social practices. To elaborate and compare these modes, recall Dworkin's account of the stages of interpretation. In the pre-interpretive stage, legal interpreters (who are also participants in the practice) identify paradigms of the social practices. Dworkin says that

> we have no difficulty identifying collectively the practices that count as legal practices in our own culture. We have legislatures and courts and administrative agencies and bodies and the decisions these institutions make are reported in a canonical way.[39]

Similarly, when judges interpret particular legal concepts, the first 'pre-theoretic' step is to identify some paradigmatic instances of application of the concept around which there is a rough consensus. Once paradigms of the area of law or particular concept have been identified, the interpreter proceeds to a second, interpretive stage, in which the core elements of the paradigms are identified, to develop an account of what the practice or concept requires.

At the interpretive stage, either a descriptive or a constructive strategy can be pursued to identify the core elements of paradigms. A descriptive approach would employ 'empirical or quasi-empirical methods'.[40] Suppose that before the Canadian Civil Marriage Act was passed in 2005, judges in Canada needed to interpret the meaning of laws related to the (secular) concept of marriage to work out whether they applied to non-traditional domestic partnerships. Also suppose that traditional opposite sex unions were taken as the paradigms of marriage. A descriptive approach to identifying the core elements of the paradigm would have asked how the term 'marriage' *was actually used* in Canadian legal practice. If 'marriage' as it was actually used referred exclusively to opposite sex unions, a descriptive approach would have concluded that being an opposite sex union was a core element of marriage. Alternatively, judges could have adopted a constructive mode. Dworkin argues that the interpretation of social practices is 'essentially concerned with purpose not cause'.[41] A social practice 'does not simply exist but has value ... it serves some interest

---

[39] Dworkin (n 12) 91.
[40] S Haslanger, 'What Are We Talking About? The Semantics and Politics of Social Kinds' (2005) 20(4) *Hypatia* 10–26.
[41] Dworkin (n 12) 52.

or purpose or enforces some principle'.[42] The constructive mode is normative and justificatory rather than descriptive, and requires that interpreters articulate and defend a substantive account of the purpose of the legal category being interpreted.[43] Before 2005 in Canada, the constructive mode would also have presupposed a pre-interpretive consensus that the paradigms of marriages were opposite sex unions. However, it would have employed normative reasoning about the purpose of marriage to identify the core elements of the paradigm. Was the purpose to encourage procreation and promote 'traditional' family values, or was it to provide official recognition of people's intimate domestic partnerships and regulate the benefits and obligations associated with these partnerships? On the latter understanding of purpose, there is no principled reason for restricting marriage to opposite sex unions, because the latter is not a core feature of the paradigm. The constructive mode corresponds to what Sally Haslanger calls an 'ameliorative project', namely one that 'seek[s] to elucidate not only the concepts we have but aim[s] to improve them in the light or our legitimate purposes'.[44] The concept 'marriage' is ameliorated when we understand it in a way that better promotes the purpose of marriage in a secular society. Thus, whereas a descriptive strategy may be limited to describing a concept *we actually have* and might for instance restrict marriage to opposite sex unions, by focusing on the purpose of marriage, an ameliorative approach permits the introduction of an improved legal concept.[45]

This constructive or ameliorative mode is not only possible but *required* in legal interpretation. Recall the point emphasised above that communities of interpretation rarely if ever provide univocal answers to questions of interpretation. The background social practice 'deliver[s] disputed factual claims, or ambiguous textual meanings, or conflicting possible courses of action'.[46] The descriptive mode will often be ineffective to resolve such controversies. I briefly outline five examples of common phenomena that are encountered in legal interpretation that call for the constructive rather than the descriptive mode: *unforeseen circumstances, abstract principles, vagueness and semantic indeterminacy; evolving social concepts*, and *disagreement within interpretive communities*. As Hart famously put it, norm-governed systems like law contain interstices, or 'gaps'.[47] Some of these arise due to the application of legal rules

---

[42] ibid 47.
[43] Julie Dickson describes constructive interpretation as 'evaluative and justificatory:' J Dickson, 'Methodology in Jurisprudence: A Critical Survey' (2004) 10 *Legal Theory* (2004) 117–56. Thomas Bustamante makes a similar point that interpretive legal concepts are 'neither purely descriptive nor purely evaluative' in ch 14 in this volume.
[44] Haslanger (n 8) 230.
[45] I provide more extended discussions of descriptive and constructive modes in N Stoljar, 'Waluchow on Moral Opinions and Moral Commitments' (2009) 3 *Problema. Anuario de Filosofía y Teoría del Derecho* 101–32, and of ameliorative legal concepts in Stoljar (n 2).
[46] Roberston (n 4) 284.
[47] Hart (n 10).

to new and unforeseen circumstances. Consider the External Affairs Power of the Australian Constitution. In 1901 when the Australian Constitution was adopted, the understanding of the Power was quite narrow; the federal government was authorised to legislate only in areas concerning traditional foreign affairs, such as borders, national security or territorial waters. It was unforeseen at that time that Australia would incur obligations under international treaties on (eg) racial discrimination and the environment. An interpretive question arose of whether 'external affairs' permitted federal legislation to incorporate these obligations into domestic law. A descriptive mode of interpretation is inadequate to decide the issue, because it is limited to empirical description of actually held views about the meaning of 'external affairs'. A constructive mode, which theorises about the constitutional function of the External Affairs Power, is needed. The second common phenomenon is that of legal clauses and principles that are couched in abstract language, for instance 'equality under the law' or 'liberty'. In applying abstract principles to concrete circumstances, it will often be necessary to theorise about the purpose of the principle rather than simply describe how it has been applied in the past. For instance, the Canadian Charter's non-discrimination clause (section 15) protects people in explicitly listed categories from discrimination. To decide whether the clause applies to people who fall outside these categories, we need to articulate the substantive purpose of the clause. Third, as Hart also pointed out, because general terms are employed in legal regulations, linguistic vagueness is an ever-present phenomenon in legal interpretation. General terms have 'core' and 'penumbral' applications:[48] for instance, a regulation prohibiting the transport of vehicles across state lines includes the general term 'vehicle'. While the regulation clearly applies to core instances of vehicle (private cars, buses, taxis, etc), it is indeterminate whether it applies to borderline or penumbral cases. Is an aeroplane a vehicle? To interpret the regulation, the purpose of prohibiting interstate transport of vehicles will have to be considered; our understanding of 'vehicle' will have to be refined (ameliorated) according to whether promoting the regulation's purpose would be advanced by treating aeroplanes as vehicles. Fourth, legal concepts often track *social* concepts, the content of which evolves over time. As explained above, constructive interpretation will be needed to answer questions about evolving socio-legal concepts like that of marriage. Fifth, it is common for there to be significant disagreement within social practices and for practices to contain both 'orthodox' and 'heterodox' accounts of core features of the practice.[49] In contradicting 50 years of established constitutional precedent, the decision of the majority in the recent US Supreme Court case of *Dobbs* (overruling *Roe v Wade*) ran counter to the orthodox approach to legal reasoning in Anglo-American legal systems. The decision failed to uphold the values of stability and predictability that are central to the idea of

---

[48] Hart (n 10).
[49] Haslanger (n 24).

the rule of law in liberal democracies. Legal practice therefore is not univocal, and future interpreters will have to resolve such disagreements using the constructive mode.

In summary, I have suggested that both descriptive and constructive modes of interpretation are open to interpreters within social practices. However, the constructive mode is needed because the descriptive mode will offer only partial and incomplete responses to many interpretive questions. In particular, legal practices are gappy: the formal features of legal texts and rules generate indeterminacies that often cannot be resolved by employing the descriptive mode. Similarly, constructive interpretation is required to respond to disagreements and conflicts within the history and cultural discourse that constitute background legal practice.

IV. FISH'S ARGUMENTS AGAINST CONSTRUCTIVE INTERPRETATION

In addition to the methodological critique that we have already considered, there are two independent arguments in Fish's work against constructive interpretation. First, he implicitly rejects Dworkin's analysis of constructive interpretation as conceptually equivalent to imposing a purpose because he claims that interpretation is necessarily intentionalist: 'it cannot proceed independent of intention [although] it also true that intentions are themselves interpretively produced and therefore cannot serve ... as a check on interpretive activity'.[50] Second, Fish claims that constructive interpretation or the 'injunction to search for the best justification of a decision' is trivial or empty and devoid of 'positive content'.[51] In a discussion that draws a parallel between the know-how required for playing baseball and that required for judging within an interpretive legal practice, Fish says:

> That is why Dworkin's repeated injunction to arrive at the 'best' judgments we possibly can and be the best judges we can possibly be sounds so strange. One wants to say, with Dennis Martinez, 'what else could we be or do except what, according to our lights, was the best?' That is, someone whose sense of appropriateness includes a firm conviction of what is and is not obligatory and what is and is not responsible judicial behavior will not have to look elsewhere for his convictions or for an understanding of what would be the 'best' thing to do. 'Be the best you can be' finally means nothing more than 'act in the way your understanding of your role in the institution tells you to act'.[52]

According to Fish, the project of constructing a best decision has positive content only if it is conceived as a rhetorical 'strategy for presenting a decision after it has already been made'.[53]

[50] Fish (n 2) 296.
[51] ibid 392.
[52] ibid 391.
[53] ibid 392.

Neither of Fish's arguments against constructive interpretation is successful. Let us first consider his intentionalism, which relies on a conceptual argument offered by the literary theorists Steven Knapp and Walter Benn Michaels.[54] They claim that 'intentionless meaning' is an incoherent notion. Knapp and Michaels consider the difference between 'texts', which are meaningful, and patterns in the sand washed up by the tide that look like the stanza of a poem. They posit that although patterns in the sand may look like texts that have meaning, in fact they are not, because only marks (or sounds) made by intentional agents who intend them to mean something *have* meaning. Fish agrees: '[a]ll interpretation is intentional – assuming as the ground of its possibility a purposeful agent who has produced its object'.[55] As others have pointed out, Knapp and Michaels' thought experiment does not establish their conclusion. Even when people know for certain that marks are *not* the products of an intentional agent – consider marks that are produced by a computer that is a 'random letter generator' – it is possible for them to attribute meaning to such marks by drawing on the conventional meanings of their language.[56] In other words, there are 'two senses of "textual meaning" …: meaning intended by an author for a text and meaning ascribed or supplied by a reader'.[57] Even if we assume for the sake of argument that Fish is correct that the attribution of meaning to marks requires an interpreter to make a causal assumption that they were produced by an intentional agent and are not gibberish, it does not follow that the only meaning that can be attributed is the author's intended meaning. There are many common examples – slips of the tongue, typographical errors, and sarcasm or irony – that establish that there is a distinction between author's intended meaning and conventional semantic meaning. Competent speakers of a language, once having made the putatively necessary causal assumption, can attribute meaning based on either what the author intended the text to mean or the conventional semantic rules of the language. It appears therefore that 'intentionless meaning' is possible, contrary to the conclusions of both Knapp and Michaels, and Fish. Constructive interpretation is not ruled out on the basis that interpretation is essentially intentionalist.

Fish's second argument is that constructive interpretation is devoid of positive content. He says that requiring an interpreter to '"Be the best you can be" finally means nothing more than "act in the way your understanding of your role in the institution tells you to act"'.[58] In the remainder of the chapter, I explicitly defend the approach of constructive interpretation by developing three responses to this criticism. First, Fish's suggested parallel between interpreters and players of baseball (or some other game) mischaracterises Dworkin's position. Second, although Dworkin's defence of his own position treats constructive

---

[54] S Knapp and WB Michaels, 'Against Theory' (1982) 8 *Critical Inquiry* 723–42.
[55] Fish (n 2) 296.
[56] Livingston and Mele (n 13) 934.
[57] ibid 935.
[58] Fish (n 2) 391.

interpretation as inseparable from a number of associated claims, these claims are in fact independent and do not have to be endorsed as a package. Constructive interpretation is in fact more defensible as a theory of legal interpretation once extracted from the associated claims. Third, the positive content of constructive interpretation emerges when we understand it as a legal version of 'conceptual amelioration'.[59] When Dworkin identifies the 'object of interpretation' he usually refers to legal texts (statutes or constitutions) or practices (areas of law such as constitutional law or legal systems such as the common law). However, within these practices or texts, the objects of interpretation are typically particular legal concepts – marriage, equal protection, constitutional privacy, legal personhood, external affairs – and these are ripe for conceptual amelioration.

Fish thinks that the parallel between competent judges and competent baseball players (like Dennis Martinez) reveals that constructive interpretation is devoid of content: 'what else could [competent players or judges do] except what, according to [their] lights, was the best?' This characterisation of Dworkin's position is misleading, however. It assumes that constructive interpretation requires interpreters to engage in a process of interpretation to the best of *their* ability. Instead, Dworkin argues that constructive interpretation requires the interpreter to 'impose meaning' to make the object of interpretation the best that *it* can be:

> The form of interpretation we are studying–the interpretation of a social practice– is like artistic interpretation ...: both aim to interpret something created by people as a distinct entity from them ... Roughly, constructive interpretation is a matter of imposing purpose on an object or practice in order to make of it the best possible example of the form or genre to which it is taken to belong.[60]

As argued above, we can agree with Fish that competent interpretation within a practice presupposes skill or know-how that has become second nature through a process of enculturation (mindshaping). In this sense, the skill of judging is analogous to that of playing a game. Notice that the skill or know-how that is displayed in judging or playing games need not be unreflective or instinctual but could involve critical reflection '*within* the routines of a practice'.[61] Nevertheless, constructive interpretation is *not* an injunction to interpreters to exhibit the best possible know-how or critical interpretive skill. Rather, it requires the interpreter to constitute the object of interpretation as 'the best that it can be'.

---

[59] Haslanger (n 8).
[60] Dworkin (n 12) 52.
[61] S Fish, *There's No Such Thing as Free Speech: and it's a good thing too* (Oxford, Oxford University Press, 1994) 304; quoted in Robertson (n 4) 285–86. For another argument that Fish and Dworkin share the view that interpreting the norms of a social practice involves know-how or practical ability, see Bustamante (n 43). On Bustamante's account, the difference between Fish and Dworkin is that the former adheres to a narrow 'instrumental' pragmatism (in Robert Brandom's sense) whereas Dworkin proposes a more 'normative' pragmatism.

Hence constructive interpretation is *not* the legal parallel of an empty request to Dennis Martinez to play baseball in the best way he can. Indeed, far from Dworkin's position being devoid of content, it could fairly be accused of being overly broad and of having *too much* content. Dworkin's elaboration of constructive interpretation includes several ambitious claims: that it is *essentially* constructive, and that it is applicable to artworks and literary texts as well as to social practices. According to Dworkin, the law is analogous to a 'chain novel' that is written in instalments by different authors yet displays an underlying thread that is taken up and developed by each subsequent author. To identify the underlying thread of a particular area of law, constructive interpretation 'instructs' judges to posit that the chain of law has been written by a single author – 'the community personified'.[62] A problem for Dworkin's exposition of his own view is that several of the features of constructive interpretation that he endorses seem implausible. For instance, if I am right that descriptive and constructive modes of interpretation are both available, legal interpretation cannot be *necessarily* constructive. It *could be* pursued in the descriptive mode. Further, even if it is true that legal interpretation and artistic interpretation both occur within social practices that are governed by natural constraints, there are still important differences between them. One of the key differences is that social practices like law and courtesy contain systems of norms that direct our behaviour, so interpretation within these practices often concerns 'what [the] tradition or practice actually requires in concrete circumstances'.[63] Concepts that are interpreted within such social practices typically have a social function 'in organizing our lives together and in shaping our self-understandings to engage fluently in the practices that enable coordination'.[64] Haslanger considers how the concept 'family' organises the social practices that involve domestic relationships: 'to have a family-concept is (roughly) to have a cluster of mechanisms for processing information *about the coordination of domestic life*, e.g., intimacy, sex, raising of children, economic partnership, intergenerational transfers of traditions and property'.[65] In contrast, the interpretation of art or literary works neither directly concerns what is required of us in concrete circumstances nor plays a role in coordinating aspects of daily life. Interpretations of the novel *Pride and Prejudice* may illuminate or even offer new understandings of the moral concepts of pride or prejudice. The concepts may shape the self-understandings and coordinate the behaviour of the characters *in the novel* (and may indirectly influence our own self-understandings) but they do not materially affect our circumstances as literary interpreters or have a social function around which we coordinate our activities. Hence, whereas constructive interpretation – interpretation that requires normative reasoning to

---

[62] Dworkin (n 12) 225.
[63] ibid 46.
[64] Haslanger (n 8) 250.
[65] ibid (emphasis added).

articulate a 'best' purpose or social function – is a plausible account of social practices containing systems of norms that direct our behaviour, it might not be a convincing account of literary or artistic interpretation. Fortunately, we do not have to take a position here on whether it applies to literary or artistic interpretation, because the various claims that Dworkin makes in the course of his elaboration of constructive interpretation need not be treated as a package.

What then is the positive account of constructive interpretation that responds to Fish's claims that it is devoid of content? Notice first that, although objects of interpretation can be whole social practices (like those of law or courtesy), typically interpreters within these practices are considering the meaning of particular *concept*s, for instance marriage, privacy, legal personhood, external affairs, equal protection etc. As I just argued, the concepts that are interpreted within social practices apply to concrete circumstances and have a social function around which we coordinate. Constructive interpretation corresponds to *conceptual amelioration* of these concepts: it seeks to identify the social function of the concept and to promote this function by offering newer and better understandings of the concept. Haslanger explains conceptual amelioration with respect to the concept 'family', the social function of which is to manage domestic life:

> For many generations, in the United States at least, the concept family conveyed a specific informational content: it included a husband, his (same-race) wife, and her biological offspring. This social formation was legally and culturally entrenched. Other ways of arranging domestic life, although acknowledged, were either unimaginable ... or were tolerated only insofar as they mimicked the dominant formation (adoption, step-families, unmarried and mixed-race couples with children). 'Childless' couples didn't really count as families (note: 'when are you going to start a family?'). At this point, heterosexual bionormative nuclear families (HBNFs) constitute one kind of family, but it is broadly recognized that families include domestic arrangements made by adoption, donated gametes, families with single parents, same-sex, trans and genderqueer parents, unmarried parents, and extended families of various kinds. I believe that conceptual amelioration has occurred, both as a result of pressure by social movements and by the development of reproductive technology, i.e., the informational content of the term 'family' has changed, due to a change in the social conditions. More ways of organizing domestic life have become normalized.[66]

The concept 'family' has been ameliorated in both an epistemic and a semantic sense. There is epistemic amelioration because 'there are more ways of organizing domestic life that in HBNFs, even in the actual world, and those who confined their understanding of family to HBNFs were mistaken'.[67] There is also semantic amelioration because the evolution of how to understand 'family'

[66] ibid 251.
[67] ibid.

introduces 'new informational content' about how to manage domestic life: 'the partition of logical space communicated changes when we include more kinds of domestic arrangements as families'.[68] Haslanger argues that, despite these shifts, it is not the case that a brand-new closely related concept has been formed, because the social function of the concept we are talking about (family) remains the same. Hence, as she puts it, conceptual amelioration involves 'going on, not in the same way'.[69]

Broadly, constructive interpretation corresponds to conceptual amelioration of legal concepts. It does not seek only to *describe* the legal concepts to which we are actually committed but rather posits modified or new understandings of their content by employing normative reasoning to consider how the concept would best serve its social function. (Recall the discussion of marriage in the last section.) Dworkin's initial discussion of courtesy implicitly reveals that constructive interpretation involves both epistemic and semantic amelioration. Courtesy has a purpose or social function – to facilitate respectful, polite (and harmonious) interpersonal relations – and in making decisions about the content of courtesy, interpreters have to employ normative theorising to evaluate this purpose. Dworkin says that 'this assumed point acquires critical power, and people come to demand, under the title of courtesy, forms of deference previously unknown or to spurn or refuse forms previously honoured'.[70] Hence, constructive interpretation involves epistemic amelioration because an outcome of the constructive interpretation of courtesy is to generate 'previously unknown' understandings of the concept of deference. It also expands the possibilities within logical space of what we mean by 'deference' and hence corresponds to semantic amelioration. Like the constructive interpretation of courtesy, legal constructive interpretation is epistemically and semantically ameliorative. The question arises of whether it is also *morally* ameliorative. At the beginning of the chapter, I said that, on Dworkin's view, the constraints delivered by constructive interpretation are moral. They are derived from the moral principles implicit in the history of a legal practice and a current interpretation should preserve coherence or integrity with those moral principles. However, contrary to this position, making the content of a legal concept the 'best that it can be' need not always correspond to moral amelioration. The normative reasoning that interpreters employ in the constructive mode is not necessarily moral because some legal concepts have non-moral social functions around which we coordinate. For instance, legal systems often contain provisions that are primarily regulatory, such as those concerning trade or external affairs. Non-moral evaluative reasoning may be required to answer questions concerning the purpose these regulatory concepts are aiming to achieve. On the other hand, the social purpose of concepts in Bills of Rights in

---

[68] ibid.
[69] ibid 230.
[70] Dworkin (n 12) 48.

liberal democracies is to tie societies to the 'mast' of abstract moral principles. Bills of Rights attempt to ensure that rights are entrenched even in circumstances in which future majorities might be tempted to override them.[71] The social function of concepts like liberty in Bills of Rights is also a moral one, and the constructive interpretation of such concepts will require interpreters to advance 'the best' moral reading of such concepts.[72] Hence, in such cases, legal constructive interpretation will exemplify epistemic, semantic and *moral* amelioration.

V. CONCLUDING REMARKS

I have argued in this chapter that constructive interpretation is a substantive position that is available to interpreters within the social practice of law. It involves legal conceptual amelioration and hence is not empty or devoid of content. The chapter has not addressed the reasons one might have for adopting one theory of interpretation over another, so it has not offered a direct defence of constructive interpretation.[73] There are however advantages of Dworkinian constructive interpretation over Fish's position. Constructive interpretation offers judges and other legal interpreters a framework for advancing better interpretations of legal concepts. It also provides important critical and theoretical tools to characterise some past judicial decisions as mistaken or incorrect, not necessarily because they are morally wrong, but because they are bad interpretations of the law. This is important because, as I have argued, the meanings we attribute to legal texts and concepts *matter* due the way the law functions in our daily lives. A glaring example is the recent decision of the US Supreme Court in *Dobbs* that overruled the established precedents of *Roe* and *Casey*. From the perspective of the constructive interpretation that I have defended here, this is a terrible *interpretive* decision:[74] it contracts rather than expands the informational content conveyed by the relevant clauses of the US Constitution and hence is not semantic amelioration. It transports us back to a pre-1973 world in which it was not known that a right to abortion could be constitutionally protected, and hence it is the opposite of epistemic amelioration. And in failing to protect reproductive rights, it fails to promote the best understanding of the moral purpose of the US Constitution.

---

[71] Waluchow (n 32).

[72] I make a more extended case for why an ameliorative project is required in the legal context in Stoljar (n 8) and N Stoljar, 'In Praise of Wishful Thinking. A Critique of Descriptive-Explanatory Theories of Law' (2012) 6 *Problema. Anuario de Filosofía y Teoría del Derecho* 51–79.

[73] For a comparison of different theories of interpretation, see N Stoljar, 'Interpretation, Indeterminacy and Authority: Some Recent Controversies in the Philosophy of Law' (2003) 11 *Journal of Political Philosophy* 470–98.

[74] The decision is criticisable even from a *descriptive* perspective as interpretation in the descriptive mode would have affirmed the concept of privacy to which US constitutional practice *actually was* committed at the time *Dobbs* came before the court.

In contrast to the critical power of constructive interpretation, Fish's position (as Robertson puts it) is that 'a competent legal practitioner ... does not need any additional guidance to know how to perform properly'.[75] His account has little to offer in response to cases like *Dobbs*. In principle, he has two avenues of analysis: either the majority judges 'performed properly' within the natural constraints of legal practice, or their interpretation was not legally 'competent' because they were in fact guided by a sectarian religious position derived from another practice in which they were also situated. But it will be impossible to empirically verify which alternative to adopt because the judgment is couched in legal language that makes it appear that the majority was operating competently in accordance with the rules of the constitutional game, even if they were not. This may not matter for the other interpretive games that both Fish and Dworkin treat as analogous to law. There is usually not much at stake when competent interpreters disagree over the meanings of literature or artworks. However, while this lack of theoretical power may be consonant with another Fishian methodological position that I did not address in the chapter (encapsulated in the phrase 'against theory'), it is unsatisfying to those who care about evaluating judicial decisions as genuinely better or worse interpretations of the law.

---

[75] Robertson (n 4) 265.

Part Three

Pragmatism and Interpretive Communities

11
Revisiting the 'Fish-Dworkin Debate'

DENNIS PATTERSON

I. INTRODUCTION

THE DEBATE BETWEEN Ronald Dworkin and Stanley Fish generated a great deal of interest at a time when 'interpretation' was all the rage. Then, everyone was reading turgid texts on hermeneutics and trying to figure out how an enterprise like literary criticism might have something to do with law. Although literary theory is Stanley Fish's line of work, Ronald Dworkin certainly assimilated the spirit of the age. In addition to his noteworthy contribution of the distinction between fit and justification,[1] his use of the literary metaphor of the 'chain novel'[2] was a singular contribution to our understanding of legal practice.

In this chapter, I reprise the debate between Fish and Dworkin but I do so from a vantage point neither would endorse. Having written a great deal about both of them, I wanted to come back to the debate by emphasising something that neither would accept: their similarities. I think both Fish and Dworkin and, indeed, much of the commentary at the time, was the product of an era that has largely been left behind in legal philosophy. Defenders of Dworkin have tried to sustain his metaphysical realist credentials while Fish has carried the torch for a more normatively contested approach to the enterprise.

I try to accomplish two things in this chapter. First is to give a rendering – hopefully accurate – of how each theorist motivates his account of legal practice with a view of interpretation.[3] I locate the place of interpretation in each

---

[1] R Dworkin, *Law's Empire* (Cambridge, MA, Harvard University Press, 1986) 65–8.
[2] ibid 228–38.
[3] Mark Greenberg has recently published an account of 'Legal Interpretation'. See M Greenberg, 'Legal Interpretation', *The Stanford Encyclopedia of Philosophy* (Palo Alto, CA, Fall edn, 2009) plato.stanford.edu/entries/legal-interpretation/ (accessed 22 February 2022). Greenberg's discussion of legal interpretation is marred by his misconstrual of what he takes to be the 'constitutive aim' of legal interpretation. Anxious to promote his 'Moral Impact Theory of Law', Greenberg misconstrues the Standard Picture of Law and with it the role of interpretation in law. The main details of Greenberg's 'Moral Impact Theory' can be found in M Greenberg, 'The Moral Impact Theory of Law' (2014) 123 *Yale Law Journal* 1288. On the shortcomings of Greenberg's theory vis-à-vis the Standard Picture, see B Watson, 'In Defense of the Standard Picture: What The Standard Picture Explains That The Moral Impact Theory Cannot' (2022) 28 *Legal Theory* 59–88.

account and show how it is central to their mutual understanding of law. I then point out why interpretation is a poor place to locate the centre of one's account of law. My argument is drawn from the Wittgensteinian tradition and some of the philosophers with whom I have made common cause against the centrality of interpretation in law. In reprising this view, I hope to renew and reinvigorate my initial critique of the work of Dworkin and Fish.

II. INTERPRETATION

As I look back on the exchanges between Dworkin and Fish, I am reminded primarily of what I noticed about both of their views: the similarities. Each is committed to the view that legal practice is a matter of 'interpretation'. Of course, they differ over the meaning of that term but there is no doubt that each is deeply committed to the idea that the core experience of any participant in law is that of interpretation. The core commitment of each is to a picture of law and legal argument wherein the exercise of individual interpretive agency is the most salient aspect of participation in legal practice. I shall briefly summarise their views.

In *Law's Empire*, Dworkin develops the idea of law as interpretation with a three-step process. As he outlines it, interpretation passes through three stages of 'constructive interpretation':

(1) The preinterpretive stage is the point at which 'the rules and standards taken to provide the tentative content of the practice are identified'.[4]
(2) The interpretive stage is the point 'at which the interpreter settles on some general justification for the main elements of the practice identified at the preinterpretive stage'.[5]
(3) The postinterpretive or reforming stage is the point at which the individual interpreter 'adjusts his sense of what the practice "really" requires so as better to serve the justification he accepts at the interpretive stage'.[6]

It is important to remember that, for Dworkin, every case requires all three stages of constructive interpretation. The methodology is the same, whether the case be easy or hard. Dworkin explains:

> We have been attending mainly to hard cases, when lawyers disagree whether some crucial proposition of law is true or false. But questions of law are sometimes very easy for lawyers and even for nonlawyers. It 'goes without saying' that the speed limit in Connecticut is 55 miles an hour and that people in Britain have a legal duty to pay for food they order in a restaurant. At least this goes without saying except in very

---

[4] Dworkin (n 1) 65–6. As Dworkin states, the word 'preinterpretive' is 'in quotes because some kind of interpretation is necessary even at this stage'.
[5] ibid 66.
[6] ibid.

unusual circumstances. A critic might be tempted to say that the complex account we have developed of judicial reasoning under law as integrity is a method for hard cases only. He might add that it would be absurd to apply the method to easy cases – no judge needs to consider questions of fit and political morality to decide whether someone must pay his telephone bill – and then declare that in addition to his theory of hard cases, Hercules needs a theory about when cases are hard, so he can know when his complex method for hard cases is appropriate and when not. The critic will then announce a serious problem: it can be a hard question whether the case at hand is a hard case or an easy case, and Hercules cannot decide by using his technique for hard cases without begging the question.

> This is a pseudoproblem. Hercules does not need one method for hard cases and another for easy ones. His method is equally at work in easy cases, but since the answers to the questions it puts are then obvious, or at least seem to be so, we are not aware that any theory is at work at all. We think the question whether someone may legally drive faster than the stipulated speed limit is an easy one because we assume at once that no account of the legal record that denied that paradigm would be competent. But someone whose convictions about justice and fairness were very different from ours might not find that question so easy; even if he ended by agreeing with our answer, he would insist that we were wrong to be so confident. This explains why questions considered easy during one period become hard before they again become easy questions – with the opposite answers.[7]

Importantly for Dworkin, the third stage of interpretation is where all the action takes place. The salient point is that it is the individual interpreter who must do the work of finding the right answer. This is a lonely exercise, one that is self-reflexive. Dworkin describes the process as 'a conversation with oneself, as joint author and critic'.[8] It is because the final stage of interpretation is one where the conversation is not in concert with others (eg, fellow jurists) that Dworkin characterises this as 'Protestant Interpretation.' Thus:

> What is law? Now I offer a different kind of answer. Law is not exhausted by any catalogue of rules or principles, each with its own dominion over some discrete theater of behavior. Nor by any roster of officials and their powers each over part of our lives. Law's empire is defined by attitude, not territory or power or process. . . . It is an interpretive, self-reflective attitude addressed to politics in the broadest sense. It is a protestant attitude that makes each citizen responsible for imagining what his society's public commitments to principle are, and what these commitments require in new circumstances. . . . Law's attitude is constructive: it aims, in the interpretive spirit, to lay principle over practice to show the best route to a better future, keeping the right faith with the past.[9]

Dworkin's commitment to constructive interpretation is a natural corollary of his view of interpretation generally. Interpretation is the way we make sense of

---

[7] ibid 353–54.
[8] ibid 58.
[9] ibid 413.

the world. Dworkin's example of this is his account of what happens when we understand speech: 'We interpret the sounds or marks another person makes in order to decide what he has said.'[10] Dworkin's affinity for interpretation is carefully calibrated with his three stages argument and his metaphor of the chain novel. Each of these methodologies distil his great contribution to the literature, the distinction between fit and justification.[11] As competing accounts of past institutional decisions are weighed and evaluated, individual judges and lawyers have to make their case for inclusion of their preferred rendering of the past.

Let us now turn to Stanley Fish. Like Dworkin, Fish is deeply committed to the notion that we cannot understand without first interpreting. As he puts the matter: 'I hold, the text, while always there, is always an interpreted object.'[12] Fish's views on law are motivated by his account of the act of reading. We shall consider that first and then turn to his interesting approach to an old chestnut of a case.

Fish privileges the reader to such an extent that he is best known as the purveyor of 'Reader Response Theory.'[13] Objectivity, Fish avers, is 'a dangerous illusion'.[14] Meaning does not reside in a text but rather in the reader: the reader creates the meaning of the text. As Fish puts it: 'The meaning of an utterance, I repeat, is its experience – all of it – and that experience is immediately compromised the moment you say something about it.'[15]

Fish's view, one that many found hyper-subjective, was subject to withering criticism as a solipsistic account of the act of reading. In reaction, Fish modified his account of interpretation with the idea of 'interpretive communities'. He wrote: '[M]eanings are the property neither of fixed and stable texts nor of free and independent readers but of interpretive communities that are responsible both for the shape of a reader's activities and for the texts those activities produce.'[16]

The idea of an interpretive community was advanced to solve the problem of solipsism that pervaded Fish's original expression of the idea. Moving from

---

[10] ibid 50.

[11] For discussion, see L Solum, 'Fit and Justification' (*Legal Theory Lexicon*, 19 September 2021) lsolum.typepad.com/legal_theory_lexicon/2004/04/legal_theory_le_1.htm (accessed 24 February 2022).

[12] S Fish, *Doing What Comes Naturally: Change, Rhetoric, and the Practice of Theory in Literary and Legal Studies* (Durham, NC, Duke University Press, 1989) 563.

[13] See E Freund, *The Return of the Reader: Reader-Response Criticism* (London, Methuen, 1987) 90–2.

[14] S Fish, *Is There a Text in this Class: The Authority of Interpretive Communities* (Cambridge, MA, Harvard University Press, 1980) 43.

[15] ibid 65. Everything, it seems, is fodder for interpretation:

> The point is a simple one: All shapes are interpretively produced, and since the conditions of interpretation are themselves unstable – the possibility of seeing something in a "new light," and therefore of seeing a *new* something, is ever and unpredictably present – the shapes that seem perspicuous to us now may not seem so or may seem differently so tomorrow. This applies not only to the shape of statutes, poems, and signs in airplane lavatories, but to the disciplines and forms of life within which statutes, poems, and signs become available to us (Fish (n 12) 302).

[16] ibid 322.

individuals to communities of individuals, each possessed of an interpretive matrix for reading texts, rescued the idea that the reader is the locus for an account of textual meaning.[17]

I mentioned Fish's discussion of a jurisprudential chestnut and that is *Riggs v Palmer*.[18] As we all know, *Riggs* took up the question whether Elmer Palmer could inherit his grandfather's estate having brought about the latter's demise by poison. The majority answered in the negative, resting their judgment on the principle 'No person should profit from his own wrongdoing.' The dissent argued for a 'literal' reading of the New York Statute of Wills and in favour of Elmer's claim.

Never one to disappoint, Fish transcends the conventional discussion of the case and gives it his own unique take on what was at stake. Here is his account:

> If it is assumed that the purpose of probate is to ensure the orderly devolution of property at all costs, then the statute in this case will have the plain meaning urged by the defendant; but if it is assumed that no law ever operates in favor of someone who would profit by his crime, then the 'same' statute will have a meaning that is different, but no less plain. In either case the statute will have been literally construed, and what the court will have done is prefer one literal construction to another by invoking one purpose (assumed background) rather than another.[19]

---

[17] Although Fish bristles at the mention of his name, John Ellis highlights some of the problems with Fish's revamped account of interpretive meaning. See JM Ellis, *Against Deconstruction* (Princeton, NJ, Princeton University Press, 1989). Ellis suggests that Fish ultimately commits himself to views incompatible with essential doctrines of Reader-Response criticism. Ellis explains:

> Stanley Fish. . . has long since committed himself to the initial assertions of reader-response criticism and. . . continues to do so but, by changing his position a number of times, has struggled with the kinds of unacceptable consequences of those assertions that I have set out in this chapter. But his latest reformulation [Fish (n14)], which is offered as if no more than a refinement, amounts in fact to his abandoning its essentials completely. His most recent version, then, involves the postulation of interpretive communities, with assumptions and conventions that guide interpretation; this, in his view, allows communication to take place and so rescues him from the consequences of earlier formulations. Now it is, of course, true that a text means nothing without conventions shared by the speakers of the language concerned, but to acknowledge this *fully* would, as Fish sees, abolish his reader-response position: if readers are guided by the rules of language, they do not have the freedom envisaged by reader-response theory, and so the text together with its relation to the linguistic system can be the place to which disputes are appealed after all, contrary to the statement by Fish that I cited. In order to continue to cling to his reader-response position, then, Fish continues to deny that it is sharing a language and 'knowing the meanings of individual words and the rules for combining them' that is involved in communication but, instead, a 'way of thinking, a form of life'. But this direct denial that the shared rules of language makes [sic] communication possible is surely bizarre, and the distinction he makes here is certainly untenable. Oddly enough, Fish's language here recalls Wittgenstein's, but in using it Wittgenstein was pointing out precisely that a language with its rules, conventions, and agreements *is* a way of thinking and form of life! ibid 121, n 6 quoting Fish (n 14) 303 (emphasis in original) (citation omitted).

[18] *Riggs v Palmer* 22 N.E. 188 (N.Y. 1889).
[19] Fish (n 14) 280.

The sentences have their meaning as a function of the presuppositions (ie, interpretive assumptions) brought to bear on the text. Those assumptions are, as it were, the lens through which the text acquires its meaning.

I am not convinced that Fish is right here. I have argued previously to this effect:

> The most obvious deficiency with Fish's account of what is at stake in *Riggs* is that both the majority and dissent recognize *not* that only one purpose informs the statute but that there are competing purposes in play. The problem is not to isolate one purpose over others; rather, the problem is that both purposes are perfectly valid juridical values, and given the fact that they conflict, a choice has to be made as to which is the overriding value. Thus, the problem is not that the majority and dissent are working from *different* grids of intelligibility. The problem is that each is trying to make sense of the question posed against *the very same grid*. What they disagree over is how lexically to order the competing juridical values.[20]

I think Fish's view has deeper problems than the one just identified. Over 30 years ago,[21] Fish and I debated the question whether there is a deep contradiction in his idea of the interpretive community and how he uses it to motivate his claims about readers and texts. I shall discuss two issues. The first uses Fish's own method against his view. The second identifies an incoherence in the idea of 'interpretive community' as Fish employs it.

As I have explained in detail elsewhere,[22] Fish employed the notion of an interpretive community to avoid the many criticisms of his view to the effect that it was simply solipsistic.[23] When one becomes a member of an interpretive community, one's reading of texts is a function of one's training and acculturation. One achieves membership in a community when one passes 'through a professional initiation or course of training,'[24] the effect of which 'is to homogenize persons who were disparate and heterogeneous before entering – and becoming inhabited by – the community's ways'.[25]

Becoming a member of an interpretive community means assimilating the habits and mores of the group. In reading texts, one brings to bear not one's personal agenda (that is solipsism) but the assumptions of one's interpretive community for '[i]t is these assumptions and categories that have been internalized in the course of training, a process at the end of which the trainee is not

---

[20] D Patterson, *Law and Truth* (Oxford. Oxford University Press, 1996) 115 (citations omitted).

[21] The relevant texts are: D Patterson, 'The Poverty of Interpretive Universalism: Toward the Reconstruction of Legal Theory' (1993) 72 *Texas Law Review* 1; S Fish, 'How Come You Do Me Like You Do? A Response to Dennis Patterson' (1993) 72 *Texas Law Review* 57; D Patterson, 'You Made Me Do It: My Reply to Stanley Fish' (1993–4) 72 *Texas Law Review* 67.

[22] See Patterson (n 20). Chapter 6 of ibid is devoted to a discussion of Fish. All the details for my claims are spelled out there.

[23] ibid 120 and 120 fns 125, 126.

[24] Fish (n 21) 58.

[25] ibid.

only possessed *of* but possessed *by* a knowledge of the ropes, by a tacit knowledge that tells him not so much what to do, but already has him doing it . . .'[26] Thus, 'thinking like a lawyer' is a matter of assimilating the discursive habits of the interpretive community of lawyers.

All of this sounds both familiar and uncontroversial. The problem is how one explains disagreement *within* an interpretive community. Fish has never been able to solve this problem. Agreement, Fish maintains, 'is not a function of particularly clear and perspicuous rules; it is a function of the fact that interpretive assumptions and procedures are so widely shared in a community that the rule appears to all in the same (interpreted) shape'.[27] But if the judges in *Riggs* are part of the same interpretive community, they should bring the same interpretive assumptions to bear on their reading of the New York Statute of Wills. But they do not. So, are they members of different interpretive communities? You see the problem.[28]

The bottom line is that the idea of an interpretive community is, in Fish's hands a notion at war with itself. On a 'homogeneous conception' of the idea, everyone in an interpretive community shares assumptions which they bring to bear on their objects of interpretation. That is the bit about everyone being assimilated to the practice in the same way with the same methodologies. But then there is a second conception, one we might term 'pluralistic'. Consider what Fish says about the two positions in the *Riggs* case:

> If it is assumed that the purpose of probate is to ensure the orderly devolution of property at all costs, then the statute in this case will have the plain meaning urged by the defendant; but if it is assumed that no law ever operates in favor of someone who would profit by his crime, then the 'same' statute will have a meaning that is different, but no less plain. In either case the statute will have been literally construed, and what the court will have done is prefer one literal construction to another by invoking one purpose (assumed background) rather than another.[29]

The majority and dissenting opinions are separated by differences in interpretive assumptions. Does that mean they are in different interpretive communities? That is what it comes to. The whole point of the concept of interpretive community is to ground the authority of particular readings outside of the text

---

[26] Fish (n 12) 127.
[27] ibid 122. See also ibid 300: '[C]onstraints [on interpretation] will not inhere in the language of the text (statute or poem). . . but in the cultural assumptions within which both texts and contexts take shape for situated agents'.
[28] As I put the matter:
> When it comes to explaining the nature of disagreement in a practice such as law or literary criticism, Fish's dilemma is to account for disagreement without subdividing the community of lawyers or critics into a congeries of interpretive communities. My contention is that Fish has not accomplished this task. In short, I believe that Fish's appropriation of the idea of an interpretive community fails to escape the criticisms leveled against previous formulations of his view. (Patterson (n 20) 125).

[29] Fish (n12) 122. See also text quoted above at n 27.

and in the community of readers. However, as Jonathan Culler observes, this formulation is

> an exceedingly weak descriptive move, which leaves us with a large number of independent communities unable to argue with one another: some readers read one way – say, Fishian readers – others read another way – say, Hirschian readers – and so on, for as many different strategies as we can identify. . . [T]his conception. . . separates us into monadic communities . . . .[30]

What began as a solution to a problem has turned into its own dilemma. The notion of an interpretive community cannot explain disagreement in a practice when the premise is that the practice is identified by shared methodologies for interpreting texts and other cultural materials. Culler is right that Fish's interpreters wind up being (Leibnizian) interpretive monads.[31] The reason is that Fish never really explains how agents can share interpretive strategies and still disagree in a way that keeps them in the same practice. Fish is not alone in this error.

III. INTERPRETATION LEADS ASTRAY

Fish and Dworkin are united in their view that legal practice is best viewed as an interpretive enterprise. In this way, they are one in their belief that understanding – whether it is law or the speech of another – depends on the activity of interpretation. This idea – that all understanding is interpretation – is pervasive in today's intellectual culture. Alas, the idea is fundamentally flawed. As I suggested long ago, because Fish and Dworkin share this view, their legal theories are defective.[32]

The idea that all understanding involves interpretation starts with Nietzsche. In *The Will to Power*, Nietzsche articulates his 'perspectivism' in clear and bold terms. He writes:

> 'Everything is subjective,' you say; but even this is interpretation. The 'subject' is not something given, it is something added and invented and projected behind what there is. – Finally, is it necessary to posit an interpreter behind the interpretation? Even this is invention, hypothesis.
>
> In so far as the word 'knowledge' has any meaning, the world is knowable; but it is interpretable otherwise, it has no meaning behind it, but countless meanings. – 'Perspectivism'.

---

[30] J Culler, *On Deconstruction: Theory and Criticism After Structuralism* (Ithaca, Cornell University Press, 1982) 68.

[31] Astutely, Postema makes the same observation about Dworkin. See GJ Postema, '"Protestant" Interpretation and Social Practices' (1987) 6 *Law and Philosophy* 283:

> While there is much language in Law's Empire that suggests otherwise, the details of Dworkin's theory of interpretation – with which he sought 'to throw discipline' over the 'mysterious' and 'unstructured' idea of 'law as craft' – threaten to reduce participants in a common practice to windowless social monads. (ibid 301 quoting Dworkin (n 1) 10).

[32] See Patterson (n 20) chs 5 and 6.

It is our needs that interpret the world; our drives and their For and Against. Every drive is a kind of lust to rule; each one has its perspective that it would like to compel all the other drives and accept as a norm.[33]

I have argued elsewhere that Nietzsche's view on interpretation spawned two lines of philosophical thought in the hermeneutical tradition.[34] That intellectual history is not necessary to the point I want to make about Dworkin and Fish and I shall not go into detail here. Following Vincent Descombes,[35] I want to make the case that the very idea that one cannot understand without first interpreting is a deeply flawed notion. It is this idea that unites the views of Dworkin and Fish. It is equally implausible for each and, as such, undermines their claim that their view enhances our understanding of law. Quite the contrary.

The argument against the notion that all understanding is the product of interpretation is, of course, taken from Wittgenstein. As I have elsewhere made the case,[36] Wittgenstein famously argues that the idea of understanding grounded in interpretation is a non-starter. Although he advanced two arguments for this claim in *Philosophical Investigations*,[37] the most well-known argument is the infinite regress argument. He wrote:

> This was our paradox: no course of action could be determined by a rule, because any course of action can be made out to accord with the rule. The answer was: if any action can be made out to accord with the rule, then it can also be made out to conflict with it. And so there would be neither accord nor conflict here.
>
> It can be seen that there is a misunderstanding here from the mere fact that in the course of our argument we give one interpretation after another; as if each one contented us at least for a moment, until we thought of yet another standing behind it. What this shows is that there is a way of grasping a rule which is not an interpretation, but which is exhibited in what we call 'obeying the rule' and 'going against it' in actual cases.
>
> Hence, there is an inclination to say: any action according to the rule is an interpretation. But we ought to restrict the term 'interpretation' to the substitution of one expression of the rule for another.[38]

For Wittgenstein, the linguistic sense of signs resides in practices. Meaning arises out of the intersubjective use of linguistic symbols the sense of which is a function of their shared use in practices. Everything from texts, signposts and

---

[33] F Nietzsche, *The Will to Power* (W Kaufmann ed, W Kaufmann and RJ Hollingdale trans, New York, Random House, 1967) 267.

[34] D Patterson, 'Postema, Dworkin and the Question of Meaning' in T Bustamante and TL Decat (eds), *Philosophy of Law as an Integral Part of Philosophy: Essays on the Jurisprudence of Gerald J. Postema* (Oxford, Hart Publishing, 2020).

[35] V Descombes, 'Nietzsche's French Moment' in L Ferry and A Renaut (eds), *Why We Are Not Nietzscheans* (Robert de Loaiza tr, Chicago, University of Chicago Press, 1997).

[36] Patterson (n 20).

[37] Meredith Williams makes the case for two arguments about rule-following in M Williams, *Wittgenstein, Mind and Meaning* (London, Routledge, 1999) 157–187.

[38] L Wittgenstein, *Philosophical Investigations* (GE Anscombe tr, Oxford, Blackwell, 2001) 201.

numbers all have meaning in virtue of their use in practices. The key to learning meaning is acquiring the repertoire of behaviours that accompany the use of signs in practices. Meaning is, at bottom, a social phenomenon and not the product of interpretation, individual or otherwise.

It is vitally important to understand that Wittgenstein does not rule out interpretation: far from it. What he rejects is a *foundational* place for interpretation in a proper account of linguistic meaning. The point cannot be made any clearer than the way Descombes articulates it. Hermeneutics puts the operation of interpretation between signs and meaning. The difference between the wild and sober dimensions of hermeneutics is a function of what is built into 'interpretation'. It can be 'politics' (Foucault and Derrida) or 'prejudice' (Gadamer). What unites both dimensions of the hermeneutic perspective is the foundational or constitutive role of interpretation in the production of meaning.

Like Heidegger, Gadamer, Foucault and Derrida, Fish and Dworkin think that something must come between signs and meaning. That something is 'interpretation'. As Descombes reminds us, what is lost in the hermeneutical point of view is a crucial distinction, that between understanding and interpretation. This is the difference between directly accessible meaning (understanding) and meaning that is accessible only by way of inference (interpretation). Understanding 'is not a mental episode parallel to the reading of the printed signs'.[39] Rather, it is the demonstration of a capacity.

What, you might ask, is wrong with privileging interpretation in the way Fish and Dworkin do? Many people do it in their work, why can't they? The person who best answers this question is Gerald Postema.[40] Taking his cue from Wittgenstein, Postema shows how Dworkin fundamentally misunderstands the nature of legal practice. The misunderstanding, as Postema makes admirably clear, is philosophical in nature. Dworkin's characterisation of legal practice evinces a fundamental misunderstanding of the enterprise. In short, Dworkin's view obscures when it should enlighten.

Postema uses Wittgensteinian's trope of understanding as embedded in social practices to great effect. Understanding a practice is 'mastery of a discipline'. Ability is a matter of 'shared capacity'. Disagreement – especially interpretive disagreement – takes place against the background of a world of 'common meanings'. 'Conflict always presupposes consensus',[41] and so on.

IV. THE VANTAGE POINT OF THE PRESENT

The great debate in legal philosophy has been between positivists and antipositivists. Dworkin, of course, is the arch antipositivist. But Fish is as well, albeit in

---

[39] Descombes (n 35) 81.
[40] See Postema (n 31).
[41] ibid 316–18.

a completely different way than Dworkin. And yet, as I have said throughout this chapter, they each share a premise in their accounts of legal practice, the notion that all understanding of law is the product of interpretation. This claim, I have argued, is profoundly mistaken.

As I have argued previously,[42] most legal questions require no interpretation. There are easy cases and they are easy for a reason: any competent lawyer will marshal the same legal materials and quickly come to the same conclusion. Similarly, there is pervasive agreement among lawyers, judges, and officials over what law requires. Fish and Dworkin would have us believe that this pervasive agreement is the product of Baroque machinations of how best to interpret legal materials. But, as I have argued, there are no such machinations.

Perhaps Dworkin and Fish think that most lawyers are wrong about legal practice. Perhaps the thought is that the entirety of the legal profession is systematically incorrect about what they are doing. Perhaps we are all always engaged in a three-step program of constructive interpretation or proceeding from the unspoken premises of our interpretive community, however understood. A theory of law has to both explain how lawyers agree and how they disagree. We could employ Occam's Razor in choosing an explanation but that is just a rule of thumb. Better to look at the ways in which lawyers decide what to dispute and how those disputes are resolved. Those argumentative practices have to figure in any explanation of legal practice.[43] Otherwise, one is simply engaged in a seminar room fantasy.

V. CONCLUSION

What can one learn from the Fish/Dworkin debate? As with so many debates in philosophy, declaring a winner is a fraught enterprise. Each scored some good points and, at the end of the day, few minds were changed. The exchanges between the two were mostly indirect but it was clear that despite all the dust flying, they had at least one central claim in common. It is to that aspect of their debate that I have written this chapter. The lack of consensus at the time of the Fish/Dworkin debate remains. All we can hope for is a measure of clarity about what we disagree about.

---

[42] Patterson (n 20) 92–4.
[43] A particularly compelling example is Watson (n 3). In this article, Watson explains why Mark Greenberg's 'Moral Impact Theory' fails to explain the law as we find it and, for that reason (and others), it fails.

12

Almost Naturalism: The Jurisprudence of Ronald Dworkin

DAN PRIEL*

I. UP IN THE AIR, IT'S ALL IN THE GAME

STANLEY FISH MUST count himself lucky: He was an English professor when universities still cared about English professors. And so, by all accounts, he got to fly a lot. I wonder sometimes whether in the hours he spent in the air, Fish ever thought about airplanes, and especially about what it is that keeps them flying. I think about this when I read his critical comments on others. Because ultimately, when one gets down to it, whether it is Richard Posner, or Richard Rorty, or David Irving, Fish makes one point.[1] With the persistence of a batting ram hurled at a castle's gate, and with about as much subtlety, his point is this: there is no escaping the discourse, the language game. Evaluation is only possible within a particular discourse. Reality (sorry, 'reality') is refracted through a discourse. 'It's all in the game.'[2]

Back when postmodernism was a thing, this excited a lot of people, and enraged a lot of others. It appears more tiresome now, especially when reading several of Fish's essays one after the other. Oh, here we go again.[3] By the fifth time, you identify a pattern. Fish starts with a friendly summary of his target, showing that they get it. They recognise that meanings are contextual, that arguments and ideas emerge from within a discourse, that language is a game within whose bounds we all play. But then, inevitably, comes the fatal conceit: Fish's target makes a point indicating that something matters to them beyond the game, that we are not just playing a game, but that something beyond the game is at stake. Big mistake! This is where Fish comes in with the same retort.

---

* I thank Thomas Bustamante for his comments on an earlier draft.
[1] *cf* D Lodge, *Small World* (London, Penguin, 1985) 200 ('It's a wonderfully adaptable paper').
[2] S Fish, *There's No Such Thing as Free Speech, and It's a Good Thing, Too* (Oxford, OUP, 1994) 230.
[3] Or in Fish's own words: 'My critique of Greenawalt is, finally, just like my critique of everyone else.' S Fish, *The Trouble with Principle* (Cambridge, MA, Harvard University Press, 1999) 220.

The target failed to grasp the full implications of their own view: trying to go beyond the game is just another move within the game. There is no escaping the game.

When it's all a game, Fish's supposedly scandalous claims begin to look different. When he says that there is no such thing as free speech, *and it's a good thing too*, he does not really mean by it what you might think he does. All he means to say is that any meaningful freedom requires constraints. And this turns out to be a much less radical idea, one that was made, for example, by Lon Fuller decades before him, without the extravagant language.[4] (I guess this shows that Fish was better at the game than Fuller.) Fish gave 'free speech' a different meaning from the one given to it by those who champion it and then proceeded to talk about his own idiosyncratic definition. Labelling *that* 'free speech' has allowed him to sound provocative without really being provocative.

But airplanes are not a game, and what keeps them in the air is not just another practice, equally political and equally dependent on 'faith' as other practices.[5] I will bet good money that if offered the choice between an airplane built using the practice of aviation engineers and another one built on another one, Fish would choose the former every single time; and not just because that was the practice that he, as a upper-middle class American was socialised into. He would have done so, because he enjoyed playing the game, and wanted to keep playing it. Because to play the game one must stay alive. And that is not just a game.

But then, what is it? In one essay, Fish proclaimed to 'have some knowledge' on 16 different topics, from sixteenth- and seventeenth-century English literature via contract law to American television shows.[6] But though 'the American academy' was first on his list, I am not familiar with any serious discussion by him of the place of the faculties of science and engineering within the academy. For all his mockery for intellectuals and their ugly Volvos,[7] Fish was very much like other humanities intellectuals of his era, with little interest in science and technology, beyond treating them as just another practice. He was, of course, an avid user of their products, but because those who made these products did not participate in the game – in his game – they remained transparent to him.

One time, Fish had to face up to physical reality. Following Alan Sokal's famous hoax, Fish published an indignant op-ed in the *New York Times*.

---

[4] See D Priel, 'Lon Fuller's Political Jurisprudence of Freedom' (2014) 10 *Jerusalem Review of Legal Studies* 18, 20–21. Before him, one finds this point also in F Nietzsche, *Beyond Good and Evil* (Marion Faber tr, Oxford, OUP, 1998) 188.

[5] Fish (n 2) 202, 211. Fish spells out the implications of this view: scientific objectivity is the product of greater consensus because certain assumptions 'are simply not in dispute for reasons of history, disciplinary politics, societal expectations, etc'. ibid 205; also 25, 201; S Fish, *Doing What Comes Naturally: Change, Rhetoric, and the Practice of Theory in Literary and Legal Studies* (Durham, NC, Duke University Press, 1989) 298.

[6] S Fish, 'One More Time' in GA Olson and L Worsham (eds), *Postmodern Sophistry: Stanley Fish and the Critical Enterprise* (Albany, NY, SUNY Press, 2004) 265, 265–66.

[7] See Fish (n 2) 273.

Recognising that the audience for this piece called for playing a different game than the one he played on the pages of *Critical Inquiry*, Fish struck a conciliatory tone:

> What sociologists of science say is that of course the world is real and independent of our observations but that accounts of the world are produced by observers and are therefore relative to their capacities, education, training, etc. It is not the world or its properties but the vocabularies in whose terms we know them that are socially constructed – fashioned by human beings – which is why our understanding of those properties is continually changing.[8]

That is not quite what some sociologists of science have said, and you do not need to take my word for it.[9] In fact, it is not quite what Fish had said before.[10] But even in this piece, Fish could not quite bring himself to say, let alone explain, what it was about science that explained its success in providing a true(r) description of reality. Despite scientists' situatedness, their prejudices, their politics, it was their practice, and only their practice, that could keep airplanes from falling to the ground.

On all this, Dworkin was seemingly very far from Fish. Dworkin distanced himself from '"post-modernism" and "anti-foundationalism" and "neo-pragmatism" and other facets of a 'fashionable intellectual style'. Dworkin was on the side of science, objectivity, reality, truth.[11] The testiness of his exchanges with Fish looks like clear evidence of how far apart their positions were. Yet, Dworkin was closer to Fish than one would surmise from reading their works. Dworkin dismissed foundationalism (what he called 'Archimedeanism') and often argued – in a manner bearing more than a passing resemblance to Fish's arguments – that all attempts to present certain arguments as external to a practice must be understood as moves from within the practice. In the end, for Dworkin too there was no escaping the game.[12]

---

[8] S Fish, 'Professor Sokal's Bad Joke', *The New York Times* (21 May 1996) A23, reprinted in S Fish, *Think Again: Contrarian Reflections on Life, Culture, Politics, Religion, Law, and Education* (Princeton, NJ, Princeton University Press, 2015) 93. Fish still said that 'the distinction between baseball and science is not finally so firm' (ibid 94), but the tone of the essay, and the attitude toward science, is clearly different from what one finds in his other writings.

[9] See B Latour, 'Why Has Critique Run out of Steam? From Matters of Fact to Matters of Concern' (2004) 30 *Critical Inquiry* 225.

[10] Fish (n 3) 439, where Fish is clear that the 'strong thesis of anti-foundationalis[m]' is 'the only thesis worth taking seriously'. See also Robertson (n 12) 36–38, for a collection of quotes by Fish on science.

[11] See R Dworkin, 'Objectivity and Truth: You'd Better Believe It' (1996) 26 *Philosophy and Public Affairs* 87, 89 (cited as Dworkin, 'Objectivity'); and targeting Fish in R Dworkin, *Justice in Robes* (Cambridge, MA, Harvard University Press, 2006) 43–48 (cited as Dworkin, *JR*).

[12] R Dworkin, *Law's Empire* (Cambridge, MA, Harvard University Press, 1986) 78–85, 266–71 (cited as Dworkin, *LE*); Dworkin, 'Objectivity' (n 1) 89–94. Fish noticed this similarity. In an otherwise hostile review of *Law's Empire*, Fish singled out the 'excellent ten pages' arguing that all critique is internal. See Fish (n 3) 370. Alas, Fish then made his signature move, contending that Dworkin committed the very error he warned against in the rest of his book. ibid 371. It is also notable that one commentator used distinctly Dworkinian language to describe Fish's views: 'we

There is, of course, one important difference between Dworkin and Fish. Fish does not believe in the power of ideas, whereas Dworkin believed in little else. Fish is the champion of spontaneous 'just doing it', Dworkin the believer in theoretical reflection and its ability to improve practice.[13] For Fish, pragmatism means that there is nothing beyond the practice; that, in turn, means that theoretical reflection on the practice must either be understood as part of the practice or is irrelevant to it. The professional baseball player, the top-flight lawyer, and the moral philosophers should all take a page from the aspiring pianist asking for directions to Carnegie Hall.

But if we take seriously Fish's stance, then he cannot even criticise those who engage in the activities he considers pointless, for the only way for him to understand what they are doing is as a manifestation of the practice, in which case his own critique is an external critique that they should ignore. To paraphrase Dennis Martinez's sentence that Fish made famous, 'what else could they do?'[14] Theorising is much part of the practice, and thus telling people they are wasting their time when engaging in it in the hope of improving the practice, is itself an external observation on their practice. (Once you learn how to play Fish's game, you can play it on anyone, even on Fish.)

To make the same point differently, if everything that happens, and especially the countless examples of legal theorising (in judicial opinions, in academic articles, in popular media) confirms Fish's account, then it is vacuous. Just as he did with free speech, Fish's argument rests on subtly changing the term of the debate in such a way as to produce an irrefutable account which cannot be disconfirmed by any evidence. To salvage Fish's ideas from vacuity, we can try and read him as suggesting that reflection and deliberation are useless or even counterproductive.[15] Understood in this way, Fish is advancing a testable hypothesis. And while there is some support for the claim that in certain contexts deliberation can lead to worse performance,[16] there are many counterexamples that undercut Fish's hypothesis. To continue on my earlier theme, science – which is a form theorising – provides a host of examples disproving Fish's claim.[17] It also raises a more general question that Fish never grapples

---

cannot subject all of our beliefs to skepticism because we cannot achieve an Archimedean position outside of our beliefs from which we could scrutinize them all'. See M Robertson, *Stanley Fish on Philosophy, Politics and Law: How Fish Works* (Cambridge, CUP, 2014) 26.

[13] For the argument that even here Dworkin and Fish may be closer to each other than they seem see ch 9 in this volume.

[14] See Fish (n 3) 372.

[15] See ibid 388 ('theory is superfluous').

[16] See G Gigernzer, *Gut Feeling: Shortcuts to Better Decision Making* (London, Penguin, 2008). Fish will be especially fond of Gigernzer's example of catching a flying ball. See ibid 9–12.

[17] Given Fish's fondness for baseball examples, he could benefit from M Lewis, *Moneyball: The Art of Winning an Unfair Game* (New York, WW Norton, 2003) especially chs 4, 8; *cf* N Silver, *The Signal and the Noise: Why So Many Predictions Fail – but Some Don't* (London, Penguin, 2012) ch 3. Part of the problem is that when Fish disparages 'theory' he never seems to think of empirical science.

with. To argue, as Fish does, that we find ourselves captured within an inescapable practice that shapes how we see things and what we think, leaves him incapable of explaining why one practice – science – succeeded where others failed to understand and transform the external reality outside its discourse.[18] If, as Fish has argued, objectivity is nothing but a contingent and temporary consensus by members of a particular (powerful) community, it must be just an odd coincidence that planes stay in the air.

Acknowledging physical reality put Dworkin on firmer ground, but it also had its weak points. For if science is a successful model of a practice capable of discovering objective truths, it is natural to think that we should adopt its methods to answer all other questions. This idea, which I take to be central to philosophical naturalism, was a position that Dworkin rejected. In his writings on objectivity and truth of moral and political discourse, Dworkin resisted this idea. The methods of science, he said, should be confined to the domain of factual inquiry, not for the wholly different inquiry about how we should live.

This debate that Dworkin had with Fish seemed to have passed with little commentary from most legal philosophers. As far as they were concerned, their debate about the nature of law had little or no bearing on these questions. Perhaps they even felt that in the debate over objectivity of morality, they were on the same side as Dworkin. What Dworkin's jurisprudential adversaries did not appreciate is how Dworkin's discussions of these issues are relevant for understanding his jurisprudential views. For it is in his exchanges with Fish that helps bring to light his philosophical presuppositions and how different they are from those of most of his jurisprudential adversaries. In short, understanding Dworkin's position on objectivity helps in understanding his critique of legal positivism, and also why his own view was so deeply misunderstood.

II. DWORKIN'S JURISPRUDENTIAL PRAGMATISM

A friend once told me, that a friend had once told him, that Dworkin had once told him that his work was an attempt to apply Quine's ideas to the legal domain. I provide the provenance of this story, as I cannot vouch for its veracity. However, there is some direct evidence for this idea, coming from Dworkin himself. In a letter to Neil Duxbury, he wrote of his strong belief that 'Quine, with whom I studied as an undergraduate, and other American philosophers of language and mind, had a more direct influence on me than any academic lawyer.'[19] And for

---

[18] For an attempt to tackle this question see RA Posner, *The Problematics of Moral and Legal Theory* (Cambridge, MA, Harvard University Press, 1999) chs 1–2. For his effort, Posner too received the Fish treatment. See Fish (n 2) 209–14.

[19] Letter from Ronald Dworkin to Neil Duxbury (12 June 1992) 1. I thank Neil Duxbury for supplying me with a copy of the letter.

what it is worth, Dworkin was memorable enough to Quine that he mentioned him in a letter to Lon Fuller.[20]

These anecdotes do not amount to an argument, they are (at best) leads, but I think they are important leads because they suggest a different way of understanding Dworkin's project, and a more profound way of understanding his rejection of legal positivism. I want to suggest that the most fundamental philosophical difference between Dworkin and most other analytic legal philosophers with whom he sparred was that he adopted a pragmatist approach to jurisprudence, whereas they did not.

It may seem odd to call Dworkin a pragmatist, as he rarely if ever discussed any of its 'classic' exponents and dissociated himself from many self-styled contemporary legal proponents, most notably Posner and Fish.[21] In *Law's Empire*, 'pragmatism' is the name Dworkin gave to one of the approaches to law that he considered and rejected before presenting his own law-as-integrity.[22] But pragmatism is notoriously ambiguous and Dworkin distancing himself from some of its sense does not imply the rejection of all. In fact, upon examination Dworkin's links to pragmatist philosophy are noteworthy, and to some extent have been noted.[23] I am particularly interested in the relationship between Dworkin's ideas and Quine's,[24] which have so far received relatively little attention.[25]

To see how Dworkin's arguments echo Quine's brand of pragmatism, one can look at the way Dworkin framed what he considered the most basic

---

[20] See letter from WV Quine to Lon L Fuller (26 November 1953) 2 (Lon Fuller Papers, Harvard Law School Library).

[21] Dworkin, *JR* (n 11) chs 2–3. Fish (n 2) 215, characteristically, disavows the label, but clearly accepts the anti-foundationalist message and chastises others for not carrying it to its logical conclusion.

[22] See Dworkin, *LE* (n 12) ch 5. The hallmark of what Dworkin called 'pragmatism' is forward-looking consequentialism. ibid 155–56, 159–60; Dworkin, *JR* (n 1) 21. Posner (rightly) dismissed this as a misrepresentation of the views of actual pragmatists. See RA Posner, *Law, Pragmatism, and Democracy* (Cambridge, MA, Harvard University Press, 2003) 338.

[23] See H Nye, 'Staying Busy While Doing Nothing? Dworkin's Complicated Relationship with Pragmatism' (2016) 29 *Canadian Journal of Law and Jurisprudence* 71; TL Decat, 'Inferentialist Pragmatism and Dworkin's Law as Integrity' (2015) 8 *Erasmus Law Review* 14. Neither work mentions Quine, who is central to my discussion below.

[24] On Quine's relationship with pragmatism see HJ Koskinen and S Pihlström, 'Quine and Pragmatism' (2006) 42 *Transactions of the Charles S. Peirce Society* 309; P Godfrey-Smith, 'Quine and Pragmatism' in G Harman and E Lepore (eds), *A Companion to W.V.O. Quine* (New York, Wiley Blackwell, 2014) 54. I am not particularly wedded to the label, so if Dworkin, Quine (or both) do not count as 'real' pragmatists, so be it.

[25] Brief remarks on some similarities between Quine and Dworkin are found in CL Barzun, 'Justice Souter's Common Law' (2018) 104 *Virginia Law Review* 655, 688; J Coleman, 'Incorporationism, Conventionality, and the Practical Difference Thesis' in J Coleman (ed), *Hart's Postscript: Essays on the Postscript to The Concept of Law* (Oxford, OUP, 2001) 99, 125 fn 42. A more critical discussion is B Leiter, *Naturalizing Jurisprudence: Essays on American Legal Realism and Naturalism in Legal Philosophy* (Oxford, OUP, 2007) 230–32.

jurisprudential question, which for him was not the more familiar 'What is law?' or 'What are the criteria of legal validity?', but rather, 'What makes it the case that a given legal proposition is true?' No less significant is how he answered this question. The standard way of thinking about jurisprudence, especially common among legal positivists, is foundationalist in nature. It presupposes that the question 'what is law?' has one answer, discovered by philosophical reflection, and that this philosophical inquiry enjoys logical priority over legal questions (what is the law in Germany?), sociological questions (why people obey the law?), and normative questions (should this law be followed?).[26]

The dominance of the foundationalist project among legal philosophers has led many to assume that Dworkin adopted it as well. Consequently, his challenges to legal positivism were 'translated' into the foundationalist framework of legal positivism with one small change: Dworkin was read as arguing that morality is one of the criteria of legality. This was a misunderstanding of the thrust of Dworkin's challenge from the start, a fact that became abundantly clear only a few years later when Dworkin repudiated the entire foundationalist picture.[27] Yet, for decades afterwards Dworkin's critique has been presented as limited to the question of criteria of legality.

Dworkin's pragmatism rejects the assumption that legal philosophers' questions are distinct from (and prior to) those of lawyers. Dworkin dismissed the idea that there is a unique philosophical question ('what is law?'), insisting instead that this theoretical question is just a more abstract formulation of the practical questions arising in concrete cases. Dworkin also denied that (legal and moral) truth is the product of correspondence between reality and its representation, seeing it instead as in some respect constructed. Finally, he believed that every belief, if pressed by enough other beliefs, can be questioned. This possibility of revising even seemingly foundational ideas is itself an illustration of the pragmatic stance, of the way that coherence is the product of human effort to *bring* our beliefs into a coherent scheme.

Dworkin made only a few references to Quine in his writings,[28] but Dworkin was always rather stingy with his citations to others. Despite the paucity of references, it is not difficult to see similarities between the ideas just mentioned and Quine's. Dworkin contrasted 'utopian' political philosophies that started from 'first principles' with his own project geared toward integrity that worked within

---

[26] For examples of endorsement of this view see J Raz, 'The Purity of the Pure Theory of Law' (1979) 35 *Revue Internationale de Philosophie* 441, 442; J Gardner, *Law as a Leap of Faith: Essays on Law in General* (Oxford, OUP, 2011) 275–76. In a somewhat different way, this view is also found in Scott J Shapiro, *Legality* (Cambridge, MA, Harvard University Press, 2011) 25.

[27] R Dworkin, *Taking Rights Seriously*, rev edn (Cambridge, MA, Harvard University Press, 1978) 76 (cited below as Dworkin, *TRS*).

[28] ibid 164–65; R Dworkin, *A Matter of Principle* (Cambridge, MA, Harvard University Press 1985) 169–70 (cited below as Dworkin, *AMP*).

an existing political structure which is 'evolutionary rather than axiomatic'.[29] In other words, we do not start with foundations from which we derive further true proposition, but always begin our inquiry *'in medias res'*.[30] The Quinean echoes are evident in remarks like '[a] legal philosopher ... begins his work enjoying a fairly uncontroversial preinterpretive identification of the domain of law, and with tentative paradigms to support his argument', which is then further analysed with the aim of making it more coherent.[31] The other side of this view is that global scepticism is incoherent: 'Skepticism', said Dworkin, 'must be built up from belief of some kind; it can't be skeptical ... all the way down', a view rather similar to one expressed by Quine.[32] And just as Quine emphasised that 'no statement is immune to revision', Dworkin wrote that 'it is part of our common political life, if anything is, that ... any decision about the distribution of any good ... may be reopened, no matter how firm the traditions that are then challenged, that we may always ask of some settled institutional scheme whether it is fair'.[33]

These points are perhaps all tied together to a broader commitment to the continuity between philosophy and practice. Dworkin denied any clear separation between law and jurisprudence, stating that '[j]urisprudence is the general part of adjudication, silent prologue to any decision at law',[34] Quine argued for a similar continuity between science and epistemology.[35] And just as for

---

[29] Dworkin, *LE* (n 12) 164; *cf* WV Quine, *Theories and Things* (Cambridge, MA, Harvard University Press 1981) 67 (repudiates any 'first philosophy prior to natural science').

[30] This expression is found in GJ Postema, 'Melody and Law's Mindfulness of Time' (2004) 17 *Ratio Juris* 203 208–10, whose overall jurisprudential approach resembles Dworkin's in many ways. *Cf* WV Quine, 'Reply to Paul A. Roth' in LE Hahn and PA Schlipp (eds), *The Philosophy of W.V. Quine*, expanded edn (Chicago, IL, Open Court, 1986) 459, 461. A clear example of a foundationalist's failure to understand this philosophical position for what it is, is John Gardner's disparaging remark (naming Postema and clearly taking aim at Dworkin as well) that its proponents treat legal philosophy as 'the back-room activity of identifying what is good or bad about legal practice'. Gardner (n 26) 24. This characterisation does not even qualify as a caricature.

[31] Dworkin, *LE* (n 12) 92; *cf* Quine (n 29) 72 ('The naturalistic philosopher begins his reasoning within the inherited world theory as a going concern. He tentatively believes all of it, but believes also that some unidentified portions are wrong. He tries to improve, clarify, and understand the system from within. He is the busy sailor adrift on Neurath's boat.').

[32] Dworkin, 'Objectivity' (n 11) 88; *cf* WV Quine, 'The Nature of Natural Knowledge' in S Guttenplan (ed), *Mind and Language* (Oxford, Clarendon, 1975) 67, 67 ('Illusions are illusions only relative to a prior acceptance of genuine bodies with which to contrast them.').

[33] WV Quine, 'Two Dogmas of Empiricism' (1951) 60 *Philosophical Review* 20, 40; Dworkin, *AMP* (n 28) 219; see also Dworkin, *TRS* (n 27) 164–65; *cf* DH Souter, 'Harvard Commencement Remarks', available at news.harvard.edu/gazette/story/2010/05/text-of-justice-david-souters-speech/ ('our cases can give no answers that fit all conflicts, and no resolutions immune to rethinking when the significance of old facts may have changed in the changing world'). Interestingly, Souter's intellectual background, like Dworkin's, traces to ideas percolating at the Harvard philosophy department around the same period. See Barzun (n 25) 689–91.

[34] Dworkin, *LE* (n 12) 90.

[35] WVO Quine, *Word and Object* (Cambridge, MA, MIT Press, 1960) 275–76 ('The philosopher's task differs from the others'... in detail, but in no such drastic way as those suppose who imagine for the philosopher a vantage point outside the conceptual scheme he takes in charge. There is no such cosmic exile'); Quine (n 33) 43 ('Ontological questions ... are on a par with questions of natural

Dworkin, jurisprudence was not concerned with the pursuit of knowledge for its own sake but was connected to the practical question of the justification of coercion, for Quine the ultimate justification of the pursuit of knowledge was the practical desire to stay alive.

III. DWORKIN FOR NATURALISTS?

Apart from filling a gap in intellectual history, these similarities are interesting because Quine is considered one of the leading lights of twentieth-century naturalistic philosophy and almost synonymous with a rather strong program of naturalising epistemology. Now, if Quine is a naturalist, and Dworkin modelled his ideas after Quine's, there is perhaps room for finding some kind of alliance between Dworkin and jurisprudential naturalists. At first, this may look like a hopeless attempt at naturalism by proxy, since Dworkin is not quite the name that springs to mind when thinking about naturalism in jurisprudence. For one, in what is often taken to be the most fundamental jurisprudential divide, between legal positivism and natural law theory, Dworkin is usually placed in the latter category. And as natural law theory is often seen, with some basis, as hostile to naturalism,[36] the case for seeing Dworkin as an anti-naturalist seems open and shut. But both pillars of the argument are shaky: on the natural law side, one can reconstruct natural law theory in naturalistic terms;[37] and a closer inspection, the relationship between Dworkin and 'standard' natural law theory is tenuous at best.[38]

There are better reasons for a naturalist to take issue with some of Dworkin's ideas, and I will consider them below. I make this point early on, so that the discussion that follows not be misunderstood for the claim that Dworkin was a naturalist. Nevertheless, I believe the links already noted between Dworkin's jurisprudence and Quine's philosophy are of interest for jurisprudential naturalists. I will focus on three interrelated ideas: the rejection of conceptual analysis, a pragmatist account of law and morality as practices, and a coherentist account of law. In addition to explaining why aspects of Dworkin's work are amenable to jurisprudential naturalists, they further bolster my claim in the previous section of the similarities between Dworkin and Quine.

---

science'); WV Quine, *Ontological Relativity and Other Essays* (New York, Columbia University Press, 1969) 82–83; WV Quine, *The Ways of Paradox and Other Essays*, rev edn (Cambridge, MA, Harvard University Press, 1976) 253 (epistemology is 'not logically prior … to common sense or to the refined common sense which is science').

[36] JL Coleman, *The Practice of Principle: In Defence of a Pragmatist Approach to Legal Theory* (Oxford, OUP, 2001) 214.

[37] See D Priel, 'The Possibility of Naturalistic Jurisprudence: Legal Positivism and Natural Law Theory Revisited' (2017) 32 *Revus* 7, 21–24.

[38] Dworkin's references to natural law theory are brief and not particularly friendly. See, eg, Dworkin, *LE* (n 12) 35–36.

A. Rejection of Conceptual Jurisprudence and the Search for the Boundaries of Law

Relatively late in his career, Dworkin explicitly stated that he found conceptual jurisprudence a pointless, uninteresting and unimportant exercise,[39] but I think what he said there was merely a more explicit statement of what had been his view all along. One rather obvious piece of evidence in support of my contention is that if you search in Dworkin's writings you will not find anywhere any statement about criteria of legality or anything that resembles the kind of conceptual inquiry that legal positivists have placed at the centre of jurisprudence.[40] One conceptual view often attributed to him – that morality is always a criterion of legality (making Dworkin a conceptual natural lawyer) – is one that he dismissed in a manner no different from legal positivists: 'Many lawyers ... believe that the progressive income tax is unjust ..., but none of them doubts that the law of these countries does impose tax at progressive rates.'[41] Beyond this, from very early on Dworkin refused to play the 'what is law?' game on conceptual legal philosophers' terms. When he finally answered it in the concluding paragraph of *Law's Empire*, his answer does not address any conceptualist questions over criteria of validity.[42]

Though the arguments Dworkin offered in support of his dismissal of the conceptual enterprise were rather brief, and in my view incomplete, they are remarkably similar to those made by naturalists. It is worth reviewing briefly some of Dworkin's critical comments about conceptual jurisprudence and those of avowed naturalist (and harsh Dworkin critic) Brian Leiter.[43] Leiter begrudgingly acknowledged that Dworkin dismissed the debate about the boundaries of law. But rather than seeing him as an ally in the futile and misguided search for the conceptual boundaries of law, Leiter distanced himself from Dworkin's arguments, arguing that they rest on 'a wild fabrication of the

---

[39] See Dworkin, *JR* (n 11) 5, 185–86, 213, 240.

[40] It is true, as Thomas Bustamante pointed out to me, that in *TRS* (n 27) vii, Dworkin says that a theory of law 'must be normative as well as conceptual'. Even here, however, the idea is spelled out quite differently from the way it is understood by legal positivists, since Dworkin makes it clear that the conceptual and the normative questions are interdependent. ibid viii. As explained further in the text, Dworkin has shown no interest in the standard conceptual question of the criteria of legal validity.

[41] Dworkin, *LE* (n 12) 36. In a later book, Dworkin flipped the example. See Dworkin, *JR* (n 1) 5 ('The rates of taxation in the United States are now manifestly unjust, but the propositions that describe these rates are nevertheless true'). In brief remarks on whether the Nazis had law, Dworkin considered it as a verbal question dispute that depended on one's perspective. See Dworkin, *LE* (n 12) 103–04. This shows that if understood as competing views about the criteria of legal validity, Dworkin dismissed both legal positivism and natural law theory.

[42] Dworkin, *LE* (n 2) 413.

[43] See B Leiter, 'The Demarcation Problem in Jurisprudence: A New Case for Skepticism' in J Ferrer Beltrán et al (eds), *Neutrality and Theory of Law* (Cham, Springer, 2013) 161. As Leiter has also drawn on Quine's ideas, the similarity of their views is unlikely to be coincidental.

positivist position', namely that 'the positivist solution to the Demarcation Problem entails claims about how judges should decide particular cases'.[44] This is not true. Dworkin's arguments did not rest on the consequences of the demarcation but challenged the plausibility of the enterprise itself. Like Leiter, Dworkin argued that what law is cannot be articulated by a set of essential criteria; both described the enterprise as 'scholastic'.[45] As part of his attempt to give some credit to the work of legal philosophers who engaged in the demarcation problem, Leiter suggested that it was 'practical consideration[s]' such as what to do when facing morally objectionable laws that 'animate[d] interest in the Demarcation Problem'.[46] This is remarkably similar to Dworkin's suggestion – strenuously resisted by most legal positivists – that legal positivism is (or at least used to be) motivated by practical considerations.[47]

Dworkin and Leiter used virtually identical language to explain why the search for the essential features of law is misguided. Here is Dworkin: 'Legal systems are not natural kinds ... that have essences. They are social kinds: to suppose that law has an essence is as much a mistake as supposing that marriage or community has an essence.'[48] Concepts of this kind do not have an 'essential nature ... given by physical or biological structure or something comparable'.[49] Writing a few years later, here is Leiter: 'law is not a natural kind like water or wolverine, since it has no distinctive micro-constitution, one that could be specified by one of the natural sciences'.[50] Just like Dworkin considered law to be an 'interpretive concept' Leiter argued that law is a 'hermeneutic concept'. Both agreed that such concepts have a history and a sociology but no unchanging set of essential features. Dworkin called to stop the 'waste of time' involved in much of jurisprudence and 'take up instead how the decisions that in any case will be made should be made'. Leiter issue a similar call to 'abandon the Demarcation Problem in favor of arguing about *what ought to be done*'.[51]

These similarities are not accidental. They are a product of a similar commitment to the idea that what belongs to the practice is itself a practical

---

[44] Leiter (n 42) 173–74. Incidentally, at least some positivists have argued that the demarcation problem is relevant for precisely the reason Leiter described as a 'fabrication'. See, eg, Shapiro (n 26) 25.
[45] Dworkin, *JR* (n 11) 213, 240; Leiter (n 43) 174; see also D Priel, 'The Boundaries of Law and the Purpose of Legal Philosophy' (2008) 27 *Law and Philosophy* 643, 683–85.
[46] Leiter (n 43) 174.
[47] Dworkin, *JR* (n 11) 211; Dworkin, *LE* (n 11) 115–16. Leiter sides here with Dworkin against vehement denials that there are any practical motivations behind the search for law's boundaries. See, eg, Gardner (n 26) 183–85.
[48] R Dworkin, 'Hart and the Concepts of Law' (2006) 119 *Harvard Law Review Forum* 95, 95.
[49] Dworkin, *JR* (n 11) 3; see also ibid 215–16.
[50] B Leiter, 'Naturalized Jurisprudence and American Legal Realism Revisited' (2011) 30 *Law and Philosophy* 499, 514.
[51] Dworkin, *JR* (n 11) 36; Leiter (n 43) 174.

matter subject to debate and revision, and not a matter of a priori philosophical determination. As explored below, they are significant not only for situating Dworkin's critique of legal positivism, but for understanding his proposed alternative.

B. A Pragmatist Account of Law and Morality

What about Dworkin's positive agenda? Here, it might be thought that Dworkin's 'moralistic' account of law, together with his robustly metaphysical view of morality, is where he and the naturalist part ways.

Not so fast. Contrary to the widely received view according to which Dworkin was a moral realist who believed that both law and morality are a matter of discovery, Dworkin unequivocally rejected these ideas. In both law and morality Dworkin denied that there are any answers 'out there', hidden in some hidden 'celestial books'.[52] Against this, Dworkin presented the 'constructive model' of morality, which views morality as a communal enterprise created and recreated by participants in the practice. In this model, people have a 'responsibility to fit the particular judgments on which they act into a coherent program of action'. Unlike the natural model, the constructive model does not assume that there is a pre-existing moral order to describe.[53] We strive for coherence *not* because we assume (based on what?) that this is a property of morality in some metaphysical sense. On the contrary, we strive to make morality (and law) coherent *because* there is no external morality to match. We strive for coherence as part of a *human* effort to make our reasons for action part of a broader scheme. A mere personal opinion has no force, unless it is embedded in an interpretation of the practice and shown how it fits in it.

One way of seeing the congruence of Dworkin's thought with naturalism is the extent to which he accepted Mackie's critical arguments about the objectivity of morality. Mackie argued that moral discourse has the appearance of objectivity but that it is grounded in error, since it refers to objects that do not exist.[54] Dworkin fully accepted that there are no 'Platonic' or 'transcendent' moral facts.[55] It follows that if the only way to account for moral objectivity were by appealing to the existence of such entities, Mackie's error theory would be correct. Dworkin's challenge to Mackie was that, in effect, he stopped his inquiry too early, because he thought the only way to account for objective morality was by thinking of it in terms similar to physical reality.

---

[52] Dworkin, *AMP* (n 33) 167; Dworkin, *TRS* (n 7) 216, 337.
[53] Dworkin, *TRS* (n 27) 160. For a detailed exposition of how Dworkin's views fit this conception of law see D Priel, 'Making Sense of Nonsense Jurisprudence', ssrn.com/abstract=3696933.
[54] See JL Mackie, *Ethics: Inventing Right and Wrong* (London, Penguin, 1978) ch 1.
[55] Dworkin, *AMP* (n 33) 138; Dworkin, 'Objectivity' (n 1) 109–10.

But there is more to reality than that. In one place, Dworkin railed against the belief that

> [i]f moral or aesthetic or interpretive judgments have the sense and force they do just because they figure in a collective human enterprise, then such judgments cannot have a 'real' sense and a 'real' truth value which transcend that enterprise and somehow take hold of the 'real' world.[56]

This approach purports to explain the objectivity of morality not in terms of correspondence to external reality but in terms internal to discourse.[57] Political morality is a never-ending practice, the practice of making our different attitudes coherent and objective. Improving our practice by making our moral beliefs more coherent, by aligning them with a community's past and future, is not an inherent feature of morality (that is, a remnant of the Platonism that Dworkin rejected), but the product of human effort.[58]

In such an account the relationship between law and morality is in some ways much deeper than even those who think of morality as a criterion of legality. Law is one of the central places where a community engages in moral deliberation. It is instructive that Dworkin did not see law as striving toward the perfection of morality; rather, he explained morality by analogy to the common law.[59] On this view, what counts as correct in the common law is not the correspondence of a given legal rule to some external standard, but the extent to which it fits within a larger scheme of principles, themselves derived from past cases. And for Dworkin, the same is true of morality as well. Law appears in this account not as a separate domain that imitates morality, but as one of the main places where humans engage in the enterprise of constructing morality.[60]

---

[56] Dworkin, *AMP* (n 3) 174.

[57] Dworkin, 'Objectivity' (n 11) 89, 103–05.

[58] Contra S Hershovitz, 'Integrity and Stare Decisis' in S Hershovitz (ed), *Exploring Law's Empire* (Oxford, OUP, 2006) 103, 114, 115, who attributes to Dworkin the view that 'we demand integrity because, whatever doubt we have about particular moral views, we are confident that the demands of morality are coherent ....We want the state (and derivatively, its courts) to act in accord with a single, coherent set of principles for the same reason we want individuals to do so'. But for Dworkin, coherence is a constraint imposed on the deliberations of a *political community*. Dworkin explicitly stated that he 'supplied no reason for thinking that the constructive model offers a good account of private moral reasoning', because he is 'unclear that any form of coherence theory, whether based on the constructive or natural model, would be adequate for that'. Dworkin, *TRS* (n 27) 353; see also ibid, 163; R Dworkin, 'Justice for Hedgehogs' (2010) 90 *Boston University Law Review* 469, 476–77.

[59] See Dworkin, *TRS* (n 27) 160. This makes Dworkin a proponent of what Postema called 'common law theory', albeit with a protestant twist. See GJ Postema, 'The Philosophy of the Common Law' in JL Coleman and SJ Shapiro (eds), *The Oxford Handbook of Jurisprudence and the Philosophy of Law* (Oxford, OUP, 2002) 588; see also D Priel, 'Not All Law Is an Artifact: Jurisprudence Meets the Common Law' in L Burazin et al (eds), *Law as an Artifact* (Oxford, OUP, 2018) 239; Priel (n 3), part IV.(A).

[60] See Dworkin, *AMP* (n 33) 170; R Dworkin, *Justice for Hedgehogs* (Cambridge, MA, Harvard University Press, 2011) 92 (cited as Dworkin, *JH*); and also Dworkin, *JR* (n 11) 264 fn 7, where Dworkin talks about concepts becoming interpretive. For a detailed discussion of this idea see Priel (n 53), part III.(d).

This is obviously a contested understanding of morality and law, but it reflects a genuine effort to explain certain features of moral discourse – its ubiquity and inescapability, its appearance of objectivity, and its surface-level cognitivism – without invoking any non-natural entities. Morality on this view is a thoroughly communal enterprise, one in which in one way or another we all participate in constructing.

C. Coherentism

That Dworkin is a coherentist is not news. There are two facets to his legal coherentism, although they may be just two ways of expressing the same idea. First, he is a coherentist with respect to legal knowledge (and thus also justification); second, coherence is a political requirement that should guide legislators and judges. In the first sense, it helps to contrast his view with the standard positivist picture. Legal positivism, with its search for criteria of validity, was a foundationalist view, an attempt to identify the properties that all laws have independently of any practical question. By contrast, in the most canonical statements of his position, Dworkin explained that what counted as law could not be separated from the substantive question of the content of law: 'According to law as integrity, propositions of law are true if they figure in or follow from the principles of justice, fairness, and procedural due process that provide the best constructive interpretation of the community's legal practice.'[61]

To see the difference between the two views, it might be helpful to compare two visual metaphors. A popular visual metaphor for Kelsen's legal positivism is as a pyramid of norms, where each legal norm gains its normative force from a norm higher up in the hierarchy.[62] Municipal bylaws are laws in virtue of powers to make law granted by a national legislature, whose own powers come from a constitution. At the apex of the pyramid is the basic norm. In the complete Kelsenian picture, states' law-making powers are derived from international law; and, at the other end, contracts are fitted into this picture as delegated law-making powers granted to individuals. Thus, in the most ideal version of Kelsen's account, all legal norms of all legal systems are ultimately derived from a universal basic norm. Importantly, the pyramid is 'formal' (or in Kelsen's term, 'dynamic') in the sense that the content of 'lower' legal norms is not a matter of deduction from higher legal norms. Hart's picture is not nearly quite as neat as Kelsen's. Hart also stressed his account's empirical, sociological, foundations against Kelsen's hypothetical ones. But for Hart, legality is a foundationalist idea: a norm is legal to the extent that it is recognised, directly or indirectly, by the rule of recognition.

---

[61] Dworkin, *LE* (n 12) 225.
[62] The 'pyramid' metaphor did not originate with Kelsen himself, but it is based on his ideas. See H Kelsen, *General Theory of Law and State* (Cambridge, MA, Harvard University Press, 1945) chs 10–11.

Dworkin treated the common law as the model for all law and occasionally described it using the old metaphor of a seamless web.[63] In this image, a norm does not get its normative force from norms higher up in the pyramid but from its place within a network of other mutually supporting norms. It is not that all legal norms are the same, but the strength of a norm does not derive (just) from its formal hierarchical position, but from the strength that its content derives from other norms in the network. This means that the 'validity' of each norm constantly changes as other legal concepts are being reinterpreted, as disparate doctrines are seen as examples of more general ones, as previously powerful concepts are slowly being abandoned. Revisiting even Dworkin's earliest critiques of legal positivism with this in mind, one sees that what he termed 'legal principles' were not simply legal rules employing vague terms but legal standards that gain their normative force from the support they give, and the support they gain, from disparate parts of the law.

The constructive account of morality described above is likewise a rejection of foundationalism in the moral domain:

> Ethics is a complex structure of different goals, achievements, and virtues, and the part each of these plays in that complex structure can only be understood by elaborating its role in an overall design fixed by the others. Until we can see how our ethical values hang together in that way, so that each can be tested against our provisional account of the others, we do not understand any of them.[64]

It is true that Dworkin rejected the 'preposterous' idea that moral truth was a matter of 'coherence for its own sake', but he still maintained that the aim is to achieve 'as much coherence *as we can command*'.[65] This ties to the second, political aspect of Dworkin's pursuit of coherence, which is directly connected to the constructive account of morality that Dworkin presents: if morality were a matter of an external reality we discover, it would be perfectly possible to imagine conflicts within it. When morality is our own work, incoherence is a sign we have not worked hard enough on reconciling them.[66] Coherence is the product of practical reflection, not a description of external reality.

Of course, a naturalist need not be a coherentist, but, once again, the similarities between Dworkin's view and Quine's brand of coherentism are evident. Dworkin's rejection of Archimedeanism is of a piece of Quine's point that there is 'no ... cosmic exile' and that he 'can scrutinize and improve the system from within, appealing to coherence and simplicity'.[67] Just as Quine argued that there is no set of formal criteria we can use to identify true propositions of fact, there is no set of criteria for identifying true propositions of law. In the words of

---

[63] Dworkin, *TRS* (n 27) 115. Quine, of course, spoke of the web of belief. See WV Quine and JS Ullian, *The Web of Belief*, 2nd edn (New York, Random House, 1978); *cf* Quine (n 3) 39 (the totality of knowledge is 'a man-made fabric').
[64] Dworkin, *JR* (n 1) 160–61.
[65] ibid 162 (emphasis added).
[66] ibid 110–11; *cf* Dworkin, *LE* (n 12) 134–35.
[67] Quine, *Word and Object* (n 35) 275–76.

Dworkin '[t]here is no paradox in the proposition that facts both depend on and constrain the theories that explain them.'[68] Both Dworkin and Quine shared the view that this implies that all propositions, no matter how seemingly secure, are potentially subject to revision, by showing how a currently popular view, or a currently 'controlling' precedent, is inconsistent with deeper commitments. This is a process Dworkin called 'justificatory ascent', which may be an allusion to Quine's 'semantic ascent'.[69] Turning to metaphors again, both were fond of invoking image of Neurath's boat, the boat repaired piecemeal at sea as an apt description of the way we revise our beliefs, by holding some constant while fixing the others.[70]

IV. DWORKIN'S ANTI-NATURALISTIC TURN

So far, Dworkin appears surprisingly friendly to many of the concerns of jurisprudential naturalists. Let me stress that even as they stand, these similarities should not be taken with the view that Dworkin was simply 'applied Quine'.[71] However, the main issue where they look far apart is the question of naturalism, with Dworkin adopting an anti-naturalist stance which left him closer to Fish than he would care to admit.[72]

I mentioned earlier that Fish did not say much about science and technology, and that when he did, he was not quite consistent. Dworkin was the same. On the few occasions that he did speak of the sciences, he kept science apart from his own concerns. In a short essay published in 1977, Dworkin dismissed the usefulness of empirical, statistical studies for deciding questions of principle. In explaining why, Dworkin distinguished between 'causal' and 'interpretive' judgments. He explained that the causal judgments are often made using statistical methods, which are far removed from the 'ordinary vocabulary' of judges, whereas interpretive judgments 'must be framed in the critical vocabulary of the community' and are grounded in 'shared understandings that reinforce each other'.[73] Dworkin did not follow this observation with a call for lawyers

---

[68] Dworkin, AMP (n 3) 169; cf WV Quine, *Theories and Things* (Cambridge, MA, Harvard University Press, 1981) 23.

[69] Compare Dworkin, JR (n 12) 52–53 with Quine, *Word and Object* (n 35) 272–73.

[70] Dworkin, LE (n 12) 111, 139; Dworkin, JR (n 11) 161. Quine used this metaphor repeatedly. For an example see n 30.

[71] One issue on which the two may look far apart is that Quine's naturalised epistemology was primarily a descriptive account whereas Dworkin's main concern was justificatory. The 'descriptive' reading of Quine used to be widely accepted and is the one found in Leiter (n 5) 35–36. However, there are good exegetical reasons to be doubtful about it. See R Sinclair, 'Quine on Evidence' in G Harman and E Lepore (eds), *A Companion to W.V.O. Quine* (New York, Wiley Blackwell, 2014) 350, 360–62 and *passim*; M Greenberg, 'Naturalism in Epistemology and the Philosophy of Law' (2011) 30 *Law and Philosophy* 419, 429–32.

[72] This point parallels some of the criticism in Leiter (n 25) 230–32.

[73] R Dworkin, 'Social Sciences and Constitutional Rights – The Consequences of Uncertainty' (1977) 6 *Journal of Law and Education* 3, 6; cf Fish (n 8) 113–14 (computers don't have the human capacity to understand).

to improve their knowledge of statistics; rather, he argued against the use of statistical evidence in constitutional cases. Already here he hinted at an idea that became explicit later: that the causal and the interpretive constituted two separate domains.[74]

Why did Dworkin adopt such a view? In the strictly biographical sense of the question, I have no idea. But if we ask this question in terms of its fit within Dworkin's overall view, they make sense; it is, in fact, an almost inevitable escape route from an otherwise unpalatable conclusion. As mentioned, Dworkin resolved the problem of objectivity of law and morality by arguing that we should understand it not in terms of correspondence to external reality but by reinterpreting them as claims within the discourse. But if we accept Dworkin's claims about the invalidity of external criticism unless reinterpreted as internal criticisms, Dworkin appears open to the charge that this line of argument leads to absurd conclusions: one must interpret 'external' claims against the existence of god(s) as 'internal' theological claims about divine demands or attributes. And those who dismiss astrology as nonsense would have to be understood as denying that next week, if you are not careful, you may get into an argument with your boss.

As a result, Dworkin, whose argument were intended as a challenge to 'postmodernism', looked perilously close to such views. To escape this fate, Dworkin cut up the world into two domains:

> Since astrology and orthodox religion, at least as commonly understood, purport to offer causal explanations they fall within the large intellectual domain of science, and so are subject to causal tests of reliability. Since morality and the other evaluative domains make no causal claims, however, such tests can play no role in any plausible test for them. We do need tests for reliability of our moral opinions, but these must be appropriate to the content of these opinions.[75]

It is here that Dworkin parted ways with Quine and opted for a view closer to that of anti-naturalist pragmatist Hilary Putnam.[76] In his response to Sokal, Fish employed a surprisingly similar strategy:

> [Sokal] thinks that the sociology of science is in competition with mainstream science – wants either to replace it or debunk it – and he doesn't understand that

---

[74] Dworkin, *JR* (n 11) 76–77. Notably, Dworkin denied there the distinction between law and morality as separate domains. See ibid 34–35. Quine wrote almost nothing on ethics. For a few opaque remarks on the relationship between ethics and science see Quine (n 68) 63–64.

[75] Dworkin, 'Objectivity' (n 11) 120; see also ibid 128 ('Morality is a distinct, independent dimension of our experience, and it exercises its own sovereignty'); Dworkin, *JR* (n 11) 76–77 (distinguishing between the domain of moral sociology, anthropology and psychology and the 'conceptually distinct' domain of 'morality itself').

[76] There are striking similarities between Putnam's 'internal realism' and Dworkin's anti-Archimedean objectivity. See H Putnam, *Realism with a Human Face* (Cambridge, MA, Harvard University Press, 1990) chs 1–2, 9–11, and especially H Putnam, *Reason, Truth and History* (Cambridge, CUP, 1981) 49–56. The connection is also noted in T Bustamante, ch 14 in this volume, 264–266. This does not mean their views were identical. *Cf* H Putnam, 'Replies' (1995) 1 *Legal Theory* 69, 75–77 (spelling out problems with Dworkin's view).

it is a distinct enterprise, with objects of study, criteria, procedures and goals all of its own ....Just as the criteria of an enterprise will be internal to its own history, so will the threat to its integrity be internal, posed not by presumptuous outsiders but by insiders who decide not to play by the rules or to put the rules in the service of a devious purpose.[77]

For both Dworkin and Fish this was a strategically useful distinction. By insisting that the domain of science is completely separate from the evaluative domain, Dworkin got himself a quick fix against one potential challenge. Based on these view Dworkin could also argue that no findings about how humans got to form their moral beliefs (the environment one grew up in, human evolutionary history) has any bearing on any moral question we need to answer.[78] But there was a price to pay. In effect, Dworkin established two senses of objectivity, perhaps even two accounts of truth, each relevant for its own domain.[79] For Fish, his response meant he could (when convenient, ie during academic debates) say that he did not doubt the reality of science, and perhaps also (here I am being speculative) answer to his own satisfaction the question of why, even though science was only one discourse among many, he would only set foot in planes built using the discourse of science.

Dworkin and Fish's views are not identical, but they face related problems. At bottom, both re-introduced the distinction between internal and external statements about morality, which both were adamant on dismissing. By insisting on the existence of boundaries to *any* domain and the inapplicability of standards external to it, Fish also adopted a stance inconsistent with his views elsewhere.[80] Fish has to admit that science has managed to develop methods that, however imperfectly realised by all-too-human scientists, have been successful in capturing reality better than others so that now, thanks to science we know more about the world than people did 300 years ago. Denying that, he would be bound to say that his preferred mode of aerial transportation is just a matter of 'traditions of inquiry and demonstration [he] currently ha[s] faith in',[81] and then, I suppose, also be forced to say that methods developed within other 'traditions' are different but not worse.

In a similar fashion, by arguing that morality does not belong to the domain of facts or that it makes no causal claims, by arguing that morality, unlike science,

---

[77] Fish (n 8) 95. A more self-serving reason to favour such a divide is that it allows one to remain ignorant about science.
[78] See Dworkin, *JR* (n 11) 77–78, Dworkin, *JH* (n 60) ch 4, 443, fn 6.
[79] *Cf* Dworkin, *JH* (n 60) 82. There are hints that Dworkin has doubts about Quine's view with respect to science but thinks they make sense with respect to morals. See Dworkin, *JH* (n 60) 154–55.
[80] To be clearer: it will not do to say that it is those 'within' the practice who draw these boundaries, when the very question of the existence (or location) of these boundaries is contested. Is there any other standard for belonging to the domain of the social studies of science than getting published in *Social Text*? No one would have doubted Sokal's membership if his essay – without a single word altered – had been published in earnest. To insist on any other standard would implicate Fish in precisely the views he has made a career on denouncing.
[81] Quoted in Robertson (n 12) 24.

is a 'matter[] of argument, not evidence',[82] Dworkin made external statements about morality. Rather than suggesting that we interpret scientific claims about the natural history of our moral practices 'internally' (his proposed solutions to 'external' metaethical claims), he delegated them to a different domain. This is a surprising move for someone who once said that 'the distinction between substantive arguments within and skeptical arguments about social practices, is … a fake'.[83] To posit the separate domains of evidence and argument, Dworkin had to adopt an Archimedean view that stands outside both, polices their boundaries, and classifies statements whether they belong to one domain or the other.

Thus, in order to maintain the validity of external criticism of religion, Dworkin had to place it in the domain of evidence and outside the domain of argument, which is not necessarily how people engaged in religious discourse understand it. And by describing the moral domain as one of argument, Dworkin considered morality a form of rational debate. Some empirical studies have questioned this assumption. These studies have shown that moral deliberation and debate do not always lead to convergence, reconciliation, or to getting closer to the truth. Instead, it often leads to greater polarisation.[84] This is clearly an argument about moral practice, but it could also be interpreted as an argument within it and may have impact on first-order moral deliberation. By contrast, empirical studies on the perceived objectivity of moral discourse show that people are not equally objectivist about all moral issues, for example with respect to contested moral questions or when they learn that a different view is widely accepted in some alien societies.[85] I understand Dworkin's claims about one right answer to legal and moral questions is not to be a metaphysical one ('the truth is out there'), but one derived from observations about moral discourse ('this is how we treat moral questions'). But these studies suggest that Dworkin's observation may not be true. More significantly, they challenge the viability of the sharp distinction between the two domains. The 'sociological' observation that some moral questions do not seem resolvable or are not amenable to demonstrable rational argument has an effect on moral argument. People rely on 'external' observations *about* moral discourse for internal judgments within the discourse.

The shakiness of the distinction can be seen from observing at the debate between Dworkin and Fish. Their main bone of contention was about the

---

[82] Dworkin, *JH* (n 60) 82.
[83] Dworkin, *AMP* (n 8) 174.
[84] See, eg, RS Baron et al, 'Social Corroboration and Opinion Extremity' (1996) 32 *Journal of Experimental Social Psychology* 537; although see H Mercier and H Landemore, 'Reasoning Is for Arguing: Understanding the Successes and Failures of Deliberation' (2012) 33 *Political Psychology* 243, 252–53, citing conflicting studies and considering the conditions under which deliberation can depolarise.
[85] See, eg, GP Goodwin and JM Darley, 'The Psychology of Meta-Ethics: Exploring Objectivism' (2008) 106 *Cognition* 1339; GP Goodwin and JM Darley, 'Why Are Some Moral Beliefs Perceived to Be More Objective than Others' (2012) 48 *Journal of Experimental Social Psychology* 250; H Sarkissian et al, 'Folk Moral Relativism' (2011) 26 *Mind and Language* 482.

usefulness of deliberation, discourse, and argument. To which domain does this question belong? If it is a question *about* morality, then Dworkin should have humbly stated that this was an empirical question on which he is not qualified to offer an answer. But his engagement with the question, partly because *he believed it could affect moral discourse*, suggests he considered this question as relevant *to* morality.

Interestingly, a naturalist may find this idea useful: empirical work on morality has moved away from earlier accounts of moral intuitions as selected-for instincts and acknowledges the complexity of the domain of morality. Such work recognises that societies may develop and thrive with different moral codes, that societies could adopt norms that have deleterious effects on the community, or fail to adopt norms that could prevent their demise.[86] Especially important in this context is that such accounts have come to recognise is the central place of moral deliberation and debate – fragmented, convoluted, contradictory, cacophonous, noisy, and, crucially, one that changes through time – as part of moral reality.[87] Thus, a naturalistic approach may incorporate precisely the 'interpretive' elements of moral discourse that led Dworkin to posit the two separate domains.[88] One idea such accounts could take from Dworkin's work is the centrality of legal institutions on the development of moral ideas.

V. CONCLUSION: OUTSIDE THE GAME

When the debates between Dworkin and Fish took place, they must have seemed mighty important and the differences between them significant. With time, their differences appear less important than their similarities. Perhaps Dworkin and Fish's main similarity is that both were engaged in what Frederick Crews called 'theoreticism': 'frank recourse to unsubstantiated theory, not just as a tool of investigation but as antiempirical knowledge in its own right'.[89] Fish would undoubtedly retort, 'Don't blame me! I always mocked these grand theorists,

---

[86] Climate change may be one such case where this is happening on a global scale. See T Pölzler, 'The Effects of Morality Against Climate Change' in R Garner and R Joyce (eds), *The End of Morality: Taking Moral Abolitionism Seriously* (London, Routledge, 2017) 202; see also J Diamond, *Collapse: How Societies Choose to Fail or Survive* (London, Penguin, 2005) ch 14 and throughout the book.

[87] See H Mercier and D Sperber, *The Enigma of Reason* (Cambridge, MA, Harvard University Press, 2017); K Sterelny, *The Evolved Apprentice: How Evolution Made Humans Unique* (Cambridge, MA, MIT Press, 2014).

[88] One such example is Sterelny (n 7) 155–62. Another is found in P Kitcher, *The Ethical Project* (Cambridge, MA, Harvard University Press, 2011). Kitcher's book takes seriously the role of the community in the never-ending construction of the 'ethical project'. It is not without to the present discussion that Kitcher called his approach 'pragmatic naturalism'. ibid 7–8; P Kitcher, 'Pragmatic Naturalism' in MI Kaiser and A Seide (eds), *Philip Kitcher: Pragmatic Naturalism* (Berlin, Ontos, 2013) 15.

[89] F Crews, 'In the House of Big Theory' *New York Review of Books* (29 May 1986) 30.

telling them their work is useless.' But Fish did not base his claims about the uselessness of theory to practice on empirical evidence; as a good theoreticist, he based them on casual observations drawn from (among other things) watching baseball. In fact, if I am right, he was in some respects the most extreme of theoreticists. With his distinction between the domain of fact (causation, evidence) and the domain of value (argument) Dworkin restricted his theoreticism to the latter; Fish was not as modest, in effect, seeking to subject the domain of evidence to his own domain of (anti-)theoreticist argument. (I told you one can do a Fish on him too.)

One of the most important intellectual developments since these debates took place is the extent to which the domain of argument has been invaded by the domain of evidence. That is the message of naturalism, and naturalistic jurisprudence in particular, that both Fish and Dworkin missed.

13

Interpreting Community: Agency, Coercion, and the Structure of Legal Practice

NICOLE ROUGHAN AND JESSE WALL*

I. INTRODUCTION

BOTH FISH AND Dworkin are often characterised as theorists of law-as-interpretation: each uses his particular understanding of interpretation expansively, to explain the character of the wider practice of law. For Fish, legal practice entails the rhetoric of force. For Dworkin, it entails the justification of force. Embedded in their ensuing disputes over legal practice – as interpretation – are competing understandings of the agents and the structure of either 'interpretive communities' (for Fish) or 'communities of principle' (for Dworkin). In this chapter, we argue that a central disagreement between Fish and Dworkin – about the relationship between agency, interpretation, and coercion – can be addressed by posing the question of *who does what in a community of interpreters?* This requires an interrogation of both practice and agency in community.

Fish and Dworkin disagreed about the relationship between agency, interpretation, and coercion in legal practice. For Fish, interpretation is itself coercive, and cannot be self-reflective. When it comes to interpretation he explains that:

> In the end we are always self-compelled, coerced by forces – beliefs, convictions, reasons, desires – from which we cannot move one inch away.
>
> Another way to put this is to say that while there are constraints on the will and therefore on interpretation those constraints are *internal* to the will and do not provide a point of reference independent of it.[1]

---

* Parts of this work draw upon Nicole Roughan's draft manuscript, *Officials*, in progress for OUP. Both authors are grateful for research assistance from Kiraan Chetty.
[1] S Fish, *Doing What Comes Naturally: Change, Rhetoric and the Theory of Practice in Literary and Legal Studies* (Durham, NC, Duke University Press, 1989) 250.

In contrast, Dworkin argues that interpretation requires reflective agency, if it is to justify law's coercion. Hence, Dworkin challenged Fish's 'crucial assumption that an interpretive practice cannot be self-conscious and reflexive'.[2] Dworkin was concerned that Fish's account:

> ... leaves actual interpretive practice flat and passive, robbed of the reflective, introspective, argumentative tone that is, in fact, essential to its character .... [Fish] still wants, in other words, to picture lawyers and judges ... supplying justifications for these rules only if asked, and then just by repeating empty phrases they memorized in law school, idle justifications that have nothing to do with their actual practice, except to impress like hydraulics textbooks on a plumber's shelf.[3]

In this chapter, we explain how both theorists, in different ways, offer a 'flat' structure of interpretive community. Section II examines both Fish's reductive and Dworkin's expansive accounts of legal practice as interpretation. In section III we turn our critical attention to Fish and his attempt to jettison the elements of agency and coercion that Dworkin considers to be 'essential' to the character of legal practice. Accepting that these elements are essential, we then assess what it means to belong to an interpretive community that is both animated by reflective agency and burdened by coercive practices. To preserve the agency and to justify the coercion that Dworkin emphasises in a 'community of principle', we will argue in section IV that a 'community of principled interpreters' must be marked by hierarchical and differentiated role responsibilities, in ways that Dworkin's 'protestant interpretation' and 'political responsibility' fail to explain.

II. INTERPRETATION: RHETORIC OR JUSTIFICATION?

A. Legal Practice as Interpretation

Both Fish and Dworkin use 'interpretation' as an umbrella term to explain aspects of legal practice beyond the search for semantic meaning. Emphasising interpretive aspects of legal practice is a technique used by Fish to narrow our focus and limit our attention to the linguistic foundations of legal practice, and used by Dworkin to broaden our focus away from legal rules and institutions to confront their foundations in political morality.

Understood strictly, 'interpretation' is the activity of 'identifying legal reasons that support a conclusion as to the meaning that is to be ascribed to a legal communication'.[4] This differs from the further activity of legal

---

[2] R Dworkin, 'Pragmatism, Right Answers, and True Banality' in M Brint and W Weaver (eds), *Pragmatism in Law & Society* (Boulder, Westview Press, 1991) 380.
[3] ibid 387.
[4] T Endicott, 'Interpretation and Indeterminacy: Comments on Andrei Marmor's *Philosophy of Law*' (2014) 10 *Jerusalem Review of Legal Studies* 48.

reasoning, of 'finding rational support for legal conclusions ... as to what is to be done according to law'.[5] It is a further activity, since legal reasoning (identifying what ought to be done according to the law), includes the tasks of specifying the requirements of abstract legal standards, and qualifying (or extending) the scope of legal standards, and resolving conflict between legal standards. These tasks can only be performed once we have a 'conclusion as to the meaning that is to be ascribed to a legal communication' (ie once we have *interpreted* the law). Both Fish and Dworkin conflate this distinction, insofar as they explain the activity of legal reasoning as an interpretive task. The equivocation between interpretation and legal reasoning, by itself, does not concern us here, but makes us wary of a further equivocation, examined below, between interpretation and 'legal practice'.

Fish and Dworkin have distinct motivations for describing legal reasoning as an interpretive practice. These motivations stem from different ways of understanding the point or purpose of legal practice. For Fish, presenting all legal reasoning as if it is a merely interpretative practice 'give[s] us ways of re-describing limited partisan programs so that they can be presented as the natural outcomes of abstract impersonal imperatives'.[6] This follows from Fish's particular view of 'practices'. In his view, 'there is no reason for any discipline or enterprise to exist except for what is brought into the world by the possibility of its practice'.[7] The law (as a practice) exists 'because people desire predictability, stability, equal protection, the reign of justice, etc., and because they want to believe that it is possible to secure these things by instituting a set of impartial procedures'.[8] According to Fish, law meets these demands duplicitously, instead deploying:

> a set of ramshackle and heterogeneous resources in an effort to reach political resolution of disputes that must be framed (this is the law's requirements and the public's desire) in apolitical and abstract terms (fairness, equality, what justice requires).[9]

For Fish, the practice of law is a political practice that, in order to sate the appetite for predictability, stability, and impartiality, presents itself as a linguistic one. And if the practice of law is to be presented as a linguistic practice, then judges ought to appear to be merely interpreting impersonal imperatives, and in doing so, perform the 'prime judicial obligation' of 'continuity' and 'the rule of law'.[10]

---

[5] T Endicott, 'Legal Interpretation' in A Marmor (ed), *Routledge Companion to Philosophy of Law* (London, Routledge, 2012) 110.
[6] S Fish, 'Almost Pragmatism: The Jurisprudence of Richard Posner, Richard Rorty, and Ronald in M Brint and W Weaver (eds), *Pragmatism in Law & Society* (Boulder, Westview Press, 1991) 71.
[7] S Fish, *There's No Such Thing as Free Speech: And It's a Good Thing, Too* (Oxford, OUP, 1994) 141.
[8] ibid 213.
[9] ibid 209.
[10] Fish (n 1) 137.

Now, we might be able to accept a repackaging of 'legal reasoning' as interpretation. That is, if legal reasoning (identifying what ought to be done according to legal standards) is reasoning about text-based legal standards, then interpretation (imputing meaning to text) will always form an operative part of the task of legal reasoning. In contrast, we will reject a further equivocation by Fish, of equating 'legal practice' with interpretation. There is more to legal practice than interpretation in Fish's linguistic sense of concern for meaning. As we shall see, at issue between Fish and Dworkin is whether the law is a coercive practice, and if so, whether that makes the interpretation of law a political and justificatory practice or merely a rhetorical exercise.

Dworkin has more robust aspirations for the possibilities of legal practice, which he interprets to have a special moral and political importance. It is a cornerstone of Dworkin's theory (and his response to legal positivism) that law is best understood as an argumentative social practice, providing tools for the contestation of rules for behaviour, and for rights and duties. The distinctive constructive point of the practice (as interpreted) is to justify the coercive practices of political institutions without apologising for those practices. As Dworkin characterises (what he argues to be) the best interpretation of the practice of law:

> the most abstract and fundamental point of legal practice is to guide and constrain the power of government in the following way. Law insists that force not be used or withheld, no matter how useful that would be to ends in view, no matter how beneficial or noble these ends, except as licensed or required by individual rights and responsibilities flowing from past political decisions about when collective force is justified.[11]

Dworkin's theory of 'integrity' then tells us what law must be like if the application of force, through law, is to be justified. Integrity is a continuing ideal which requires that legal interpretation continually re-engage in the task of justifying political acts. It does so by holding on to what is valuable about what has passed in a particular tradition, for a particular political community, but insisting that it be defended afresh if it is to be carried forwards. It operates, in Dworkin's account, as an expression of the foundational egalitarian value. As he argues, 'government must act to make the lives of those it governs better lives, and it must show equal concern for the life of each'.[12] Only under the aegis of legal practice as 'constructive interpretation' – can the law continually engage in the task of justifying state coercion consistently with equal concern for all. For him, reflectively understanding, interpreting, and indeed furthering the point of the practice is crucial to the practice itself, ie those who do (and thus also theorise) law are engaging its point.

---

[11] R Dworkin, *Law's Empire* (Cambridge, MA, Belknap Press, 1986) 93.
[12] R Dworkin, *Sovereign Virtue: The Theory and Practice of Equality* (Cambridge, MA, Harvard University Press, 2000) 128; a Dworkin elaborates the 'abstract egalitarian attitude' in '*Sovereign Virtue* Revisited' (2000) 110 *Ethics* 106, 112.

B. Interpretation in Community

Both theorists situate the interpretive practice of law in a community. Specifically, their interests in community invite attention to both the agents who make up a community, and the structures or institutions through which they do things together. This allows us to consider what both theorists consider to be the 'community' of those engaged in legal practice.

Let us start with Fish again. For him, the law requires interpretation because law (as the text, or object) has no meaning that is independent of the activity of interpretation. But nor can the individual interpreter be the progenitor of meaning. 'Interpretive communities' are then introduced to collapse the dichotomy between object (the text) and the subject (the individual interpreter). As Fish explains, it is these 'interpretive communities, rather than either the text or the reader, that produce meanings'.[13] To be in an interpretive community is to 'share interpretive strategies not for reading but for writing texts, for constituting their properties'.[14] Elsewhere these strategies are described as 'tacit knowledge', a 'way of thinking, a form of life' or 'a structure of assumptions'.[15]

The law therefore requires interpretation in community because any meaning that can be attributed to the law relies upon these 'shared interpretive strategies' that 'exist prior to the act of reading and therefore determine the shape of what is read'.[16] Fish, at this point in *Is There a Text*, offers a totalising account of what it means to belong to an interpretive community. When Fish is offering his account of 'interpretive communities' he explains that they are 'made up of those who share interpretive strategies not for reading texts but for writing texts, for constituting properties'.[17] He then immediately adds:

> Even this formulation is not quite correct. The phrase 'those who share interpretive strategies' suggests that individuals stand apart from the communities to which they now and then belong .... I will make the point that since the thoughts an individual can think and the mental operations he can perform have their source in some or other interpretive community, he is as much a product of that community (acting as an extension of it) as the meanings it enables him to produce.[18]

An interpretive community is a totalising community in the sense that these 'shared strategies' compel a meaning. In Fish's own words:

> [Not] only is there always a gun at your head; the gun at your head is in your head; the interests that seek to compel you are appealing and therefore pressuring only to the extent they already live within you, and indeed are you.[19]

---

[13] S Fish, *Is There a Text in This Class? The Authority of Interpretive Communities* (Cambridge, MA, Harvard University Press, 1980) 14.
[14] ibid.
[15] ibid 303–04.
[16] ibid 14.
[17] ibid 14.
[18] ibid 14.
[19] Fish (n 1) 520.

It would be easy, here, to conclude that the law's agents have no agency. We might think that if Fish 'believes that persuasion – e.g., rhetoric – is coercion' then he 'holds that human agents have strikingly little freedom in these matters'.[20] If we are inescapably embedded in our interpretive communities, and if it these communities that shape the 'structure of assumptions that produce meaning', then any given interpreter is a mere conduit for the 'way of thinking' that the community represents. There is, however, further nuance to add. The activity of interpretation still requires interpreters, and any interpreter still has a task to do. In legal reasoning, the task is 'to construct and reconstruct [the] abstract shape [of particular decisions and statutes] and then to characterise and decide the present case in a way that makes of it a confirmation or extension of that same shape'.[21] As Fish continues to explain:

> Such an interpretation is creative without being wilful since he is guided by something independent of him, and he is constrained without being slavishly so since the something that guides him is something he must construct.[22]

Whilst the interpreter cannot escape the totalising pressure of the interpretive community, the act of interpretation can still be liberating since 'Fish leaves it to individuals to decide on the actual pattern (or chaos) of choices' and, in doing so, 'Fish has reinstated [the individual] in their role as the prime and privileged makers of meaning and history'.[23] There is still an interpreter making use of the interpretive strategies that enable meaning.

In contrast to Fish's community of rhetoric and shared meaning, Dworkin's is a community of justification and argumentative reflection. Dworkin grounds his theory of law as a theory of law for a political community – understood to include all those who are subject to the law and other political acts of the polity. In a 'bare' sense, a political community is a community of persons sharing a particular history of institutionalised and concrete practices of power, but a 'true' political community is one in which there are shared norms that express reciprocal relations of equal concern among members.[24] Such a 'community of principle' does not simply arrive at and apply conventional rules for communal living, but also commits to understanding them as expressions of standards carrying the values of integrity.[25] Dworkin understands the obligations that result from those standards (so interpreted) as associative obligations owed between members in virtue of their membership.[26] According to Dworkin, 'a

---

[20] A Wolfe, 'Algorithmic Justice' in D Cornell and M Rosenfeld (eds), *Deconstruction and the Possibility of Justice* (New York, Psychology Press New York, 1992) 365.
[21] Fish (n 1) 363.
[22] ibid.
[23] AC Hutchinson, 'Part of an Essay on Power and Interpretation (With Suggestions on How to Make Bouillabaisse)' (1985) 60 *New York University Law Review* 850, 870.
[24] Dworkin (n 11) 198–205.
[25] ibid 243, 214.
[26] ibid 206. This characterisation of political obligation as associative obligation has drawn sustained analysis and critique. See, eg, AJ Simmons, 'Associative Political Obligations' (1996) 106

political society that accepts integrity as a political virtue thereby becomes a special form of community, special in a way that promotes its moral authority to assume and deploy a monopoly of coercive force'.[27]

It is important, both for Dworkin and for our examination of the Fish/Dworkin debate, that Dworkin's community of principle is neither a situational community, nor a trained/disciplined community, nor a self-selecting community of interpreters of meaning. Quite the opposite. It is a cornerstone of Dworkin's theory that there is no sharp (Hartian) division between the political morality applying to officials and subjects: both are bound by the values and principles (of integrity).[28] Moreover, one typically finds oneself in a community of principle (indeed on Dworkinian thinking one would hope to be a member of a community of principle) involuntarily. Subjects of law in a community of principle bear associative political obligations even when they do not personally endorse the shared norms.[29]

For present purposes, it is key that Dworkin's community of principle operating in accordance with integrity is also (though in a sense distinct from Fish's) an interpretive community. All participants in the community bear interpretive responsibilities, and must engage as individuals in interpretive practices. Dworkin spells out the interpretive effort of a participant in a practice, who is 'trying to discover his own intention in maintaining and participating in that practice [...] finding a purposeful account of his behavior he is comfortable in ascribing to himself'.[30] In the context of a community of principle, this requires that individuals reflect on the community's 'past political acts' to see how they ought to be carried forwards in a participant's own behaviour. It acknowledges that some interpretation will go awry, but these interpretations will progressively be worked out through the argumentative tools that the practice of law provides. In that process, the participant in the practice contributes towards the aggregate content of the shared norms that are to be applied to themselves and other members.

As Dworkin explains in a much-cited passage at the end of *Law's Empire*:

> Law's empire is defined by attitude, not territory or power or process. *We studied that attitude mainly in appellate courts, where it is dressed for inspection, but it must be pervasive in our ordinary lives if it is to serve us well even in court.* It is an interpretive, self-reflective attitude addressed to politics in the broadest sense. It is a protestant attitude that makes each citizen responsible for imagining what these commitments require in new circumstances. The protestant character of law is confirmed, and the

---

Ethics 247–73. Dworkin's conception of associative obligations among members, as an instance of role obligations, arguably obscures the hierarchical differentiated role obligations that also obtain in such a community. *cf* Michael Hardimon, who distinguishes role and associative obligations in M Hardimon, 'Role Obligations' [1994] *Journal of Philosophy* 41, 335–36.

[27] Dworkin (n 11) 188.
[28] See analysis from D Kyritsis in *Shared Authority: Courts and Legislatures in Legal Theory* (Oxford, Hart Publishing, 2004) 145–47.
[29] Dworkin (n 11) 211–215.
[30] ibid 58.

creative role of private decisions acknowledged, by the backward-looking, judgmental nature of judicial decisions, and by the regulative assumption that though judges must have the last word, their word is not for that reason the best word.[31]

This is the core statement of Dworkin's 'protestant' account of interpretation, understood as an individual's own best reading of the meanings on offer within a practice. As Dworkin puts it, integrity 'asks the good citizen, deciding how to treat his neighbor when their interests conflict, to interpret the common scheme of justice to which they are both committed in virtue of citizenship'.[32] The equal concern and respect required of the public institutionalised applications of force in a community of principle is also a requirement of its members' private interpretive practices. The interpretive norms generated by participants as members of the wider community, are moral and political norms, rather than the norms of technical or disciplined legal reasoning. That approach preserves the agency of members in a community of principle. Their involuntary associative responsibilities to others in their community both preserves and justifies space for subjective judgment about what the community's practices mean (and therefore require). In order for no one to have power over others, integrity makes interpreters of us all.

Dworkin's image of the individual interpreter not only highlights the interpretive burden upon private persons, but also the individualised character of judicial interpretation. In Dworkin's account of adjudication, the individual judge wielding interpretation within her judicial role must bring her own best assessment to the interpretive task.[33] The individualised interpretive pursuit is exemplified in the work of judge Hercules, whose constructive interpretive method is supposed to carry forwards his best interpretation of the legal rules, principles, and institutions in his tradition. Judging itself institutionalises his own best efforts, his own interpretations of the practice. Yet in Dworkin's scheme, the community's background moral and political norms do the lion's share of the justificatory work required when choosing between different available interpretations of concrete political acts. This integrated structure of interpretation separates Dworkinian interpretation from more formal or technical disciplinary notions, including more technical notions of coherence and consistency with past decisions.

For both Fish and Dworkin, the 'interpretive community' (with its shared background and political norms) is nonetheless a source of constraint for the individual agent. However, they give opposing accounts of how an individual *is* (Fish) or *becomes* (Dworkin) constrained. As Robertson explains, for Fish

---

[31] Dworkin, *Law's Empire* (n 11) 413, our emphasis, which is explored at section IV.A below.
[32] Dworkin, *Law's Empire* (n 11) 189–90.
[33] See R Dworkin, *Justice in Robes* (Cambridge, MA, Harvard University Press, 2008), *Law's Empire* (n 11), and R Dworkin, 'Hard Cases' (1975) 88 *Harvard Law Review* 1057 for different formulations. On judges 'wielding power in service of conscience', see R Dworkin, 'The Judge's New Role: Should Personal Convictions Count?' (2003) 1 *Journal of International Criminal Justice* 11.

the interpreter 'is constituted by local embeddedness and so can never stand outside the constraints that come with embeddedness';[34] whilst for Dworkin, an interpreter becomes 'constrained by the moral and political background of the law' through the exercise of constructive interpretation consistent with an ideal of integrity.[35]

On Fish's account, the agency of the judge or adjudicator is narrowed down to an 'interpretive agency'. Whilst it is never possible to stand outside the shared structure of assumptions that enable meaning, at the same time, the act of interpretation can reconstruct, recharacterise, and recontextualise, what those assumptions require by way of meaning. In this way Fish preserves some agency – some creativity that is short of wilfulness – that is only a limited interpretive agency, not a deliberative agency. Unlike some of his critical contemporaries, Fish maintains that it is not possible to be deliberative about the background scheme of moral and political assumptions that enable the interpretation of law. To start, it is not possible to identify, and correct, biases or ideologies; any shift in background assumptions is a shift from one partisan view in favour of another. Moreover, and more importantly, if the interpreter were to try and re-examine, evaluate, or challenge, the shared structure of assumptions that enable an interpretive practice, then the interpreter is no longer engaged in that practice, but some other practice 'of literary criticism or of continental philosophizing'.[36] It is not possible to be both participant and observer, so either the interpreter participates in the practice of interpretation, or the observer reflects upon the act of interpretation.

We need not accept this further explanation for why reflective agency is a departure from legal practice. As we have forewarned, it rests upon a narrow construction of legal practice as an exhaustively interpretive practice, whereas legal practice extends beyond linguistics and a concern for meaning. To understand why, we need to turn to 'coercion' – and to both Dworkin's and Fish's use of the term.

III. LAW'S COERCION

A. Nettles and Dandelions

Let us return to the gun that, for Fish, is both 'at your head' and 'in your head'. Describing interpretation as coercive appears as a rhetorical manoeuvre by Fish that side-lines concern for the physically coercive nature of legal practice, where the force in the head of law's agents gets applied to the bodies of its subjects.

---

[34] M Robertson, *Stanley Fish on Philosophy, Politics and Law: How Fish Works* (Cambridge, Cambridge University Press, 2014) 254.
[35] ibid.
[36] Fish (n 1) 369.

When a judge sentences a criminal defendant, adjudicates on the custody of a child, or interprets criminal codes or contractual terms, the judge is exercising the ability to modify the behaviour of another person. Whatever else it is, it is a coercive power, since the behaviour of another is modified through the threat or application of physical force; defendants may be imprisoned, children may be relocated, property may be seized. If so, then it is easy to commit to the 'general critical principle that the use of legal coercion by any society calls for justification as something *prima facie* objectionable'.[37] We might further agree with the claim that '[t]he three most general and important features of law are that it is normative, institutionalized and coercive'.[38]

Dworkin grasps the nettle of law's coercive force. As he explains:

> Day in and day out we send people to jail, or take money away from them, or make them do things they do not want to do, under coercion of force, and we justify all of this by speaking of such persons as having broken the law ... Even in clear cases ... we are not able to give a satisfactory account of what that means, or why that entitles the state to punish or coerce ....[39]

In comparison, 'force', under Fish's analysis, is a rhetorical or persuasive power. For him, '[f]orce is simply, a (prejorative) name for the thrust or assertion of some point of view'.[40] It is 'already a repository of everything it supposedly threatens – norms, standards, reasons, and yes, even rules'.[41] In his reinvention of force, coercion and compulsion, Fish is adopting the terminology of legal philosophy whilst ignoring the field's efforts to distinguish and relate different concepts of control.

Fish's account of 'force' is developed in response to Hart (not Dworkin). He takes aim at Hart's 'linguistic' foundations of law in *The Concept of Law*; at Hart's hope that determinate language (that has an 'authoritative mark') can differentiate 'the mere temporary ascendancy of one person over another' from the practice of law.[42] Fish then runs the CLS playbook to argue that Hart's faith in language is misplaced. Rather than referring the interpreter to what is relevant, the interpreter 'simply beats the text into a shape which will serve his own purpose' and 'makes the text refer to whatever is relevant to that purpose'.[43] Now, if the judge was performing the role of a literary critic, then there are only dandelions to grasp. That is to say, if the law only has linguistic foundations, then the idea that the interpreter is beating the text – of the criminal code or *Paradise Lost* – into shape carries no sting with it.

---

[37] HLA Hart, *Law, Liberty and Morality* (Oxford, Oxford University Press, 1963) 20.
[38] J Raz, *The Concept of a Legal System* (Oxford, Oxford University Press, 1980) 3.
[39] R Dworkin, *Taking Rights Seriously* (Cambridge, MA, Harvard University Press, 1977) 15.
[40] S Fish, 'Force' (1988) 45 *Washington and Lee Law Review* 883, 899.
[41] ibid 900.
[42] HLA Hart, *The Concept of Law*, 3rd edn (Oxford, OUP, 1961) 24.
[43] R Rorty, *The Consequences of Pragmatism* (Minnesota, University of Minnesota Press, 1982) 151.

Nonetheless, Fish suggests that from his deconstruction of Hart's gunman writ large, he can identify a pattern: 'a mechanism is proposed with the claim that it will keep force ... at bay; and in each instance force turns out to be to the content of the mechanism designed to control it'.[44] Language, logic, procedure, and rules are mechanisms which attempt, but all fail, to convert power and temporary ascendency into something else – something lawful. These mechanisms can be rhetorically successful where they can satisfy the need for a 'way of neutralizing interest so that the decisions generated by the system will not be the product of any partial or partisan point of view'.[45]

We know that (for Fish) the impartial point of view is not possible. The problem that Fish seizes upon is that 'rhetoric is by definition the forceful presentation of an interested argument'.[46] In this way, 'rhetoric is another word for force'.[47] Hence, the mechanism for successfully converting force into legality is itself forceful. Fish can then create this neat feedback loop: 'force is already inside the gate because it *is* the gate'.[48] This looping is only possible because we have two different meanings of 'force' in circulation.

Compare Fish's own rhetorical flair with the 'general critical principle' (above). In 'Force' we again encounter his two guns:

> [....] the force of law is always and already indistinguishable from the forces that it would oppose. Or, put the matter another way, there is always a gun at your head. Sometimes the gun is, in literal fact, a gun. Sometimes it is a reason, an assertion whose weight is inseparable from some already assumed purpose ... Whatever it is, it will always be a form of coercion, of an imperative whose source is an interest which speaks to the interest in you.[49]

This demonstrates the need to be (at the very least) tighter with our language. A judge may be 'constrained' by sentencing guidelines, but she is not (physically) constrained in the way that the defendant that stands before her might be; a judge may be 'compelled' by the applicable law to grant primary care to a parent, but not in the way that the parent losing custody is compelled; and a judge may act under the inescapable 'force' of the substantive partisan agendas that she advances, but that is distinct from the coercive power and force that she wields over subjects. These may all, however, appear to Fish as mere interpretations of our community's shared languages of coercion. The more potent response is to look more closely at the agents who are both participating and implicated in Fish's interpretive community, and what they do to each other. The implication of finding force everywhere, undifferentiated between rhetoric and violence, is to flatten legal practice itself by collapsing distinctions between its agents and its subjects.

---

[44] Fish (n 40) 895.
[45] ibid 896.
[46] Fish (n 40) 895–986.
[47] ibid 896.
[48] ibid 898.
[49] ibid 898.

Returning to the direct contest between Fish and Dworkin, if we accept that legal practice is: (i) a physically coercive practice – in which some agents apply and some agents receive force –; and (ii) that there are differences between the force internally constraining the judge and the force that judge applies externally, then we must reject Fish's claim that an interpreter who seeks to reflect upon the political foundations of the practice is no longer engaged in the practice. On the contrary, it this 'reflective, introspective, argumentative tone that is, in fact, essential to [the] character' of legal practice.[50] Before we can declare a win for Dworkin on this point, however, we must consider Fish's fall-back position: that the reflective tone is just a good rhetorical device rather than genuine deliberation. We argue below that this relies upon a particular understanding of 'theory', one that Dworkin does not adopt.

B. Theory and Reflection

Fish does not deny that judges are conscious of the coercive consequences of their decisions, reflect on their institutional role in applying power over others, and seek to justify their decisions. But when judges reason along these lines, they are (according to Fish) merely being Sophists. They are engaging in rhetorically persuasive techniques 'to sell that decision to the legal audience being asked to consume it'.[51] It can only be sophistry because (according to Fish) the explanations and justifications that the judge seeks to provide belong to a different – theoretical – discipline. However, Fish assumes that a reflective practice is a theoretical one. Consider how he denies that reflection is constitutive of legal practice:

> [A]s a practice judging is one of those that include as part of its repertoire self-conscious reflection on itself, and therefore it seems counterintuitive to say that such reflection – such theorising – is not to some extent at least constitutive of what it is reflecting on: but that is just what I will be asserting ....[52]

Using the power of the em-dash, the move from reflection to theorising is very quick. And if Dworkin was not the target here (instead some more orthodox account of theory), the equivocation might otherwise go unnoticed. The problem is that both Fish and Dworkin have different understandings of how theory relates to practice, and neither of them are orthodox.

Put briefly,[53] Dworkin is critical of any attempt 'to distinguish the first-order claims of lawyers in legal practice from second-order philosophers' claims about

---

[50] Dworkin (n 3) 387.
[51] Robertson (n 34) 268.
[52] Fish (n 1) 378–79.
[53] See J Wall, 'On Hating and Despising Legal Philosophy' (2021) 46 *Journal of Legal Philosophy* 29.

how first-order claims are to be identified and tested'.[54] For Dworkin, there is no methodological separation from the practice of reasoning or interpretation from the requirement of deliberation and justification.

Fish agrees with Dworkin on *one* important (and unorthodox) methodological point. Like Dworkin, he rejects the idea that we can move between ordinary discourse with its 'thick texture of particular situations with their built-in investments, sedimented histories, contemporary urgencies', and metadiscourse that is somehow 'purified of such particulars and inhabited by large abstractions'.[55] We can, *pace* Dworkin, construct a metadiscourse about our ordinary discourse, and the metadiscourse can be different in substance from the ordinary discourse. However, because different discourses require different sets of background assumptions – distinct preoccupations, methods and aims – the metadiscourse cannot 'give us some special purchase on the questions [in the ordinary discourse] that we find most difficult to address'.[56] As Ripstein explains, 'Fish does not aim to provide a guide to [the practice of] interpretation, because he denies that any such guide is possible.'[57]

Hence, Fish believes that justifications are ultimately idle rhetoric because no practitioner can bridge the gap between theory and practice; or the gap between judging and reflection. Dworkin, however, denies that there is a gap., On this point, the debate ends with an impasse.[58]

If, however, we are to engage with Dworkin – on his methodology – then 'theory' constructs a meta-discourse that is not different in substance from the ordinary practice. If so, then interpretation is not detached and theoretical – it is reflective, introspective, and argumentative. However, as we shall see below, Dworkin's attempt to disperse this reflective and introspective task of interpretation individually across a community of principle, notwithstanding its unevenly coercive implications, risks leaving the role of the interpreter flat and under-differentiated.

IV. INTERPRETING COMMUNITY

A. A Community of Principled Interpreters?

Both Fish and Dworkin treat participants in interpretive legal practice as insiders to an integrated structure in which individuals are all interpreters. In both accounts, interpretation is overrun with agents, but short on authority as well

---

[54] R Dworkin, 'Hart's Postscript and the Character of Political Philosophy' (2004) 24 *Oxford Journal of Legal Studies* 1, 20.
[55] S Fish, 'Theory Minimalism' (2000) 37 *San Diego Law Review* 761, 762.
[56] A Ripstein, 'Introduction: Anti-Archimedeanism' in A Ripstein (ed), *Ronald Dworkin: Contemporary Philosophy in Focus* (Cambridge, Cambridge University Press, 2007) 5.
[57] ibid 17.
[58] Dworkin (n 11) 198–201.

as representative agency. Such a flat structure of interpretive practice, in its community, suits Fish just fine – amplifying his claim that interpretation is a rhetorical practice of power shaped by disciplinary not moral norms – but it arguably should not suit Dworkin at all, given his own account of interpretation's role in justifying the coercive imposition of the community's standards. While Fish's interpretive community ultimately offers no justificatory claim, Dworkin's community of principle needs to bear out the claim that it makes.

To distinguish (while relating) the interpretive characteristics and implications of Dworkin's political community of principle and Fish's interpretive community of rhetoric and meaning, we will call Dworkin's '*a community of principled interpreters*'. Our terminology aims to capture that, for Dworkin, a community of principle involves participants, as members of that community, interpreting its standards in accordance with the value of integrity, while judging others' and their own behaviour accordingly. It is a community that needs to be understood as a polity, replete with hierarchies, roles, and differentiated responsibilities among its members to enable their lives in public together, overlaying and differentiating their common participation in practices of interpretation.[59]

Recall Dworkin's account of individualised 'protestant' interpretation harbours a dispersed structure of interpretive responsibility that on the face of it, does not appear communal at all. As Postema pointed out in an early reply to this aspect of *Law's Empire*, the individualised pursuit of interpretation appropriately captures the individual responsibility borne by interpreters for the interpretive work that they do, but fails to capture the intersubjectivity of interpretation. According to Postema, Dworkin's account, 'makes interpretation of social practices insufficiently practical, insufficiently intersubjective, and thus insufficiently political'.[60] Postema argues, instead, that the generation of principles and meaning, as shared social practices, require reciprocal aspects of interpretation; the interpretation of social practices is a public activity. Postema then highlights a mismatch between Dworkin's approach to interpretation and the understanding of the point of law that is carried in his theory of law as integrity: 'while [Dworkin] regards the activity of the practice as public and collective, he seems to regard the enterprise of understanding that activity as private and individual'.[61] This 'ignores the interactive, public character of the practical reasoning demanded by integrity'.[62]

---

[59] This focus, and the bulk of this section, presents ideas elaborated in more detail in Nicole Roughan's draft manuscript, *Officials* (forthcoming).

[60] GJ Postema, 'Protestant Interpretation and Social Practices' (1987) 6 *Law and Philosophy* 283, 301.

[61] ibid 288–89.

[62] GJ Postema, 'Integrity: Justice in Workclothes' in J Barley *Dworkin and His Critics: With Replies by Dworkin* (Oxford, Blackwell, 2004) 291, 295–96.

Other scholars (including other contributors to this volume) have examined in detail the Dworkin/Postema exchange on interpretation as the search for the meaning of social practices, which help to situate Dworkin's position in relation to Fish's theories of interpretation as meaning.[63] Our primary interest here, in contrast, is on the impact of the individual/communal debate on understanding the practice of interpretation as justification. If interpretation is to carry justificatory potential and burdens, contributing to the justification of the use of force in and for a community rather than mere rhetoric, then (as Postema argues) the practical reasoning that is 'demanded by integrity' requires reflection with others, not mere self-reflection upon others' practices.

There are ways of reading Dworkin to address these concerns. For instance, Bustamante finds the necessary sociability within the object of interpretation, namely, within the practice of law. Dworkin's interpretation takes place as a theory of the argumentative practice of law, and so 'an interpretive claim is not just a claim about what other interpreters think'.[64] The task of justification carried by the practice of law *as integrity*, moreover, can only be understood as a communal task, using the value of integrity as an other-regarding standard, one that only makes sense as a kind of search for coherence with what others do/have done. So understood, the sociability of the practice, and its point, requires reflective intersubjective interpretation, not the aggregation of practices of individualised interpretation. Such a rescue plan doubles down on Dworkin's idealism, so that the interpretive ideal (protestant though it is), is understood to be practiced not just in any situational community, nor a specialised community around a disciplined practice, but within an ideal community of principle. In that context, members of the community are bound to one another by associative obligations, which extend to the ways in which they must pay each other equal concern and respect when engaging in interpretation of their shared standards. Interpretation must then be other-regarding and reciprocal, even in the hands of individual interpreters.[65]

---

[63] See, eg, D Patterson, 'Can We Please Stop Doing This?: By The Way, Postema was Right' in P Banaś, A Dyrda and T Gizbert-Studnicki (eds), *Metaphilosophy of Law* (Oxford, Hart Publishing, 2016); T Bustamante, 'Revisiting the Idea of Protestant Interpretation: Towards Reconciliation between Dworkin and Postema' in T Bustamante and TL Decat (eds), *Philosophy of Law as an Integral Part of Philosophy: Essays on the Jurisprudence of Gerald J. Postema* (Oxford, Hart Publishing, 2020) 113; T Bustamante, 'Is Protestant Interpretation an Acceptable Attitude Toward Normative Social Practices? An Analysis of Dworkin and Postema?' (2021) 66 *The American Journal of Jurisprudence* 1.

[64] Dworkin (n 11) 63. And at 410: 'Judges should decide what the law is by interpreting the practice of other judges deciding what the law is.' For analysis see Bustamante, 'Is Protestant Interpretation' (n 63).

[65] R Dworkin, *Justice for Hedgehogs* (Cambridge, MA, Harvard University Press, 2011) 312, 319–20; and see Bustamante, ibid.

B. Political Responsibility, Interpretive Responsibility, and the Judicial Role

Our concern here is that, even if we can interpret Dworkin's community of principle to meet much of what Postema demands of him in respect of the intersubjective object of interpretation, the rescue package still fails to capture the structural element of publicity that is in our view most significant for the justificatory branch of the challenge to individualised interpretation. The critique of Dworkin's account of protestant interpretation is not merely a challenge to its individualism (and so not merely answered with the account of reciprocity that Dworkin himself came to adopt), that is found within the ideal of integrity, but to its structure. Protestant interpretation is anti-hierarchical. It appears to saddle all interpreters – private citizens and public officials – with the same interpretive task of offering their best reading of what the community's standards require. How could such a flat and generic structure of interpretive responsibility serve in a justification for the use of force by some, in the name of a community, against others?

To address that concern we need to read further into Dworkin – forwards and backwards from protestant interpretation and communities of principle – to track something of his notion of roles, and in particular, to find an account of the role of judicial (and other official) interpreters. In conceiving of both the individuality and general dispersal of interpretive practices and interpretive responsibilities, rejecting hierarchies in favour of a reciprocity-affirming ideal of integrity, did Dworkin mean to deny that public and private agents contribute very differently to the overall practice of interpretation as it operates to support law's justification for coercion? Do judges and citizens have the same – or a differentiated – interpretive responsibility within the practice in which they all participate?

This requires more Dworkin exegesis and engagement with commentators than is possible here. In brief, however, consider Bustamante's reading, in which 'interpretive responsibility *rejects* the idea of *asymmetry* in authority. If the law is to be authoritative upon us, it is because of the acknowledgments and commitments we make when we participate in the game of giving and asking for reasons'.[66] Bustamante suggests that in Dworkin's account, 'we make critical practical judgments and by making these judgments keep the law in force when we earn the recognition of other participants in the same practice, who play the same critical role in the game of giving and asking for reasons'.[67] Roughly put, our objection is that if the judge and citizen are to be understood as being engaged in the same practice at all, it is (at least) as much a coercive as a reason-giving practice, and very far from a game. Alternatively, if judges and citizens are engaged in different practices, then we need an account of the relation between

---

[66] Bustamante, ibid (n 63) 11. Emphasis in original.
[67] ibid.

them. In either case, the account needs to differentiate rather than assimilate or generalise the interpretive responsibilities entailed in the respective roles of interpreters applying and interpreters subject to the law.

Though Dworkin is typically read to reject a Hartian emphasis on an official/subject divide, he accepts that in political community there are individuals who 'have special roles and powers, enabling them to act, singly or together, on behalf of the community as a whole'.[68] Such acts are the concrete, institutional political actions that provide the foreground rules and principles of the tradition under interpretation. Individual interpreters then look through these acts into the background understandings and principled outworking of the wider community's practices, formed through members' individualised interpretations, which are constrained only by the ideal of integrity itself. In contrast, judges and other bearers of representative roles carry an additional burden under Dworkin's 'doctrine of political responsibility', which requires that they 'must make only such political decisions as they can justify within a political theory that also justifies the other decisions they propose to make'.[69] Moreover, the doctrine requires 'articulate consistency', requiring judges to give reasons for their decisions that can be rendered consistently with past decisions.[70]

The notion of political responsibility is under-developed in Dworkin's larger body of work, perhaps because it rings a little too close to positivistic notions of convergence of behaviour among officials. Of all the ways in which Dworkin's account stands as a challenge to Hart, the centrality of the individual judge – and her sense of the morally best interpretation of the legal tradition in which she operates – is arguably the most foundational. Unlike his arguments surrounding distinctions between rule and principle, or between theoretical and empirical disagreement, the account of the solo Herculean judicial interpreter directly opposed Hart's notion of convergent behaviour of officials holding the internal point of view towards whatever their own practices generate as a rule of recognition.[71] It would hardly do for Dworkin to elaborate too much, or place too much weight upon, an obligation of judges to pursue consistency with one another's reasoning or decisions.

However, when Dworkin did take roles seriously – exploring the role of the judge and the very possibility of role obligations – his account arguably assumed (without committing to) an understanding of officiality. The famous passage (cited above) from the end of *Law's Empire* is sometimes cited with an ellipsis in place of our added emphasis: 'Law' s empire is defined by attitude, not territory or power or process. *We studied that attitude mainly in appellate courts, where it is dressed for inspection, but it must be pervasive in our*

---

[68] Dworkin (n 65) 342.
[69] Dworkin (n 39) 87.
[70] ibid 88.
[71] These represent two bedrock views of the role of the official of the law, and of the significance of the official in legal theory. They are explored in Roughan's *Officials* manuscript, see esp. ch 4, 'Taking Roles Seriously'.

ordinary lives if it is to serve us well even in court ....' Dworkin's sustained efforts to defend his account of interpretation, and its generality, may obscure that this part of the passage speaks to the relation *and thus the distinction* between court practices and the practices of the rest of us 'in our ordinary lives'. The passage suggests how official and private agents' interpretations work together, but it can only be understood that way by attending to their distinctive and respective forms of agency.

Dworkin's invocation of the interpretive enterprise requires a distinction between judicial and private interpreters, even as both kinds of agents engage in interlocking interpretive enterprises. It reveals the importance of 'the creative role' of private decisions (and decision-makers) being acknowledged by those who have the 'final' word. Yet what judges do, in their interpretive work, is 'dressed up', 'in robes'.[72] The dressing up itself may be read as shorthand for an assumption of role differentiation that is crucial for the justification of law's coercive force. It is important, moreover, that the judges are dressed up not for show (as they might be for Fish), but 'for inspection'. With the robes comes the representation of officiality, including practices of enforcement and application of their preferred interpretations, as well as the accountability that comes with publicity.[73]

However, while we might seek to read ideas of officiality and a differentiated judicial role into Dworkin's account, a truly Dworkinian account could only offer interpretations of such roles and the content of their interpretive responsibilities. For Dworkin, the judicial role itself needs to be constructively interpreted. Dworkin articulates that judicial practice requires the 'interpretation and reinterpretation of responsibility'.[74] There is:

> [a] deep dynamic that explains large and small shifts among schools and vogues of interpretation: the shared assumption of responsibility to a practice together with different assumptions about what that responsibility now demands. Judges, historians and literary critics all take themselves to have responsibilities, roles to play given by the traditions of some genre. Their theories of those responsibilities are as much creative, and are even more evidently in conflict, than the discrete interpretations they propose in light of those theories.[75]

Dworkin's all-embracing interpretivism thus precludes determining the role obligations that would enable judges to administer the differentiation that is encapsulated in the publicity requirement at the core of Postema's objection. Instead, for Dworkin, role obligations fall out of the tradition itself

---

[72] As Dworkin emphasised to the extent of embedding it in the title of an essay collection: Dworkin, *Justice in Robes* (n 33). That collection, however, offers very little direct discussion of the significance of roles (or robes).

[73] Postema, above; and on officiality see N Roughan, 'From Office-Holding to Officiality' (2020) 70 *University of Toronto Law Journal* 231; and on accountability see K Rundle, 'Office and Contracting-Out: An Analysis' (2020) 70 *University of Toronto Law Journal* 1.

[74] Dworkin (n 65) 143.

[75] ibid 142.

(as interpreted), and will be genuine obligations if their content is consistent with the core principle of equal concern for dignity. Such interpretivism, however, precludes conditioning law's justificatory claims upon the normative content of the judicial role, eg by linking official role obligations to those of the subject.[76] For Dworkin, responsibility is owed 'to a practice', not to those subject to its applications of coercion, while reciprocity is owed between members in a community of principle, rather than between differentiated subjects and officials.[77]

Our critique here emphasises the need for a distinction and relation between the private and public interpretive practices in which participants in legal practice are engaged, if we are to make sense of Dworkin's claim that law as integrity to justify law's imposition of coercion. Arguably, to operate his account of a community of principle – replete with integrity – in a way that can justify coercion, Dworkin needs a fuller account (perhaps a Fuller account) of the roles of officials. At the very least, it needs to attend to the hierarchical structure that is built into the very notion of the public official – replete with representative agency, claims to authority, and applications of collective power over persons – to emphasise the communality rather than the commonality of interpretation in a community of principle.

The argument from publicity captures that a community can only be understood as a community of principle if there are roles for different participants complete with delineated responsibilities and empowerments owing across each side of these different roles. Flattening interpretive roles within a community denies both the meaning and the normative impact of the political acts that law is supposed to justify, taking the justification of coercion much closer to an account of the rhetoric of justification. Without interpretations constrained by the structure and ideals of publicity, and not just by the tradition of legal practice as interpreted by its agents, the community of principle operates as a community of force, in which the loudest or most virulent interpretations will prevail. In such a community, justification reduces to rhetoric.

V. CONCLUSION

We have argued that Fish and Dworkin both reductively characterise the relationship between agency, interpretation, and coercion, and they do so in a similar way, by flattening the structure of interpretive practice. This takes some of the

---

[76] As Postema's own work does, along broadly Fullerian lines of reciprocity, see Postema, 'Law's Ethos: Reflections on a Public Practice of Illegality' (2010) 90 *Boston University Law Review* 1847, 1182: law's ethos takes effect in 'a community of mutual faithfulness to differentiated but interconnected responsibilities, the voluntariness of which lies not in its origin, but in reciprocity of its demands, responsibilities, and protections'; Compare L Fuller, *The Morality of Law* (New Haven, CT, Yale University Press, 1969); L Fuller, 'Positivism and Fidelity to Law: A Reply to Professor Hart' (1958) 71 *Harvard University Law Review* 630.

[77] Dworkin (n 65) 143.

sting out of Dworkin's critique of Fish, by moving Dworkin's own account of law's justification of force closer to an account of law's forceful rhetoric.

Fish would agree with Dworkin that 'Judges, historians and literary critics all take themselves to have responsibilities, roles to play given by the traditions of some genre' and that what those responsibilities require are themselves subject to interpretation.[78] But since it is not possible to be both participant and observer, the judge, historian, or critic, may participate in the practice of interpretation (of their roles), and an outside observer may then reflect upon their act of interpretation. The interpreters, themselves, cannot be reflective about their own practice, not even the practice of interpreting their responsibilities. As we have seen, this renders a legal practice that is 'flat and passive', and places rhetoric in place of justification.

Whilst Dworkin can grasp the nettle and help us understand why judges ought to be attentive to their responsibilities, his own account renders a practice that is flat and under-differentiated, inviting rhetoric to take the place of justification. As we have explained, his account of the individualised practice of interpretation needs to explain those role obligations and powers that separate official from private interpretations, and attend to their respective or relative justificatory impacts in a structure of interpretive responsibility. Diluting by generalising interpretive responsibilities – so that we are all interpreters now – does not cut it, when some of us are stung by the interpretations applied by others.

---

[78] Dworkin (n 65) 142.

14
Fish versus Dworkin: A Comparison between Two Versions of Legal Pragmatism

THOMAS BUSTAMANTE*

I. INTRODUCTION

THIS CHAPTER IS aimed at three desiderata. First, to show how the critical exchange in the 'Fish-Dworkin debate' was a turning point in Dworkin's philosophy of law, which provides the background of the model of 'law as integrity'. Second, to show that despite the similarities between Fish's and Dworkin's interpretive jurisprudences, there are important differences between the two. Third, to discuss Dworkin's response to Fish.

In section II, I explain the impact of the Fish-Dworkin debate on Dworkin's work. In sections III and IV, I distinguish two versions of philosophical pragmatism: a narrow pragmatism, endorsed by Fish, and a broad version, endorsed by Dworkin. The difference between these two is that only the former is committed to instrumentalism and to the thought that the judgments we make to understand the content of contested concepts come naturally to us, instead of deriving from a rational assessment. In section IV, I criticise Fish's narrow pragmatism. In section V, I explore a conventionalist reply to this critique (based on Fish's account of interpretive communities) and offer a counterargument to this reply. In section VI, I analyse Dworkin's response to Fish, which claims that the law is a special kind of social practice where the objectivity of interpretive assertions depends on its ability to satisfy a normative point, which is the task of interpreters to make explicit and apply to justify their judgments about the content of law.

---

* I would like to thank Thiago Decat, Margaret Martin, Brian Bix, Dan Priel, and Alma Diamond for their insightful comments on previous versions of this chapter, and the National Council for Scientific Development (CNPq) for funding part of the research that led to this chapter (Grants # 423696/2018-1 and # 306284/2020-0).

II. FROM METAPHYSICS TO PRAGMATICS: DWORKIN MEETS FISH

In the Introduction to *Taking Rights Seriously*, Dworkin asserts that a general theory of law must be both 'normative' and 'conceptual'. He presents us with a series of divisions within these branches. The normative branch, for instance, should comprise 'a theory of legislation, of adjudication, and of compliance', which examine the law from the 'standpoints of a lawmaker, a judge, and an ordinary citizen'.[1] In Dworkin's early jurisprudence, there are several ways in which the conceptual and the normative parts of a general theory of law are interdependent. Moreover, a sound theory of law should make sense not only of that interdependence but also of the connections between the general theory of law and 'other departments of philosophy', which establish further relations between the normative and the conceptual part.[2]

All of this points to a more complex and ambitious research agenda than the limited domain of questions usually asked within the tradition of Anglo-American legal philosophy, but still shares with Hart the methodological assumption that conceptual and normative inquiries are *different endeavours* and that one can distinguish between the activities of *describing* and *evaluating* the law. The argument of *Model of Rules I*, for instance, assumes that 'when we ask what law is and what legal obligations are, we are asking for a theory of how we use those concepts and of the conceptual commitments our use entails'.[3] Hart's jurisprudence fails not because it adopts a 'second-order' or 'metaphysical' standpoint to describe the law,[4] but only because the framework it provides is 'an inadequate conceptual theory'.[5]

In the first essay of the Fish-Dworkin debate, however, the interpretive methodology applied in *Law's Empire* is fully developed and Dworkin becomes aware that his jurisprudence must depart also from the conceptual framework that characterises the analytical method of Hart's legal positivism. Contrary to the predominant reading among Dworkin's positivist interpreters, the argumentative move that distinguishes *Taking Rights Seriously* from *Law's Empire* is *not* the substitution of the argument from principles (which claims that Hart cannot explain the legal status of some norms that are valid because they are 'a requirement of justice or fairness or some other dimension of morality')[6] by the argument from theoretical disagreement (which claims that the rule of recognition cannot explain the judicial disagreements about the 'grounds of law' or the facts that make something a legal norm).[7] The argument from theoretical

---

[1] R Dworkin, 'Introduction' in *Taking Right Seriously*, 2nd edn (Cambridge, MA, Harvard University Press, 1978) vii, vii–viii.
[2] ibid viii–ix.
[3] R Dworkin, 'Model of Rules I' in *Taking Rights Seriously* (n 1) 14, 15.
[4] ibid 22.
[5] Dworkin (n 1) xii.
[6] Dworkin (n 3) 22.
[7] R Dworkin, *Law's Empire* (Cambridge, MA, Harvard University Press, 1986) 3–6.

disagreement is not an innovation of *Law's Empire*, since it already figures in *Model of Rules II*.[8]

The central innovation of *Law's Empire* was the view that law is interpretive because the propositions we use to describe the law are *neither purely descriptive nor purely evaluative*, but rather a more complex sort of statement that 'combines elements both of description and evaluation but is different from both'.[9] At the core of Dworkin's newer philosophy lies what he described in the exchange with Fish as the 'aesthetic hypothesis', which holds that our legal judgments are like our judgments about the meaning of an artistic work. 'An interpretation of a piece of literature', Dworkin contends, 'attempts to show which way of reading (or speaking or directing or acting) the text reveals it as the best work of art'.[10]

A crucial assumption in this construction is the distinction between 'interpreting' and 'inventing' an artistic work. 'Interpretation of a text attempts to show *it* as the best work of art *it* can be, and the pronoun insists on the difference between explaining a work of art and changing it into a different one.'[11] A theory of interpretation must contain, therefore, 'a subtheory about identity of a work of art in order to be able to tell the difference between interpreting and changing a work'.[12] The point of that subtheory is to provide a 'right-wrong picture of interpretation', ie, 'a picture which supposes that interpretation may be sound or unsound, better or worse, more or less articulate'.[13]

Dworkin argues that the right-wrong assumption is not 'a picture philosophers impose on interpretation from outside', but is rather a 'part of the practices that constitute the institution of interpretation' and figures, in fact, 'at the center of that practice'.[14] The requirement of *integrity*, with its two dimensions of 'fit' and 'justification', provides 'the *formal* structure for all interpretive claims'.[15] Nevertheless, Dworkin insists, 'the idea of interpretation cannot serve as a general account of the nature or truth value of propositions of law, *unless* it is cut loose' from any 'associations with speaker's meaning or intention', for otherwise it becomes again another version of legal positivism.[16]

With these constructions, Dworkin moved away from the domain of the 'descriptive' or 'conceptual' claims he advanced to criticise Hart. The assumption

---

[8] R Dworkin, 'Model of Rules II' in *Taking Rights Seriously* (n 1) 46, 57. For the view that the emphasis on theoretical disagreement is the distinctive feature of Dworkin's later argument, see S Shapiro, 'The "Hart–Dworkin" Debate: A Short Guide for the Perplexed', in A Ripstein (ed), *Ronald Dworkin* (Cambridge: Cambridge University Press 2007) 22.
[9] R Dworkin, 'How Law is Like Literature' in *A Matter of Principle* (Cambridge, MA, Harvard University Press, 1985) 146, 147.
[10] ibid 149.
[11] ibid 150.
[12] ibid 150.
[13] R Dworkin, 'My Reply to Stanley Fish (and Walter Benn Michaels): Please Don't Talk about Objectivity Any More' in WJT Mitchell (ed), *The Politics of Interpretation* (Chicago, University of Chicago Press, 1983) 287, 289.
[14] ibid.
[15] Dworkin (n 7) 58–59.
[16] Dworkin (n 9) 148.

that there is an 'internal structure'[17] in interpretation brings Dworkin right into Fish's province, because both scholars assume that

> interpreters are constrained by their *tacit awareness* of what is possible and not possible to do, what is and is not a reasonable thing to say; and [that] it is *within* those same constraints that they see and bring others to see the shape of the documents to whose interpretation they are committed.[18]

There are at least three points of agreement between Dworkin and Fish: first, what makes interpretation a distinct 'mode of knowledge' is the absence of an external or Archimedean point to which the interpreter can appeal in order to understand that practice;[19] second, in order to interpret the practice one must grasp the *implicit* part of the practice (*either* a 'point or value'[20] or some principle that has not 'been recognized explicitly',[21] for Dworkin, *or* a set of 'assumptions' that 'constitute [the] roles' of a participant in a legal practice,[22] for Fish); third, to understand the norms and concepts employed in the practice an interpreter must make a *judgment* to determine the content of the 'earlier decisions within that practice'.[23]

Nevertheless, there is a disagreement about how that judgment is undertaken and whether there is a way to constrain that judgment without appealing to something outside the practice. While Fish believes that to think 'within a practice' means 'to have one's very perception and sense of possible and appropriate action issued "naturally" – without further reflection – from one's position as a deeply situated agent',[24] Dworkin offers us a 'doctrine of political responsibility' that requires, in its most general form, 'that political officials must make only such political decisions as they can justify within a political theory that also justifies the other decisions they propose to make'.[25] The gist of this doctrine is that it 'condemns a style of political administration that might be called, following Rawls, intuitionistic',[26] and demands, instead, a rational or articulate *consistency* in the 'application of the principle relied upon'.[27] It aims to provide, thus, an '*intellectual* constraint' in which the 'structured and complex mix of different kinds of beliefs and convictions' enables these beliefs and convictions

---

[17] Dworkin (n 13) 294.
[18] S Fish, 'Working on the Chain Gang: Interpretation in Law and Literature' in *Doing What Comes Naturally* (Durham, NC, Duke University Press, 1989) 87, 98.
[19] Dworkin (n 9) 148.
[20] ibid 160.
[21] Dworkin (n 7) 247.
[22] S Fish, 'Almost Pragmatism: The Jurisprudence of Richard Posner, Richard Rorty, and Ronald Dworkin' in M Brint and W Weaver (eds), *Pragmatism in Law and Society* (Boulder, Westview Press, 1991) 47, 62.
[23] Dworkin (n 9) 159.
[24] S Fish, 'Dennis Martinez and the Uses of Theory' in *Doing What Comes Naturally* (n 18) 372, 386–387.
[25] R Dworkin, 'Hard Cases' in *Taking Rights Seriously* (n 1) 87.
[26] ibid.
[27] ibid 88.

to act as 'checks' on others. Although 'no single of these is absolutely foundational, in the sense of absolutely privileged', Dworkin thinks that '*as a system* these convictions ... check and constrain one another in a variety of ways'.[28]

It is precisely this idea of an 'articulate consistency' that is challenged in Fish's critique, inasmuch as Fish believes that nothing but the 'historical experience of practice' is fit to perform a critical role within that practice.

'The internalized "know-how" or knowledge of "the ropes" that practice brings is sufficient unto the day and no theoretical apparatus is needed to do what the practice is already doing, that is, providing the embedded agent with a sense of relevancies, obligations, directions for action, criteria, etc.'.[29] The problem of Dworkin's jurisprudence, Fish contends, is that it misunderstands the 'nature' of interpretation, because Dworkin is looking for constraints that cannot be drawn from within the practice:

> The distinction between explaining a text and changing it can be no more maintained than the others of which it is a version (finding vs. inventing, continuing vs. striking out in a new direction, interpreting vs. creating). To explain a work is to point out something about it that had not been attributed to it before and therefore to change it by challenging other explanations that were once changes in their turn. Explaining and changing cannot be opposed activities (although they can be the names of claims and counterclaims) because they are the same activities. Dworkin opposes them because he thinks that interpretation is itself an activity in need of constraints, but what I have been trying to show is that interpretation is a *structure* of constraints, a structure which, because it is always and already in place, renders unavailable the independent or uninterpreted text and renders unimaginable the independent and freely interpreting reader. In searching for a way to protect against arbitrary readings (judicial and literary), Dworkin is searching for something he already has and could not possibly be without.[30]

There is a lot to spell out in this long quotation, which calls for two correlated critical observations.

The first observation is that Fish's understanding of the distinctions embedded in Dworkin's 'right-wrong' image of adjudication (eg, finding vs. inventing, continuing vs. striking out in a new direction, interpreting vs. creating, explaining vs. changing, and so on) is less radical than his inflated rhetoric makes it seem. As Fish adduced in his second response to Dworkin, he does not mean to 'deny the distinction between continuing and inventing', but rather to point out that, 'as in the case of explaining versus changing, the distinction is interpretive' and that '*because* the distinction is interpretive',[31] it can *neither* be fixed by the

---

[28] R Dworkin, 'Pragmatism, Right Answers, and True Banality' in Brint and Weaver, *Pragmatism in Law and Society* (n 22) 357, 377 (emphasis added).
[29] Fish (n 24) 388.
[30] Fish (n 18) 98.
[31] S Fish, 'Wrong Again' in *Doing What Comes Naturally* (n 18) 103, 109 (emphasis added).

text or by other constraint to which the interpreter might appeal, *nor* allow for an objective assessment by an independent interpreter.[32]

Why does Fish think that interpretive distinctions cannot constrain the understandings and the intellectual activities of the members of an interpretive practice? This question takes us to the heart of the disagreement between Dworkin and Fish, because Dworkin replies that Fish's supposition that the right-wrong picture presupposes a theory of meaning in which 'meanings are "just there" or "self-executing" or "independent" or "already in place" in the text' derives from a *tacit endorsement* of a '"copy" theory of truth, about what the world *would have to be like* in order to make the right-wrong picture appropriate'.[33]

Although Dworkin is sometimes criticised for not revealing the sources of his philosophical insights, this time he explicitly disclosed that the purpose of his analogy between law and literature was 'pragmatic'[34] and cited Hilary Putnam immediately after the sentence in which he attributes to Fish that 'copy' (or, more technically, 'correspondence') theory of truth.[35] Putnam's critique against correspondence theories of truth is an objection to 'metaphysical realism', a doctrine which assumes that 'the world consists of some fixed and totally mind-independent objects', such that 'truth involves some sort of correspondence relation between words or thought-signs and external things and sets of things'.[36] In contradistinction to that *'externalist'* philosophical perspective, he advocates a pragmatic or *internalist* perspective that holds that the question *'what object does the world consist of?* is a question that it only makes sense to ask *within* a theory or description'.[37] Putnam defines *truth*, therefore, as 'some sort of (idealized) rational acceptability – some sort of ideal coherence of our beliefs with each other and with our experiences *as those experiences are themselves represented in our belief system* – and not a correspondence with mind-independent "states of affairs"'.[38]

Dworkin's endorsement of Putnam's theory of truth as acceptability explains not only his disagreement with Fish about the possibility of making sense, within the context of an interpretive practice, of the distinction between 'interpreting' and 'inventing' a given work, but also of a more ambitious and controversial thesis that Dworkin avers in *Law's Empire*: that legal theory 'is the general part of adjudication, silent prologue to any decision at law'.[39] There is no discontinuity between theory and legal practice because there are no 'criteria

---

[32] ibid 108.
[33] Dworkin (n 13) 290 (emphasis added).
[34] ibid 291.
[35] H Putnam, *Reason, Truth, and History* (Cambridge, Cambridge University Press, 1981) ix, cited in Dworkin (n 13) 290.
[36] Putnam (n 35) 50.
[37] ibid.
[38] ibid 50–51.
[39] Dworkin (n 7) 90.

or ground rules' that a lawyer can follow 'for pinning legal labels onto facts'.[40] In other words, 'no firm line divides jurisprudence from adjudication or any other aspect of legal practice', because 'legal philosophers debate about the general part, the interpretive foundation any legal argument must have', while 'any practical legal argument, no matter how detailed and limited, assumes the kind of foundation jurisprudence offers'.[41]

It is in light of this absence of a qualitative distinction between theory and practice that we should understand the Dworkinian view that legal theory can perform the *utterly practical* task of providing a set of 'paradigms' that can 'give shape and profit to interpretive debates about law'.[42] Although 'no paradigm is secure from challenge by a new interpretation that accounts for other paradigms better and leaves that one isolated as a mistake', the interpretive paradigms developed by a constructive and interpretive theory are fit to 'anchor interpretations',[43] providing a 'plateau of rough consensus' to answer 'whether and why past political decisions' can supply a justification for the use of force, and then provide 'a unifying structure for the conception as a whole'.[44]

Let us consider some of Dworkin's controversial notions. The thoughts that 'judges develop a particular approach to legal interpretation by forming and refining a political theory sensitive to those issues on which interpretation in particular cases will depend; and then they call this their legal philosophy';[45] or that 'a legal philosopher's theory of law is not different in character from, though it is of course much more abstract than, the ordinary legal claims that lawyers make from case to case';[46] or that 'we cannot climb outside morality to judge it from some external Archimedean tribunal, any more than we can climb out of reason itself to test it from above';[47] or that 'you cannot think about the correct answer to questions of law unless you have thought through or are ready to think through a vast over-arching theoretical system of complex principles';[48] or several other Dworkinian quotes an attentive reader can pick and choose, are all dependent on Putnam's idea that '*theory selection always presupposes values*', despite the insistence of logical positivists and empiricist philosophers who are 'determined to shut their eyes' to this indisputable fact.[49] Furthermore,

---

[40] ibid.
[41] ibid.
[42] ibid 91–92.
[43] ibid 72.
[44] ibid 109.
[45] Dworkin (n 9) 161–162.
[46] R Dworkin, 'Hart's Postscript and the Point of Political Philosophy' in *Justice in Robes* (Cambridge, MA, Harvard University Press, 2006) 140, 141.
[47] R Dworkin, 'Objectivity and Truth: You'd Better Believe It' (1996) 25 *Philosophy and Public Affairs* 87, 128.
[48] R Dworkin, 'In Praise of Theory' in *Justice in Robes* (n 46) 49, 50.
[49] H Putnam, *The Collapse of the Fact-Value Dichotomy and Other Essays* (Cambridge, MA, Harvard University Press, 2002) 31.

the hypothesis of a direct influence of Putnam in Dworkin's jurisprudence becomes almost irresistible when we consider Dworkin's argument that interpretive concepts must be interpreted in light of its 'point or value',[50] which assumes that the legal domain is impregned with the kind of concepts that Putnam described as 'thick' ethical concepts, like the concepts of 'generous', 'cruel', 'liberty', 'just', 'duty', 'equal', and so on, in which the *entanglement* between facts and values make these concepts 'non-factorable' into a 'purely descriptive component' and a 'purely evaluative component'.[51]

None of the Dworkinian quotes in the previous paragraph are inconsistent with the assumption that theory construction is an activity *within* the practice, because Dworkin's contention is that the constraints that make a difference in interpretation are provided by the 'history or shape of a practice',[52] for it is the practice that 'sets the conditions of interpretation'.[53] We develop our theories to justify the practice from bottom up, since the kind of justification required by the practice is bound up with a history of interpretations and a concrete set of assumptions about the principles we are asked to explain. 'Any legal argument is vulnerable', therefore, to what Dworkin calls a 'justificatory ascent'.[54] The activity of building a theory for the justification of a particular claim moves from concrete to more abstract principles, because we often 'can only inspect and reform our settled views the way sailors repair a boat at sea one plank at a time, in Otto Neurah's happy image'.[55] Part of the role of that theory, Dworkin argues, is to remain faithful to the law by reconstructing and applying the principles that despite being implicit the legislators *endorsed through the enactment* of legislative texts.[56]

I can come, now, to the second observation on the long quote from Fish cited some paragraphs above, which refers to the claim that 'In searching for a way to protect against arbitrary readings (judicial and literary), Dworkin is searching for something he already has and could not possibly be without.'[57] As a reader familiar with the Fish-Dworkin debate will realise, this contention is the same argument that Fish would deploy a few years later, in response to *Law's Empire*. Fish's argument in *Still Wrong After All These Years* is that the interpretive positions Dworkin offered as alternatives to 'law as integrity', namely 'conventionalism' and 'legal pragmatism', are not merely unattractive but impossible to occupy. 'Conventionalism', insists Fish, 'is not a possible form of action because for one to be able to "perform" it – to "do" conventionalism – it

---

[50] Dworkin (n 9) 160.
[51] Putnam (n 49) 31. See also, on Dworkin's reliance on Bernard Williams and Hillary Putnam to reply to Rorty's pragmatism, Dworkin (n 28) 361.
[52] Dworkin (n 7) 52.
[53] ibid 64.
[54] Dworkin (n 48) 52–53.
[55] Dworkin (n 7) 111.
[56] R Dworkin, 'Reflections on Fidelity' (1996) 65 *Fordham Law Review* 1799, 1815.
[57] Fish (n 18) 98.

would have to be the case that language, at least in some of its instantiations, can set limits for its own interpretation'.[58] This hypothesis presupposes, for Fish, precisely the 'plain-fact' view that Dworkin is at pains to rebut. 'Legal pragmatism', in turn, is equally unavailable because to be a 'legal pragmatist' (in the sense Dworkin criticises in *Law's Empire*) one would have to be 'not bound by any sense of obligation to history'[59] and lack any 'underlying commitment' to a 'fundamental conception of public justice'.[60] The problem with this interpretive conception would be that 'the very ability to formulate a decision in terms that would be recognizably legal depends on one's having internalized the norms, categorical distinctions, and evidentiary criteria that make up one's understanding of what the law is'.[61] Given that a judge's ability to make a legal judgment is an acquired capacity to respond to values that 'do not exist independently of socially organized activities but emerge simultaneously with the institutional and conventional structures within which they are intelligible',[62] Fish comes to the following apparently shocking conclusion:

> *Whatever shape that [interpretive] story then has will be a principled shape; that is to say, it will be a shape that reflects a commitment to law as integrity.* What this means is that 'law as integrity' is not the name of a special practice engaged in only by gifted or Herculean judges, but the name of the practice engaged in 'naturally' – without any additional prompting – by any judge whose ways of conceiving his field of action are judicial, that is, by any judge.[63]

Recall that, according to Dworkin, the reasons for Fish's explicit denial of the possibility of a right-wrong picture of legal interpretation are his implicit demand for a correspondence theory of truth and his conviction that the objectivity of legal judgments cannot be vindicated without committing to metaphysical realism. Since no internalist philosophy can provide a sound conception of objectivity, there seems to be no such a thing as 'objectivity' or an interpretive 'truth'.

Fish's account of interpretation claims to be offering, therefore, only a 'pragmatist *account* of the law', ie, a pragmatism which argues that 'the law works not by identifying and then hewing to some overarching set of principles or logical calculus, or authoritative revelation, but by deploying a set of ramshackle and heterogenous resources in an effort to reach political resolutions of disputes that must be framed ... in apolitical and abstract terms'.[64] He resolutely rejects, however, to provide any 'pragmatist *program* of law', ie, a pragmatism which supposes that some *normative consequence* follows from

---

[58] S Fish, 'Still Wrong After All These Years' in *Doing What Comes Naturally* (n 18) 356, 357.
[59] ibid 360.
[60] Dworkin (n 7) 189.
[61] Fish (n 58) 360.
[62] S Fish, 'Anti-Professionalism' in *Doing What Comes Naturally* (n 18) 215, 232.
[63] Fish (n 58) 367–368 (emphasis in original).
[64] Fish (n 22) 56–57.

the pragmatist account and thus becomes 'unfaithful to its own first principle – which is to have none – and turns unwittingly into the foundationalism and essentialism it rejects'.[65]

Dworkin and Fish have disparate positions on whether 'theories' or 'principles' are able to control legal interpretation because they are committed to different versions of philosophical pragmatism. It is because they undertake different sets of pragmatic commitments that they end up with contrary and mutually exclusive conceptions of law, rationality, and interpretation. It is to these pragmatic commitments that I will now turn my attention.

III. NARROW AND BROAD VERSIONS OF PHILOSOPHICAL PRAGMATISM

It might be tempting to think that Fish accepts that a practitioner in an interpretive practice is 'free to confer on an utterance any meaning he likes'.[66] To resist this temptation, one should be careful to avoid the impression that Fish's pragmatism requires the performative contradiction of understanding legal interpretation as a social practice without any social norms. Fish rejects this idea because he believes the role of interpreters is fixed by a set of 'assumptions' that establish professional competences and 'institutional forms of lives'.[67] Fish's impression that the meaning of texts 'comes naturally' derives from the fact that what makes an interpreter capable of understanding them is that she shares with other participants a bundle of '*assumptions* about the direction from which they could possibly be coming',[68] which are 'understood to be relevant in relation to purposes and goals that are already in place' in an interpretive community.[69] Fish cannot be read, thus, as accepting that a practice of interpretation is not driven by norms, because he explicitly relies on social norms and assumptions to determine the ways in which interpretive judgments are performed.

But there is an important difference between Dworkin and Fish, which lies on the description of how judges *react* to these norms and what these norms *entitle* judges (and perhaps other practitioners) to do. While Dworkin constantly reminds us that interpretation is a rational and reflective exercise, in which the 'articulate consistency' of principles and the 'abstract justification' of theories are internal demands of the practice, Fish repeatedly says that the correct or appropriate interpretation is that which *immediately* comes to the mind of a trained practitioner.[70] By the same token, while Dworkin insists that 'lawyers

---

[65] ibid 57.
[66] S Fish, *Is There a Text in this Class? On the Authority of Interpretive Communities* (Cambridge, MA, Harvard University Press, 1982) 303, 310.
[67] ibid.
[68] ibid 316.
[69] ibid 318.
[70] ibid 318 (emphasis in original).

and judges are working philosophers of a democratic state',[71] in the sense that it is part of the judicial job to construct a sound justification for their decisions on the basis of the 'embedded theories'[72] or 'underlying principles'[73] found in the practice, Fish counter-argues that the judge is in the same position of a baseball player who is told to 'Throw strikes and keep'em off the bases', because there is nothing else to say or recommend to him (besides, perhaps, a few encouraging words) that would actually improve his intuitive job.[74]

Although most – if not all – participants in the judicial practice acknowledge a requirement of *public justification* of legal decisions, Dworkin and Fish understand this justification in different ways. Dworkin thinks only decisions '*licensed* or *required* by rights and responsibilities flowing from the past political decisions' are authorised,[75] whereas Fish describes this requirement as mere 'rhetoric' or 'theory-talk'.[76]

Fish depicts the task of justification as an add-on to a purely intuitive judgment. This amounts to a version of Legal Realism's 'argument from conclusion to premises', reinstating a familiar debate, within that tradition, about how to interpret Dewey's distinction between the 'logic of inquiry' (the intuitive process by which we approach an object, make it concrete, and grasp it in order to '*find* statements, of general principle and of particular fact, which are worthy as premises') and the 'logic of justification' (the backward process by which we check our insights in light of rational principles, working from general premises to particular conclusions).[77] As Gerald Postema summarised it, the Legal Realist's 'argument *from* conclusion' or of 'judicial window-dressing' is characterised by the following three-step process: first, 'grasping and making sense of the facts and arriving at a hunch concerning the right way to deal with it (the right conclusion)'; second, 'working back from this conclusion to plausible premises to support it'; and third, 'working in reverse down from principles back to the conclusion, usually in the public form of a written judicial opinion'.[78]

As Postema points out, this model was interpreted (inside the Legal Realist tradition) in different ways: while Hutcheson and Frank regarded that process as 'passive and unresponsive',[79] because judges 'really decide cases by feeling, and not by judgment; by "hunching" and not by ratiocination',[80] such that

---

[71] R Dworkin, *Justice for Hedgehogs* (Cambridge, MA, Harvard University Press, 2011) 414.
[72] Dworkin (n 48) 52.
[73] Dworkin (n 7) 210.
[74] Fish (n 24) 372.
[75] Dworkin (n 7) 93.
[76] Fish (n 24) 389–390.
[77] J Dewey, 'Logical Method and Law' (1924) 10 *Cornell Law Review* 17, 23.
[78] GJ Postema, *Legal Philosophy in the Twentieth Century: The Common Law World* (Dordrecht, Springer, 2011) 119.
[79] ibid 119–120,.
[80] JC Hutcheson, 'The Judgment Intuitive: The Function of the "Hunch" in Judicial Decision' (1929) 14 *Cornell Law Quarterly* 274, 285. See also J Frank, *Law and the Modern Mind* (Stevens and Sons, 1949) 100–117 and the discussion in Postema (n 78) 81–139, especially 95–98, 118–121.

the rational justification appears only in the opinion, as a persuasion strategy, Llewellyn regarded the third element as an 'active process of *reasoning*'[81] and 'an integral component of the process (not just a final, unimportant stage)'.[82] The activity of justification, for Llewelyn, provides a 'public check upon his [the judge's] work', that develops in the following way: 'while it is possible to build a number of divergent logical ladders up out of the same classes and down again to the same dispute, *there are not so many that can be built defensibly*'.[83]

It is not difficult to see that Fish is supporting the intuitionist interpretation of Dewey suggested by Hutcheson and Frank, instead of the more plausible interpretation suggested by Llewelyn. What appears to be central in Fish's argument is not the question whether the process of interpretation is free or constrained (since Fish does not dispute that the inquiry is informed by social norms), but rather the role that justification plays in the interpretive task of determining the content of legal concepts. Fish's scepticism about the distinction between 'inventing' and 'interpreting', like his discussion about the need of constraints by theory or justification, is actually a *distraction*, because the gist of the Fish-Dworkin debate is a controversy over, first, the status and role of the *implicit* norms we use to understand the sense of explicit concepts, and, second (and perhaps more importantly), *whether* these norms make the practice a *reflective* and *rational* enterprise.

Jeremy Waldron, for instance, forcefully advocates that the argumentative and reflective character of the practice of law is an implicit demand of the duty to justify a judicial decision, and consequently a normative demand of the *rule of law*, acknowledged as binding both by officials or institutions in charge of adjudication, and by citizens or individuals subjected to the governance of law.[84]

Hence, the Fish-Dworkin debate is a disagreement about the character of the implicit norms practitioners use to orient their decisions and about the reflective or intellectual character of the practice of legal argumentation. I believe that the best way to explain the difference between Fish's and Dworkin's interpretive jurisprudences is with a distinction presented by Robert Brandom between two senses of philosophical pragmatism, namely a *narrow* version that can be described as a philosophical school 'centered on evaluating beliefs by their tendency to promote success at the satisfaction of wants' (practiced by the 'classical American triumvirate of Charles Peirce, William James, and John Dewey'), and a *broad* or *extended* version that can be classified as a 'movement centered on the primacy of the practical' (initiated by Kant and continued in the twentieth century not only by the supporters of the narrow version but also by

---

[81] Postema (n 78) 121.
[82] ibid 120.
[83] K Llewellyn, *The Bramble Bush* (Oceana, 1951) 73.
[84] J Waldron, ch 3 in this volume.

Quine, Sellars, Davidson, Rorty, and Putnam).[85] Brandom explains the difference between these two versions through five pragmatic commitments, four of which are shared by the two versions and one of which is endorsed only by the narrow one. While Fish is a textbook example of the narrow version, Dworkin is a member of the broader one.

Let us begin with the four commitments that the narrow and the broader versions of pragmatism share.

The *first* and most basic pragmatic commitment is what Brandom calls a 'methodological' pragmatism, that is, the thought that the point about semantics is defined by the pragmatic use we make of the concepts a semantic theory purports to explain. On Brandom's vocabulary, pragmatics is the 'systematic or theoretical study of the *use* of linguistic expressions', whereas semantics is the study of the '*contents* they express or convey'.[86] To be a pragmatist in the methodological sense is to conceive 'semantics as answering to pragmatics in the sense that pragmatic theory supplies the explanatory target of semantic theory – and hence is the ultimate source of *criteria of adequacy* according to which the success of that theoretical enterprise is to be assessed'.[87] As Michael Dummet explains in a passage quoted *in verbis* by Brandom, this requires that a semantic theory '*gets its point* from a systematic connection between the notions of truth and falsity and the practice of using those sentences'.[88]

The *second* commitment is a 'semantic' pragmatism, that is, the assumption (endorsed by the philosophy of language developed under the influence of the later Wittgenstein) that the point of departure of any semantic analysis must be 'the way practitioners *use* expressions that makes them *mean* what they do'.[89] By employing a sentence or a linguistic utterance in the context of a social practice, practitioners can be regarded as undertaking a pragmatic commitment about correct and incorrect ways to use and understand that sentence.[90]

The *third* commitment is what Brandom calls a 'fundamental pragmatism', that is, the thought that *knowing-how* has an explanatory priority over *knowing-that*. The only way to render explicit conceptual contents intelligible, Brandom affirms, is 'against a background of implicit *practical abilities*'.[91]

---

[85] RB Brandom, *Perspectives on Pragmatism: Classical, Recent, and Contemporary* (Cambridge, MA, Harvard University Press, 2011) 56.
[86] ibid 57.
[87] ibid 58–59.
[88] M Dummet, *Frege: Philosophy of Language*, 3rd edn (Cambridge, MA, Harvard University Press, 1993) 413 (emphasis added).
[89] Brandom (n 85) 61.
[90] It is not easy to distinguish between methodological and semantic pragmatism, but the difference is important because the latter implies something more than the former, which is the assumption that the order of explanation begins with the practice, that is, with the understandings and conditions of correct or incorrect employment of a concept that are in fact used and embedded in that practice. ibid 63.
[91] ibid 65 (emphasis added). For an argument that also leads to the conclusion that Fish and Dworkin are fundamental pragmatists, see N Stoljar, ch 10 in this volume. Stoljar correctly notices, in addition, that Dworkin's 'constructive' interpretation is distinct from Fish's account of

The driving force of this pragmatic commitment is an objection to Platonist intellectualism, which substitutes the appeal to first principles or idealistic values by the thought that the responsibilities of a rational agent can be described as 'task responsibilities' to *take* something as meaningful, *commit* to the ascription of meaning one does by using a concept, and *attribute* to the hearer (or to other participants of a social practice, who accept similar responsibilities) an entitlement to use that concept in the same way.[92]

I believe that this 'fundamental pragmatism' is particularly important in the context of the Fish-Dworkin debate, because it is probably the most telling aspect to differentiate projects of Fish and Dworkin, on the one side, from the 'conceptual' or analytical mainstream of contemporary jurisprudence, on the other side. Fundamental pragmatism, as Brandom defines it, precludes an 'exclusively *intentional* vocabulary' to describe the use of language.[93] Since Fish and Dworkin are fundamental pragmatists, they both believe that the content of the law is not determined through a correspondence-theory of truth that acknowledges a practice-independent meaning detained by the text itself.[94] They define interpretation as a *practical capacity* possessed by the participants of the legal practice, which Dworkin described in his early works as a 'sense of appropriateness'.

It is this 'sense of appropriateness' that allows an interpreter to determine when to treat a particular norm or principle as belonging to the legal practice. For Dworkin, Hart's pedigree test for legal validity is insufficient because it does not work for the legal principles underlying difficult cases like *Riggs* and *Henningsten*, which were not decided according to an explicit and discrete legal rule. 'The origin of these as legal principles', Dworkin asserts, 'lies not in a particular decision of some legislature or court', but in the '*sense of appropriateness* developed in the profession and the public over time',[95] which accounts for the 'continued power' of these principles over us.[96]

But how does this 'practical capacity' or 'sense of appropriateness' emerge? This question brings us to the *fourth* commitment of philosophical pragmatism, which Brandom calls a *normative pragmatism* (or a pragmatism about norms).[97] A discursive social practice cannot provide the distinction between 'correct' and 'incorrect' applications of the explicit rules accepted by participants without

---

interpretive communities because it is 'ameliorative', in the sense that 'it seeks to identify the social function of the concept and to promote this function by offering newer and better understandings of the concept'. ibid 193.

[92] RB Brandom, *Reason in Philosophy: Animating Ideas* (Cambridge, MA, Harvard University Press, 2009) 52.

[93] Brandom (n 85) 66.

[94] See, for instance, S Fish, 'There is No Textualist Position' (2005) 42 *Stanford Law Review* 629, 633, where Fish suggests that it is impossible to pull apart texts, their historical contexts, and intentions because 'they go together, and are inseparable from one another'.

[95] Dworkin (n 3) 40.

[96] ibid.

[97] Brandom (n 85) 67–70.

presupposing *implicit norms* against the background of which they must be read.

To grasp the full significance of normative pragmatism to the understanding of legal concepts, it is necessary to dig into a technical discussion of Wittgenstein's argument of regress. According to Wittgenstein, if we grant that the meaning of concepts is fixed by rules, we must reject the claim that the content of these rules is determined through 'interpretation', on the pain of falling into an infinite regress. To avoid this regress, there must be 'a way of grasping a rule which is not an interpretation, but which is exhibited in what we call "obeying a rule" and "going against it" in actual cases'.[98] But we should be careful not to be tricked by an ambiguous use of words. Wittgenstein's regress argument is *not* an argument against interpretation in Dworkin's or Fish's sense, because Wittgenstein defines 'interpretation' in a peculiar and very distinctive way. To interpret a rule, for Wittgenstein, is to posit a meta-rule for fixing its meaning.[99] Hence, when Wittgenstein objects to 'interpretation' in the context of the regress argument, he is offering an argument against the kind of rule-rationalism that postulates 'rules all the way down'. He is arguing, in other words, that participants in linguistic practices have shared standards of correctness to distinguish between appropriate and erroneous applications of a given rule. Rules provide, for Wittgenstein, a justification for our claims and for the knowledge we purport to have; our ability to grasp a concept is in part explained by our capacity to understand and apply these rules. Nevertheless, there comes a point in which the postulation of conceptual rules must stop because the exigency to provide a justification comes to an end.[100]

It is only with Wittgenstein's 'regress problem' in mind that we can grasp the significance of normative pragmatism. One can find in the literature two different paths to explain Wittgenstein's escape from the regress: the first is a *regularist* reading, and the second is an *inferentialist* reading of Wittgenstein's argument.

On the regularist reading, we appeal to regularities of responses of rule-users to determine what counts as a correct application of a rule. If I ask you to 'please pass the salt', your understanding 'is made manifest in the *act* of passing the salt, and the act is a criterion for having understood the utterance'.[101] The need for interpretation arises only when the utterance requires *clarification*, which arises when a concept is 'vague or otherwise opaque'.[102] As Patterson argued, 'the key to learning meaning is *acquiring the repertoire of behaviours* that accompany

---

[98] L Wittgenstein, *Philosophical Investigations*. Trans, GEM Anscombe (Blackwell, 1958) §201.
[99] This is what Wittgenstein means with his assertion that 'we ought to restrict the term "interpretation" to the *substitution* of one expression of the rule for another'. ibid §201.
[100] L Wittgenstein, *On Certainty*, trans D Paul and GEM. Anscombe (Blackwell, 1969), §§191–192.
[101] D Patterson, 'The Poverty of Interpretive Universalism: Toward the Reconstruction of Legal Theory' (1993) 72 *Texas Law Review* 1, 21.
[102] ibid.

the use of signs in practices'.[103] Lawyers and participants in linguistic practices can understand a legal concept, therefore, *without making further inferences* or undertaking 'interpretive' (in Dworkin's sense of 'critical' or 'reflective') work. But this account of legal understanding is not correct.[104]

If we adopt an inferentialist response to Wittgenstein's regress argument, we can resort to something more than automatic responses and regularity of behaviour to escape the regress, and accept a *normative pragmatism*. Unlike the 'regularist' explanation of understanding that is usually offered in response to the argument of regress (which supposes that 'a norm implicit in a practice is just a pattern exhibited by behavior'), normative pragmatism explains the implicit norms that make the explicit rules of the practice intelligible in terms of *attitudes* of the practice's participants, ie, in terms of acknowledgments, attributions, endorsements and recognitions of *commitments* by the users of implicit norms that define the appropriate conditions for application of concepts.[105] What distinguishes merely perceptual or sensorial behaviour, which is the sort of activity of intelligent sentient creatures, from the distinctively rational action of sapient creatures like us is the fact that only the latter can treat these norms as *reasons*, instead of mere regularities that we repeat because of habits or natural dispositions. We act *rationally* and we understand *correctly* when we place ourselves under the authority of rational norms.

IV. FISH'S INSTRUMENTAL PRAGMATISM

It is only when we consider the fifth pragmatic commitment described by Brandom, the one accepted by the 'classical' or *narrow* version of pragmatism, that we can grasp the gist of the disagreement between Dworkin and Fish.

---

[103] D Patterson, 'Dworkin, Postema, and the Question of Meaning' in T Bustamante and TL Decat (eds), *Philosophy of Law as an Integral Part of Philosophy: Essays in the Jurisprudence of Gerald J. Postema* (Oxford, Hart Publishing, 2020) 141, 143.

[104] One way to show that it is not correct without necessarily endorsing the inferentialist solution adopted here is to attribute to Patterson an *over-reading* of Wittgenstein. Patterson's analysis of legal reasoning fails because he assumes that Wittgenstein's account of linguistic meaning guarantees the 'correctness' or the 'achievement of consensus' in every legal case. BH Bix, *Law, Language, and Legal Determinacy* (Oxford, Oxford University Press, 1993) 45–46. 'The jump from the grammar of language to "the grammar of law" implies', according to Bix, that, 'analogous to Wittgenstein's discussions of meanings and mathematical series, the definitions of legal terms and the moves within the legal discourse cannot sensibly be challenged and are not in need of further justification' (ibid 47). This jump is a mistake because it fails to grasp the argumentative aspect of legal practice that is particularly salient in hard or controversial cases. Unlike some conventional forms of ordinary language, 'legal practice, locally and generally, *is* subject to criticism and *is* in need of further justification' (ibid 49). Bix is correct in his criticism of Patterson and in the demand of justification for legal rules and legal concepts, especially in hard cases. Nevertheless, I believe that the inferentialist response is more interesting because it preserves Wittgenstein's insight that there are *unstated* or *implicit* norms which define the content of explicit assertions. This insight is useful not only to understand how language works, but also how law, or any other rational normative practice, works.

[105] RB Brandom, *Making it Explicit* (Cambridge, MA, Harvard University Press, 1994) 28.

Narrow pragmatism accepts all of the four pragmatic commitments described in the previous section: first, 'by giving pride of place to habits, practical skills, and abilities, to know-how in a broad sense', they accept fundamental pragmatism; second, by accepting that 'the point of our talk about what we mean or believe is to be found in the light it sheds on what we *do*, on our habits, our practices of inquiry, of solving problems and pursuing goals', they accept a methodological pragmatism; third, by taking that the meaning of our utterances and beliefs must be explained in terms of 'the role those utterances and beliefs play in our habits and practices', they endorse semantic pragmatism; fourth, by resorting to norms implicit in social practices, they attach to normative pragmatism.[106]

The difference is the kind of norms to which they resort, because narrow pragmatists focus 'exclusively on *instrumental* norms' to determine what counts as a performance 'better or worse' or 'correct or incorrect'.[107] Everything turns, Brandom summarises, on 'the agent's success in securing some end or achieving some goal':

> This is the kind of norm they see as implicit in discursive practice, and (in keeping with their semantic pragmatism) as the ultimate source of specifically semantic dimensions of normative assessments such as truth. They understand truth in terms of usefulness and take the contents possessed by intentional states and expressed by linguistic utterances to consist in their potential contribution to the *success* of an agent's *practical enterprises*. Peirce, James, and Dewey are at base (though not always, and not in every respect) *instrumental* normative pragmatists.[108]

One of the reasons for the classical pragmatist's subscription to instrumental norms is the apparent facility with which it manages to reconcile its insights on the role of implicit norms with the naturalism endorsed by its proponents. The instrumental interpretation of norms eliminates the apparent mystery of discursive practices and the attribution of conceptual contents by the participants in these practices.

A central feature of narrow pragmatism is its endorsement of a previous (Humean) version of Davidson's 'belief-desire' model of rational explanations. According to this model, to give a rational explanation is to provide a causal explanation: 'A reason rationalizes an action only if it leads us to see something the agent wanted, desired, prized, held dear, thought dutiful, beneficial, obligatory or agreeable.' To hold that an agent acted *for a reason*, therefore, is to characterise his action as '(*a*) having some sort of pro attitude towards actions of a certain kind', and '(*b*) believing (or knowing, perceiving, noticing, remembering) that his action is of that kind'.[109] Given that the 'pro attitude'

---
[106] Brandom (n 85) 70–71.
[107] ibid 71.
[108] ibid.
[109] D Davidson, 'Actions, Reasons, and Causes' in *Essays on Actions and Events* (Oxford, Oxford University Press, 1980) 3–4.

described in '*a*' is described in terms of 'desires, wantings, urges, promptings, and a great variety of moral views, aesthetic principles, economic prejudices, social conventions, and public and private goals and values in so far as these can be interpreted as attitudes an agent directed towards actions of a certain kind',[110] we can call this account a *belief-desire model* of rationalisation.

According to Brandom, narrow pragmatism identifies *true beliefs* by their capacity to satisfy a desire, leading us to a semantic theory 'based on the pragmatic distinction between a desire's being satisfied and its not being satisfied'. In addition, it determines when a desire is satisfied according to a *'felt satisfaction'* of that desire.[111] Like an animal can recognise that something 'itches' and then that something removes that itch and satisfy its desire to stop scratching, one can hope to build a model of 'content-attributions' in that way, according to the following scheme:

> Desires motivate behavior, and permit the sorting of behavior into that which does and that which does not satisfy, fulfill, or eliminate the desire. In the context of those desires, beliefs can be imputed as implicit in the behavioral strategies an organism adopts to satisfy them. The beliefs will concern how things are, and so what effects can be expected to ensue from various sorts of performance. *The success or failure of those strategies then permits assessment of the truth or falsity of the beliefs.*[112]

Narrow pragmatists suppose, in short, that 'true beliefs' are those that successfully satisfy one's desires. But there are at least three problems with this approach.

The first problem with this strategy, according to Brandom, is that it incurs on what Sellars has called the 'Myth of the Given', because it falsely assumes that 'felt satisfaction' is all we need to motivate our behaviour and to *know* what counts as '*evidence* for or against the truth of a belief'. It endorses a 'paradigm of givenness' because it assumes that the desires that play a part in determination of true beliefs are immediately accessible to our perception, discharging us of the requirement to attribute 'conceptually articulated contents' to the states we unreflectively apprehend as desired. This strategy is fragile because the desires 'felt' or 'implicit in behavioral strategies' have little to offer in the rational process of fixating reliable beliefs. These desires lack complexity and cannot be regarded as having *intentional* content, for they cannot 'play a role as premises in practical reasoning' or 'engage inferentially' with beliefs.[113] An immediate consequence of this approach is that it does not explain the possibility of *mistakes* in one's rational judgments about one's beliefs: 'The notion

---

[110] ibid 4.
[111] Brandom (n 85) 73.
[112] ibid (emphasis added).
[113] ibid 74.

of *felt satisfaction*, or relief from a motivating pressure, includes an element of immediacy as *incorrigibility*[114] that prevents it from counting as a rational process to understand the world.

The second problem of this version of pragmatism (which is closely related to the first) is that it fails to discriminate between 'felt' desires and the 'more complex' desires that figure in an assessment of the world by a rational creature who seeks for a way to act and situate herself in the world. It is only the latter type of desire that, together with actions and reasoning, might be fit to permit the 'imputation' of a belief.[115] Desires that can count as motivating intentional actions have a more complex structure than felt desires, since desires of the former type do not come automatically and are not detached from a rational appreciation of one's situation and the objective reality one is set to explain. The classical pragmatist's reliance on successful behavioural responses to perceived needs in order to define the truth of a certain belief is, therefore, wrong also for a '*structural*' reason, because it misses the crucial point that the 'essentially *inferential* articulation of conceptual content' implies that it is not possible to '*isolate* the contribution a belief makes to the success of practical undertakings based on it'.[116] In other words, 'a true belief conduces to practical success only in the context of a set [or perhaps more properly, a system] of *true* background beliefs',[117] which cannot be known in isolation because there is 'no noncircular way to state or eliminate this condition' while devising a program to distinguish between a true and a false belief.[118]

But that is not all. A third problem of the belief-desire model, as Joseph Raz observed, is that any plausible explanation of the role of desires in practical reason requires '*reasons* for satisfying desires' which inevitably '*transcend the self-imposed boundaries of the approach*', because no desire should be taken as 'inherently worthy of satisfaction'.[119] Desires that are fit to count as plausible candidates to justify an action or belief inevitably 'track' or 'instantiate' *values* that allow a rational appreciation of the situation in which they apply. Reasonable desires – like, for instance, the 'philosophical' desire for knowledge – are different from 'urges' precisely because they 'do not have a felt quality' and arise, instead, from the belief that there are *reasons* to act in a certain way.[120] The belief-desire model appears to be struck, therefore, by the following dilemma: if the values presupposed in order to attribute normativity to a desire 'do not rest on desire alone, then there are values whose normative force is independent of being desired, and without them the belief-desire

---

[114] ibid 75.
[115] ibid.
[116] ibid.
[117] ibid 76.
[118] ibid.
[119] J Raz, *Engaging Reason* (Oxford, Oxford University Press, 1999) 52 (emphasis added).
[120] ibid 54.

approach does not make sense, whereas with them it is no longer the belief-desire approach'.[121]

I believe these failures of the belief-desire model are devastating for Fish's ambition to explain the practical capacities of judges and law practitioners without the *right-wrong* picture of adjudication Dworkin's constructionism is struggling to vindicate. It tells us where Fish goes wrong in his assessment of Dworkin's 'law as integrity' or the alternative models of 'conventionalism' and the commonsensical, Posner-like, version of '*legal* pragmatism'. It is precisely Fish's endorsement of the unmediated relation between 'felt desires', successful responses, and truth that leads him to conclude that Dworkin's 'law as integrity' is an inevitable way of conceiving the practice of adjudication (or 'a position that one not could fail to put in practice')[122] and that when a trained interpreter is set to determine the content of a legal concept 'whatever shape that story then has will be a principled shape'.[123]

Fish partakes in the philosophical vice of incorrigibility that Brandom ascribes to classical pragmatism because he believes a trained interpreter or an 'initiated student', who has 'thoroughly internalized the distinctions, categories, and notions of relevance and irrelevance that comprise "thinking like a lawyer", cannot see anything *but* the practice'.[124]

This problem was accurately identified in Nigel Simmond's analysis of Fish's jurisprudence in this book. Consider Fish's definition of 'force', presented somewhat obscurely in the context of an inquiry into the 'force of law':

> Force is simply a (pejorative) name for the thrust or assertion of some point of view, and in a world where the urging of points of view cannot be referred for adjudication to some independent tribunal, force is just another name for what follows naturally from conviction. That is to say, force wears the aspect of anarchy only if one regards it as an empty blind urge, but if one identifies it as *interest aggressively pursued*, force acquires a content and that content is a complex of goals and purposes, underwritten by a vision, and put into operation by a detailed agenda complete with steps, stages, and directions. Force, in short, is already a repository of everything it supposedly threatens – norms, standards, reasons, and yes, even rules.[125]

According to Simmonds, 'force', in Fish's account, 'is not a discrete presence', like some usual explanations that identify 'force' with 'coercion' might suggest, but a much more comprehensive concept that appears to 'encompass everything, and assumes a distinct character only as the mark of a gaping *absence*'.[126] What is missing in Fish's overarching notion of force, Simmonds tells us, is the role of *reason* to understand the law. Fish cannot distinguish, like Raz did in the

---

[121] ibid 52.
[122] Fish (n 58) 361.
[123] ibid 367.
[124] ibid 364.
[125] S Fish, 'Force' (1988) 45 *Washington and Lee Law Review* 883, 899–900.
[126] NE Simmonds, ch 4 in this volume, 67 (emphasis added).

passages quoted a few paragraphs above, between *urges* and *rational desires*. His endorsement of the belief-desire model is incapable to explain one of the most *natural* and distinctive capacities of human beings, which is the capacity to act for reasons and to articulate these reasons to justify or criticise a behaviour, whenever a need for justification comes about. Simmonds grasped this problem better than any other commentator of Fish's work:

> Is the critical face of reason really so distinct from its mundane aspect in our ordinary practices of reasoning? Might our practices not themselves call into being a critical standard by reference to which any instantiation of reasoning (including those self-same practices) can be judged? Might the basis of reason not be found in those 'structures of thought and language' (mentioned by Hart) which render us mutually intelligible and render the world intelligible to us? Fish would doubtless object that such structures merely consist of such things as convictions, desires, prejudices and other mutable and historically contingent aspects of 'force': they are merely aspects of the gun at our head, which turns out to be our head (as he memorably puts it). But some human convictions (or, if you like, 'prejudices') are themselves the expression of our mutual recognition, and constitutive of our status as responsible agents. If they are, in some sense, a gun at our head, they are also the basis of a mode of being that gives that imagery (of guns and coercion) its force: for they are the basis of our freedom and responsibility, and our status as moral persons. A rich and complex strand of philosophical thought (including such highly diverse figures as Fichte, Hegel, T.H. Green, Strawson and Darwall) explores these ideas. We discern, within that strand of thought, the way in which structures that we have ourselves created may transform us, rendering our beliefs and actions answerable to critical, but nevertheless human, standards.[127]

Fish's account of the practice is implausible, therefore, because it cannot explain the force and the role of reason in interpretive practices. While I write this chapter, for instance, the United States Supreme Court announces a judgment overruling one of its most important precedents in the past 50 years, *Roe v Wade*,[128] and disavowals its historical holding that the right to privacy enables women to have an abortion at their own discretion during the first trimester of pregnancy. Several lawyers across the world unambiguously claim the decision to override *Roe* is a legal *mistake* (since the Court on these lawyers' view is, to paraphrase Dworkin, striking out the chain of law in a new direction) and accuse the Court of mistakenly deconstructing a set of doctrinal concepts that rest on an overarching legal principle of 'autonomy' that can be drawn either from the 'Fourteenth Amendment's concept of personal liberty and restrictions upon state action', or from the Ninth Amendment's notion that there are unenumerated rights reserved to the people, which shall not be construed as exceptionable by an act of Congress.[129] The new decision cannot fit the history of the Court's practice, these lawyers submit, because the principle that justifies and explains

---

[127] ibid 69–70 (footnotes omitted).
[128] *Roe v Wade*, 410 U.S. 113 (1973).
[129] *Roe*, 410 U.S. at 153.

decisions like *Roe* is a central part of the constitutional practice and provides a justification also for a larger array of decisions about related topics like sexual identity, the use of contraceptives, the unconstitutionality of statutes banning sodomy and homosexuality, the right to marry and constitute a family according to one's own preferences and ethical values, and so on.

How can we *make sense* of these lawyers' beliefs that the decision is wrong, or that it is pushing the practice in a direction not faithful to the institutional history or the scheme of values the US Constitution is said to endorse? If we stick to the narrow version of philosophical pragmatism, that Fish subscribes to, the only resource to which we can appeal in order to explain these lawyers' beliefs is the *felt need* or the *unexamined* judgments of first impression these lawyers make, which is nothing more than an unarticulated set of feelings that cannot be placed in a network of beliefs and commitments inferentially articulated and consistently systematised. By endorsing Fish's pragmatism, a lawyer loses part of an important capacity *claimed* and *implicitly acknowledged* by any competent participant of the practice, which is the capacity to explain, assess, respond, evaluate, and justify these kinds of judgments in order to determine whether the speaker is entitled to them, and whether they are authorised by the internal structure of norms that turns the practice into a rational or argumentative endeavour and is normatively postulated as an internal exigency of fidelity to the rule of law. This is a bad mistake (Dworkin argues) because 'anyone who is blind to the critically argumentative and reflexive character of intellectual practices will understand almost nothing else about them'.[130]

Fish's assertion that interpretive distinctions (like the distinction between interpreting and inventing) 'can't be used to settle anything' is described by Dworkin as a 'casebook example of Wittgenstein's diagnosis of philosophical bewitchment', because Fish's contention that all claims to correctness or objectivity must be confined to a meta-level that cannot play a part in the justificatory reasoning of an insider is a priori committed to the implausible idea that 'an interpretive theory cannot be self-conscious and reflexive'.[131] This assumption is unsound because it imposes upon the practice an interpretation of its character that no serious participant can endorse, which describes the practice as 'unreflective and automatic'. Once the activities of making judgments inside the practice and attempting (but, according to Fish, always failing) to produce objective reports of the practice in an external level are separated, both activities are misunderstood: the separation 'abandons interpretive theory to the external metalevel of invented enemies, and leaves actual interpretive practice flat and passive, robbed of the reflective, introspective, argumentative tone that is, in fact, essential to its character'.[132] In other words, Dworkin contends, 'Fish

---

[130] Dworkin (n 28) 378.
[131] ibid 380.
[132] ibid.

dramatically underestimates the complexity of the internal structure of practices people quite naturally fall into', and forgets that interpretive practices like law, morality, and perhaps other things that we do, 'are more argumentative than throwing a forkball'.[133]

V. A CONVENTIONALIST REPLY

Have I made a fair assessment of Fish's pragmatic account of interpretation in the previous section? One may argue that I did not.

A supporter of Fish could concede that his argument against Dworkin is mistaken, and that his critique of the distinction between interpreting and inventing a law is actually a *red herring*,[134] but still insist that there is something to retain in Fish's approach to interpretation of social practices. The reason for this insistence is that Fish is happy to accept both that the judgments of the participants in these practices are informed by a set of assumptions or implicit norms embedded in the practice, and that these norms entail that 'interpretation is a *structure* of constraints' that 'renders unimaginable the independent and freely interpreting reader'.[135]

As I argued at the beginning of the previous section, it is precisely that supposition that prevents the interpreter from being 'free to confer on an utterance any meaning he likes',[136] and that allows us to classify Fish's understanding (despite his resistance to endorse any 'pragmatist program') as a kind of *normative pragmatism*.

There are traces of this argument in Fish's writings, especially in the passages where he is developing his positive view of interpretive practices, instead of replying to Dworkin. In his account of interpretation in literature, for instance, Fish argued that 'literature ... is a conventional category', because 'what will, at any time, be recognized as literature is a function of a communal decision as to what will count as literature'.[137] The content of the practice of literature 'proceeds from a collective decision as to what will count as literature, a decision that will be in force only so long as the community of readers or believers continue to abide by it'.[138] To interpret a text or the content of a work within the practice, one appeals to a *shared sense* that comes not from the individualised sensibilities and perceptions of an interpreter, but from 'the interpretive community of which he is a member'. In other words, 'it is interpretive communities, rather than either the text or the reader, that produce meanings and are responsible

---

[133] ibid 382.
[134] Dworkin (n 28) 379.
[135] See above, text cited above n 30.
[136] Fish (n 66) 310.
[137] ibid 10.
[138] Fish (n 66) 11.

for the emergence' of the 'formal features' to which one appeals to interpret a text. As Fish explicitly acknowledges in this argument, although there is no 'mechanical and algorithmic procedure by means of which meanings could be calculated and in relation to which one could recognize mistakes', there is still a sense in which one can say, from the internal point of view of the practice, that there are reasonable or unreasonable interpretations because 'language is always perceived, from the very first, within a *structure of norms*'.[139]

Fish is offering us, with this line of reasoning, something that he explicitly claimed it is not possible to provide, that is, an 'internalist' or 'interpretive' version of Dworkin's 'right-wrong image' of adjudication. In effect, Fish is now advocating for an 'interpretive positivism' (as Dworkin labelled it in a later work),[140] because he resorts to the interpretive conventions accepted by a community of interpreters to determine the ways in which texts and political decisions that figure in legal practice shall be read. He appears to endorse, in other words, Dworkin's *conventionalism*, which is the same position that he argued in response to Dworkin it is impossible to occupy.[141]

In this conventionalist account, it is the reliance on interpretive conventions endorsed by a *community of interpreters* that allows Fish to avoid the regularist explanation of understanding, that 'is committed to identifying the distinction between correct and incorrect performance with that between regular and irregular performance'.[142]

But is this solution really an *alternative* to the regularist explanation, that I rejected in section III (when I attributed to Dworkin and Fish a normative pragmatism)?

To understand the norms of the practice that fix the manners by which practitioners can respond to the practice and perform any move in its language-game, we would have to look, in Fish's conventionalism, to the dispositions developed and shared by a *community*, instead of the desires and intuitions of a particular reader. Interpretive conventions are now the product of *regularities of communal assessment* and of a sense of appropriateness developed by a *group* that shares an understanding about the practice and its central concepts.

The problem of this solution, as Brandom explains, is that this strategy is vulnerable to the same challenge that applies to the strategy of appealing to a practitioner's intuitions to interpret a given concept.[143] If conceptual rules are characterised as correctly or incorrectly employed only in terms of the assessments, responses and endorsements undertaken by the 'community to which

---

[139] ibid 318 (emphasis added).
[140] Dworkin (n 46) 178–183.
[141] Fish (n 58) 357–358.
[142] Brandom (n 105) 28.
[143] See above, section IV.

the individual belongs',[144] it becomes impossible for the *community* to make a mistake.

By following the 'communal' dispositional route to avoid Wittgenstein's regress, Fish is in no better shape than the original formulation of the dispositional response, because this 'communal' dispositional strategy fails *either* because the idea of 'communal assessments, endorsements, or verdicts' is a *fiction* (for things like 'judgments' or 'assessments' are done by *individuals*, rather than collective entities) *or* because it lacks a criterion for assessing the judgments made by the community itself (for there is no conceptual space for irregularity, or for the community to *violate* a norm).[145] The same problem of incorrigibility that we identified in Fish's critique of Dworkin crops up again, although in a slightly different form. We are stuck with two disturbing alternatives: either we describe implicit norms in terms of natural dispositions (no matter if these are dispositions of individuals or a community of speakers) that regularly appear in the community's judgments, or we secretly rely on further norms that the community employs to assess the correctness of the application of explicit norms. While the first alternative fails because it depends on an implausible reduction of normative statuses (or conceptual norms) to behavioural dispositions, the second fails because it falls back into the regress that Wittgenstein attempted to resolve in the first place.

This is not a mistake Dworkin's 'law as integrity' would make, because as Dworkin explained in the light of his example of the interpretation of controversial aspects of the practice of courtesy, 'even if we assume that the community is a distinct person with opinions and convictions of its own, a group consciousness of some sort, that assumption only adds to the story a further person whose opinions an interpreter must judge and contest, not simply discover and report'.[146] As a consequence, Fish's conventionalist account of interpretive communities, which he develops while constructing his own account of the implicit norms of interpretive practices, is in no better shape than the intuitionistic and antitheoretical assumptions of the narrow or instrumentalist pragmatism that he endorses in his criticism of Dworkin's philosophy of law, because a subscriber of the communal dispositional explanation 'must still distinguish ... between the opinion the group consciousness has about what courtesy requires, ... and what he, the interpreter, thinks courtesy really requires'.[147]

Fish's account of interpretive communities fails because it cannot avoid the *burden of judgment* that each participant in an interpretive community must carry in order to understand the law. What is missing in Fish's account, therefore, is a sound justification of the implicit norms that fix the propriety conditions for interpreting a legal concept.

---

[144] Brandom (n 105) 37.
[145] ibid 38–39.
[146] Dworkin (n 7) 65.
[147] ibid.

As Simon Blackburn noticed in a direct comment on Fish's critique of Dworkin, Fish can be presented as a 'counterpart to Rorty',[148] because, like the latter, the former begins with a very bold statement (eg, that there is no way to distinguish between 'interpreting' and 'inventing' a law) and then adopts a rhetorical strategy that gradually deflates the premise with which the argument began: 'the whole issue becomes slightly deflated. What presents itself as a wholesale revolution now looks like a damp squib':

> When Rorty first substituted the goal of consensus for the goal of truth, we shuddered at the outrageous image of someone valuing *après*-truth chitchat in the coffee-house above serious work in the library or the laboratory. It is this that was so shocking. But now it turns out that there is a qualification for membership of the coffee-house. The talkers in the coffee-house are to be masters of the library or the laboratory, just as the legal interpretive community includes only masters of the constitution and of precedent.[149]

Fish's account of interpretation is based on an attribution of *authority* to interpretive communities, ie, to the members of that interpretive community, in order to determine, as a group, the conventional norms that define the content of the assertions a competent participant in a legal practice can utter and use.

The most important question, however, is left unanswered: *How* can we *make sense* of the difference, that Rorty qualifies in response to his critics as a 'serious and important distinction', between a 'frivolous' and a 'serious' assertion of an expert in the coffee-house?[150] Or, in a more legalistic vocabulary, how can we make sense of the distinction, that even Fish is committed to retain (for as long as it is understood as an 'interpretive' distinction, ie a distinction acknowledged and used within the practice, by its participants), between 'explaining' and 'changing' a legal norm? In order to answer this type of question, 'we have to postulate an interpretive community that has the *ability* to winnow out those who are not really curious whether p or who are not serious in their inquiry whether p or not trustworthy in reporting whether p',[151] which requires an attachment to epistemic norms the status of which cannot be merely conventional, it they are to perform a proper critical role.

Given that it is a rational assumption that even the community of interpreters can (sometimes) make mistakes, and that Fish cannot explain this assumption, Fish has not managed to construct a solution to the argument of regress. We should look to Dworkin, to check if he did a better job.

---

[148] S Blackburn, *Truth – A Guide for the Perplexed* (London, Penguin Books, 2005) 162.
[149] ibid 163–164.
[150] R Rorty, 'Response to Dennet' in RB Brandom (ed), *Rorty and His Critics* (Oxford, Blackwell, 2000) 101, 104–105.
[151] Blackburn (n 148) 165.

VI. DWORKIN'S RESPONSE TO FISH: THE LAW AS A SPECIAL NORMATIVE PRACTICE

Here are some words from a song every reader of this chapter will recognise:

> So, so you think you can tell
> Heaven from hell?
> Blue skies from pain?
> Can you tell a green field
> From a cold steel rail?
> A smile from a veil?
> Do you think you can tell?[152]

One could suppose that these are the sort of questions no sensible interpreter is used to answering, because her perception and familiarity with these concepts and phenomena will almost always *automatically* ground her judgment. Intuition and natural capacities are all we need.

But what if these are not the only kind of questions we must answer? What if there are *special* practices in which our sensibility is not enough, because the questions asked *within* these practices are inherently dependent on *rational* or *reflected* judgments? Perhaps this is the case of law, as Dworkin responded to Fish's objection that it is impossible to offer objective answers to interpretive legal judgments.

Consider the demand for objectivity in legal reasoning. Although Dworkin maintained in *Justice for Hedgehogs* that 'we cannot defend a theory of justice without also defending, as part of the same enterprise, a theory of moral objectivity' (and that 'it is irresponsible to try to do without such a theory'),[153] Dworkin also affirmed in his first response to Fish that the question of objectivity, as formulated by Fish, 'is a fake because the distinction that might give it meaning, the distinction between substantive argument within and skeptical arguments about social practice, is itself a fake'.[154]

How can we reconcile the claims that it is irresponsible to attempt to answer questions of justice without a theory of objectivity and that the question of objectivity is a fake?

Dworkin is endorsing in the first claim an account of 'domain objectivity', ie, of how to make acceptable or justified assertions inside a particular domain, whereas he is rejecting, in the second claim, an account of 'metaphysical objectivity' (in the same spirit that he rejected a correspondence theory of truth). What avoids a contradiction between these sentences is Dworkin's assertion, in the first claim, that the theory of objectivity we need for a theory of justice is 'part of the *same enterprise*' of constructing an account of justice, as well as his

---

[152] R Waters and D Gilmour, 'Wish You Were Here' in Pink Floyd, *Wish You Were Here* (Columbia Records 1975).
[153] Dworkin (n 71) 8.
[154] Dworkin (n 13) 300.

assumption, in the second quotation, that it does not make sense to combine, like some notable philosophers do,[155] substantive statements *within* the practice and sceptical statements *about* it.

On Dworkin's view, the problem of objectivity is not presented as a metaphysical problem, because 'whether moral judgments can be objective is itself a moral question, and whether there is objectivity in interpretation is itself a question of interpretation'.[156] Even if Dworkin's critics are correct to point out that he begs some metaethical questions because his denial of an austere metaethics can be understood as another metaethical undertaking, the only kind of scepticism that might undermine a practitioner's claim to objectivity will be a scepticism *within* the practice we are considering.

The concept of objectivity required for justifying the idea of objectivity presupposed by Dworkin comprises the notion of 'epistemic objectivity', that is, the view that people can be objective about certain features 'if they are, in forming or holding opinions, judgments, and the like, ... properly sensitive to factors which are epistemically relevant to the truth or correctness of their opinions or judgments'.[157] But there is more. It encompasses, in addition, a type of 'domain objectivity', which recognises not only 'certain structuring features' common to different domains,[158] but also some special responsibilities in the inquiry inside its own domain.[159]

An important condition for any objective domain is what Raz named the 'relevance condition', which requires that a domain contains 'facts or other considerations which are reasons for believing that they are or are likely to be true or correct'. Raz believes that depending on the domain of thought the 'reasons for holding a thought to be true or false are of a large variety of kinds'.[160] There is a large set of features, in each domain, that account for the appropriateness of the reasons in the domain. The objectivity of a domain need not presuppose 'either a priori or self-evident or incorrigible understanding' of the reasons which are relevant in the domain. It is satisfied, instead, with the assumption that the thoughts which belong to this domain 'allow for the application of judgments based on reasons' and 'that there can be reasons of an appropriate kind'.[161]

Dworkin believes that the feature of law that makes it a special practice, or the law's internal 'relevance condition', is that legal interpretation is a *purposive* activity, 'not just in vocabulary of its claims but in the standards of its success'.[162] The 'interpretive attitude' Dworkin recommends toward a legal rule

---

[155] See the discussion of 'external' scepticism in Dworkin (n 47) 94–129, and Dworkin (n 71) 40–68.
[156] Dworkin (n 13) 301.
[157] J Raz, *Engaging Reason* (Oxford, Oxford University Press, 2009) 119.
[158] GJ Postema, 'Objectivity Fit for Law' in B Leiter (ed), *Objectivity in Law and Morals* (Oxford, Oxford University Press, 2001) 99, 105.
[159] Raz (n 157) 122–123; Postema (n 158) 105–107.
[160] ibid 124.
[161] ibid 125.
[162] Dworkin (n 71) 152.

must assume, first, that this rule 'does not simply exist but has value', in the sense that it 'serves some interest or purpose or enforces some principle', and, second, that legal requirements 'are not necessarily or exclusively what they have always been taken to be but are instead sensitive to that point, so that the strict rules must be understood or applied or extended or modified or qualified or limited by that point'.[163] Without this interpretive attitude, one cannot come to an understanding of law.

To grasp this argument, we must beware of a subtle but important distinction. While the point of the practice of law 'can be stated independently of just describing the rules that make up the practice',[164] it is still the case that this point is embedded in the practice and can be made explicit with a rational judgment of the kind participants in the practice are routinely required to make.

What makes law special is the fact that the point of law – as Dworkin expects his readers to agree – 'is to establish a justifying connection between past political decisions and present coercion'.[165] There must be a special way to argue about law, an institutionalised argumentative process that enables officials to justify their coercive acts of legal enforcement in a morally and politically legitimate way. Legal judgments are conceived as a special kind of judgment in a sense analogous to the 'artificial' rationality of classical common law jurisprudence. 'The rules of common law' were not, in that traditional jurisprudence, made in the way Bentham assumed statutes are promulgated – ie, by enactment of a command – but rather more like the 'rules of English grammar' which are 'regularly taken up, used in deliberation and argument, and followed in practice'.[166] In other words, 'the law ... was not a structured set of authoritatively posited, explicit directives, but of rules and ways implicit in a body of practices and patterns of thinking "handed down by tradition, use, [and] experience"'.[167]

The notion of an 'artificial reason' for law allowed Postema to claim that these common lawyers had a *distinctive* jurisprudence, that resorted simultaneously to the seemingly conventionalist notion that the common law is a 'custom of the realm',[168] and to the natural law view that common law is 'nothing else but common reason'.[169] Although the classical common law jurisprudence, 'even in its heyday, did not mature into a full-fledged philosophical theory',[170] it

---

[163] Dworkin (n 7) 47.
[164] ibid 47.
[165] Dworkin (n 7) 98.
[166] GJ Postema, 'Classical Common Law Jurisprudence (Part I)' (2002) 2 *Oxford Commonwealth Law Journal* 155, 166–167.
[167] ibid 167. The quote inside the quotation is from W Blackstone, *Commentaries on the Laws of England* (Oxford, Clarendon Press, 1765–69) vol 1, 17.
[168] J Davies, 'Irish Reports' in A Grosart (ed), *The Works in Verse and Prose (including Hitherto Unpublished Mss) of Sir John Davies* (Blackburn, 1869–76) vol 2, 251–252, cited in Postema (n 166) 168.
[169] H Finch, *Law, or a Discourse Thereof* (AM Kelly Publishers, 1969) 75, cited in Postema (n 166) 176.
[170] Postema (n 166) 156.

organised the concepts of custom and reason in a 'broad' pragmatism of the sort that Brandom suggested and I described in sections III and IV.

For the common law notion of 'artificial' reason, 'custom was always subject to the test of reason, but reason was embodied in the common practices of law'.[171] According to Postema, this claim to an 'artificial reason' allows us to characterise the jurisprudence practiced by these historical lawyers as a 'third theory' of law, like John Mackie assessed Dworkin's intermediary position between legal positivism and classic natural law.[172]

I believe that the common law's notion of artificial rationality is similar to Dworkin's idea that legal practice is interpretive in a *distinctive* way, which is different both from 'conversational' interpretation (or the kind of interpretative task we take up when we want to make sense of the intention of a speaker) and from the kind of reasoning we engage in the domain of science (which Dworkin called a 'scientific interpretation' in *Law's Empire*[173] but reformulated later to claim that it is not a proper form of interpretation, because science, he came to believe, is an intellectual domain in which truth has nothing to do with purposes or interpretive points).[174]

Dworkin's account of constructive interpretation can be read as an endeavour to make sense of the common law maxim that the law can 'work itself pure', since it 'has its own ambitions' and contains an internal scheme of principles that enables its inconsistencies and mistakes to be *corrected* throughout that interpretive process.[175] The model to which Dworkin subscribes is like classical common law in that it distinguishes between 'positive law (the law in the books, the law declared in the clear statements of statutes and past court decisions)' and the 'full law' (which comprises also the 'set of principles of political morality that taken together provide the best interpretation of positive law').[176] It is the job of a *critical* interpreter, thus, to put that interpretive process into motion, or to *make the law objective* by making explicit the 'set of principles' that provides the 'best interpretation of positive law' while providing the 'best justification available for the political decisions the positive law announces'.[177]

By revisiting classical common law, Dworkin explained the argumentative or *self-critical* character of legal practice. Although it is commonly thought that common law jurisprudence is a conservative theory of law, Dworkin was able to give it, as Dan Priel aptly acknowledged, 'a critical twist'[178] to explain the role

---

[171] GJ Postema, 'Classical Common Law Jurisprudence (Part II)' (2003) 3 *Oxford University Commonwealth Law Journal* 1, 1.
[172] Postema (n 171); J Mackie, 'The Third Theory of Law' in M Cohen (ed). *Ronald Dworkin & Contemporary Jurisprudence* (Lanham, MD, Duckworth, 1984) 161.
[173] Dworkin (n 1) 49–53.
[174] See Dworkin (n 71) 153.
[175] R Dworkin, 'Law's Ambitions for Itself' (1985) 71 *Virginia Law Review* 173.
[176] ibid 176.
[177] ibid.
[178] D Priel, 'Making Sense of Nonsense Jurisprudence' (2020) *Osgoode Legal Studies Research Paper*, dx.doi.org/10.2139/ssrn.3696933, 56.

of *reason* in law, which is precisely the aspect of the practice of developed legal systems that was missing in Fish's work.

VII. CONCLUSION

Dworkin and Fish agree that, in order to interpret the law, citizens and legal practitioners resort to implicit norms that enable them to identify correct and incorrect applications of legal concepts. Nonetheless, Fish's narrow pragmatism is implausible because it commits to the belief-desire model and to the view that these norms are always instrumental norms. Dworkin's jurisprudence is a better interpretive theory of law because it is more apt to explain the role of *reason* in legal judgments.

Dworkin's response to Fish endorses the classical common law view that the law is a *special domain* where judgments can be defended and criticised according to an artificial rationality, which relies on embedded principles instead of transcendental metaphysics or mysterious mental states. This is a plausible account of methodological objectivity in the legal domain, although I believe (but cannot argue for it here)[179] that it can be extended to develop a general and more ambitious theory of meaning, that is not limited to the adjudication of legal cases in common law.

---

[179] I am glad that my colleague Thiago Decat took up this task in his chapter in this book. See also T Bustamante and TL Decat, 'Semantic Theories and Interpretation: A Critique of Michael S. Green's "Dworkin's Fallacy"' in T Gizbert-Studnicki, F Poggi, and I Skoczeń (eds), *Interpretivism and the Limits of Law* (Cheltenham, Edward Elgar, 2022) 176.

15

Making it Objective: Dworkin, Inferentialism, and the CLS Critique

THIAGO LOPES DECAT

I. INTRODUCTION

THIS CHAPTER BUILDS on an argument developed by Thomas Bustamante in the previous chapter of this book and attempts to provide an inferentialist answer to Fish's objection that Dworkin's right-wrong picture of adjudication fails because no objective answer to legal problems is at reach. According to Fish, it makes no sense to distinguish, within interpretive legal practices, between interpreting and inventing (or explaining and changing) a legal text.[1] Bustamante's chapter responds to this charge, to defend Dworkin's distinction, and compares Fish's and Dworkin's accounts of law and interpretation. It argues that Fish and Dworkin offer two different versions of pragmatism: while Fish endorses a 'narrow' (or instrumental) pragmatism, Dworkin commits to a 'broad' (or inferentialist) pragmatism. It suggests that the differences between Dworkin and Fish derive from the fact that the latter endorses a Humean version of the belief-desire model of rational action, which produces an impact on Fish's account of imputation of beliefs. Since Fish subscribes to a merely instrumentalist conception of knowledge, he fails to explain the role of rationality in legal assessments and to provide a standard of correctness for legal decisions.[2] It is because of this failure that Fish argued that it is not possible, for a legal practitioner, to occupy the two positions that Dworkin described as alternatives to 'law as integrity',[3] namely a *conventionalist* account of interpretation (that regards as legally binding only the rules explicit in an official's authoritative pronouncements), and a *pragmatist* account (that 'denies that past political decisions in themselves provide any justification for either using or withholding the state's coercive power', instructing judges and

---

[1] S Fish, 'Working on the Chain Gang: Interpretation in Law and Literature' in *Doing What Comes Naturally* (Durham, NC, Duke University Press, 1989) 87.
[2] See also NE Simmonds, ch 4 in this volume.
[3] See, for all, S Fish, 'Still Wrong After All These Years' in *Doing What Comes Naturally* (n 1) 356.

other officials to adjudicate legal cases according to their capacity to promote a collective good).[4]

I believe that the general argument of Bustamante's chapter is correct and reinforces Dworkin's conclusion that Fish's account of interpretive practices provides a passive and intuitionistic account of interpretation, compromising the argumentative or critical dimension of the value of the rule of law.[5] Nevertheless, Bustamante does not yet provide a fully articulated answer to the questions whether Dworkin has a more successful account of interpretation, and, more specifically, whether his 'right-wrong' picture of adjudication can resist the criticism that it is unable to provide an internal structure capable to deliver correct or acceptable legal judgments. It is to these questions that I turn my attention now.

I examine in this chapter an argument that is available to Dworkin, but he did not adduce in his replies to the objections presented by Fish. The counterargument that Dworkin presented to Fish's criticism was, as noticed in Bustamante's chapter, that there is a *special type* of objectivity appropriate to the legal domain. The law is a distinctive type of interpretive practice, in which the truth-claims of interpretive propositions are responsive to a normative point that underlies the explicit decisions of past political authorities. Nonetheless, I would like to examine a more general inferentialist argument about the rationality of communicative social practices, which (I suppose) is fully consistent with Dworkin's theory of legal interpretation but was not explicitly endorsed by Dworkin in his account of law, morality, and interpretation.[6]

Although I am convinced that Dworkin's argument about the special character can be successful, I argue that it can sometimes be vulnerable to an objection presented by the supporters of Critical Legal Studies, according to which the law of certain jurisdictions – like, it is argued, the US – is an incoherent compromise of inconsistent ideologies, in which 'law as integrity' cannot do its interpretive work because the 'articulate consistency' among principles presupposed by Dworkin's theory of adjudication is an unachievable goal. This is an empirical argument, and while it is likely that the law of most contemporary legal systems does not confirm this empirical hypothesis, I concede (alongside Dworkin) that there is no conceptual argument against the possibility of incommensurable interpretations in the legal domain.

---

[4] R Dworkin, *Law's Empire* (Cambridge, MA, Harvard University Press, 1986) 151.
[5] R Dworkin, 'Pragmatism, Right Answers, and True Banality' in M Brint and W Weaver (eds), *Pragmatism in Law and Society* (Boulder, Westview Press, 1991) 357, 380.
[6] Although Dworkin did not offer an inferentialist argument explicitly, he could have offered it, for it is entirely consistent with his own writings and is probably the best way to make sense of some central claims that he makes in his debate with Fish. See, for instance, T Bustamante and TL Decat, 'Semantic Theories and Interpretation: A Critique of Michael S. Green's "Dworkin's Fallacy"' in T Gizbert-Studnicki, F Poggi, and I Skoczeń (eds), *Interpretivism and the Limits of Law* (Cheltenham, Edward Elgar, 2022) 176; TL Decat, 'Inferentialist Pragmatism and Dworkin's Law as Integrity' [2015] *Erasmus Law Review* 14; and TL Decat, *Racionalidade, Valor e Teorias do Direito* (Belo Horizonte, D'Plácido, 2015).

This possibility is one of the reasons why the more general argument, provided by Brandom's inferentialism, can be more successful than Dworkin's actual response to Fish. I present, thus, an inferentialist reading of Dworkin's jurisprudence, that makes it not only more resistant to Fish's and the CLS's critiques, but also more capable to explain some important aspects of modern legal systems, like the role of reason in legal judgments.

The chapter is divided into four sections. In section II, I analyse a response that Dworkin actually gave to Fish, which holds that law is an 'interpretive' practice in a distinctive sense, whereas in section III I respond to an objection presented by CLS and furnish an inferentialist response to Fish (that Dworkin did not articulate explicitly but was available to him). I clarify two Hegelian aspects of the inferentialist semantic theory that I believe are required to make sense of Dworkin's claim to objectivity in the normative domain. First, the notion of 'progress' in rational judgments and, second, the social aspect of normative practices. Section IV concludes.

II. FROM FISH'S CRITIQUE TO CLS: DWORKIN'S VIEW OF THE LAW AS A SPECIAL NORMATIVE PRACTICE

Dworkin argues in response to Fish that the law is a special domain with an internal structure that provides its distinctive standards of objectivity. This is a general argument underlying several passages of *Law's Empire*, and probably Dworkin is right about that. Nevertheless, perhaps someone may think Dworkin's jurisprudence cannot meet the interpretive challenges this understanding of law as a special practice entails.[7] In effect, Dworkin's claim that the law is a special domain relies on the *contingent* empirical assumption that the law has a kind of content that allows an objective assessment by the participants in interpretive practices, instead of comprising a set of conflicting and incompatible values that cannot be interpreted in the rational and consistent way Dworkin would want us to try.

Dworkin is aware of this possibility when he considers situations where 'internal' scepticism prevails, but he is confident that these are not numerically significant cases and for the most part 'law as integrity' is a sound interpretive method to provide an acceptable justification for legal decisions. In effect, Dworkin presupposes a concept of objectivity similar to that of classical common lawyers, which can be classified as a 'moderately' domain-specific notion of objectivity. On this view, 'while it is possible for specific conceptions of objectivity to differ, they share certain generic or structuring features'[8] like some

---

[7] I thank Thomas Bustamante for discussing this challenge with me, inviting me to comment on his chapter in this book, and encouraging me to offer this printed response to the challenge.
[8] GJ Postema, 'Objectivity Fit for Law' in Brian Leiter (ed), *Objectivity in Law and Morals* (Oxford, Oxford University Press, 2001) 99, 100–101.

of the features discussed in Bustamante's chapter. Particularly important among these features is the possibility of 'assessments of the *correctness* or *validity* of judgments', and the assumption that despite the possibility of disagreement and agreement 'there is some ground for hope of moving from the one to the other on the basis of the reasons that support the judgments'.[9]

It is precisely this assumption that is denied by the advocates of Critical Legal Studies, or CLS, who claim that Dworkinian integrity is unachievable because the law 'is a patchwork quilt, as it were, of irreconcilably opposed ideologies', which are all fit to 'play a significant part in the public debate of our political culture' and are inevitably 'replicated in the argument of [any] judicial decision'.[10] Objectivity is always out of reach, CLS scholars suppose, not only because settled law 'is the transitory and contingent outcome of ideological struggles among social factions in which conflicting conceptions of justice, goodness, and social and political life get compromised, truncated, vitiated, and adjusted',[11] but also because these ideological and social tensions crop up again in adjudication.

According to the CLS scholar Duncan Kennedy, for instance, legal norms in American legal practice are but a provisory settlement of a persistent and fundamental conflict between two general and incommensurable tendencies or 'visions of humanity and society', namely a *communitarian* tendency towards 'altruism' and a *liberal* tendency towards 'individualism'.[12] Although Kennedy's more recent scholarship nuances (and is not entirely consistent with) his previous understanding of this tension, in that he now struggles to establish a neat distinction between 'legislation' and 'judicial lawmaking' and argues that the latter 'works within and seeks to be faithful to law',[13] one can argue that the CLS objection (in its original form) creates a dilemma for Dworkin because his constructivism only can offer a sound reply to the objection 'at the cost of cutting loose of the idea that the community is in some sense already committed to a coherent and principled position which the Dworkinian lawyer has a responsibility to unearth'.[14] According to Jeremy Waldron, who is not a CLS scholar but thinks Dworkin did not respond appropriately to their arguments, Dworkin's jurisprudence faces a tension because the method it employs to deliver a rational and objective decision – constructive interpretation – does not work if there is no minimum level of integrity, *already in place*, among the 'commitments of the

---

[9] ibid 107–108.
[10] A Altman, 'Legal Realism, Critical Legal Studies, and Dworkin' (1986) 15 *Philosophy & Public Affairs* 205, 222.
[11] ibid 221.
[12] D Kennedy, 'Form and Substance in Private Law Adjudication' (1976) 89 *Harvard Law Review* 1685.
[13] GJ Postema, *Legal Philosophy in the Twentieth Century: The Common Law World* (Dordrecht, Springer, 2011), 237, commenting on D Kennedy, *A Critique of Adjudication (Fin de Siècle)* (Cambridge, MA, Harvard University Press, 1997).
[14] J Waldron, 'Did Dworkin Ever Answer the Crits?' in S Hershovitz, *Exploring Law's Empire: The Jurisprudence of Ronald Dworkin* (Oxford, Oxford University Press, 2009) 155, 156.

community' that Dworkin applies to make 'coherent sense of the existing legal materials'.[15]

If the *Crit*s are correct in their diagnostic that the law is composed of a 'messy, rich in compromises, exceptions and contradictions' patchwork of norms, then Dworkin would be vulnerable to a serious concern: 'One would have to be naively optimistic – to the point of some sort of Hegelian faith in the cunning of reason – to believe that these [constructive interpretive] processes yield a single determinate structure of principled reasons'.[16]

Dworkin responded to this argument on several occasions, and the answer was always the same. In response to Waldron, he acknowledged that 'if no-eligible-interpretation situations were systemic in American law the pursuit of integrity there would be silly', but argued that Waldron offers no example of that kind of conflict and that Kennedy (the most prominent CLS scholar) 'does not even claim, let alone try to illustrate, an endemic no-eligible-interpretation situation in American law'.[17] It is the *Crit*, Dworkin replies, that bears the burden of proving that these incommensurable conflicts exist. Moreover, given the impossibility of demonstrating that no such conflicts exist, we must 'await actual supposed examples'. There is nothing to say in response to CLS, Dworkin argues, because 'we cannot be sure, before we look, that constructive interpretation can produce integrity in any particular area of law. But we have no reason to think, in advance, that it cannot'.[18] As Dworkin argued also in response to the challenges of incommensurability presented by John Mackie[19] and Neil MacCormick,[20] any argument in support of incommensurability cannot be a 'conceptual' argument that supposes that 'you can see in advance, just by understanding the concepts involved, that you can't compare the two cases', because the question of incommensurability is a *practical*, rather than ontological, problem.[21] The absence of a conceptual argument against incommensurability (either in law or in morality) should not be a serious concern. Although Dworkin presupposes 'a conception of morality other than some conception according to which different moral theories are frequently incommensurable',[22] we can still have a sound moral system if there are not too many moral conflicts, and there seems to be nothing in the structure of moral or legal judgments that force us to presuppose that assumption.

---

[15] ibid.
[16] ibid 163.
[17] R Dworkin, 'Response' in *Exploring Law's Empire* (n 14) 291, 300.
[18] ibid 304.
[19] J Mackie, 'The Third Theory of Law' in M Cohen (ed), *Ronald Dworkin & Contemporary Jurisprudence* (Lanham, MD, Duckworth, 1984) 161, 165.
[20] N MacCormick, 'On "Open Texture" in Law' in P Amselek and N MacCormick (eds), *Controversies about Law's Ontology* (Edinburgh, Edinburgh University Press, 1991) 72, 74–75.
[21] R Dworkin, 'On Gaps in the Law' in *Controversies about Law's Ontology* (n 20) 84, 89.
[22] R Dworkin, 'A Reply by Ronald Dworkin' in *Ronald Dworkin & Contemporary Jurisprudence* (n 19) 247, 272.

Although I cannot argue for that position here,[23] I believe Dworkin is correct in this response, and that incommensurability is not a serious problem in the legal domain if we treat the value of 'integrity' (or, more recently, his assumption of the unity of value) as an interpretive goal, ie, as something we *strive towards* by taking up a moral responsibility of knitting our values together and explaining how more abstract values feed into concrete ones. Integrity is a pragmatic methodological requirement that we need to *achieve* objective judgments about value propositions, instead of a metaphysical requirement that we assert under the assumption of a correspondence theory of truth.

Unlike Fish, Dworkin is not committed to a metaphysical concept of objectivity (that follows from a correspondence theory of truth), because the kind of objectivity that matters is a methodological one, for 'true', 'valid', or 'acceptable' statements are only those that we can *make objective* through reasoned judgments that display *fidelity* to the scheme of principles we use law as integrity to understand.

Law as integrity can be interpreted as committed to the idea of *progress* and to the thought that within a concrete normative practice the participants of interpretation can *put into motion* the process that, when the law succeeds in its claim to legitimacy, 'yields a single determinate structure of principled reasons'. Although some would think that CLS has shown that this is a naïve form of optimism because it believes in 'some sort of Hegelian faith in the cunning of reason',[24] perhaps there is something in Hegel that can come to our rescue, for it is in the contemporary forms of philosophical inferentialism (which relies partly on Hegel) that we can find an argument that provides a better Dworkinian response to Fish, one that does not depend only on some empirical features of positive law, because it is based on an inquiry into general features of rationality and social practices instead of resorting only to domain-specific features of any particular legal system. Brandom's Hegelian account of rational social practices seems to suggest, in this sense, that some of the features Dworkin (and others) regarded as special to law (or common law) are actually general aspects of rationality, of which Fish appears to be unaware.

III. INFERENTIALISM AND THE RATIONAL STRUCTURE OF NORMATIVE SOCIAL PRACTICES

A. Inferentialism: A General Outlook

Before addressing the topic of how a (partly) Hegelian account of social practices may equip us with the tools to simultaneously give an appropriate response to

---

[23] But see T Bustamante, 'Between unity and incommensurability: Dworkin and Raz on moral and ethical values' (2022) 13 *Jurisprudence* 169.
[24] See Waldron's argument on the text above n 14.

Fish's criticisms of 'law as integrity' and eschew the empirical objections of the *Crits*, it is important to show why such a take on the rationality of social practices is needed in the first place. To do so, however, will require an explanation of the inferential rationality instantiated by social linguistic practices, such as law, and of the ways in which this model of rationality is incomplete and insufficiently critical (in Kant's sense of revealing the conditions of possibility of the subject of investigation) so as to invite complementation by a Hegelian historical rationality.

Brandom developed *inferentialism* in part as a general semantic theory that explains the conceptual contents of linguistic expressions and performances in terms of the inferential articulation of the contents of commitments undertaken and entitlements claimed (as well as attributed to others) by participants of linguistic practices. This semantic theory, however, is also understood as an aspect of the rationality of linguistic practices in general. On this view, to be *rational* is to take part in the language game of making and challenging *assertions*, which are put forward as reasons to believe something is true.

Brandom argues rational social practices can be properly understood only in relation to a general 'game of giving and asking for reasons', since the propositional contentfullness of expressions and linguistic performances advanced by participants in other language games, including institutionalised explicitly normative ones like law, are dependent on the inferential articulations that define their roles in the basic language game of assertion:

> Utterances and states are propositionally contentful just insofar as they stand in inferential relations to one another: insofar as they can both serve as and stand in need of reasons. Conceptual contents are functional inferential roles. ... So long as one can assert (put something forward as a reason) and infer (use something as a reason), one is rational.[25]

The bulk of the inferences that Brandom takes as articulating and constituting conceptual contents of expressions and performances are not, nevertheless, logical or formal inferences, but *material* ones. They are tokenings of norms determining the correct use of expressions in terms of entitlement to employ and commitments to endorse other propositions. What makes them *material inferences* is the fact that they are acceptable inferential transitions because of the *content* and not the form of the propositions involved. Instead of formal inferences like 'every man is mortal; Smith is a man; hence, Smith is mortal', they are inferences like 'A is over B; hence, B is under A', or 'it is raining outside; hence, the streets are wet', or yet 'Martha is dead; hence, Martha is not breathing'.

This inferentialist conception of rationality, according to which being rational is to be able to produce and consume reasons by operating with structures that can play the roles of premises and conclusions in reasoning, embeds

---

[25] RB Brandom, *Tales of the Mighty Dead* (Cambridge, MA, Harvard University Press, 2002) 6.

semantics in a normative *pragmatics*[26] that is committed to the assumptions that: (i) a semantic theory of meaning should be regarded as 'answering to pragmatics in the sense that pragmatic theory supplies the explanatory target of semantic theory – and hence is the ultimate source of *criteria of adequacy* according to which the success of that theoretical enterprise is to be assessed' (that Brandom classified as a 'methodological' pragmatism);[27] and (ii) that these criteria of adequacy are implicit in the 'the way practitioners *use* expressions that makes them *mean* what they do' (that Brandom classified as a 'semantic' pragmatism).[28]

On this account:

> Nothing is recognizable as a practice of giving and asking for *reasons* … unless it involves undertaking and attributing *commitments*. And those commitments must stand in *consequential* relations: making one move, undertaking one commitment must carry with it further commitments … commitments whose contents follow from the contents of the first commitment. Further, a practice of giving and asking for reasons must be one in which the issue of one's entitlement to a commitment one has undertaken (or that others attribute) can arise. And those entitlements, too, must stand in consequential relations: entitlement to one move can carry with it entitlements to others.[29]

The inferentialist conception of linguistically structured social practices understands a rational practice – one in which participants consume and produce reasons – as concerning the question of the participants' entitlement to the commitments they have undertaken or that others have attributed to them. Hence, according to Brandom, 'to take or treat someone in practice as offering and deserving reasons is to attribute inferentially articulated commitments and entitlements'.[30]

Although a reader not familiar with inferentialism might find Brandom's deontic vocabulary too technical, and perhaps removed from the ordinary arguments lawyers and judges employ in their daily activities, there is an emerging literature in jurisprudence that applies Brandom's philosophy to understanding the practice of law.[31] In effect, Brandom's refinement of the structure of

---

[26] On Brandom's vocabulary, pragmatics is the 'systematic or theoretical study of the use of linguistic expressions', whereas semantics is the study of the 'contents they express or convey'. RB Brandom, *Perspectives on Pragmatism: Classical, Recent, and Contemporary* (Cambridge, MA, Harvard University Press, 2011) 57.
[27] ibid 58–59.
[28] ibid 61. See also, for Fish's position, T Bustamante, ch 14, section II in this volume.
[29] Brandom (n 25) 7.
[30] ibid 6.
[31] See, in addition to my own works cited at n 6, L Marchettoni, 'From Hart to Dworkin via Brandom: Indeterminacy, Interpretation, and Objectivity' in G Villa Rosas and J Fabra (eds), *Objectivity in Jurisprudence: Legal Interpretation and Practical Reasoning* (Cheltenham, Edward Elgar, 2022) 127; L Marchettoni, 'Brandom on norms and objectivity' (2018) 19 *Critical Horizons* 215; M Klatt, *Making the Law Explicit: The Normativity of Legal Argumentation* (Oxford, Hart Publishing, 2008).

argumentative social practices can make sense of some concepts which are very useful for legal philosophy, like Wil Waluchow's distinction between the 'moral opinions' and 'moral commitments' accepted in the practice of constitutional law: while the locution 'moral opinions' describes 'moral views that have not been critically examined so as to achieve reflective equilibrium', the expression 'moral commitments' express 'those that have'.[32] True moral commitments, according to Waluchow, are those that resist after a careful reflection under an interpretive scheme. On this account,

> It's the commitments, not the beliefs, that are said to be true – although those who believe that moral sentences express propositions to which truth values can be assigned will hope that their beliefs share this property as well. Following Rawls, we can say that our moral opinions sometimes conflict with our moral commitments.[33]

Although Waluchow does not make explicit reference to Brandom, he admitted in a recent interview that Brandom's account of the inferential relations among commitments is 'very agreeable' and 'perfectly coincident with the approach that I defend'.[34] In effect, it is the distinction between moral opinions and moral commitments that allows Waluchow to explain, for instance, the possibility that the *majority*, or perhaps the *whole community* can be wrong about a particular aspect of the constitutional morality it endorses. In the context of the criticisms received by the Canadian Supreme Court, for instance, Waluchow explained this possibility in the following way:

> When Court decisions are criticized for being out of sync with the moral views of citizens, the focus is almost always on some widespread moral *opinion* that is at odds with the court's ruling. The focus is almost never on the general principles and values to which most citizens are actually committed.... When judicial recognition of same-sex marriage is criticized for being against the moral beliefs of Canadians, the reference is almost always to moral opinions. These are moral opinions that, upon reflection, flatly contradict fundamental beliefs, principles, values, and considered judgments that enjoy widespread, if not universal, currency within the community, and they introduce significant evaluative dissonance. They are also opinions that are inconsistent with any reasonable interpretation of the Charter and the many judicial decisions made in its name.[35]

As Bustamante argued in an analysis of Waluchow's jurisprudence, despite the differences of Waluchow and Dworkin with regards to methodology and the nature of law, Waluchow's acknowledgment of the relevance of *implicit commitments* in constitutional interpretation places his constitutional theory in

---

[32] WJ Waluchow, *A Common Law Theory of Judicial Review: The Living Tree* (Cambridge, Cambridge University Press. 2007) 224.
[33] ibid.
[34] T Bustamante, S de Matos, and ALS Coelho, 'Interview with Professor Wil J. Waluchow' in *Law, Morality and Judicial Reasoning: Essays on W.J. Waluchow's Jurisprudence and Constitutional Theory* (Dordrecht, Springer forthcoming).
[35] Waluchow (n 32) 225.

the same neighbourhood of Dworkin's model of 'law as integrity', and it is their tacit endorsement of the *inferential semantics* made explicit by Brandom that establishes their common ground.[36]

B. Deontic Scorekeeping and Relations Among Commitments

The activities of meaning attribution and acknowledgment can be described as a kind of 'deontic scorekeeping' (in Brandom's vocabulary) of the commitments and entitlements that can be ascribed to the participants in the practice. To participate in the practice, a member should have in mind her own score and the score of other participants in the same game: 'Competent linguistic practitioners keep track of their own and each other's commitments and entitlements. They are (we are) *deontic scorekeepers*.'[37]

Since Brandom takes the pragmatic significance of making a claim or assertion as being the undertaking of a commitment to its content and inferential consequences, and since the inferential relations that articulate the content of an assertion can be altered by the endorsement of another commitment, 'Speech acts ... alter the deontic score; they change what commitments and entitlements it is *appropriate* to attribute, not only to the one producing the speech act, but also to those to whom it is addressed.'[38] This deontic scorekeeping requires *each of the participants* in social practices to act as a *rational* participant therein, keeping two ledgers: the first comparing the antecedents and the consequences of the interlocutor's commitments with other commitments and entitlements the scorekeeper attributes to her, and the second comparing those deontic statuses with commitments and entitlements the scorekeeper acknowledges herself.

The two kinds of deontic statuses – commitments and entitlements – can find themselves in three sorts of inferential consequential relations that guide the activity of recording and adjusting the deontic score.

First, they may be articulated along *commitment-preserving relations*, which can be described as a translation in deontic scorekeeping and material inference vocabulary of traditional logical and deductive relations. Consider the following example: since Wittgenstein wrote the *Tractatus* in the trenches of the First World War, anyone committed to Wittgenstein being the greatest Austrian philosopher would be committed, knowingly or not, to the greatest Austrian philosopher having written his first book in the trenches of the First World War.

---

[36] T Bustamante, 'Waluchow and Dworkin's Disagreement on Legal Theory, Precedent and Adjudication: A Family Affair' in *Law, Morality and Judicial Reasoning* (n 34).
[37] RB Brandom, *Making it Explicit* (Cambridge, MA, Harvard University Press, 1994) 142.
[38] ibid (emphasis added).

Second, deontic statuses may also be articulated along *entitlement-preserving* relations, which are extensions of inductive relations of classical logic to material inferences. Brandom clarifies this possibility with the following example:

> Since falling barometric readings correlate reasonably reliably (via a common cause) with the stormy weather ahead, one who is both entitled and committed to the claim that the barometric reading is falling has some reason entitling commitment to the claim that stormy weather is ahead.[39]

Finally, the third type of inferential consequential relations, namely *incompatibility relations*, are extensions to material inferences of modal relations. Because the practice is sustained by the engagement of *rational agents*, who must master the inferential articulation of the norms of the practice, we need to master the incompatibilities between these norms in order to understand the *mistakes* of the agents that purport to engage with the practice. In other words, we must 'use the relation between commitment and entitlement ... to get a grip on a *material* notion of negation, or better, incompatibility'.[40] Two claims are incompatible if, from the perspective of the scorekeeper, 'commitment to one precludes entitlement to the other'.[41] This is the consequential relation that sustains, for example, the inference from the claim that an object is wholly red to the claim that it cannot be wholly white.

This inferential conception of rationality also encompasses another important feature: a redefinition of the role of logical and of explicitly practical normative vocabulary. Understanding both semantics and rationality in terms of 'material inferential articulation of commitments and entitlements' inaugurates a new way of explaining the relation between logic and rationality: 'instead of seeing conformity with logical truth as what rationality consists in, one can see logical vocabulary as making possible the explicit codification of meaning constitutive inferential relations'.[42]

Logical vocabulary – specially conditionals – has the expressive function of allowing speakers to *say explicitly* through claims what in the absence of conditionals they could only do, namely, endorse or reject material inferences by means of non-linguistic practical behaviour:

> Prior to the introduction of the conditional, for instance, one can implicitly take or treat the material inference ... from p to q as a good or a bad one, endorsing or rejecting it in practice. Once a suitable conditional is available, though, one can explicitly *claim that* p entails q.[43]

---

[39] Brandom (n 25) 8.
[40] Brandom (n 37) 160.
[41] Brandom (n 25) 8.
[42] ibid 9.
[43] ibid.

Logical locutions have therefore an *expressive* function. They make material inferential relations explicit in the form of claims, that is, the kind of things we can ask and offer reasons for and against.

Brandom sees an analogous expressive role being played by explicit normative vocabulary regarding practical material inferential relations. These are relations that specify the ways in which transitions from doxastic commitments (ie, commitments acquired in the making of assertions) to practical commitments (ie, commitments to do something) are structured.[44]

According to Brandom, there are three types of practical inferences that can allow an inference from doxastic commitments to practical inferences: *instrumental oughts*, *institutional oughts*, and *unconditional oughts*.

Consider the following example of an *instrumental* ought. In the same way that the conditional 'if p then q' makes the commitment of a person who endorses the conditional to the propriety of the inference from p to q explicit, 'expressions of preference or desire show up as codifying commitment to the propriety of patterns of practical inference'.[45] For instance, someone's desire to stay warm *expresses* a commitment to the propriety of inferences like the inference from 'only wearing a jacket will keep me warm' to 'I shall wear a jacket'.

In a similar way, a statement of obligation associated with a specific *institutional* status can play the same roll of expressing the commitment of the utterer to the propriety of a pattern of practical inferences. This institutional pattern of practical inference differs from expressions of preference in a relevant aspect, however, since 'the latter is binding only on those who endorse the preference in question, while the former is binding on anyone who occupies the status in question ... regardless of their desires'.[46] As an example, the statement of obligation 'judges ought to be impartial towards the parties to the litigation' licenses inferences from 'doing X would not be acting impartially' to 'I shall not do X', ie, it makes the endorsement of the material inferential transition explicit.

Finally, *unconditional oughts* can codify in an explicit way the endorsement of practical material inferences understood to be binding on everyone, regardless of desires and institutional statuses, by the person who endorses them. For instance, the statement of obligation 'one ought not to be cruel' licenses inferences from 'doing X would be cruel' to 'I shall not do X'.

Brandom avoids Humean and Kantian assumptions of a rational priority for the first and third of these patterns of practical reasoning, because his inferentialist picture is committed to the claim that 'all of these "oughts" – the

---

[44] Inferential transitions from doxastic commitments to practical ones may strike some as an enthymeme since Hume's law seems to block this inferential move. Brandom develops a sophisticated argument to circumvent this conclusion based on the fact that practical material inferences are non-monotonic. I cannot address the issue here, but for a complete exposition see chr 2 of RB Brandom. *Articulating Reasons* (Cambridge, MA, Harvard University Press, 2000).

[45] Brandom (n 25) 10.

[46] ibid 11.

instrumental, the institutional and the unconditional – are in the most basic sense *rational* oughts, since they codify commitments to patterns of practical reasoning'.[47]

In an inferentialist reading, when someone makes a judgment or utters a statement, she commits herself to the propositional content of this judgment or linguistic performance. However, since the meaning a person attaches to her own performances depends on the *inferential articulation* of the content of commitments recently acknowledged with that of other normative statuses, and since the making of a new speech act or judgment has the pragmatic meaning of *undertaking* a new commitment capable of altering the normative score of that person, judging and speaking involve a responsibility to do something, a kind of *task responsibility*, namely 'the responsibility to *integrate* the judgment into a *unity of apperception*'.[48] To do so is to integrate new endorsements into a coherent whole composed of the person's previous endorsed commitments.

This successive integration involves activities destined to fulfil three different responsibilities. The first is a *critical responsibility* that demands eschewing materially incompatible commitments: 'This means rejecting candidate judgments that are incompatible with what one is already committed to and responsible for, or relinquishing the offending prior commitments.'[49] The second, *ampliative* responsibility, requires that one extracts the material inferential consequences from old and new commitments by conjoining them with each other: 'Each commitment gives one reason to accept others' in the sense that 'one has already implicitly committed oneself to them by acknowledging the commitment from which they follow'.[50] The last, *justificatory* responsibility, asks of us to be prepared, in the sense of being willing to offer reasons for the commitments we endorse (that is, to show which other commitments entitle us to the new ones). Each of these three component task responsibilities has the aim of turning the whole body of our commitments consistent, complete, and warranted, respectively.

Since Brandom believes that, regarding the task responsibilities one undertakes in judging and uttering, 'there is a parallel story about endorsing a practical maxim', the similarity between this integrative specification of responsibilities involved in scorekeeping and Dworkin's conception of interpretation comes to light. Consider, for instance, Dworkin's suggestion that constructive interpretation can be divided in three stages: a pre-interpretive stage, in which rules and legal materials are tentatively identified; an interpretive stage, at which the interpreter identifies the general justification of the materials identified in the first stage; and a post-interpretive stage, or 'reforming stage', at which the interpreter

---

[47] ibid.
[48] RB Brandom, *Reason in Philosophy: Animating Ideas* (Cambridge, MA, Harvard University Press, 2009) 36.
[49] ibid.
[50] ibid.

'adjusts his sense of what the practice "really" requires so as better to serve the justification'.[51]

If we translate the experimental data to be gathered in the first stage of the constructive interpretation of law (and to be effectively interpreted in the second stage) into the vocabulary of inferentialism, those political and judicial decisions become nothing more than *institutional oughts* to be integrated into a consistent, warranted, and complete whole in face of the need of undertaking a new practical commitment forced on interpreters by a new set of circumstances of action. It is possible to see the force of critical responsibilities in what Dworkin describes as our intuitive aversion to checkerboard laws and in our common expectation that the state, speaking for the community, does it in a single and consistent voice.[52]

By the same token, the fulfilment of ampliative responsibilities is what is at stake when an interpreter extracts implicit rights and duties from the set of conceptions of political morality principles or values that best justify the practice as a whole, and not only from the plain meaning of explicit past political decisions. She is then precisely unearthing implicit practical commitments as conclusions from premises found in the explicit commitments that the practice, considered as a whole, undertook.[53] The *justificatory responsibility* of giving reasons for new practical commitments when it is required, by pointing to yet other commitments that entitle the interpreter to the new one, is precisely what is fulfilled by what Dworkin calls a 'justificatory ascent':

> We reason from the inside-out: we begin with discrete problems forced upon us by occupation or responsibility or chance, and the scope of our inquiry is severely limited, not only by the time we have available, but by the arguments we happen actually to encounter or imagine. A judge, reasoning from the inside out will rarely find either the time or the need to undertake long, laborious research or argument. Sometimes, however, he will.[54]

Perhaps we can summarise this point in the following way:

> Dworkin's claim is not that understanding is never possible without constructive interpretation. It is, instead, based on two ideas: first, that it is not always the case that understanding is possible without it; and second, that all norms and concepts are interwoven (such that it is possible to resort to the interlocking network of norms when disagreement emerges about the content of individual norms, because this interlocking network explains even the concepts we are able to grasp intuitively or without controversial argument). In other words, Dworkin is committed to the view that legal arguments are potentially vulnerable to a justificatory ascent.[55]

---

[51] Dworkin (n 4) 65–66.
[52] ibid 183.
[53] ibid 96.
[54] R Dworkin, 'In Praise of Theory' in *Justice in Robes* (Cambridge, MA, Harvard University Press, 2009) 49, 54–55.
[55] T Bustamante, 'Is Protestant Interpretation an Acceptable Attitude Toward Normative Social Practices? An Analysis of Dworkin and Postema' (2021) 66 *American Journal of Jurisprudence* 1, 24.

The Dworkinian concept of 'justificatory ascent' dovetails nicely with the more detailed account of this justificatory task responsibility that Brandom describes in *Making it Explicit* as the '*default and challenge structure of entitlement*'. When discussing the aspect of entitlement attribution of linguistic practices, the author identifies the risk of an account of social practices incurring in a kind of infinite regress, namely a regress of entitlements: 'What gets the process off the ground? What gives these … mechanisms something to work with in the first place, so that chains of vindication can come to an end?'[56] Brandom's answer to this problem is to turn one more time to his fundamental pragmatic commitment that allows him to see normative statuses, not only commitments but also entitlements, as implicit in social practices:

> Those practices need not be – and the ones that actually confer content on our utterances are not – such that the default entitlement status of a claim … is to be guilty until proven innocent. … [A] grounding problem arises in general only if entitlement is never attributed until and unless it has been demonstrated. If many claims are treated as innocent until proven guilty – taken to be entitled to commitments until and unless someone is in a position to raise a legitimate question about them – the global threat of regress dissolves.[57]

Brandom believes this second position regarding the default entitlement status of a claim is sensible for the same anti-cartesian reasons found in Peirce's early writings.[58] Doubts too need to be justified if they are to be in a position to challenge entitlements to commitments. The question of which of our commitments requires vindication is a matter of the practical attitudes adopted towards them by the participants of the social practice. Some commitments, doxastic and practical, are frequently treated by practitioners as ones to which people are prima facie entitled. It is the case of simple claims such as 'People have noses' or of practical commitments such as 'I ought to eat now'. Even they can have their status as justified questioned, but these questions will need to have some justification in order to have a stand to impugn entitlement. As Brandom summarises the point:

> Practices in which that status [being entitled] is attributed only upon actual vindication by appeal to inheritance from other commitments are simply unworkable; nothing recognizable as a game of giving and asking for reasons results if justifications are not permitted to come to an end.[59]

The *default and challenge structure of entitlement* aims to show, therefore, that frequently, and as a matter of social practice, when a commitment is attributed to an interlocutor by a deontic scorekeeper, entitlement to it is also attributed by default.

---

[56] Brandom (n 37) 176.
[57] ibid 177.
[58] See CS Peirce, 'The Fixation of Belief' (1877) 12 *Popular Science Monthly* 1–15.
[59] Brandom (n 25) 177.

It is possible to see this same structure of default entitlement to commitments in Dworkin's explanation of an interpreter's justificatory ascent:

> My claim ... is that legal reasoning presupposes a vast domain of justification, including very abstract principles of political morality, that we tend to take that structure as much for granted as the engineer takes much of what she knows for granted, but that we might be forced to reexamine part of the structure from time to time, though we can never be sure, in advance, when and how.[60]

This sketch of how linguistic social practices look when seen from the vantage point of an inferential semantics (embedded in a normative pragmatics) enables me to take, in the next section, the last theoretical step to complete this picture, which requires an incursion into Brandom's Hegelian explanation of the attitudes and responsibilities of participants in a rational social practice.

C. Specifying the Content of Dworkin's (and Brandom's) Interpretive Responsibility

It becomes clear, from the summary exposition of the inferential rationality of social practices offered in this section, that the specification of the meaning-constitutive inferential relations between propositions in normative terms makes our judgments and actions the kind of things we are *responsible* for. And we are responsible for them in a distinctive way, captured by the notion of task responsibility. Judgments and actions express commitments of knowers and agents, and something must determine what we commit to by judging and acting in certain ways. Even if the deontic score is kept by an interlocutor or an observer of behaviour in action, the recording she makes is guided by the content she identifies in these activities, that is, it is guided by its conceptual content. Brandom makes this theoretical proposal clear: 'As I am suggesting that we think of them, concepts are broadly inferential norms that implicitly govern practices of giving and asking for reasons.'[61] In this sense, Brandom follows Kant in understanding concepts as rules:

> The norms or rules that determine what we have committed ourselves to, what we have made ourselves responsible for, by making a judgment or performing an action, Kant calls 'concepts'.[62]

All concepts, including those concepts Dworkin calls interpretive and Putnam and Williams call 'thick' ethical concepts, are for Brandom 'rules determining what is a reason for what'.[63] And here lies the problem. Inferential rationality

---

[60] Dworkin (n 54) 56.
[61] Brandom (n 48) 120.
[62] ibid 115.
[63] ibid 14.

is a conception of rationality that adopts, although it is not restricted to it, the central Kantian idea that rational beings are norm-sensitive beings, both in their theoretical and practical endeavours. When one asks, however, how to understand what it presupposes, namely, the existence of conceptual norms available and adequate to the particulars to which they apply, it becomes clear that it uncritically presupposes a set of norms inferentially articulated as an activity already in progress. It remains unanswered, if an innate explanation is no longer accepted, what makes the existence of determinate conceptual norms possible, that is, what users of concepts must do to establish and submit themselves to such norms. Brandom understands this questioning as the last in a series of increasingly critical questions about the semantic assumptions of rationality.

The solution Brandom finds to this problem is to embed inferential rationality and semantics in a Hegelian historical conception of rationality. This conception understands the rationality of social practices 'as consisting in a certain kind of reconstruction of a tradition'.[64] This reconstruction has a characteristic expressive function, since it 'exhibits [the tradition or practice] as having the expressively progressive form of the gradual, cumulative unfolding into explicitness of what shows up retrospectively as having been all along implicit in the tradition'.[65]

Although this conception of rationality shares with Kant the inferentialist idea that being rational is being a concept user and that rationality consists in being subject and sensitive to conceptual norms, which requires being able to correctly characterise particulars under the universals they really fall under, it has the comparative advantage of explaining the availability of determinate norms (determinate concepts) that guide the process. As Brandom explains it, for Hegel, as well as for Kant, 'concepts are norms for judgment', since they 'determine proprieties of application to particulars of terms that, because of the normative role they play in such judgments, expresses universals'.[66] Hegel, however, as Brandom reads him, thought that 'the *only* thing available to settle *which* universal a word expresses is the way that word – and others linked to it inferentially – has *actually* been applied in *prior* judgments'.[67]

To illustrate the answer Brandom thinks Hegel gave to the question of how past uses of concepts determine what we ought to do with them in the future, that is, what we have to do to subject ourselves to determinate conceptual norms, the author points to the *rational activity* of judges in a common law tradition. Brandom believes that this activity instantiates the Hegelian historic-expressive rationality that consists in 'retrospectively picking out an expressively progressive trajectory through past applications of a concept, so as to determine

[64] Brandom (n 25) 12.
[65] ibid.
[66] ibid 13.
[67] ibid.

a norm one can understand as governing the whole process and so project into the future'.⁶⁸ Brandom believes a slightly idealised version of this judicial activity provides us with an interesting model to understand the rationality of social practices because all one can employ to determine the limits of applicability of a concept is the set of decided cases acknowledged as precedents: 'there is no explicit initial statement of principle governing the application of legal universals to particular sets of facts – only a practice of applying them in always novel circumstances'.⁶⁹ Since, in this model, concepts get their contents exclusively from the history of their past applications, a judge must – to fulfil his justificatory task responsibilities which have an institutional coating but logically precede it – *rationalise* her decision as the next step in that tradition or practice, 'by so selecting and emphasizing particular prior decisions as precedential that a norm emerges as an implicit lesson'.⁷⁰ In finding the norm (that determines the universal) applicable to the case (the particular), the judge 'must make the tradition cohere, must exhibit the decisions that have actually been made as rational and correct, given the norm she finds is what has implicitly governed the process all along'.⁷¹

It is difficult to ignore the resemblance of this description of the judicial model Brandom chooses to exemplify the Hegelian historical rationality guiding the institution and application of conceptual norms to Dworkin's conception of the constructive interpretation oriented to integrity. The exhibition of a decision as correct and rational for being a continuation of a tradition or practice is just another name for the normative force orienting the chain novel of law. But the resemblance does not stop there. Brandom understands this process as rational in a structured way since the justifiability of the application of a concept in a decision is obtained by presenting 'an expressively progressive genealogy of it'.⁷² The presentation of this 'expressively progressive genealogy', however, is dependent on a particular *attitude*, once 'it is insofar as one *takes* the tradition to be rational, by a Whiggish rewriting of its history, that one *makes* the tradition be and have been rational'.⁷³ The same kind of *progressive performative attitude* is an element of the interpretive attitude that gets Dworkinian constructive interpretation off the ground.⁷⁴ It is by treating legal practice as valuable and coherent that an interpreter committed to 'law as integrity' *makes* it be and have been valuable and coherent. Both linguistic practitioners and Dworkinian

---

[68] ibid.
[69] ibid.
[70] ibid.
[71] ibid 14.
[72] ibid.
[73] ibid.
[74] Dworkin's 'protestant interpretation', for instance, can be construed as an attempt to specify the responsibilities *each participant* (including not only judges and officials but also anyone who can make an interpretive claim) must undertake to participate in the discursive game of giving and asking for reasons. See Bustamante (n 55) 9–11.

interpreters are, in a way, in the same Hegelian business of 'finding a norm by making a tradition' and 'giving it a genealogy' that is, of giving contingency the form of necessity, in the Kantian sense of being in accordance with a norm.[75]

If this is correct, as we believe it is, Dworkin's conception of constructive interpretation oriented towards integrity is but an instance, regarding Brandomian *institutional oughts*, of this *rationality as systematic history*. Understanding it in these terms has three major advantages, in the context of the discussions developed in the other sections of this chapter.

First, it backs the interpretation of Dworkin's theory of interpretation as a contemporary version of the common lawyers' idea of an 'artificial' rationality internal to legal practice. In their writings, as in Brandom's and Dworkin's, the interpretive resources to perfect, correct, and improve the practice can be found *inside* the practice. No recourse to an Archimedean point of view is postulated or needed.

It is no casualty that Dworkin interprets some of the traditional assumptions of classical common law (like the claims that there is a 'law beyond law' implicit in legal practice,[76] and that the law 'works itself pure' through a continuous search for integrity)[77] and natural law jurisprudence (like the claim that 'what the law is depends in some way on what the law should be')[78] in a *critical way*, reversing the apparently conservative character of these theories of law.[79]

Second, the presentation of how linguistic social practices look, when redescribed through the lenses of inferential and historical rationalities, makes available a better reply (perhaps a compelling reply) to the criticisms levelled against integrity-based interpretation in law by the *Crits*. As I reported in section II, the CLS's criticism to Dworkin was based on a controversial empirical description of two supposedly incompatible ideologies underlying each approximately half of the law. *Ad argumetandum tantum*, even if they were right in that description, it would not be the case that the Whiggish attitude of trying to give contingency the form of necessity, ie, of trying to find a norm by making a tradition, is inappropriate. Although Dworkin recognises the possibility of an internal scepticism about a proposition of law, he accepts that possibility only as an outcome of, instead of cause for disregard of, the search for integrity.

Furthermore, this rational-historic frame underlying legal practice suits it because of its linguistic structure, having a reach that stretches beyond the legal domain. Since this rational framework is part of a general semantic theory (the other side of the coin of a theory of rationality, according to Brandom), its legal instantiation is *not* vulnerable to differences in the contents of municipal

---

[75] Brandom (n 25) 14.
[76] Dworkin (n 4) 400.
[77] ibid 404–405.
[78] R Dworkin, 'Natural Law Revisited' (1982) 34 *University of Florida Law Review* 165.
[79] D Priel, 'Making Sense of Nonsense Jurisprudence' (2020) *Osgoode Legal Studies Research Paper*, dx.doi.org/10.2139/ssrn.3696933, 56.

legal systems. Dworkin's jurisprudential ideas can be regarded as applicable, therefore, beyond the boundaries of common law legal systems.[80] A complete criticism of it would have to mobilise specialised arguments against inferential semantics.

Third, understanding 'law as integrity' as an instance of historic-expressive rationality still leaves room to understand legal practice as a *special* normative practice, preserving the insight (of Raz, Postema and others) that there are certain standards of objectivity *specific* to the legal certain domain. The normative goal of *turning a past into a history* is compatible with different 'genres' of narratives amounting to a systematic history, each distinguished by its own internal justifying functions and values, and compatible with the existence of different proposals of reconstruction inside each special practice, proposals that are made possible by the different perspectives of deontic scorekeepers in the practice.

Nevertheless, perhaps there is room for an objection. Given what was said in this section so far, it would not be unreasonable to question if, despite the apparent similarities between Brandom's semantic and rationality theories, on one hand, and Dworkin's theory of legal interpretation, on the other, our argument has not gone too far. Wouldn't this approach reduce practical norms to conceptual ones? Would Brandom himself agree with this interpretation?

I believe those questions can be answered in a way that reinforces the interpretation proposed here. In his paper answering Habermas' criticisms to *Making it Explicit*, for instance, Brandom claims: 'Habermas is right to detect sympathy for an assimilation of normativity in general to specifically conceptual normativity (as I think Kant and Hegel do).'[81] This may sound strange, especially to readers that have Humean inclinations in the theory of action. To make it work, Brandom needs a theory of action that explains how motivating reasons can be understood in terms of modifications in the deontic score the agent keeps of her own commitments and entitlements. I will not be able to address the issue here, but such a theory can be found in the second chapter of *Articulating Reasons*.[82]

There are no grounds for doubting Brandom himself would agree with an inferentialist reading of Dworkin's theory of law. In his paper *A Hegelian Model of Legal Concept Determination*, Brandom presents his evaluation of Dworkin's theory of law, with focus on his idea of the chain novel: 'It is clear that this model is getting at something important about case law (and about common

---

[80] For a specific argument that Dworkin's and Brandom's theories of law 'are powerful not only with respect to common law but also with respect to civil law', see also S Arnold, 'The Chain Novel and Its Normative Fine Structure in Civil Law and Common Law: *Dworkin, Brandom* and Law's Normativity' in N Bersier, Christoph Bezemek and F Schauer (eds), *Common Law-Civil Law: The Great Divide?* (Dordrecht, Springer 2022) 29.
[81] RB Brandom. 'Facts, Norms, and Normative Facts: A Reply to Habermas' (2000) 8 *European Journal of Philosophy* 3, 371.
[82] Brandom (n 44) 79–96.

law, which is case law all the way down).'[83] But despite that positive impression, Brandom considers Dworkin's model stricken with 'extreme generality' and providing not a full account of the rationality of the process of applying and instituting norms, but 'only the form of an account'.[84] Brandom then sets out to explain the normative fine structure underlying Dworkin's chain novel:

> My suggestion is that the diachronic, historical species of Hegel's generic reciprocal recognition model of the institution of normative statuses by normative attitudes specifies a substantive structure of authority and responsibility that fills in the normative fine structure gestured at but not supplied by Dworkin's chain novel metaphor.[85]

There is little ground for suspicion, therefore, that Brandom's semantics is not fit to supply the fine structure of argumentative practices that is required to explain the interpretive endeavours and the critical standards demanded by Dworkin's right-wrong image of the practice of legal adjudication.

D. On the Social Aspect of Legal Practice

I attempted to carry out part of that enterprise (of specifying this fine structure) in the previous paragraphs of this section. It remains to be seen what Brandom has to say about the social dimension of the process of interpretation, application, and institution of legal norms. Brandom believes Hegel's theory of recognition holds the key to understanding the simultaneous application and institution of conceptual legal norms we find in Dworkin's theory of legal interpretation. He believes this Hegelian model is both a way of bridging the is/ought gap, allowing a weak naturalist explanation of norms, and recognising that normative status or norms are real entities, not mere epiphenomenal appearances derived from normative attitudes, as radical expressivist or relativist metanormative theories suppose. The central idea is that 'normative statuses are *social* statuses'.[86] Normative statuses such as commitments and entitlements, albeit real, are not part of the furniture of the world, they are products of a human activity: 'it requires us practically to take or treat each other *as* responsible and authoritative for us to *be* responsible and authoritative'.[87] However, the institution of normative statuses by normative attitudes is not a voluntaristic or solipsistic affair. Talking about Hegel's primary normative status, the status of *selfhood*, understood as the status of those who are subjects of normative statuses, ie, capable

---

[83] RB Brandom. 'A Hegelian Model of Legal Concept Determination: The Normative Fine Structure of the Judges' Chain Novel' in G Hubbs and D Lind (eds), *Pragmatism Law and Language* (London, Routledge, 2014) 31.
[84] ibid.
[85] ibid.
[86] ibid 28.
[87] ibid.

of undertaking responsibilities and exercising authority, Brandom explains that 'it is necessary and sufficient to be a normative subject that one is recognized as such by those one recognizes as such. When recognitive attitudes are in this way reciprocal, they institute a genuine normative status: selfhood.'[88]

According to this idea, the attitude of recognising others has an inherent reciprocal nature, since *recognising* another person is *attributing* to her the authority to recognise others as well as the original recogniser himself. If this person whose authority was attributed by the original recogniser, together with other persons he recognised, exercise in turn their authority to recognise him, that original recogniser is thereby constituted as a *self*. Brandom summarises this process in the following way: 'being able to *be* responsible (a normative status) depends on others *holding* one responsible (a normative attitude)'.[89] The same structure is found in the institution of a more prosaic normative status, such as being a good philosopher or being a judge. One important outcome of the institution of normative status by normative attitudes presenting the structure of reciprocal recognition is that the status is not determined by the attitude of a single person: 'it is up to each agent whether to undertake a commitment or to claim an entitlement. But what the status that is instituted determinately *is* is up to those one has made oneself responsible to by recognizing them.'[90]

This Hegelian account of the structure of reciprocal recognition is useful to understand legal practices because it provides a way to explain how we can be entitled to the claim that judges (or, perhaps more generally, interpreters) are responsible *for the law*, on one hand, and *to the law*, on the other hand. The sense in which judges are responsible for the law is the outcome of the fact that there is nothing to guide the application of legal concepts except the history of previous applications to particular cases. The judge in charge of a case selects the cases she treats as precedential, the features of facts she considers relevant for the decision, and formulates a rationale for the decisions she makes. In doing so, she establishes precedents to which judges of future cases are potentially answerable. By doing all this, the deciding judge of the present 'exercises authority over both the content of the legal concepts being applied and, thereby, over the decisions of future judges'.[91] At the same time, the deciding judge is responsible to the content of the concept she applies in the decision, and which she inherited from the tradition. Since the application of legal concepts in decisions can find its justification only in the authority conferred to previous applications and decisions (or, in other words, since all the deciding judge has to determine the boundary of the concept's application is the meaning conferred on the legal term by those decisions), she is bound by the authority of previous judges.

---

[88] ibid.
[89] ibid.
[90] ibid 29.
[91] ibid 32.

So far, what has been said shows how judges located in the past can *exercise authority* over the content of the law and thereby over future judges located ahead of them in time. However, these future judges exercise a reciprocal authority over the content of the law, and consequently over judges located before them in the chain of judicial decisions. For each judge has the authority to revise precedents established by prior judges, constructing rationales that show certain previous applications of legal concepts as mistakes that reduce, instead of increase, the coherence of the tradition of application of legal concepts. These judges are then, like their colleagues, as responsible *for* the law as they are responsible *to* the law.

All these reciprocal authorities and responsibilities of participants in the judicial practice of applying legal concepts come together to synthesise norms for present cases, provided these normative relations instantiate the appropriate recognitive structure. What is needed is a bundle of normative attitudes capable of sustaining the process of sequential integration of new commitments into a constellation of previous ones, and in doing so instituting a legal conceptual norm. Brandom describes the process in these terms:

> Each deciding judge recognizes the authority of past decisions (and so of the contents they both acknowledge and help institute) over the assessment of the correctness of the decision being made. That judge also exercises authority over future judges, who are constrained by that judge's decisions, insofar as they are precedential. But the currently deciding judge is also responsible to (and held responsible by) future judges, who can (by their practical attitudes) either take the current decision (and rationale) to be correct and precedential, or not. For the current judge actually to exercise the authority the decision implicitly petitions for recognition of, it must be recognized by future judges. And if that precedential authority *is* recognized by the later judges, then it is real (a normative status has been instituted by those attitudes), according to the model of reciprocal recognition.[92]

IV. CONCLUSION

I conclude that Dworkin's interpretivism is well equipped to resist Fish's critique of the key distinctions Dworkin needs to establish the legitimacy and objectivity of legal claims (distinctions between 'finding' and 'inventing'; 'continuing' and 'striking out in a new direction', 'interpreting' and 'creating', 'explaining' and 'changing', and so on). The inferentialist and Hegelian detailing of the normative fine structure of constructive interpretation, summarised in the last section (and subsections therein), provides the key to understand the resolutely *holistic* and *social* character of the inferential semantics underlying both Brandom's description of linguistic practices, and the internal structure of argumentation that Dworkin postulated in his account of law as 'law as integrity'. To uphold

---

[92] ibid 33.

a non-foundationalist and interpretive character for legal practices, like Fish and Dworkin do, one must make sense of the task responsibilities comprised in the practice of interpretation and of the role played by the *implicit norms* which define this task. One must explain, in other words, how to make these implicit elements explicit and through this process of 'cumulative unfolding into explicitness' (to paraphrase Brandom again) *make* our apparently controversial judgments *objective*, in Dworkin's sense. This requires us to show that these are judgments we are *entitled* to make in a rational normative practice, because we can show that they are *worthy of being accepted* in virtue of their inferential relations to other judgments a responsible interpreter must accept. Part of the responsibility of interpreting legal concepts and past political decisions (that stem from the institutional history of a political community) is the responsibility to make *critical* and *reflective* judgments about the content of these legal materials, within the game of giving and asking for reasons in which the interpreter participates. It is that responsibility that enables one to understand how the norms implicit in the internal structure of normative legal practices make certain interpretations 'correct and incorrect', 'consistent and inconsistent'. Given the impossibility of completely closed technical vocabularies, which is even more pronounced in the case of practical normative vocabulary, this is not only a task of judges and political officials, but a capacity any *responsible* interpreter of a legal text is entitled to have and required to possess.

Part Four

Implications

16

Dworkin, Fish, and Radically Defective Constitutions

SANFORD LEVINSON*

I. INTRODUCTION

THOUGH I AM flattered at having been asked to participate in this retrospective review of the famous set of exchanges between Ronald Dworkin and Stanley Fish, I must also confess to being uncertain about what I have to offer. It is true that, as someone much influenced by what we might now describe as the 'early Fish', I argued that one could understand better the controversies over 'constitutional interpretation' by becoming familiar with the extraordinarily rich debates occurring within the field of what was being labelled 'literary theory'.[1] Whether or not I was myself interpreting Fish exactly as he intended – a question that itself sets up an obvious question and possible paradox – I certainly was convinced by his emphasis on the importance of 'reader response' and the concomitant role of the reader, as a member of what Fish labelled an 'interpretive community', in actively constructing the meaning of *any* given text as a crucial insight.

This was also the time when he published his classic book *Is There a Text in This Class?*[2] The role of the 'interpreter' became not so much to discover the singular immanent meanings 'within' a truly 'authoritative' text, whether a novel, poem, or legal text, but, instead, in effect to become a co-creator of the text in terms of the meanings to be ascribed to it. There were no longer 'Framers' who sent messages that interpreters would try to decode and then implement; instead, the reality is that the Constitution was continually being 'reframed' by decisions of those with interpretive authority, even if, for rhetorical reasons, the interpreters claimed to be the faithful servants of the text and/or the Framers.

---

* As always, I am grateful to Jack Balkin and Mark Graber for their helpful comments on an earlier draft

[1] S Levinson, 'Law as Literature' (1982) 60 *Texas Law Review* 373–403, reprinted in S Levinson and S Mailloux, *Interpreting Law and Literature* (Evanston, Northwestern University Press, 1988).

[2] S Fish, *Is There a Text in This Class?* (Cambridge, MA, Harvard University Press, 1982).

Given that different readers would generate (or 'create' or 'invent' or 'impose') different meanings, this was viewed as supporting arguments about so-called 'textual indeterminacy', a view that I certainly identified with.[3] It simply seemed to me foolish to believe that the questions generated by the US Constitution, the primary focus of my scholarly endeavours, presented unique solutions, which would have to be accepted by everyone else, to what Robert Jackson famously referred to as both its 'majestic generalities' and 'cryptic words', each of which is an apt reference to the Fourteenth Amendment and, in fact, much else of the Constitution.

Fish has recently published, as part of an online symposium focusing on my own work on constitutional interpretation, an extremely helpful synopsis or 'retrospective' of what he calls 'the theory debates of the 1980s'.[4] He says that they revolved around the central question of 'what if anything constrains interpretation?' Is it plausible, in the words of Cole Porter, that 'anything goes' when offering interpretations or, as a matter of fact, are interpreters necessarily 'constrained', ie, limited in the range of their possible interpretations? Can we therefore distinguish better from worse – or, even more to the point, 'true' from 'false' interpretations, precisely because the former remained within the necessary constraints? As a matter of fact, no one was really arguing that 'anything went'. Or, perhaps more accurately, anyone arguing such a position had to confront the obvious pragmatic reality that all arguments, especially within what were tellingly called 'disciplines', had limits – constraints. But then the vital question became, in Fish's words, 'What is the source of these constraints?' Some argued that they resided in such things as 'the text, rules,

---

[3] The term 'indeterminacy', as Ronald Dworkin argued in 'Objectivity and Truth: You'd Better Believe It' (1996) 22 *Philosophy & Public Affairs* 87–139, differs importantly from 'uncertainty'. The latter suggests an empirical reality that might, given further developments, be resolved. The former is a more ontological condition where there can never be resolution; or, even if there is an ontological 'right answer', our epistemological deficiencies may assure that we will never in fact attain it. I can understand the philosophical difference among these concepts, but I am not sure about the practical difference. It is certainly true that the debates often featured the word 'indeterminacy'. Would they have taken significantly different directions had they instead emphasised only the 'uncertainty' of many legal concepts? I doubt it. In both cases, presumably, there was the practical need for at least provisional resolution and, therefore the possibility that any such resolution would be basically by fiat, where a Humpty Dumpty-like figure simply claimed the authority to make the words mean whatever he wished them to mean. Some in the US have assigned that role to the Supreme Court. 'We are under a Constitution', Charles Evans Hughes, later to serve as both an Associate and Chief Justice of that Court, asserted, 'but the Constitution is what the judges say it is'. Although often quoted, almost no one takes this view seriously as a matter of constitutional or legal theory. Among other things, it seemingly makes it impossible to assert that 'the judges' are ever mistaken, given that there is no independent point of judgment outside the members of the Court themselves. And, of course, deciding what it means to be a 'judge' itself raises profoundly important questions. Antonin Scalia, for example, accused his colleagues on occasion of 'not behaving like judges'. If we could agree in fact on what exactly it means to 'act like a judge', then Hughes's comment might have a quite different implication than simply accepting as 'law' any decision issued by someone occupying an office of 'judge'.

[4] S Fish, 'The Theory Debates of the 1980s: A Retrospective', *Balkinization (Guest Blogger)*, 22 June 2022, balkin.blogspot.com/2022/06/the-theory-debates-of-1980s.html.

authorial intention, the moral foundation of the law, the structure and conventions of practice, divinely revealed truths'. The ultimate point, though, was that 'In order to have constraints must you first have a theory? If so, what kind of theory – linguistic, formalist, economic, natural law, pragmatist, feminist, postmodernist, realist?' The interpreter brought the theory to the enterprise of interpretation, so that, understandably enough, many of the debates, which could turn quite bitter, turned on determining what interpretive theories made most sense. Theories in effect create meanings we ascribe to texts – or, indeed, to the world more generally. And, to put it mildly, there was no consensus on what single theory was best – or 'true'.

Still, Fish emphasises, by way of chiding presumed partisans of 'indeterminacy', we always at all times operate within webs of constraints; that is, the words and sentences of legal documents are not floating in some garden of pure isolated abstraction, waiting for us to give them meaning in the way that Adam named the animals at Eden, but, instead are part of suitably complex communicative systems that we come to in the first place because we are embedded in communities that have taught their members to believe that what they mean is important. I still think it fair to say that 'meanings' comes from the perceptions of the relevant communities and not 'from the texts themselves'. Not only might the relevant community itself be quite divided on the meanings of key texts, but it is also a key lesson of legal history, like all history, that meanings change over time. As a matter of fact, one interpretive community can lose its intellectual authority as anyone emerges and wins converts. And, over time, the new would-be hegemonic community will find itself faced with challengers. Uneasy lies the heads of those who wear crowns.

Even before encountering Fish, though, I was certainly disinclined, given my initial training as a political scientist, to give much credit to the famous 'right answer' thesis associated especially with what might also now be described as the 'early Dworkin'. For Dworkin it was essential to recognise that the model judge – the idealised and totally fictitious Hercules – was endeavouring to find – and presumably *could* find – the uniquely correct 'right answer' to any given legal conundrum. As a fledgling academic at Princeton, before entering the legal academy, I reviewed his early collection of essays, *Taking Rights Seriously*, which included, of course, his classic view of the tasks presented when confronting what he called 'hard cases'. Even for the hardest of cases, there was always, at least in theory, a singular answer, in the specific sense that a proper judge was never confronted with the law 'running out' and therefore having to make an essentially wilful decision manifesting ultimately her own preferences rather than the commands of the law.[5] As a political scientist, I found this implausible in the extreme, for the empirics of actual decision-making obviously revealed

---

[5] See S Levinson, 'Taking Law Seriously: Reflections on "Thinking Like a Lawyer"' (1978) 30 *Stanford Law Review* 1071–1109 (review of Ronald Dworkin, *Taking Rights Seriously*).

often bitter disagreements among presumably conscientious judges. The explanation for such differences seemed to reside in what Felix Frankfurter, in his own essay in the initial *Encyclopedia of the Social Sciences*, called the ideological 'pictures' that resided in the heads of the justices. That is, it was ultimately impossible to separate 'law' from 'politics' and, therefore, the contingent personae of the adjudicators.

Within political science, of course, this led to the development of what came to be called 'attitudinalism', where judges were conceived of basically as 'politicians in robes', with 'law' as such having little, if anything, to do with actual decisions. If they were 'constrained', it was only by a prudential sense of what they could get away with, rather than by a sense of obedience to the rules laid down. One need not have gone entirely down that road. One might concede that 'law' is in some sense a 'reality' in the work life of a judge inasmuch as it is perceived, phenomenologically, as a genuine 'constraint' on what is proper. This is true especially in what might be called 'easy cases' where any real conflict concerns determining the 'facts' in the case rather than the 'law' that presumably organised the facts. But this was not true of 'hard cases' where both 'the facts' and 'the meaning of the law' could easily be contentious. Nor, incidentally, was it self-evident which were 'easy' and which were 'hard' cases. That distinction, too, was determined by interpretive communities and not the inherent properties of language.[6] At least some 'easy cases' would turn into 'hard cases' because of changes in the polity or even, perhaps, because of changes in 'legal theory'.[7] That was the context within which Dworkin was writing and was disputing, although, to my knowledge, he never directly addressed any of the relevant literature in political science. Walter Murphy's book, *Elements of Judicial Strategy*, published in 1973, was presumably never on Dworkin's (or Hercules's) reading list.[8]

One might, of course, interpret the 'right answer' thesis to mean only that *any* interpreter of any text, whether a poem, a musical score, a dramatic script, or a law, would try conscientiously to come up with what was, all things considered, the 'best answer' with regard to resolving the particular problems that one

---

[6] See S Levinson, 'What Do Lawyers Know (And What Do They Do With Their Knowledge)? Comments on Schauer and Moore (1985) 58 *Southern California Law Review* 441–58; 'On Interpretation: The Adultery Clause of the Ten Commandments' [1985] *Southern California Law Review* 719–25, reprinted in A Aarnio and N MacCormick (eds), *Legal Reasoning, Vol II* (New York, New York University Press, 1992), 323–29.

[7] Consider an example raised in Texas in July, 2022. Is a woman cited for driving alone in a 'high occupancy vehicle lane', which requires at least two passengers, entitled to plead that the fact that she is pregnant means that she meets the requirement, since the foetus is a 'person' who should be recognised as such for the purposes of this traffic law? I suspect this would not have been taken at all seriously several years ago; it would have been an 'easy case'. Today, though, because of the Supreme Court's decision overruling the notion that there is a constitutional right to an abortion, this assertion has already generated some respectful comment that suggests that it may no longer be an 'easy case'.

[8] W Murphy, *Elements of Judicial Strategy* (Chicago, University of Chicago Press, 1973).

was presented with at Time T and situation S. It would seem strange if those charged with 'interpretation' of any of these varieties of texts would pronounce themselves as truly indifferent to seeking the 'best' answer. But it was not clear to me then, and it is not clear to me now, that that 'concession', as it were, announced anything more than a trivial phenomenological truth. The point is that 'all things considered' would, for judges like Richard Posner or Steven Breyer, quite overtly include decisions as to what would best serve the overall interests of the polity. Posner initially found the answer in economics, Breyer in forms of technocracy. Only Posner, an intellectual adversary of Dworkin, would dare write one book titled *Overcoming Law* and another one scoffing at the utility of legal theory, but one suspects that he spoke for many at least in the privacy of their chambers.

Furthermore, As Jack Balkin and I argued in 1991,[9] the task of an isolated reader of a poem differed greatly from, say, the director of a play or the conductor of an orchestra concerned, among other things, with the actual abilities of the actors and musicians available to work with and the expectations of a potential audience that would have to buy tickets and encourage their friends to do so as well. It was chastening to realise that in many productions of *King Lear* in the eighteenth and nineteenth centuries Cordelia lived, because audiences were simply too depressed at the truly tragic ending. To be commercially successful, the director had to anticipate the reactions of the audience. Anyone interested in the historical actuality of Shakespeare as performed would have to take this into account, whatever we today might think of the 'fidelity' of such performances to the initial text. And, crucially, one had to presume that the 'interpretive community' of theatre directors and actors, not to mention critics, found it altogether acceptable to revise texts, even of the immortal Bard, when revision could provide comfort instead of despair for the audience.[10]

The essay that Balkin and I wrote was couched as a review of a book on the 'authentic performance' movement in music, which we likened to the burgeoning insistence during the Reagan Administration that 'originalism' provided a royal road to achieving legal 'right answers'. Did 'authentic performance' require playing only on period instruments or taking every single repeat indicated in a musical score, perhaps explicable because, quite obviously, no pre-twentieth-century audience could ever hope to hear a piece of music again simply by putting (at least in what we can now recognise as *our* 'old days') a record in a phonograph and placing a needle on it? As a matter of fact, repeats are now usually regarded as, at most, suggestive rather than mandatory, and few

---

[9] J Balkin and S Levinson, 'Law, Music, and Other Performing Arts' (1991) 139 *University of Pennsylvania Law Review* 1597–1658.

[10] See J Balkin and S Levinson, 'Interpreting Law and Music: Performance Notes on "The Banjo Serenader" and "The Lying Crowd of Jews"' (1999) 20 *Cardozo Law Review* 1513–72 (concentrating especially on changes in lyrics). We certainly are aware that almost no one today puts on productions of Shakespeare's plays that include literally every scene and word that he wrote.

performers insist on playing Beethoven sonatas on pianofortes of the kind available in Vienna, with their more limited range of notes than modern pianos. Does that teach a valuable lesson about the general notion of 'interpretive fidelity'?

Balkin and I argued as well that the task – the phenomenological reality – of any actual judge, unlike Hercules, was far different from that of an isolated reader concerned only with trying to figure out, say, the role of Satan in *Paradise Lost*.[11] An 'isolated reader', assuming we can agree on what that term might actually mean, is very different from, say, a vulnerable assistant professor concerned with achieving tenure or even an ambitious tenured professor eager to 'move up' the prestige ladder. Either might wish to offer truly 'audacious' interpretations, sincerely believed to be correct ways of understanding the given text; but both might also legitimately be worried about the possibility that 'audacity' will be interpreted by others as 'foolhardiness' or worse. This is certainly true as well of the position of any public official called a 'judge'.

Hercules is an extraordinarily odd judge, seemingly the sole member of an apex court who never had to be concerned with anyone else when deciding a case. 'Compromise' was not a significant part of Dworkin's vocabulary, perhaps because Hercules was unencumbered by other immediate judicial colleagues whose votes might be vital to attaining a necessary majority or 'inferior' judges charged with implementing his decree. There were also no 'superior' judges who might hear an appeal challenging Hercules's opinion. There was similar indifference to the non-judicial readers of an opinion. Would they in fact comply with it and, if so, exactly why? Could they be presumed to be faithful servants (again, assuming we knew exactly what this means) of Hercules, happily implementing whatever rule (or standard) he happened to lay down? Or is it possible that, for whatever reasons, they disagreed with the mighty Hercules and quite self-consciously looked to ways to work around any presumed commands issued by that mighty presence? Such disagreement might be generated, incidentally, because Hercules famously believed that 'taking rights seriously' required an indifference to the actual consequences of any such taking.

II. 'LEGITIMACY' AS A CONSIDERATION FOR (ACTUAL) JUDGES

The political scientist James Gibson has famously suggested that 'legitimacy is for losers', by which he means that one can expect that winners in a given adjudication will rarely question the decision and be more than happy to proclaim its legitimacy. That will be left up to potentially unhappy losers, and 'legitimacy' can be measured perhaps by the extent to which they will in effect be 'good

---

[11] Fish, of course, made his initial mark within the world of literature and such literary theory by his writings on Milton and, especially, *Paradise Lost*.

sports' and say, as Al Gore famously did in December 2000, that it was his duty, as a loyal American, to accept the fact that the Court had spoken in *Bush v Gore*, whatever his private opinion might be of the quality of the decision in terms of its reasoning or of the consequences in terms of its having in effect brought the election to an abrupt end with the de facto election of George W Bush as president.[12] Thus Hercules seemed to preside in Dworkin's imagination as a god-like character, having no genuine colleagues or superiors and presumably believing that the only role of underlings was to offer obedience. He would have no need to read Murphy's *Elements of Judicial Strategy* because he simply had no cause to think strategically. He would simply declare what the right answer was, and everyone else would presumably comply.

The Dworkinian model of judicial behaviour never really made much sense to me, even if I was willing to accept the picture of judges trying conscientiously to achieve an 'all things considered, best' solution to the cases before them. But, to put it mildly, that did not in the least provide anything that might be called determinative answers or even explain why one should accept as binding answers that one found problematic or even repugnant.

No doubt one reason for my scepticism was having been socialised into the operative reality of the American legal system and the presence of almost omnipresent disagreement that exists within it. Within the US, but unlike, say, the European Court of Justice or a few other national judicial systems, judges are permitted to write dissenting opinions, as well as 'concurring' opinions that, even while agreeing with the majority's decisional outcome, might well go on to castigate the reasoning by which the majority got there. Germany originally barred dissent, but then, perhaps as what was then West Germany was demonstrating its political maturity, chose to allow them beginning in 1971. Built into the American 'interpretive community' of judges is this possibility – and most certain reality – of conflict and dissent. It is hard to take entirely seriously the more grandiose notions of 'rule of law', as contrasted with 'the rule of particular judges' when judges sign opinions and feel altogether free to accuse their colleagues of what could easily be interpreted as incompetence or outright bad faith in interpreting the Constitution. I can only wonder what students in countries that suppress dissent, or students of contemporary European law, come to believe about the possibility of challenging 'the law' as enunciated by courts, but I suspect they have a more 'formalistic' notion of law than do almost all Americans.

---

[12] It is worth noting in this context that the Court, when overruling earlier decisions, increasingly seems willing to refer to defects in reasoning that presumably rob the earlier case of any presumptive validity. See the recent opinion by Justice Alito in the *Dobbs* case that overrules *Roe*, in part because of such defects. Alito had earlier offered the same rationale for overruling a 40-year-old precedent in *Janus v American Federation of State, County, and Municipal Employees, Council 31*, 585 U.S ___ (2018). But, of course, the Court seemingly expects everyone else to defer to badly reasoned decisions. Surely that cannot be because *only* the Court has the intellectual capacity to recognise something as 'badly' rather than 'well' reasoned.

It is a fundamental reality of the American legal experience that both A and not-A are offered by equally competent and legally skilled judges as answers to legal conundra. To be sure, it is a phenomenological reality that we often prefer one answer to the other, but we are kidding ourselves if we truly believe that our preferred answer is the 'one true' answer and that those who differ are either incompetent or in bad faith. At least prudentially, practicing lawyers were well advised to accept a version of the Holmesian understanding of law and attempt to 'predict' what judges faced with a certain legal problem would decide (whether or not they necessarily agree with the predicted resolution).

Dworkin was not ignorant of the fact of legal disagreement. I think it fair to say, though, that he ultimately regarded it as irrelevant, a mere empirical reality that had no genuine jurisprudential implications. Did the demonstrated 'uncertainty' over the correct legal answer mean that there was 'in fact' no such answer waiting in the wings, as it were, to be found if one were only diligent enough? The answer for him appeared to be no. One can agree that Dworkin offered some genuine insights as to how a legal interpreter might approach the materials. It seems undoubtedly true, for example, that almost no actually functioning judge is so positivistic as to be indifferent in all cases to the presence of overarching 'principles' that temper what a naïve reader might believe to be the 'clear meaning' of an unadorned text. To the extent, say, that Hercules's adversary 'Herbert', ie, HLA Hart, did not recognise the importance of such principles in his own legal theory, that did indeed seem to be a deficiency. I do not know that anyone today denies the existence of 'unwritten' aspects of law, including constitutional law, that must be taken into account when giving meaning to the documents. Paradoxically or not, perhaps Dworkin's most enthusiastic promoter right now – ie, in 2022, nearly a decade after his death in 2013 – is Harvard law professor Adrian Vermeule, a bitter critic not only of legal positivism but also of 'liberalism' more generally. Vermeule would have us basically junk the Enlightenment-oriented program of liberalism in favour of returning to what he calls a 'common-good' constitutionalism that he identifies with the ancient tradition of natural law and, just as importantly, the teachings of the Roman Catholic Church. But that does not prevent him from citing Dworkin as a proto-natural lawyer[13] with many good lessons to teach benighted modern positivists.

Similarly, even if one ultimate rejects, on Benthamite grounds, any particular veneration for precedents, it is desirable to pay attention to them and try to achieve a reasonable 'fit' among those precedents that one *does* respect simply because one believes they continue to display a certain degree of wisdom or, even if not particularly wise, at least have become widely accepted and have generated a certain degree of reliance within the legal community on their continued legitimacy. Those precedents, it is worth pointing out, are very

---

[13] See A Vermeule, *Common Good Constitutionalism* (Oxford, Polity Press, 2022) 188–89.

different from ones that one regards as deeply wrong in terms of what might be called 'legal craft' and, more relevantly, counter-productive or even truly evil in their social consequences.[14] Why should one ever seek 'fit' with *those* precedents or offer adherence to them as justifications for continuing what one might well describe as an 'evil' practice? But this reduces Dworkin to the role of a sagacious advice-giver, similar perhaps to Polonious, rather than the truly transformative jurisprudential figure that he certainly aspired to be (and was treated as being throughout his life).

III. IS 'LAWYERING' DIFFERENT FROM 'JUDGING'?

It is worth emphasising that Dworkin, and Fish as well at least inasmuch as much of his own writing was spurred by his desire to critique Dworkin's arguments, focused exclusively on judges and the presumptive constraints operating on them. But 'judging' is only one form of lawyering, and relatively few lawyers ever become judges. Dworkin never addressed the phenomenological reality of the overwhelming number of actual practicing lawyers, who are self-consciously trying to serve the interests of those who have hired them as what is well termed 'advocates'. Or, for that matter, one can think of the vast number of lawyers who serve in legislatures or other similar positions. To put it simply (though I hope not simplistically), lawyers generally use ostensibly legal arguments as instrumental weapons. They are, ultimately, rhetoricians, with no duty at all to believe that the arguments they convey to judges or juries – or perhaps to their legislative colleagues – are the 'right answers' in any sense other than that it serves the interest of the client, which may include one's constituents or the causes to which one is committed. And 'professors' of law – an interestingly ambiguous term – must generally, at least in the US, teach their students the rhetorical techniques of successful advocacy rather than simply convey their own opinions as to which decisions are 'correctly' decided and which are 'mistakes' that students should simply ignore.

This, of course, was the point made by Plato over two millennia ago in the *Gorgias* dialogue, where the title figure, the leading sophist of his era, admitted that the essence of the skills he taught his own students was to make the 'lesser' argument appear, to the adjudicator, the 'greater'. There is a 'hermeneutics of suspicion' built into any consideration of any argument presented by lawyers: what interests, or clients, are they serving, whatever their high-minded assurances might be that they are simply endeavouring to serve the public good? It is, to put it mildly, difficult to discern the limits – the 'constraints' – that lawyers feel when called upon to represent clients. The law itself says

---

[14] See, eg, MA Graber, *Dred Scott and the Problem of Constitutional Evil* (Cambridge, Cambridge University Press, 2008).

that lawyers are forbidden to make 'frivolous' arguments, but it is notoriously difficult, pragmatically, to identify the boundary lines between what might be called an implausible-but-makeable-argument and one that can be legitimately condemned (and even sanctioned by fines) as 'frivolous'.[15] A client ought to be told that there is a minimal likelihood of winning a given case, but that does not at all prevent the client from saying 'go ahead' or the lawyers from offering the 'best arguments' available even if they are privately believed to be weak arguments indeed. But, who knows, perhaps the golden-tongued lawyer will in fact persuade the non-too-bright judge that the client *does* deserve to win, legally, and that result would presumably redound to the lawyer's benefit.

It is one thing for a profession to be divided about what is the singular 'right' answer to a legal problem; it is something else to be unable even to be able to identify with confidence what are unequivocally 'wrong' and 'frivolous' answers and fully to license the 'zealous' presentation of what lawyers themselves believe to be weak, but presentable, arguments. But it is also the case, as Balkin and I have suggested, that over time some answers that once appeared 'frivolous' or, in a term much used by Balkin, 'off the wall', become at least 'on the wall' and, in some instances, become so embedded within the way 'we' now think about law that to challenge them would itself be viewed as 'frivolous'.

Fish has been a vigorous critic of those who believe there is an alternative to rhetoric, called, say, Platonic 'truth', which is presumably some kind of genuine and verifiable correspondence with the ontological forms of reality, whether of triangles or morality. Fish is identified, rightly or wrongly, with the 'postmodernist turn' in American intellectual life, characterised, among other ways, by a critique of the presence of foundations for one's pronouncements that would entitle one to say that they 'corresponded' with reality as it really was. I can say that another profound influence on my own thoughts about law was Thomas S Kuhn's *The Structure of Scientific Revolutions*, which, along with other books by Norwood Hanson, Steven Toulmin, and Paul Feyerabend, attempted to destroy the faith in what was called the 'correspondence theory of truth'.[16] As pragmatists argued, we in effect created our own truths; the best we could do is to present our own arguments and to explain why we held the relevant views. But it never added anything to say, at the end, 'And besides, everything I've said is true' because it corresponds with the truth of a theory-free 'reality'. Richard Rorty in his *Philosophy and the Mirror of Nature*, (in)famously declared that there was nothing really interesting to say about 'truth'.[17] (It should be clear that that is different from a confident pronouncement that 'there exist no truths', which is an ontological statement that generates well-known paradoxes.) It is unlikely, I believe, that Dworkin

---

[15] See S Levinson, 'Frivolous Cases: Do Lawyers Really Know Anything at All?' (1986) 24 *Osgoode Hall Law Journal* 353–78.

[16] TS Khun, *The Structure of Scientific Revolutions* (Chicago, University of Chicago Press, 2012).

[17] R Rorty, *Philosophy and the Mirror of Nature* (New Jersey, Princeton University Press, 1981).

entertained such post-modernist views.[18] Fish helped to create them, and I certainly accepted them.

Many might describe Dworkin as less 'cynical' than some might view Fish as being, but, perhaps, that is only to establish that the former are Platonists who fully accept the Socratic critique of sophistic casuistry. But even if that is the case, one can maintain that lack of cynicism only by avoiding any confrontation with the actualities of lawyering. And, of course, if, like most political scientists, one views judges themselves as having their own idealised pictures of the world, their own ideological preferences, then it is impossible to escape the belief that judicial reasoning itself is also 'motivated', even if not by the simple desire to win a case for an overt client. Balkin and I distinguished between what we called the 'high politics' present in all judges and the 'low politics' – ie, a partisan commitment to a particular political party or leader – that may be absent in many, if not most, judges and the presence of which we might well identify with corruption. But that is different from looking for judges without any priors at all regarding the best way to organise our complex society. So it remains the case, after more than 40 years, that I remain far more in the camp of Stanley Fish (whom I am also honoured to call a friend) than of Ronald Dworkin (whom I interacted with several times, albeit rather distantly), at least if one is focusing on the issues of most interest to most academic lawyers and judges.

IV. 'INTERPRETING' AN UNHAPPY LEGAL PAST

However, several things have happened over these 40 years – and, even more relevantly, perhaps, in the past couple of decades – that have made me less involved in these interpretation wars from the past. One has to do with the extent to which the 'interpretation wars' from years ago all tended to focus only on *contemporary* legal controversies, often cases before the US Supreme Court. Dworkin himself, of course, was a regular contributor to the *New York*

---

[18] Though see Dworkin (n 3), in which, he perhaps 'entertains' such views, but does not seem inclined to bring them home and introduce them to his family. He concedes, for example, that 'post-modernism' and 'anti-foundationalism' have come to 'dominate … fashionable intellectual style', particularly in what he calls 'the unconfident departments of American universities', including 'art history English literature, and anthropology', and including 'law schools as well'. ibid 87. It is obvious that Dworkin does not want to join this particular 'fashionable' intellectual community. But, as suggested, the essay seems primarily driven by the desire to distinguish an ontological (and, he argues, dubious) theory of 'indeterminacy', which presumably precludes even the theoretical possibility of 'right answers' to moral questions, and a far more plausible theory of empirical 'uncertainty' that leaves open the possibility of discovering the right answers that ontologically exist. That being said, it is difficult by this point in Dworkin's noted intellectual tergiversations to see precisely what is ultimately different from Dworkin's and Fish's positions with regard to any 'foundations' that might underlie Hercules's confident pronouncements. It was at this point that Dworkin started analogising law to a 'chain novel', though Fish happily ridiculed the idea that there would, in actual practice, be only one best way to continue a group novelistic project of the kind that Dworkin envisioned.

Review of Books, where he could be counted on to offer his own ruminations about leading decisions issued by the Court particularly involving rights. Given the move rightward by the Court over Dworkin's career, many of his essays were quite critical of the Court. He also played an active role in criticising the valorisation of 'originalism' as a privileged method in both the decisions and the books written by such figures as Antonin Scalia and Robert Bork. All of these were important and often convincing, especially to those of us who rued the direction of the Court in general and the increasing influence of Scalia and Bork in particular. One can have no doubt at all that Dworkin, were he alive, would be apoplectic about the US Supreme Court's recent decision in the *Dobbs* case, erasing constitutional protection for abortion. He would certainly have denounced its purported reliance on 'originalism' to generate constitutional meaning.

But I think he would have difficulty simply rejecting Justice Alito's insistence that his loyalty was to his reading of what the Constitution, correctly understood, required, coupled with complete indifference to public opinion or dire predictions about potential consequences of the decision. One need not deny Justice Alito's 'good faith' in order to disagree with his particular reading of the Constitution and, even more strongly, to believe that the social consequences may well be disastrous. But, of course, Hercules, too, denied that predicted social consequences were a proper part of what went into determining 'right answers', not least, one might suggest, because it is totally unclear that there is anything in legal training that equips one to be a particularly competent commentator on the actual impact of different public policies.

It is understandable that contemporary cases dominate our interest, as they did with Dworkin. And it is important to recognise the at times limited domain of those cases. Frank Michelman, for example, had famously suggested, in a *Harvard Law Review* article tellingly titled *Protecting the Poor Through the Fourteenth Amendment*, that that Amendment could legitimately be read in effect to instantiate a great deal of Rawlsian concern for the less-well-off in American society.[19] And there were a number of Supreme Court cases in the late 1960s and early '70s that, read broadly, could suggest that Michelman was correct not only in his abstract theory, but also in terms of predicting the direction that the Supreme Court was going, especially inasmuch as it was being influenced by the Justice for whom he had clerked, William J Brennan. But the appointment of several new justices by Richard Nixon brought an end to that judicial project. It was also at this time that American 'liberals' and the national Democratic Party became 'neo-liberals', with greater faith in markets and less overt concern for distributive justice and, just as importantly, the political groups that might be

---

[19] F Michelman, 'Protecting the Poor Through the Fourteenth Amendment' (1969) 83(1) *Harvard Law Review*.

advocating such redistribution in the direction of the 'working class' or other marginalised groups.[20]

For all of Dworkin's interest, in some of his writings on an 'insurance society' and the general conundra surrounding the notions of economic equality, he did not in fact believe that an American Hercules could legitimately read into the US Constitution any robust theory of a Michelmanian welfare state. It is striking that his formidable *Sovereign Virtue: The Theory and Practice of Equality* contains no index entry at all for Michelman.[21] One might well describe most of the book as pure political theory, having no apparent connection to legal interpretation. Dworkin might himself support the welfare state, but Hercules apparently cannot, at least within the American context. Interestingly enough, several of the concluding essays in that book, on free speech affirmative action, and 'Sex, Death, and the Courts', do opine on opinions of the Supreme Court, which only underscores the relative distinctions among these various issues in terms of their interest to Dworkin as an American jurisprude. But this, of course, is precisely to generate an all-important question about the connection, if any, between legal interpretation and moral or political theory. Dworkin had famously emphasised the importance of overarching 'principles' in understanding a legal order. But were some principles, however intellectually commendable, simply not truly 'within' a given legal order and thus unavailable to Hercules? A liberal Dworkin most certainly was, but it is not clear that he should really be described as a 'leftist', at least at that term had been used in earlier decades.[22]

Moreover, I think it is fair to say that neither Dworkin nor Fish ever displayed any serious interest in what has come to be called 'American constitutional development', which requires, among other things, close attention to the actual history of legal arguments and decisions, particularly about what one might regard as the most problematic – perhaps repugnant and even evil – aspects of our past. In the case of the US in particular, this would require paying close attention to race and, of course, the American system of highly racialised chattel slavery and then Jim Crow following the ostensible abolition of slavery in 1865. To what extent, for example, did the 1787 Constitution, correctly understood by those seeking 'right answers', offer protection for slavery and for the white supremacy on which American slavery was founded? Could, for example, even Hercules have denied that Congress was without legal authority to ban American participation in the international slave trade prior to 1808?[23]

---

[20] See R Kuttner, 'Free Markets, Besieged Citizens', *The New York Review of Books,* 21 July 2022, 12–14 (review of Gary Gerstle, 'The Rise and Fall of the Neoliberal Order: America and the World in the Free Market Era').

[21] R Dworkin, *Sovereign Virtue: The Theory and Practice of Equality* (Cambridge, MA, Harvard University Press, 2000).

[22] I owe this point to Jack Balkin.

[23] See Art I, s 9, of the US Constitution: 'The Migration or Importation of such Persons as any of the States now existing shall think proper to admit, shall not be prohibited by the Congress prior to the Year one thousand eight hundred and eight, but a Tax or duty may be imposed on

Or, if one is looking at lawyers rather than adjudicators, to what extent could describe as honourable and conscientious those lawyers who defend the broad cause of slavery and the interests of slaveowners because, after all, that was just what the Constitution required and the 'rule of law' just means that individuals are entitled to what the law allows? Perhaps they need not be view as cynical sophists, because many of them surely believed the 'better' arguments supported slavery.

To my knowledge, Dworkin addressed the reality of American slavery only once, in a review of Robert Cover's *Justice Accused* that was published in the (London) *Times Literary Supplement*.[24] Although a copious republisher of his own essays, he never chose to republish this particular one, and one might add that it is even extremely hard to track down the text, rather than simply the reference, on the otherwise ubiquitous Internet. Interestingly enough, in his essay on 'Objectivity and Truth', Dworkin several times places slavery in the same context as genocide, 'enslaving a race or torturing, a young child, just for fun, in front of its captive mother'.[25] He says that 'it is startlingly counterintuitive to think there is nothing wrong' with any of these practices. One might commend him for his moral acuity, putting to one side the truly bizarre set of qualifications that follow his denunciation of torture,[26] but nonetheless ask if this insight has any implications at all with regard to how Hercules would have had to address the specific realities of American slavery. This would not, of course, have required him to see merits to slavery that we today are blind to, but instead to say that the (im)morality of slavery was simply irrelevant to how he would have to adjudicate a given case as a conscientious judge.

Cover's project was to understand how ostensibly 'anti-slavery judges' could nevertheless rule in favour of slavery and against the claims of enslaved persons. It is easy enough to surmise why slaveowners, like John Marshall, might systematically dismiss the claims of enslaved persons. It is far harder to understand why, say, Joseph Story, from Massachusetts and certainly a critic of slavery,[27]

---

such Importation, not exceeding ten dollars for each Person.' It is of rhetorical significance that the Clause does not include the magic word 'slave' or 'enslaved person', but there is no doubt whatsoever that almost everyone at the time interpreted the Clause to refer to the 'importation' of slaves. South Carolinians applauded this protection of the slave trade, and anti-slavery delegates to the Massachusetts ratifying convention rued it, but no one at the time seriously doubted its meaning. Perhaps one should score one point for 'original public meaning'.

[24] See R Dworkin, 'The Law of the Slave-Catchers' (1975) *Times Literary Supplement*, 5 December 1975, 1437, 1437.

[25] Dworkin (n 3) 117–18.

[26] That is, would anyone argue that it would be thinkable to torture a young child (or perhaps anyone else), so long as it is not 'for fun' or not done in front of a 'captive parent'? Surely, an editor should have caught this and questioned Dworkin as to what he 'really' meant to say.

[27] Story, sitting as a circuit judge, declared with great passion and at considerable length 'that the international slave trade necessarily carries with it a breach of all the moral duties, of all the maxims of justice, mercy and humanity, and of the admitted rights, which independent Christian nations now hold sacred in their intercourse with each other'. There is no reason to believe that his critique of slavery extended only to the international slave trade, outlawed by the US Congress in 1808, so that he was comfortable with the merely domestic version of chattel slavery.

would write one of the most morally abominable opinions in American history when justifying the constitutional legitimacy of the Fugitive Slave Law of 1793 in *Prigg v Pennsylvania*.[28] So consider the fact that in 1842, the year of the decision, Story wrote to a friend, 'You know full well that I have ever been opposed to slavery. But I take my standard of duty as a judge from the Constitution.'[29] This plaint certainly seems congruent with the model of legal fidelity that Hercules would typify. 'Right answers' might not always be comforting, at least once one rejected the classical view that 'unjust laws' were not laws at all. That was never Dworkin's announced position, whatever his critiques of certain forms of legal positivism.

But the real point is that Dworkin basically maintained a silence about this extraordinarily important feature of American constitutionalism; similarly, to my knowledge, he never fully addressed the duties of South African judges in what David Dyzenhaus accurately labelled a 'wicked legal system'.[30] To a significant extent Dworkin (and Hercules) always seemed to generate, at least with regard to the issues that he wrote about as a jurisprude, what their primary liberal audiences viewed as 'happy endings'. Hercules was not the kind of doctor who delivered bad news that the patient might be suffering from a fatal disease or, at the least, needed radical surgery in order to survive.

These controversies are not of merely 'historical' interest. The US at present is wracked by a bitter debate over the nature of the US Constitution and the degree to which it should be read, at the very least, as complicit with slavery and, even more strongly, as what William Lloyd Garrison called a 'Covenant with Death and an Agreement with Hell'. Garrisonianism, paradoxically or not, entailed the proposition that fidelity to such a Constitution indeed required recognising the claims of the slaveowner against the enslaved. This, for Garrison, is why no honourable person should agree to serve as a judge. But it did not entail that Story was incorrect to believe that fidelity to his role as an honourable judge within what Dworkin often labelled 'the forum of principle' required the decision that he wrote. To absolve Story of what might be termed legal, as well as moral, culpability seems to require that one agree that the ante-bellum Constitution did indeed protect slavery and, all importantly, that Hercules too would have had to come to the same conclusion.

Quite obviously, the present US Constitution does not protect slavery, but why, exactly, would we all agree to that anodyne proposition? A positivist would simply point out that that is a result of an addition to the text of the Constitution, the Thirteenth Amendment, adopted in 1865 that fundamentally

---

[28] See S Levinson and MA Graber, 'Justice Accused at 45: Reflections on Robert Cover's Masterwork' (2022) 37 *Touro Law Review* 1851.
[29] Cited in ibid 1863–64.
[30] See D Dyzenhaus, *Hard Cases in Wicked Legal Systems: Pathologies of Legality*, 2nd edn (Oxford, Oxford University Press, 2010). See also Frederick Schauer's review of Dyzenhaus, 'The Legality of Evil of the Evil of Legality' (2011) 47 *Tulsa Law Review* 121.

transformed the legal reality of the American constitutional order. That is, to be sure, a happy result, but it certainly does not legitimise an equally happy portrayal of the prior constitutional order, which would have required even Hercules to collaborate in the oppression of enslaved persons (or else resign).

Fish easily allows one – or at least easily allowed me – to present Story, or Roger Taney in *Dred Scott*, as 'honorable judges' who offered legally plausible, albeit morally disturbing, readings of the Constitution. There were, obviously, other views that one might also view as legally plausible, even 'better' according to one's own preferred approach. But that did not license one necessarily to identify Story's or Taney's readings as offering anything other than the internally-felt 'right answers' that conscientious judges came to when faced with the profound questions raised by the 'peculiar institution' of chattel slavery as an important part of the American social and legal fabric. Perhaps equally conscientious judges might have come to different conclusions. So what? On what precise basis does one 'prefer' one opinion over the other? Is it because of what Habermas might call the ineluctable force of the better legal argument? Does one refer to those who prefer a different opinion as exhibiting cognitive deficiencies in terms of 'thinking like a lawyer'? Can one actually spell out the methods by which one can distinguish 'better' from 'worse' arguments? That, after all, was a question that consumed many legal academics in the 'interpretation wars'. I think it safe to say that supplying an answer was never Fish's goal, but it did seem to be entailed by Dworkin's overall endorsement of Herculean mastery and ability actually to achieve, rather than merely believe that she had achieved, the demonstrable 'right answer'. In my own writing and teaching, I generally resisted the temptation to supply 'right answers' in favour of simply trying to understand the predicate conditions of any given answer that might be presented.

So one explanation from my own relative lack of interest in returning to the specific debates that we associate with the 'Fish-Dworkin' controversy is that, in retrospect, they were remarkably presentist, whereas my own interests have turned more and more to trying to figure out what we can usefully say about ostensibly legal decisions made in past times and about the overarching reality of racialised chattel slavery. It may be that to criticise Fish and Dworkin for failing to write about such matters is like criticising the authors of even very good books for not having written the book one wishes they had written instead. In retrospect, one can say even of Robert Cover that he ultimate elided the issue of whether there were genuine alternatives, especially if one takes seriously the Fishian idea of 'interpretive communities' as constituting the set of truly 'thinkable ideas' and closing the Overton window to ideas viewed as not only outside the 'mainstream', but even 'utopian'. That was the very adjective that Cover himself used to describe so-called 'anti-slavery constitutionalists' who certainly existed but played no significant role within the adjudicative community of federal judges or elected national figures, including Abraham Lincoln. Going back at least to Durkheim, we have realised that one role of 'communities' is to set conditions for membership, and that is certainly true of 'interpretive communities' as well. No doubt there are interpretive communities even in twenty-first century America of professional astrologers. But none of them should expect to be hired by a contemporary American university, itself organised by reference to 'disciplines' all of which reject the plausibility of astrology and, indeed, condemn it to the ranks of 'frivolous' theories that no 'rational person' should believe or, even more, be taught. Such 'censorship', which is fact a highly unhelpful notion unless we really do adopt a theory that 'anything goes' everywhere at all times, is true within 'disciplines' as well as among them.[31] I suspect that a contemporary department within a major university is unlikely to hire today anyone who announces that she wishes to write a highly Freudian biography of a major political figure or novelist, even if such biographies were certainly acceptable in the mid-twentieth-century academy.

V. FOCUSING ON THE 'HARD-WIRED' CONSTITUTION AND ITS DEFICIENCIES

But, as television hucksters, might say, there's more! In the time since I was primarily interested in theories of interpretation and participated, albeit as a minor character, in the debates of the 1980s, I have become convinced that a pathology of at least the American legal academy is our almost obsessive focus on only certain parts of the Constitution (or of non-constitutional texts as well). That is, 'we' concern ourselves with what I have come to call the 'Constitution of Conversation',[32] which can be identified quite precisely using Jackson's comment as a template. It is indeed the 'magnificent generalities' and 'cryptic words' that dominate the consciousness of legal education. This also leads some, naturally enough, to rely on what has come to be called 'common law constitutionalism'. Wise judges within Dworkin's 'forum of principle' in essence will engage in constant updating and even what some might see as de facto amendment of the Constitution in order to bring it into conformity with what Hercules will recognise as our overarching principles that produce the 'best fit' in defining and thus justifying, in a modern catch phrase, 'who we really are'.[33] This view of 'the law' is aided because – I now believe altogether unfortunately – the legal academy, at least in the US, is in thrall to the work product of the US Supreme Court. What the justices think important is what 'we' think important to talk about with our students; concomitantly, what they ignore we feel equally free to ignore.

---

[31] Note that the first essay in one of Fish's most recent books, S Fish, *The First: How to Think about Hate Speech, Campus Speech, Religious Speech, Fake News, Post-Truth, and Donald Trump* (New York, Atria/One Signal, 2019) is entitled 'Why Censorship is a Precondition of Free Speech'.
[32] See S Levinson, *Framed: America's 51 Constitutions and the Crisis of Governance* (Oxford, Oxford University Press, 2012) 19.
[33] The most prominent proponent of 'common law constitutionalism' is University of Chicago Law Professor David Strauss. See D Strauss, *The Living Constitution* (Oxford, Oxford University Press, 2010).

Students can emerge with a quite superb understanding of contemporary judicial controversies while, at the same time, remaining appallingly ignorant of basic features of the American political system. I can only wonder if this is just another form of American exceptionalism or whether this is a reality even in other legal systems and systems of legal education across the world.

In contrast to the 'Constitution of Conversation', and its almost natural association with 'common law constitutionalism', I posit the existence of what I call the 'Constitution of Settlement'.[34] By this, I refer to what I also call the 'hard-wired' structural features of the Constitution – or perhaps of *any* written constitution – that do not lend themselves to litigation and concomitant debate about 'meaning'. It is not simply because a long string of cases has generated 'doctrines' that might be viewed as having 'settled' some dispute; rather, there was never litigation in the first place, usually because the relevant text appeared so clear that lawyers were unwilling to litigate. Frederick Schauer's valuable review of David Dyzenhaus's book on South African constitutionalism emphasises the difference between 'plain fact' constitutionalism and its 'common law' alternative. And he suggests, not surprisingly, that Dworkin in fact rejected a jurisprudence of 'plain facts', as did, for very different reasons, Stanley Fish. The Constitution of Conversation is entirely about disputed meaning – and, therefore, what 'methods of interpretation' might be useful in elucidating the best, or even one-true, meaning of the text. And, of course, one frequently sees sharp, even angry, confrontations among interpreters who disagree on the answers to such questions.

The 'Constitution of Settlement', however, poses few, if any, questions of genuine 'interpretive' difficulty. It invites 'plain fact' interpretation, not least because the relevant 'interpretive communities' will scoff at what will appear wilfully ignoring the 'commands' latent within the text. Nobody can identify with great confidence what would count as a 'frivolous argument' concerning the meaning of, say, 'equal protection of the laws'. It is, however, relatively easy to do so with regard to other parts of the Constitution that almost never come up in law school precisely because there really is 'nothing to argue about' in the particular sense that lawyers define 'argument'. I am fond, for example, of contrasting Inauguration Day – the day on which the US inaugurates a new president, who might, as at present, have defeated an extremely antagonistic opponent – with any one of the 'majestic generalities' of the Fourteenth Amendment. There is, if you will, a Dworkinian 'right answer' to the question, 'When is a new president of the United States inaugurated?' It is 'at noon on January 20 of the year following the quadrennial election'. The 'proof text' is the Twentieth Amendment to the Constitution: 'The terms of the President and the Vice President shall end at noon on the 20th day of January.' As it happens, I believe that this feature of the US Constitution is, in the modern world, highly

[34] ibid 19.

questionable, even, as we learned with regard to Donald J Trump, dangerous. But that is a question of *wisdom*; it is not a question of *meaning*. And, ironically or not, one of the precepts associated with Dworkin is that judges should be fearless in obeying the laws – ie, adopting the singular 'right answer' irrespective of the social consequences of any such decision. That is just what it meant to 'take rights seriously'. Although, as with other neo-deontological theorists, Dworkin seemed to have a potential exception for genuinely catastrophic consequences – he did not really believe that 'let the right answer be followed though the heavens fall' – that was not a feature that he highlighted.

Inauguration Day is an example of a *structural* feature of the Constitution, having nothing directly to do with 'rights', the principal focus of Dworkin's work and, for better and worse, of most 'constitutional theorists' following World War II. As I have written elsewhere, it is unclear that Dworkin, or his creature, Hercules, ever really addressed structures,[35] in part because there are rarely interesting questions of 'interpretation' attached to answering questions involving not only Inauguration Day, but also, and more importantly, the allocation of voting power in the US Senate. Almost all well-trained American lawyers regard it as completely irrelevant that the US Senate is illegitimate under almost any plausible twenty-first-century theory of representative democracy. How can one really defend the fact that the approximately 550,000 residents of Wyoming have the same two senators as the almost 40,000,000 residents of California? The explanation of this irrelevance, at least to the practicing lawyer, is simply that the text of the Constitution clearly 'ordains' equal voting power of the states in the Senate. James Madison, in discussing this section of the Constitution, referred to it as the product of a compromise, what he called a 'lesser evil', where capitulation to the smaller states demanding excessive voting power was necessary lest there be no constitution at all. Political power, not the 'force of the better argument', accounts for the US Senate (as well, for that matter, as the compromises with slavery). The 'evil' remains. It took the death of 750,000 combatants in effect to invalidate slavery; unfortunately, nothing has been done to tame the evil of the Senate. In any event, a knock-down argument to anyone asking why the Senate is not 'unconstitutional' as well as 'illegitimate' or even 'evil', is to ask, quite simply, 'What part of "two senators" do you not understand?'

This answer is relevant, of course, to Fish himself. It is, I think, undoubtedly true that most texts in actuality are subject to legitimate differences in interpretation. That is precisely what gives *Is There a Text in This Class?* its rhetorical power. The answer is 'no' if what is being asked is (something like) 'will we be reading texts that are so clear in their meaning that they are self-sufficient for the

---

[35] S Levinson, '"Reflections on What Constitutes "a Constitution": The Importance of "Constitutions of Settlement" and the Potential Irrelevance of Herculean Lawyering' in D Dyzenhaus and M Thorburn (eds), *Philosophical Foundations of Constitutional Law* (Oxford, Oxford University Press, 2016) 75–93.

interpretive enterprise'. But that does not mean that *all* aspects of the text are subject pragmatically to interpretive pirouettes. 'Two senators' or 'January 20' are among these. I can still agree with Fish that the interpretive stability of these texts is explained not by a theory of linguistics that unequivocally distinguishes 'clear' words from 'unclear' ones – only the latter of which require 'interpretation' – but, rather, by the fact that the relevant 'interpretive community' simply does not recognise the potential indeterminacy of some texts in a way that it does of the 'majestic generalities'.

Around a seminar table, one can note that the Twentieth Amendment refers only to January 20 and does not include 'within the Gregorian version of the solar calendar'; these are assumptions that are necessary to treat January 20 as genuinely hard-wired, and it can be pedagogically useful to inform students of this reality and even to suggest exotic hypotheticals where it might be crucial to indicate whether one is operating under a solar or a lunar calendar or the Gregorian or Julian version of that calendar. Does, for example, the requirement that an individual be 30 to become a US senator rule out someone who is 30 under a widely-used lunar calendar (though not in the US) but not under the solar calendar? It is a little harder to problematise 'two', but clever academics could certainly find a way, perhaps by taking account of developments in artificial intelligence. But the point is that no competent lawyer, at least at present or in the foreseeable future, would assert a claim before a judge that the Constitution, best understood as a whole, renders these particular features, because they are unwise or even illegitimate from the perspective of normative political theory, 'unconstitutional' as well. Both Fish and I admire Richard Rorty and his famous comment that interpreters often 'beat texts' into the shapes required to support their motivated arguments. But I think we also both agree that at any given moment there will be perceived limits on how much beating can take place before the beater is exiled from the relevant interpretive community. I thus often describe myself as a continuing adherent of 'textual indeterminacy'[36] with regard to the Constitution of Conversation, in part because of the continuing influence of my early reading of Fish (and others), while at the same time having become a 'mindless textualist' with regard to the Constitution of Settlement. That is because I recognise the practical power of 'what part of noon on January 20 or of two do you not recognize?'

My own personal shift of interest from the Constitution of Conversation to the Constitution of Settlement is not motivated by simple intellectual beliefs, as real as they are, that American law students (and even their professors) should pay more attention to the hard-wired structures even if that means diminishing the time spent on what it means to 'take rights seriously'. As Jack Balkin has reminded me, though, it is worth noting Dworkin's relative indifference to what

---

[36] As noted earlier, does it really matter if I substitute 'uncertainty' for 'indeterminacy'?.

might be called 'economic rights' linked to a redistributive welfare state. His endorsement of a *strong* judiciary, fearlessly willing to enforce rights against obstreperous majorities, seemingly did not extend to such economic rights (or, say, the environment). In those domains, Dworkin seemed quite content with what was often termed a highly 'restrained' judiciary that simply deferred to decisions made by the so-called 'political branches'. We do indeed live within 'marketplaces of ideas' where it is an inevitable, albeit unfortunate, truth that the opportunity cost of concentrating on A, B, or C, however interesting they may be, is an almost literally wilful ignorance of D, E, or F. Students want, and professors are happy to give them, discussions of abortion, affirmative action, and hate speech; they are less taken by the prospect of sacrificing time spent discussing these topics in order to discuss the hard-wired structures that are in fact never litigated and about which judges have almost literally nothing to say, or even, perhaps, whether medical care or education ought to be viewed as a constitutional entitlement to be enforced by judges.

In a perhaps fantasised 'old-fashioned' world, students would have taken courses on 'civics education', where they would have learned important details about the structures of the American (and perhaps even their state's) political system and why those structures are in fact important to explaining the actual outcomes of the political process. But one of the few things that most people agree on these days in the US is that 'civics education' has basically disappeared, and too many courses that do address the Constitution look only at its rights provisions. Most people, I suspect, can offer at least a broad definition of 'The Bill of Rights'; few have a desirable level of knowledge about the non-rights provisions of the Constitution or, for that matter the 'rights provisions' of many other constitutions around the world or even states within the US.

VI. LEGAL FIDELITY TO MENACING CONSTITUTIONS

But my discontent is generated by far more than my unhappiness that certain features of the Constitution are being ignored. Rather, I have come to believe that these structural aspects are, in their own ways, dangers to the maintenance of the American republic (which, therefore, has to be defined as something perhaps far different from a positivist maintenance of each and every specific structure or institution set out in the 1787 Constitution). This, I believe, is most obvious with the already mentioned US Senate. It is not simply that any political system presumptively predicated on the notion of 'one-person/one-vote' can scarcely justify the disproportionate impact of individual voters in Wyoming and California with regard to their representation in the Senate. It is also the case that the less-populated states are, overall, significantly different than the larger states. The former, almost by definition, have no large cities. The largest city in Vermont is Burlington, with a population of approximately 42,500; Wyoming's largest city, its capital Cheyenne, is home to about 65,000 people. Each would be a 'neighbourhood' in, say, Los Angeles or New York City. Indeed, even the fifth-largest city in California, Fresno, has a population (approximately 540,000) only 40,000 short of Wyoming's 580,000. Even the 15th-largest city in California, Irvine, has a population of over 250,000 people.

But the differences go well beyond sheer numbers, as important as they may be if Dworkinian 'equal concern and respect' is important in one's metric. The smaller states are also, in general, far less diverse. They tend to be significantly whiter, more rural in overall composition, more religious, and, in general, less open to what one ordinarily thinks of as 'cosmopolitanism', including the contributions that can be made by immigrants. Again almost by definition, they are unlikely to be particularly knowledgeable of, or sympathetic to, the problems facing the majority of Americans who live now in only nine of the 50 states (and who possess, therefore, only 18 of the total of 100 senators). Many visitors to the US are surprised by 'infrastructure' problems, especially if they land in one or another of America's largest airports. But it is exceedingly difficult to get senatorial approval for ambitious programs that would go 'disproportionately' (if one is measuring only per/state financing) to the minority of states where people actually live.

A spate of books has been published in the past several years that take seriously the possibility of renewed secessionism within the US; there have even been books on the prospect of 'civil war' in the US. Consider a national survey in 2021 by John Zogby that found that 46 per cent of Americans, a plurality, believed a future civil war was likely; 43 per cent thought it was unlikely, with the remainder 'not sure'.[37] Interesting enough, younger people were more likely to predict a future civil war than were older ones (53 per cent to 31 per cent. Southerners (49 per cent) and those residing in the heart of the American Midwest (48 per cent) were more worried (assuming they did not welcome the prospect) than were those living in the eastern United States (39 per cent). The political scientist Barbara Walter published in 2022, *How Civil Wars Start: And How to Stop Them*, which became a much-discussed best seller.[38] This has occurred at the same time that the US is increasingly being perceived as a 'backsliding' democracy. Thus in 2020 the Economist Magazine Intelligence Unit rated Canada as a 'full democracy', while the US entered the ranks of 'flawed democracies'.[39] Certainly nothing has happened since 2020 to lessen this presumed concern about the US. Steven Levitzky's and Daniel Ziblatt's

---

[37] Zogbyanalytics, 'The Zogby Poll: Will the US Have Another Civil War?, zogbyanalytics.com/news/997-the-zogby-poll-will-the-us-have-another-civil-war.

[38] B Walter, *How Civil Wars Start: And How to Stop Them* (London, Penguin, 2022).

[39] The Economist, *Democracy Index 2020: In sickness and in health?*, pages.eiu.com/rs/753-RIQ-438/images/democracy-index-2020.pdf?mkt_tok=NzUzLVJJUS00MzgAAAGFby0sdwqPsjIYgbgAMyUzM9Rc8s3JARxYz-IVt41hJMtGLe0NAL8z49soLtvn4ALsjT1Vi3J7pVPpStmz2IXxXIaQfMpce0NKSHJDoiQ11nUcFA.

How Democracies Die also became a best seller in many circles because of concerns about the US.[40]

To be sure, there are many different diagnoses offered to explain the apparent sickness of the US. Many of them focus on political culture and the perhaps exceptional triumph within the US of a particularly libertarian form of liberalism that limits any general commitment to what the Preamble to the Constitution calls the 'general welfare' and that Vermeule, an acknowledged anti-liberal, calls 'the common good'.[41] Many emphasise the sheer range of diverse groups and views of large numbers of people within the US and the concomitant difficulties in the way of achieving any necessary consensus (or even compromise) necessary to pass political programs. Social media, including Facebook and Twitter, have also come in for sustained attention. American elections come under critiques of their own, especially with regard to the role played by the wealthy and their ability to finance their own favourites and, at the same time, in effect drown the prospects of those unable to find wealthy backers of their own. Ironically or not, these aspects of the American election system are increasingly protected by the Supreme Court, which, in the name of the First Amendment and its capacious protection of 'freedom of expression', has invalidated a number of efforts by both Congress and state legislatures to regulate campaign financing.

But I have become especially interested in the role that might be played by the dysfunctional political structures that provide the hard-wired context within which American politics take place. These include, but are not limited to, the already named (and castigated) Senate; the electoral college that has allowed twice in the last 20 years, the election of candidates who did not even come in first in the overall vote; the ineffectiveness of the Impeachment Clause in serving as a method of holding accountable clearly deficient presidents; life tenure on, particularly, the US Supreme Court; and, finally, an unusually difficult process of constitutional amendment that has, as a practical matter, made it nearly impossible to envision any needed constitutional transformations.

What is distinctive about all of these is that lawyers as such have almost nothing useful to say about them. 'We' concentrate on what can be (and is) reasonably subject to litigation – the lawyer's mode of 'conversation', and the brute fact is that none of these deficiencies has become the subject of such 'conversation'. This is why, as already noted, Hercules (or Dworkin) never had anything interesting to say about these topics. Hercules is always interpreting an already existing Constitution and focuses his interest ultimately only on those parts of the Constitution that deal with 'rights'. To that extent, at least, there is always a 'text in this class' even if one readily agrees that the text is not self-interpreting. Even those three countries still regarded as lacking a canonical written

---

[40] S Levitzky and D Ziblatt's, *How Democracies Die* (London, Penguin, 2019).
[41] Michael Sandel has also offered for many years a less strident but also significant critique of particularly Rawlsian liberalism and an emphasis on focusing on the common good.

constitution – the UK, New Zealand, and Israel – all have dense legal cultures in which one can speak of 'conventions' and, increasingly, of certain statutes that take on the status of being 'quasi-constitutional'. Dworkin and Fish never displayed the slightest interest in what has come to be known as 'constitutional design', save perhaps for Dworkin's endorsement of the British Parliament's entrenching of certain rights. In the case of Fish, that is hardly surprising. Why would one expect him to be interested in such questions, other, perhaps, than as an ordinary citizen? Does one wish to be equally understanding (or forgiving) of Dworkin's lack of interest in institutional design in his home country?

In any event, the primary explanation for my own turn to constitutional design, instead of remaining focused on 'constitutional interpretation', is my concern that aspects of the hard-wired institutions are dangerous and very much in need of change. But change requires the discussion that is currently lacking because of our general obsession, especially within the US, with rights. Any discussion that focuses only on 'taking rights seriously' (whatever exactly that is thought to mean) will necessarily be ignoring what for me is increasingly the elephant in the room.

VII. SUPPLEMENTING 'THEORY' WITH EMPIRICAL AGREEMENT

It is scarcely the case, though, that we have reliable knowledge on the precise fit between our end goals for an admirable political system and the particular institutional means likely to achieve them. These have been essential questions for political scientists over at least two millennia. What can, at the very least, presumably be agreed, is that providing answers to these questions requires a joinder of normative political theory and high-level empirical analysis. As to the former, one must have a theory of what in fact entitles any given polity to be deemed admirable or not. Is it one that maximises some general notion of individual rights, as many liberals would argue? Or, as Vermeule argues, is it one that has a robust notion of the 'common good' that might require the erasure of many traditional liberal rights because they are found to 'corrupt' the public, which is need of a strong government that will preserve and protect a distinct public 'morality'? Vermeule certainly causes as much consternation to contemporary American 'conservatives' as to 'progressives'; he scoffs at the 'small government' libertarianism of the former even as he denounces the moral pluralism and libertarianism of the latter. One cannot 'design' a constitution for a polity unless one has some notion of its *purpose*. Perhaps this can be set out in a preamble, as is the case with the US Constitution (but which is, interestingly enough, not really treated as an operative part of the Constitution by lawyers and judges). But the idea of a 'one-size-fits-all' and absolutely 'value-neutral' constitution that can be used as a template for any and all societies is absurd.

However, as already suggested, agreement on great ends, even if that is attained, in no way assures that there will be equal agreement on how to achieve them or, even more to the point, that perceived relations between ends and means that might have been true at time X will necessarily remain true decades later. That is a basic problem, obviously, with 'originalism'. Even if one can overcome all of the hurdles in the way of ascertaining the collective intent of multi-member bodies or, as required by latter day 'originalists', the 'original public meaning' of large and diverse assemblages, that provides no warrant for assuming that the initial decisions should bind us years later. This is true even if one accepts, as I am reluctant to do, arguments like Vermeule's that values are eternal and, therefore, that there can be no 'progress' in defining what 'really' constitutes the common good or public interest. One still has to figure out what institutions are conducive to realising values, whether eternal or more historicist. Doing that requires very different skills than those found even in the most Herculean of interpreters.

Consider the very choice between relying on 'common-law constitutionalism' and its implicit valorisation of the judiciary as 'the forum of principle', in presumed contrast to the cesspool of politics that is the legislature, and what Schauer calls 'plain fact' constitutionalism that would limit the ability of judges to intervene in decisions by legislatures and executives (or, possibly, administrative agencies) unless some plain text in effect commanded such intervention. This might certainly be the case if Congress simply passed a law stating that the election of a new president would be a function of popular votes received and that inauguration would take place on, say, 1 December. Both would, from my perspective, be great improvements on the present way we do things in the US, but it is impossible, as a practical matter, to see a judiciary that would endorse them; the 'best' that one might practically hope for is that a court would engage in the Bickelian 'passive virtue' of announcing that the laws in question raised such 'political questions' as to be beyond judicial capacity.

As Schauer writes, 'the choice between a plain fact and a common law view of what judges should do is in fact a choice'. It raises a profound 'question of institutional design'. The central issue, therefore, is

> the question of the circumstances under which it is better for a society to choose one or another style of judging or to choose one or another understanding of just how legal actors should treat the rules that are made by legislatures and other governmental bodies. That this is clearly a choice should be obvious, but it is less obvious how this choice should be made.[42]

More precisely, is it a choice to be made on abstract 'jurisprudential' grounds, or must one instead have a fairly robust notion of empirical probabilities concerning the identity of those likely to be appointed judges and then, in addition, the degree to which, overall, they will exhibit greater wisdom about public policy than will legislators or executives, including bureaucrats within

---

[42] Schauer (n 30) 129.

administrative agencies? As Schauer notes, to choose common law constitutionalism is in effect to risk giving 'morally misguided judges greater resources to undercut morally enlightened legislation'.[43]

At the present moment in the US, there are relatively few people in Dworkin's political camp, ie, political liberals, who are inclined to give great respect to the undoubted 'moral' precepts that underlie in particular the reversal of *Roe v Wade* in the *Dobbs* case. Instead, there is now increasing debate about the desirability, for example, of 'packing the Court' by expanding its membership and assuring the appointment of politically compatible judges. The alternative, as demonstrated recently by Ian Ayres and Kart Kandula, is the overwhelming likelihood that the Court (Dworkins 'Forum of Principle'?) will be dominated for the rest of the lifetime of anyone likely to read this essay within ten years of its publication by conservative Republicans. Ronald Dworkin would undoubtedly be absolutely dismayed by this possibility (or, in fact, near certainty). But would he – or Stanley Fish – have anything genuinely useful to say about it, even though one would certainly expect Fish to take acerbic note of the fact that both sides in any such dispute would rhetorically present themselves as uniquely defending the abstraction known as 'the rule of law' and fidelity to the 'real' requirements of 'taking the United States Constitution seriously'?

---

[43] ibid.

17
The Problem of Immoral Integrity

LARS VINX

I. INTERPRETIVISM AND WICKED LAW

CAN LEGAL PRACTICE, as interpretive practice, fall short of the demand of integrity? Stanley Fish denies that it can. For some judicial decision to be recognisable as a judicial decision, it must, Fish argues, comply with requirements that are constitutive of legal practice, and these requirements are identical to the requirements of integrity. It follows that any legal practice must not only possess integrity; it must possess as much integrity as it could. The same must hold for any judicial decision, if that is what it is. Integrity, Fish concludes, cannot function as a standard of excellence for judicial decisions. It cannot guide a judge to one decision or another if both are possible moves within legal practice or tell us which of the two decisions will have a better claim to be legally correct.[1]

Dworkin, of course, denies that integrity is inert in this way. Integrity, for Dworkin, is a matter of degree. The quality of a legal practice depends on the extent to which it realises integrity, while the quality of an individual decision can be assessed by reference to whether it enhances or decreases systemic integrity.[2] Still, it might be argued that Dworkin's views on the relation between legality and integrity are not as far removed from Fish's thesis as it might appear. Though Dworkin denies that any legal order must exhibit perfect integrity, he endorses the view that any legal order that rewards an interpretive attitude must exhibit some degree of integrity.[3]

Integrity, for Dworkin, entails moral justification. If a system of governance possesses a degree of integrity, and thus qualifies as a bona fide instance of

---

[1] See S Fish, 'Working on the Chain Gang: Interpretation in the Law and in Literary Criticism' (1982) 9 *Critical Inquiry* 201; S Fish, 'Still Wrong After all These Years' (1987) 6 *Law and Philosophy* 401.
[2] See the description of the ideal of integrity in R Dworkin, *Law's Empire* (Cambridge, MA, Harvard University Press, 1986) 254–58.
[3] It might be argued that Dworkin's view has room for an interpretive legal practice that is interpretive while it eschews integrity. I agree with Fish (see 'Still Wrong' (n 1) 402–06) that conventionalism and pragmatism are not viable interpretive theories of adjudicative practice, as Dworkin's own critiques of these two positions suggest.

legal order, the decisions on the use of coercive force rendered by the system are at least presumptively legitimate, in virtue of being decisions rendered by that system. Where a system's decisions are not at least presumptively legitimate, it must be held to lack integrity and to fail to fully qualify as legal.[4] The standard example of such a case, of course, is Nazi Germany. In *Law's Empire*, Dworkin argues that Nazi Law might be regarded as law only in a marginal or pre-interpretive sense that does not carry justificatory connotations.[5] In *Justice for Hedgehogs*, Dworkin more boldly affirms that all or some of the rules made by Nazi authorities were no law at all since they 'did not create even *prima facie* or arguable rights and duties'.[6] We can conclude that, in Dworkin's view, a system of governance will fully qualify as legal only if it creates 'arguable rights or duties', and it will be able to do that only if it has integrity, that is, if it is possible to interpret the system as committed to underlying moral principles that have genuine justificatory force and that are consistently applied.[7]

Positivist critics of natural law theory argue that it is implausible, from a descriptive angle, to deny that Nazi Law was law. The Nazi system of governance possessed all the non-moral characteristics we associate with legality. There was a recognised legislator who enacted statutory rules. These rules were applied by courts, and they were followed, for the most part, by citizens. The system was stable and was regarded as legitimate by the bulk of the members of society, at least in the period from 1933 to 1939. The stark claim that there was no law in Nazi Germany or that some of the enactments of the Nazis failed to attain validity, on the sole ground that extremely unjust enactments do not qualify as law, disregards the facts and leads to a simplistic view of the moral problems to which wicked law may give rise.[8]

Dworkin was keen to avoid the perceived crudity of the Thomist *lex iniusta*-thesis or of the Radbruch-formula. He promised in *Law's Empire* that legal theory will 'have little trouble in making sense of that claim [the claim that Nazi law was not law] once we understand that theories of law are interpretive'.[9]

---

[4] See Dworkin (n 1) 45–86.
[5] ibid 101–08.
[6] R Dworkin, *Justice for Hedgehogs* (Cambridge, MA, Harvard University Press, 2011) 411.
[7] According to Dworkin (n 1) 96 integrity holds that 'rights and responsibilities flow from past decisions and so count as legal, not just when they are explicit in these decisions but also when they follow from the principles of personal and political morality the explicit decisions presuppose by way of justification'.
[8] The *locus classicus* is Hart's critique of Radbruch in HLA Hart, 'Positivism and the Separation of Law and Morals' (1958) 71 *Harvard Law Review* 593, 615–21.
[9] Dworkin (n 1) 101. See for further discussion of Dworkin on wicked law D Dyzenhaus, 'Dworkin and Unjust Law' in W Waluchow and S Sciaraffa (eds), *The Legacy of Ronald Dworkin* (Oxford, OUP, 2016) 131. Dyzenhaus recognises the possibility of immoral integrity, but he conceives of the problem as arising from unjust acts of legislation. In this version of the problem of immoral integrity, wicked legislation might make it impossible for judges, despite their best efforts, to develop a principled interpretation that produces morally tolerable outcomes. That judges might be part of the problem does not seem to occur to Dyzenhaus. His approach to wicked law therefore does not fit the Nazi example. The Nazi example shows that statutory law that is morally unobjectionable or even benign may come to be debased through principled wickedness in interpretive practice.

This claim on behalf of interpretivism can be read as an implicit reply to Hart's charge that positivism offers a clearer and more nuanced account of the problem of wicked law than natural law theory. This chapter will argue that Dworkin's promise is empty. Interpretivism, in the end, must either accept the positivist claim that legality is separable from morality or embrace what is in effect nothing more than an obtuse version of the *lex iniusta*-thesis. It neither adds nuance nor clarity to our understanding of wicked law.

This failure is concealed by an ambiguity in the role that the notion of integrity plays in interpretive legal theory, which I will set out to start us off.

If we accept the view that any legal order has integrity, the claim that Nazi law was a bona fide instance of law will imply that the legal order of Nazi Germany had integrity. Provided we also accept that integrity entails justification, we will be forced to conclude that Nazi law was justified, that the claims to which it gave rise, in virtue of their legality, were at least 'arguable rights and duties'. Suppose we find that conclusion unacceptable. What would be the best way to disrupt the inference to the conclusion that Nazi law was justified?

One possibility would be to deny the assumption that any instance of legal order must exhibit integrity. This response, however, is unavailable to the interpretivist. Both Fish and Dworkin argue that an interpretivist is committed to the view that any legal order, any system of governance that is fit to sustain an interpretive attitude, must possess integrity.

An interpretivist has two options to block the inference to the conclusion that Nazi law was justified. The first preserves the link between integrity and justification. The interpretivist might argue that Nazi law lacked integrity and therefore justification while holding on to the claim that any instance of legal order must exhibit integrity and therefore be justified.[10] To choose this option leads to a denial of the legality of Nazi law. The second option for the interpretivist is to claim that Nazi law, while it was not morally justified *qua* law, did not lack integrity and therefore qualified as law from an interpretivist perspective. In other words, the second option breaks the link between integrity and justification. It concedes that there may be morally perverted instantiations of integrity that have no justificatory purchase.

Dworkin, at first glance, appears to refuse to recognise the second of these two options. A system of governance will either support a constructive interpretation, which will inevitably show the system under a valid guise of moral justification, or the would-be interpreter will be compelled to abandon the

---

[10] For Dworkin, the claim of justification comes to the following: if a legal system possesses integrity, then the norms which it comprises will be presumptively binding. For any norm that belongs to the legal system in question, there will be a moral reason (though not necessarily a conclusive moral reason) for legal institutions to enforce those norms. TRS Allan argues that the link between integrity and justification is even stronger and identifies the demands of integrity with the demands of justice so that sound reasons of integrity are always both morally and legally conclusive. See TRS Allan, 'Law, Justice, and Integrity: The Paradox of Wicked Laws' (2009) 29 *Oxford Journal of Legal Studies* 705.

project of interpretation and to embrace internal scepticism.[11] A wicked system of governance, in this view, simply is not amenable to a successful constructive interpretation that would show it to qualify as an instance of legal order.

This chapter will argue that there is a possibility of morally perverted integrity and that the legal practice of Nazi Germany might be regarded as an example case. Nazi legal thought and practice was methodologically interpretivist. Nazi judges did not blindly submit to wicked statutory enactments. They were engaged, rather, in developing a constructive interpretation of the positive legal material, one that aimed to show the law of Nazi Germany in its best light, though their views as to what interpretation would show the law in its best moral light were catastrophically misguided. The conclusion to be drawn is that an interpretivist ought to admit that there is no necessary link between integrity and justification.

One might reply, in support of the attempt to preserve the link between integrity and justification, that there can be no true integrity without sound moral justification. I am inclined to agree. But this way out undercuts the claim that interpretivism offers a more nuanced approach to the problem of wicked law than legal positivism. In effect, Dworkin's interpretivist approach to wicked law offers nothing more than a needlessly obtuse version of the blunt *lex iniusta*-thesis that is associated with Radbruch and with Thomas Aquinas. The appeal to integrity adds nothing of jurisprudential or moral significance to the analysis of wicked law.

II. INTERPRETIVE PRACTICE IN NAZI GERMANY[12]

Though invocations of Nazi law are part and parcel of jurisprudential debate, the legal-philosophical perspective on the law of Nazi Germany is skewed by a focus on wicked statutory enactments which tends to neglect judicial practice in Nazi Germany. Gustav Radbruch set the tone for jurisprudential debate about Nazi law in claiming, shortly after the war, that German legal officials were disabled from putting up intellectual and practical resistance to Nazi practices by the fact that German jurisprudence of the time had been staunchly positivist. According to the German version of legal positivism, or so Radbruch argued,

---

[11] See Dworkin (n1) 78–85.
[12] Please note that my discussion in this section is limited in two key respects and does not aim to offer a comprehensive account of Nazi legal order. For one, I do not address the problem of the dual state, that is, the relation between governance by law and extra-legal power in Nazi Germany. The focus is on the operation of what Ernst Fraenkel called the normative state. See E Fraenkel, *The Dual State. A Contribution to the Theory of Dictatorship*, ed Jens Meierhenrich (Oxford, OUP, 2017). What is more, I do not discuss wartime conditions or the Holocaust. The focus is on judicial practice in peacetime Nazi Germany. For the jurisprudential significance of keeping these two periods apart see K Rundle, 'The Impossibility of an Exterminatory Legality: Law and the Holocaust' (2009) 59 *University of Toronto Law Journal* 65.

a judge was held to be under a strict obligation to apply validly enacted statutes irrespective of their substantial moral quality or catastrophic lack thereof: *Gesetz ist Gesetz*. He went on to claim that the widespread acceptance of legal positivism had favoured the Nazis in taking power and in running their regime.[13] With few exceptions, Radbruch's focus on wicked statutory law put in place by the Nazis has been uncritically adopted by jurisprudential debates on Nazi law. Legal philosophers discuss whether post war German courts might have been justified in denying the legality of certain Nazi statutes in assessing the behaviour of defendants in grudge informer cases. Fuller claimed that some or all Nazi laws lacked legal quality for their egregious violation of the principles of legality which, according to Fuller, must govern successful legislative activity. In *Law's Empire*, Dworkin imagined a judge called Siegfried valiantly grappling with the question whether to apply a discriminatory statute that denies certain defences against a claim of breach of contract to Jews while granting them to Aryans.[14] In *Justice for Hedgehogs*, Dworkin pronounced that 'the hideous Nazi edicts' – he did not specify which – were not legally valid at all, on the ground that 'the purported Nazi government was fully illegitimate, and no other structuring principles of fairness argued for the enforcement of those edicts'.[15]

What this focus on statutory law obscures is that clear examples of wicked Nazi statutes, such as the famous Nuremberg Laws, were not all that numerous. While the Nazis did set out on ambitious enterprises of legislative reform – most notably the preparation of a new criminal code, which did not, in the end, come

---

[13] See G Radbruch, 'Statutory Lawlessness and Supra-Statutory Law', translated by S Paulson and B Litschewski–Paulson (2006) 26 *Oxford Journal of Legal Studies* 1. The phrase 'Gesetz ist Gesetz' in the German original could be translated as 'the law is the law' or 'the law is whatever it is'. The most literal translation, however, would be 'statute is statute', since the German term 'Gesetz', in its core meaning, refers to statutory enactments. The position Radbruch had in mind, *Gesetzespositivismus* or statutory positivism, is the view, preponderant in the jurisprudence of the Wilhelmine Empire, that all laws are statutory enactments and that judicial decisions are to be justified by way of subsumption under statute. On the history of statutory positivism see F Wieacker, *Privatrechtsgeschichte der Neuzeit unter besonderer Berücksichtigung der deutschen Entwicklung* (Goettingen, Vandenhoeck & Ruprecht, 2016) 458–68; EW Böckenförde, *Gesetz und gesetzgebende Gewalt. Von den Anfängen der deutschen Staatsrechtslehre bis zur Höhe des staatsrechtlichen Positivismus* (Berlin, Duncker & Humblot, 1981) 210–20. The suggestion that the view of law and adjudication was generally accepted in the Weimar Republic is inaccurate. Radbruch's assessment overlooks the lively debate, the so-called *Methodenstreit*, between defenders and critics of 'statutory positivism', which had begun to influence adjudication. See M Stolleis, *Geschichte des öffentlichen Rechts in Deutschland. Weimarer Republik und Nationalsozialismus* (Munich, C.H. Beck, 1999) 153–86; PC Caldwell, *Popular Sovereignty and the Crisis of German Constitutional Law. The Theory and Practice of Weimar Constitutionalism* (Durham, NC, Duke University Press, 1997). For illuminating critical discussion of Radbruch's claim that legal positivism disposed German officials to submit to Nazi enactments see M Walther, 'Hat der juristische Positivismus die deutschen Juristen im "Dritten Reich" wehrlos gemacht?' in R Dreier and W Sellert (eds), *Recht und Justiz im Dritten Reich* (Berlin, Suhrkamp, 1989) 323 and H Dreier, 'Die Radbruchsche Formel – Erkenntnis oder Bekenntnis?' in M Borowski and SL Paulson (eds), *Die Natur des Rechts bei Gustav Radbruch* (Tuebingen, Mohr Siebeck, 2015) 1.

[14] See Dworkin (n1) 101–04.

[15] Dworkin (n 6) 411.

into force – the impact of Nazi legislative activity on German law was in fact quite limited. The courts of Nazi Germany, which had been stripped of Jews but otherwise operated with the same personnel as before, continued to apply the civil, criminal and administrative law that had been in force in the Weimar Republic. The adaptation of the retained law of the Weimar Republic to the goals of the new regime, as German language legal-historical research made clear a long time ago, took place by interpretive means.[16]

Consider the following civil case from 1938, decided by an ordinary court.[17] The farmer Jakob Juster, an Aryan, bought a milk cow from the Jewish livestock dealer Alfred Mayer. Juster gave Mayer another (less productive) cow in return and, in addition, promised to pay RM 60.70. However, Juster then refused to make payment, on the ground that the cow Mayer had sold gave less milk than promised. Mayer thereupon sued Juster for RM 60.70, plus 5 per cent interest. The court refused to enforce the contract between Mayer and Juster, on the ground that it was null and void, by appeal to section 138 of the German Civil Code, which determines that a legal transaction that is *sittenwidrig* (opposed to good morals) is to be regarded as null and void. The court upbraided Juster for having entered into a commercial transaction with a Jewish merchant, given that it was well known, or so the court claimed, that for an Aryan to do business with Jews was opposed to the interests of the German *Volk* and to the 'prevalent moral conscience of the people'. Juster could nevertheless hardly have wished for a more favourable judgment. Though the court regarded the contract between Juster and Mayer to be null and void, it also made it clear that Juster should not have to return the cow to Mayer. Mayer, the judgment pointed out, had sued for payment of RM 60.70, not for the return of the animal.

To add insult to injury, the court made a frivolous show of paying respect to the rule of law. According to the court's theory of section 138, a contract was *sittenwidrig* if it would be regarded as immoral by the ordinary person and if it is generally known that it would be so regarded. The court conceded, however, that popular opinion of what is immoral is subject to change over time. It therefore opined that if the transaction between Juster and Mayer had taken place shortly after the Nazi seizure of power in 1933, and not in 1937, the contract between the two would not have been *sittenwidrig* and would, as a result, not have been void, because popular moral opinion would not, at that time, have disapproved (or not have disapproved strongly enough) of dealmaking between Jews and Aryans. Whether a contract is void on account of its immorality must be determined by reference to the moral opinion prevalent at the time of

---

[16] See B Rüthers, *Die unbegrenzte Auslegung. Zum Wandel der Privatrechtsordnung im Nationalsozialismus* (Tuebingen, Mohr Siebeck 2017), which focuses on the application of private law in Nazi Germany. A shorter overview in I Müller, *Furchtbare Juristen. Die unbewältigte Vergangenheit der deutschen Justiz* (Edition Tiamat, 2014).

[17] Printed in I Staff, *Justiz im Dritten Reich. Eine Dokumentation* (Fisher, 1978) 161–63. Rüthers (n 16) reports numerous comparable cases.

contracting. It would not be appropriate, the court implied, to apply current moral opinion retroactively to void a contract that would not have been seen to be immoral when it was made.

Legal philosophers in Nazi Germany were only too happy to provide a legal theory to justify strategies of interpretation that deprived Jewish Germans of their legal rights. The most prominent legal theory in Nazi Germany, frequently echoed in court judgments, was all but designed to justify that strategy of interpretive adaptation. Carl Schmitt, a uniquely gifted inventor of memorable terminology, coined the name of the view: *Konkretes Ordnungsdenken* (concrete order thought).[18]

Concrete order thought might be described as an attempt to play out the notion *Recht* against the notion of *Gesetz*. Let me briefly explain.

It is difficult to translate the German word 'Recht' into English. 'Recht' might be rendered as 'law', in the sense of *the* (as opposed to *a*) law. But unlike 'law', 'Recht', like the Latin 'ius', is etymologically tied to the notion of justice. Like 'ius', 'Recht' can denote what is right or just, in either an objective or a subjective sense. Rights-talk, in German, uses the word 'Recht' in a subjective sense. A *Recht* is a claim against someone else that is, to use Dworkin's terms, properly enforceable on demand. Talk about the *Recht* in an objective sense, in turn, refers to an order or arrangement of affairs that is right. In either case, the word 'Recht' carries the connotation that the subjective claim or the objective order that is referred to has moral justification.

The word 'Gesetz', by contrast, which corresponds to the Latin 'lex', lacks that automatic justificatory connotation. 'Gesetz' can be translated as 'a law' or, more specifically, as 'statute'. A *Gesetz* is a legal norm issued by a recognised legislator. The positivism that Radbruch was concerned to assail – often referred to as *Gesetzespositivismus* (statutory positivism)[19] – is the view, in very crude abbreviation, that the law consists exclusively of statutory norms, coupled with

---

[18] The term was made popular by C Schmitt, *Über die drei Arten des rechtswissenschaftlichen Denkens* (Berlin, Hanseatische Verlagsanstalt, 1934). See also C Schmitt, 'Nationalsozialistisches Rechtsdenken' in C Schmitt, *Gesammelte Schriften 1933-1936 mit ergänzenden Beiträgen aus der Zeit des Zweiten Weltkriegs* (Berlin, Duncker & Humblot, 2021) 156–64. Schmitt's terminology was adapted by many other jurisprudes in Nazi Germany, for instance by Reinhard Höhn and Karl Larenz. See for extracts from the relevant writings of these two authors H Pauer-Studer and J Fink (eds), *Rechtfertigungen des Unrechts. Das Rechtsdenken des Nationalsozialismus in Originaltexten* (Berlin, Suhrkamp, 2019) 159–217. Larenz, after the war, managed to establish himself as a leading legal theorist and simply relabelled his jurisprudential position as a version of natural law theory, in line with the jurisprudential fashion of the time. See K Larenz, 'Zur Beurteilung des Naturrechts' in W Maihofer (ed), *Naturrecht oder Rechtspositivismus?* (Darmstadt, Wissenschaftliche Buchgesellschaft, 1962) 27. For a detailed analysis of concrete order thought in Nazi Germany see B Rüthers, *Rechtslehren und Kronjuristen im Dritten Reich* (Munich, C.H. Beck, 1989). For the impact of concrete order thought on adjudicative practice see Rüthers (n 16). For general accounts of Nazi legal theory see H Pauer-Studer, *Justifying Injustice. Legal Theory in Nazi Germany* (Cambridge, CUP, 2020); K Anderbrügge, *Völkisches Rechtsdenken. Zur Rechtslehre in der Zeit des Nationalsozialismus* (Berlin, Duncker & Humblot, 1978).
[19] See n 13 above.

the claim that judges are duty-bound to decide, whenever possible, in accordance with statutory prescription.

Statutory positivism was arguably the dominant legal theory of the Wilhelmine Empire, but it came under sustained criticism in the Weimar period, most notably from Carl Schmitt, who pursued two related lines of attack against statutory positivism. On the one hand, Schmitt, anticipating Radbruch, accused statutory positivism of mistakenly reducing legitimacy to mere legality. If any formally valid statutory prescription, irrespective of the moral quality of its content, is binding on judges as well as citizens, then statutory positivism will allow for the law to turn into a mere instrument of oppression, a top-down projection of authority. Legitimate law-making must be animated by a suprapositive idea of *Recht*.[20]

On the other hand, Schmitt argued that statutory positivism was in any case incoherent as a theory of how adjudication. In an early work that has thus far received too little attention in Schmitt scholarship, *Gesetz und Urteil (Statute and Judgment)*, Schmitt pointed out that a judge must always interpret a statute to apply it.[21] To say that a judge is bound to apply statute is to say that a judge is bound to decide in accordance with their interpretation of the meaning, scope and relevance of statute. If a legislator issued a prescription as to how statute is to be interpreted and applied, that prescription would itself stand in need of judicial interpretation. If decisions taken in legal practice are predictable, the reason is not that judicial behaviour is controlled by imposed statutory command, but rather that judges aim to make their decisions conformable to standards of interpretation accepted among their peers.

In *Gesetz und Urteil*, Schmitt claimed that the aim to achieve legal determinacy, understood as predictability of judicial decision, was the key purpose guiding in Wilhelmine judicial practice. Schmitt also argued that predictability would be achievable only on the condition that judges held to a shared view of the substance of *Recht*. Statute had to be interpreted in light of commonly accepted background principles for judicial decisions to be suitably determinate. The claim that judges are bound to statute, in other words, was replaced with the claim that judges are (or ought to be) bound to *Recht*, to what is regarded as right or legally proper. The content of *Recht* was not to be supplied by a judge's personal moral opinion, but by the socially accepted conception of proper order.[22]

---

[20] See C Schmitt, *Legality and Legitimacy*, translated by Jeffrey Seitzer (Durham, NC, Duke University Press, 2004).

[21] Now available in translation in L Vinx and SG Zeitlin (eds), *Carl Schmitt's Early Legal-Theoretical Writings. Statute and Judgment and The Significance of the Individual* (Cambridge, CUP, 2021) 39.

[22] For further analysis of Schmitt's theory of adjudication see the introduction in Vinx and Zeitlin (n 21) 1.

A socially accepted conception of order, theorists of concrete order argued, was not to be developed on the philosophical armchair. Rather, it was held to be implicit in prevalent ways of life. Society may be understood as a patchwork of established social fragments of order antecedent to positive law – the family, the church, the workplace – which form part of an encompassing people's community and endow that community with a distinctive ethics. Positive statutory law is legitimate, according to the theory of the concrete order, if and only if it expresses and helps to maintain the integrity of the concrete orders of which a society is composed. It follows that it would be wrong for judges to consider themselves bound to statute. Statute, due to the need for interpretation in the process of application cannot bind the judge. Statutory enactments are to be interpreted and applied by reference to the ethos implicit in existing concrete orders.[23]

Though statutory positivism (or what Dworkin would call 'conventionalism') is to be rejected as an incoherent account of judicial practice, in making demands that no judge could possibly follow, there is nevertheless a practical point to replacing formalist theory with concrete order thought. Judges will labour under a form of false consciousness if they wrongly believe that what they do is simply to apply statute. Judges labouring under that form of false consciousness, by clinging to crimped interpretive techniques that sustain the fiction that judicial decision-taking is determined by imposed statutory command, are likely to fail to take decisions that properly serve the goal of the maintenance of concrete order. Schmitt argued, in *Gesetz und Urteil*, that judicial decisions that appear directly to contravene existing statutory law may be perfectly legitimate, in case they are informed by a concern for the maintenance of concrete order.[24]

Schmitt's somewhat confusing views on the proper limits of judicial power and on the legitimacy of judicial review become understandable in the context of concrete order thought. Where judges are committed to a liberal ideology that commends neutrality between conceptions of the good, and where they take their job to consist in the mechanical application of statute, they will be ill-equipped to rectify mistakes the legislator may have made in giving expression to concrete order. During the Weimar Republic, Schmitt therefore argued against endowing the Supreme Court of the Weimar Republic with a power of constitutional review and attributed the role of guardian of social order to the executive.[25] But he was happy to abandon any restraint on judicial powers of

---

[23] Pauer-Studer, *Justifying Injustice* (n 18) 203–29 accordingly observes a 'moralization of law in National Socialism'.
[24] See Vinx and Zeitlin (n 21) 135–39.
[25] For a partial translation of Schmitt's *Der Hüter der Verfassung* which contains Schmitt's arguments against constitutional review see L Vinx (ed), *The Guardian of the Constitution. Hans Kelsen and Carl Schmitt on the Limits of Constitutional Law* (Cambridge, CUP, 2015) 79.

interpretation in the Nazi period, on the condition that judges were committed to Nazi ideology, which Schmitt took to be expressive of popular moral opinion.[26]

Judicial practice in Nazi Germany was profoundly influenced by concrete order thought. Talk of concrete order frequently featured in judicial decisions that set aside existing statutory norms or re-interpreted these in order to make them conformable to Nazi ideology. Radbruch's analysis of the workings of Nazi legal order was therefore misleading. The problem was not that judges who might otherwise have used the resources of the law to defend citizens against arbitrary tyranny slavishly obeyed wicked statutory enactments because their positivist education disposed them to consider such laws to be binding even if wicked. Rather, judges in Nazi Germany routinely reworked or refused to apply existing statutory norms inherited from the Weimar Republic – norms that were in themselves unobjectionable enough or even benign – in ways that allowed them to arrive at shockingly discriminatory outcomes. This tendency was visible even where courts applied the few high-profile wicked statutory enactments that are commonly treated as paradigms of Nazi legality.[27]

On the methodological level, concrete order thinkers were interpretivists. They rejected the idea that it is possible to establish the content of law by appeal to a positivist conception of the sources of law. They would have agreed with Dworkin's claim that the application of statute requires a constructive interpretation that must aim to show the law in a morally attractive light and provide justification for the coercive force that is exercised in the name of the law, though their views as to what background principles would do that were morally perverted and wrong.

In *Law's Empire*, Dworkin claimed that an interpretivist methodological approach has room for several different interpretive conceptions of the law and went on to sketch interpretive versions of a positivist and of a realist conception of law – conventionalism and pragmatism – which he contrasted with law as integrity. Stanley Fish doubts that these positions are viable options within an interpretive methodology,[28] and I am inclined to agree. At any rate, it seems clear that concrete order thought was not conventionalist. As we have seen, Schmitt rejected a conventionalist understanding of adjudication. But neither were proponents of concrete order thought pragmatists in Dworkin's sense. They did not deny that there was law and that judges were supposed to apply it. If Alfred Mayer had not been a Jew, Nazi legal thinkers would certainly have argued that he had a claim against Jakob Juster that was properly enforceable on demand.

---

[26] See C Schmitt, *Staat, Bewegung, Volk. Die Dreigliederung der politischen Einheit*, in Schmitt, *Gesammelte Schriften* (n 18) 76, 112–15.

[27] The Katzenberger case, which concerned an alleged sexual relationship between a Jewish man and an Aryan woman, is a well-known example. The judgment is printed in Staff (n 17) 178. For commentary see Müller (n 16) 144–49.

[28] See Fish, 'Still Wrong' (n 1) 402–06.

If concrete order thought was methodologically interpretivist, and if its conception of law was neither conventionalist nor pragmatist, then, it would seem, it must have been a version, albeit perverted, of law as integrity. Concrete order thought demanded that the legal material be read in light of background principles, which were themselves taken to belong to the law on the condition that they figure in a compelling constructive interpretation, and which were to show the law in what was taken, though wrongly, to be a morally attractive light. The example of judicial practice in Nazi Germany would appear to confirm the possibility of immoral integrity.

III. FISH AND NAZI INTERPRETIVE PRACTICE

As pointed out in the introduction, the interpretivist might react to this result in either of two ways: they can hold on to the view that integrity entails justification, but deny that Nazi law had integrity, which would lead to the further conclusion that Nazi law was at best a marginal or defective instance of law, or perhaps no law at all. The other option is for the interpretivist to concede the possibility of immoral integrity and to break the link between integrity and justification. Nazi law was law, from an interpretive perspective, but the claims to which it gave rise had no moral force by dint of their legality.

Which of these two options would sit better with Fish's account of integrity? The answer to this question depends on whether Fish is committed to Dworkin's idea that integrity entails justification. There are some passages in Fish's writings that might be read to intimate adherence to that view. Here is one example:

> A judge hearing *McLoughlin* might be inclined to decide against the plaintiff because she reminds him of a hated stepmother or because she belongs to an ethnic group he reviles. But think of what he would have to do to 'work' such 'reasons' into his decision. He could not, of course, simply declare them, because they are not legal reasons and would be immediately stigmatized as inappropriate. Instead, he would be obliged to find recognizably legal reasons that could lead to an outcome in harmony with his prejudices; but if he did that he would not be ruled by his prejudices, but by the institutional requirement that only certain kinds of arguments – arguments drawn from the history of concerns and decisions – be employed.[29]

Fish concludes that it is wrong for a legal theorist to be worried about the danger that judges might decide in accordance with their personal preferences rather than with integrity. If one is 'deeply enough embedded in some principled enterprise, the conflict will never be actualized because some preferences simply will not come into play'.[30] Whatever a judge may do as participant in legal practice

---

[29] ibid 412.
[30] ibid 413.

is going to 'reflect a commitment to law as integrity'.[31] Fish also characterises legal practice as animated by justice. He avers, at one point, that 'the defining characteristic of a judicial opinion would be that it presented itself as flowing from principles of justice'.[32]

Despite these passages, however, Fish rejects the view that integrity entails moral justification. How should we parse the claim that a judicial decision must appeal to 'recognizably legal reasons?' It might seem that the phrase is meant to convey that to deny a claim on ground of ethnicity could never be a recognisably legal reason, a view congenial to Dworkin's view that a legal system that exhibits integrity must treat all its subjects with equal concern and respect. But Fish makes it clear that what counts as a recognisably legal reason within some legal practice or other depends on the contingent history of that practice. He remarks that 'whenever the distinction between principle and policy is invoked, the line it draws will be bright and visible only within the assumptions of some policy that is, for the moment, so deeply in force as to be beyond challenge'.[33] He goes on to observe that challenges that shift the line between principle and policy can be raised and are sometimes successful. If that is the case, the content of integrity, of what counts as a recognisably legal reason, is liable to change over time.

Fish's account of integrity, then, poses no obstacle to the claim that Nazi law had integrity, though morally perverted. Judges and legal scholars in Nazi Germany upheld coherent (though gravely immoral) practice-internal standards of what, at the time, counted as a recognisably legal reason. Integrity, in this view, is doubly inert. It is not merely unable, as Fish explicitly argues, to provide criteria for a choice between alternative decisions that are recognisably legal. It also fails to forge a necessary link between legality and moral justification. While there can be no legal practice that is lacking in integrity as Fish describes it, we must not conclude that legal practice, morally speaking, takes care of itself. The integrity that must inevitably go along with the existence of interpretive practice does not entail moral justification. Dworkin is right to look out for a more demanding normative standard, but he is wrong to think the standard is internal to law.

IV. DWORKIN AND NAZI INTERPRETIVE PRACTICE

Dworkin's views on wicked law changed over time. The discussion of wicked law in *Law's Empire* remains ambivalent. While it seems to deny that Nazi law was a bona fide instance of legality, it also contains concessions to a positivist view that come close to admitting the possibility of perverted integrity. The later discussion of wicked law in *Justice for Hedgehogs* is less concessive to a positivist

---

[31] ibid 414.
[32] ibid 410.
[33] ibid 416.

approach, but the price it pays for that is that it collapses into an obtuse version of the classical *lex iniusta*-thesis.

To say that Nazi law was not valid law, Dworkin argues in *Law's Empire*, is to say that 'the legal practices so condemned yield to no interpretation that can have, in any acceptable political morality, any justifying power at all'.[34] Given that the political morality of the Nazis was not acceptable, we are led to the conclusion, as interpretivists, that Nazi law did not qualify as bona fide law. Dworkin concedes that a legal theorist might instead describe matters in positivist terms and claim that the Nazis had law, but law that 'lacked the features of a minimally decent system'.[35] However, Dworkin claims that this description is inferior in nuance to that given from the within the interpretive perspective. A theorist choosing the positivist description, he argues, 'would have told us less of what he thinks, revealed less of his overall jurisprudential position [...]'[36] than the theorist who told us that there was no genuine law in Nazi Germany.

According to Dworkin, 'interpretive theories are by their nature addressed to a particular legal culture, generally the culture to which their authors belong'.[37] Those who offer an interpretive theory for the legal culture to which they belong, he adds, will treat their own law as 'a flourishing example of law, one that calls for and rewards the interpretive attitude'.[38] As we have seen, Nazi legal theorists and judges would have seen their own law as a flourishing example of legality that called for the interpretive attitude. They were not driven to internal scepticism. But Dworkin does not, I think, mean to endorse the view that any legal order or practice that is regarded as a flourishing instance of interpretive practice by its participants ought to be so regarded by the legal theorist. Rather, he claims that if an interpretation of our own legal practice identifies some feature of that practice as what confers general legitimacy on legally warranted coercion, and if that feature is missing in some other legal practice, then we should deny presumptive moral legitimacy, and by implication legal quality, to that practice. In other words, it is our own interpretation of our own law, provided it does not lead us into internal scepticism, that will determine what counts as law elsewhere, not the point of view, however interpretive, of the participants in some foreign legal practice.

Dworkin, however, qualifies this account in two important respects. The first qualification claims that an interpretive theorist who considers that some foreign legal practice lacks essential characteristics of legitimacy, as they have become apparent in a constructive interpretation of 'Anglo-American law', need not 'deny that the Nazis had law'.[39] The theorist can claim instead that the Nazis

---

[34] Dworkin (n 1) 102.
[35] ibid 104.
[36] ibid 104.
[37] ibid 102.
[38] ibid 102.
[39] ibid 103.

had law, but only in a pre-interpretive sense which does not carry justificatory connotations.

Note that this claim might be understood in three different ways. The statement that the Nazis did not have law in an interpretive sense might be taken to convey that Nazi legal practice was not (or not self-consciously) interpretive, that judges, perhaps lacking in any degree of independence of political authorities, were slavishly obedient to instructions issued by those political authorities and these instructions were applied without being filtered through considerations of principle. So understood, the claim that Nazi law was not interpretive is descriptively inaccurate, as we have seen.

The claim that the Nazis did not have law in the interpretive sense might be understood to say that while the Nazis had law in a positivist sense – a system of rules recognised as law and validated by pedigree – the laws in question, due to their moral heinousness, arbitrariness or lack of consistency, were incapable of being interpreted and applied in a principled and coherent manner. This account of Nazi legal practice, reminiscent of Fuller's claim that coherence has an affinity with the good, is likewise descriptively inaccurate as applied to the legal order of Nazi Germany.

Finally, the claim that Nazi law failed to attain the quality of law in the interpretive sense might be understood to say that Nazi law lacked general justification because the political morality that guided constructive interpretation in Nazi Germany was entirely unacceptable. This latter claim is of course true. But if read in conjunction with the concession that Nazi law was law in the pre-interpretive sense, it amounts to little more than a cumbersome rephrasing of the positivist claim that Nazi law was law but too unjust to be obeyed. We might choose to express our moral condemnation of Nazi law using the language of integrity, on the ground that no system that lacks moral justification could be judged to possess authentic integrity. But the appeal to integrity will then lack any explanatory value, it will add nothing to the claim that Nazi Law was too unjust to be presumptively binding, a claim a positivist can happily endorse.

Dworkin's second concession admits that even if it is true that Nazi law was not law in the interpretive sense, it does not follow that Nazi laws could never have had any moral force. Suppose Alfred Mayer had been an Aryan, not a Jew. The law of Nazi Germany would then have given him an enforceable claim against Jakob Juster for payment of the price of the cow he had delivered. What is more, the law of Nazi Germany would, in making Mayer's claim enforceable, have aligned itself with the requirements of sound morality (just as it would have aligned itself with sound morality if it had held Mayer's claim to be enforceable irrespective of his Jewishness). There can be no doubt that a fair few of the claims that citizens of Nazi Germany held against each other under rules in force in Nazi Germany were, to speak in Dworkin's terms, properly enforceable on demand.

Dworkin's discussion of the travails of a fictional judge Siegfried in Nazi Germany further belabours that point. The reader of *Law's Empire* is invited to put themselves 'in Siegfried's shoes', to reflect on how 'a judge in the foreign system we disapprove of [...] should decide some hard case arising there'.[40] It might turn out, Dworkin claims, that 'the interpretive attitude is wholly inappropriate there' since the relevant practice 'can never provide any justification at all, even a weak one, for state-coercion'.[41] Siegfried should then be advised to ignore legislation and precedent altogether and to decide in accordance with sound morality. However, Dworkin thinks it is possible that this is not where Siegfried will end up. There may be cases, like the dispute between Mayer and Juster, in which Siegfried should find that the plaintiff's claim deserves enforcement, notwithstanding the fact that 'the system is too wicked to be justified in any overall interpretation'.[42]

Dworkin then imagines that the case at hand might be a hard case in the context of the wicked legal order because Siegfried and his fellow judges 'disagree about what, precisely, the pertinent rules of contract law are'.[43] Contractual disputes between Jews and Aryans that turned on how to read section 138 of the German Civil Code were hard cases, in precisely this sense, in the early stages of Nazi rule.[44] Dworkin opines that, due to the wickedness of the system, we cannot resolve the issue by appeal to an overall interpretation of Nazi legal practice that we take to have general justificatory purchase. Dworkin's suggestion as to how to deal with a hard contract case in a wicked legal system is to instead affirm that parties to a contract have legal rights against each other, since they 'should be protected in relying and planning on law even in wicked places'. The further question of the proper understanding of the content of contract, Dworkin claims, is an 'interpretive question' to be settled by reference to 'the point of view of the parties'.[45]

I accept Dworkin's claim that this would have been 'a sensible approach to take'[46] for the court that decided the dispute between Juster and Mayer. It would have favoured Mayer, given that it could hardly have made sense to argue that either of the parties to the contract would have assumed it to be void on account of Mayer's Jewishness. But as we have seen, the court did not act on the ground of Dworkin's sensible proposal. Dworkin goes on to argue that interpretivism can account even for that. One might ask not how Siegfried ought to decide the

---

[40] ibid 105.
[41] ibid 105.
[42] ibid 105–06.
[43] ibid 105.
[44] See Rüthers (n 16) 370–79.
[45] See Dworkin (n 1) 106–07. Hart accused Dworkin of making morally implausible claims in arguing that there might be moral reasons to enforce wicked laws. See R Dworkin, 'A Reply by Ronald Dworkin' in M Cohen (ed), *Ronald Dworkin and Contemporary Jurisprudence* (London, Duckworth, 1983) 247, 256–60, in response to HLA Hart, 'Legal Duty and Obligation' in HLA Hart, *Essays on Bentham. Studies in Jurisprudence and Political Theory* (Oxford, OUP. 1982) 127, 147–53, and compare the discussion in Dyzenhaus (n 9) 149–50.
[46] Dworkin (n 1) 107.

case to make it come out as morally acceptable as possible from our moral point of view, but rather how he ought to decide it given that he is a committed Nazi:

> If we assume he will treat his problem as interpretive, as we would do if a similar problem arose in our own law, our question remains interpretive rather than descriptive in any simpler sense. But the premises of our interpretive question have shifted again. Now we put ourselves more fully in Siegfried's shoes and interpret from the point of view of the full set of his political and social convictions.[47]

To say that this question is interpretive and not descriptive in any simple sense, presumably, is to say that once one has adopted the point of view of a committed Nazi who happens to be a judge, one can ask oneself what decisions it would be appropriate to take from that point of view. One can ask oneself what constructive interpretation of the law would show the law in its best light, what principles would best explain and justify practice, while assuming the political and moral outlook of Nazism. Had the court decided, say, to enforce Mayer's claim against Juster for payment of RM 60.70, one would, from that interpretive point of view, have had to criticise its decision for not giving proper expression to the principles of Nazism in interpreting section 138 of the German Civil Code.

These musings flatly concede the possibility of immoral integrity. And once that concession is made, the claim that the Nazis lacked law in the interpretive sense will evidently come to little more than the view that the law of Nazi Germany was so deeply immoral that one should not hold that there was presumptive moral justification for the enforcement of its norms – a claim that simply restates the positivist take on these matters in needlessly cumbersome language.

Dworkin's position in *Justice for Hedgehogs* is much less concessive to positivism. The late Dworkin embraces the view, or so it would appear, that the Nazis had no law:

> The hideous Nazi edicts did not create even prima facie or arguable rights and duties. The purported Nazi government was fully illegitimate, and no other structuring principles of fairness argued for the enforcement of those edicts. It is morally more accurate to deny that these edicts were law. The German judges asked to enforce them faced only prudential dilemmas, not moral ones.[48]

The edicts of the Nazis, Dworkin now argues, were 'too unjust to count as valid law' – a claim that he had avoided in *Law's Empire* (the discussion of wicked law in *Law's Empire* does not use the terms 'valid' and 'invalid'). Unfortunately, Dworkin does not explain how exactly we are to understand the phrase 'the edicts of the Nazis'. It might be taken to refer to all laws enacted by the Nazi Government, or perhaps to all laws that were in force in Nazi Germany (including the retained law of the Weimar Republic), or perhaps only to some laws

---

[47] ibid 107.
[48] Dworkin (n 6) 411.

enacted by the Nazis that are famous for their antisemitic and discriminatory character, such as the Nuremberg Laws.

The context of the passage would appear to suggest that Dworkin does not mean to endorse the implausible claim that all laws that were held to be force in Nazi Germany were invalid. Such a claim would be implausible even if we accepted the core thesis of the one-system picture that Dworkin defended in *Justice for Hedgehogs*, that is, the claim that legal rights are a species of moral rights, those that it is proper for legal institutions to enforce on demand. As we have seen, there must have been rights resulting from laws that were in force in Nazi Germany that it would have been morally proper for German legal institutions at the time to enforce on demand. It is therefore best to take Dworkin to claim that some enactments of the Nazis were too unjust to be legally valid.

This interpretation also fits better with the background of the quoted passage[49] – a comparison between Nazi law and the federal Fugitive Slave Acts of the antebellum US. Dworkin considers the question whether one should say that those acts were valid law, but too unjust to be obeyed, or that they were too unjust to count as valid law. He reasons that we should adopt the first of these options. The Fugitive Slave Acts, though wicked in substance, were enacted by an otherwise legitimate government whose decisions 'generally created political obligations'. This endowed the 'slaveholders' claims [to retrieve their runaway human property] with more moral force than they would otherwise have had'.[50] Dworkin hastens to add that this moral force was amply outweighed by countervailing moral reasons. No judge ought to have enforced the fugitive slave laws. But the laws were nevertheless valid, and so were the slaveholders' claims, according to the one-system picture, since there was some moral reason, grounded in systemic considerations, to enforce those claims. A similar conclusion does not, however, hold for the 'hideous edicts of the Nazis'. The latter were not issued by an otherwise legitimate government and therefore did not create any 'arguable rights and duties'. No judge ought to have felt that they had a moral reason, however weak, to apply them.[51]

Dworkin concludes by crediting the shift to the one-system picture with being able to offer more descriptive and moral nuance than a positivist account, in showing that there are different species of wicked law.[52] Some wicked law is valid law, because the claims to which it gives rise have some moral force, while other wicked law is not valid because the claims to which it gives rise altogether lack moral force. Dworkin appears to have thought that it was less implausible to deny the validity of the edicts of the Nazis than to deny the validity of the Fugitive Slave Acts in the antebellum US. To make room within the one-system

---

[49] See ibid 410–12.
[50] ibid 411.
[51] ibid 411.
[52] ibid 411.

picture for the possibility of laws that are valid because they create arguable rights but too unjust to be obeyed, all things considered, will soften the charge of descriptive implausibility against interpretivism.[53] We can now say that unjust laws of the antebellum US were valid but deny that title to unjust Nazi laws.

I must confess that I do not see how Dworkin's distinction between types of wicked law contributes to descriptive nuance or moral clarity. The contrast that Dworkin tries to draw between unjust but valid laws in the antebellum US and unjust and invalid enactments in Nazi Germany strikes me as morally confused. Are laws that establish or protect the institution of slavery less morally hideous in their substance than laws that, say, prohibit sexual intercourse or marriage between Jews and Aryans? Dworkin, one imagines, would have replied that this question misses the point. The claim that there is a difference between the two cases, he might have argued, rests on the background legitimacy (or lack thereof) of the government that made the wicked laws at issue. But this response is unhelpful. No government, however democratic or otherwise committed to upholding the rule of law, could have a power that has any moral purchase to make laws enabling some human beings to own other human beings as their property. And if to make such laws could not possibly be part of the legitimate powers of any government, then the fact that a government that enacts them is in other respects morally decent enough does not provide any reason to hold that the claims of slaveholders to recover their supposed human property are to be attributed some degree of moral force, a degree sufficient to turn them into arguable rights (and the laws that institute or protect slavery into valid laws).

I do not mean to deny that there could be (defeasible) moral reasons for a judge to enforce an unjust law that stems from the law's membership in a decent legal system. My claim is that there was no such moral reason to enforce the Fugitive Slave Acts, just as there was no such moral reason to enforce the hideous edicts of the Nazis. Background reasons of legitimacy can be relevant and provide reason for the application of substantively unjust laws only where laws are unjust but not catastrophically so. This is the sound core of Radbruch's formula.

The implications of the one-system view for the problem of wicked law, I conclude, are more straightforward than Dworkin makes them out to be. The one-system picture, in effect, leaves us with a version of the classical *lex iniusta*-thesis. Laws that pass a threshold of extreme injustice do not generate moral reasons. In the one-system picture, this will entail that such enactments are not valid laws since the fact that they were enacted by a de facto authority provides no moral reason, however weak, to enforce them. Whether this description is to

---

[53] Compare the discussion in M Greenberg, 'The Moral Impact Theory of Law' (2013-2014) 123 *Yale Law Journal* 1288, 1337–38, who is less hesitant than Dworkin to bite the bullet and to deny the legality of unjust laws. For discussion of the relation between Greenberg and Dworkin see T Bustamante, 'Law, Moral Facts and Interpretation: A Dworkinian Response to Mark Greenberg's Moral Impact Theory of Law' (2019) 32 *Canadian Journal of Law and Jurisprudence* 5.

be preferred to the positivist option which affirms the validity of wicked law is not the question of this chapter. Dworkin himself concluded that 'the ancient jurisprudential problem of evil law is sadly close to a verbal dispute'.[54] This weary conclusion all but admits that the appeal to integrity fails to add either descriptive nuance or moral clarity to discussions of wicked law.

V. FLAVOURS OF INTEGRITY

Did the legal order of Nazi Germany really exhibit integrity? The argument offered in this chapter is not intended to deny that, from a moral point of view, there is a perfectly straightforward sense in which it did not. Integrity, as described by Dworkin, is an attractive ideal of legitimacy for a legal order, sustained by a compelling constructive interpretation of Anglo-American legal traditions. Nazi legality did not instantiate that ideal. Nazi law, after all, was built on an explicit denial of the demand that a political and legal system must show equal concern and respect for all those who are subject to it. No system of governance that does that can exhibit a form of integrity that has legitimating force.

What has been suggested here is that Dworkin's morally sound ideal of integrity, the commitment to equal concern and respect, is not internal to legality. It is not internal, to be more specific, to any flourishing interpretive practice that, in the view of its participants, 'calls for and rewards the interpretive attitude'.

In *Law's Empire*, Dworkin describes law as integrity as the view that 'rights and responsibilities flow from past decisions and so count as legal, not just when they are explicit in these decisions but also when they follow from the principles of personal and political morality the explicit decisions presuppose by way of justification'.[55] This description does not rule out the integrity of Nazi legal practice – unless we add that the principles of morality embedded in that practice were substantively false or mistaken principles, in light of the practice-independent standards of justice to which we hold.

The interpretivist is left with two choices: they can either concede that evil law is valid, and may even have its own integrity, though it is a morally wicked integrity that has no justificatory purchase, or they must retreat to the blunt assertion that laws – or, for that matter, judicial decisions – that fly in the face of any morally defensible version of integrity must lack validity. In either case, interpretivism will leave everything exactly where it is.

---

[54] Dworkin (n 6) 412.
[55] Dworkin (n 1) 96.

# 18

What Makes Law? Dworkin, Fish, and Koskenniemi on the Rule of Law

DAVID LEFKOWITZ[*]

I. INTRODUCTION

WHAT MAKES LAW? So formulated, the question is an ambiguous one. On what I will call the micro-level, it asks for the successful conditions for an assertion of law, what justifies or provides the truth conditions for claims such as 'I have a legal right to ϕ' or 'you broke the law'. Much of the debate between Ronald Dworkin and Stanley Fish concerns this question; for example, the role that theory plays in actors' identification of the law, or the constraints, if any, that legal materials themselves impose on what counts as an interpretation of them. At the macro-level, the question 'what makes law?' concerns the features that distinguish a genuinely *legal* political order from other types of political order. Or, in the somewhat archaic phrase, what makes it the case that a society is ruled by law and not by men? I will argue that Dworkin and Fish agree on the answer to this question, and so too does the contemporary international legal theorist Martti Koskenniemi. Specifically, each of them identifies law with a practice of government informed by fidelity to the ideal of the rule of law, or legality. All three theorists conceive of legality as an attitude, mindset, or approach to constructing the social world, one that is most fully developed in members of the legal profession, or what is the same, those who have been habituated into a culture devoted to the ideal of government in accordance with the rule of law. And all three develop their account of law as a practice of government informed by legality by contrasting it with an instrumental or managerial approach to government.

Why include a discussion of Koskenniemi's remarks on the nature of law in a chapter of a volume devoted to the Fish-Dworkin debate? There are several reasons to do so. First, Koskenniemi's characterisation of law in terms of both a culture of formalism and a constitutional mindset nicely bridges the apparent divide created by Fish's focus on interpretive communities and the way in which

---

[*] Significant portions of this chapter were written while I was a visiting research scholar in the Department of Law at the University of Pompeu Fabra. I gratefully acknowledge their hospitality, and particularly that demonstrated by José Luis Martí.

individuals acquire a particular 'cultural lens' that informs their engagements with (some aspect of) the world, and Dworkin's focus on the protestant attitude that defines law's empire.[1] Second, neither Dworkin nor Fish have paid much attention to international law, or for that matter, to any (putative) legal order other than that of the US and England. The fact that a leading commentator on international law makes use of the same understanding of law to characterise (and critique) our existing practice of global government, and the political society it constitutes, provides some defence against an accusation of parochialism, though more is needed. Finally, though Koskenniemi regularly references (and endorses) Dworkin's account of constructive interpretation, on the whole his scholarship bears a far greater resemblance to Fish's. Indeed, their views are so much alike that an argument that one characterises law in terms of fidelity to legality provides a compelling reason to think that the other must (or should) as well.

My aim in this chapter is twofold. On the one hand, I offer readings of texts by Dworkin, Fish, and Koskenniemi to support the claim that they share an understanding of the nature of law; that is, of the features in virtue of which a practice of government counts as a legal one. My goal here is to provide insight into the views of particular theorists, and in the case of Dworkin and Fish, to emphasise a commonality in those views that may well exceed in its importance whatever differences may also characterise them.[2] On the other hand, I seek to clarify the concept of the rule of law by bringing together similar descriptions of it advanced by three prominent legal scholars. In doing so, I also aim to make a case for its superiority to other analyses of the rule of law, and for that matter, to other accounts of law. The argument is not so much an appeal to authority as it is an appeal to testimony. In their characterisation of a practice of government in accordance with the rule of law, Dworkin, Fish, and Koskenniemi help us to understand the life of the law as the experience of lawyers.

---

[1] R Dworkin, *Law's Empire* (Cambridge, MA, Harvard University Press, 1986).
[2] In truth, if we look at what each author says on his own behalf, rather than what is attributed to him by the other, less divides Dworkin and Fish than it may appear. For example, Dworkin does not advocate for the use of theory, as Fish defines it, to identify what the law is. Nor does he maintain that a text itself (eg, legal materials) constrains eligible interpretations; rather, it is the point or purpose of a practice that does so. For reasons I detail later in the main text, that is why a constructive interpretation of legal materials must meet a threshold criterion of fit if it is to qualify as the identification of existing law, rather than an act of legislation. Furthermore, Dworkin does not maintain that a lawyer – a person genuinely devoted to the ideal of government in accordance with the rule of law – might choose to substitute his own judgment of appropriate conduct for that of the political community's. Instead, Dworkin warns against the possibility, not infrequently realised, that a person who occupies a legal office – or better, a position in a government institution (a court, a police force, etc) – might fail to exhibit the virtue of a lawyer. Contra Dworkin's assertion, and at least in his more Peircean moments, Fish does not deny the possibility of right answers or true beliefs. He only denies the possibility of a perspective from which we could know with certainty what they are. This last point does point us to a genuine disagreement, however. While both theorists are value pluralists, Dworkin maintains that they fit together to form a coherent whole – values compete, but do not conflict – whereas Fish denies the unity of value thesis.

II. DWORKIN ON THE RULE OF LAW

As I read him, Dworkin maintains that a system of coercive government counts as a genuinely legal one if and only if it exhibits fidelity to a conception of the rule of law as valuable for the constitutive contribution it makes to the treatment of all its (individual human) subjects with equal concern and respect. This requires both a particular type of institutional structure, one that includes inter alia government through law and recourse to (relatively) impartial dispute resolution procedures, and a particular political culture or *ethos* on the part of both rulers and ruled that Dworkin labels law as integrity.[3] In a political community that governs itself through law properly so-called, this *ethos* regulates the community's use of coercion to uphold its members' political rights and duties. It does so by informing members' attempts to identify terms for just interaction, ie, attempts to specify those legal rights and duties members of the community should or already do enjoy, and to engage with one another on those terms. For example, judges identify those rights and duties enforceable upon demand without any further legislative action by constructively interpreting the political community's past practice of government according to the rule of law as an attempt to realise concretely a fundamental moral commitment to treating all of its members with equal concern and respect. Legal subjects instantiate such treatment by guiding their conduct according to findings of law simply because it is the law; that is, because they take the exercise of governmental power in accordance with law as integrity to be legitimate. In sum, for Dworkin, legal reasoning has a specific form; the product of such reasoning, law properly so-called, necessarily provides a moral justification for the exercise of governmental power; and legitimate government simply is government according to the rule of law informed by a proper understanding of what makes the rule of law valuable.[4]

I focus my remarks here on Dworkin's identification of law with government in accordance with the rule of law. In *Law's Empire*, he writes:

> our discussions about law by and large assume, I suggest, that the most abstract and fundamental point of legal practice is to guide and constrain the power of government in the following way. Law insists that force not be used or withheld, no matter how beneficial or noble the ends in view, except as licensed or required by individual rights and responsibilities flowing from past political decisions about when collective force is justified. The law of a community on this account is the scheme of rights

---

[3] For discussion of the institutional elements of the rule of law, see D Lefkowitz, *Philosophy and International Law: A Critical Introduction* (Cambridge, Cambridge University Press, 2020) 73–83.
[4] Dworkin presents his most complete statement and defence of these claims in Dworkin (n 1), but many are also the subject of essays collected in R Dworkin, *A Matter of Principle* (Cambridge, MA, Harvard University Press, 1985) and R Dworkin, *Justice in Robes* (Cambridge, MA, Harvard University Press, 2006).

and responsibilities that meet that complex standard … This characterization of the concept of law sets out, in suitably airy form, what is sometimes called the 'rule' of law.[5]

We might quibble with Dworkin's assumption that the rule of law concerns the *coercive* enforcement of rights and responsibilities, on the grounds that law enforcement sometimes takes the form of denying members of the political community benefits to which they would otherwise be entitled.[6] Likewise, Dworkin's claim that law concerns *individual* rights and responsibilities may be too narrow, insofar as the agents that law constitutes as bearers of rights and responsibilities may be collective ones, such as corporations and states.[7] Finally, insofar as it suggests that the rule of law concerns only the conduct of legal officials (judges, prosecutors, police officers, etc), and not that of legal subjects, this description offers an incomplete purview of government in accordance with the rule of law.[8] Nevertheless, Dworkin's claim captures two of legality's key features: it offers a regulative ideal for the exercise of political power premised on the treatment of legal subjects as bearers of rights and responsibilities, and it locates the content of those rights and responsibilities in (a constructive interpretation of) the political community's practice of holding accountable.[9]

Dworkin contrasts legality with a pragmatist approach to government, which he characterises as 'a skeptical conception of law', one that 'rejects[s] the idea of law and legal right deployed in my account of the concept of law'.[10] A pragmatist 'denies that past political decisions in themselves provide any justification for either using or withholding the state's coercive power'.[11] Consequently, she takes a strategic approach to identifying (the content of) legal subjects' rights. Rather than construing legal rights as forms of treatment to which actors are entitled even if that would be worse for the community, the pragmatist treats

---

[5] Dworkin (n 1) 93.

[6] See, eg, OA Hathaway and SJ Shapiro, 'Outcasting: Enforcement in Domestic and International Law' (2011) 121 *Yale Law Journal* 252.

[7] Note that the attribution of legal rights to collective agents is consistent with value-individualism, 'the view that only the lives of individual human beings have ultimate value and collective entities derive their value solely from their contributions to the lives of individual human beings' (CH Wellman, *Liberal Rights and Responsibilities* (Oxford, Oxford University Press, 2013) 5).

[8] That Dworkin does take fidelity to the rule of law to be a character trait that both rulers and ruled must possess if a political society is to have law comes through clearly in both his discussion of political obligation and his summative description of law as 'a protestant attitude that makes each citizen responsible for imagining what his society's public commitments to principle are, and what these commitments require in new circumstances'. Dworkin (n 1) 413.

[9] Legality, then, is only one element of a comprehensive political philosophy, or moral theory of government. It does not address questions such as 'who should exercise legislative authority, and how should they do so?' or 'what should the content of that legislation be?' Answers to those questions require normative accounts of democracy (or aristocracy, or monarchy) and of justice. Yet the concept of the person legality presupposes likely has implications for who should have the power to legislate, and what sort of laws a political community ought to have.

[10] Dworkin (n 1) 95, 160.

[11] ibid 151.

them as 'only the servants of the best future: they are instruments we construct for that purpose and have no independent force or ground'.[12]

It might be thought that what distinguishes pragmatism from legality, on Dworkin's analysis, is that the former appeals solely to the production of socially beneficial outcomes to justify the exercise of political power, while the latter maintains that individual rights sometimes trump the pursuit of social welfare. While Dworkin does reject consequentialism, or at least Utilitarianism, his complaint against legal pragmatism goes deeper, and applies equally to judges (and all legal subjects) who subscribe to a deontological morality. Dworkin's fundamental objection to a judge who accords only strategic value to past political decisions is that she fails to recognise the political community as a collective agent engaged in an ongoing effort to realise a fair and just political order. An agent devoted to legality conceives of government in accordance with the rule of law as an end in itself – the constitution of a political community premised on its members status as autonomous and responsible agents, and so bearers of genuine rights and responsibilities. In contrast, a pragmatist conceives of government as merely a means for advancing some exogenous and independently specifiable goal, such as human flourishing or human rights, construed as moral rights possessed by all agents or patients as such, independent of their membership in any particular, concrete, community. The former actor aims to identify *our* commitments, that is, the standards of right conduct the political community has identified as binding on its members as such, while the latter actor aims to give effect to *her own* judgment of the ends that government should serve, and how it should do so. Pragmatism 'says that judges should follow whichever method of deciding cases will produce *what they believe* to be the best community for the future'.[13] The contrast with legality comes through clearly in F.A. Hayek's characterisation of it, which Dworkin quotes approvingly: 'the conception of freedom under the law ... rests on the contention that when we obey laws, in the sense of general abstract rules laid down irrespective of their application to us, we are not subject to another man's will and are therefore free'.[14] Or in Dworkin's own words, the rule of law 'is not just an instrument for economic achievement and social peace [or, one might add, honouring moral rights], but an emblem and mirror of the equal public regard that entitles us to claim community'.[15]

---

[12] ibid 160.

[13] ibid emphasis added.

[14] FA Hayek, *The Constitution of Liberty* (London, Routledge, 1960) 153, quoted in Dworkin, *Justice in Robes* (n 3) 177. Kant makes the same point when he asserts that actors enjoy external freedom, or freedom as non-domination, only when they are subject to a common juridical order, a system of norms that substitutes an omni-lateral will (the political community's conception of right) for a unilateral will (each actor's conception of right). For discussion, see P Capps and J Rivers, 'Kant's Concept of Law' (2018) 63 *American Journal of Jurisprudence* 259.

[15] Dworkin, *Justice in Robes* (n 4) 74.

Though Dworkin identifies law with the concept of legality, he treats that concept as interpretive in two respects. First, agents who share the concept of legality may nonetheless disagree as to whether a particular act satisfies that standard, or what is the same, whether that act is legal. They will all concur with the claim that members of the political community as such presently enjoy all and only those rights, and are subject to all and only those duties, that 'flow from past decisions of the right sort' or 'standards established in the right way'. Yet as Dworkin observes, 'it remains to be specified what kind of standards satisfy legality's demands, and what counts as a standard's having been established in the right way in advance [of any enforcement of a right or duty]'.[16] *Conceptions* of legality offer answers to these questions. They are properly described as interpretations of the concept of legality because the identification of the standards of appropriate conduct to which the community has committed itself, as well as the content of those standards, depends on an exercise of judgment. The case for any particular conception of legality rests on a contestable normative claim regarding the value of government in accordance with the rule of law. The case for any particular assertion of law rests not only on a contestable conception of legality, but also contestable conceptions of procedural fairness and substantive justice, and contestable claims regarding the bearing those values have on the (type of) case at issue.[17]

Second, the assertion that law is essentially a practice of government informed by fidelity to the ideal of legality is also an interpretive claim. It is advanced from within the practice, one identified in terms of an existing (but always provisional) consensus on paradigms of law and legal reasoning. It purports to offer a statement of the central concept of the practice that will enable its participants 'to see their arguments as having a certain structure, as arguments over rival conceptions of that concept', or what is the same, an 'abstract description of the point of law most legal theorists accept so that [they can understand] their arguments [to] take place on the plateau it furnishes'.[18] The success of the claim that law just is a practice of government informed by the ideal of legality is a matter of how useful we find it as a way of making sense of the practice we 'pre-interpretively' and provisionally identify as law. There is, then, nothing objectionably 'metaphysical' in Dworkin's depiction of law as, essentially, a practice of coercive government informed by fidelity to the ideal of legality.

---

[16] ibid 169.

[17] That a claim is *contestable* does not mean that it is, or will be, *contested*. Yet the contestation of specific claims regarding what the law is, and what it ought to be, are pervasive. Dworkin aspires to offer an account of such contestation that shows at least some of it to be genuine disagreement, and not simply instances of agents with fundamentally different world views or ways of life talking past one another. That account requires that agents be members of a common community (or way of life) in virtue of which they can adopt a shared world view, even while disagreeing over some of its details.

[18] Dworkin (n 1) 92–3.

III. FISH ON THE RULE OF LAW

Fish's recognition that law just is the enterprise of governing informed by fidelity to legality comes through most clearly in his response to Richard Posner's proposal that society adopt instead a social scientifically informed managerial approach to government.[19] After noting that Posner's 'pragmatic program will succeed when legal concepts and terms have been replaced by economic ones', Fish observes that 'if the "intangibles" he [Posner] finds "too nebulous for progress" – justice, fairness, the promotion of dignity – are removed in favour of "concrete facts," the disciplinary map will have one less country, and where the was law there will now be social science'.[20] Relatedly, in response to Posner's criticism of judges who believe without, or even against, the evidence that the judiciary's effectiveness depends on a belief by the public that judges are finders rather than makers of law, Fish remarks that

> this particular belief is itself founding, and constitutes a kind of contract between the legal institution and the public, each believing in the other's belief about itself, and thus creating a world in which expectations and a sense of mutual responsibility confirm one another without any external support.[21]

To find law, rather than to make it, is to exercise coercive government 'only in accordance with standards established in the right way before that exercise'.[22] And as Fish rightly observes, the commitment to legality is a founding belief or structural assumption, one that serves to constitute members of the political community as creatures with dignity, in virtue of which they are entitled to fair and just treatment. Specifically, a practice of government in accordance with the rule of law presupposes that legal subjects are autonomous and responsible agents. To be an agent is to be capable of acting for reasons. A responsible agent is, in Lon Fuller's words, 'capable of understanding and following rules, and answerable for his [or her] defaults'.[23] Responsible agents can hold themselves accountable for conforming to standards of right conduct, and do the same for other actors they judge to be responsible agents. Autonomous agents are capable of acting as the authors of their own lives, of exercising some degree of control over both the ends they pursue and the means to achieving them that they adopt. In contrast, the practice of government Posner advocates presumes a conception of the person as a creature with desires or preferences in need of satisfaction.[24]

---

[19] S Fish, 'Almost Pragmatism: The Jurisprudence of Richard Posner, Richard Rorty, and Ronald Dworkin' in M Brint and W Weaver (eds), *Pragmatism in Law and Society* (Boulder, Westview Press, 1991) 47–82.
[20] ibid 62, 71.
[21] ibid 62.
[22] Dworkin, *Justice in Robes* (n 4) 169.
[23] LL Fuller, *The Morality of Law*, rev. edn (New Haven, CT, Yale University Press, 1969) 162.
[24] For an alternative reading of Fish, one that attributes to him a conception of the person closer to the one I ascribe to Posner, see T Bustamante, ch 14 in this volume.

That conception is fundamentally at odds with the one that provides the rule of law with its raison d'etre, and that is why Fish rightly concludes that Posner's program amounts not to a proposal to reform law but to replace it.

Posner maintains that law's value rests on the contribution it makes to facilitating the efficient achievement of social goals. Many features of contemporary legal practice render it highly sub-optimal as a tool for maximising social welfare, which is a primary reason Posner advocates for its replacement by an empirically informed managerial approach to government. Fish counters that Posner misconstrues the desire to which law is a response. Law emerges not because it is an efficient tool for maximising social welfare, but 'because people desire predictability, stability, equal protection, the reign of justice, etc., and because they want to believe that it is possible to secure these things by instituting a set of impartial procedures'.[25] Law, Fish maintains,

> is centrally about such things as conscience, guilt, personal responsibility, fairness, impartiality, and no analysis imported from some other disciplinary context 'proving' that these things do not exist will remove them from legal culture, unless of course society decides that a legal culture is a luxury it can afford to do without.[26]

A practice of government in accordance with the rule of law presupposes that human beings are autonomous and responsible agents. As Fish observes, it is a 'belief' or 'assumption' that cannot be argued for from within the practice, because it provides the very condition for any arguments that can be successfully advanced within the practice. This claim regarding the nature of enterprises, interpretive communities, or as I prefer, practices of holding accountable, does not entail the impossibility of a human society in which government is not premised on a conception of people as autonomous and responsible agents. But as Posner observes and Fish concurs, the emergence of such a society from one with an (always imperfect) history of government in accordance with the rule of law will require many of its officials and subjects to undergo a 'come to Bentham' experience, a conversion that substitutes one 'foundational' conception of human beings and the point or purpose of government for another.[27] It is not quite right, then, to say that a society will *decide* that a legal culture is a luxury it can do without. Rather, should such a (mass) conversion occur, a legal culture – government in accordance with the rule of law – will simply be an activity whose value people cannot grasp, a way of life they cannot imagine themselves leading.

The attribution to Fish of an essentialist claim – that law just is the practice of government in accordance with legality – may appear hard to reconcile with his professed anti-foundationalism, and his criticism of Posner for straying from

---

[25] Fish (n 19) 61.
[26] ibid 62.
[27] ibid 54.

the Pragmatist fold by advancing a foundationalist and essentialist program.[28] The tension is merely apparent, however. Anti-foundationalism, as Fish understands it, requires only the rejection of a universal vantage point, a perspective that is simultaneously a view from nowhere (practice-independent) and from everywhere (comprehensive), from which one can form indubitable beliefs, or what is the same, know that a claim is true. Posner's error, Fish maintains, is to think that (a perfected or completed) economics, or social science more generally, offers such a perspective, and so the possibility of identifying with certainty the best law and policy. Crucially, the characterisation of an interpretive community or practice of holding accountable in essentialist terms requires no commitment to a foundationalist epistemology. To the contrary, it constitutes an anti-foundationalist epistemology, one in which our grasp of the (social) world is always-already structured by certain beliefs or assumptions presupposed by any competent participant in a particular (type of) interpretive community or practice of holding accountable.[29]

Fish contends that 'what makes a field a field ... is a steadfastness of purpose, a core sense of the enterprise, of what the field or discipline is *for*, of why society is willing (if not always eager) to see its particular job done'.[30] The purpose of government in accordance with the rule of law is the constitution of a political community that treats its members (legal subjects) as autonomous and responsible agents. This essentialist claim is fully consistent with the assertion that law is contingent in two respects. First, nothing in the essentialist characterisation of law entails that any human society be governed in accordance with legality. Indeed, history clearly illustrates that political societies can persist and, along some metrics, even flourish without law.[31] Second, the regulative ideal that gives an enterprise its point or purpose is purely formal, in the sense that it is not possible to deduce any substantive claims from that ideal. So, one cannot logically derive from the ideal of government in accordance with the rule of law, or the concept of the person it presupposes, the specific forms of treatment that count as conduct exhibiting fidelity to that ideal. In part, that is due to the fact that practical reasoning consists in the exercise of judgment, a method for drawing conclusions that cannot be reduced to an algorithm (or theory, as Fish defines that term). More importantly, however, it owes to the fact that assertions of law

---

[28] ibid 57.
[29] Fish describes anti-foundationalism as an epistemology premised on 'the irreducibility of difference, ... a world in which persons are situated – occupying particular places with particular purposes pursued in relation to particular goals, visions, and hopes as they follow from holding (or being held by) particular beliefs – [and thus] no one will be in a situation that is universal or general (that is, no situation at all), and therefore no one's perspective (a word that gives the game away) can lay claim to privilege' (ibid 54).
[30] ibid 68.
[31] Note that the claim here concerns a particular approach to governing, not the possibility that a society can persist or flourish without government, or without rules, including those that constitute institutions such as courts or the monarchy.

are claims regarding the political community's commitments at that point in time, its current judgment of what the treatment of all legal subjects as autonomous and responsible agents requires. The success of any such claim depends on its uptake by other members of the political community; roughly, their concurrence with the (sometimes implicit) claim that the law (ie, their law) condones or condemns a particular act. There is no universal or Archimedean standpoint outside any particular political community's practice of holding accountable from which we can identify what fidelity to the ideal of legality truly requires. Rather, the rule of law is worked out via a practice of challenge and response, one that encompasses not only assertions of legality or illegality, but also assertions that, in asserting the legality or illegality of a particular (type of) act, an agent has substituted her own judgment for that of the political community, or what is the same, has failed to exhibit fidelity to the ideal of government in accordance with the rule of law.

None of this is to deny that there are true or right answers to questions regarding the legality, or justice, of particular exercises of political power. To the contrary, the belief that there is may well be an unavoidable presupposition of inquiry and argument. Nor does it require that we equate truth with what we take ourselves to be justified in believing. Rather, the claim is that the pursuit of truth can only be carried out within particular disciplines or interpretive communities, enterprises constituted by norms that govern what counts as a justification for actions, beliefs, feelings, etc. As Dworkin states, legality is an interpretive concept; any attempt to characterise it is a normative undertaking that necessarily embroils one in the making of first-order normative claims, such as accusing government officials of having violated that ideal. Fish draws a similar conclusion. He holds that justice, fairness, and human dignity are rhetorical constructions; their content is worked out through practices of persuasion, especially those that constitute the law. That is why he asserts that

> if we want to use notions of fairness and justice in order to move things in certain directions, we must retain disciplinary vocabularies, not despite the fact that they are incapable of independent justification, but *because* they are incapable of justification, except from the inside.[32]

It will come as no surprise when an earnest moral philosopher such as Dworkin valorises government in accordance with the rule of law. But can the same really be true of Fish? After all, he is a critic, and so his contributions to our sometimes-self-conscious experience of law focus largely on unmasking how it works, rather than inspiring devotion to it. As noted above, Fish attributes the existence of law to human beings' mistaken belief that fairness and justice can be secured by instituting a set of impartial procedures. Expanding on this claim,

---

[32] ibid 71.

Fish writes that were we to adopt Posner's managerial approach to government in place of a legal one,

> we would no longer be able to say 'what justice requires' or 'what fairness dictates' and then fill in those phrases with the courses of action we prefer to take. That, after all, is the law's job – to give us ways of redescribing limited partisan programs so that they can be presented as the natural outcomes of abstract impersonal imperatives.[33]

Passages like these have suggested to some readers that Fish conceives of law as 'merely rhetorical', in the pejorative sense that it functions as a tool that devious, or perhaps self-deceived, agents can use to manipulate others in the pursuit of their own ends. They also explain why Fish is sometime associated with the critical legal studies movement, whose members repeatedly attack the rule of law as a myth, a form of propaganda that serves to cloak practices of oppression and domination by the powerful. Yet while Fish adopts an ironic stance toward the rule of law, he is no cynic. The exercise of political power in accordance with the rule of law is not the application of practice-independent determinate standards of right conduct identifiable without the exercise of moral and political judgment. But neither is it necessarily 'mere rhetoric', the wolf of private interest and the will to power dressed in the sheep's clothing of principle.

When Fish speaks of 'limited partisan programs', I contend that he means nothing more than the conceptions of justice and fairness that particular actors bring to the task of identifying the law. Legal materials, or what is the same, the political community's past practice of identifying, applying, and enforcing standards of right conduct, do not themselves yield a determinate answer to the question of what is legally permitted, required, or forbidden in the case at hand. Rather, the answer to that question depends on the exercise of judgment, an interpretation of the legal materials that, in Dworkin's words, shows them in their best light. Such a judgment is premised on agents' (possibly implicit) conception of the point or purpose of government in accordance with the rule of law, one that is manifest in their ability to grasp what the law requires in the case at hand, and to present a reading of the legal materials that they take to demonstrate why this is the case.

Fish's account of law does suffer from certain infelicities, which may simply owe to a certain style of presentation (more invigorating than my own, but at a price), but may also or instead reflect an incomplete grasp of law, or the enterprise of government in accordance with legality. For example, the adoption of a managerial approach to government would not deprive us of the ability to present our own limited partisan programs as the natural outcomes of abstract impersonal imperatives. Rather, it would only compel us to present them in terms of what is good for human beings, instead of in terms of what persons

---

[33] ibid.

are entitled to as a matter of right. Put another way, it would substitute a perfectionist political order for a liberal or republican one. Fish correctly observes that members of a society without law would lack the 'argumentative resources that abstractions such as justice, fairness, and human dignity now stand for'. It is not clear, however, whether he fully appreciates the implication that law necessarily presupposes or constructs legal subjects as autonomous and responsible agents, as bearers of rights and duties.

It is this presupposition that explains why people want to, and in fact must, believe that 'the reign of justice' can be secured by instituting a set of impartial procedures, and in fact, can *only* be secured in this way. Government in accordance with the rule of law is the promise of a political society organised according to principles of right, one in which actors hold one another accountable by invoking norms that bind generally and unconditionally, that is, independent of any actor's interests or power. This notion of impartiality – again, one premised on a conception of legal subjects as autonomous and responsible agents – is integral to the ideal of government in accordance with the rule of law. Fish rightly criticises those who think impartial rule can be achieved without the exercise of political or moral judgment, as well as those who think it is possible to adopt a universal vantage point from which they can identify beyond any shadow of a doubt what counts as rightful conduct. But neither the necessity of moral judgment when applying the law nor a fallibilist conception of (moral) knowledge reveals the law's promise of impartiality to be merely illusory.

In his description of the law's job, Fish confuses the point or purpose of law with how law achieves that purpose. Or again, and borrowing Aristotle's terminology, Fish conflates law's formal cause, how law works, with law's final cause, what law is for. Law's job is to constitute legal subjects as members of a political society premised on a conception of legal subjects as autonomous and responsible agents. Government in accordance with the rule of law realises this goal when, or to the extent that, members of that society hold one another and themselves accountable for conformity to its existing standards of right conduct. Disputes over what those are – whether a given act is legal or illegal – are inevitable, since as Fish ably demonstrates, legal materials are indeterminate. Any assertion of law will therefore reflect the claimant's construction of the community's past political practices, yet she will advance it not in her own name but instead in the name of the community; that is, as a matter of the standards of right conduct to which *we* are already committed. This is the sense in which 'a limited partisan program' will be presented as 'the natural outcome of an abstract impersonal imperative'.[34] It also explains why, as Fish puts it, all legal histories are invented in a 'weak' sense that contrasts with discovered, but no legal history is invented in a strong sense that 'the urgency that led to

---

[34] Fish (n 19) 71.

its assembly was unrelated to any generally acknowledged legal concern'.[35] If, or as long as, an agent's assertion of law is accepted by other members of the political society, if they integrate it into the practice of holding accountable that constitutes them as a community, it will qualify as a successful example of doing law's job; that is, of constituting legal subjects as bearers of rights and duties.

IV. KOSKENNIEMI ON THE RULE OF LAW

Like Dworkin and Fish, Koskenniemi identifies law not with rules or institutions but with a particular approach to the exercise of political power, one premised on the treatment of legal subjects as autonomous and responsible agents. However, he adopts a somewhat ambivalent stance toward the phrase 'the rule of law'. At times he employs (a capitalised version of) it to refer to a genuinely *legal* approach to government that, as I will demonstrate, corresponds to the exercise of political power informed by a commitment to legality.[36] At other times Koskenniemi associates the phrase 'the rule of law' with the rule of rules, valuable solely for the contribution it makes to facilitating agents' rational planning by enabling them to predict when, where, and how officials will exercise political power.[37] He advances two critiques of the rule of law, so conceived. First, rules are indeterminate – they do not spell out the conditions for their application – so whatever certainty and stability a practice of government exhibits will owe not to the rules but to those who apply them.[38] This is the same point Dworkin and Fish press against those who think it is possible to identify what the law of a particular political community is without engaging in a value-laden interpretation of its past political practice. Second, Koskenniemi implies that predictability and the enabling of rational planning fails to get at the core of what makes government in accordance with the rule of law valuable.[39] His explanation in the passage where he makes this claim is not perspicuous, but if we look elsewhere in his corpus his reason becomes clear. While predictable government does treat subjects as agents, creatures capable of acting for reasons, it need not exhibit respect for their autonomy (their capacity to act as the authors of their own lives), nor for their sense of responsibility (their capacity to use the law to hold themselves accountable). Predictable rule is fully consistent with an instrumental approach to government, but that is precisely the form of

---

[35] S Fish, 'Working on the Chain Gang; Interpretation in Law and Literature' in S Fish (ed), *Doing What Comes Naturally* (Durham, NC, Duke University Press 1989) 94.

[36] See, eg, M Koskenniemi, 'What is International Law For?' in MD Evans (ed), *International Law*, 4th edn (Oxford, Oxford University Press, 2014) 41.

[37] M Koskenniemi, 'Constitutionalism as Mindset: Reflections on Kantian Themes About International Law and Globalization' (2007) 8 *Theoretical Inquiries in Law* 9, 25.

[38] ibid.

[39] ibid.

government that Koskenniemi seeks to contrast with law, or a specifically *legal* practice of government. In light of this critique, Koskenniemi generally eschews talk of government in accordance with the rule of law, and instead develops an account of the nature of (international) law premised on 'a culture of formalism' and 'constitutionalism as a mindset'. Labels aside, however, I contend that Koskenniemi shares the same understanding of law I have attributed to Dworkin and Fish.

Consider, first, Koskenniemi's description of a culture of formalism.[40] To say that law is formal is to say that it provides agents with a reason for action that does not depend on their particular interests or prudential goals, what (they believe) is good for them, or what (they believe) will make them happy.[41] To engage in a *legal* practice of government, then, is to employ general rules for action that apply unconditionally to hold oneself and other members of the relevant community or society responsible. So understood, law (or legal reasoning) contrasts with instrumentalism, which predicates reasons for action on agents' interests or prudential goals. The reasons for action agents have depend on their particular interests, and the means available to them to advance or satisfy those interests. Whereas instrumentalism provides actors with strategic reasons for action, law provides them with rights and responsibilities. It does so by constituting them as members of a single, common, juridical community, as agents and subjects of law. As Koskenniemi writes,

> the form of law constructs political adversaries as equals, entitled to express their subjectively felt injustices in terms of breaches of the rules of the community to which they belong no less than their adversaries – thus affirming both that inclusion and the principle that the conditions applying to the treatment of any one member of the community must apply to every other member as well.[42]

As a 'social practice of accountability, openness, and equality', a culture of formalism constitutes 'a culture of resistance to power'.[43] In any political society where such a culture flourishes, might cannot make right. Or put another way, where fidelity to legality is a basic belief or assumption that structures how its members conceive of their relations to one another, both as fellow citizens and as rulers and subjects, it will not be possible to justify one's conduct to oneself or to others in purely instrumental terms, that is, in terms of power and interest. Rather, every public act will need to be justified in *legal* terms, by reference to a

---

[40] For a reading of Koskenniemi that contrasts a culture of formalism with a culture of legality, rather than treating the former as just another name for the latter, as I do, see J Brunnée and SJ Toope, 'The Rule of Law in an Agonistic World: The Prohibition on the Use of Force and Humanitarian Exceptions' in W Werner et al. (eds), *Koskenniemi and His Critics* (Cambridge, Cambridge University Press, 2015).
[41] Koskenniemi (n 36) 40–1.
[42] ibid 41.
[43] M Koskenniemi, *The Gentle Civilizer of Nations: The Rise and Fall of International Law 1870–1960* (Cambridge, Cambridge University Press, 2001) 500.

general rule that applies unconditionally to members of the political community as such, and therefore agents will be able to demand treatment that is theirs by right, even where they lack the power to give others a prudential reason to treat them that way.[44] Moreover, by framing the enterprise of government in terms of rights and duties, justice and fairness, and respect for human dignity – in short, by invoking norms that presuppose a conception of political subjects as autonomous and responsible agents – a culture of formalism or legality provides resources that agents can use to resist oppression or domination.

> Notions such as 'peace', 'justice', or 'human rights' … give voice to individuals and groups struggling for spiritual or material well-being, fighting against oppression, and seeking to express their claims in the language of something greater than their merely personal interests.[45]

As Fish would say, law provides actors with rhetorical resources, a grammar that actors can use to contest their treatment. They do so by, in Dworkin's terms, advancing a novel constructive interpretation of the political community's past practice, or in Fish's terms, presenting a rewriting of the community's history, that shows the treatment in question to be inconsistent with the community's other commitments.

That is not to say that power has no influence on what is treated as right. Government, including government in accordance with the rule of law, inevitably serves 'to advance the values, interests, and preferences that those in dominant positions seek to realize in the world'.[46] Indeed, like Fish, Koskenniemi construes every finding of law as 'a *hegemonic* act in the precise sense that though it is partial and subjective, it claims to be universal and objective'.[47] Necessarily, any human judgment of what 'we' take to be required as a matter of right (an assertion of a general and impartial norm) will be partial, in two senses of that term. First, the experience it reflects will always be a limited one that comprehends neither all the possible circumstances in which human beings must determine 'how to go on', nor all the value-laden perspectives from which human beings engage with the natural and social world. Put another way, no culture or practice of holding accountable is complete in the sense that those who participate in it possess a fully worked out conception of what follows from the regulative ideal that provides the culture or practice with its point or purpose. That Herculean task lies not only beyond the ability any individual human being but of any community of human beings, even one that extends across many generations (which is to say, one that is constituted by, and so realises, a tradition).

---

[44] Of course, the content of jurisdictional concepts such as 'public act', 'legal official', and 'citizen' are also open to contestation, and indeed, specific examples of their contestation often figure centrally in both emancipatory and reactionary narratives of a political community's historical quest to realise the rule of law.
[45] Koskenniemi (n 36) 44.
[46] ibid 48.
[47] ibid 43.

And human beings can and do create and sustain a plurality of practices of holding accountable premised on different regulative ideals, or on vastly different concrete understandings of what follows from a shared but highly abstract regulative ideal. Hence Koskenniemi's caution against, and denouncing of, 'false universals'.[48] Second, judgments of what is required as a matter of right are inevitably coloured by judgments of what is good, for me, for mine, or for all humanity. The 'distortion' this introduces owes not simply to human beings' inevitably limited experience of what is good for (creatures like) them, but to the germ of instrumentalism, of strategic or means-end reasoning, it implants in an enterprise that purports to offer an alternative to instrumentalism.[49] Even government in accordance with the rule of law will favour certain conceptions of justice and fairness over others, and which one triumphs (vis-à-vis a particular exercise of political power, at a particular point in a political community's history) will inevitably be shaped by officials' and subjects' conceptions of the good life. The doubly-partial nature of moral judgment accounts not only for disagreement over what the law is (or should be), but also the tendency of those whose view is not realised in the practice of government to describe the triumphant view pejoratively as *political*, the exercise of power to advance a private conception of the good at the expense of fidelity to public right.

Formalism requires that government be exercised in accordance with general rules that apply unconditionally. As Kant, Kelsen, and others have recognised, however, rules do not spell out the conditions of their own application.[50] Rather, 'every rule needs, for its application, an *auctoritatis interposition* that determines what the rule should mean in a particular case and whether, all things considered, applying the rule might be better than resorting to the exception'.[51] It is not the presence of rules (including those constitutive of institutions such as courts) that determine whether a society is governed in accordance with legality, but the 'mindset' of those who administer them; that is, those who interpret the rules, or what is the same, who judge what the rules entail in a particular case. Legality obtains when, or to the degree that, authoritative determinations of what the law is are made by lawyers. Like Fuller, Dworkin, Fish and I maintain, Koskenniemi uses the term 'lawyer' to refer to members of a profession whose primary allegiance is to the ideal of government in accordance with the rule of law. 'The idea of a universal law needs servants that define themselves [as] administrators (instead of inventors) of universal standards – the class of lawyers. The traditions and practices of this class are significant only to the extent they remain attached to the "flat, substanceless surface" of the law'; that

---

[48] See, eg, M Koskenniemi, 'International Law and Hegemony: A Reconfiguration' (2004) 17 *Cambridge Review of International Affairs* 197.
[49] Koskenniemi (n 36) 41.
[50] Koskenniemi (n 37) 9–11.
[51] ibid 10.

is, to general rules that apply unconditionally.[52] The culture of formalism is comprised of the 'sensibilities, traditions and frameworks, [and] sets of rituals and self-understandings among institutional actors' that together define the legal profession. That profession, like all enterprises, exists in virtue of its distinctive point or purpose, one that Fuller aptly describes as 'the enterprise of subjecting human conduct to the governance of rules' that do not 'tell a man what he should do to accomplish specific ends set by the law giver, [but instead] furnish him with baselines against which to organize his life with his fellows ... [and provides] a framework with which to live his own life'.[53]

Individuals become lawyers via habituation, by learning to think or reason the way that lawyers do. This involves becoming proficient (at least) in the use of various professional techniques lawyers employ to identify the law, those rights and responsibilities that members of the political community are entitled to have enforced on demand, without the need for any legislation. Yet as Koskenniemi observes, 'while the culture of formalism is a necessary though often misunderstood aspect of the legal craft, as a historical matter, it has often provided a recipe for indifference and needs to be accompanied by a live sense of its political justification'.[54] The acquisition of specifically legal forms of reasoning (as opposed to, say, economic ones) without a sound grasp of legality's point or purpose can easily lead to a form of rule worship, or a 'bureaucratic spirit'.[55] Thus, if lawyers and the larger political society to which they belong wish to retain and strengthen its practice of government in accordance with the rule of law, it is imperative that they learn to properly appreciate its nature and value. Where the rubber of general norms hits the road of specific cases, government in accordance with the rule of law requires not merely *techne* but *phronesis*.

---

[52] Koskenniemi (n 36) 42.
[53] Fuller (33) 106; LL Fuller, *The Principles of Social Order: Selected Essays of Lon L. Fuller*, KI Winston (ed) (Durham, NC, Duke University Press 1981) 234.
[54] Koskenniemi (n 36) 45.
[55] ibid.

19
Is Hercules a Natural?

MARGARET MARTIN*

JUDGING, STANLEY FISH insists, is like playing baseball. You just hit the ball. Those who know how to do it just *know*. To do something *naturally* is to internalise the requirements that make a practice what it is. The normative power that typically accompanies the use of the term is lost with this usage. The normative dimension of the idea of 'natural' is evident in both everyday discourse and philosophical debates. When we say, 'she is a natural', we typically mean she is good at the skill in question and that she appears able to carry out the task successfully and with relatively little effort. The term is also commonly used to suggest a preferable state of affairs. For instance, to say that it is 'natural' to want to have many friends is to suggest that it is a good worth pursuing.

Philosophers in the contractarian tradition have an acute awareness of the power and implications of this term. They wield it to persuade their audience of the kind of social order that would be ideal – a type of order that best reflects our 'natural' tendencies. Often, thinkers call for a return to the 'state of nature', but not always. For instance, Thomas Hobbes argues that our natural condition, which is defined by perpetual conflict, is one that we should promptly exit. Civil society, as he envisions it, is only marginally more attractive than the state of nature, but this is precisely his point: we are supposed to accept personal subjugation to the sovereign in order to secure peace.[1] John Locke, on the other hand, revises this picture. He carves out a space for individual conscience but concedes that when citizens are granted a greater degree of freedom, there is an increased risk of civil war.[2] Trade-offs of this kind are inevitable. Jean-Jacques

---

*I am grateful to Thomas Bustamante for his excellent comments on an earlier draft of this chapter.

[1] T Hobbes, *Leviathan* (first published 1651, London, Penguin, 1985) ch 17.

[2] See Ross Harrison's discussion on this point in R Harrison, *Hobbes, Locke, and Confusion's Masterpiece* (Cambridge, Cambridge University Press, 2003) 169. Unlike Hobbes, Locke famously defends the right to revolution. See J Locke, *Two Treatises of Government*, P Laslett (ed) (New York, Mentor Books, New American Library, 1965) ch 3.

Rousseau, who was preoccupied with this need for trade-offs, blames *Nature* for our predicament:[3]

> Whatever these origins [of speech and of society] may be, from the little care taken by Nature to bring Men together through mutual needs and to facilitate their use of speech, one at least sees how little it prepared their Sociability, and how little it contributed to everything Men have done to establish Social bonds.[4]

Here, Nature is personified. She is responsible for the fact that we need each other, but she is also responsible for how hard we must work to live together. While Nature has endowed us with the capacity for speech, for instance, it takes effort to develop this capacity. Even when a language is shared, there is no promise of mutual understanding. The very features that are typically thought to set human beings apart from other creatures, and are often lauded as such, also serve as obstacles that threaten the establishment of a viable social order.

Fish, in his book *Doing What Comes Naturally*, turns this tradition on its head. He intentionally robs the word 'natural' of its normative force, while collapsing its complex history into a single, timeless idea: those who participate in a practice do so *naturally*.[5] This is so even when we are dealing with a complex practice at the apex of a hierarchy of power, like judging. To the extent that judges believe they are choosing between options, they have failed to see that the path is set by the assumptions that inform their view of things – assumptions that are not of their choosing. Fish's usage of the term counters Rousseau's in an important sense: we have the mere appearance of freedom and, therefore, the mere appearance of choice. We are already bound from within, just as other animals appear to be. Fish is part of a long line of philosophers who insist that we can only move from one cave to another.[6] There is, so to speak, no exit.

Despite appearances, it is not Fish but Dworkin who attempts to manufacture an escape from the history of political thought. Dworkin is generally considered one of John Rawls's heirs, but he seems to want to shed this association, and indeed all others. Gregory C. Keating, in his review of *Law's Empire*, remarks that the work is both 'undeniably important and irritatingly illusive'.[7] Dworkin is illusive, Keating argues, because he 'recasts the entire legal theory

---

[3] Nelson Lund remarks, 'If one had to identify a single central preoccupation in [Rousseau's] works, it might be these trade-offs.' N Lund, 'Adam Smith on Rousseau and the Origin of Language' (2022) 48 *Interpretation* 209, 237.

[4] JJ Rousseau, *Discourse on The Origins of Inequality (Second Discourse)* in RD Masters and C Kelly (eds), *The Collected Writings of Rousseau, Vol 3*, JR Bush et al (trans) (Hanover, Dartmouth College, 1992) 1, 33–34.

[5] S Fish, 'Still Wrong After all These Years' in *Doing What Comes Naturally: Change, Rhetoric, and the Practice of Theory in Literary and Legal Studies* (Durham, Duke University Press, 1989) 356–71.

[6] S Fish, 'Anti-Foundationalism, Theory Hope, and the Teaching of Composition' in *Doing What Comes Naturally: Change, Rhetoric, and the Practice of Theory in Literary and Legal Studies* (Durham, Duke University Press, 1989) 345.

[7] RH Pildes, 'Dworkin's Two Conceptions of Rights' (2000) 29 *Journal of Legal Studies* 309, 310.

in a new vocabulary without making commensurate changes in the theory's content'.[8] In the preface to *Law's Empire*, Dworkin announces, 'I have made no effort to discover how far this book alters or replaces positions I have defended in earlier works.'[9] He also tells his reader that he will not locate his account in the broader debate. That is, he will not 'compare [his] views with those of other legal and political philosophers, either classical or contemporary'; nor will he explain the extent he has 'been influenced by or [has] drawn on their work'.[10] Once unmoored from the past, Dworkin manages to make himself a far harder target at which to take aim.

To see Dworkin's account clearly, it must be placed on the arc of philosophical thought. From Dworkin's perspective, the older debate about the natural condition of humankind appears to be a relic that may be of interest to historians but not necessarily to philosophers. The question, it seems, has shifted. Political theorist John Dunn argues that, in recent times, questions about the requirements of distributive justice have eclipsed questions of political obligation.[11] Dunn bemoans this shift in focus as it presupposes that this fundamental question has been definitively solved.[12] In what follows, I will suggest that Dunn is correct to worry. Dworkin's account of the political obligation, sketched very quickly in *Law's Empire*, is neither fully developed nor defended. Lost is any sense of the struggle involved in the establishment and maintenance of social order. Dworkin does not attend to the need for trade-offs, but this does not mean such trade-offs are unnecessary. Instead, Dworkin offers an ideal vision of liberal democracy that may prove to be too demanding to be realisable, despite appearances to the contrary.

It is Fish's critique of *Law's Empire* that enables this broader worry to become visible. Fish is correct to argue that Dworkin moves, almost imperceptibly at times, between the claim that judges are always 'naturally' aiming to realise the ideal of 'law as integrity' (that is, they do so simply by engaging in the interpretive act) and the claim that judges *should* choose to realise this ideal as it is the best interpretive option available to us. Fish famously concludes that Dworkinian integrity is, in fact, indistinguishable from Fish's own account: judges do not have interpretive choices, but instead, they do what they do naturally. Instead of following Fish down this path, I will resurrect interpretive possibilities that are latent in *Law's Empire*. For instance, I will argue that Fish's critique of *Law's Empire* reveals that the value of 'protected expectations' does not rise and fall with 'conventionalism', as Dworkin suggests. Once this point

---

[8] Pildes (n 7) 526. This, I suspect, is why Fish readily recycles his older criticisms of Dworkin. See Fish (n 5) 356.
[9] R Dworkin, *Law's Empire* (Cambridge, MA, Harvard University Press, 1986) iii.
[10] Dworkin (n 9) ii.
[11] J Dunn, *The History of Political Theory and Other Essays* (Cambridge, Cambridge University Press, 1996) 3.
[12] Dunn (n 11) 3–4.

comes into view, so does an important question: to what extent is Dworkinian integrity wedded to the ideal of protected expectations? Or more generally still, what kind of sacrifices are involved when one opts to pursue integrity?

I will argue that the answer to these questions will differ depending on whether one is thinking about common law rights or Charter rights. Dworkin, of course, has the former in mind, but he presupposes that legal rights take a single form (this is yet another assumption he shares with Fish). Following Nigel Simmonds, I argue that the introduction of Charter rights has a corrosive effect on traditional legal rights, which are central to the common law tradition. In the course of exploring Simmonds's argument, it becomes clear that Dworkin's own account of political obligation, sketched briefly in *Law's Empire*, is marred by the same tension Fish has identified. Dworkin, once again, finds himself perched uncomfortably on the horns of a dilemma: if citizens naturally interpret the law in accordance with integrity, then Dworkin's account is indistinguishable from Fish's; conversely, if integrity is a demanding ideal that one must choose to pursue, Dworkin is telling us what citizens should aspire to be, rather than what interpretation already requires. Dworkin's brief discussion of the practice of courtesy veils this deep ambiguity. Once the problem is made visible, so too is the power of Fish's critique.

To begin this inquiry, it is useful to once again explore the term 'natural'. This time, however, I will return to an older way of thinking about the term, which has been largely overlooked by the history of philosophy, namely, Aristotle's. This discussion will highlight the complex legal and customary practices that comprise social order, thereby setting the stage for the broader discussion to follow. I will then call attention to the failure of Fish and Dworkin to attend to the customary order. Dworkin's discussion of the practice of courtesy is flawed in ways that haunt his account of judging and his account of social order – a point that traces back to Fish's critique. *Law's Empire* places integrity in its best light but, as it turns out, not its clearest.

I. NATURE, CUSTOM AND LAW: A RETURN TO ARISTOTLE

James Bernard Murphy argues that thinkers in the history of philosophy operate within the 'natural/conventional divide', including thinkers like Hobbes, Locke and Rousseau. While this particular debate will not wholly disappear given how entrenched it has become, Murphy's point is that the popular dichotomy between *nature* and *convention* is false: 'the concept of convention collapses the important distinction between tacit social order of custom and the individually designed order of stipulation'.[13] This becomes clear once the deep

---

[13] JB Murphy, 'Nature, Custom and Reason as Explanatory Principles in Aristotelian Political Science' (2002) 64 *The Review of Politics* 469, 476. See Aristotle's *Politics* 1332a38.

ambiguity at the heart of this familiar dichotomy is exposed: 'when something is described as conventional we do not know if the claim is that it was deliberated stipulated or that it arose spontaneously'.[14] Thus, instead of redeploying this flawed dichotomy, Murphy turns to Aristotle's tripartite distinction between the order of nature (which is biological), the order of custom and the stipulated order of law.

Murphy's point (and, indeed, Aristotle's) is that there are three types of order that operate as a 'nested hierarchy' in the sense that 'every social institution or practice has a natural, customary, and stipulated dimension'.[15] According to this account, 'nature' is understood as 'the set of physical, chemical, and biological processes'.[16] It refers to the law of gravity, for example, and to involuntary behaviours, such as blinking. The order of nature also includes capacities that may or may not be fully developed, such as speaking, singing or reasoning. A law student may have the capacity to reason like a lawyer, for instance, but this capacity may not be fully developed. After all, there are good lawyers and not-so-good lawyers. When Fish argues that lawyers do what they do naturally, he collapses these two categories into one – it is far from clear that this move works.[17]

While it is easy to assume that the order of nature is the order of brute facts, this would be an error. The order of nature enjoys a degree of plasticity that is easily overlooked. For instance, technology, which plays an increasingly important role in human biology, does not fit easily within either the customary order or the stipulated order. While technological interventions are intentional (stipulated), what qualifies as science depends on cultural norms and theories of scientific knowledge, which shift over time. The 'natural' dimension of our social order is itself a complex concept that, on occasion, incorporates the 'artificial' within itself. The difference between Fish and Aristotle, however, is that only the latter will affirm the superiority of certain paradigms over others; Fish denies our ability to make these judgements.[18] Fish also includes the customary order within the category of 'natural'. For Aristotle, this move should be resisted.

---

[14] Murphy (n 13) 476. Murphy is not a legal positivist. He argues that the positivist's mistake is to limit the realm of jurisprudence to the positive law. Instead, he distinguishes between law as a 'species of order' and jurisprudence as an 'explanation of law'. The latter requires a consideration of all three kinds of order, according to Murphy. See JB Murphy, 'Nature, Custom, and Stipulation in Law and Jurisprudence' (1990) 43 *The Review of Metaphysics* 751, 761. The key point is that Dworkin's account is not defined away by the use of these terms because Dworkin retains his commitment to the dimension of 'fit'.

[15] Murphy (n 13) 480.

[16] Murphy (n 14) 755.

[17] In other words, we have the distinction between 'lawyer by trade' (factual observation) and lawyer proper (ie, one who does the job well). This is a distinction that traces back to Plato. See Plato, *Republic*, Book 1, 340d.

[18] Fish (n 5) 371.

Custom, Murphy argues, has its own distinct logic, which is rarely attended to.[19] He explains that the customary order 'is the product of human action but never wholly the execution of any design'.[20] Given that the customary order is in constant flux, legal norms will continually interact with it in complex ways. How (or whether) any given legal norms will be taken up by the populace, or how a given legal norm will be understood through time, is not something that is within the control of judges or legislators (or, indeed, anyone). Given the degree of complexity that is present in the interaction of the stipulated order and the customary order, it is easy to understand why many theorists overlook this interaction or the customary dimension of order altogether. Attending to this dimension of a legal system can easily impede a theorist's attempt to offer crisp concepts that can lay claim to universality. To overlook the customary dimensions of order, however, leads theorists into error: 'Severed from its roots in custom, legal stipulation is often seen as arbitrary and willful.'[21] Murphy adds that the stakes are not simply theoretical, given that authoritarian impulses are fostered by this kind of thinking.[22] For Murphy, but not for Fish, theory has consequences.

The viability of Fish's claim about the consequences of theory – recall that he argues that there are none – will depend on whether or not he is able to condense all three dimensions of order into his thesis that judges do their jobs 'naturally'. Is this claim plausible considering Murphy's discussion? While I will not address this question in full, it is useful to see how Fish deals with the customary dimension of order. More important for the purposes of this chapter is how Dworkin deals with customary practices. Dworkin's discussion of courtesy contains the same ambiguity that Fish identifies in his discussion of integrity. This ambiguity veils the nature of the choices that face the interpreter of the practice and, in turn, the legal philosopher.

II. ACCOUNTING FOR CUSTOM

Recall that Fish argues that law is like baseball. Notice, however, that customs play a different role in baseball than in law. Baseball is an autonomous practice

---

[19] Murphy (n 14) 757. Gerald Postema is one clear exception. See GJ Postema, 'Custom, Normative Practice, and the Law' (2012) 62 *Duke Law Journal* 707. The difference between Murphy's work and Postema's is that Murphy treats the customary dimension of order as separate from law – he rejects the idea of 'customary law'. See Murphy (n 14) 751.

[20] Murphy (n 13) 480.

[21] Murphy (n 14) 755. Murphy adds that there is a second kind of error: while those writing in the positivist tradition tend to limit the domain of jurisprudence to only that of stipulation, others collapse the stipulated dimension of order with custom, which can obscure the differences between the two types of order. Murphy (n 14) 757.

[22] Murphy (n 14).755. Notice that the worry pertains to a kind of thinking (or a disposition towards the world) and not a program for deciding cases.

insofar as the norms apply to the game and remain largely untouched by a society's shifting customary practices. While the rules of baseball have changed over the years, most changes are carried out intentionally by those who oversee the game.[23] Conversely, legal norms necessarily interact with the shifting customary order. The customary norms that inform the practice of judging will also shift, thereby indicating that the 'game' is not necessarily stable through time. Fish does not deny this. However, it is not clear that he can easily accommodate these kinds of changes. For instance, when a judge decides to rely on a hypothetical set of facts instead of the facts before them, is this something they do *naturally*, even if this technique had never been used before?[24] Or is this 'new' interpretive approach the result of a choice linked to the desire to arrive at a certain outcome and, in the process, expand the domain of power judges have? Judges, unlike baseball players, can alter the rules of the game for themselves in the act of playing the game precisely because they participate in stipulating the norms that are then to be followed. Judges are the umpires, not the batters, and the rules of the game are pliable.[25] Fish's favoured analogy hides this point from view.

Dworkin also struggles to navigate the customary order. Like Fish, he assumes that interpreting the law is akin to interpreting a practice. Unlike Fish, Dworkin assumes that there is a standard against which interpretations can be measured, which is the source of legitimacy for interpretations. Even if one is sympathetic to Dworkin's view, Fish is nevertheless correct to worry that Dworkin assumes a degree of interpretive freedom that is unavailable to the interpreter. Consider Dworkin's discussion of courtesy, whereby peasants are expected to take their hats off for nobility.[26] Dworkin argues that once we move from a condition of 'unstudied deference' to a 'runic order', participants inevitably adopt what he calls the 'interpretive attitude'.[27] When this attitude takes hold, we assume that the practice has value and that its value is wedded to its perceived point.[28] We then interpret the requirements of the practice in reference to what we take to be its point. When discussing the interpretive process, Dworkin worries that the interpreter may overstep the bounds of permissible interpretations and invent a new practice.[29] This, however, is impossible.

Any interpretation of a customary practice like courtesy is only meaningful against a shared, intersubjective understanding of the practice. If, for instance, an individual refuses to remove her hat when it is expected, a message of dissent

---

[23] *The Baseball Almanac* tracks such changes: www.baseball-almanac.com/rulechng.shtml.
[24] See *R v Smith* [1987] 1 SCR 1045.
[25] Fish concedes this point in his critique of HLA Hart's *The Concept of Law* found in the chapter titled 'Force'. See Fish (n 5) 504. For an excellent analysis of 'Force', see NE Simmonds, ch 4 in this volume.
[26] Dworkin (n 9) 47.
[27] ibid.
[28] ibid.
[29] Dworkin (n 9) 66.

is communicated. Alternatively, a participant can opt to partake in this practice because she believes it is what she should do or simply to ensure that she keeps her head below the parapet. Either way, a message of compliance is communicated. The key point is that there are only two potential paths of action before her, and these two options – compliance or rebellion – have meanings that emerge from the intersubjective nature of the practice, which is beyond her interpretive control. Dworkin's fear that a participant might strike out in a new direction only arises if he begins with an isolated individual and proceeds to canvass all imaginative possibilities. However, once the interpreting subject is placed within the context of the practice, there are only two options. Even acts of rebellion are structured by conventions.[30] In short, while the shape of the practice will change over time, it does not follow that the individual, at any point, is at risk of going beyond the practice.

Here we have arrived at the gist of Fish's critique: Dworkin vacillates between offering interpretive options on the one hand and insisting that we are all Dworkinian interpreters on the other.[31] Notice that these two options re-emerge when we consider the practice of courtesy alongside Dworkin's famous claim that participants must put the practice in its *best* light (Dworkin calls this 'constructive interpretation'). What does 'best' mean in this context? If, for example, Dworkin is leaving it up to each interpreter to determine what they think is best, then the term 'best' has no independent meaning, and Fish is right. However, if the term 'best' does have a meaning independent of the interpreter, then what precisely is the standard? How do we determine who is and who is not placing the practice in its best light?

Dworkin's response to this query moves his account uncomfortably close to Fish's. Dworkin maintains that 'each individual is trying to discover his own intention in maintaining and participating in that practice ... in the sense of finding a purposeful account of his behaviour that he is comfortable in ascribing to himself'.[32] The interpreting subject appears to be the only one who can determine the best path forward. After all, only the interpreter can discern the nature of her emotional response to the options in question.[33] Dworkin quietly

---

[30] N Frye, *The Educated Imagination and Other Writings on Critical Theory 1933–1963*, G Warkentin (ed) (Toronto, University of Toronto Press, 2006) 466.

[31] See, especially, Fish (n 5).

[32] Dworkin (n 9) 58. When Dworkin considers interpretation more generally, he insists that it is 'not in the sense of retrieving his mental state'. Dworkin (n 9) 58. That is, when interpreting, we do not seek to discern the intentions of the author. This shift in focus makes sense if we notice that we are moving from the customary order, where practices do not have a single author, to the stipulated one, where laws will be the product of intention (but are not necessarily grasped by considering the posited dimension of law alone or by assuming that simply because law is part of the stipulated order, intentions are central to the interpretive task).

[33] Postema is also worried about this passage. See GJ Postema, '"Protestant" Interpretation and Social Practices' (1987) 6 *Law and Philosophy* 283, 288. For a response to this critique, see T Bustamante, 'Revisiting the Idea of Protestant Interpretation: Towards Reconciliation between Dworkin and Postema' in T Bustamante and TL Decat (eds), *Philosophy of Law as an Integral Part of Philosophy: Essays in the Jurisprudence of Gerald J. Postema* (Oxford, Hart Publishing, 2020) 113.

rules out another plausible interpretive possibility by placing the individual (and her comfort level) at the centre of his example. An interpreter may opt for the uncomfortable path because she views the practice as having social value. Courtesy, after all, takes many forms and, like other practices of civility, can foster peaceful relations between strangers and political adversaries alike.[34] Dworkin's choice of example hides these considerations from view, which helps him secure his core claims in the minds of his readers. Dworkin's readers, after all, will likely view the act of removing hats in the presence of nobility as an antiquated practice. They will not immediately wonder whether it has social value; rather, they are likely to sympathise with Dworkin's imagined interpreter of the requirements of courtesy who may feel uncomfortable showing deference to members of the aristocracy. While Dworkin ignores the shared values that may be found in inherited customs of this kind, he nevertheless harnesses the shared assumptions of his reader to secure his central narrative. It is a narrative of progress, and the individual is at the centre of the action.[35]

Notice that Dworkin's discussion of courtesy operates as a fable that reinforces his central narrative: we begin in a moment of history dominated by unthinking obedience, and as a result of the introduction of the interpretive attitude, individuals can harness their critical capabilities to break free from antiquated customs, thereby claiming their agency. The contrast between Dworkin's narrative and Fish's is stark. For Fish, there is no such thing as the empowerment of the individual or progress of this kind. The interpreting agent cannot suddenly break free from her interpretive chains with or without Dworkin's help. We can only move from one set of chains to another, from one set of interpretive constraints to another. The background assumptions, according to Fish, are in our heads.[36] These assumptions produce the world that we see.

Dworkin, on the other hand, gives scant attention to these assumptions. In *Law's Empire*, he explains the preconditions that must hold if his interpretive approach is going to work:

> [The participants] must, to be sure, agree about a great deal in order to share a social practice. They must share a vocabulary ... They must understand the world in sufficiently similar ways and have interests and convictions sufficiently similar to recognize the sense in each other's claims, to treat these as claims rather than just noises. That means not just using the same dictionary, but sharing what Wittgenstein called a form of life sufficiently concrete so that one can recognize sense and purpose in what the other says and does, see what sort of beliefs would make sense of this diction, gesture, tone, and so forth. They must 'speak the same language' in both senses of that phrase. But this similarity of interests and convictions need hold only

---

[34] See J Waldron 'Civility and Formality' in A Sarat (ed), *Civility, Legality, and Justice in America* (New York, Cambridge University Press, 2014) 46–68.
[35] Dworkin, in my view, is echoing the liberal story of progress. For a different view on the idea of progress in the context of Dworkin's theory, see T Decat, ch 15 in this volume.
[36] Fish (n 5) 520.

to a point: it must be sufficiently dense to permit genuine disagreement, but not so dense that disagreement cannot break out.[37]

Here Dworkin concedes that hovering behind his interpretive theory are assumptions about the nature of the political order, including assumptions about the customary dimension of the social order. Dworkin does not tell us whether these conditions have been met, nor does he explain what it would require for these conditions to be met. If these conditions prove to be demanding, so too is Dworkin's account: his theory will be reserved for the few societies that meet the relevant threshold of the right degree of 'similarity of interests and convictions'. If, however, these preconditions are easily satisfied, then Dworkin begins to look a lot like Fish. We have returned, once again, to the foundational ambiguity identified by Fish. This deep ambiguity is easily overlooked: by moving quickly through this discussion, Dworkin invites readers to presuppose that the preconditions for the realisation of integrity are already in place.

We find a similar problem at what is arguably the core of *Law's Empire* – Dworkin's discussion of integrity. As mentioned, it is Fish who spies this problem: Dworkin holds out integrity as the best option, but given that pragmatism and conventionalism ultimately collapse, this leaves only Dworkin's own account of interpretation left standing. Dworkin must join Fish, or he must offer viable alternatives. While Fish insists Dworkin's only option is the former, I will explore the second possibility. Once faced with a viable alternative, it becomes clear that Dworkin must give more content to his own account, which will involve making some difficult political and philosophical choices.

III. CONVENTIONALISM, PRAGMATISM AND INTEGRITY: THE ILLUSION OF INTERPRETIVE OPTIONS?

In *Law's Empire*, Dworkin contrasts his preferred approach to legal interpretation, law as integrity, with two alternatives. He famously labels these less desirable options 'conventionalism' and 'pragmatism'. Each interpretive option is underpinned by different conceptions of justice. The conventionalist judge, Dworkin explains, endorses the value of 'protected expectations': she looks to apply pre-existing black-letter law whenever possible in order to ensure that individuals can know what is expected of them in advance. Justice, in this instance, comes in the form of fair notice. Conversely, Dworkin argues that the pragmatist judge has a utilitarian conception of justice in mind; Dworkin argues that he is wholly concerned with the future.[38] Justice, according to this view, is not a matter of ensuring there is a degree of consistency with precedent or existing legislation but involves determining what is best going forward.[39] The pragmatist judge is

---

[37] Dworkin (n 9) 63–64.
[38] Dworkin (n 9) 151.
[39] ibid.

a committed utilitarian and, unlike Dworkin, is sceptical about the existence of rights. Dworkin rejects both options in favour of 'law as integrity'.

Dworkin's imagined judge, Hercules, occupies the middle position: he is not overly wedded to past practice, but unlike the pragmatist judge, he is not wholly forward-facing. Judges who embrace integrity seek to identify a 'coherent set of principles about people's rights and duties' that inform the system in question.[40] This is the backwards-facing dimension of 'fit'. They will then proceed to offer the 'best constructive interpretation of the political structure and legal doctrine of their community'.[41] This is the normative dimension of 'justification', which serves to bring the past forward while simultaneously placing it in its best moral light.

Upon closer inspection, however, it becomes apparent that Fish is right. Dworkin only offers *one* viable option: his own. Fish argues, 'although conventionalism begins by insisting on severe indeed positivistic constraints, it ends in a vision of constraints entirely left behind'.[42] In other words, '[t]he trouble with [conventionalism] is that it commits Dworkin to both of the positions he wants to avoid: strict conventionalism and freewheeling pragmatism'.[43] Conventionalism presupposes a text that can be applied without interpreting it, while pragmatism gives judges complete freedom to strike out in a new direction. Fish calls into question both possibilities. Even those who are not committed to Fish's brand of interpretation can see that Dworkin's dichotomy is a false one.[44] Tellingly, even Dworkin concedes that conventionalism is untenable, insisting that only pragmatism offers a challenge to his position.[45]

Dworkin is happy to concede the internal collapse of conventionalism because it marks a significant victory for his account over his positivist rival. The conventionalist judge is the normative incarnation of Hart's account of adjudication found in *The Concept of Law*; thus, the fall of conventionalism is the fall of Hart's account of adjudication.[46] When placed beside *The Concept of Law*, *Law's Empire* has notable persuasive power. However, when *Law's Empire* is viewed through the lens of Fish's critique, this point of strength is transformed into a potential weakness. The problem is not simply

---

[40] Dworkin (n 9) 255.
[41] ibid.
[42] Fish (n 5) 356.
[43] Fish (n 5) 362.
[44] Fish notes that Dworkin quickly 'checked himself', thereby indicating that he sees the problem that Fish has identified: In *Law's Empire*, Dworkin writes, 'It does not follow ... that an interpreter can make of a practice or a work of art anything he would have wanted it to be .... For the history or shape of a practice or object constrains the available interpretations of it.' Dworkin (n 9) 52. While this is certainly the case, it is not a point that Dworkin takes seriously in his discussion of conventionalism or in his earlier discussion of courtesy. Instead, Dworkin continues to offer imaginative possibilities, conceived by the subjective interpreter, as if they were real options.
[45] Dworkin (n 9) 150.
[46] M Martin, 'Method Matters: Non-Normative Jurisprudence and the Re-Mystification of the Law' in JL Fabra-Zamora and G Villa (eds), *Elucidating the Concept of Law: Contemporary Disputes* (New York, Springer, 2021) 53–72.

that conventionalism collapses from within but also that pragmatism is equally implausible. Fish argues, 'pragmatism's route to inadequacy is even shorter in Dworkin's story, for a pragmatist's first principle is that there are no first principles, merely the judge's opinion as to what, at any moment, is the best thing to do'.[47] Pragmatism, Fish explains, 'forsakes even the possibility of linking up with a history that principle has informed'.[48] Given that it is impossible to start anew, the fear is that Dworkin has offered readers a straw man. While Dworkin had set out to warn his readers about the dangers of conventionalism and pragmatism, 'since these are not forms of possible judicial practice, the warning is unnecessary'.[49] Only integrity is left standing.

Fish sees this double collapse as evidence that Dworkin shares his view. However, there is another possibility worth canvassing. It is possible that Fish has simply revealed Dworkin's flawed rhetorical strategy.[50] Dworkin makes it *appear* as if integrity is the only attractive option by making sure it is the only viable one while still giving us the illusion of choice. What if there are other options that are more plausible than the ones Dworkin offers readers? One interpretive alternative is hiding in plain sight. While conventionalism's collapse is supposed to signal the futility of any appeal to the ideal of protected expectations, this conclusion is too hasty. Dworkin's central example, *Riggs v Palmer*, gives the impression that integrity is a panacea.[51] *Riggs* gives us everything we could hope for from a case without the need for trade-offs.

In *Riggs*, we learn that a grandson has been convicted of murdering his grandfather. He had hoped to secure his inheritance. The question before the court was whether he is entitled to his inheritance given that this possibility was not expressly prohibited by black-letter law at the time. Despite the silence of the positive law, the majority held that the grandson is not entitled to his inheritance, citing the principle that 'no one should profit from his own wrong'.[52] Conversely, the dissent in *Riggs* appealed to a positivistic conception of law that separates private law from public law:

> I cannot find any support for the argument that the respondent's succession to the property should be avoided because of his criminal act when the laws are silent. Public policy does not demand it, for the demands of public policy are satisfied by the proper execution of the laws and the punishment of the crime.[53]

---

[47] Fish (n 5) 356. Dworkin argues that pragmatism rejects 'any form of consistency with the past'. See Dworkin (n 9) 95. Judges are encouraged to 'act on their own views'. Dworkin (n 9) 152.

[48] Fish (n 5) 357. Recall that Fish insists that judicial decisions are inevitably connected to the past via 'principle', which is itself a produce of rhetoric. He sees his position as identical to Dworkin's idea of integrity, but he does not view it as one choice among many, but what judges do 'naturally'.

[49] I will revive a version of pragmatism below, but I nevertheless share Fish's view that Dworkin has constructed a 'straw man'.

[50] Fish rejects the distinction between rhetoric and mere rhetoric that I am employing here: 'another word for anti-foundationalism is rhetoric'. Fish (n 5) 347.

[51] Dworkin (n 9) 20.

[52] ibid.

[53] *Riggs v Palmer* 115 NY 506, available at www.nycourts.gov/reporter/archives/riggs_palmer.htm.

Dworkin argues that *Riggs* represents the triumph of integrity over conventionalism.[54] An appeal to principle, not the application of positive law, was determinative in this case. Significantly, what Dworkin does not draw our attention to is the fact that it is the opinion of the majority, not the dissent, that realises the value of protected expectations.[55] This value does not rise and fall with conventionalism as Dworkin suggests.

The judicial appeal to principle, in this case, is parasitic on a more foundational legal and moral norm; namely, that murder is wrong. Allowing for the possibility of inheritance in this instance would strike most as morally wrong and legally absurd. For this reason, the appeal to principle does not disrupt the expectations generated by customary norms; rather, the appeal to principle re-enforces pre-existing ideas of how the law should operate. Why, after all, would any society let a convicted murderer inherit the money that motivated the crime? Notice, also, that the seemingly expansive principle – that no one should profit from his own wrong – is given juridical force in a very narrow context.[56] This is further evidence that the principle in question will not disrupt the existing normative landscape. Instead, it reinforces the public commitment to a shared idea of what justice requires in this case, while ensuring that a perverse incentive structure does not become part of the law. When *Riggs* is in our line of sight, it appears as if a judge who is committed to integrity is also committed to the value of protected expectations. It also appears as if integrity is on the side of common sense and justice. Can integrity deliver everything?

In the preface of *Law's Empire*, Dworkin admits that his theory will, at times, generate controversial decisions, even though the examples he relies on in *Law's Empire* do not illustrate this point. Fish is likely right that Dworkin's chosen examples are 'flat and uninteresting'.[57] I suspect this is by design. The message quietly but consistently delivered is that integrity arrives without the need for unpalatable trade-offs, or with an attachment to any political baggage that might alienate a portion of his readership. While it is possible that, at least in the context of common law rights, Dworkin can deliver on this promise, it is unlikely that he can do so in the context of Charter rights. It is far from clear that Hercules can attend to the value of protected expectations while also pursuing the single right answer.

---

[54] Dworkin (n 9) 16. The positive law has not 'run out' as conventionalists suppose; the principle in question is part of American law.
[55] For a discussion of additional examples of this kind, which are largely drawn from the works of Lon F Fuller, see M Martin, *Judging Positivism* (Oxford, Hart Publishing, 2014) 135–141.
[56] NE Simmonds, 'Constitutional Rights, Civility and Artifice' (2019) 78 *Cambridge Law Journal* 175, 191. In this paper, Simmonds is challenging Robert Alexy's account.
[57] Fish (n 5) 369.

IV. HAS THE GAME CHANGED? CHARTER RIGHTS AND RIGHT ANSWERS

Is adjudication one kind of interpretive 'game', as Fish argues? Is there only one kind of interpretive approach that seeks to identify right answers that are moral in nature? In what follows, I will suggest that adjudication takes at least two forms, but only one of these forms – traditional common law reasoning – is consonant with the idea of legal rights. Neither Fish nor Dworkin attend to this difference, which may prove to be significant from the perspective of theory and practice.

While there is no theory-independent way of thinking about the common law, nevertheless, Gerald Postema's discussion of what he calls the 'paradox of precedent' addresses a common misconception. Postema states, 'in common-law practice, precedent is said to be binding, albeit not absolutely.'[58] The problem frequently noted by critics is that 'precedent seems to claim our allegiance when it least deserves it'.[59] That is, its binding character is most apparent in cases that involve less-than-ideal outcomes. When the outcomes are commendable, it is unclear whether it is the prior case or the moral argument that is doing the work. It is tempting to explain the puzzle as follows: 'according to common law practice, we are committed to the view that decision-makers are *morally required to follow morally incorrect principles*'.[60] Postema rejects this characterisation of the problem. He opts, instead, to restate the question.

Postema maintains that 'morally speaking, prior decisions ... are relevant and often decisive for the proper decision of present cases'.[61] Crucially, he adds that this is so 'even if the prior decisions are themselves open to reasonable objection'.[62] The paradox dissolves when we come to see that the debate between judges in the courtroom is not about 'whether past decisions alter the present decisional landscape but rather how and to what extent they do so'.[63] In other words, '[t]he controversy is not about whether the best decision in the present case can be found by ignoring the past-determined context of the case, but rather about how to understand and account for the normative relevance of the past'.[64] Precedent is the near-invisible centre of gravity of common law decision-making, which, in turn, means that the past anchors current practice. Does precedent always operate in this fashion?

Simmonds argues that the introduction of Charters of rights marks a shift in the practice: precedent matters little insofar as outcome-based

---

[58] G Postema, 'Integrity: Justice in Workclothes' (1996–97) 82 *Iowa Law Review* 821.
[59] ibid.
[60] ibid.
[61] ibid.
[62] ibid.
[63] ibid 822.
[64] ibid.

reasoning is popularised.⁶⁵ If Simmonds is right – and I will argue that he is – this will have implications for both Fish and Dworkin.

For Fish, this means that judging is not *one* game, but is at least two different games that resemble each other yet are, nevertheless, distinct. To borrow Fish's analogy, common law adjudication would be akin to baseball, while Charter adjudication would be a game that looks like baseball but is not quite the same game. While Fish may wish to argue that Simmonds is simply marking the emergence of a new 'interpretive community', it is nevertheless worrisome that Fish's theory does not prompt us to identify, or reflect upon, such changes in judicial practice. If we assume that judges do what they do naturally, it is unclear why we would be interested in pursuing inquiries of this kind. (Notice that the normative dimension of the term 'natural' has quietly re-emerged: if things cannot be otherwise, we may be tempted to accept them as they are.) This posture, if adopted, helps to solidify normative structures and practices that comprise any given social order. Theory, it turns out, may have consequences after all.

Dworkin, of course, has always been worried about such consequences. He does not endorse Fish's foundational commitments, so for him, Simmonds's critique of Charter adjudication presents a unique challenge. Once Dworkin's account is placed alongside Simmonds's critique, it is hard for Dworkin to avoid the political waters that seem remote in *Law's Empire*. To see this point, it is imperative to explore how Charter adjudication differs from common law adjudication. The first notable difference pertains to the question being posed in court. Judges are asked to determine whether a piece of legislation is constitutional – to establish whether a given law is consistent with the broadly worded freedoms articulated in the document before them. It is far from clear that Postema's vision of precedent is operating in the background of Charter cases. Rather, Simmonds argues, we find a process of reasoning that is markedly different.⁶⁶

In most jurisdictions, Simmonds rightly notes, courts carry out what is referred to as the proportionality analysis.⁶⁷ This involves weighing the interests of the individual claimant against competing interests that inform the particular law being challenged. This process of reasoning often flattens out what is, in reality, a complex web of interrelated values and practices, customs and conventions. Judges are often asked to focus on a single legal norm in relation

---

⁶⁵ Simmonds, as we shall see, does not argue that there is no connection to the past at all, only that judges are not attending to the need to preserve 'workable rules'. Significantly, his position is Fullerian, not Hartian, so he does not fall prey to Dworkin's critique of conventionalism. See NE Simmonds, *Law as a Moral Idea* (Oxford, Oxford University Press, 2006).
⁶⁶ One might argue that the lack of clarity can be attributed to the fact that Charters are fairly new additions to the legal landscape. Eventually, the argument goes, precedents will accumulate, and, in time, the patterns found in the common law will be reproduced in the constitutional context. While this is possible, there are notable features of current practice that suggest this hope may very well be misplaced.
⁶⁷ Simmonds (n 56) 188.

to a discrete set of interests in order to assess the perceived value of the law in question. This process of 'balancing' frequently makes it appear as if the court is making a simple, surgical intervention in a relatively static social environment – an intervention that is presented as an 'improvement'. The technocratic language used fosters the illusion of control, an illusion that is itself buttressed by a sense of moral certitude exhibited by judges in many cases. Simmonds adds that the case-by-case reasoning process that has taken hold in the context of Charter rights has become popular in non-Charter contexts, thereby eroding traditional legal rights (and, hence, the role of precedent).[68] Simmonds is doubtful that a course correction in the judicial sphere is on the horizon: 'Are we to ignore the possibility that judges may not wish to lay the shackles of law back on their own limbs, having once tasted the pleasures of political power without political responsibility?'[69]

A Dworkinian might reply that Dworkin is not a fan of proportionality. While this no doubt true, Simmonds's fundamental concern is with the outcome-driven approach, which *happens* to take the form of proportionality in most jurisdictions. This outcome-centred approach weakens the traditional conception of precedent and the corresponding conception of legal rights. The problem is that Charters of rights encourage judges to adopt a case-by-case approach to judicial decision-making. The pursuit of the 'right answer' undercuts the idea that the content of our legal rights should be identifiable in advance.[70] In other words, Charter rights are legal rights in name alone. It is, of course, indisputable that judges cannot 'justify decisions by reference to non-universalisable features of the case (such as the date on which it was decided) since a requirement of universalisability is inherent in the very idea of justification'.[71] However, this does not secure a meaningful place for precedent (or, therefore, for the traditional conception of legal rights). Judges can, and often do, 'justify their decisions by reference to complex assemblages of universalisable features, so that no workable rule which is likely to apply in future cases will emerge'.[72] By focusing on the specific features of a given case, judges fail to carry

---

[68] ibid 190.
[69] ibid.
[70] One of the most controversial parts of *Law's Empire* is, in this sense, Dworkin's endorsement of Gadamer's idea that '[u]nderstanding always involves something like applying the text to be understood to the interpreter's present situation'. See HG Gadamer, *Truth and Method*, J Weinsheimer and D Marshall (trans) (New York, Continuum, 2004) xxvii. According to Dworkin, this inseparability between interpretation and application is a 'crucial point'. Dworkin (n 9) 55. For an argument that this undermines the possibility of objectivity in interpretation, see D Patterson, 'The Poverty of Interpretive Universalism: Toward the Reconstruction of Legal Theory' (1993) 72 *Texas Law Review* 1. For a response, see Bustamante (n 33) 121–23.
[71] Simmonds (n 56) 190.
[72] ibid. I doubt Dworkin would disagree with this point, but the question is how he can navigate this issue. On this point, *Law's Empire* is unclear. The key differences between Simmonds and Dworkin will come to light as the comparison proceeds.

out their 'lawyerly *responsibility* to develop and articulate workable rules'.[73] Put differently, it is far from clear (and, in fact, unlikely) that precedent operates as the silent centre of gravity in the sphere of Charter rights.

Once Dworkin's single-right-answer thesis is situated in the context of Charter rights, his account can easily be seen to foster habits of thought that reinforce this outcome-orientated approach that Simmonds is criticising. This is true regardless of whether or not Dworkin rejects 'balancing' in favour of another approach. The problems identified thus far are rooted in the nature of the question posed and not simply in the method of reasoning typically deployed. When judges seek a single right answer, they are not necessarily seeking to articulate a set of workable rules. Or, in Postema's language, judges will not necessarily be attending to the normative significance of past decisions in an attempt to locate a new case in that pre-existing matrix of norms (customary and legal). An example can help to elucidate the stakes in this particular debate.

In *Ward v Quebec*, the Supreme Court of Canada held in a 5–4 decision that comedian Michael Ward did not violate the Quebec Charter when he told an offensive joke.[74] If *Ward* operates like a typical precedent in the traditional sense, we could presume that this decision secures freedom of speech for comedians going forward.[75] This conclusion is too hasty. It is, after all, easy to bring a new human rights complaint against a different comedian insofar as courts are willing to see each complaint as a singular act that brings novel harms to be weighed against the potential benefits of free speech. If the court adopts this approach, they are signalling a willingness to seek what they take to be the single right answer in the case before them rather than deciding in advance whether or not the state will patrol speech in comedy clubs. Unsuspecting individuals may face legal processes that could last for years, regardless of the outcome of any given case. The law would no longer be securing a degree of freedom from state interference. Instead, the courts, in the name of rights, would engage in *ad hoc* decision-making on a case-by-case basis, which is the antithesis of legal rights, as Simmonds forcefully argues.[76] Put differently, judges appear willing to sacrifice the value of protected expectation in order to secure what they take to be the morally best answer. If this proves to be the favoured path, then the exercise of state power will increasingly be used in ways wholly unconstrained by law.

There is further evidence that Dworkin cannot sidestep contentious political and philosophical issues in the context of Charter rights: Simmonds is very clear that his critique springs from a traditional liberal vision of the social order that

---

[73] ibid.

[74] *Ward v Quebec* (Commission des droits de la personne et des droits de la jeunesse) [2021] SCC 43 (CanLII), canlii.ca/t/jk1tl.

[75] *Ward* is not a typical case: the Supreme Court of Canada denied standing to the Quebec Court of Appeal instead of addressing the substantive issue. This does not alter the analysis above as judges can still proceed in a case-by-case fashion.

[76] On this point, also see G Webber, 'On the Loss of Rights' 16/2013 LSE Law Working Papers, file:///Users/margaretmartin/Downloads/SSRN-id2272978.pdf.

advocates the separation of 'the right' from 'the good'.[77] Simmonds acknowledges that the right and the good can never (and should never) be treated as wholly separate in thought; nevertheless, the complete fusion of the right with the good in the legal sphere should be resisted.[78] In societies like our own, which are marked by persistent disagreements about the nature of justice, this older liberal vision of the social order provides a workable solution. According to this account, the state leaves questions of the good for citizens to determine for themselves; citizens will not, therefore, be beholden to another's worldview, religious or otherwise. Simmonds, like the other writers in the tradition, is deeply sceptical of the 'politics of perfection', largely because of 'the ease with which dreams can become nightmares'.[79] For this reason, '[r]ights must not be made conditional upon their virtuous exercise, nor dissolved into a goal-oriented focus upon the attainment of desirable states of affairs'.[80] Dworkin does not appear to attend to, or endorse, this famous separation.

There is another element at the heart of Simmonds's account that is notably absent in Dworkin's – namely, a deep appreciation of the customary order and, specifically, the practices of civility. Recall that Dworkin quietly prioritises individual agency over collective practices in his discussion of courtesy. Instead of searching for the right answer, traditional legal rights, combined with the practices of civility, serve as the practical touchstones that serve both to bind people together and to guide them in their daily interactions. These inherited practices do not stand in the way of the realisation of the liberal democratic order; rather, these practices constitute the democratic order as Simmonds sees it.[81] Practices of civility allow for the expression of mutual respect, or what Simmonds calls 'civic friendship'.[82] From the perspective of Charter reasoning, however, such practices often appear antiquated – like remnants of a previous age that are obstacles to the realisation of human rights. The question is not simply about Dworkin's posture towards traditional legal rights, but Simmonds also invites us to reflect on our posture towards the past more generally.

Simmonds is not simply worried about the decline of traditional rights in the face of the popularity of Charters of rights. He also fears that the habits of thought cultivated by Charter adjudication shapes our attitudes toward the past. Simmonds writes:

> Not everything of value needs to be an unmediated expression of natural reason: custom, shared attachment and habituation will always play a large part.

---

[77] Simmonds (n 56) 181.
[78] ibid 176.
[79] ibid 179.
[80] ibid.
[81] ibid 186.
[82] Simmonds (n 56) 193. Simmonds allocates legal rights a key role in the process of fostering civic friendship.

The somewhat accidental inception of our practices will generally long precede our reflective understanding of their significance. But the attainment of that understanding does not convert our civil and political practices into mere applications of abstract principle. Indeed, they are to a large extent the groundwork of such principles, in detachment from which the principles themselves cannot be grasped or applied. We are the heirs of a complex history, and such spiritual depth as we possess is ours only in consequence of that history.[83]

The law is an important part of our shared inheritance. The past should not be viewed as an obstacle to the realisation of rights rather than the locus of law's authority. As Postema notes above, this does not require unthinking deference but a careful consideration of the normative weight that ought to be afforded to precedent.[84] Simmonds lays the blame for this fundamental misunderstanding with thinkers who begin their analyses with abstract ideals and seek to apply these ideals to the world in hopes of improving it. Rawls is one such thinker; Dworkin may prove to be another.

V. DWORKIN'S EMPIRE

Dworkin begins with a theory of legal interpretation in the courtroom, but he extends his account beyond this narrow starting point. By offering a view of how citizens ought to reason with rules, he offers a fleeting glimpse into his understanding of the social order as such. Lost, however, is any sense of the nature of the trade-offs required in any given account of the ideal organisation of society.

In a well-known passage in *Law's Empire*, Dworkin argues that political obligation is not simply a matter of 'obeying discrete political decisions'; rather, participants must adopt a 'protestant' attitude. This involves adopting a posture of 'fidelity to a scheme of principles' that recognises that 'each citizen has a responsibility to identify, ultimately for himself, as his community's scheme'.[85] Dworkin assumes that *all* participants seek 'articulate consistency' in the legal system as a whole; everyone must seek to establish how to go forward in light of the dual requirements of *fit* and *justification*. In Dworkin's hands, legal reasoning is democratised. Law is not its own kind of special reasoning that requires training; rather, it is a kind of moral reasoning that we all have the capacity to engage in, and according to Dworkin, it is our responsibility to do so. In this

---

[83] ibid 183.
[84] Postema (n 58) 821.
[85] Dworkin (n 9) 190. Murphy offers us another way to see this this argument. Dworkin is setting up the positivist picture, which treats the stipulated dimension of legality as if it exhausts the field; Dworkin amends the picture by turning to the customary dimension of practice. The question is whether his account becomes only about custom and not about the relation between custom and the stipulated order.

brief passage, Dworkin offers us an account of the social order, albeit one that is treated as a fact that does not stand in need of further elaboration or defence. To see the problem with his account, we must return to Fish's critique of integrity.

Recall, for a final time, that Fish identifies a deep ambiguity at the heart of *Law's Empire*. Dworkin is not clear about whether we *always* inevitably interpret the law (or a given practice) as *integrity* requires or whether we must choose to do it. Dworkin appears to say both things at once, which gives readers the impression that he is both illuminating the existing structures of interpretation while simultaneously explaining the normative source of their legitimacy. Disagreement, according to this model, springs from human fallibility: while consensus is the aim, many will inevitably fail in their attempt to get it right. Once this ambiguity in Dworkin's account is explored in further detail, Dworkin is forced to decide whether he is offering an ideal account of what law *ought* to be or whether he is aligned with Fish. Neither of these options is likely to hold appeal.

To see this point, consider yet another rift between Dworkin's account and Simmonds's, which is now visible. Dworkin democratises legal reasoning while Simmonds affirms a much older vision of legal reasoning. For Simmonds, the artificial reason of the common law is central to the account of legal rights he is defending. Simmonds reminds us that 'artificial' was not used by common lawyers in the tradition to suggest that the reasoning was 'fake'; rather, it signalled the 'potentially admirable work of human ingenuity'.[86] Simmonds adds that this account of legal reasoning endorsed by the common lawyers was criticised for being elitist.[87] It is a specialist kind of reasoning that is available only to those who have been trained in the profession.[88] Citizens do not imitate the reasoning of the judge, nor are they expected to.[89] Legal norms, if properly integrated into the customary order, can provide the requisite guidance in day-to-day life. Simmonds, like those who defend this particular vision of the liberal polity, takes citizens as he finds them. He is not telling us that legal reasoning *should* be specialised. Rather, he is simply accounting for a readily identifiable feature of practice.[90]

Dworkin, on the other hand, removes the distinction between citizen and judge, and the outcome is an idealised vision of the community, which may prove far harder to realise than Dworkin suggests. As mentioned, Dworkin expects all of us to attempt to imitate Hercules, insisting that we have the responsibility to

---

[86] Simmonds (n 56) 177. Simmonds names Rawls as the thinker who suggests that artificial reasoning is 'fake'. As Murphy notes, we come to see artificial reason as arbitrary only if the customary structures are omitted from consideration (even though they are never omitted from practice). See Murphy's discussion of Hobbes and Kelson in relation to this point in Murphy (n 14) 765.
[87] Simmonds (n 56) 177.
[88] This is a point that Fish will likely agree with.
[89] It does not follow that law's authority is located in the positive law alone. See Simmonds (n 65) ch 6.
[90] Fish also treats legal reasoning as a specialised kind of reasoning.

do so. The first obstacle that stands in the way of attempts to democratise legal interpretation is the fact that judges are in a different position than citizens when the risk of state-imposed sanctions is considered. Judges, according to Dworkin, aim to justify the use of coercion. Conversely, citizens, in many instances, may act in a manner that takes into account the risk of sanction. Citizens are not simply considering whether to bow to the king, for example; they may often have to reflect on whether it is wise to rebel or comply. The 'best' interpretation may accommodate this variable. Holmes-inspired prudence is a live interpretive possibility, and it is one that Dworkin does not take seriously enough.[91]

Dworkin appears to sidestep the problem by assuming that the interpretation of the stipulated order of legality is identical to the interpretation of customs in day-to-day life. Only then does the risk of sanction fade into the background. However, it is still far from clear that citizens are imitating Hercules when they interpret various practices. The relevant question, then, is not merely whether citizens *should* mimic Hercules but whether they *do so*. After all, only if it turns out to be easy for citizens to mimic Hercules can Dworkin be understood as illuminating features of existing legal systems rather than proposing an ideal. The sole example offered in *Law's Empire* is courtesy. Consequently, it is useful to revisit this example one last time.

Above I argue that Dworkin's discussion of courtesy operates as a fable. By offering a simple narrative, readers are given the impression that everyone becomes engaged in 'constructive interpretation' as soon as the 'interpretive attitude' takes hold. In other words, we are told that we are all 'naturally' Dworkinians. This idea seems credible in the context of courtesy precisely because Dworkin indicates that 'comfort' is the relevant metric. The ability to determine one's comfort level is something done with relative ease – it is something individuals do *naturally*, so to speak. Hercules, however, does not look to mere 'comfort' when seeking to justify the use of coercive force. He looks to the dimensions of *fit* and *justification*. That is, he utilises a particular kind of moral theory in order to place the relevant legal resources in their best moral light. Hercules has knowledge of the relevant precedents and statutes. He also has a deep understanding of the principles that a given society is committed to. This aim, again, is to realise 'articulate consistency' in reference to this fairly extensive set of resources. The goal, or the hope, is that the process leads the interpreter to a single right answer, which has objective status. The task, it seems, is Herculean.

Dworkin's bind is now visible: the more demanding the interpretive activity becomes, the less plausible Dworkin's conception of the social order becomes. While it is reasonable to assume that judges will have the requisite legal resources and the necessary training to utilise them, it is far less plausible to assume that

---

[91] Fish rejects pragmatism: I follow Fish only to the extent that I agree with him that Dworkin offers a straw man when he discusses pragmatism. In many ways, my discussion of Charter adjudication involves the revival of pragmatism in a plausible (but worrying) form.

citizens will have the needed resources or the requisite training to mimic Hercules (it is not a matter of failing to achieve the end sought; I am calling into question the idea the citizens are pursuing the end Dworkin has in mind). By quietly replacing 'comfort' with 'integrity', Dworkin urges readers to conclude that we are all born with the ability to reason like Hercules, but this is only plausible *if* comfort is Hercules's metric.[92] If most citizens do not have the requisite training or resources, membership in Dworkin's imagined community will be reserved for a select few who do.[93] The non-hierarchical conception of community has collapsed into its opposite. While his non-hierarchical account of community is appealing to many, it may prove quite difficult to realise in practice.

The utopian dimension of Dworkin's thought is apparent in Dworkin's brief remarks about protestant interpretation. Here, he unites a commitment to individual freedom (which takes the form of interpretive freedom) and community. He does not, for instance, suggest that the interpretive freedom granted to individuals will threaten to undermine social cohesion, although his critics express this worry.[94] There is no apparent trade-off. Perfection, it seems, is within our reach. While thinkers in the history of philosophy grapple with the tension between freedom and order, Dworkin, in a few short sentences, defines it away. This is likely the source of Dunn's dissatisfaction with the tradition ushered in by Rawls and reimagined, at least in part, by Dworkin. For Dunn, the point of studying the history of political thought 'is to struggle to win from often inaccessible and refractory seams, the materials for grasping the possibilities and dangers of the human world, as this still confronts us'.[95] The goal is to see the trade-offs, not to erase them.

To see the stakes in philosophical debates, including this one, it is useful to return to a very old idea about the nature of freedom that is rarely discussed. Theologian John S Dunne compares Hegel's state-centred approach to individual freedom to a far less familiar account of freedom proposed by Pericles. Dunne writes:

> For Hegel freedom is appropriation of the self while for Pericles it is appropriation of the past. For Hegel slavery is alienation from the self while for Pericles it is alienation from the past. It is the difference between placing ultimate value on the self that passes through life and placing it on the life through which the self passes.[96]

---

[92] Following Murphy, it is probably better to think of lawyerly reasoning as a natural capacity that may or may not be realised depending on whether the needed training is given to the individual in question, and whether the individual has the requisite capacities to realise the skillset.

[93] The size of the community of responsible citizens will turn on empirical data.

[94] Dunn (n 11) 76. See also NE Simmonds, 'Protestant Jurisprudence and Modern Doctrinal Scholarship' (2001) 60 *Cambridge Law Journal* 271, 292–95. For a response arguing that Dworkin's account of protestant interpretation reflects the interpretive responsibility of any participants in a public practice of argumentation, see T Bustamante, 'Is Protestant Interpretation an Acceptable Attitude Toward Normative Social Practices? An Analysis of Dworkin and Postema' (2021) 66 *American Journal of Jurisprudence* 1, 9.

[95] Dunn (n 11) 27.

[96] JS Dunne, *The City of the Gods: A Study in Myth and Mortality* (Notre Dame, University of Notre Dame Press, 1965) 97.

Pericles invites us to see ourselves as transient beings living in and passing through communities – communities that do not simply shape the individuals, but, in an important sense, constitute them.[97] The aim of philosophy, then, is not to abstract ourselves out of history, nor is it to conceive of ourselves as fully bound by it. Both competing temptations ought to be resisted, not least because they easily engender a misplaced sense of superiority (in the first case) or a sense of hopelessness (in the second). Rather, the real worry is that the movement between these two extremes can obscure a third possibility – namely, that our inherited order, which is largely customary, is itself a source of freedom rather than an obstacle to its realisation.[98] While Pericles's account of freedom may not seem intuitive or 'natural', his point is placed in its sharpest light when we take note of the intergenerational impact that follows when people are intentionally disconnected from their past.

It does not follow that all customs should be embraced, or that the existing case law should be venerated. The point, again, is to see the trade-offs clearly and to proceed with caution. To the extent that philosophy can help to cast light on the complexity of a given matter, this alone does not bring about change. Failing to see the issues clearly, however, leaves everything to chance.[99] When viewed in this light, it becomes evident that philosophy may have consequences after all, and it is worth attending to this possibility.

---

[97] This is likely an idea Fish can affirm.
[98] It does not follow that Hegel is wrong. There is more than one path to tyranny.
[99] For a discussion of this theme, see M Martin 'Persuade or Obey: *Crito* and the Preconditions for Justice' in S Bertea (ed), *Contemporary Perspectives on Legal Obligations* (London, Routledge, 2020) 153–172.

20

Interview with Professor Stanley Fish

THOMAS BUSTAMANTE AND MARGARET MARTIN

Thomas Bustamante: Professor Stanley Fish, it is a pleasure and an honour to do this interview and to have a chance to discuss with you some of the points raised by the several contributions of this book. We would like to begin with a question about the historical context in which some of your ideas were shaped. Your debate with Ronald Dworkin in the early 1980s has been widely discussed in the literature. It is rare that events like this are discussed. Do you have any recollections of this event? Could you describe how you met Dworkin and what your relationship with him was like?

Stanley Fish: Sure, I was invited to this conference at the University of Chicago, which had many celebrated people like Julia Kristeva, Gayatri Spivak, Stanley Cavell, Stephen Toulmin, a whole bunch of what then would be thought of as A-List academics. Some of the contributors were offering papers, and the rest of us were asked to comment on one of the papers. Three of us at Johns Hopkins – Walter Benn Michaels, Michael Fried (art historian) and I – all wanted to respond to Dworkin's paper. We were all very eager to respond to that effort. But for some reason that I've now forgotten, I won. So, I got the chance to respond to Dworkin at the University of Chicago conference. Dworkin gets up and presents a twenty-five-minute summary of his position impeccably, without notes, coherently, brilliantly, while I stood up ready to demolish it. I got two sentences out of my mouth when Dworkin seized one word in the second of my sentences and asked me to clarify it because it could have meant more than one thing. So I did that. Then I got two more sentences out of my mouth, and he did the same thing. By that time, as we say in sports, I was 'off my game'. It got worse and worse. It was as if he put me in one of these revolving doors that you find in large buildings, and I was just going round and around and around … until I got into his sights, and he shoots me with another one. I kept on going. And I felt that I was entirely destroyed by this. I felt that I was falling down on the ground bleeding, much as in that poem by Shelley. But as I fell to the ground, metaphorically, I said to myself, and I really do remember this moment: 'I am going to get that fucker in print'! So that's the start of the relationship. I had never met Dworkin before, although I had, of course, read his work. Another noteworthy thing about that conference was that Dworkin, along with the rest of us, was in the conference room all day. And at night, there were regular banquets or meals. There was no time to do anything but be a participant in the conference. But, nevertheless, Dworkin managed to submit an expenses bill in the thousands, which includes his having flown over from England in the Concorde, when there was a Concorde. So immediately this gained my admiration [laughs]. He was someone who really knew how to work the system. The rest of us hadn't spent forty cents on a Diet Coke, which was what it cost then, and he had managed to get expenses in the thousands. So that was my introduction to Dworkin, and then I wrote my first Dworkin piece, 'Working on the Chain Gang', which was a reference, of course, to his very provocative and influential chain-novel theory of the law. And then he came back, and I came back, and he came back again, and I came back, and according to somebody who made a count, there were ten exchanges between the two of us which lasted about a decade.

During the course of that decade, had I met him socially? Not at all. But I did meet him professionally, and one time when I met him professionally was when I was in New York teaching at Columbia University. He was then teaching at NYU, and he called me on a late Friday afternoon to ask me if I would appear in his seminar so we could discuss some of the issues that divided us. And I said: 'Of course, when is your seminar?' He said: 'Monday'. This is typical Dworkin: he's not going to give me much time to prepare. So, fine, I come to this seminar on Monday, which is populated not only by Dworkin's students but by many members of the faculty and others who have heard about this and wanted to see the contest that would ensue. And Dworkin got up and said – I can remember this so vividly: 'Some of my friends and colleagues have wondered why I would invite Stanley Fish to join me in this seminar since he and I have had so many differences in print'. And he went on to say: 'But why should not there be personal amity between two persons, two scholars, who happen to disagree on intellectual matters? Certainly, it is the case that these two scholars can meet, debate vigorously and still remain perfectly amiable and friendly'. That was Dworkin's first move, which I would label 'taking the high ground', which he did very effectively. And I stood up and said something that I'll have to explain after I report what it is. I said: 'Of course Professor Dworkin is correct. There should be no reason for persons who disagree intellectually, even on a number of matters, to feel a personal animosity toward one another. And besides, what could there be but amiability between two nice Jewish boys from Providence, Rhode Island?' Now, if you ever saw Dworkin – Did you? [Margaret Martin: 'yes'; Thomas Bustamante: 'not in person'] – you'd notice that Dworkin was a dandy. He was always dressed impeccably, often in a three-piece suit with a watch-chain and a foulard in his pocket, with a slightly British accent – I guess a slightly 'Britishised' accent. The last thing that he would like to think of himself as was a 'nice Jewish boy from Rhode Island'. We grew up on the corner from each other, although he was ten years my senior, so I never knew him. That's one of those accidents in history, and it's also an illustration both of the kind of skills that Dworkin exhibited and of my tendency to be a counterpuncher.

And this even has a theoretical payoff. This is not one of the questions you asked, but I'll answer it for free. People sometimes ask me: 'What is the Fish-position? Is there a school of Fish, without the joke attached to the phrase? Can you be a Fishian?' My answer is: 'Not really'! You can be a Dworkinian, you can be a Hartian, you can follow and approve the legal theories of Bruce Ackerman, or Brian Leiter, or Jeremy Waldron, or somebody like that. But what I often do is unpack other people's arguments. Of course, I build some of my own positions. But the unpacking of the other person's argument is at least 60% of what I do. That's what I meant when I characterized myself as a 'counterpuncher'. And a counterpuncher is never going to be someone who forms a school. So, I would say that's one reason – though perhaps not the only reason – why I believe that Dworkin's presence and influence in the profession is much greater than mine, because he has a positive theory to offer. He writes large books like *Law's Empire*, *Justice for Hedgehogs*, and others, which present that theory, while I write little essays, or sometimes middle-sized essays, demonstrating why such-and-such a position doesn't hold up.

The last time I saw Dworkin was a year before his death. I was teaching at Cardozo Law School, in New York, which is only five or six blocks away from the NYU Law School, so we lived in the same neighbourhood again. He had one of those little townhouses on a cobbled street in Greenwich Village, which is extremely rare. It is perfectly appropriate that he had that kind of house because he was that kind of grandly outsized figure. So I meet him in a 'dry-cleaner' establishment, which was halfway between his house and my apartment. I brought in a shirt that I wanted to have cleaned. It was a perfectly ordinary blue Oxford button-down shirt. And I took it in and asked the person: 'How much to clean this shirt?' And he said: 'Forty-six dollars'. And I said: 'I only paid twelve for it [laughs], so I'm not going to want it cleaned'. At that moment, Dworkin walked in. Of course this was Dworkin's dry-cleaner. And he immediately urged me to stick with this dry-cleaner because they were the absolute best. I'm sure they were the absolute best, and I'm also sure that Ronald Dworkin never in his life bought a shirt that cost twelve dollars. How's that?

Thomas Bustamante: Not surprising.

Stanley Fish: But he was a grand character. And a total influential and important and major figure. I'm very sorry that he's not here to engage in our conversation.

Margaret Martin: I will say, Professor Fish, that your work, as you know, also spans various genres. All my students who studied English literature, when I mentioned the book, understood who you were, but they didn't know who Dworkin was. Your work is quite impressive, and they were really stunned that we have managed to engage with you about your ideas.

Stanley Fish: Well, there are people in the legal world that don't know that I had an earlier life in the literary world. I happened to move into legal studies, you know, in the late seventies, after having worked in literature and literary studies since 1960.

Margaret Martin: May I ask what prompted you to move from literature to law?

Stanley Fish: The short answer is basketball. I used to play basketball with a friend of mine, Walter Benn Michaels, whose name I mentioned before, and another friend who was then a member of the University of Maryland Law School, Kenneth Abraham, who is now at the University of Virginia Law School and an expert on insurance law. In between games, when we were sitting down, probably because we had lost – these are three-on-three games – we would talk about work, and it turned out that there was an intersection between the kind of work that he was interested in, in legal studies, and the kind of work that Walter and I were doing in literary studies. The intersecting point was the idea of interpretation and notions of evidence, demonstration and validation, interpretive authority and other things that were attached to the word 'interpretation'. So we decided that the three of us would teach a course, which is what academics always do when they kind of know something but don't know enough about that something. We thought: 'Let's teach a course and figure out'. And that's what we did. One semester we would teach at the University of Maryland Law School, and then on next time we would teach it at Johns Hopkins's English department, where both Walter and I were members. So that's what we did. I got very taken with the legal issues, and became more and more interested in them. I ended up teaching an adjunct course at the University of Maryland Law School after Ken had already moved to the University of Virginia. This was in the late 70s. Then in 1984, when my wife and I were both offered senior positions at Duke University, I was also at the same time offered a position in the Law School, because by that time I had published a bunch of pieces, including some parts of the Dworkin debate, that had attracted the notice of some legal faculty. So, by 1985 I was a member both of the Law School and of the Humanities department, and I kept on teaching in both and became more and more involved in questions in law, starting off by teaching contracts at Duke, and then moving into First Amendment and other areas. So that's how that went.

Margaret Martin: So, we'll stay on the sports theme. Thomas and I are curious whether Dennis Martinez has ever come across your views.

Stanley Fish: I haven't the slightest idea. I'm afraid I have no knowledge of any kind of Martinez, except as a pitcher who was, for many years, as you may or may not know, a drunk. But then he recovered and became a very good pitcher, pitched a no-hitter and pitched very well. But, other than that, I didn't know him at all. I wish I had. I don't know what I would have said, or whether he would have been interested in talking to me.

Margaret Martin: Why did you choose Dennis Martinez over any other athlete?

Stanley Fish: When I saw this report at the New York Times, it just struck me immediately. I had used an athletic example before, back in the 60s, when there was a journeyman outfielder for the Baltimore Orioles, whose name I forgot. But, anyway, he was one of those fill-ins, someone who could play several positions, so the Orioles kept him on, and the most that he had ever hit in a season were two or three home runs. Then, suddenly, in the beginning of a new season, in the first week or two he hits five home runs. And so the sportswriter went to him – Pat Kelly, that was his name – and said: 'What's happened to you? Did you change your stance, choke up on the bat, get a bat of a different weight, or something like that'? And he said: 'I'm born-again Christian'. In other words, what changed was that he was 'born again': Christianity, and the spirit that flowed through it, was the answer, so that he was entirely convinced that his newfound batting province was the result of the Spirit of the Lord working in him. The sportswriter expressed irritation, to say the least. He said: 'I couldn't get Kelly to talk about his achievements', this was his phrase, 'in strictly baseball terms'. And the reason that I locked on to this example was because obviously for Kelly, 'strictly baseball terms' was not a category. That is, the sportswriter was suggesting: 'there is your athletic skill over here, and your religious beliefs over there, and they can't have an intimate relationship', whereas Kelly was saying: 'not only do they have an intimate relationship, but they are also indistinguishable'.

That was one of the early formulations, on my part, of what an interpretive community is like. By being 'born again', Kelly had internalised the ambitions, hopes, beliefs, tenants, doctrines, the whole package of a community, which I would later call an 'interpretive community', and he saw everything that he did and everything that he saw in its light. That was one of the early glimpses, for me, of that idea. Like everyone else in the literary theory at the time – this was like the late 50s and early 60s – I was looking for a way of talking about interpreting poems that neither assumes that poems declare their own meanings – because if that were the case, there would be no need for anybody to be in the literary interpretation business – nor supposes that it could be the case that a poem meant anything that a reader wanted it to mean. So, like everyone else, I was looking for some way of accounting both for the variability of meanings proposed for this or that poem, and for the fact that that variability was not wide open but was finite and at least partially constrained. That's where the interpretive community idea began to emerge, and I realised that the mistake was to think of a stand-alone interpreter facing a stand-alone object and trying to figure out what's inside it, needing a bridge which we might call 'interpretation' to get from his apparent present perception to a deeper understanding of the object. And now, finally, I said: 'the assumed independence of the reader from the poem he or she is reading is what must be challenged', and argued instead: let's think of both poem and the reader – and I didn't have the phrase then, but I do now – within an 'interpretive community'. Hence, the reader of the poem is himself or herself not free in the sense of being able to impute any meaning to the poem he or she prefers, and nor was the poem a free-standing object waiting for someone to offer the right interpretation of *it* to *it*. Instead, the interpretive community model began to think of both the poem and the reader – this is the phrase I later used – as community property.

Thomas Bustamante: Before moving on to more particular aspects of your debate with Dworkin, let's talk a little more about interpretive communities.

Dennis Patterson, for instance, makes a very specific argument in his chapter of the book, where he says that you moved from a view that you held at the beginning of your career, called a 'reader-response view', which is accused of being solipsistic, to a conventionalist account centred on 'interpretive communities'. Are these notions really inconsistent, as he claimed? Did you change your views over time, or did your critics misunderstand this point?

Stanley Fish: I did [change my view]. With respect to that issue, I should add that six years ago, Dennis invited me to give a series of talks in Italy, so I'm very grateful to him for that. My views on the reader-response theory you are talking about changed. And in fact, the book 'Is There a Text in This Class?' reports on this change in the last four chapters and in the Introduction. What changed is that I started talking about the reader, but the obvious question to which, at first, I had no answer was 'What reader? Who is this reader?' So I came up with the notion of the 'informed reader', because I had to escape the charge of solipsism, the charge that I was just talking about myself as a reader and presenting myself as the guide to interpretive correctness. Hence, I invented somebody called the 'informed reader'. But who is the 'informed reader'? Well, the informed reader, let's say of 'Paradise Lost', since at that time I was working strongly on the poetry of Milton, would be someone who had read Milton, who knew something about the seventeenth century, who is well-versed in Theology and Reformation Theology, and well-versed in the difference between what we would now call Anglican Theology, Episcopalian Theology and Dissenting Theology, that is some version of Puritan Theology; someone who would know something about the political events that were important in Milton's life – he was born in 1608 and died, I believe, in '74 – like the Commonwealth Revolution, led by Cromwell, the Restoration of Charles II, and so on. My informed reader would have to know, and know it in a very deep way, the classical writings of Greek and Roman literature, and the major renaissance writings in Italian literature, and a couple of things in French. So that's the informed reader. I constructed that reader and tried to ask the question 'What is the experience of that reader going to be like when he or she picks up one of these poems and starts to process it?' The informed reader is obviously a construct. It's not me, it's not you, or [any] of us. It's a construct. And that means that, in some sense, it's a creation of convention; it's something that I, at that time, imagined. Now, the informed reader, as I then constructed him, has a kind of relationship to the 'reasonable man' often put forward in cases. The idea of the 'reasonable man', for example, is central to Justice O'Connor's 'coercion test' for [the First Amendment's] 'establishment clause' violations. When she wants to ask if the 'reasonable man' would, looking at this display of, say, a religious item at a courthouse, think that this was an endorsement by the state of religion, the reasonable man is regarded as a construct. My informed reader was also a construct. So there was a definite change from just talking about a reader, and not specifying who that reader was, and therefore inviting the accusation that that reader was just me and I'm just universalising my own experience, to talking about the informed reader.

To give an example, Milton's pastoral elegy, 'Lycidas', a great poem, starts with the words 'Yet once more'. Now, what I would say, and did say, about 'Lycidas', is that 'yet once more' is a signal to the informed reader that this poem is going to be one of a long series that began with Theocritus's First Idyll, written in third-century BCE Alexandria, and then a whole series of pastoral elegies that went through Virgil, various Christian authors like Edmund Spenser and so forth. 'Yet once more' says: 'Here I am again', this lyric singer bewailing the death of a young poet, knowing that someday another young poet will be bewailing my death. That's what the informed reader, as I described him, would know and would understand the moment the first three words of 'Lycidas' were encountered. Now, if you gave 'Lycidas' today to a group of freshmen students, you wouldn't have a chance. It would take a lot. I once taught 'Lycidas' to freshmen students, at Hopkins, and spent a whole semester teaching them how to read the poem, which meant introducing them to vast areas of English literature, history, theology, art and so forth. At the end, they could do it, of course, because they have been made into what I would then call an informed reader.

Thomas Bustamante: There are people who believe your account of interpretive communities is at odds with your endorsement of legal originalism. But in one of our conversations, you clarified that you are an 'intention-originalist', not a 'text-originalist'. Could you elaborate on this distinction and on how it hangs together with your views about interpretive communities?

Stanley Fish: Well, as you know, at least until recently there were three accounts of legal interpretation available in the field: originalism, which has two versions (textualism and intentionalism), and the living constitution. The difference between originalism, in either of its versions, and living constitutionalism is the direction in which you look. Originalism, in both of its forms, looks backward to the past to find a perspective that will control or rule or govern the present in order to understand the present fact situation, while living constitutionalism picks up the stick at the other end and asks a very different question: not 'How can we judge this case so that it fits with past precedents?', but rather 'How can we judge this case in a way that will allow the country, the democracy, the republic, to move forward in a better fashion?' So rather than being backward-looking, living constitutionalism is forward-looking. It is not that living constitutionalism won't make use of the constitution, it's just that they will 'bring in' bits of the constitution when these bits seem to be useful to the project of deciding the present case in a way which advances the interest of justice, democracy and so forth. The constitution makes an appearance in living constitutionalism, but it is not controlling, as it is in both the intentionalist and the textualist versions of originalism.

Now, intentionalism begins by challenging the object of the textualist's attention. In other words, in order for textualism to get started, it must be assumed that most of what we want to know about a text can be derived by just looking at the text in and of itself, studying the words and identifying the meanings they would have historically acquired at the time of production and then proceeding on the basis of that lexical history to issue a reading of the text. What an intentionalist would say is that 'there is no text to look at, independent of the assignment or assumption of intention'. That is a radical statement, so radical that even though I've said that many times to many textualists, they don't understand it. But you can understand it perhaps by way of an analogy. Let's say you're in the American West, as it is grandly conceived, and you see some smoke arising from a hill somewhat distant from you. There are two things you can decide: you can decide that the smoke is just a natural effect of a fire, or you could decide that the smoke was a signal, and if the smoke was a signal, that means that it's been used to send a message and the task is then to figure out what the sender of the message had in mind, what the signals, now understood to be intentionally produced, are telling you. For a textualist, the smoke, independently of whether or not it's being sent intentionally, is a possible repository of meaning. For an intentionalist, that makes no sense whatsoever! In other words, in order to identify something as a text, you have to have identified it as something purposely designed to send or communicate a message, and the text won't perform that identification for you. This is the big thesis that Larry Alexander has been preaching for years: the text won't tell you what the intention within which it was produced is, won't even tell you if it's a text.

Textualists have to believe that the text will tell you what the intention behind it is, and, in fact, Scalia said that exactly. He said that if a text is carefully crafted, its intention will be built into that well-crafted artifact. But the intentionalist will reply: 'No, that's wrong. There's no such a thing as a text independently of the assumption of intention; there's no such a thing as a *text* standing there as an independent object, of which you then can or not make something depending on how successful your interpretive efforts are'. So that's a very large difference, which I summarised in the claim that the trouble with textualism is that it doesn't have an object on which to operate, because textualism assumes a text standing there independently, and then an inquiry into what it means and, therefore, in some sense, into what was intended. The assumption of intention comes first, the text second; no assumed intention, no text.

To answer the second part of your question, that is obviously related to the little story I told a while ago about why I thought up the idea of interpretive communities, because, again, it had been assumed that you have this poem, over here, which had its own features, characteristics, and then you had this reader, over there, and the reader had only some kind of mental capacity for trying to determine what these features were. So, in other words, the old story assumed two independent entities, and the problem was how to get them together in a fruitful way. But I'm saying: 'No, no. Both the poem and the reader were intelligible only within the space of an interpretive community'. I trust that you can see the relationship between that and intentionalism, as opposed to textualism, because textualism goes back to the old interpretive picture of an independent text and independent reader, and the need for something to bridge the distance between them to bring them together, something like, to go back to Dworkin, an 'interpretive theory'. But that's not the case, as I've said, because what is the case is that you're situated within a world of intentions and purposes that are themselves functions of what I later came to call an interpretive community, or other people would call an 'arena of practice', or a 'paradigm', or a 'lifeform', or Nelson Goodman [would call] a 'way of worldmaking', or an 'episteme', a 'habitus', in Bourdieu's word, or a 'Gestalt', or something also related to Michael Polanyi's notion of 'tacit knowledge'. All those positions, which have been elaborated in different terms by the scholars and theorists I've just named, share the idea of a world of social practices which is already complete although capable of changing. It is already complete in the sense that it comes with items, with aspirations, with objects, with projects, with tasks, with rules, with conventions, with ways of determining if something is right or wrong, correct or mistaken. It's a very rich notion, I think, and it was developed by all of the scholars that I have named a moment ago, although in slightly different ways.

Thomas Bustamante: There are critics who think the idea of interpretive community is a bedrock assumption that your theory needs, but your theory does not permit any bedrock assumptions. Perhaps a sceptic can argue that you are faced with the following difficulty. First, if everything can be interpreted, the notion of interpretive community is itself interpretive and we can never be sure whether we are agreeing with one another, or we are actually misunderstanding each other's point. Second, if …

Stanley Fish: Let's stop at that. Neither of you is old enough to remember this or to be interested in it, but there used to be a series of programs, on American TV especially, called 'variety shows', where you had a singer, you had a joggler, you had a dog act, you had flamenco dancers, whatever, and then a presiding impresario like Ed Sullivan or somebody like that. Now, often one of the acts that continually showed up in these programs was two people who are engaged in a conversation – I'm not going to be able to reproduce this with an example, but I'll give you the general practice and you could choose the example for me – that begins with a certain subject matter of some kind, which the speaker intends in one way, but his interlocutor hears it in another way. But neither, at the moment, is aware of the difference, so they keep on going, and each of them says things which seem perfectly reasonable in terms of his or her understanding of the interpretive contours of the situations, whereas the other person hears it as also perfectly reasonable, so that they go through a conversation at length, lasting a number of minutes, and at the end walk away perfectly satisfied with what is transpired but each of them has entirely different notions of what transpired. This didn't sound funny or comic as I rehearsed it, but it was comic when these people would do it, because what makes it work as a performing event is that the audience is privy to a long sequence of misunderstanding which keeps on going and going further. So, to get back to your point, it is possible that you and I could walk away from the conversation we are having quite satisfied with the resolution but each of us has a different understanding of what that resolution and its meaning were.

The next question is: 'Is there a way to test for this?', that is: 'Can you invoke some measure or standard?', and the answer is 'no'. What you could do if you suspected that this was happening is to get the two persons back and say: 'ok, you understood X by that first thing, while you understood Y', and they could both say: 'I did'. But the understanding that you now are confessing to is as much an object of interpretation as the confusion it is attempting to dissipate. This is not to say that all conversations, or most conversations, have this shape. But they sometimes do. This [the following example] can't be true for you, but it is true for me: I've been married for forty-five years, and there are conversations like that, where two parties talk about entirely different matters. Milton, in *Paradise Lost*, 'Book IX', depicting a quarrel between Adam and Eve, provides a textbook example of how two people could go on talking past each other even though they are within two inches of each other. Does that answer your question, Thomas?

Thomas Bustamante: I think it does.

Stanley Fish: It [that kind of communicative misunderstanding] is certainly possible. Another way to put this is: although interpretation can be stopped by any number of ways (you can say: 'that's enough! We have to finish the job, after all'; in other words: 'we have to get on with the business of whatever it is'), there's nothing inherent in the production and hearing of language which will lead us to a method that will give us absolute certainty of what was said.

Thomas Bustamante: Let's come now to the second part of the question. If disagreements can only be explainable within an interpretive community, as you suggest, it can be the case, the critic may say, that there are no common paradigms or interpretive conventions from which one can proceed in order to avoid a subjective or discretionary judgment. Is your account of interpretive community equipped to respond to this challenge?

Stanley Fish: First of all, remember, I've told you [before the interview] not to use the word 'subjective', because 'subjective' is not part of anything that I've ever written. In fact, a very good criticism of my work would be that it doesn't leave any room for an individual's subjective creativity, or leaves very little, if any, room. That would, I think, be a proper criticism. But let me invite you, once again, if you pardon me, to ask the question again. I'm not sure I got it entirely.

Margaret Martin: Let me try it. Maybe it will be a follow-up to your answer. Your answer still presupposes the possibilities of coming or not coming to a communal understanding. With your work, I always look for something to hold on to, and the thing I try to hold on to, of course, slips away [Stanley Fish laughs], which is part of the power of your work. But then I'm always trying to figure out what to hold on to, or if there's something to hold on to. If there isn't, what are the implications of having nothing to hold on to? Or, if there is, what is it and how do you establish the thing to hold on to? So, if you go back to your answer, can I hold on to the possibility of 'right' or 'wrong' active communication between, say, Thomas and I, so that we either understood each other or didn't, even if we can never perfectly figure that out? Is there still something more that seems to be at issue in interpretation, that could possibly serve as bedrock?

Stanley Fish: I'll give you the short answer, then a long one. The short answer is: 'There's no bedrock'. But anti-foundationalism doesn't mean the absence of foundations. It doesn't even mean the absence, ultimately, of objective, universal foundations. It just means that even if there are objective universal foundations, we don't have any access to them, because we are linguistic, situated creatures. Our access to the universal is always through the limited perspectives that are ours by virtue of education in geography, history, language, code and so forth. But then the next step is to say: 'Having said that, what has been taken away?' And here is what has been my thesis throughout the years: 'Nothing'! It's not the case that the bedrock is one day taken away from the world by Jacques Derrida or Stanley Fish or Thomas Kuhn or Michel Foucault. Bedrock has never been around. Of course, this is something that has been said in different ways by Thomas Hobbes a long time ago, by the Greek atomists at an even longer time ago, and by many theorists of biblical interpretation, in the fifteenth, sixteenth and seventeenth centuries. There are no foundations to which you can have recourse in order (a) to come up with a right answer, and (b) to absolutely and permanently disqualify any answer that has already been offered. But, nevertheless, there are those foundations – and I don't hesitate to call them 'foundations' – that come along with well-developed practices. 'Well-developed practices' is just another phrase that I can substitute for 'interpretive communities'. What is a well-developed practice? A well-developed practice is one that comes equipped, as I said a little while ago, with the categories, presumed obligations, a list of tasks that have to be accomplished along with a list of tasks that have been accomplished, a set of resources that are available for discussing and disputing a matter and so forth. That's a well-developed practice. It is well-developed in the sense that embedded practitioners are persons whose consciousnesses are already equipped with all of the above. Interpretive communities' members don't consult assumptions, protocols, notions of evidence and so forth. They are *constituted* by those notions. So, an interpretive community's member looks at the field of whatever it might be and already sees all of the configurations in place. Again, to use the example of a sport, if you walk into a baseball field or onto a basketball court, you already not only see the objects, but also know what they mean and why they are there. In basketball, you don't have to ask: 'What's that ten-foot thing sitting there with what looks like some kind of configuration of cotton fibres on a ring?' You don't have to answer it, since you know what it is, and you know what you're supposed to do and you know what the possibilities are, right? Not only do you know how to play. As you know, Margaret, I'm sure, since you played at a level higher than any I have played, the worse thing to do, the way you can really get hurt, is not when you play someone incredibly more skilled than you are, but when you play someone who doesn't know anything about the game. If you are a player of the game, you know that someone could be here, someone could be there, someone could be going backdoor, someone could be looking at the weak side, someone could be doing this and that ... You can move in ways that, then, find you in an intelligible position. But if you know nothing about the game, you are likely to hit somebody. You know what I mean, don't you?

Margaret Martin: Yes, of course. Your description of basketball is what those in the philosophy faculty where I was a member would say every day: 'What is that thing that you throw that other thing in? And why do you do it?'

Stanley Fish: So there we are. We are equipped with all of this. Now, does that mean that every move that we make is predetermined or scripted in advance? Of course not. Within any interpretive community, there are always rules for dispute. I spoke to Thomas the other day about a dispute that occurred in Milton studies, which is: 'Is *Paradise Regained* a "brief epic"?' Well, how many people can understand that question? Only the people who are readers of Milton, who know the history of Milton criticism, who have read a very important work by the Harvard Miltonist lately deceased Barbara Lewalski, who wrote a book called *Milton's Brief Epic*, and so forth. Disagreement is not an innocently or neutrally observed fact; it is an achievement and is unavailable as an achievement to non-community members. So people could say: 'yes, it is a brief epic' or 'no, it isn't a brief epic', or someone could say 'I don't believe in the category of brief epic'. All of those are possible ways of disagreement, but they are disagreements within the interpretive community's assumptions in which there are places for these ideas like poem, epic and so forth. Is that clear enough?

Margaret Martin: Yes.

Stanley Fish: There's always a possibility of disagreement. Now, is there a possibility of agreement to the extent that all disagreement seems to have ceased or to have been defeated? The answer is yes, but it's only going to be temporary. When I came into the profession, in the late 50s and early 60s of the twentieth century, there were two things you weren't supposed to do: you weren't supposed to talk about readers, and you weren't supposed to talk about the biography of authors. One was called the 'affective fallacy', and the other was called the 'intentional fallacy', and they were put into authoritative place by two people, Monroe Beardlsey and William Wimsatt, in two essays, one called 'The Intentional Fallacy' and the other called 'The Affective Fallacy'. And Wimsatt was a teacher of mine. So, when I entered the profession, those were not things that you did. In response to my little mantra 'Is this the kind of thing we do around here?', talking about readers and talking about biographies of authors was not. What you talked about (this was, of course, the 'new criticism' or 'close reading' school of literary criticism) was the text. That was a general agreement, so you could be engaged in a conversation about a poem with other scholars and might say something and someone would say: 'Well, that's just the intentional fallacy'. And that would be what Richard Rorty would call a 'conversation stopper'. But, once you set up the situation like that, whether it's literature, history, law, this is an invitation to bright young eager scholars to undo the apparent, almost universal or at least disciplinary-wide, agreement on a matter. So, a bunch of people – and I was one of them – started in 1964 to commit the affective fallacy. When I wrote my book *Surprised by Sin: The Reader in Paradise Lost*,

I was committing the affective fallacy by doing what you're not supposed to do. But I did it, and I got away with it. And it became the most influential book in Milton criticism of the last seventy-five years, without a doubt. Then, after I'd done that, I began to commit the intentional fallacy. And I'm still doing it today.

So, I built my whole career on moving out of a situation where there were two things that you weren't supposed to do, and everyone agreed that you weren't supposed to do them. After the end of doing them and arguing for them until there was a revolution, although this might be too grand a word, at the end the fallacy was to think that the text was a stand-alone, independent object. That is now the fallacy. Hence, the whole position that 'fallacy is over here', while the 'tried and true way over there', or vice-versa, remain positions that are still there and will always be there. It's just that they shifted. This is, of course, often what happens in legal history, in cases where a doctrine that was declared not to be one that we can take seriously then becomes acceptable, usually first through powerful dissent by members of the Supreme Court. After a while, the dissenters become members of the majority. That's how it happens in practice, whether we are talking about interpretation of a poem, how to decide a case, how to describe an event in history or how to characterise the habits of a primate tribe, if you are an anthropologist and so forth. That's what we do, at least what we academics do. And one can also say that, in a larger sense, that's what culture does. What happens in the culture – and this is a kind of Rortyan point – is that certain vocabularies, which were regarded as inappropriate or not weighty in any way, become introduced in forceful ways – those forceful ways can vary – until, at a certain point, things that no one would have been saying are now things that everyone is saying, and things that everyone was saying twenty years ago are things that you wouldn't be caught dead saying!

One of the things about watching movies, as I do, from the 1930s, 40s, and 50s, is that you see in the movies all these assumptions, some racial, ethical and religious assumptions about persons, a host of assumptions which seemed to the persons making these assumptions just common sense are now gone, and we have a new common sense, which is used to expose and demonise all the old assumptions. If you agree with me, that's what happens in cultural and political change, which are intertwined in obvious ways, then the idea of an interpretive community makes sense. It is the way in which norms, protocols and standards are simultaneously in place and capable of being altered. Now, what would alter them? That, of course, is an empirical question. You can never tell what's going to be the trigger that signals that a new way of thinking has taken over from the old. But it does happen, and it happens by routes that you can analyse after the fact, but you can't predict them and you can't design them. And part of what people do when they want to cling to the category of the 'bedrock' is that they want to both predict and be able to design the next, so that the effect will be assured. There's nothing more common in politics, whether in your country or my country, than someone acting to introduce a policy that is designed to improve a situation over here, but then finding that an unintended consequence or a whole set of problems arise over there.

When in 2015 the Supreme Court decided the *Obergefell* case, constitutionalising same-sex marriage, one of the things that Justice Roberts said in his dissent – and predicted, quite correctly – is that there will now be a conflict between this newly given constitutional right to same-sex marriage, and older rights like the right of free association and other rights. Based on these rights, some persons will not want to acknowledge same-sex unions and will want to open restaurants or operate bakeries which do not serve same-sex marriages or do not bake cakes for same-sex marriages. Now, that's the kind of thing that always happens, and then the whole thing keeps on going, and keeps on going. So my picture is simultaneously a picture of a kind of stability, which is provided by the general outlines of the interpretive community to which most of the people who are operating within them conform, because it's part of their ways of thinking, and then [there's] the myriad of ways in which ways of thinking can be altered. Does that make any sense at all?

Margaret Martin: Yes. I can agree with that narrative, but I want to press on something else. I've always tried to get my head around this idea of 'no consequences'. If I take what you've just said seriously in light of your antifoundationalism, then I would be foolish, I think, to write a paper saying that the new way or the old way of thinking after the Supreme Court's judgment was 'better' or 'right' or 'true'. Is that it?

Stanley Fish: No, no. I disagree with that. [pause] Perhaps you can explain further. What would prevent you from saying that my view is incompatible with that?

Margaret Martin: You are suggesting that we just have this changing of the paradigms over time, that we can't control it and that we can't stop it, but we always want to control it and we want to use theory to control it. I agree with that instinct in the impulse, and I do see it everywhere as well. But if I take you seriously, in reference to your claims about truth, then any claim I make to say this is the better way, whichever side I choose to defend, would be a truth-claim that is within a paradigm that can never be established. So, if I really believed your anti-foundationalism position, and I'm always tempted by it, then I think I would have to do my work differently.

Stanley Fish: That's interesting. You expect too much of anti-foundationalism. Anti-foundationalism is just the answer to a set of traditional questions in philosophy. It is not in any way a recipe for living, or for doing anything. If you are an anti-foundationalist, and I'm a foundationalist, and we are both serving on the same court and looking at the same case, we could easily come to the same conclusions despite the differences in our large philosophical position, and the reverse is true. Let's say you and I agreed entirely about foundationalism and anti-foundationalism and truth and convention and all the rest. We could still disagree vehemently on how to read a present fact-situation. That's what I mean when I say that your general epistemological position doesn't have any effect whatsoever on your performance in particular situations. And nor would it have the effect of making you distrust your judgments, as you suggested. I gave you, a few moments ago, part of an analysis of the first three words 'yet once more' [in Milton's 'Lycidas']. I do a whole chapter on that in the book *Professional Correctness*. Now, I am confident that I am right about how 'yet once more' functions in the poem. I am confident, therefore, on what kind of reading follows from my analysis of those three words. So, I'm saying that my reading of that first three words is true or correct. It's not true 'for me', it's not true 'for me and my friends', or 'the people on my department'. It's just true. However, is it the case that there is a mechanism or a measure by which I could demonstrate that truth to all rational persons in the world? The answer is no.

You have to live with two things: a) I'm absolutely certain that my reading of this line from Milton is correct; b) I'm also absolutely certain that people as well-educated, or even better educated than I am, could come out with another reading. The fact that all those other readings were in contradiction to mine would only mean, from my point of view, that error is always possible – that is, that there are people who, despite their education and fine minds, can make mistakes. When I hold to a reading as true, why do I hold to that? Because I'm doing literary criticism, or I'm doing legal analysis, either one. When I say, for example, the Establishment Clause [in the American Constitution's First Amendment] has been read out of the constitution since 1947 in the first Establishment Clause case, *Everson*, I'm giving you a reading of the Establishment Clause from 1947 to the present, and I can back it up with all kinds of evidence and cases and so forth. But I know people who also write on law and religion who don't hold that view at all. Now, I hold that view, not because I am either a foundationalist or because I am an anti-foundationalist. I hold that view because I've looked at the cases, I've figured out what was going on, I've come to a conclusion about what these various opinions delivered by Justices amount to, I'm able to cite chapter and verse, as is my opponent. And that's what I rest on: the analytical, empirical work that I've done, not on any big ideas I have about the objectivity or the absence of objectivity or foundations or the absence of foundations. Can you see?

Margaret Martin: I do, and I always find it a compelling claim. But let me ask you in the way that we phrased at the end because it gets at that meta level, if there is such a thing. We think this claim is interesting. The worry, of course, is that if people agree with you, the activity of judging may not change, but philosophy might. So, even if you are right that the judges keep doing what they are doing and literary critics do what they do, will philosophers keep doing what they do – or even should they? Insofar as philosophy is committed to finding distinctions in the world and arguing for the reality of certain distinction, are you suggesting that, perhaps, that particular game [philosophy] is a little more pointless than we would like to think?

Stanley Fish: What exactly do you mean by pointless? Is the game of literary criticism pointless? Well, yes and no. Sure it is, from a certain perspective. If I say, for instance: 'This is the right reading of *Paradise Lost* or Milton's 'Lycidas', or Bunyan's *Pilgrim's Progress*, one of my favourite texts and so forth', and then somebody else says: 'no, that one is the right reading', what's the point of that exercise? The point of that exercise is, for me, to persuade someone else that my understanding of this poem or this novel or this epic is the correct one. What, then, hangs on that, independently of the conversation between two or more persons interested in these texts? The answer is 'nothing'. Hence, it is pointless if you are looking for a point that goes beyond the aspirations and pleasures of the particular interpretive community game. In other words, someone can say to me – and I would agree: 'Look, the idea of an interpretive community doesn't do anything to topple capitalism or to undo patriarchy. Interpreting poems doesn't do anything to put food in people's mouths'. I have to say: 'That's absolutely right'. Then the next step is: 'Therefore it's pointless'. I'll say: 'No, that's not its point'. Its point is to get a better understanding of some of these extraordinary pieces of verbal art that we have long appreciated. Why is this so moving? Why does this text seem so powerful? Why is this painting so overwhelming when we see it? What's going on there? The answer is that it is a particular practice. Philosophy is also.

As far as judges are concerned, consider this example. There was a case called *Washington v. Glucksberg*, which was the assisted suicide case in Oregon and has an interesting relationship to the *Dobbs* case, which overruled *Roe*. In that case, the Justices decided that assisted suicide is not a constitutional right, and in doing so they rejected, pretty much, the set of arguments that later won the day in the same-sex marriage cases. They rejected the argument, to use Justice Blackmun's vocabulary, that one should be free or have a liberty to order one's own intimate affairs. They rejected that argument in favour of the argument which we now see revived in *Dobbs*, that for there to be a constitutional right it must be either named in the constitution, or be embedded for a long time, in a sustained way, in our judicial traditions. That's what they did. Now, a bunch of famous political philosophers, including Dworkin, Scanlon, Nozick, Rawls, Judith Jarvis Thomson and somebody else – but that's already a heck of a list! – wrote a *Philosophers' Brief*, which argued for the liberty to order one's own intimate affairs, including the liberty to decide how one wishes to die. The Justices of the Supreme Court paid no attention to that brief. Why? Because they were judges and not philosophers. And this is a big difference between Dworkin and me, since he thinks judges are or should be philosophers, finally. In the best of all possible worlds, all the judges would be like his judge Hercules, which means that all the judges would be like Ronald Dworkin. That's what he thinks.

But the Supreme Court in *Washington versus Glucksberg* said: 'Here's our legal tradition, here's the arguments, here's such and such counter-arguments', and then they decided on legal grounds. You decide what a poem means on literary critical grounds. Well, this is quite different from *using* a poem. A poem can be used in a political effort. There was a book called 'Chariot of Wrath', written by G Wilson Knight in the early forties; and what it did was to appropriate 'Paradise Lost' for Allied propaganda. It re-read 'Paradise Lost' in the context of World War II, then being fought, to assign Hitler the role of Satan, while

Churchill was assigned the role of hero, and so forth. It interpreted the great 'Book VI', which is the book on the war between the angels in *Paradise Lost*, into an allegory of the war between Allied forces and Rommel's tanks in North Africa, and so forth. Now, that was not literary criticism. It was politics. What happened? Well, World War II was won, thankfully, although we are seeing glimmers of a new one, and that piece of literary criticism passed away. No one responded. The game returned to its usual forms.

So, philosophy – I always say this – is an academic discipline and not a natural kind. What philosophers do is lots of fun. I do it myself. I engage in it. I think it's calisthenic, it can feel almost athletic, and it's wonderful to see the people who are really good at it. You can say, 'Jeez, that was a great argument!' or 'I see that!' or 'Now we see the death knell of realism!' or 'Now we see the death knell of conventionalism!' or 'Now we see the death knell of relativism!' or whatever it is that has just been slammed. And then the game takes another turn. But what, meanwhile, has happened in the world outside the philosopher's seminar? Nothing. Absolutely nothing.

I've had that conversation with the Chairman of the Philosophy Department at the Hebrew University. I was teaching at the University of Texas Law School, in the spring of 2022, and I went to a seminar in the Philosophy Department given by this guy, and he was talking about a particular branch of law and said that philosophical arguments are not the right thing to bring into that branch of law. I tried to get him to extend his argument to say that philosophical arguments are the wrong thing to bring in *anywhere*, except if you're in a philosophy seminar! All I mean is that philosophy has no consequences. It does not mean that ideas have no consequences. Ideas have huge consequences. If I have the idea that women should receive equal pay for equal work, or that there should be acknowledgments of ways in which women have been shut out from this or that kind of work, that's an idea that has *legs*, because it can lead to legislation. But if I have a big, totally persuasive argument against pragmatism, for example, and everyone has applauded me, and I get whatever awards there are given in the philosophy realm, the next question is the same question that I put in the literary criticism seminar: What is this going to do to put food in people's mouths or to stop certain forms of tyranny from expanding? Nothing whatsoever. I often put it in this way on my work on higher education: 'The academy, love it or leave it. Don't love it because you think that the work you do in it is going to have a beneficial and large effect on the world outside the academy. If you harbour those hopes, they will always be disappointed, and you will always be accusing your fellows of having betrayed the enterprise'. Now, you should stay in the academic world and perform academic work because you like it, because it presents problems that interest you and you get both a kind of pleasure in it and satisfaction out of trying to work them out! That's it. There's nothing else to say.

Margaret Martin: I'd like to ask Thomas if he wanted to defend Dworkin.

Stanley Fish: Well, there's a lot of things about Dworkin that I could defend.

Thomas Bustamante: Ok, but there's one point that appeared in the book, a central disagreement between you and the more Dworkinian chapters of the book.

Stanley Fish: Which ones?

Thomas Bustamante: For instance, Waldron's. Dworkin is trying to make sense of a distinction between, on the one hand, making your own responsible judgment in order to assign meaning to a concept or to understand a normative concept like liberty and, on the other hand, deferring to the interpretation of others.

Stanley Fish: I've never said one should defer to the interpretation of others. There's nothing in my work that advises anyone to defer to the interpretation of others. And I want to ask you the question: What do you mean by 'your own responsible judgment'? What the hell does that mean? What's the content of that?

Thomas Bustamante: Well, let me try to elaborate. I think that his point is that judgments are things made by people, not by communities.

Stanley Fish: No, wrong, wrong. It's made by people, but not by people independent of their having themselves formed by communities. In other words, you keep trying to reinvent the person who stands outside the community or practices in which he or she is embedded. You're always looking for that. I know you by now! You are always looking for that Archimedean place where you can stand outside. This doesn't mean that you don't have [the category of] judgments. It doesn't mean that judgments cannot be offered or disputed or argued about or changed or anything like that. It just means that you're never going to find a place that is independent of the ways of thinking that constitute your very consciousness and your perceptions for that matter. You're never going to find that. If that's what you're looking for, you can look from now to the end of time.

Thomas Bustamante: Does that mean that the community can never be wrong?

Stanley Fish: Sure. Well, there are two answers to that question. One is that the kind of communities I'm talking about are 'well-developed practices', with histories and mechanisms for self-revision – that is, mechanisms which lead, for example, to the *Dobbs* decision. A lot of people would believe – I know that you don't, Thomas – that *Dobbs* is a decision that was a mechanism of correction – that is, it corrected something that was going wrong in this part of American jurisprudence since roughly 2003, in *Lawrence versus Texas*, and that now *Dobbs* comes back and reasserts the appropriate perspective. The internment of the Japanese – I mentioned to you this the other day – during the years of World War II, something that was approved by a Supreme Court Decision called *Korematsu versus United States*, has now been totally repudiated, so much to the extent that the government itself has issued an apology. *Brown versus Board of Education* is a deliberate and explicit overruling of *Plessy versus Fergusson*, again, using legal arguments, although lots of Brown's critics didn't think that the arguments were legal enough. The kinds of interpretive communities that

I'm thinking about have within them built-in mechanisms for recognising and correcting their mistakes. But your question is another one. Your real question is the same question you always ask! Your real question is: 'Ok, but how can we decide from outside the community that its judgment was wrong?', and the answer is 'you can decide that from within another community, but not from a vantage point outside any community'. So, let's take the *Dobbs* decision. I've said something to you at the end of our last conversation [not recorded]. I didn't know whether it registered one way or the other with you. I said, look: 'Let's take these two instances of legal history. *Dobbs* overrules *Roe v. Wade*, and *Brown v. Board* overrules *Plessy v. Fergusson*'. I'm saying: 'Same thing! That's exactly the same thing'! What you want, Thomas, is a way of saying: 'yeah, but one overruling was right and true, while the other overruling was wrong and bad', right? You want to be able to say that.

Thomas Bustamante: I want to be able to say that while exploring some sort of internal structure within the community, in a way that doesn't need to get out of it.

Stanley Fish: You can do it, but all that it will do is provoke counterarguments from the other side. Other conservative legal academics, many of whom I know, like Larry Alexander or Steven Smith, of the same San Diego Law Faculty, or Eugene Volokh of UCLA, will be ready to respond. You can elaborate an argument which says 'no, this was the wrong decision for the following reasons', and the guys on the other side will say 'no, this was the right decision for these reasons, and it's the one that has corrected wrongs that have been too long allowed to have a place in our culture'. Sure, you have a dispute [between these views]. But that's not what you're after. You're after some measure which could come in and allow one to say, 'Look, overruling *Plessy v. Fergusson* was right, whereas overruling *Roe v. Wade* was wrong'. You're never going to get that. You can make arguments within the tradition of the community. There were lots of people, when *Brown v. Board of Education* was first published, who disagreed with the decision, including many who were on the left and who were very much in favour of [desegregation], as Herbert Wechsler said when he wrote his famous essay 'Towards Neutral Principles'. He liked the result – he would rather live in a world where *Brown v. Board of Education* was the rule rather than a world in which *Plessy v. Fergusson* was the rule – but he couldn't see how *Brown v. Board of Education* was a coherent and legitimate legal holding. If you want to distinguish between *Brown v. Board of Education* overruling *Plessy*, and *Dobbs* overruling *Roe v. Wade*, how would you do it?

Thomas Bustamante: Could I say that there is a claim to reciprocity and equality embedded in the structure of law? In other words, I might say that the mere fact of legality comprehends some sort of egalitarian morality that would allow me to say it.

Stanley Fish: You could, and then all the Republican lawyers, all the people who go back to the debate that surrounds the Federalist Papers will say, 'This is not a Democracy. This is a Republic', and you'll also be running up against a tradition which was championed by Scalia, who was also an extraordinarily smart guy. Scalia said over and over again that what he wanted to do was to take the court out of the business of making large moral/philosophical decisions because, he said, 'that's the business of legislators', and that was his position throughout the arguments about same-sex sex and same-sex marriage: 'Let's have these questions decided legislatively rather than having the court pronounce on them on the basis of the latest cultural fashion'. So, you can make the argument that you are about to make, Thomas, and it might be a very powerful argument. But that wouldn't stop the argument on the other side.

Thomas Bustamante: Well, let me restate, without necessarily subscribing to it, an argument that Dworkin makes. One of your positions that produced strong reactions among the critics is the observation that lawyers and practitioners cannot help but apply 'law as integrity', because this is what they do naturally. Does this mean that interpretive judgments are intuitive and passive, as Dworkin accused them of being under your account?

Stanley Fish: Not at all! First of all, this is a genuine question: 'What do you think "law as integrity" means'?

Thomas Bustamante: Law as integrity, for me, is a method of discriminating between right and wrong decisions. I think that the two requirements in law as integrity, fit and justification, are two facets of the same general requirement. What makes law as integrity, as I read it, an attractive idea is the exigency of consistency. There is consistency with past political practices.

Stanley Fish: What he calls 'articulate consistency', which I'm all in favour of.

Thomas Bustamante: And there also is consistency in justification. So inconsistency is a mistake, and that's all that Dworkin demands.

Stanley Fish: I know you've heard this argument, Thomas, and it did not make any impression on you, but I'll try it again.

Thomas Bustamante: Ok.

Stanley Fish: Inconsistencies are asserted – they are not self announcing – and can always be challenged. Dworkin goes wrong in his checkerboard theory, for example, when he says things like 'if you are a congressman devoted to X, and known to be a champion of X, and yet you're voting for policy Y, you are going to have to give up one or the other. You're either going to have to say: "No, I can't vote for this", or acknowledge that your position has changed'. That's not true. This is what the whole mechanism of distinguishing a case in law is for. You say, 'well, yes', and this happens again and again: 'This case is really not totally analogous with the case that you are comparing it with. Instead, here are the distinctions that make this case different and therefore I can make my decision without violating or undermining my position'. In other words, what I'm trying to say is that 'articulate consistency', in which I believe, is a rhetorical achievement. And by that I mean that when it is accomplished, it is because the arguments you're able to make put together two pieces of your judicial or lawyerly practice, and make them hang together. The two pieces, whatever they are, don't have an independent shape. We are back to 'poem' and 'reader'. We are back to 'text' and 'intention'.

It's all the same. They don't have an independent shape. Consistency or inconsistency are not natural facts, they are facts that are argued for, and since argument is always capable of failure – it is always possible that argument cannot be fitted together – it is possible that a perceived inconsistency will not be able to be reconciled by this particular lawyer/jurist/theorist. But then someone will come along, some bright young man or some bright young woman, fresh out of Oxford or Yale Law School or somewhere, who has figured out a way to put together what everyone thought could not be put together, and will therefore turn an inconsistency into an articulate consistency. It's easily done. Well, not exactly easily done. It requires a lot of work. It's not necessarily the case that it will happen. But it can happen. So I believe in articulate consistency, but I believe in it as a rhetorical accomplishment and not as something that depends on the independent existence of two positions, one of which is inconsistent with the other. That's the work that lawyers always do. In fact, lots of law cases and many law review articles have that form: 'It has often been thought that the doctrine of X is incompatible with the practice of Y. But I am going to show that in fact they can be perfectly consistent'. How many law review articles have you seen that begin that way? Does that register with you?

Thomas Bustamante: It does, but another idea immediately comes to mind, which is the idea that this argument can fail. How do we know when it fails? You accept that persuasion is the test.

Stanley Fish: Sure, sure.

Thomas Bustamante: Can we have anything else?

Stanley Fish: Persuasion is a very big category. It's not a small thing. Remember, I explained the other day the whole tradition of classical and medieval and renaissance rhetoric, in which persuasion is a huge machine which encompasses everything that I'm talking about in interpretive communities. It's what Kuhn argues in *The Structure of Scientific Revolutions* when he says that the scientific theory that wins out is not the one that matches the independent facts of the world, but the one that is persuasive to the relevant community, which is the community of scientists in his case. So, Kuhn repudiates the idea of scientific progress, in the sense that every time we come up with a description that has been accepted by many, we are closer and closer to the goal that Francis Bacon aimed at the beginning of the seventeenth century. He says: 'What we need is a complete description of all the operations of nature', and he thought it could be done in six generations. Francis Bacon was a very smart guy, but of course we now know it hasn't been done, and we should know, if we think about it, that it's never going to be done. This is Kuhn's point, which I fully agree with: the way scientific argument proceeds is winning over a number of the relevant practitioners in the enterprise to a point of view, and then that point of view for a while becomes the reigning point of view and acquires the status of a 'paradigm'. For a long time, perhaps, it will remain so, until it is challenged, and anomalies begin to be pointed out, and their weight increases until suddenly there is a period of revolution when it's not clear what things are like. Then it settles down again, in a different way. That's the way it is. That's how it is in science, in literature, in law, in history, you name it. That's the way it is!

When I persuade someone, in the context of literary criticism, or legal studies, or history, in order to do so, I have to marshal huge masses of evidence, I have to make complicated arguments, I have to take into account counter-arguments, I have to imagine the objections to what I'm saying and I have to be able to give responses to those objections. That's the stuff of persuasion. As I was saying to you the other day: never use the word 'mere' in front of the word 'rhetoric' – 'mere' rhetoric, 'mere' persuasion, etc. For persuasion is the entire game. Is there another game that could possibly win? Sure, it's the game from the God's eye point of view. Are you a God? I'm not. Are you a God, Margaret? I doubt it.

Margaret Martin: The debate is really, as you said, about the God's eye perspective. But if I were to try to adjudicate this discussion, I'd take it that in reference to Dworkin's position, in general, what you're saying is: 'It's true that there is no truth'. I know that you take the anti-Archimedean position on, but just for the sake of getting it on the book, can you respond to this?

Stanley Fish: That's perilously close to Habermas's performative contradiction, and as I've said in print, and will repeat now, any reference to Habermas which is positive is enough to disqualify the person who makes it. Look, it's a 'gotcha' game. Think of this as a tennis match. I'm translating the idea of anti-foundationalism versus foundationalism into a tennis match. Let's say an anti-foundationalist and a foundationalist are playing a tennis match. When can either win the game? The answer is: the anti-foundationalist cannot win the game.

Only the foundationalist can win the game. How? By 'lobbing' a ball over the net, labelled 'foundation'. Then the anti-foundationalist has to hit it back, having demonstrated that it is not a foundation. It is itself just a particular, powerful product of anti-foundational, rhetorical, disciplinary success. If you as a foundationalist get one ball over the net, labelled foundation, and I can't hit it back: you've won. But I can never win. All I can do is stand there and keep on hitting back the foundationalist ball that you have sent over to me. Now, a friend of mine who used to be the chairman of a philosophy department of the NYU, Paul Boghossian, is a realist in a philosophical sense, and therefore a foundationalist. He says: 'Ok, how many people in the room believe that it is ok for people to murder infants for no reason at all?' Nobody raises her hand. And, therefore, he says: 'Ok, the game is over'. Can you see the way it works? Now, of course, someone could elaborate it in a better way. But what he's saying is that there are certain kinds of things or activities or practices that everyone condemns. There are evil or unacceptable deeds, on the one hand, and entirely good deeds, on the other hand. He's saying – and he's right – that as long as you got one ball over the net, then you can build a foundationalist world on that one. And what an anti-foundationalist can do in response to this is to – I hate to use this word, and I'm happy that've gone almost three hours without using this word – 'deconstruct' – that's the word – what has been sent over the net. Does that make sense?

Finally, I'm not caught in a contradiction, because I'm not making a claim, except the claim that for anything that you point to me as a foundation, I'm going to be able to show to you or make an argument that it isn't. And the moment that I fail in that claim, I lose.

Margaret Martin: Would you say, in a sense, both sides have a 'gotcha' argument, in the way you present? In a sense, the foundationalist has a 'gotcha' argument too, with which I've struggled as a PhD student, because I've read your books initially. Every time I've had an argument against anything you've said, I've realized that you would get me in that way. So, there's a way in which there is no neutral place to stand between the two positions, there's no way to arbitrate or adjudicate the debate. The best that you can do is to take people on your team.

Stanley Fish: What do you mean by taking people on your team?

Margaret Martin: You can persuade me or Thomas does. Whoever persuades me, I end up on that team, but that's all there is to it. So, I either believe I'm searching for an Archimedean point that I can use (even though I recognise that not everybody is going to agree, so consensus won't be a sign that it exists or doesn't exist), or, on the other side, I could deconstruct the argument, or use psychology to say that that desire is misplaced or the search is misplaced.

Stanley Fish: Well, I don't know about the part of the search being misplaced. As I have explained in a recent and still unpublished piece,[1] the desire for a foundation, the desire to have a fulcrum, an Archimedean point, a bottom line, bedrock, to use the word that you used before, is understandable, and it's hard to get rid of it. Rorty claimed that he had got rid of that desire himself. He claimed that he learned how to do it without certain words like 'truth', and so on. But I'm not sure I believe he did it, because the appeal is finally a theological one. You want to believe that there's a point of view that transcends all of our points of view: no matter what sets of practices we subscribe to, no matter what religion or non-religion we profess, what political philosophy we adhere to or don't, there must be something that can judge. But the fact is that there isn't. Not that there isn't, finally. Perhaps now we see through a glass darkly, and someday, face to face. But not now. That's the whole point of the essay on 'Impossible Things' I've just cited. Not now. We are all human and situated. And being human and situated, we have certain powers and abilities. But the ability to find a point outside of, and independent of, human perceptions and practices is not an ability that is ours.

---

[1] Stanley L. Fish, 'Impossible Things: Blind Submission, Legal Realism, Textualism, Corpus Linguistics, Critical Legal Studies, Anti- professionalism, Interdisciplinarity, Consciousness Raising, Transparency, Artificial Intelligence', manuscript on file with authors.

Thomas Bustamante: Can I ask a final question? The more I hear you, the more I find that, in the end of the day, there are more similarities between you and Dworkin than disagreement, because he also would claim that he is not a foundationalist. He would say that the principle of integrity, understood as articulate consistency, is part of the practice; it's a central element of the practice. So, our final question is this: In the end, what is the big difference? What remains as a disagreement between you and Dworkin?

Stanley Fish: Well, it can be identified in Dworkin's phrase 'the weak constraints of practice'. Both he and I believe that practice comes along with constraints, with protocols, with resources and so forth, and that we are responsible to those constraints not by an act of will but because we are embedded in that set of constraints. But Dworkin then believes that some other constraint, which he calls 'theory', is necessary. He believes that because the constraints of practice are weak – I don't believe they are weak, but he does – there's the need of an articulate overarching theory of the kind that Hercules could develop. And I'm saying: 'No, you don't need that'. You already have everything that you want in phrases like 'articulate consistency' or, as he says in another place, 'sense of appropriateness', which is another value that I would espouse. You have all that you need in that. The desire for theory is always a desire, again, for the Archimedean point. So that's the big difference between us. I find very attractive many of the Dworkinian positions, especially when he talks about the 'moral reading' of the constitution, which says that we are all together in the same long-standing journey and adventure, something that began in the late eighteenth century – he is, of course, speaking about the American tradition – and that it is our job to continue and enrich and deepen that tradition of representative democracy, and we're going to be able to do that by recognising our place in the continuing story and desiring to continue that story, rather than striking off in an entirely new direction. I think that is absolutely correct, and I think that it is also inspiring. I just don't think that he needs all the theoretical machinery that he seems to desire, because, as I've said a few moments ago, he wants to be a philosopher of the kind that offers all of the non-philosophers in the world the help that they surely need. It would be better, in Dworkin's view, if everyone were a philosopher, which in my view, would be a kind of nightmare.

Thomas Bustamante: Wonderful. Thank you. I think we can finalise and stop the recording.

Stanley Fish: Let's stop the recording and get out on the basketball court.

Index

accountability 42, 45, 47, 91, 356, 376
action, theory of 310
adjudication 111–14, 118
  adjudication in Nazi Germany 13, 346–61
  articulate consistency 292
  atheoretical generation, claim of 111–13
  Charter rights adjudication 384, 394–9
  judging 43, 47, 384, 394–9
  legal interpretation 170–2
  right-wrong image of adjudication 263–4, 267, 292, 311
  virtue ethics 111–13
agency
  coercion 239–40, 257–8
  community of principle 240
  constraints 246–7
  deeply situated agents, judges as 109
  institutional context 23
  interpretive communities/interpretive community 239–40, 243–7, 249, 251–2, 256–8
  legal interpretation 206, 239–40, 257–8
  rational agents 188
  rule of law 369–77
Amaya, Amalia 112–13
ameliorative interpretation 10, 185, 193, 197, 199–201
ampliative responsibility 303–4
analogy, role of *see also* chain novel analogy; Dennis Martinez (Fish's anti-theory hero)/baseball analogy; *Hercules* (Dworkin's imagined judge) analogy
  analogical argument 145–6, 148, 154, 157
  Cave, prisoner from the 72
  disanalogies 146–8, 151–7
  literary interpretation 144–57
analytical jurisprudence 12, 186, 189
Annas, Julia 107–11, 114–18
anti-foundationalism 3, 219, 415, 418–19, 426
  coherentism 189
  epistemological anti-foundationalism 189

  Fish, interview with 415, 418–19, 426–7
  legal interpretation, constraints on 3, 185–6, 189–90
  metaphysical anti-foundationalism 189
  natural law/naturalism 219
  rule of law 370–1
anti-theory 160, 283
Aquinas, Saint Thomas 344–6, 355, 350
Archimedean jurisprudence 119, 121, 123–9, 138, 219, 231, 235, 265
argumentation
  internal structure 313–14
  interpretive communities/interpretive community 242, 244–5, 253
  legal interpretation 168, 177, 242, 244–5
  pragmatism 270, 287
  social practices 298–9
Aristotle 4, 21, 49, 104, 374, 384–6
articulacy 114, 117, 255, 263, 292
artistic interpretation 198, 202, 261
atheoretical generation, claim of 100–1, 102, 103–4, 111–13
attitudinalism 320
Australian Constitution, External Affairs Power of 194
authentic performance movement in music 321–2
authority
  attribution 284
  authoritative legal texts, interpretation of
  cases governed by 31–2, 33
  cases not governed by 32–3
  integrity, law as 8, 126–8
  interpretive communities/interpretive community 211–12, 251–2, 254, 257, 284
  judging 38, 65
  judicial review 44
  legitimacy 135–6
  moral authority 56–7, 59, 63, 123–4, 245, 350
  past, judges located in the 313
  power 62
  precedent 58
  rational norms 274

430 *Index*

recognition 312
rhetoric 92–3, 95, 317
rights 399
rule of law 43

Balkin, Jack 321–2, 327, 336–7
baseball analogy *see* Dennis Martinez (Fish's anti-theory hero)/baseball analogy
belief-desire model of rationalisation 11, 275–80, 289
beliefs *see* convictions/beliefs/prejudices
Bentham, Jeremy 287, 324, 370
Bills of Rights in liberal democracies 200–1, 337
Blackburn, Simon 284
board games, problems with rules of 75–6, 77, 93
Brandom, Robert 11–12, 270–8, 282–3, 288, 293, 296–314
Bustamante, Thomas 253–4, 294, 299–300

Canada
  Charter, non-discrimination clause in 194
  Civil Marriage Act 2005 192–3
  full democracy, as 338
  moral opinions 299
  Ward v Quebec 397
Cave, prisoner from the 72
chain novel analogy 28–9, 406
  judging 78, 80, 103–4, 109, 112
  legal interpretation 198, 205
  legal positivism 28
  literary interpretation 2, 142, 144–57
  semantic theory 311
Charter rights adjudication
  advance, identification of rights in advance 396
  balancing approach 396–7
  Bills of Rights in liberal democracies 200–1, 337
  Canada, *Ward v Quebec* decision in 397
  interpretive communities 395
  name only, rights in 396
  outcome-based reasoning 394–7
  past, attitudes towards the 398–9
  precedent 394–7
  right answers 384, 394–9
  single-right answer thesis 393, 397

social order 397–8
traditional legal rights, effect on 384, 398–9
Civil Rights Act of 1964 (United States) 174
CLS (Critical Legal Studies/Crits) 12, 84, 89–90, 94, 248, 292–7, 373
coercion of law
  force 245–6, 257, 344, 352, 355, 357, 401
  gun at your head or gun in your head 66, 69, 243, 247, 249, 279
  integrity, law as 33, 137, 344
  interpretive communities/interpretive community 247–54, 257–8
  justification 37, 248, 250–1, 257–8, 291
  legal interpretation 162
  legal practices 247–51
  legitimacy 344
  naturally, doing something 4, 401
  objectivity 291–2
  past political decisions 37, 287
  rhetoric 244, 247–50, 257–8
  rule of law 365–6, 369
  sanctions 52
Cohen, Mathilde 115–17
coherence
  anti-foundationalism 189
  coherentism 223, 225, 228, 230–1
  integrity, law as 123–7, 132–8
  interpretive communities/interpretive community 210, 246
  moral coherence 132, 231
  naturally, doing something 391
  Nazi Germany, interpretive practice in 356
commitments and entitlements 300–6, 311, 372, 377
common law *see also* precedent
  artificial reason, notion of an 287–8
  classical common law 287–9, 293, 309–11
  constitutionalism 334, 341–2
  judging 114
  legal reasoning 127
  morality 229
  natural law/naturalism 229, 231, 287, 309
  rationality 307, 309
  rights 384, 394–5, 400
  working itself pure, as 175–6, 288, 309
communitarianism 294

concepts
    conceptual amelioration   197
    contested concepts   259
    doctrinal concepts   279
    interpretive concepts   227, 266–7, 352, 372
    political concepts   43
concrete order thought   349–53
conservative theory of law   288–9
Constitution of United States *see* United States Constitution
constitutionalism
    common good constitutionalism   324, 334, 341–2
    interpretation   334, 341–2
    living constitutionalism   411
    plain fact constitutionalism   334, 341
constraints
    agents   246–7
    external/internal constraints   250
    fit and justify thesis   125–6, 128, 132
    integrity, law as   144
    interpretive constraints   10, 80, 183–202, 246–7, 318–20
    judging   125–6, 128, 132
    legal interpretation   99–139, 141–57, 159–81, 183–202
    legal theory   38–9
    morality   162
    natural constraints   10, 184–5, 187–92, 198, 202
    pragmatism   40, 263, 270
    social constrains   181–2
constructive interpretation/'constructive' interpretation   14, 206–8, 215
    constraints   10, 181, 184–5, 189–90, 192–202
    Critical Legal Studies (CLS)   294–5
    Hercules (Dworkin's imagined judge)   161–3, 164–6, 173–4, 176
    inferentialism   303–4
    instrumental pragmatism   278
    integrity, law as   242, 308–9
    Nazi Germany, interpretive practice in   345–6, 352–3, 355–6, 361
    objectivity   291, 303–4, 309, 313
    pragmatism   288
    rule of law   364, 366, 377
conventionalism *see also* conventionalism and pragmatism
    alternative models   278
    protected expectations   383–4, 390

conventionalism and pragmatism   10, 46, 187, 190–1, 266–7, 281–4, 287–8
    axis of fit   30–1
    authoritative legal texts, interpretation of   33–4
    concrete order thought   352
    defendants' rights argument   33–4
    future, concerns with the   390–1
    Hercules (Dworkin's imagined judge)   132–3, 162, 391
    instrumental pragmatism   278
    integrity, law as   14, 30–1, 137, 266–8, 291, 390–3
    interpretive communities/interpretive community   259, 283
    invention and interpretation, distinction between   281
    judging   14, 390–3
    legal positivism   30, 391–3
    literal meaning   22
    natural law/naturalism   30
    naturally, doing something   14, 390–3
    Nazi Germany, interpretive practice in   351, 353
    objectivity   291, 298
    protected expectations   392–3
    semantic pragmatism   298
    soft conventionalism   137
    subjectivity   190–1
conversational interpretation   288
convictions/beliefs/prejudices   8, 29, 88, 269–70
    belief-desire model of rationalisation   11, 275–80, 289
    established practices and beliefs   51–2
    force   51–4, 64, 66–7, 69, 71–2
    literary interpretation   144
    pragmatism   262–3
courtesy, practice of   384, 386, 387–9, 398, 401
Cover, Robert   330–2
critical interpretation   288
Critical Legal Studies (CLS)/crits   12, 84, 89–90, 94, 248, 292–7, 373
Culler, Jonathan   212
culture   12, 23, 188, 192, 339, 364, 377
customary practice
    accounting for custom   386–90
    common law   287–8
    courtesy, practice of   384, 386, 387–9, 398, 401

flux, as in constant 386
naturally, doing something 384–90, 393, 398, 400–1, 403
rebellion, acts of 387–8, 401
stipulated order of law, interaction with 386–7

Davidson, Donald 271, 275
default and challenge structure 305
democracy 63–4, 399–401
'Dennis Martinez and the Uses of Theory' article. Fish, Stanley 8, 99–118
Dennis Martinez (Fish's anti-theory hero)/ baseball analogy 99–118, 159–81
  about a practice and within a practice, rejecting distinction between 8, 102–5
  adjudication, theories of 111–14, 118
  Annas 107–11, 114–18
  atheoretical generation, claim of 100–1, 102, 103–4, 111–13
  customary practices 386–7
  Hercules (Dworkin's imagined judge) 9, 112, 159–81
  inauthentic explanation, claim of 100, 101–2, 103, 104–5, 111, 113–17
  interview with Fish 408–9
  judging and distinction between practice and theory 41–2, 47–8, 100, 102–18, 269
  legal interpretation 9, 112, 159–81, 195–8
  MacIntyre 105–9, 111, 113, 118
  natural law/naturalism 220, 237
  naturally, doing something 386–7, 395
  practice and theory, interplay between 8, 99–118
    atheoretical generation, claim of 100–1, 102, 103–4, 111–13
    inauthentic explanation, claim of 101–2, 103, 104–5, 111, 113–17
    judging, distinction as applied to 100, 102–5
    reflection 107–9
    standards of excellence 106–7
    thinking within a practice and thinking with a practice 102–5
  routine and skill distinguished 107–11, 220
  thinking within a practice and thinking with a practice, contrast between 8, 102–5

virtues
  ethics 99, 105–14, 117–18
  jurisprudence 99, 118
  skill, virtue as a 107–11, 114–15, 117
deontic scorekeeping 300–6
Descombes, Vincent 213–14
descriptive interpretation 185, 192–5, 198
developed practices 415, 422
Dewey, John 269–70, 275
difference, irreducibility of 86
disagreement 45–7, 193–4, 211–12
disanalogies 146–8, 151–7
discourse-centred approach 18
dissenting opinions 127, 164–5, 323–4
distributive justice 328–9, 383
Dobbs ruling (United States) 189, 194–5, 201–2, 279–80, 328, 342, 420, 422–3
'Doing What Comes Naturally'. Fish, Stanley 169, 178, 382
Dunn, John 383
Dunne, John S 402
Dworkin, Ronald *see also Law's Empire*. Dworkin, Ronald; *Hercules* (Dworkin's imagined judge) analogy
  adversaries, attitude to 5–6
  anti-naturalistic turn 225, 232–6
  Fish and Dworkin
    first on-stage encounter of 7, 405–6
    Fish, interview with 14, 405–28
  Hart 5, 186, 255, 260–2, 324
  historical context of Fish-Dworkin debate 1–2, 7, 27–34
  Justice for Hedgehogs 5, 9, 122, 128, 177, 285, 344, 347, 354–5, 358–9, 407
  'Law as Interpretation' article 27–30, 78–82, 144
  legal pragmatism 11–12, 259–89
  'My Reply to Stanley Fish' article 29–30
  revisiting the Fish-Dworkin debate 205–15
  Taking Rights Seriously 27, 260–1, 319

essentialism 268, 370–1

family, concept of 199–200
felt satisfaction, notion of 276–7
fidelity, duty of 13, 280, 342, 263–5, 337–40, 368–72, 331–2, 399

Fish, Stanley
   Dennis Martinez and the Uses of Theory' article   8, 99–118
   '*Doing What Comes Naturally*'   169, 178, 382
   Dworkin and Fish
      first on-stage encounter of   7, 405–6
      interview with Fish   14, 405–28
   'Force' article   8, 51–74, 249, 278
   Hart   5, 55–69, 248
   historical context of Fish-Dworkin debate   1–2, 7, 27–34
   'How Come You Do Me Like You Do' article   10
   interview   14, 405–28
   Is There a Text in This Class?   243, 410
   'The Law Wishes to Have a Formal Existence' article   53, 91
   legal pragmatism   11–12, 259–89
   legal theorists to Fish, reactions of   8, 75–95
   revisiting the Fish-Dworkin debate   205–15
   'Still Wrong After All These Years' article   7, 266
   'Working on the Chain Gang' article   28–30, 406
   'Wrong Again' article   29
Fiss, Owen   83–5, 190–1
fit and justify thesis
   backward-facing dimension   391
   instrumental pragmatism   277
   integrity, law as   30, 125–6, 128, 131–2, 144, 261, 424
   judging   112, 125–6, 128, 132
   legal interpretation   78–9, 125–6, 162, 176, 183, 205, 207–8
   literary interpretation   144, 152–3
   naturally, doing something   399, 401
   precedent   325
   threshold requirement of fit   126
force *see also* 'Force' article. Fish, Stanley
   coercion   245–6, 257, 344, 352, 355, 357, 401
   collective force, justification of   40
   convictions/beliefs/prejudices   51–4, 64, 66–7, 69, 71–2
   force of law   1, 249, 278
   gun at your head or gun in your head   66, 69, 243, 247, 249, 279

interpretive communities/interpretive community   11, 239, 242, 245–6, 257
justification   11, 40, 64–5, 239, 352, 357
legitimacy   344, 355
meaning   52–3
monopoly of coercive force   245
'Force' article. Fish, Stanley   8, 51–74
   coercion   52, 66, 249, 278
   convictions/prejudices   52–4, 64, 66–7, 69, 71–2
   demands backed by threat of violence   56–9
   distinctions between domain of force   54
   established practices and beliefs   51–2
   force, meaning of   52–3
   general rules, governance by   61, 63
   Hart and the gunman   55–9, 61–3
   Hart's theory of law   55–66
   interests aggressively pursued   52–3, 278
   laws and reasons   62–6
   legal interpretation   59–63
   legal positivism   58–61, 66, 68, 72
   legal reasoning   8, 52, 55, 60, 65–74
   masking force, law as   56
   moral reason   59–61
   norms, standards, reasons and rules   8, 53–4, 59–61
   opposing/resisting force, law as   54–5, 66–7
   power   52, 55, 58–60, 62–5, 69, 72–4
   reasons   62–7
   rule of law   54, 63
   rule of recognition   61, 64–5
   sanctions   52, 64–5
   social practices   8, 73–4
   systematisation and perfection of force   52
   threat or use of violence   52–3
   transcendence of reason   8, 51, 68–70, 73
   violence   52–3
formalism   11, 78, 82, 91, 376–9
Foucault, Michel   10, 214, 415
foundationalism *see also* **anti-foundationalism**
   Archimedeanism   219, 231
   Fish, interview with   426–8
   legal interpretation   185–7, 189, 214
   natural law/naturalism   219, 223, 230–1
   pragmatism   268
   rhetoric   189
   rule of law   370–1
Frank, Jerome   172–3, 269–70

freedom 367, 381–2
  constraints 218
  free speech 218, 339, 397
  freedom of conscience 136
  gun at your head or gun in your head 69
  integrity, law as 130
  intellectual freedom 126
  interpretive freedom 131, 387, 391, 402
  legal realism 28
  past, alienation from the 402–3
  political obligations 135
  radical freedom 80
Fugitive Slave Act of 1793 124, 331, 359–60
Fuller, Lon 218, 222, 257, 347, 356, 369, 378

generosity, virtue of 114–15
Germany *see* Nazi Germany, interpretive practice in
government, identification of law with 365, 372–9
Greenberg, Mark 128–9
grounds of law 260–1
gun at your head or gun in your head 66, 69, 243, 247, 249, 279
gunman analogy (Hart) 55–9, 62–3

Habermas, Jürgen 70, 310, 332, 426
habits 107–8
hard cases 137, 147, 186, 206–7, 319–20, 357
Hart, HLA 5, 55–69, 186, 193–4, 230, 245, 248–9, 255, 260–2, 272, 279, 324, 345, 391, 407
Haslanger, Sally 193, 198–200
Hegel, GWF 70, 279, 293–7, 306–13, 402–3
Hercules **(Dworkin's imagined judge) analogy**
  Dennis Martinez (Fish's anti-theory hero) 9, 112, 159–81
  integrity, law as 3, 30–1, 124, 132–7
  Judge Ralph thought experiment 164–7, 171
  legal interpretation 9, 112, 159–81, 186, 207
  naturally, doing something 14, 163, 165–6, 171, 391, 393, 400–2
  right answer thesis 112, 319, 321–3
  United States Constitution 319, 321–4, 329, 331–3, 335, 339, 341
  values and principles of judges 172–3, 178

hierarchical and differentiated role responsibilities 11, 240, 257
historical context of Fish-Dworkin debate 1–2, 27–34
  authoritative legal texts, interpretation of
    cases governed by 31–2, 33
    cases not governed by 32–4
  Fish, interview with 405–28
  integrity, law as 27–31, 33–4
  post-mortem on Fish-Dworkin debate 31–4
  summary of debate 27–31
Hobbes, Thomas 3, 381, 384, 415
homogenization 210–11
'How Come You Do Me Like You Do' article. Fish, Stanley 10
Hume, David 291, 302–3, 310
Hutcheson, JC 269–70

imagined communities 402
immoral integrity, problem of 343–61
  coercive force, use of 344
  degree, integrity as a matter of 343
  interpretivism and wicked law 343–6
  legality, relation between integrity and 343
  moral justification 343–4
  Nazi Germany, interpretive practice in 12, 13, 344–61
  perfect integrity 343
  systemic integrity 343
impartiality 56, 63, 68, 365, 370, 274, 377
impersonality 56, 63
implicit norms 11–12, 289, 314
  explicit rules 44–5, 47–8, 270, 274
  natural law/naturalism 275, 283
  objectivity 314
  social practices 272–3, 281
inauthentic explanation, claim of 100, 101–2, 103, 104–5, 111, 113–17
individualism, liberal tendency towards 294
inferences
  broad/inferentialist pragmatism 291
  commitments, relations among 300–6
  inferentialism 12, 273, 291–3, 296–306, 313
  linguistic practices, rationality of 297–8, 305
  material inferences 297, 301–3
  objectivity 12, 273, 291, 293, 296–306, 313
  rationality of social practices 12, 297–8, 306–8

semantic theory 293, 297–8, 300–1, 309–10
social practices 296–9, 305–8
task responsibilities 303–6
unconditional oughts 302–3
understanding 214
infinite regress argument 213
inside-outside dichotomy 172, 174, 304
instrumentalism 12, 259, 274–81, 283, 289, 291, 302–3, 309
integrity, law as 3–5, 119–39
  ambiguity 386, 390
  Archimedean jurisprudence 29, 119, 121, 123–9, 138
  authority 8, 126–8
  coercion 33, 137
  coherence 123–7, 132–8
  common sense 393
  community of principle 130–1
  constructive interpretation 242, 308–9
  conventionalism and pragmatism 14, 30–1, 137, 139, 291, 390–3
  Critical Legal Studies (CLS) 292–7
  degree, integrity as a matter of 343
  doctrinal theory, as 27–8
  fit and justify thesis 30, 125–6, 128, 131–2, 144, 261, 424
  Hercules (Dworkin's imagined judge) 3, 30–1, 124, 132–7
  immoral integrity, problem of 12, 13, 343–61
  inclusive integrity 134
  inferentialism 297, 300
  institutional actions, response to 9, 120
  internal and external viewpoints, boundary between 138
  interpretive communities/interpretive community 242, 245–6, 252
  interpretive practice 13, 346–61
  judging 4, 23, 125–8, 132, 252, 257
  justice and fairness 122–7, 134, 137, 393
  Justice for Hedgehogs, Dworkin 122, 128
  justification, connection with 13, 261, 344–6, 353–7, 361
  legal interpretation 8–9, 13, 78–9, 119–38, 160, 162–3, 178, 181
  legal positivism 28–9, 122–4, 133, 139
  legal practices 119–20, 125, 135, 138
  legal theory 82–3
  morality 9, 13, 119–39, 181, 343–61
  natural law/naturalism 223–4
  naturally, doing something 14, 383–4, 400, 402
  Nazi Germany, interpretive practice in 13, 346–61
  obedience to law 121–2
  objectivity 291, 293–5, 308–10
  perfect integrity 343
  political morality 9, 119–20, 122, 124–5, 127, 132
  pragmatism 259, 261, 266–8, 278, 283
  precedent 120, 134–7
  preconditions 390
  pre-interpretive legal materials 30–1
  protected expectations 384, 392–3
  protestant interpretation and legal practice 127, 129–36, 138
  pure and inclusive integrity, distinction between 134
  rule of law 122, 136, 365
  sacrifices, types of 384
  systemic integrity 343
  trade-offs 392–3
  wicked law 124, 343–6
intellectual practice, law as a 9, 160, 163, 167–9, 171, 178
intention (intentionalism)
  authorial intention 29–30
  Fish, interview with 411–12
  intentionalism 195–6
  intentionless meaning 196
  legal interpretation 32, 80–1, 195–6
  legislators, of 165
  postmodernism 32
  reader response view 32
  textual interpretation 411–12
internalisation of practices 264, 267, 282
  Dennis Martinez (Fish's anti-theory hero) 41
  interpretive communities/interpretive community 210–11
  judging 80
  naturally, doing something 381
  objectivity 267
  social contexts 187–8
interpretation *see also* **interpretive communities/interpretive community; legal interpretation; literary interpretation; Nazi Germany, interpretive practice in; objectivity; subjectivity**
  interpretive constraint 10, 80, 183–202, 246–7, 318–20

interpretive freedom 387, 402
interpretive theories 21, 35, 141, 265, 280, 289, 319, 355, 413–14
interpretivism 6, 12, 256–7, 343–61
inventing and interpreting, distinguishing 291
literary interpretation
nature of interpretation 1
political morality 125–6
practices 292–3
responsibility, content of interpretive 306–11
stages of interpretation
   interpretive 126, 164, 192, 206, 303
   post-interpretive 164, 303–4
   pre-interpretive 38, 192, 303
textual interpretation 2–3, 129, 184, 186, 242, 318–19, 336, 411–12
interpretive attitude 286–7, 355, 387, 389, 401
interpretive communities/interpretive community 82, 239–58
agency 239–40, 243–7, 249, 251–2, 256–8
argumentation 242, 244–5, 253
assimilation 210–11
authority 211–12, 251–2, 254, 257, 284
Charter rights adjudication 394–7
coercion of law 239–40, 247–53, 254, 257–8
coherence 210, 246
conditions for membership 332–3
consistency with past decisions 246
constraints 246–7
constructive interpretation 242
conventionalism and pragmatism 259, 283
disagreement 193–4, 211–12
exile 336
Fish, interview with 409–23
flat structure of an interpretive community 240, 252, 257–8
force 11, 239, 242, 245–6, 257
Hercules (Dworkin's imagined judge) 161, 171, 173, 176, 178–80, 246, 255
hierarchical and differentiated role responsibilities 11, 240, 254, 257
homogenization 210–11
integrity, theory of 242, 245–6, 252–3, 257
internalization 210–11
judging 250–1, 254–7, 323
justification of force 11, 239, 252–3, 257

legal interpretation 83–4, 191–4, 239–40, 257–8
legal practice as interpretation 239–42, 244–5, 247, 250–1, 253, 257
legal reasoning as an interpretive practice 240–2
morality 245
objectivity 291–314
political community 244–5, 252
political responsibility 11, 240, 254–7
pragmatism 259, 281–4
principled interpreters, a community of 239–40, 245–6, 251–4, 257–8
protestant interpretation 11, 240, 245–6, 252, 254
Reader Response Theory 317, 321
reflective agency 240
rhetoric 11, 239–42, 244, 251–2
rule of law 241, 363–4, 370–1
self-reflection 239, 245, 253
social practices 183–4, 252–3
structure of legal practice 239
subjectivity 246
tacit knowledge 184, 211, 243
textual interpretation 242
United States Constitution 323, 332–3, 335–6
intuition 13, 269–70, 282–3, 285, 292
invention 120–1, 125, 261, 270, 281, 284, 291
is/ought distinction 71, 122–3, 311
Is There a Text in This Class? Fish, Stanley 243, 317, 335–6, 410

Jackson, Robert 86, 318, 333
judging *see also Hercules* (Dworkin's imagined judge) analogy
accountability 91
adjudication 43, 47, 384, 394–9
atheoretical generation, claim of 103–4, 111–13
chain novel analogy 78, 80, 103–4, 109, 112
Charter rights adjudication 384, 394–9
coercion 4, 246, 252, 254–7
constructive interpretation 198
constraints 38–9
conventionalism and pragmatism 14, 390–3
dissenting opinions 127, 164–5, 323–4
fit and justify thesis 125–6, 128, 132
guidance, judges' need for 79, 82

inauthentic explanation, claim of   103–5, 113–14
independence   356
integrity, law as   4, 23, 125–8, 132, 252, 257
interpretive communities/interpretive community   254–7, 323
justification   126, 257, 269
lawyering as different from judging   325–7
legal interpretation   198, 207
legal practices   18, 23–4, 188–9
legal theory   38–9, 43–4, 78–82, 87–8, 91, 93
legitimacy   322–5
naturally, doing something   3, 14, 382–3, 387, 400–1
political responsibility   254–7
practice and theory, interplay between   2, 22, 100, 102–18
pragmatism   269–70, 390–3
professional excellence   106–7
professional training and experience   23, 80, 109, 179, 210, 399, 401–2
psychological bias   23–4
reasoning within and about legal practices   8, 18–25, 102–5#
reasons
    articulate consistency   255
    practice and theory, distinction between   103, 104–5, 111, 113–17
    rhetoric   93, 102–3, 104–5, 114
    role   254–7
sanctions   401
self-reflection   48, 102, 104–7, 109–10, 112–13, 115, 117
Siegfried (imaginary judge)   347, 356–8
statutes   125, 294
stipulated order of law   387
subjectivity   3–5, 183
Supreme Court of the United States   166, 173, 327–9, 333–4, 339
unconstrained judges, problem of   18, 23–4, 78–82, 84–5
United States Constitution   319–20, 331–2, 337
values   43, 49, 103, 109–10, 172–3, 178, 267
virtue ethics   111–14, 117
wicked legal system, duties of judges in a   331

jurisprudence
Judge Ralph thought experiment   164–7, 171
jurisprudence *see* legal theory/jurisprudence
justice and fairness
    distributive justice   328–9, 383
    integrity, law as   122–7, 132, 134, 137, 393
    legal positivism   124
    morality   125
    Nazi Germany, interpretive practice in   347, 358
    normative practice, law as a special   285–6
    political morality   122
    pragmatism   260
    procedural fairness   162
    rule of law   368, 372–3, 378
    unjust laws as not being   331
Justice for Hedgehogs. Dworkin, Ronald   5, 9, 122, 128, 177, 285, 344, 347, 354–5, 358–9, 407
justification
    coercion   37, 248, 250–3, 257–8
    force   11, 40, 64–5, 239, 352, 357
    Hercules (Dworkin's imagined judge)   391, 401
    inferentialism   303–5
    integrity, connection with   13, 261, 344–6, 353–7, 361
    interpretive communities/interpretive community   252–3, 257
    judging   126, 269
    legal theory   85, 91
    moral justification   343–4
    political decisions   269, 288
    pragmatism   266, 270
    rhetoric   251, 257–8
    social practices   76–7

Kant, Immanuel   270–1, 297, 302, 306–10, 378
Keating, Gregory C   382–3
Kelsen, Hans   230, 378
Kennedy, Duncan   294–5
Kletzer, Christoph   70
Knapp, Steven   196
know-how   11
knowledge *see* tacit knowledge
Koskenniemi, Martti   13, 363–4, 375–9
Kuhn, Thomas S   326, 415, 425

438 Index

'Law as Interpretation' article. Dworkin,
    Ronald 27–30, 78–82, 144
'The Law Wishes to Have a Formal Existence'
    article. Fish, Stanley 53, 91
Law's Empire. Dworkin, Ronald 13, 27,
    33–4, 407
  constructive interpretation 163
  conventionalism and pragmatism 14, 22,
      30–1, 46, 390–3
  fidelity, duty of 399
  fit and justify thesis 78–9, 399
  Hercules (Dworkin's imagined judge) 124,
      161–2, 168, 170
  integrity, law as 14, 27, 30–1, 33–4, 46,
      78–9, 120, 122–4, 383–4
  interpretive communities/interpretive
      community 245–6, 252, 255–6
  legal interpretation 36, 143–4, 186, 206–7,
      390
  legal theory 36–7, 46, 78–9, 82
  literary interpretation 143–4
  natural law/naturalism 222, 226
  naturally, doing something 382–4, 389–93,
      400–1
  Nazi Germany, interpretive practice in
      344–5, 347, 352, 354–8, 361
  political obligations 383, 399
  pragmatism 30–1, 39–40, 260–1, 264–7,
      288
  protestant interpretation 399
  reasoning within and about legal
      practices 22
  rule of law 365–6
  scepticism 18–19
  special normative practice, law as a 293
learning, impossibility of 180–1
legal formalism 11, 78, 82, 91, 376–9
legal interpretation 12, 205–15, 324, 329
          see also constructive interpretation/
          'constructive' interpretation; legal
          interpretation, nature of constraints
          on; literary interpretation;
          objectivity; subjectivity
  adjudication, theory of 170–2
  agency 206
  anti-foundationalism 3, 185–6, 189–90
  argumentation 168, 177
  authoritative legal texts, interpretation
      of 31–4
  causal and interpretive judgments,
      distinction between 232–3
  chain novel analogy 205

coercion 162
constitutional interpretation 334, 341–2
constraints 99–139, 141–57, 159–81,
    183–202
conversational interpretation 288
critical interpretation 288
Dennis Martinez (Fish's anti-theory
    hero) 9, 159–81
dissenting judgments 164–5
ex ante law 142, 147–8, 150–7
expansive account 240
fit and justify thesis 78–9, 125–6, 162, 176,
    183, 205, 207–8
foundational role of interpretation 214
hard cases 206–7
Hercules (Dworkin's imagined judge) 9,
    132, 159–81, 207
inside-outside dichotomy 174
integrity, law as 8–9, 13, 119–38, 160,
    162–3, 178, 181
intellectual practice, law as a 9, 160, 163,
    167–9, 171, 178
intention 32, 80–1, 195–6
internal/external forms of argument 160,
    168–71, 175–7
interpretative stage 206–7
interpretivism 12, 343–6
intuitions and implicit dispositions,
    interpretation as relying on 9–10
invention 281
Judge Ralph thought experiment 164–7,
    171
judging 172–3, 178, 207
Law's Empire. Dworkin 206–7
legal positivism 159, 161, 163, 214–15, 288
legal practices 36, 120–1, 159–81, 187–9,
    192, 195, 212–15, 239–42, 247, 257
legal theory 8, 33, 36–7, 79, 83–5
literal interpretation 22, 161, 209
methodology 160, 167–9, 171, 177–8
moral principles 1, 8–9, 119–26, 183–5,
    198, 200–1, 329
naturally, doing something 163, 165–6,
    171, 387, 390, 399, 401
Nazi Germany, interpretive practice in 13
objectivity 20, 161–2, 292
past, law as an exercise in interpreting
    the 78–9
plain fact interpretation 334, 341
political practice 241–2
post-interpretative/reforming stage 33,
    206–7

pre-interpretive stage   192, 206–7, 303
progress in law   166, 174–6
protestant interpretation   207, 252
purposive activity, as   286–7
Reader Response Theory   208
reasoning within and about legal
    practices   8, 18–25, 102–5
reductive account   240
rhetoric   160, 170, 173
rule of law   241, 363
scientific interpretation   288
signs and meanings   213–14
social practices   12, 212–13
subjectivity   161–2, 165, 208, 212–13
tacit knowledge   163
three-step process   206–8, 215
understanding   9, 10, 12, 212–15
values   59–60, 130, 293, 304
wicked law   343–6
Wittgensteinian tradition   206, 213–14
legal interpretation, nature of constraints on   183–202
abstract principles   193
ameliorative interpretation   10, 185, 193, 197, 199–201
analytical jurisprudence   186, 189
anti-foundationalism   185–6, 189–90
artistic interpretation   198, 202, 261
best interpretation   181, 195, 197–8, 201
Bills of Rights in liberal democracies   200–1
chain novel analogy   198
constructive interpretation   10, 181, 184–5, 189–90, 192–201
cultural practices   188, 192
descriptive interpretation   185, 192–5, 198
disciplining rules   190–1
fit and justify thesis   183
foundationalism   185–7, 189
Hercules (Dworkin's imagined judge)   159–81, 186
insider expertise   188
integrity, law as   119–39, 181
intentionalism   195–6
interpretive communities   10, 184, 191–4
judging   183, 188–9, 198
legal practices   187–9, 192, 195
literary interpretation   141–57, 184, 198, 202
methodological perspective   184–90, 202
moral constraints   183–5, 198, 200–1

natural constraints   10, 184–5, 187–92, 198, 202
objects of interpretation   197, 199
paradigms   192
positive account of interpretation,
    repudiation of   184
pragmatism   187, 190–1
pre-interpretive stage   192
radically unconstrained interpreters   187
self-conscious deliberation   192
semantic indeterminacy   193
social concepts, evolution of   193–4
social contexts, internalisation of   187–8
social practices   181–4, 188–95, 198–200
stability and predictability   194–5
subjectivity   183, 185, 190–2
tacit guidelines   184
textual interpretation   184, 196
three modes of interpretation   190–5
unforeseen circumstances   193–4
vagueness   193–4
legal positivism
anti-positivism   129, 214–15
best interpretation   288
coherentism   230–1
conventionalism and pragmatism   30, 391–3
creating and applying law, distinction
    between   6
force   58–9, 68, 72
full law and positive law distinguished   288
gunman analogy (Hart)   58–9
integrity, law as   28–9, 122–4, 132–3, 139
is/ought distinction   122–3
justice and fairness   124
legal interpretation   159, 161, 163, 214–15, 288
legal realism   28–9
legal reason   68
natural law/naturalism   11, 221–8, 230, 288, 344
naturally, doing something   392–3
Nazi Germany, interpretive practice
    in   344–7, 349–58
pragmatism   30, 260–1
slavery   331–2
statutory positivism   349–52
legal practices   7–8
coercion   247–51
commitments and entitlements   311
descriptive interpretation   195

440 Index

Hercules (Dworkin's imagined judge) 159–81
integrity, law as 119, 120, 125, 135, 138
interpretive communities/interpretive community 247–51
invention 120, 125
judging 18, 23–4, 188–9, 343
legal interpretation 36, 120–1, 159–81, 187–9, 192, 195, 212–15, 239–42, 247, 257
literary interpretation 146
natural law/naturalism 225
normative legal practices 293, 314
objectivity 314
political morality 124–5
pragmatism 263, 288–9
proposition 'Λ'/peculiarity of legal practice 35–8, 43, 45–6, 48
protestant interpretation 127, 129–36, 138
recognition, Hegel's theory of 311–13
social aspects 293, 311–13
social welfare, maximisation of 370
special normative practice, law as a 293–6, 310
structure of legal practice
thinking within a practice/thinking with the practice 8, 17–25, 102–5, 163, 188, 262
understanding 5
legal pragmatism, comparison between Fish and Dworkin's versions of 259–89
argumentation, practice of legal 270, 287
articulate consistency, idea of 263
artificial reason for law 287
artistic interpretation 261
belief-desire model of rationalisation 11, 275–80, 289
broad pragmatism 259, 268–75, 288
common law 287–9
constraints 263, 270
constructive interpretation 288
conventionalism 266–7, 281–4, 287–8
correctness or validity of judgments 294
differences between Fish and Dworkin 259, 264, 268–9
distinctive interpretation 288
Dworkin's response to Fish 259
essentialism 268
externalist/internalist philosophical perspective 264–5
foundationalism 268
fundamental pragmatism 11, 271–2, 275
implicit norms 11–12, 270, 273, 283, 289
instrumental pragmatism of Fish 259, 274–81, 283, 289
integrity, law as 259, 261, 266–8, 278, 283
internal structure to interpretation 261–2
intuition 269–70, 282–3, 285, 292
interpretive attitude 286–7
interpretive communities 12, 281–4
inventing and interpreting, difference between 270, 284
judging 269–70
justification 266, 270
legal positivism 260–1
legal practices 263, 288–9
legal realism 269–70
literary interpretation 261, 264
metaphysics 260–8, 285–6, 289
methodological pragmatism 271, 275, 289
narrow pragmatism 259, 268–74, 276, 283, 288–9
normative practice, law as a special 285–9
normative pragmatism 11–12, 272–4, 275, 281–2
objectivity 267, 280, 285–9, 292
reason in law, role of 289
regress argument 273–4, 283
regularist reading of understanding 273–4
rhetoric 263, 269, 284
right-wrong image of adjudication 263–4, 267, 292
rule of law 270
semantic pragmatism 271, 275–6
similarities between Fish and Dworkin 259, 262
social practices 268, 271–3, 275, 285
special normative practice, law as a 285–9, 292
structure of norms 282
tacit awareness 262
truth, theory of 264, 267, 272
Wittgensteinian 273–4, 280, 283–4
legal realism 11, 28–9, 84, 228, 269–70
legal reasoning 9, 17–25
arguing within a practice 18–25
barriers or walls 55, 60, 65
common law 127

critical role of legal theory 51–74
democratisation of legal reasoning 399–401
force 66–74
illusion, as an 68
impartiality and independence 68
interpretive practice 240–2
judging 18, 23–4
legal interpretation 18, 19–21, 23
moral reason, law grounded in 59–61
outcome-based reasoning 394–7
practical reasoning 303
role of reason in law 289
thinking within a practice/thinking with the practice 8, 17–25, 102–5, 163, 188, 262

legal theory/jurisprudence
accountability 42, 47
analytical jurisprudence 12, 186, 189
anti-theory 160, 283
Archimedean jurisprudence 119, 121, 123–9, 138, 219, 231, 235, 265
baseball analogy 41–2, 47–8
conceptual theory of law 225, 226–9, 260
conservative theory of law 288–9
Critical Legal Studies (CLS) 84, 89–90, 94
critical role 7, 17–95
disagreement 45–7
distinctive jurisprudence 287
Fish, legal theorists reaction to 8, 75–95
  agenda, law's need for an 93–5
  alternatives, lack of 76–7, 88–90
  Fiss 83–5
  guidance 21–2
Hart's theory of law 55–65
judging 78–82, 87–8, 91, 93
  appointment, nomination and confirmation 43–4
  constraints 38–9
  unnecessary for judges, as 35–49
justification 85, 91
law and reason 51–74
originalism 7, 31–2, 84–5, 321, 328, 341, 411–12
practice and theory, interplay between 8, 99–118
proposition 'Λ'/peculiarity of legal practice 35–8, 43, 45–6, 48
reasoning within and about (legal) practices 8, 18–25, 102–5
redundant, legal theory as 8, 76

rhetorical, legal theory as 8, 49, 76–7, 88, 90–5
Rule of Law 8, 35–7, 43–4, 47–9
truth, theory of 264, 267, 272
us to ourselves, explaining 35–49
who needs theory 42–4
without theory, whether law could do 93–5
legality, principle of
fidelity, duty of 368, 369, 372
government, practice of 363, 370–1
instrumental approach to government 363, 376, 378
integrity, law as 343
managerial approach to government 363, 373
morality 226, 229
natural law/naturalism 223
Nazi Germany, interpretive practice in 344–5, 347, 350, 353–5, 361
rule of law 13, 363–79
legitimacy of law
coercive force, use of 344, 355
judging 322–5
Nazi Germany, interpretive practice in 350–1, 355–6, 360–1
nihilism or illegitimacy, fear of 86, 87–8
Leiter, Brian 226–7, 407
linguistic practices 141, 297–8, 300, 305–6, 309, 313–14
literal interpretation 22, 161, 209
literary interpretation 3, 9, 141–57
  analogy, role of 144–57
  coercion 248
  chain novel analogy 2, 142, 144–57
  constructive interpretation 198
  constraints 184, 198, 202
  disanalogy 146–8, 151–7
  fit and justify thesis 144, 152–3
  interpretive communities/interpretive community 2, 248
  legal interpretation and literary interpretation, analogy between 9, 142–4
  linguistic meaning 141
  local law 153–6
  pragmatism 261, 264
  precedent 141–2, 153, 156
  Reader Response Theory 317
  reasons for judgments, written 155
living constitutionalism 411
Locke, John 381, 384

MacCormick, Neil 116, 295
MacIntyre, Alasdair 105–9, 111, 113, 118
Mackie, John L 228, 288, 295
MacKinnon, Catharine 173–4
marriage, purpose of 192–3
Martinez, Dennis *see* Dennis Martinez (Fish's anti-theory hero)/baseball analogy
material inferences 297, 301–3
McLoughlin case 132, 137, 353
meaning, account of 10
metaphysical arguments
  assumptions 7
  anti-foundationalism 189
  morality 228, 235
  objectivity 285–6, 296
  pragmatism 260–8, 289
  reasoning within and about legal practices 17, 24
  right answer thesis 12
  scepticism 19
Michaels, Walter Benn 196, 405, 408
mindshaping 188, 192, 197
Moore, Michael 23–4, 42, 44, 111
moral principles *see also* virtue ethics
  ambiguity in connection with law 9, 120–2
  ameliorative interpretation 201
  authority 56–7, 59, 63, 123–4, 245, 350
  coherence 132, 231
  commitments 299, 365
  common law 127, 229
  deonotological morality 367
  error theory 228–9
  foundationalism 231
  incommensurability 295
  institutional actions 9, 120
  integrity, law as 13, 122–39, 181, 343–61
  justice and fairness 122, 125
  justification 343–4
  legal interpretation 1, 8–9, 119–26, 183–5, 198, 200–1, 329
  legal practice 124–5
  legal realism 11, 228
  metaphysics 228, 235
  natural law/naturalism 225, 228–30, 233–6
  Nazi Germany, interpretive practice in 344–61
  objectivity 228–30, 233–5, 292, 296, 299
  political morality 9, 119–20, 122, 125–7, 132
  pragmatism 228–30
  precedent, morally mistaken 33

rule of law 365, 378
scepticism 18, 19–20
similarity, criteria of 125
thick ethical concepts 11, 266, 306–7
values 1, 59–60, 138, 280, 299
Mullendert, Richard 7
Murphy, James Bernard 384–6
Murphy, Walter 320, 323
'My Reply to Stanley Fish' article. Dworkin, Ronald 29–30
Myth of the Given 276

Nagel, Thomas 5, 67–8
natural constraints 10, 184–5, 187–92, 198, 202
natural law/naturalism 1, 11, 217–37
  anti-foundationalism 219
  anti-naturalistic turn of Dworkin 225, 232–6
  Archimedeanism 219, 231, 235
  boundaries of law, search for 226–8
  causal and interpretive judgments, distinction between 232–3
  coherentism 223, 225, 228, 230–2
  common good constitutionalism 324
  common law 229, 231, 287, 309
  conceptual jurisprudence, rejection of 225, 226–8
  conventionalism and pragmatism 30–1
  Dworkin, jurisprudence of 217–37
    boundaries of law 226–8
    coherentism 223, 225, 228, 230–2
    conceptual jurisprudence, rejection of 226–9
    law and morality, pragmatist account of 228–30
    pragmatism 221–5, 228–30
  foundationalism 219, 223, 230–1
  integrity, law as 223–4
  jurisprudential pragmatism of Dworkin 221–5
  legal positivism 11, 221–8, 230, 288, 344
  legality, criteria of 223
  morality 11, 225, 228–30, 233–6
  Nazi Germany, interpretive practice in 344–5
  neo-pragmatism 219
  objectivity 84, 221, 228–30, 233–4
  postmodernism 217–19, 233
  power 58–9
  practices, law and morality as 225
  pragmatism 217–37

proxy, naturalism by   225
Quine   11, 221–6, 231–3
realism   11, 228
social practices   235
naturally, doing something   381–403
  ambiguity   386, 390
  appearance of freedom and choice   382
  Aristotle's tripartite distinction   384–6
  best interpretation   388–9, 401
  baseball   386–7, 395
  biological order of nature   385
  Charter rights adjudication   384, 394–9
  coercion   4, 401
  common law rights   384, 394–5, 400
  conventionalism   14, 383–4, 390–3
  contractarian tradition   381
  courtesy, practice of   384, 386, 387–9, 398, 401
  customary practices   384–90, 393, 398, 400–1, 403
  democratisation of legal reasoning   399–401
  fit and justify thesis   399, 401
  Hercules (Dworkin's imagined judge)   391, 393, 400–2
  integrity, law as   14, 383–4, 400, 402
  judging   3, 14, 38–9, 163, 165–6, 171, 382–4, 387, 394–401
  Law's Empire. Dworkin   14, 382–4, 389–93, 399–401
  legal interpretation   163, 165–6, 171, 387, 390, 399, 401
  natural/conventional divide   384–5
  nested hierarchy of order   385
  peace, subjugation to sovereign as a price of   381–2
  pragmatism   14, 39, 390–3
  preferable state of affairs, natural as suggesting a   381
  protestant interpretation   399, 402
  single-right answer thesis   393, 397
  social order   385, 399–402
  state of nature   381
  stipulated order of law   385–7
  technological interventions   385
  trade-offs   381–3, 392, 399, 403
Nazi Germany, interpretive practice in   13, 346–61
  1933–1939   344
  arguable rights and duties, creation of   344–5, 360
  coercive force   352, 355, 357
  concrete order thought   349–53
  constructive interpretation   345–6, 352–3, 355–6, 361
  conventionalism and pragmatism   351, 353
  Fugitive Slave Acts (US), comparison with   359–60
  independence from political authorities, judges' lack of   356
  justice and fairness   347, 358
  justification and integrity, connection between   13, 344–6, 353–7, 361
  legal positivism   344–7, 349–58
  legality, principle of   344–5, 347, 350, 353–5, 361
  legitimacy   350–1, 355–6, 360–1
  methodological approach   352–3
  moral principles   344–61
  natural law/naturalism   344–5
  Nuremberg Laws   347–8, 359
  pragmatism   352–3
  Recht and *Gesetz*, notions of   349–50
  rule of law   348
  Siegfried (imaginary judge)   347, 356–8
  socially accepted conception of proper order   350–1
  statutory positivism   349–52
  theory as answering to practice   12
  Weimar Republic   348, 350–2, 358
  wicked law   13, 344–6, 354–61
  wicked statutory enactments   346–51
  Wilhelmine Empire   350
neoliberalism   328–9
nervous shock, damages for   132
Neurath's boat   232
Nietzsche, Friedrich   212–13
nihilism   86, 87–8
normative practice, law as a special   285–9
normative pragmatism   11–12, 272–4, 275, 281–2
normative theory of law   260
Nuremberg laws   347–8, 359

obedience to law   121–2
objectivity   4, 20, 121, 161–2, 291–314
  anti-foundationalism   3
  classical common law   293, 309–11
  coercion   291–2
  commitments, relations among   300–6
  constructive interpretation   303–4, 309, 313
  critical interpretation   288

Critical Legal Studies (CLS) 12, 292, 293–7
deontic scorekeeping 300–6
domain objectivity 12, 285–6
epistemic objectivity 286
Hercules (Dworkin's imagined judge) 161–2
implicit norms, role of 314
inferentialism 12, 291, 293, 296–306, 309, 313
integrity, law as 291, 293–6, 308–10, 313–14
instrumentalist concept of knowledge 291
interpretive communities/interpretive community 291–314
interpretive practice 292–3
interpretive responsibility, content of Dworkin's 306–11
inventing and interpreting, distinguishing 291
metaphysics 285–6, 296
methodological objectivity 296, 299
morality 221, 228–30, 233–4, 292, 296, 299
natural law/naturalism 221, 228–30, 233–4
pragmatism 267, 280, 285–9, 291, 298
rationality in law, role of 291, 308–11, 314
Reader Response Theory 208
relevance condition 286–7
right-wrong image of adjudication 292, 311
semantic theory 293, 297–8, 300–1, 309–14
social aspect of legal practices 293, 311–13
social practices 292, 296, 306, 309
special normative practice, law as a 293–6, 310
values 73, 161, 296
obligations *see also* political obligations
role obligation 245, 255–8
statement of obligations 302
officials 153, 207, 215, 255–8, 262
coercion 287
commitments 125
conduct of legal officials 366
consistency with past conduct 39
conventionalism and pragmatism 292
integrity, law as 4, 123, 126–8, 135–6
internal point of view 64–5
morality 245
Nazi Germany, interpretive practice in 346–7
official/subject divide 255
political officials 314
protestant interpretation 254
reasons for decisions 116
rule of law 366, 375, 378
self-interest 62, 64–5
open mind, keeping an 71, 72
originalism 7, 31–2, 84–5, 321, 328, 341, 411–12

paradigms 126, 192
Parker-Chandler thought experiment 149
the past
alienation 402–3
backward-looking character of law 37
coercion 36, 287, 291
fit and justify thesis 162
judging 37, 38
legal interpretation 78–9
political decisions 12, 35–6, 287, 291–2
unhappy legal past, interpreting an 327–33
Peirce, Charles S 270, 274, 305
Pericles 402–3
Plato 3–4, 72, 228–9, 272, 325–7
political community
interpretive communities/interpretive community 244–5, 252, 255
rule of law 367–9, 372–3, 377, 379
political obligations
associative political obligations 245–6
distributive justice 383
integrity, law as 136
naturally, doing something 399
social order 383
political responsibility
coercion 11, 240, 254–7
interpretive communities/interpretive community 254–7
pragmatism 262
positivism *see* legal positivism
Posner, Richard 13, 39, 48, 217, 278, 321, 369–73
post-interpretive/reforming stage 126, 206–7, 303
Postema, Gerald J 130, 214, 252–7, 269, 287–8, 310, 394–5, 397, 399

postmodernism 7, 27, 29, 32, 34, 217–19, 233, 326–7
practice and theory, interaction between 8, 12, 99–118, 269 *see also* Dennis Martinez (Fish's anti-theory hero)/baseball analogy; naturally, doing something
  atheoretical generation, claim of 100–1, 102, 103–4, 111–13
  causal relationship 22
  driving to work/playing the piano, distinction between 107–9, 220
  inauthentic explanation, claim of 101–2, 103, 104–5, 111, 113–17
  judging 2, 100, 102–5
  learning, impossibility of 180–1
  practice, definition of 105–6
  reasoning within and about legal practices 8, 18–25, 102–5
  reflection 107–9
  routine and skill distinguished 107–11
  standards of excellence 106–7
practices *see also* customary practice; internalisation of practices; legal practices; Nazi Germany, interpretive practice in; social practices
  developed practices 415, 422
  linguistic practices 141, 297–8, 300, 305–6, 309, 313–14
pragmatism *see also* conventionalism and pragmatism; legal pragmatism, comparison between Fish and Dworkin's versions of
  agency, coercion, and the structure of legal practice 239–58
  broad/inferentialist pragmatism 291
  commitments and entitlements 302
  comparison between two versions of legal pragmatism 259–89
  correspondence theory of truth 326
  default, as 39–41
  Dworkin's attitude to pragmatists 5–6
  fundamental pragmatism 11, 271–2, 275
  inferentialism 298
  instrumental pragmatism 275, 283, 291
  interpretive communities/interpretive community 239–58
  methodological pragmatism 298
  morality 228–30
  narrow/instrumental pragmatism 291
  natural law/naturalism 217–37

  naturally, doing something 39
  neo-pragmatism 219
  normative pragmatism 11, 272–5, 282
  objectivity 291–314
  past political decisions as justification for coercion 291
  postmodernism 326
  rule of law 366–7, 371
  semantic pragmatism 298
precedent
  binding character 394
  consistency 246
  fit and justify thesis 325
  integrity, law as 120, 133–7
  legal interpretation 9, 125
  legitimacy 324–5
  legal theory 141–2, 153, 156
  morally mistaken precedent 33
  naturally, doing something 394–5, 401
  outcome-based reasoning 394–7
  paradox of precedent 394
  ratio decidendi 141–2
  reciprocity 313
pre-interpretive stage 28–9, 33, 34, 38, 192, 206–7, 303
prejudices *see* convictions/beliefs/prejudices
professional training and experience 23, 80, 109, 179, 210, 399, 401–2
progress in law 166, 172, 174–6
proportionality analysis 395–6
protected expectations 383–4, 390, 392–3, 397
protestant interpretation
  hierarchical and differentiated role responsibilities 11, 240, 254
  individualised protestant interpretation 246, 252
  interpretive communities/interpretive community 245–6
  legal interpretation 207
  legal practice 127, 129–36, 138
  naturally, doing something 399, 402
  rule of law 364
purposive interpretation 286–7
Putnam, Hilary 11, 233, 264–6, 271, 306–7

Quine, WVO 11, 221–6, 231–3, 271

Radbruch formula 344–7
Radbruch, Gustav 344–7, 349–50, 352, 360
radically unconstrained interpreters 187

rationality/reason
  agents 301
  belief-desire model of rationalisation 11, 275–80, 289
  common law 287, 307, 309
  Hegelian historical conception 307–8
  human practice 67–8
  linguistic practices 297–8, 305
  oughts 303
  progress, notion of 293
  role in law 291, 308–11, 311
  social practices 12, 292, 296–8, 306–8
  transcendence of reason 8, 51, 68–70, 73
  unreason distinguished 68–9
  values 67, 70, 272, 276–7, 293
Rawls, John 186, 188, 262, 299, 328, 382, 399, 402, 420
Raz, Joseph 42, 65, 144, 277–9, 286, 310
Reader Response Theory 32, 208, 317–18, 321–2
reason *see* rationality/reason
reasoning *see* legal reasoning
reasons
  articulate consistency 255
  force 62–7
  judgments, written reasons for 155
  legal, reasons must be 23–4
  practice and theory, distinction between 103, 104–5, 111, 113–17
  rule of law 115
  sanctions 64–5
  written judgments 102, 104, 114–17
rebellion, acts of 387–8, 401
reciprocity 257, 312–13
recognition, Hegel's theory of 293, 311–13
regress argument 213, 273–4, 283–4
regularist reading 273–4
responsibility
  ampliative responsibility 303–4
  critical responsibility 303
  hierarchical and differentiated role responsibilities 11, 240, 257
  individual rights and responsibilities 366
  interpretive responsibility 254–7, 306–11
  justificatory responsibility 303–5
  political responsibility 11, 240, 254–7, 262
  task responsibilities 303–6
rhetoric
  authority 92–3, 95, 317
  coercion 244, 247–50, 257–8
  Critical Legal Studies (CLS) 248
  foundationalism 189

intellectual practice, law as a 160
interpretive communities/interpretive community 244, 247–51, 252, 257–8
judging 49, 93, 102–3, 104–5, 114
justification 251, 257–8
lawyering as different from judging 325–6
legal reasoning 160, 170, 173
legal theory 8, 49, 76–7, 88, 90–5
pragmatism 263, 269, 284
professors of law 325
rule of law 373, 377
sophistry 250
United States Constitution 317–18
Riggs v Palmer 209–12, 272, 392–3
right answer thesis
  Hercules (Dworkin's imagined judge) 112, 319, 321–3
  lawyering as different from judging 326
  metaphysical fiction 12
  reasoning within and about legal practices 20
  single-right answer thesis 393, 397
  United States Constitution 319–23, 326, 331–2, 334–5, 337, 340
rights
  Bills of Rights in liberal democracies 200–1
  Charter rights adjudication 384, 394–9
  defendants' rights argument 33–4
  free speech 218, 339, 397
  interpretation 4
  Ninth Amendment's concept of rights (US Constitution) 279
  Recht and *Gesetz*, notions of 349–50
  rule of law 366
  traditional legal rights, effect of Charter rights on 384, 398–9
Robertson, Michael 190–1, 202, 246–7
Rorty, Richard 13, 19, 217, 271, 284, 326, 336, 416–17, 427
Rousseau, Jean-Jacques 381–2, 384
routine and skill distinguished 107–11
rule of law 363–79
  adjudication 43
  agency 369–77
  anti-foundationalism 370–1
  coercion 365–6, 369
  commitments 372, 377
  constructive interpretation 364, 366, 377
  Critical Legal Studies (CLS) movement 373

culture 364, 377
fidelity, duty of 13, 280, 342, 363–5, 368–72
force 54, 63
formalism, culture of 376–9
foundationalism 370–1
government, identification of law with 365, 372–9
gunman analogy 63
impartiality 365, 370, 374, 377
individual rights and responsibilities 366
integrity, law as 122, 136, 365
international law 13, 364
interpretive communities/interpretive community 241, 363–4, 370–1
judging 37, 43, 323
justice and fairness 368, 372–3, 378
Koskenniemi 13, 363–4, 375–9
legal officials, conduct of 366
legal practices 241, 370
legal theory 8, 35–7, 43–4, 47–9
legality, principle of 13, 363–79
morality 365, 378
nature of law 363–4
Nazi Germany, interpretive practice in 348
political community 367–9, 372–3, 377, 379
political power, exercise of 373, 375
powerful, as domination by the 373
pragmatism 270, 366–7, 371
proposition 'Λ' 45–6
protestant interpretation 364
reasons 115
rhetoric, law as 373, 377
rule of rules 375
United States Constitution 330, 342
value, as a 43, 63, 377
rule of recognition 61, 64–5, 230
rules
disciplining rules 84, 190–1
exceptions to binding rules 62
games, rules of the 10
interpretive communities/interpretive community 2
rule of rules 375
shared 65
wicked rules as valid law 124

sanctions 52, 64–5, 401
Scalia, Antonin 31–2, 48, 328, 412, 424

Scanlon, Thomas 5, 6, 420
scepticism 10, 18–20, 286, 292–4, 355
Schauer, Frederick 334, 341–2
Schmitt, Carl 349–52
science and technology 217–21, 224, 232–5, 288, 385, 425–6
scientific interpretation 288
self-reflection
interpretive communities/interpretive community 239, 245, 253
judging 48, 102, 104–7, 109–10, 112–13, 115, 117
semantic theory
amelioration 200–1
chain novel analogy 311
indeterminacy 193
inferentialism 293, 297–8, 300–1, 306–8
linguistic practices 313–14
objectivity 293, 297–8, 300–1, 309–14
pragmatism 271, 275–6, 298
sense of appropriateness 195, 272, 282, 428
shared assumptions 2, 7, 256, 389
Siegfried (imaginary judge) 347, 356–8
signs and meanings 10, 213–14
Simmonds, Nigel E 278–9, 384, 394–8
single-right answer thesis 393, 397
skill
driving to work/playing the piano, distinction between 107–9, 220
legal interpretation 12, 212–13
routine and skill distinguished 107–11
virtue as a skill 107–11, 114–15, 117
slavery 329–32
social media 339
Sokal, Alan 218–19, 233–4
social order 383–5, 390, 397–402
social practices 2, 4–5, 12
argumentation 298–9
commitments and entitlements 300, 305
conventionalism and pragmatism 281
coordination among participants 188
courtesy, practice of 384, 386, 387–9, 398, 401
force 73–4
inferentialism 296–9, 305–8
interpretive communities/interpretive community 252–3
justification 76–7
legal interpretation 181–4, 188–95, 198–200
linguistic practices 306, 309
natural law/naturalism 235

objectivity   292, 296, 306, 309
pragmatism   11–12, 268, 271–3, 275, 281, 285
purpose of practice, understanding the   25
rationality   12, 292, 296–8, 306–8
solipsism   208–10
Solum, Lawrence   111–13
South Africa   331, 334
stages of interpretation
  interpretive   126, 164, 192, 206, 303
  post-interpretive   164, 303–4
  pre-interpretive   38, 192, 303
state of nature   381
'Still Wrong After All These Years' article. Fish, Stanley   7, 266
stipulated order of law   385–7
subjectivity
  intention of legislation   165
  interpretive communities/interpretive community   246
  judging   183
  legal interpretation   165, 183, 185, 190–2, 208, 212–13
  value judgments   3–5
subjects   245, 247, 249, 257, 311, 354, 365–78
sublimation   68–9, 71–2

tacit knowledge
  implicit to explicit, from the   44–5, 47
  interpretive communities/interpretive community   184, 243
  legal interpretation   163, 184, 211
  pragmatism   262
  truth, discovering the   23–4
Taking Rights Seriously. Dworkin, Ronald   27, 260–1, 319
technological interventions   385
textualism   2–3, 129, 184, 186, 242, 318–19, 336, 411–12
theoreticism   236–7
theorizing (about a practice)   8, 100–1, 103
theory *see also* legal theory/jurisprudence; practice and theory, interaction between
  consequences of   82, 169, 176, 386, 395
  rhetorical nature of   8, 49, 76–7, 88, 90–5
  theory hope   89
thick ethical concepts   11, 266, 306–7
thinking within a practice/thinking with the practice   8, 17–25, 102–5, 163, 188, 262
Thomist *lex iniusta* thesis   344–6, 355, 360

threshold requirement of fit   126
trade-offs   381–3, 392, 399, 403
tradition
  Charter rights on traditional legal rights, effect of   384, 398–9
  contractarian tradition   381
transcendence   8, 51, 68–70, 73
truth, theory of   264, 267, 272

unconstrained judges, problem of   18, 23–4, 78–82, 84–5
understanding   5, 9, 10, 12, 212–15, 273–4
unforeseen circumstances   193–4
United States *see also* United States Constitution
  abortion   189, 194–5, 201–2, 279–80, 328, 342, 420, 422
  Civil Rights Act of 1964   174
  Constitution   201, 279–80
  Dobbs ruling   189, 194–5, 201–2, 279–80, 328, 342, 420, 422–3
  Fugitive Slave Act of 1793   124, 331, 359–60
  literal interpretation   209–10
  New York Statute of Wills   209
  privacy, right to   279
  race   422–3
  Riggs v Palmer   209–12, 272, 392–3
  Roe v Wade, overruling   189, 194–5, 201–2, 279–80, 328, 342, 420, 422
  Supreme Court   166
    Dobbs ruling   189, 194–5, 201–2, 279–80, 328, 342, 420, 422
    Fish, interview with   417–18
    same-sex marriage   418
United States Constitution   317–42
  1787 Constitution   329, 337
  amendments   339
  American constitutional development   329
  analytical jurisprudence   12
  attitudinalism   320
  backsliding democracy, US as a   339
  best fit   333
  Bill of Rights   337
  civil war, prospect of a   338
  common law constitutionalism   334, 341–2
  Constitution of Conversation   333–4, 336–7, 339
  Constitution of Settlement (hard-wired structural features)   12–13, 334, 336–7
  constraints on interpretation   318–20

design of constitutions   340–1
elections and campaign financing   339
Electoral College   339
empirical agreement, supplementing theory with   340–2
Equal Protection Clause   27–8
Establishment Clause   419
fidelity, duty of   331–2
First Amendment on free speech   339
fit and justify thesis   340
flawed democracy, as   338–9
Fourteenth Amendment   27–8, 32, 279, 318, 328, 334
framers   317
hard cases   319–20
hard-wired constitution and its deficiencies   333–7, 339–40
Hercules (Dworkin's imagined judge)   319, 321–4, 329, 331–3, 335, 339, 341
Impeachment Clause   339
Inauguration Day   334–6
institutional design, domain of   12
interpreters   317–19
interpreting an unhappy legal past   327–33
interpretive communities   332–3, 335
judging   319–20, 331–2, 337
lawyering as different from judging   325–7
legal fidelity to menacing constitutions   337–40
legal interpretation   324, 329
legal positivism   331–2
legitimacy as a consideration for judges   322–5
natural law/naturalism   324
neoliberalism   328–9
Ninth Amendment's concept of rights   279
originalism   32, 321, 341
political culture, flaws in   339
political science   317–20, 327, 340
Preamble   339
race   329
reader response   317–18, 321–2
rhetoric   317–18
right answer thesis   319–23, 326, 331–2, 334–5
rights provisions   337, 340
rule of law   330, 342
secessionism   338
Senate, evil of the   335–6, 337–9
slavery   329–32

social media   339
South Africa   331, 334
structural features of Constitution   335, 337
Supreme Court   166, 173, 327–9, 333–4, 339
  life tenure   339
  packing the Court   342
Taking Rights Seriously. Dworkin   319
textual indeterminacy   318–19, 336
Thirteenth Amendment   331–2
Twentieth Amendment   334–6
unjust laws as not being laws   331
welfare state, reading in theory of a   328–9, 337

values   1, 3–4, 66–7, 70–3, 299, 304, 310, 368
  agency   276
  common good or public interest   341
  customs   389
  family values   193
  integrity, law as   134, 160, 244–5, 296
  internal/external values   168, 310
  judging   43, 49, 103, 109–10, 172–3, 178, 267
  legal interpretation   59–60, 130, 293, 304
  moral values   1, 59–60, 138, 280, 299
  objectivity   73, 161, 296
  political   43, 122, 124
  proportionality analysis   395–6
  rationality   67, 70, 272, 276–7, 293
  rule of law   43, 63, 377
  subjective values   3–5, 191
  theory selection   265–6
  United States Constitution   280
veil of ignorance   186
Vermeule, Adrian   324, 339–41
violence   52–3, 56–9
virtue ethics   99, 105–14, 118
  adjudication, theories of   111–13
  atheoretical generation, claim of   111–13
  generosity   114–15
  habits   107–8
  judging   111–14, 117
  legal interpretation   99–118
  routine and skill distinguished   107–11, 114
  skill, virtue as a   107–11, 114–15, 117

Waldron, Jeremy   7–8, 270, 294–5, 407, 422
Waluchow, Wil J   299–300
Ward v Quebec   397

wicked law   13, 124, 331, 344–6, 354–61
Williams, Bernard   5, 306
Wittgenstein, Ludwig   9, 19–20, 41, 206, 213–14, 271, 273–4, 280, 283–4, 300, 389

'Working on the Chain Gang' article. Fish, Stanley   28–30, 406
written judgments   102, 104, 114–17
'Wrong Again' article. Fish, Stanley   29

Milton Keynes UK
Ingram Content Group UK Ltd.
UKHW022359300823
427780UK00005B/175